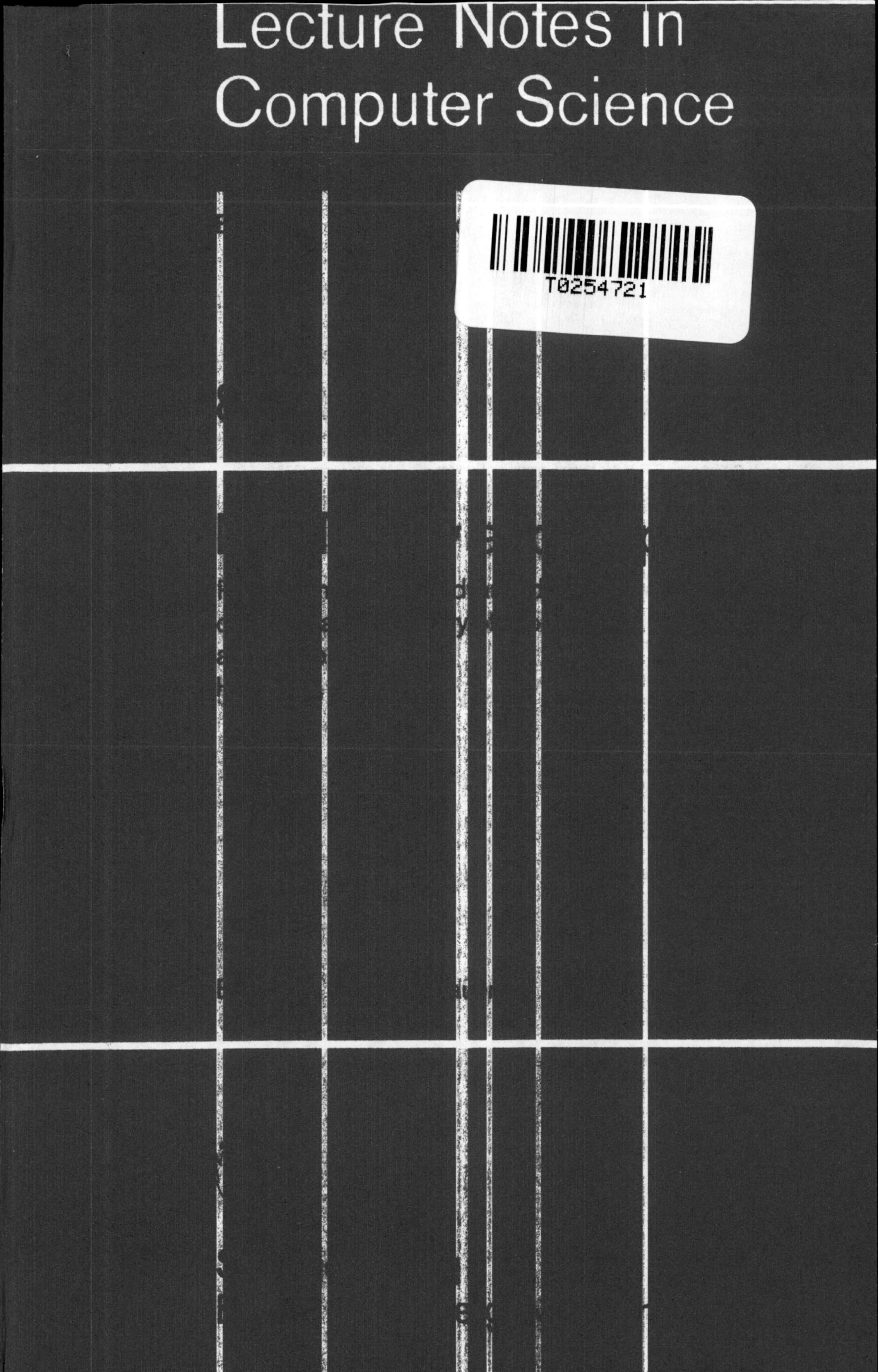
Lecture Notes in
Computer Science
T0254721

Lecture Notes in Computer Science

Vol. 1: GI-Gesellschaft für Informatik e.V. 3. Jahrestagung, Hamburg, 8.–10. Oktober 1973. Herausgegeben im Auftrag der Gesellschaft für Informatik von W. Brauer. XI, 508 Seiten. 1973.

Vol. 2: GI-Gesellschaft für Informatik e.V. 1. Fachtagung über Automatentheorie und Formale Sprachen, Bonn, 9.–12. Juli 1973. Herausgegeben im Auftrag der Gesellschaft für Informatik von K.-H. Böhling und K. Indermark. VII, 322 Seiten. 1973.

Vol. 3: 5th Conference on Optimization Techniques, Part I. (Series: I.F.I.P. TC7 Optimization Conferences.) Edited by R. Conti and A. Ruberti. XIII, 565 pages. 1973.

Vol. 4: 5th Conference on Optimization Techniques, Part II. (Series: I.F.I.P. TC7 Optimization Conferences.) Edited by R. Conti and A. Ruberti. XIII, 389 pages. 1973.

Vol. 5: International Symposium on Theoretical Programming. Edited by A. Ershov and V. A. Nepomniaschy. VI, 407 pages. 1974.

Vol. 6: B. T. Smith, J. M. Boyle, J. J. Dongarra, B. S. Garbow, Y. Ikebe, V. C. Klema, and C. B. Moler, Matrix Eigensystem Routines – EISPACK Guide. XI, 551 pages. 2nd Edition 1974. 1976.

Vol. 7: 3. Fachtagung über Programmiersprachen, Kiel, 5.–7. März 1974. Herausgegeben von B. Schlender und W. Frielinghaus. VI, 225 Seiten. 1974.

Vol. 8: GI-NTG Fachtagung über Struktur und Betrieb von Rechensystemen, Braunschweig, 20.–22. März 1974. Herausgegeben im Auftrag der GI und der NTG von H.-O. Leilich. VI, 340 Seiten. 1974.

Vol. 9: GI-BIFOA Internationale Fachtagung: Informationszentren in Wirtschaft und Verwaltung. Köln, 17./18. Sept. 1973. Herausgegeben im Auftrag der GI und dem BIFOA von P. Schmitz. VI, 259 Seiten. 1974.

Vol. 10: Computing Methods in Applied Sciences and Engineering, Part 1. International Symposium, Versailles, December 17–21, 1973. Edited by R. Glowinski and J. L. Lions. X, 497 pages. 1974.

Vol. 11: Computing Methods in Applied Sciences and Engineering, Part 2. International Symposium, Versailles, December 17–21, 1973. Edited by R. Glowinski and J. L. Lions. X, 434 pages. 1974.

Vol. 12: GFK-GI-GMR Fachtagung Prozessrechner 1974. Karlsruhe, 10.–11. Juni 1974. Herausgegeben von G. Krüger und R. Friehmelt. XI, 620 Seiten. 1974.

Vol. 13: Rechnerstrukturen und Betriebsprogrammierung, Erlangen, 1970. (GI-Gesellschaft für Informatik e.V.) Herausgegeben von W. Händler und P. P. Spies. VII, 333 Seiten. 1974.

Vol. 14: Automata, Languages and Programming – 2nd Colloquium, University of Saarbrücken, July 29–August 2, 1974. Edited by J. Loeckx. VIII, 611 pages. 1974.

Vol. 15: L Systems. Edited by A. Salomaa and G. Rozenberg. VI, 338 pages. 1974.

Vol. 16: Operating Systems, International Symposium, Rocquencourt 1974. Edited by E. Gelenbe and C. Kaiser. VIII, 310 pages. 1974.

Vol. 17: Rechner-Gestützter Unterricht RGU '74, Fachtagung, Hamburg, 12.–14. August 1974, ACU-Arbeitskreis Computer-Unterstützter Unterricht. Herausgegeben im Auftrag der GI von K. Brunnstein, K. Haefner und W. Händler. X, 417 Seiten. 1974.

Vol. 18: K. Jensen and N. E. Wirth, PASCAL – User Manual and Report. VII, 170 pages. Corrected Reprint of the 2nd Edition 1976.

Vol. 19: Programming Symposium. Proceedings 1974. V, 425 pages. 1974.

Vol. 20: J. Engelfriet, Simple Program Schemes and Formal Languages. VII, 254 pages. 1974.

Vol. 21: Compiler Construction, An Advanced Course. Edited by F. L. Bauer and J. Eickel. XIV. 621 pages. 1974.

Vol. 22: Formal Aspects of Cognitive Processes. Proceedings 1972. Edited by T. Storer and D. Winter. V, 214 pages. 1975.

Vol. 23: Programming Methodology. 4th Informatik Symposium, IBM Germany Wildbad, September 25–27, 1974. Edited by C. E. Hackl. VI, 501 pages. 1975.

Vol. 24: Parallel Processing. Proceedings 1974. Edited by T. Feng. VI, 433 pages. 1975.

Vol. 25: Category Theory Applied to Computation and Control. Proceedings 1974. Edited by E. G. Manes. X, 245 pages. 1975.

Vol. 26: GI-4. Jahrestagung, Berlin, 9.–12. Oktober 1974. Herausgegeben im Auftrag der GI von D. Siefkes. IX, 748 Seiten. 1975.

Vol. 27: Optimization Techniques. IFIP Technical Conference. Novosibirsk, July 1–7, 1974. (Series: I.F.I.P. TC7 Optimization Conferences.) Edited by G. I. Marchuk. VIII, 507 pages. 1975.

Vol. 28: Mathematical Foundations of Computer Science. 3rd Symposium at Jadwisin near Warsaw, June 17–22, 1974. Edited by A. Blikle. VII, 484 pages. 1975.

Vol. 29: Interval Mathematics. Procedings 1975. Edited by K. Nickel. VI, 331 pages. 1975.

Vol. 30: Software Engineering. An Advanced Course. Edited by F. L. Bauer. (Formerly published 1973 as Lecture Notes in Economics and Mathematical Systems, Vol. 81) XII, 545 pages. 1975.

Vol. 31: S. H. Fuller, Analysis of Drum and Disk Storage Units. IX, 283 pages. 1975.

Vol. 32: Mathematical Foundations of Computer Science 1975. Proceedings 1975. Edited by J. Bečvář. X, 476 pages. 1975.

Vol. 33: Automata Theory and Formal Languages, Kaiserslautern, May 20–23, 1975. Edited by H. Brakhage on behalf of GI. VIII, 292 Seiten. 1975.

Vol. 34: GI – 5. Jahrestagung, Dortmund 8.–10. Oktober 1975. Herausgegeben im Auftrag der GI von J. Mühlbacher. X, 755 Seiten. 1975.

Vol. 35: W. Everling, Exercises in Computer Systems Analysis. (Formerly published 1972 as Lecture Notes in Economics and Mathematical Systems, Vol. 65) VIII, 184 pages. 1975.

Vol. 36: S. A. Greibach, Theory of Program Structures: Schemes, Semantics, Verification. XV, 364 pages. 1975.

Vol. 37: C. Böhm, λ-Calculus and Computer Science Theory. Proceedings 1975. XII, 370 pages. 1975.

Vol. 38: P. Branquart, J.-P. Cardinael, J. Lewi, J.-P. Delescaille, M. Vanbegin. An Optimized Translation Process and Its Application to ALGOL 68. IX, 334 pages. 1976.

Vol. 39: Data Base Systems. Proceedings 1975. Edited by H. Hasselmeier and W. Spruth. VI, 386 pages. 1976.

Vol. 40: Optimization Techniques. Modeling and Optimization in the Service of Man. Part 1. Proceedings 1975. Edited by J. Cea. XIV, 854 pages. 1976.

Vol. 41: Optimization Techniques. Modeling and Optimization in the Service of Man. Part 2. Proceedings 1975. Edited by J. Cea. XIII, 852 pages. 1976.

Vol. 42: James E. Donahue, Complementary Definitions of Programming Language Semantics. VII, 172 pages. 1976.

Vol. 43: E. Specker und V. Strassen, Komplexität von Entscheidungsproblemen. Ein Seminar. V, 217 Seiten. 1976.

Vol. 44: ECI Conference 1976. Proceedings 1976. Edited by K. Samelson. VIII, 322 pages. 1976.

Vol. 45: Mathematical Foundations of Computer Science 1976. Proceedings 1976. Edited by A. Mazurkiewicz. XI, 601 pages. 1976.

Vol. 46: Language Hierarchies and Interfaces. Edited by F. L. Bauer and K. Samelson. X, 428 pages. 1976.

Vol. 47: Methods of Algorithmic Language Implementation. Edited by A. Ershov and C. H. A. Koster. VIII, 351 pages. 1977.

Vol. 48: Theoretical Computer Science, Darmstadt, March 1977. Edited by H. Tzschach, H. Waldschmidt and H. K.-G. Walter on behalf of GI. VIII, 418 pages. 1977.

Lecture Notes in
Computer Science

Edited by G. Goos and J. Hartmanis

84

Net Theory and Applications

Proceedings of the Advanced Course
on General Net Theory of Processes
and Systems
Hamburg, October 8–19, 1979

Edited by Wilfried Brauer

Springer-Verlag
Berlin Heidelberg New York 1980

Editor

W. Brauer
Fachbereich Informatik, Universität Hamburg
Schlüterstraße 70, 2000 Hamburg 13

Course Directors

Wilfried Brauer
Universität Hamburg

Carl Adam Petri
Gesellschaft für Mathematik und Datenverarbeitung mbH Bonn

Brian Randell
University of Newcastle upon Tyne

AMS Subject Classifications (1979): 68-06, 68B20, 68B10, 68C99, 94A99, 93A99
CR Subject Classifications (1978): 1.1, 4.0, 5.20, 6.0

ISBN 3-540-10001-6 Springer-Verlag Berlin Heidelberg New York
ISBN 0-387-10001-6 Springer-Verlag New York Heidelberg Berlin

PREFACE

Complex organizations and their behaviours cannot be adequately described by classical sequential system models; the problems related to concurrency of actions of different subunits, to conflicts between local and global goals to limitations of resources, to different levels of exactness of descriptions, to different types of interfaces between different types of machines and different types of users, to different types of information flows etc. necessitate new approaches. C.A. Petri realized this already in the early sixties and developed what is now called Petri nets and moreover the general net theory of processes and systems. But only since a few years, since the practical problems in informatics and its applications have made the need for such a theory of non sequential processes and systems more obvious, an evergrowing number of informaticians have joined the field and have contributed to the development of the theory or have applied it to practical problems.

I believe that net theory will become one important part of the theoretical foundations of informatics and, as well, a very useful engineering tool for many parts of informatics and its applications. But up to now Petri net theory is not known widely and well enough in the community of informaticians. And at least until the beginning of the Advanced Course on General Net Theory of Processes and Systems even within the relatively small group of net theorists and net users communication was not too good. During the course we learned that net theory is much more diverse with respect to topics, models, notions and notations as well as with respect to the way it is pursued and developed than it was known to anyone before.

We had much more applications for participation then we could accept. Finally there were 114 participants (including lecturers) from 17 countries. They came from universities and research centres, from computer industry and from users. A great need for more contacts, more information was felt. Thus, during the course the special interest group "Petri Nets and Related System Models" of the Gesellschaft für Informatik (GI) decided to change its "Rundbrief" into a newsletter (publication language English) which will now serve as an international forum for the quick exchange of informations on the further development of the field (For information write to H.-J.Genrich). Already in the preparation phase of the course(in particular in a one week preparatory seminar) we (the lecturers and the course directors) paid great attention to meet, among others, the following goals

- to be as comprehensive as possible,
- to find a consistent and widely adopted terminology and notation,
- to present coherent, non-redundant course material.

Nevertheless the actual experience during the course lead to many improvements of the material which is now presented in these proceedings.

The course was the first occasion to present net theory and its applications to a wider public and this volume is the first and rather comprehensive publication on that topic.

One part of the course material is not included into this book, but it is available from GMD:

A Bibliography of Net Theory
by E. Pless and H. Plünnecke

It comprises already almost 100 pages and will be updated constantly.

There was one extra invited talk, given by Dr. G. Plotkin, Department of Artificial Intelligence, University of Edinburgh, on "Petri Nets and Denotational Semantics" whereG. Plotkin gave a short introduction to denotational semantics and discussed the following topics:

- nets as syntax
- nets as semantic values (computations)
- nets as domains (types of computations).

The main points of this lecture are contained in

Nielsen, M.; Plotkin, G.; Winskel, G.: Petri Nets, Event Structures and Domains

in: G. Kahn (ed.) Semantics of Concurrent Computation, LNCS Vol. 70, Springer-Verlag, Berlin 1979, pp 266-284.

At the third day of the course, the Department of Informatics of the University of Hamburg awarded the degree of honorary doctor of sciences to one of the lecturers - to Konrad Zuse, who designed and constructed the first fully functioning program-controlled digital computer, who developed already in 1945 a very high level algorithmic language, the "Plankalkül", and who still contributes to the development of informatics and its applications. The lectures given at the festive colloquium on that occasion and some more informations on Zuses work will be published as a special monograph by the Springer-Verlag.

I very much hope that this course and these proceedings contribute to an intensification of research on non-sequential processes and systems and to a wider use of net theory.

Hamburg, February 1980

Wilfried Brauer

ACKNOWLEDGMENTS

The Advanced Course on General Net Theory of Processes and Systems was held under the auspices of and financed by the Commission of the European Communities and the Minister for Research and Technology of the Federal Republic of Germany.

The course was organized by the Department of Informatics of the University of Hamburg in cooperation with the Institute for Information Systems Research of the Gesellschaft für Mathematik und Datenverarbeitung m.b.H. Bonn (GMD).

But the course would not have taken place and would not have been so successful if not quite a number of other institutions and of persons had supported the organisers in many ways or had worked with enthusiasm,ardour and perseverance for the course.

In the name of the course participants I would like to thank them all particularly - but I can only name a few of them here:

The two other Course Directors: C. A. Petri, B. Randell

The lecturers: E. Best, H.-J. Genrich, C. Girault, M. Jantzen, K. Lautenbach, J. D. Noe, H. Oberquelle, S. S. Patil, C. A. Petri, G. Plotkin, G. Roucairol, R. M. Shapiro, J. Sifakis, P. S. Thiagarajan, R. Valk, K. Zuse

Those who were mainly involved in the organization and whom I personally would like to give my sincere thanks:

Dipl.-Inform. G. Friesland, chairman of the organization committee in Hamburg who was in charge of all organizational aspects of the planning, preparation and running of the course and often had to act as a substitute of the Course Directors.

Dr. H. Fuß, GMD, who was in charge of the organisation of the preparatory seminar in April 1979 in the GMD and of the printing of the course material which was done by GMD.

Mrs. G. Mercker, head of the administration of the Department of Informatics of the University of Hamburg, who was responsible for all administrative, especially all financial affairs.

Dipl.-Kfm. C.-H. Schulz, who was as a part-time employee my general secretary and executive and had to do almost everything since all the others involved could work for the course only in their spare time.

CONTENTS

INTRODUCTION TO GENERAL NET THEORY

C.A. Petri
GMD Bonn

The aim of this course is to present a comprehensive framework which provides a firm formal basis for the numerous recent efforts to adapt the highly specialized theory of "transition nets" originated in 1960 to a wide range of applications.

Results of typical efforts of this kind will be presented during this course, especially from the area of computer science. Along with these presentations, a thorough introduction to the concepts and to the mathematical tools of a more general theory of nets will be given, in order to enable participants and readers to make effective use of the theory in existing and possible further applications, and also to view the diverse examples before a common background and in a single context.

By far the greatest part of current literature on nets [1] refers to "special net theory", as we shall call the above-mentioned restricted theory which is concerned with the flow of countable resources through nets, that is, through structures which resemble graphs, in which the various flows are on the one hand coordinated (e.g. synchronized) and on the other hand branched and merged. The interplay between synchronization and branching/merging may be graphically represented in a way which is easily understood by the non-specialist, and it permits numerical treatment of bottleneck- and deadlock problems and also of some questions about safety of operation and about conflict.

An informal but typical example for this stage of theory is given in Fig.1. It describes (part of) an arrangement as might be encountered in industrial production :

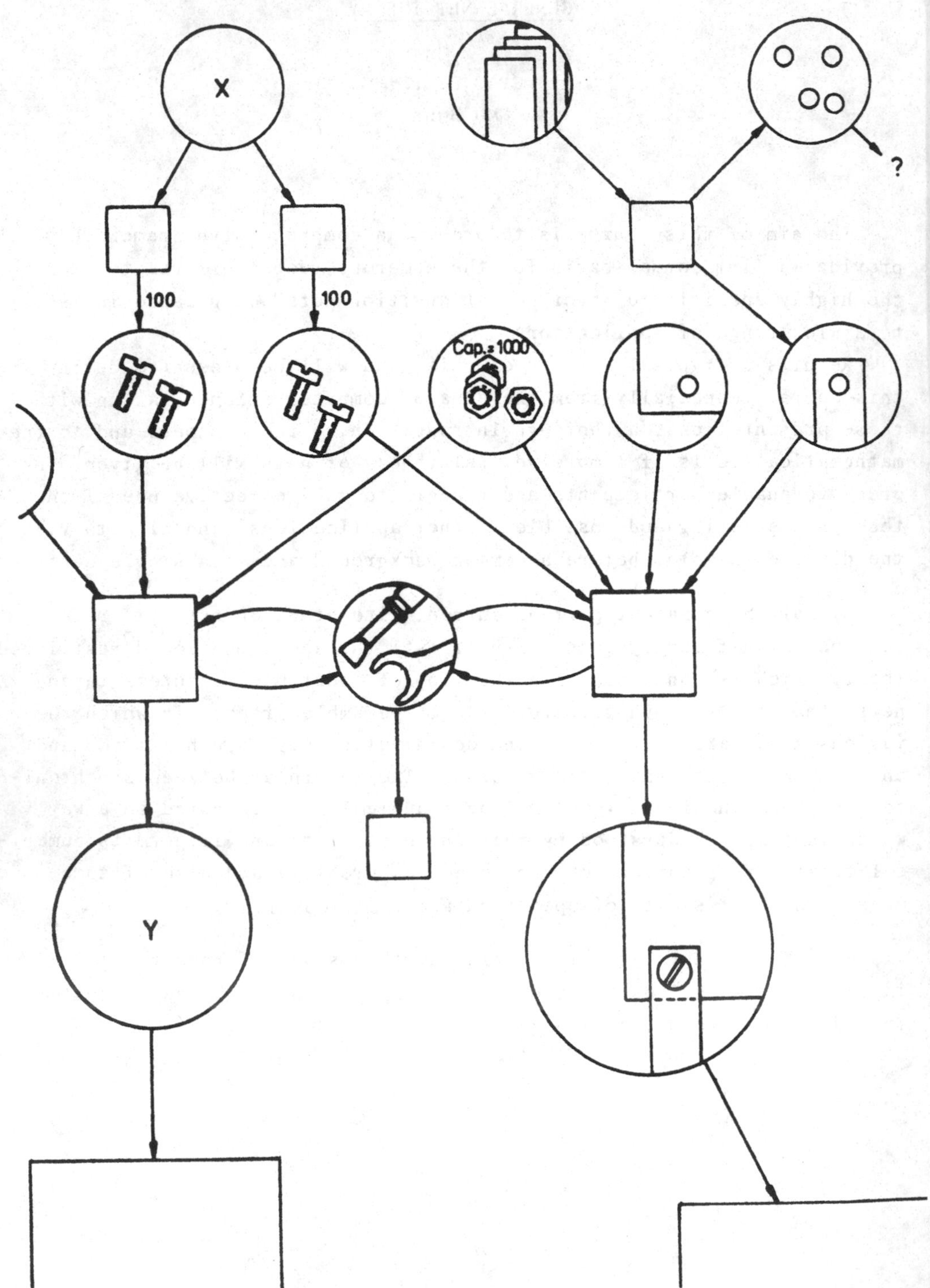

Fig. 1 : A production schema

The rectangular □ symbols denote production activities such as transport, assembly or disassembly (example: punching); the circular ○ symbols denote places at which resources may be temporarily stored. The arrows ⟶ denote the directed relation of immediate accessibility; it is important to explain that they do not denote channels through which resources can flow; they are not assumed to have any material physical existence.

All □ ○ ⟶ symbols may carry inscriptions of a pictorial kind or taken from some formal or natural language. Some inscriptions relate the schema to real-world circumstances, others indicate the number of resources available at a place in an assumed case, or the number or resources needed in each instance of a certain activity, still others may indicate common features of distinct items or a detailed specification of an item.

In this way, <u>special net theory</u> treats a <u>single</u> net and the flow phenomena in this net, for each instance of application. Its practical limitations lie in the exclusive treatment of flow problems at a very low and detailed level. It is very difficult to even represent a net with thousands or millions of elements without making mistakes; it is practically impossible to explore the unknown behaviour of a system described in this way, or to verify all its intended behavioural characteristics by simulating and evaluating all processes which can occur in the system. Even with nets of less than 16 elements, one may have to give up understanding their workings by hand simulation. Nevertheless, the mere attempt to do so gives a basic understanding of the intricacies of concurrency and of local phenomena such as conflict and confusion. -

The development of <u>general net theory</u> was started in 1970 with the aim to overcome the limitations just mentioned. General net theory is not concerned with single nets; rather, the entities under consideration are relations between nets, operations and functions on the class of nets, transformations of nets, and most notably "net morphisms". <u>Net morphisms</u> are functions from one net into another which respect connectivity and orientation. They are of special interest in reasoning about systems and processes if they preserve other net properties as well, or if they interconnect very large and very small nets.

The following example is, at first sight, utterly trivial (Fig.2) :

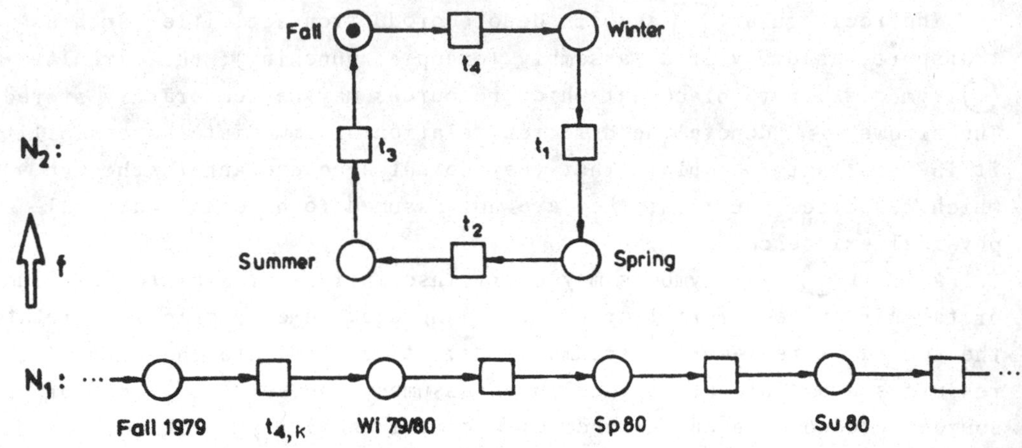

Fig. 2 : The change of seasons

The function f , a net morphism, maps the "very large" (infinite?) net of occurrences of seasons onto a "small" net which can be understood at a glance : $f : N_1 \longrightarrow N_2$.

Let us call the net elements denoted by ◯ symbols "state elements" or S-elements and those denoted by □ symbols "transition elements" or T-elements .

Several conceptual and formal questions arise here, in spite of the apparent simplicity of the example :

1. The net N_1 (and therefore f) is not fully specified. We shall have to devise a means for recursive definition of nets; not restricted to this example, of course.
2. If N_1 is a chain of infinite length, it is just a mathematical construct which can be derived by "unfolding" the net N_2 , and is not an object of our experience. If we insist upon its reality, it means that we insist upon an eternal existence of the system N_2 , without beginning and without end.
3. If N_1 is to be a finite chain, we have to ask whether it begins resp. ends with an S-element or a T-element. (If N_1 is to be subjected to the same rules as the "condition-event-system" N_2 , its begin and end must consist of S-elements). The length of the chain then is either a matter of observation, or it expresses our scope of concern, as in the given example.
4. A typical occasion to extend our scope of concern arises when we shift our attention from the elements of a set X to sets of such ele-

ments, i.e. to the subsets of X . In doing so, we move to a different conceptual level, and the number of objects to be distinguished rises from n to 2^n . Therefore, if we define as "natural orders of magnitude" G_o , G_1 , ... G_n ... by

$G_o := G(o) := O$; $G_{n+1} := G(n+1) := 2^{G(n)}$; $g := G^{-1}$

we have suitable milestones to describe one main purpose of net morphisms : to decrease or increase the scope of concern by an order of magnitude.

This is not obvious or compelling in the example of Fig.2; but $G_5 = 65536$ is surely a reasonable scope of concern for N_1 , and $G_4 = 16$ for N_2. (In practice, there has never yet been occasion to use G_9).

5. The function f - once it is defined, along with N_2 - shall be called a <u>process</u> which can occur in the <u>system</u> N_2 . N_1 is the <u>process domain</u> (of f); note that f may be defined by suitable inscriptions to the elements of N_1 , but a chain without such inscriptions shall not be called a process; rather, it is the domain structure of many quite different processes.
6. Conditions such as "summer", "winter" etc. certainly have a <u>duration</u>, commonly speaking. What about the <u>changes</u> (transitions) between conditions? Do they also have duration? Depending on educational background, many different incompatible answers are given :

   a. All changes have a non-zero duration
   b. Changes take up all time
   c. All changes have zero duration
   d. All changes are states of uncertainty about the holding of conditions
   e. The concept of duration is not applicable to changes.

   Each of these opinions has been extensively used and defended, often with ideological vehemence. Net theory does not adopt one of these opinions a priori, but seeks to reconcile them by showing how they are interconnected and how a correct and useful part is contained in each.
7. The discussion of duration of changes is not mere hairsplitting, since its outcome <u>decides</u> the question how the apparatus of logic is to be applied to propositions of changing truth value; it <u>determines our logic of change</u> in this sense. Examples : If "winter" is recognized as a <u>condition</u> (propos. of changing truth value), does it comprise the transitions into winter and out of winter? We have indicated by the notation in Fig.2 that we choose to <u>define</u> the answer to be "no" : we want to talk of transitions as of enti-

ties in their own right, not just as of relations between conditions. This is a characteristic of the approach of net theory. But then the question arises : is "not-winter" also a condition in the system? If so, does "not-winter" comprise all four transitions t_1 - t_4 , or just t_2 and t_3 , or no transitions at all? Is there a condition "winter or spring", "winter or summer", "winter and spring"? Are we justified in asserting that, within our scope of concern, it is "winter or spring or summer or fall" at all times?

Consistent answers to all of these questions, which have to be left open at this stage, will appear from a theory of concurrency, but not in terms of time-points and durations, which are not well defined concepts in the operational sense.

Net theory will treat times as clock readings, and will treat clocks on an equal footing with other system components : subject to malfunction and destruction, serving a purpose and requiring maintenance.

This non-idealizing attitude is also a main concern in the development of net theory : most assuredly for the sake of sound applications and not for philosophical reasons.

Let us sum up here all of the main concerns of general net theory, by listing the areas of problems to the solution of which this theory seeks to contribute :

A1	Interconnection between many conceptual "levels"
A2	Concurrency (partial independence of occurrences)
A3	Limitation of (all) resources
A4	Finding the most relevant concepts on each level
A5	Respecting imprecision of measurement, ubiquity of noise
A6	Bridging the gap between "discrete" and "continuous" models

A1 will be topic of a separate section. The tool offered in this problem area is the category of nets, comprising all net morphisms.

A2 will also need a separate section. Knowledge of the properties of concurrency is indispensable when constructing systems without central control or global observability of all details. The following example may illustrate the point. It shows an imperfect execution of a plan to extinguish a fire by carrying water from a remote source via a bucket chain involving a number of people, even the general manager (since no central control is necessary for the execution of the plan) and the otherwise observing and theorizing scientist (no observation promotes the execution of the plan, under the given circumstances).

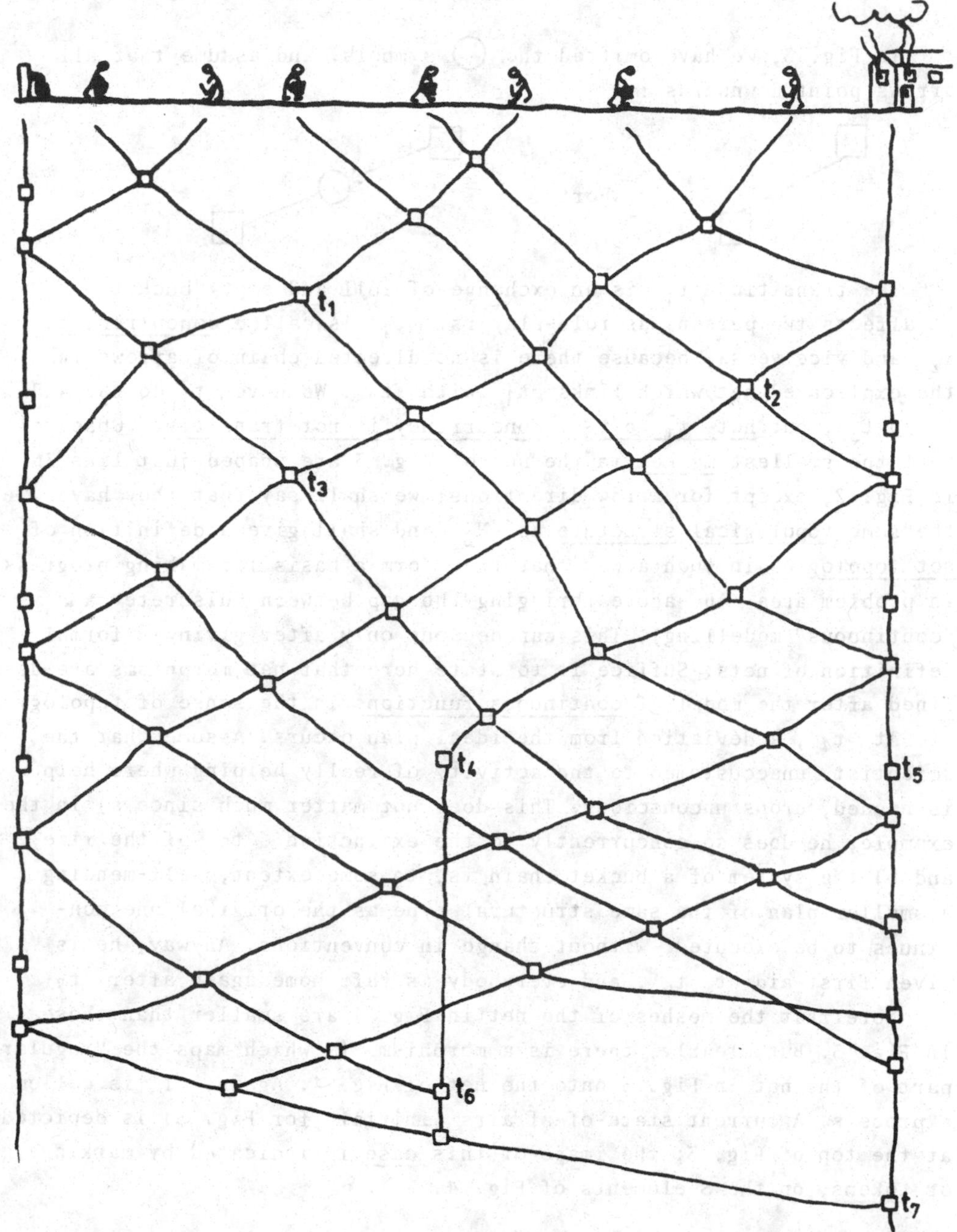

Fig. 3 : Partial history of execution of a plan

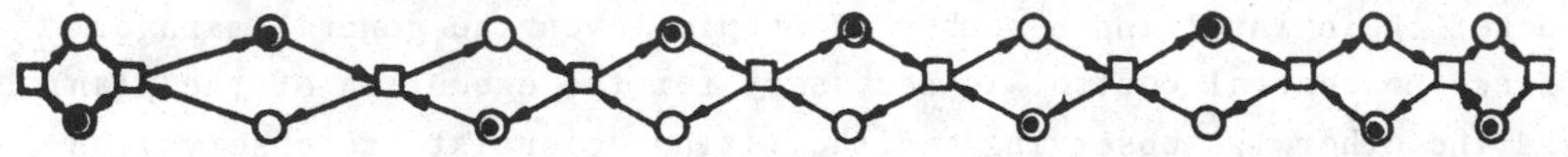

Fig. 4 : The plan of which Fig. 3 is an imperfect execution

In Fig. 3, we have omitted the ○ symbols, and assume that all arrows point downwards :

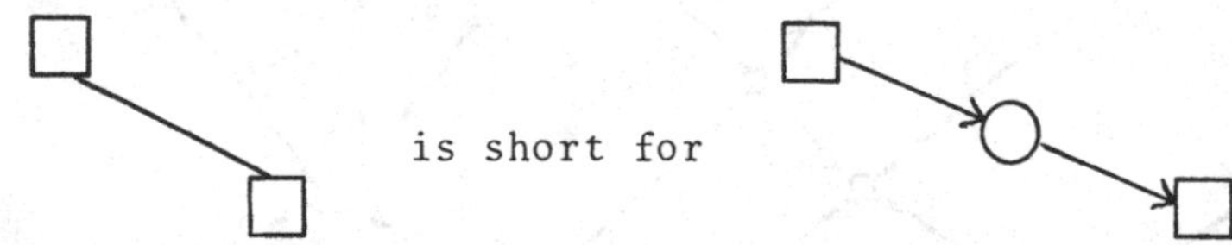

The transition t_1 is an exchange of full and empty bucket; it affects two persons as role-players. t_1 is called concurrent to t_2 and vice versa, because there is no directed chain of arrows in the explicated net which links t_1 with t_2 . We have t_1 co t_2 and t_2 co t_3 , but not t_1 co t_3 . Concurrency is not transitive. Observe that the smallest meshes in the net of Fig. 3 are shaped just like N_2 in Fig. 2, except for arrow directions; we shall say that they have the same topological structure as N_2 and shall give a definition of net topologies in such a way that they form a basis for making progress in problem area A6 above (bridging the gap between "discrete" and "continuous" modelling). This can be done only after giving a formal definition of nets. Suffice it to state here that net morphisms are defined after the model of continuous functions in the sense of topology.

At t_4 , a deviation from the ideal plan occurs. Assume that the scientist, unaccustomed to the activity of really helping where help is needed, drops unconscious. This does not matter much since a) in the example, he does so concurrently to the extinction t_5 of the fire, and b) the system of a bucket chain is, to some extent, self-mending : a smaller plan of the same structural type as the original one continues to be executed, without change in conventions. Anyway, he is given first-aid at t_6 , and everybody is safe home again after t_7 .

Note that the meshes of the net in Fig. 4 are smaller than those in Fig. 3. But clearly, there is a morphism f which maps the "regular" part of the net in Fig. 3 onto the net of Fig. 4. Again, f is called a process. A current state-of-affairs (initial, for Fig. 3) is depicted at the top of Fig. 3; the image of this case is indicated by markings, or tokens, on the S-elements of Fig. 4. -

The fact that all <u>resources are limited</u> should be recognized by every realistic theory of systems and processes (<u>A3</u>). This goes without saying, and becomes tautological if we define "resources" as those entities which can, by being scarce in a given situation, impede the reaching of a goal. Energy, materials, manpower are obviously resources. Time and space are also often referred to as resources, and rightly so, though not in a formal sense. Net theory seeks to go a step further by taking the "resource-type" character of space-time as fundamental and constitutive for the space-time concept. Final results of this approach do not yet exist, but the spirit of the approach should be kept in mind when translating classical system descriptions into net-theoretical ones. It should not be regarded as a defect of net theory that some geometrical and kinematic concepts are not readily expressed in terms of nets.

Rather, <u>information</u> will be the resource of main interest in net theory, because its usage is more complex and much more general than the usage of other resources; indeed, information usage is a prerequisite of usage of other resources, but little is known about it. We do have e.g. hydrodynamics and electrodynamics in a satisfactory degree of perfection, but no remotely comparable "information dynamics". To indicate the approach of net theory in this respect, we state here that we shall treat (define) <u>information as that kind of resource which is used to resolve conflicts</u>. We shall introduce formally an "axiom of local determinacy"; to the extent this axiom is valid in the world we live in, we are able to assert that "information is always somewhere but never everywhere" as a basic relation between information and space-time.

It is a point of special importance that the <u>absence</u> of certain entities or phenomena (in a given context) is also to be treated as a resource. This point has first been recognized in full depth by Anatol HOLT. Obvious examples are the absence of toxic substances in a biological context; absence of noise for ideal transmission of messages; also, the whiteness of paper (absence of previous printing) makes such paper a resource beyond the availability of paper material. But many resources of this kind are hidden to the untrained mind and do not yet have a name. E.g. several different resource types which fall under the heading "omission of an activity" have to be distinguished because they have different properties. -

Relative to a given goal, some resources appear to be unlimited in supply. In classical logic, in pure mathematics and in part of computation theory, the supply of "white paper" and of time is (implicitly) taken to be unbounded; from the standpoint we take in net theory, this means precisely that shortages of these resources are outside the scope of concern of those scientific activities, in the sense we have used when discussing Fig. 2. Note that in computation theory, the scope of concern has been narrowed down in this way just in order to detect the limitations of another "resource" : computability. Once this goal has been achieved, the proper thing to do is to shift or to widen again the scope of concern. (Again, the development of computation theory is an example that this is being done).

A final remark about resources : It is not true that limitation of resources is just a fact to be deplored. In everyday-experience as well as in net theory, we find many examples that scarcity of resources may have an advantage. Its impact on the choice of more realistic goals is only a superficial, though important, aspect; the reader can easily find more specific examples. Abstractly speaking, the artificial well-structured limitation of resources is one of the main tools to establish an organization - possibly the only one. -

Re A4 : Finding the most relevant and appropriate concepts on each level of process or system description, is a task which cannot be readily explained without doing it. We use the word "level" in an informal sense only. We recognize that the notion of an objective arrangement of lower and higher levels of thinking into a series is not a sound one, but is sometimes helpful in teaching.

In this spirit, Fig. 5 should be regarded as intuitive and somewhat arbitrary, except that we shall provide a sequence of formal constructions from level 0 up to level 3 and beyond. These constructions can serve, in a general way, as a schema for stepping up to "higher" levels, and for analysing and defining (vague) higher-level concepts in terms of lower-level concepts.

We regard a concept of some level as appropriate if it is related in an understandable and precise way to the concepts of neighboring levels. Therefore, a concept can be called "appropriate" only relative to the chosen structuring of levels.

Levels 4 to n-2 refer to computer science matters, level n-1 to administrative and business matters where organizations and procedures are fairly well defined, at least for the modest purpose of mere description.

The concepts of channel, agency, role and activity named at this level have been chosen in such a way that it becomes possible to go far beyond description on this level. Again, this can be done only by recognition of at least one additional level n .

Level number:	Typical concepts:	
n:	Interests (of groups, individuals...)	Restrictions (natural, legal, economic...)
n-1:	Channels (for resources, messages...)	Agencies (institutions, offices...)
	Roles (of people, artefacts...)	Activities (belonging to each role)
n-2:	Global reliability	Performance
n-3:	Data bases	Computer architectures
. . . .	. . .	
	Protocols	Operating systems
	Files	Tasks
	Records	Statements
	Machine words	Machine instructions
. . .	if, and, assignment, identifier, value ...	
4:	NAND-gates , delays , clocks ... transistors , diodes , oscillators ...	
3:	"Stations","flux" ; (as used in low level information flow graphs)	"Transfers","influence"
2:	Conditions Synchrony (as used in condition-event systems and transition nets)	Transitions "Enlogy"
1:	Occurrences and their partial order in time (Occurrence nets)	
0:	Concurrency structures ("ropes")	

(Levels n-2 to 4: Computer Science)

Fig. 5 : A sequence of conceptual levels concerning computer science, its foundations and certain applications

The fact that precision and explicitness are not always welcome on level n (with regard to interests, intentions, recognition of restrictions) puts a definite limit to useful formalization on level n-1 and, at closer inspection, on all lower levels. For the rest, it can observed in Fig. 5 that with increasing level number, our classical formal tools become less and less useful or successfully applicable.

While on the subject of concepts and formalization, we cannot proceed without a bit of formalism : the concepts named in Fig. 5 have been chosen, wherever possible, such that they can be related to the carrier sets (S) and [T] of a net.

A net can be defined in many structurally equivalent ways (see the Dictionary in these proceedings). We chose the one which is used most in the literature. A triple (S,T;F) will be called a net, iff S and T are disjoint nonempty sets with a relation F between them such that every element of S and T occurs in the relation F :

Net (S, T; F) :$\Leftrightarrow$	
1.	$S \cap T = \emptyset$
2.	$S \cup T \neq \emptyset$
3.	$F \subseteq (S \times T) \cup (T \times S)$
4.	$\mathrm{dom}(F) \cup \mathrm{cod}(F) = S \cup T$

Fig. 6 : The (S,T;F)-form of a net

Note that it follows from Fig. 6 that both S and T are non-empty, that F is non-empty, and that no element of S or T is isolated in terms of F .

Examples : Every directed multigraph is a net (S,T;F) = (Arcs, Vertices; Incidence-relation) iff it has no isolated vertices.

$(S,T;F) = (\mathbb{R},I;F)$ is a net where $\mathbb{R}$ is the set of real numbers, I the set of finite connected open intervals over $\mathbb{R}$, and

$$(r,i) \in F \;:\Leftrightarrow\; r \in \mathbb{R} \wedge i \in I \wedge \bigvee r' \in \mathbb{R} : i = \{x \mid r < x < r'\}$$
$$(i,r) \in F \;:\Leftrightarrow\; i \in I \wedge r \in \mathbb{R} \wedge \bigvee r' \in \mathbb{R} : i = \{x \mid r' < x < r\}$$

A non-example : A net is not a bipartite graph because the triple (S,T;F) is ordered : S and T play different roles. If (S,T;F) is a net then (T,S;F) is also a net, but a different one, and not necessarily isomorphic to (S,T,F) , as with the nets

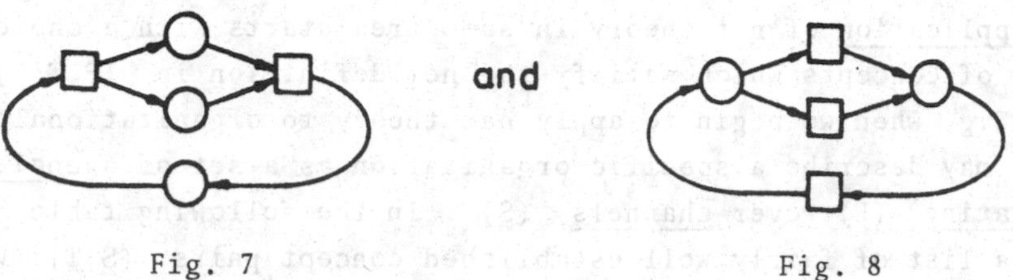

Fig. 7 Fig. 8

which are called duals of each other; whereas the bipartite graph (F, $\{S, T\}$; incidence-relation) is the same for both nets.

The reason we have to insist that nets are not structurally equivalent to bipartite graphs is this : Once we have chosen to associate S-elements with the concept of "state" and T-elements with the concept of "transition" as in our first example (Fig. 1), we have no longer a choice how to associate other suitable pairs of mutually "dual" concepts with S and T ; e.g. chemical substances (elements or compounds) and chemical reactions can be consistently associated with S and T in this order. When we form new pairs of concepts such as "channel" and "agency" (for analysing organisatorial problems), the way to classify them under S resp. T carries an essential part of meaning and is a prerequisite for establishing the conceptual interconnection between neighboring levels within one science, and also for the transfer of structural knowledge between different sciences.

Net theory is mainly concerned with computers and information handling, but has drawn many ideas about structure and organization from other areas, mainly from areas where computers are applied: Fig. 9. Some feedback to those areas has occurred (see [1] and these proceedings); much more of this interdisciplinary transfer is under investigation.

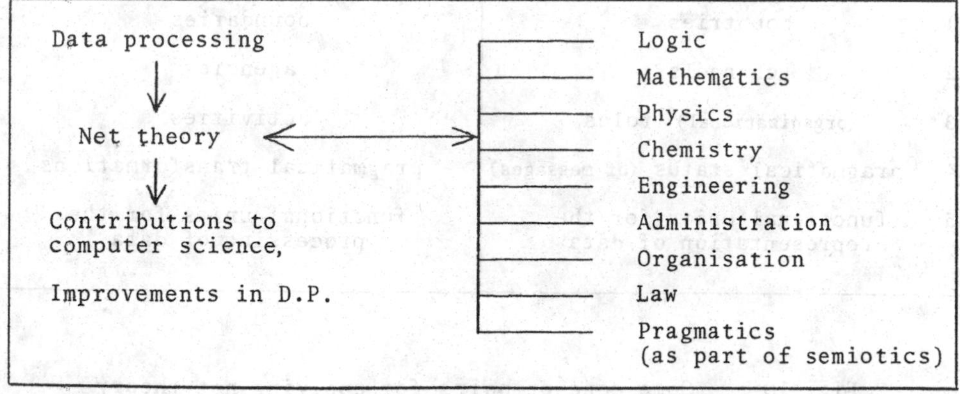

Fig. 9 : Evidenced interdisciplinary connections of net theory

An application of net theory in some area starts with a choice of a triple of concepts which satisfy the net definition in (S,T;F) form, Fig. 6. E.g. when we begin to apply net theory to organizational problems, we may describe a specific organization as a set of agencies (T) communicating (F) over channels (S). In the following table Fig. 10, we give a list of fairly well established concept pairs (S,T) which are suitable for this purpose. The meaning of the corresponding relation F is not given in the list. It is easy to find when the meaning of S and T is understood, but often difficult to verbalize concisely.

	S	T
o	state-elements	transition-elements
1	states	transitions
2	conditions; "places"	events
3	conditions	facts
4	open singletons	closed singletons
5	structural types	constructions
6	log. statements	dependencies, deductions, proofs
7	chem. substances	chem. reactions
8	languages	translators
9	stations (in information flow nets)	transfers
1o	product types	production activities
11	countries	boundaries
12	channels	agencies
13	(organizational) roles	activities
14	pragmatical status (of messages)	pragmatical transformations
15	functional units for the representation of data	functional units for the processing of data

Fig. 10 : Some concept pairs for applying net theory

The entries in the list Fig. 10 are in arbitrary order, numbered for reference only. They are not intended to show that net theory has many and diverse applications : a comparable list for graph theory might have hundreds of entries. Rather, all entries of concepts are closely interrelated by net theory : e.g. knowledge about condition-event-nets yields definite useful rules for the analysis of channel-agency nets. Another example : the existence of a "1-mesh"

as a subnet of a given net means

in chemistry : s is a catalyst in catalytic reaction t
in logic : t is a tautology containing „s ⇒ s"
in mathematics : t is a theorem about the structure class s
in condition-event-systems: s or t is not atomic
in graph theory: a selfloop exists at vertex t
in pragmatics : the change in pragmatical status of messages in s by t is neglected. (t might be a READ or COPY operation)

So we can learn about pragmatics by studying the theory of catalytic reactions, learn about catalytic reactions by studying the logic of change, etc. From some connections we cannot learn much, but in principle always something.

The concept pair "data/processing" is not in the list because it has many facets. Some of these facets are subsumed in the entries 2, 3, 5, 6, 8, 9, 10, 12, 15, and - most importantly - 14.

To assign a pragmatical status to each instantiation of a piece of "data" is useful and appears to be necessary to establish a strict bond between messages and purposes. This bond is well acknowledged and respected e.g. in banking and in the handling of "sensitive" data, but not in a formal sense. A pragmatic status can be described as a place where messages can reside; the input and output transitions denote the activities by which a message can enter resp. leave that place. In genaral, such activities do not consist in a mere transport of one message from its pragmatic status into a new one; rather, they consist in transforming a bundle of messages belonging to one another into a new bundle. E.g. an order is not transported correctly from the status "to be executed" to the status "executed" without doing something else in that same act. The simplest feature immediately expressed in a pragmatic net is accessibility, through the relation F . Accessibility can mean a legal right to access, or the physical possibility of access. The next step for developing a useful formal calculus for pragmatics is, to express legal rights in terms of physical possibilities. This can be done by employing the formalism of "multiple enlogic structure" through the distinction of legal cases, illegal cases and non-cases. We shall not follow this up here.

A5 and A6, the problem areas at the end of our list, are closely connected. In a good modelling technique, imprecision of measurement should be respected from the beginning. Concerning net theory, we take the standpoint that this imprecision is not only a consequence of our poor abilities to distinguish by direct or indirect observation, but that it is inherent in the nature of the measuring process itself and in our relation to the objects we measure. We regard measurement processes not as basic to the theory and not as lying outside of the theory, but rather as complicated processes of information flow, influenced by noise, i.e. by unaccounted-for information; and we enquire into the combinatorial structure of these processes. Also, we have reason to propose, as a result of this enquiry, a new type of measuring scales [2] which has a bearing on the treatment of measurement results.

We shall respect the presence of noise to the greatest possible extent : all information flow nets (level 3 in Fig. 5) will be constructed exclusively from "noisy channels" for transmission of bits. The concept of "noisy channel" can be explicated by a net morphism on level 2 (of Fig. 5) in terms of conditions and events, as an injection of intended transmission into physically possible (noisy) transmission :

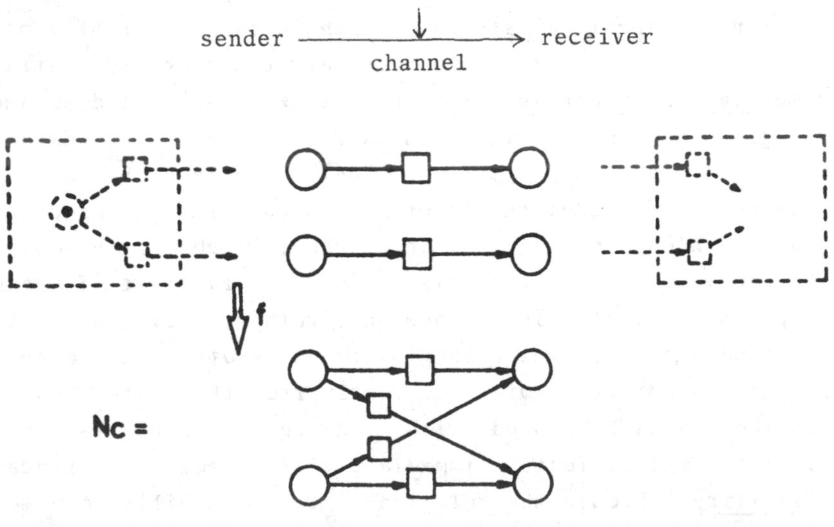

Fig. 11 : Explication of "noisy channel"

All level 3 nets will be composed (by quotient formation) out of level 2 nets of the structure of Nc (in Fig. 11); they are operationally equivalent with the class of all distributed, self-synchronizing binary switching networks with memory. Nc can also be described as a 4-mesh with the same topology as the cycle of seasons (Fig. 2) :

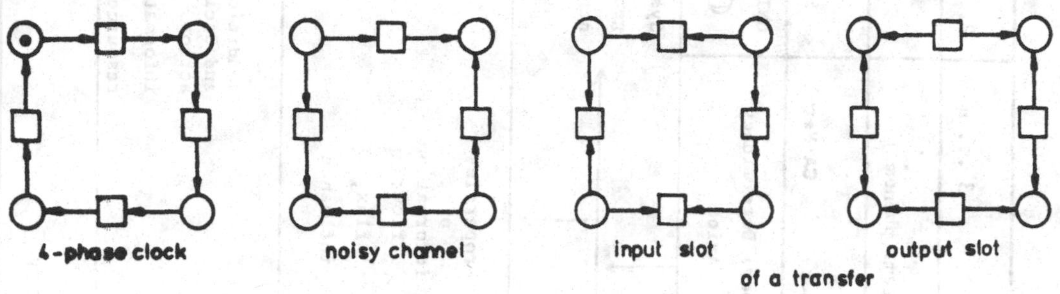

Fig. 12 : Meshes for composing level-3 nets

Slots will be explained elsewhere in these proceedings.

Re A6 : As a final problem area for net theory we mention the striving to bridge the gap between so-called discrete and continuous types of modelling (Fig. 13).

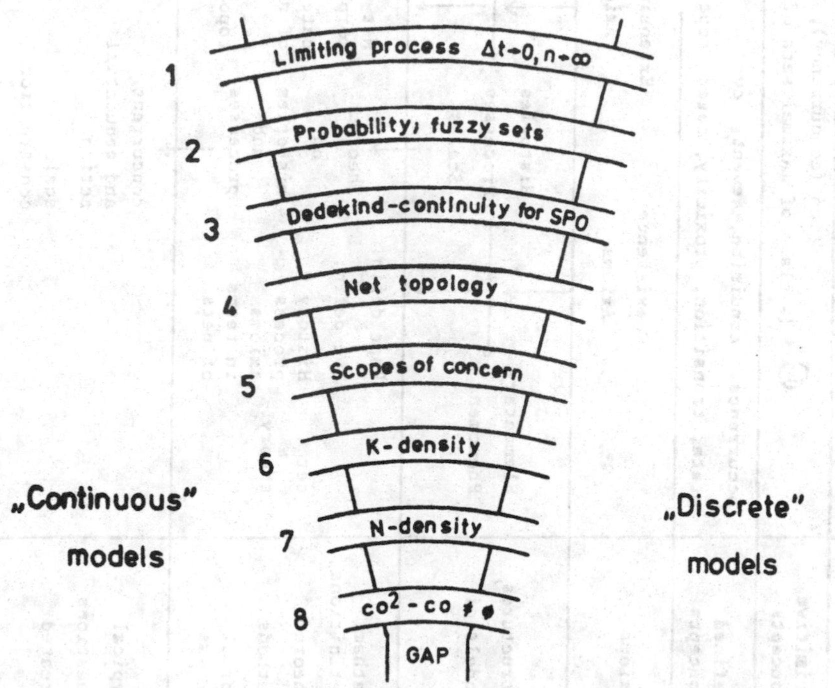

Fig. 13 : Bridges between continuous and discrete models

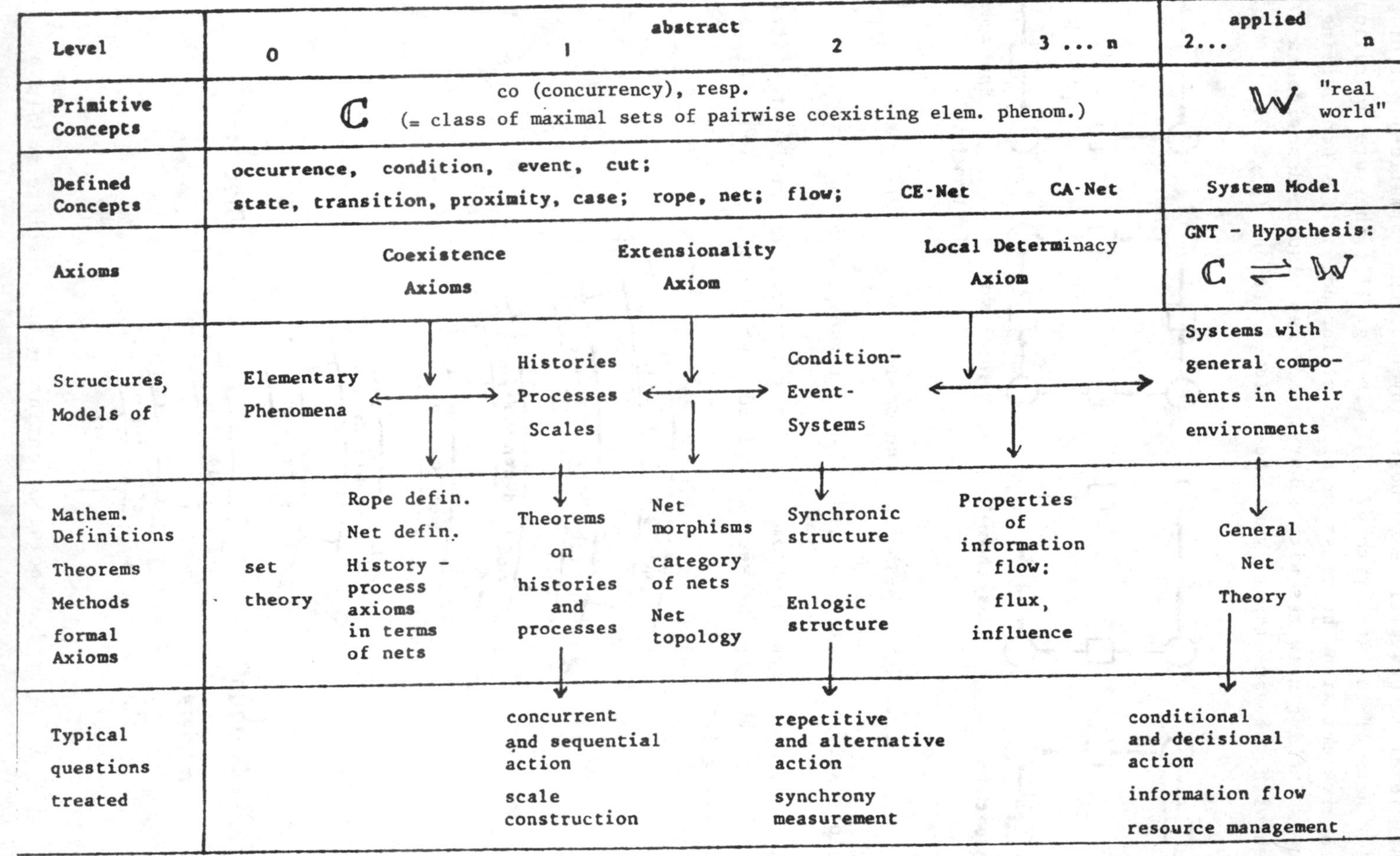

Fig. 14 : Outline of General Net Theory

Bridges 1 and 2 are the well-known classical ones. They span the gap where it appears widest, so they are difficult to cross. Net theory has, up to now, built six additional bridges 3 - 8. It remains to be seen how much load they can carry. They are strict formal constructs, presented here in an informal way. Giving up the assumption that concurrency is transitive when a process description is sufficiently detailed (bridge 8) takes a single inconspicuous formal step, and is a matter of course in relativity theory. Yet it appears to be a most difficult step to many workers in other fields, and is often violently attacked. We shall content ourselves, in this course, with pointing out the formal consequences of this step, to the extent that they seem important for past and future applications.

In conclusion, we give without further explanation the present status of the conceptual framework for the development of general net theory : Fig. 14. It might serve to guide the reader through the formal aspects of the material presented in this course; it should be revisited after taking notice of this material.

The aim of this introduction has been to sketch in broad strokes the landscape of net theory. It reflects the perspective with which the author wishes to view this theory and its applications. In the body of the introduction, results have been claimed but the claims have not been substantiated. Concepts have been named but they have not been sufficiently explained. These matters will be attended to in the course material proper. But beyond this, this introduction may have raised a mixture of high hopes and grave doubts in the mind of the reader. He should be aware that a long hard road with many bends and pitfalls will have to be traversed before these hopes can be fulfilled and the doubts dispelled. Our introduction is to be viewed as an invitation to the reader to join in the undertaking of this difficult journey.

References

[1] Pless, E. and Plünnecke, H.: A Bibliography of Net Theory. First edition 31. August 1979 ISF-Report 79.04 Selbstverlag GMD, 1979

Available at this course, or from the authors, GMD, Postfach 1240, D-5205 St Augustin

[2] Petri, C.A.: Modelling as a Communication Discipline. in: Measuring and Evaluating Computer Systems. Ed.: H.Beilner and E.Gelenbe. North Holland Publishing Company, 1977

Those informatics students in Hamburg who worked part-time for the course, in particular B. Heinemann who not only acted as the main assistant to the organizers, Friesland and Schulz, but was also one of the tutors of the working groups formed by the course participants, and was, moreover, our course photographer.

We were particularly thankful to the Department of Mathematics of the University of Hamburg which allowed us to use its new building with all its facilities even during the first week of the semester.
special thanks are due to
- the President of the University of Hamburg and the university administration,
- the Senator for Science and Research of the State of Hamburg,
- the board of directors and the administration of the GMD.

Several participants, in particular some from non-EC countries, would not have been able to come and several items on the course program which contributed considerably to the well-being of the participants would not have occured if we had not got generous grants from
Arthur Andersen & Co. G.m.b.H., Hamburg
Axel Springer-Verlag, Hamburg
Burroughs G.m.b.H., Eschborn/Taunus
Control Data G.m.b.H., Frankfurt/Main
Digital Equipment, Hamburg
Eppendorfer Gerätebau, Netheler & Hinz G.m.b.H., Hamburg
Gesellschaft für Mathematik und Datenverarbeitung m.b.H., Bonn
IBM Deutschland G.m.b.H., Stuttgart
Philips G.m.b.H. Forschungslaboratorium, Hamburg
Siemens Aktiengesellschaft, München
Universität Hamburg

Last but not least, many thanks to the Springer-Verlag for publishing these proceedings in the LNCS series.

Wilfried Brauer

ELEMENTS OF GENERAL NET THEORY

H.J. Genrich, K. Lautenbach, P.S. Thiagarajan
Institut für Informationssystemforschung (ISF)
Gesellschaft für Mathematik und Datenverarbeitung
Schloss Birlinghoven, D-5205 St.Augustin 1

Abstract

Some of the main features of a theory of systems in which the concept of concurrency plays a central role are presented. This theory is founded upon a systems model called condition/event-systems (CE-systems).

In order to enrich the language concerning CE-systems, three types of completions are carried out. Completion w.r.t. information flow enables us to explicate conflict resolution and brings the notion of information into the theory. T-completion and S-completion lead to a systematic classification of all system invariants, the enlogic structure and the synchronic structure of CE-systems. The relationship between logic and net theory obtained through the enlogic structure is further exploited in a number of different ways. Similarly, the concept of synchronic distance is generalized and applied more directly to the study of systems.

From the point of view of applications, it is important to develop a family of net based models. Two such models are exhibited, bipolar synchronization sytems and predicate/transiton-nets. The question as to what is meant by a family of net based models is is studied by presenting the category of nets.

Contents

0. PREFACE

Increasingly often, digital computers are called upon to play roles which consist of more than just computing, in strict isolation, a mathematical function. In many instances, they form an integral part of a much larger system. It is not obvious what kinds of concepts, tools and techniques ought to be developed to explicate and facilitate the use of computers in such environments. That there exists an urgent need for doing so is, however, obvious.

Net theory is the outgrowth of one approach to studying information processing systems in this light. It is slanted towards those instances where a computer derives its functional identity from being part of a larger organizational system. Or, stated differently, net theory is particulary directed towards modelling and analyzing information processing systems whose dominant task is to establish a desired pattern of information flow among a collection of concurrently acting human and technical agents. Hence in the vocabulary of the theory, terms such as coordination, synchronization, safety, concurrency, conflict, etc. will appear more often than the terms that are frequently encountered within the theory of computation.

Net theory is 'open-ended', constantly growing, and composed out of a number of different lines of research. This can be ascertained by merely glancing through this volume. From the very beginning, a large amount of effort has gone into the study of Petri nets with particular emphasis on the 'token game' associated with these nets. A second major line of research, however, has concentrated on developing a coherent set of concepts, tools, and techniques to study the organizational problems that are 'solved' by information processing systems. The resulting theory is called General Net Theory - a generalization of the 'special' net theory of the token game.

In this paper we present the major features of general net theory, together with a selection of our own research efforts in this area. A good deal of our knowledge in this field is due to our association with C.A. Petri at ISF. Petri initiated general net theory in 1962 [44] and, over the years, has identified a number of the fundamental constructs of the theory: Information flow (1962 [43], 1965 [45]), net morphisms (1973 [46]), enlogic and synchronic structure of condition/event-systems (1975 [48]), axioms of concurrency (1978 [50]). We have also been fortunate to have been able to interact with A.W. Holt over a period of years.

Now for a quick sketch of what we consider to be the major elements of general net theory: The basic system model is called the condition/event-system model (chapter 1). To enrich the formal vocabulary concerning systems, three kinds of 'completion' are carried out on the basic model. Completion w.r.t. information flow gives rise to information flow graphs (chapter 2). T-completion and S-completion lead to the enlogic structure and to the synchronic structure of condition/event-systems (chapter 5). The enlogic structure establishes the first link between net theory and logic which can be further strengthened (chapter 6). The synchronic structure provides a fundamental metric for condition/event-systems which can be usefully generalized and applied (chapter 7). In practice, a number of net based models will have to be formulated and studied. Two such models that we have developed are called bipolar synchronization systems (chapter 3) and predicate/transition-systems (chapter 4). The conceptual framework for interrelating the various net models that may arise is provided by a suitably chosen category of nets, and (net) morphism diagrams defined within this category (chapter 8).

These are the elements of general net theory that will be discussed in this paper. A more detailed description of the organization of the paper is given towards the end of chapter 1. The interested reader will also find a more elaborate discussion of the motivations and aims of general net theory in the contribution of C.A. Petri in this volume entitled "Introduction to General Net Theory".

We should like to conclude this preface with an apology. Our paper is a first attempt at providing a synthesis of work carried out over an extended period of time by a group of people at ISF. Due to the variety of the material reported as also due to the differing tasks of the three authors, we have not been able to achieve a uniform style of presentation. In a future, similar but more ambitious, effort we hope to do much better.

1. CONDITION/EVENT-SYSTEMS

1.0. Introduction

The aims of this chapter are twofold. Firstly, to precisely define the class of systems which are the objects of study within net theory. We do this by formulating a formal model of this class of systems. This model is called condition/event-systems. Our second aim is to point out the kinds of conceptual, descriptive and mathematical tools that a theory of condition/event-systems will have to contain. This will motivate and justify the tools and techniques of net theory that are presented in the subsequent chapters. The organization of this chapter is as follows: In the next section we informally outline the general considerations that have guided the formulation of our model. In section 1.2, the condition/event-systems model is presented and the fundamental situations that can arise in these systems are pointed out. In section 1.3 we sketch the requirements that an adequate theory of these systems will have to meet. Most of the material presented here has been taken from [46,48].

1.1. Conditions and Events

Conditions and events are the two fundamental concepts that we start with in our study of systems. Usually, the behaviour of a dynamic system is specified by means of a state space and the transition rules which determine the set of possible future states, given a present state. In our approach, a 'state' is described by means of those conditions which hold concurrently in that 'state'. Such a (maximal) set of conditions holding while nothing changes is called a case. (We have deliberately chosen a new name in order to avoid unnecessary misunderstandings because a case is an entity which is distributed in space and time; we do use the term state but in a more restricted sense.) Thus we have a set of conditions B and certain subsets of conditions which form the set of cases C: $c \in C \Longrightarrow c \subseteq B$.

A basic unit of changes in the holdings of conditions which leads the system from one case to another is specified by an event. Consequently, we have a set of (elementary) transition rules, E, transforming cases into cases; E is the set of events.

In the modelling of a system, B, C and E and their interrelationships can be chosen in a variety of ways. The choices regarding B and E however are _not_ independent choices. This point is an important one but shall not be worked out at this occasion. Instead, we shall concentrate on displaying that there indeed are choices. To do this, we first collect together our informal remarks concerning what, in our theory, a system is composed of:

Definition: A _case transition model_ of a dynamic system is a quadruple (B,C,E,r) where

1) $B = \{b_1, b_2, \ldots\}$ is the set of _conditions_,
2) $K = \mathcal{P}(B)$ is the set of _constellations_ (all the conceivable combinations of conditions) and $C \subseteq K$ is the set of _cases_ (the possible combinations of conditions),
3) $E = \{e_1, e_2, \ldots\}$ is the set of _events_ (elementary changes),
4) $r \subseteq C \times E \times C$ is the relation of _reachability by an event occurrence_.

By placing different restrictions on the r relation we can obtain different system models. Up to now three possibilties have been explored in some depth. Two of these lead to system models called _Assignment Systems_ [58] and _Loosely Coupled Systems_ [61]. In this paper, we will confine our attention to the third approach which is guided by the requirements of general net theory. The principle upon which our approach is based may be termed as the _principle of extensionality_ and it can be stated as follows:

Defintion: A case transition model (B,C,E,r) satisfies the _principle of extensionality_ if there exist two functions $pre: E \to K$ and $post: E \to K$ (where for $e \in E$, pre(e) is denoted by $\bullet e$ and post(e) by $e \bullet$) such that:

1) $\forall (c_1, e, c_2) \in r: c_1 - c_2 = \bullet e \wedge c_2 - c_1 = e \bullet$
2) $\forall e \in E: \bullet e \cup e \bullet \neq \emptyset$
3a) $\forall c \in C \forall e \in E: [\bullet e \subseteq c \wedge e \bullet \cap c = \emptyset \implies \exists c': (c, e, c') \in r]$
3b) $\forall c \in C \forall e \in E: [\bullet e \cap c = \emptyset \wedge e \bullet \subseteq c \implies \exists c': (c', e, c) \in r]$
4) $\forall e_1, e_2 \in E: [\bullet e_1 = \bullet e_2 \wedge e_1 \bullet = e_2 \bullet \implies e_1 = e_2]$

For an event e, $\bullet e$ is the set of _pre-conditions_ and $e \bullet$ the set of _post-conditions_ of e. _Whenever_ e occurs, the conditions in $\bullet e$ cease to hold and the conditions in $e \bullet$ begin to hold. This is stated by 1) in our definition. As a consequence, the pre- and post-conditions of an event are disjoint. 2) states that the occurrences of an event must cause _some change_ in the condition holdings. For an event e, its _concession_, i.e. its chance to occur, in a case c is determined solely by the presence of $\bullet e$ and the absence of $e\bullet$ in c. Correspondingly, the issue of whether an occurrence of e could lead to the case c is determined solely by the absence of $\bullet e$ and the presence of $e\bullet$ in c. 3a) and 3b) reflect these considerations. Finally, an event is completely characterized by its extension, i.e. by the changes in the condition holdings produced by its occurrences. This is stated in 4).

It is easy to prove the consequences of the principle of extensionality stated below:

Theorem: Let (B,C,E,r) be a case transition model which satisfies the principle of extensionality, and let $(c_1,e,c_2) \in r$. Then
$\forall c_3,c_4 \in C: [c_1-c_2=c_3-c_4 \wedge c_2-c_1=c_4-c_3 \Longrightarrow (c_3,e,c_4) \in r]$

Theorem: Let (B,C,E,r) be a case transition model which satisfies the principle of extensionality. Then

1) $(c_1,e,c_2) \in r \Longrightarrow c_2=(c_1-\bullet e) \cup e\bullet$
2) $(c_1,e,c_2),(c_1,e,c_3) \in r \Longrightarrow c_2=c_3$
3) $(c_1,e,c_2),(c_1,e',c_2) \in r \Longrightarrow e=e'$
4) $[(c_1,e,c_2),(c_3,e',c_4) \in r \wedge c_1-c_2=c_3-c_4 \wedge c_2-c_1=c_4-c_3] \Longrightarrow e=e'$

The principle of extensionality leads to the formulation of the condition/event-system model as we will soon see. Before we will impose some additional restrictions on B, C and E.

Firstly we reject the possibility that the transition rules can assume knowledge of the 'global system state'. We shall require that all changes (in condition holdings) that are possible in a system be composed out of definite, indivisible, local changes called events. Secondly, we reject the possibility that the applications of the rules of changes (event occurrences) can be a function of the ticks of a universal discrete clock. Rather we shall demand that the composition of event occurrences be by sequence and concurrency.

Turning now our attention to C, we shall require it to be 'large enough' to enable us to predict the future behaviour of a system and to reason backwards concerning the past behaviour of the system. We feel that this is imperative for developing a complete image of information flow and its application in areas such as error correction and error recovery. To say precisely what 'large enough' means, the concept of a step is needed.

Let (B,C,E,r) be a case transition model which satisfies the principle of extensionality. Recall that this means that an event e is characterized completely by the (pre- and post-)conditions affected by its occurrences. Moreover, the concession for e in a case c is determined solely by the presence of •e and the absence of e• in c. In fact, generalizing, we will say: If $e \in E$ and $k \in K$ such that $\bullet e \subseteq k$ and $e \bullet \cap k = \emptyset$, then e has concession in the constellation k.

The notion of a step can now be stated. A step consists of the concurrent occurrences of a set of events:

Definition: Let (B,C,E,r) be a case transition model which satisfies the extensionality principle. Let $k_1, k_2 \in K$ and $\emptyset \neq G \subseteq E$. Then k_1 can be transformed into k_2 in one step by an occurrence of G, and we denote this as $k_1[G>k_2$, if the following conditions are met:

1) Each $e \in E$ has concession in k_1;
2) $\forall e_1, e_2 \in G$: $[e_1 \neq e_2 \implies \bullet e_1 \cap \bullet e_2 = \emptyset \wedge e_1 \bullet \cap e_2 \bullet = \emptyset]$;
3) $k_1 - k_2 = \bigcup \bullet e | e \in G$ and $k_2 - k_1 = \bigcup e \bullet | e \in G$.

We note here briefly that this definition enforces the resolution of conflicts between events which may singly occur in k_1 but have a precondition or postcondition in common. (We will have to say more about conflicts later).

Using this definition we can define reachability in one forward step to be the binary relation $R1 \subseteq K \times K$ where:

$$R1 = \{k_1, k_2 | \exists G \subseteq E: k_1[G>k_2\}$$

We are now prepared to say precisely what we mean by 'C should be large enough'. Namely, the set of cases $C \subseteq K$ should be such that:

1) If $c_1 \in C$ and $(c_1, c_2) \in R1$ then $c_2 \in C$
2) If $c_1 \in C$ and $(c_3, c_1) \in R1$ then $c_3 \in C$
3) If $(c_1, c_2) \in R1$ then $(c_1, c_2) \in (R1 \cup R1^{-1})^*$
4) If $k \in K - C$ and $c \in C$ then $(k,c), (c,k) \in R1$

Stated differently, C is an equivalence class of the full reachability relation $R = (R1 \cup R1^{-1})^*$. We will justify our choice of R1 and hence R to characterize the 'fullness' of C after introducing the system model that we are after. Our purpose here has been to merely give an informal sketch of our approach to the study of systems and introduce some basic terminology.

1.2. Condition/Event-Systems

Using the ideas introduced in the previous section, we shall now define a condition/event-systemm as a quadruple (B,E;F,C) first informally and then by stating formally the restrictions on the sets B,E,F and C.

Basically, for Σ = (B,E;F,C) to be a condition/event-system, B,E,F and C should meet the following requirements:

1) The triple (B,E;F) is a net and F, the flow relation, is used to specify the extension of each event in E. It is necessary to eliminate multiple representations of an event because of the extensionality principle. On the other hand, it is convenient to eliminate multiple representations of a condition, for nothing is gained by permitting this. Hence (B,E;F) is required to be a simple net.
2) Every case $c \in C$ is a set of conditions; $c \subseteq B$ and $C \subseteq \mathcal{P}(B)$. There are no 'hidden parameters' in the description of a case.
3) Every event has concession, i.e. a chance to occur, in some case. If a supposed 'event' does not have concession in any case, it can never occur. We can remove it from E. (It will appear in a different set - when we consider all conceivable changes - and will play an important role in system specification.)
4) Every case is reachable from every other case in a finite number of (forward and backward) steps. No constellation which is not a case is reachable from a case. No case can be reached from a non-case constellation. (Ken(C,R) is the succinct form that is used for saying all this.)

We can now, at last, launch into formal definitions:

Definition: A (directed) net is a triple N = (S,T;F) where:

1) $S \cap T = \emptyset$
2) $S \cup T \neq \emptyset$
3) $F \subseteq (S \times T) \cup (T \times S)$
4) $dom(F) \cup codom(F) = S \cup T$.

S is the set of S-elements and T is the set of T-elements. $X = S \cup T$ is the set of elements of N. F is called the flow relation and the elements of F are also referred to as arcs. Often F is viewed as being composed of two binary relations. Namely:

1) $Z = F \cap (S \times T)$ (the target relation)

2) $Q = F^{-1} \cap (S \times T)$ (the source relation)

In diagrams, S-elements will be drawn as circles ◯ and T-elements as boxes □. If $(x,y) \in F$, then there will be an arrow from x to y.

We now introduce a useful notation which we have already used (more or less informally). Let $N = (S,T;F)$ be a net and $x \in X$ $(= S \cup T)$. Then,

$\bullet x = \{y \mid yFx\}$ (the pre-set of x)

$x\bullet = \{y \mid xFy\}$ (the post-set of x)

Definition: Let $N = (S,T;F)$ be a net. Then N is simple if

$\forall x,y \in X: [\bullet x = \bullet y \wedge x\bullet = y\bullet \implies x = y]$

We can now at last present our system model formally:

Definition: A condition/event-system (CE-system) is a quadruple $\Sigma = (B,E;F,C)$ where:

1) $(B,E;F)$ is a simple net. B is the set of conditions, E the set of events. ($(B,E;F)$ is a CE-net.)

2) $C \subseteq K$ is a non-empty set of cases where $K = \wp(B)$ is the set of constellations.

3) For each event $e \in E$ there is a case $c \in C$ such that $\bullet e \subseteq c$ and $e\bullet \cap c = \emptyset$. (Every event has concession in some case in C.)

4) C is an equivalence class of the full reachability relation R:

4a) $R = (R1 \cup R1^{-1})^*$;

4b) $R1 \subseteq K \times K$ is given by
$(k_1,k_2) \in R1$ iff $k_1[G>k_2$ for some non-empty $G \subseteq E$;

4c) Let $k_1,k_2 \subseteq K$, $\emptyset \neq G \subseteq E$. Then $k_1[G>k_2$ if

1) $\forall e \in G$: e has concession in k_1,

2) $\forall e_1,e_2 \in G$: $\bullet e_1 \cap \bullet e_2 = e_1\bullet \cap e_2\bullet = \emptyset$,

3) $k_1 - k_2 = \bigcup \bullet e \mid e \in G$ and $k_2 - k_1 = \bigcup e\bullet \mid e \in G$.

Let $(B,E;F,C)$ be a CE-system. Now, given B,E and F, to specify C, it is sufficient to indicate one arbitary element $c \in C$ ($C = [c]$). In diagrams, we will indicate c by a marking: We place a token on each of the circles which correspond to the conditions that hold in c. Using these conventions, an example of a CE-system is shown in fig. 1.1.

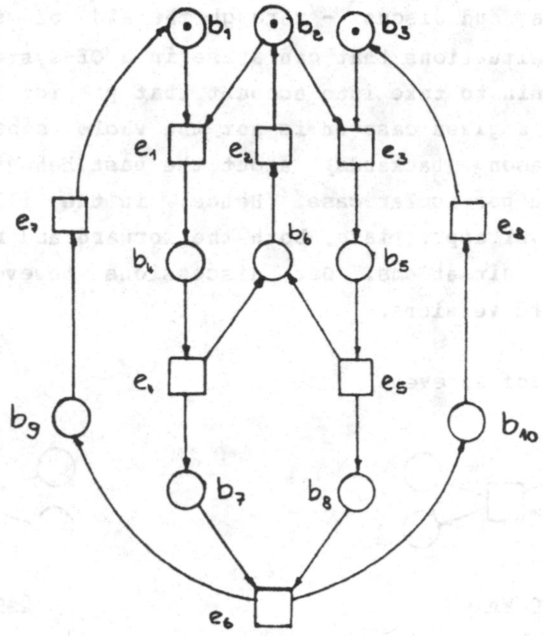

Fig. 1.1

Let $\Sigma=(B,E;F,C)$ be a CE-system. It follows from the definitions that:

1) Every condition holds in at least one case and does not hold in at least one case ($\forall b \in B \exists c,c' \in C:[b \in c \land b \notin c']$).
2) The underlying net $(B,E;F)$ is <u>pure</u>: $(x,y) \in F \implies (y,x) \notin F$.

We characterize C through the notion of a step rather than through the occurrence of a single event due to a number of reasons. Two of the reasons can be pointed out here. Firstly, one might be interested in the 'sequential distance' $d(c_1,c_2)$ between two cases c_1,c_2 if it exists: $d(c_1,c_2) = \mathrm{Min}[n \mid (c_1,c_2) \in R1^n]$. Secondly, in the definition of $(B,E;F)$ we do not require B and E to be finite sets. Hence, in general C will be 'full' only if we allow changes comprising an infinite number of concurrent occurrences of events. The appropriate restrictions to finite cardinalities will arise naturally when we consider <u>processes</u> and <u>occurrence nets</u> which appear later. Instead of R we might have considered a second equivalence relation: $R' = (R1)^* \cup (R1^{-1})^*$. But then, in general, $R' \subseteq R$ and we would like our system model to be as general as possible.

We now display and discuss - through the aid of illustrations - the fundamental situations that can arise in a CE-system. In doing so, we have once again to take into account that predicting the behaviour of a system from a given case on is not the whole story. Often, one has also to reason (backards) about the past behaviour of a system that has led to a particular case. Hence, in the illustrations, we will show, wherever appropriate, both the forward and reverse forms of the fundamental situations. Our discussions however, will centre around the forward versions.

1) <u>Concession</u> (of an event)

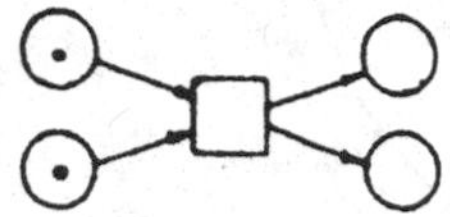

<u>Forward</u> <u>Backward</u>

2) <u>Occurrence</u> (of an event)

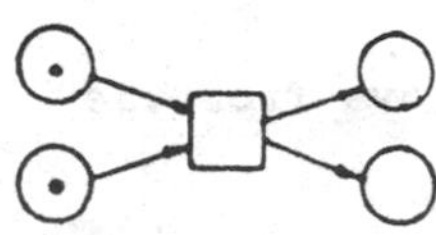

<u>Before</u> <u>After</u>

If in a case c, two events e_1, and e_2 have concession and $\bullet e_1 \cap \bullet e_2 = e_1\bullet \cap e_2\bullet = \emptyset$ then e_1 and e_2 can occur <u>concurrently</u> in c. Hence, in general a case is transformed into a new case by a <u>partially</u> ordered set of occurrences of events and conditions. We will address this point in more detail towards the end of this section. In fig. 1.1, in the case $\{b_9, b_2, b_{10}\}$ both e_7 and e_8 can occur concurrently.

3) <u>Contact</u> (of conditions)

<u>Forward</u> <u>Backward</u>

All pre-conditions and some post-conditions of an event hold concurrently (in a case).

Contact is often refered to as an <u>unsafe</u> situation in higher level descriptions. It is one of the characteristics of net theory in that it describes and solves safety problems. At the basic and most detailed level of description - namely the CE-system description - a contact situation might or might not have harmful consequences. This depends purely on the way in which the conditions and events have been chosen to reflect reality. What is certain however is, at a contact situation the involved event does <u>not</u> have concession. It can not occur. This reflects our view that an event is to be identified purely through the set of conditions that cease to hold (the pre-conditions) and the set of conditions that begin to hold (the post-conditions) as a result of an occurrence of the event. The system shown in fig. 1.1 is free of contact.

4) <u>Conflict</u> (of a pair of events)

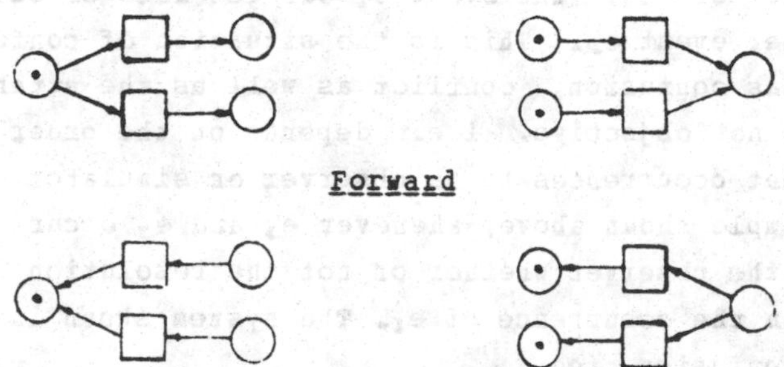

<u>Forward</u>

<u>Backward</u>

Two events are in conflict in a case if they both have concession but have at least one pre- or post-condition in common. If two events are in conflict in a case, then in that case, either one of them may occur but <u>not both</u>. Thus an implicit part of our transition rule is: The change in a condition-holding that takes place as part of an event-occurrence belongs uniquely to this occurrence. In fig. 1.1, in the case shown, e_1 and e_3 are in conflict.

The information required to resolve a conflict is to be supplied from the environment of the system. Stated differently, every CE-system which has conflict is to be thought of as being part of a larger conflict-free CE-system which is complete w.r.t. information flow. The formal version of this statement is the axiom of local determinacy for CE-systems and will be stated in chapter 2.

In general, it is difficult to explore the structure of the 'full' system if a given system contains confusion:

5) Confusion

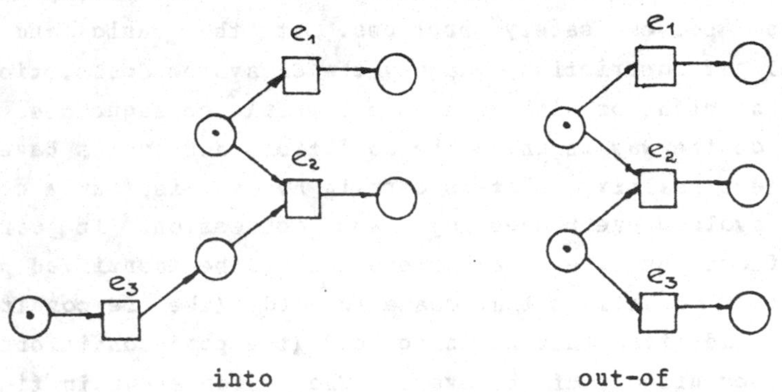

into out-of

In a case c, the events e_1 and e_3 can occur concurrently. Through the occurrence of e_3, the event e_1 can get into or out of conflict with yet another event e_2. This is the situation of confusion. In a system which has confusion, conflict as well as the attendent flow of information is not objective, i.e. depends on the order imposed to concurrent event occurrences by an observer or simulator.

In the example shown above, whenever e_1 and e_3 occur concurrently, it depends on the observer whether or not the resolution of a conflict was involved in the occurrence of e_1. The system shown in fig. 1.1 can give rise to confusion, too.

Confusion is due to a subtle and intimate relationship between causality, concurrency and conflict. Many of the existing approaches to concurrency may be roughly characterized as: Concurrency equals 'parallelism' equals all possible (sequential) interleavings of 'parallel' actions. Here the problem of confusion simply does not arise. In net theory however, where concurrency roughly means causal independence, confusion certainly arises. The reader who suspects that this merely reflects a drawback of net theory should consult [28] to see that in at least one other - radically different - approach to concurrency, the phenomenon of confusion arises. More importantly, in real systems, confusion is certainly present as evidenced in the literature concerning arbiters, synchronizers and the 'glitch' phenomenon [4,42].

We suspect that in order to deal effectively with the problem of confusion, one needs to arrive at a fresh and formal notion of measurement. We are however, at this stage not prepared to pursue this any further. To return to the more modest aims of this chapter, the various basic situations that we have described, together enable a CE-system to give rise to a rich variety of behaviour. We shall now briefly discuss what constitutes the behaviour of a CE-system.

Briefly stated, the behaviour of a CE-system consists of all the processes it can give rise to. A process is a partially ordered set of occurrences of events with the attendent holdings of conditions which transforms a case of the system into another (possibly the same) case of the system. For example, the net shown in fig. 1.2 is a process of the system shown in fig. 1.1.

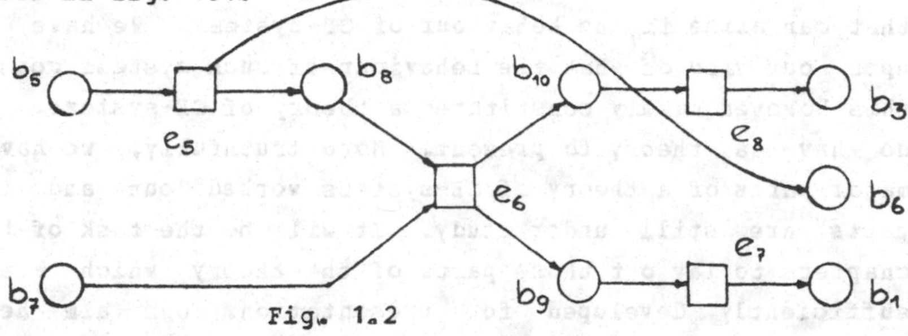

Fig. 1.2

It transforms the case $\{b_5, b_7\}$ into the case $\{b_1, b_3, b_6\}$. A formal definition of the set of processes associated with a CE-system will be given in chapter 5. Two important features concerning our notion of behaviour can however be mentioned here and they are brought out by the example shown in fig. 1.2. Firstly, we use the same language namely the language of nets to describe both systems and the processes that can run on these systems. Secondly, even the most elementary description of behaviour such as the one shown in fig. 1.2 is composed out of partially-ordered occurrences of events and conditions.

With reference to this example, the question whether e_7 occured before or after - or simultaneously with - e_8 is, within net theory, considered to be ill-stated. Regarding this process, it is true that two different observers may report two alternative descriptions namely the two event sequences e_5, e_6, e_7, e_8 and e_5, e_6, e_8, e_7. What we do insist upon however is - and quite reasonably so - that <u>these alternatives of description do not constitute alternatives of system behaviour</u>. Alternatives of system behaviour have to do with conflict, conflict-resolution and information flow.

The processes that are supported by CE-systems are members of a class called <u>non-sequential</u> processes or <u>occurrence nets</u>. Non-sequential processes play a crucial role in the axiomatic foundations of net theory. The seminal work on these processes is to be found in [47] and further results have been reported in [3]. Elsewhere in this volume (in the contributions of Petri and Best) the reader will find more detailed information concerning non-sequential processes.

1.3. Requirements for a Theory of CE-Systems

We have, at this stage, a formal model of the class of systems that net theory is concerned with. We know what the basic situations are that can arise in the behaviour of CE-systems. We have also touched upon our view of what the behaviour of such systems consists of. All this however hardly constitutes a theory of CE-systems. But then, we do have a theory to present. More truthfully, we have some of the major parts of a theory of CE-systems worked out and the remaining parts are still under study. It will be the task of the succeeding chapters to lay out those parts of the theory which are at present sufficiently developed for presentation. Our aim here is to put forward a rationale for the particular way in which the theory of CE-systems has been (and is being) pursued at the Institut für Informationssystemforschung (ISF).

A theory of systems based on the CE-system model, will have to meet many requirements. Among these, some of the more important ones are:

1) The concept of information in the context of conflict-resolution should have a firm formal basis. It should be possible to identify, analyze and quantify the flow of information across the system-environment boundary and through the system.

Information flow graphs are the formal objects that have been formulated with this purpose in mind. Chapter 2 contains the basic material concerning information flow graphs and their role within net theory.

2) Very often, the CE-system description of a 'real' system will be far too detailed and hence very cumbersome to handle, due to the sheer size of the description. Hence, tools are needed which allow systems, and more importantly different aspects of system behaviour, be described at different levels of abstraction.

Three of the succeeding chapters deal with this very important issue. These three chapters differ widely from each other in style and contents. However, they have all been influenced by the same consideration. Namely - and this is one of the central features of net theory - to look for a uniform and coherent language for describing systems and processes at various - not necessarily hierarchial - levels. Moreover, the different descriptions should be chosen such that it is possible, at least in principle, to relate them to each other in a systematic fashion. In this connection, the CE-system description will play the role of a connecting bridge. For this reason, we will often refer to it as the basic interpretation and say that it provides the basic representation of systems.

In chapters 3 and 4 we present two concrete examples of higher-level nets as representation tools. In both these chapters, we indicate how to obtain the basic (CE-system) representation, starting with the higher-level representation. In chapter 8 , one of the more formal chapters of this paper, we use the category of nets and morphisms defined within this category, to give a precise mathematical formulation for our approach to dealing with the crucial issue of multi-level descriptive tools and their (net) semantics.

3) It is necessary to correctly and effectively reason about the behaviour of CE-systems. Conventional tools of logic are however not directly applicable, since they are designed for dealing with static truth values.

One half of chapter 5 explains how the classification of all the T-forms associated with a CE-system leads to the notion of a fact . Facts are, in effect, invariant assertions concerning condition holdings. Chapter 6 shows how this simple idea can be exploited to considerably improve our ability to represent and reason about dynamic systems.

4) The CE-system model neither recognizes nor appeals to a universal sequential time scale. In the absence of this convential and classical metric, we need net-based metrics for measuring and tuning the behaviour of systems modelled by nets.

Once again, one half of chapter 5 explains how the classification of all the S-forms associated with a CE-system gives rise to the metric called synchronic distance . In chapter 7, we illustrate through detailed examples this metric's potential as a tool for dealing with performance issues.

To conclude, an adequate and applicable theory of (concurrent) systems based on the CE-system model will have to meet very many requirements. We have chosen to try and fulfill, what we feel are some of the more important and urgent needs that the theory will have to meet.

These choices have defined the lines of research that we have pursued and are pursuing. The results that have been obtained so far along these different but closely related lines of research are presented in the following chapters.

2. INFORMATION FLOW IN CONDITION/EVENT-SYSTEMS

2.0. Introduction

In this chapter, we will introduce the concept of information and information flow and discuss its role within our systems theory. It may well be that our usage does not square with mental images that the reader associates with the terms 'information' and 'information flow'. This is not a serious problem because we are not interested in discussing here questions of the form: What is information?

We shall use these terms - as much as possible - in a technical sense to describe certain formal concepts that arise in our theory. It is these concepts which will be the focus of attention here. We feel that these concepts, however they may be named by different people, are important and deserve careful study.

We shall start with the issue of conflict resolution in CE-systems. In the next section, the axiom of local determinacy is stated and explained. This axiom is a formal expression of our understanding of how conflicts are resolved in CE-systems and brings in the notion of information into the theory. Roughly speaking, in our view information is what resolves conflicts. This will lead us to formulate that conflict-free CE-systems are closed w.r.t. information flow, and the completion of a CE-system w.r.t. information flow should yield a conflict-free CE-system.

In section 2, we introduce a special kind of conflict-free CE-systems called information flow graphs. In section 3, information flow graphs are viewed as interesting formal objects in their own right and some of their known properties are presented. In this light, information flow graphs may be looked upon as the first example of a higher level net model in this paper.

In the last section, using this model, we will explain two important aspects of information flow called flux and influence.

2.1. The Principle of Local Determinacy

In the preceeding chapter where we presented the CE-system model, we introduced the notion of concession denoting a situation in which an event has a chance to occur. We have seen that in a situation in which two events e_1, e_2 have singly concession, it is essential to distinguish between the two alternatives: Either e_1 and e_2 may occur <u>concurrently</u> (in <u>one step</u>), or e_1 and e_2 are in <u>conflict</u>, i.e. when one event occurs the other looses concession. Formally:

<u>Definition</u>: Let $\Sigma = (B,E;F,C)$ be a CE-system, and $c \in C$ be a case of Σ in which two events e_1, e_2 (singly) have concession: $(\bullet e_1 \cup \bullet e_2) \subseteq c$ and $(e_1\bullet \cup e_2\bullet) \cap c = \emptyset$. Then

1) e_1 and e_2 may occur <u>concurrently</u> in c, iff
   $(\bullet e_1 \cap \bullet e_2) = (e_1\bullet \cap e_2\bullet) = \emptyset$
2) e_1 and e_2 are in <u>conflict</u> in c, iff
   $(\bullet e_1 \cap \bullet e_2) \cup (e_1\bullet \cup e_2\bullet) \neq \emptyset$

If no conflict situation arises in Σ - if Σ is <u>conflict-free</u> - then any given 'initial' case of Σ completely determines the future behaviour of Σ. If the same holds also for looking into the past, i.e. for the reverse system, then we will say that Σ has the 'local determinacy' property. Formally:

<u>Definition</u>: Let $\Sigma = (B,E;F,C)$ be a CE-system.

1) Σ is called <u>conflict-free</u> iff there is no case $c \in C$ in which two events are in conflict.
2) Σ is said to possess the <u>local determinacy property</u> iff both Σ and its reverse, $\Sigma^{-1} = (B,E;F^{-1},C)$ are conflict-free.

Fig. 2.1 shows a simple CE-system. In the case shown by the 'initial' marking, there exist - concurrently - two conflict situations, one for events e_1 and e_2 and one for e_3 and e_4. In this case, we are not able to predict how these conflicts will be resolved. In a subsequent case, however, when either of the four events e_5 to e_8 may occur we are able to 'postdict' how the conflicts were resolved. The system now contains <u>information</u> which was not present in the initial case. Thus, we conclude that <u>the resolution of conflicts generates information</u>.

Once this usage of the term "information" being accepted, we are confronted eith several consequences.

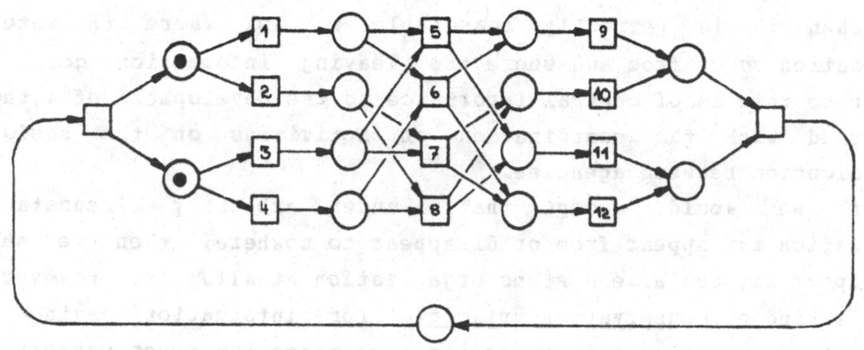

Fig. 2.1

First, we would like to quantify the 'amount' of information generated. The basic unit of information shall be the bit denoting the quantity of information generated by a single one-out-of-two choice. Thus, in our example, by the step from the initial case to the subsequent case mentioned before, two bits - of information - are generated.

Other units, for one-out-of-n choices with $n > 2$, may be derived from the unit bit in many different ways. For example, a sequence of two choices may produce a 'trit' (one-out-of-three), a choice between choices a 'quadrit' (one-out-of-four), and so on.

The second, and most inportant, question we are confronted with is: Where does the information come from? - provided we answer positively the 'meta-question' whether that is a meaningful question at all.

When we continue with the simulation of the CE-system of fig. 2.1 we see that by the next action (one out of events e_5, e_6, e_7, e_8), the two bits being present before will be consumed and two new bits be produced. (Information is transported and transformed.) Then, in the subsequent step (the decision between e_9 and e_{10} concurrently with the decision between e_{11} and e_{12}), all information 'gets lost', i.e. nothing is left in the system of the information supplied by the initial decisions. While we could trivially predict which of the events e_9 and e_{10} and of e_{11} and e_{12} would occur next, the two pairs of events are in backward conflicts afterwards.

So we may say that information enters the system, is transported and transformed in the system, and eventually leaves the system again.

But then it is perfectly reasonable to ask where the entering information comes from and where the leaving information goes. The answer to this is of central importance to the development of a theory concerned with the coordination of activities on the basis of communication between agencies.

If we would accept that, under arbitrary circumstances, information may appear from or disappear to nowhere, then we should not expect any reliable systems organization at all. If, however, we state a kind of <u>conservation principle</u> for information saying that information can flow and change its appearance but never can get lost or created from nothing, then conflicts and their resolution become a matter of how the system under consideration is cut out of a larger whole which is <u>complete</u> w.r.t information flow. Or, in other words, systems which do not have the local determinacy property must have an <u>evironment</u> from which information is supplied or into which it disappears.

The formal expression of this conservation principle for information flow in CE-systems is the

<u>Axiom of Local Determinacy</u>: The union of a CE-system Σ and its environment $Env(\Sigma)$, regarded together as a new (larger) CE-system $(\Sigma \cup Env(\Sigma))$ has the local determinacy property.

In practice, it may be very difficult to verify that a given CE-system Σ satisfies the axiom of local determinacy. In particular, when Σ gives rise to <u>confusion</u> (which we brieflv discussed in the previous chapter), a correct representation of that part of the rest of the universe which constitutes the necessary $Env(\Sigma)$ may be impeded by, e.g., the limitation of resources.

For us, accepting the principle of local determinacy for CE-systems means that completion w.r.t. information flow is an important, and in many cases, interesting task within the theory of CE-systems.

The first and rather early result of work inspired by the idea that information flow must obey certain conservation principles [43] was the formulation of a higher-level system model called <u>information flow graphs</u> [45]. This model will be the subject of the subsequent sections.

2.2. Information Flow Graphs

The easiest way to get along with priciple of local determinacy seems the formulation of a class of system models which, by definition, have the local determinacy property and thus are already complete w.r.t. information flow. Synchronization graphs, e.g., which will play an important role in the next chapter have this property.

For our purposes it is important to be able to trace the flow of effects of decisions and to observe mutual influences of decisions. So we try to find a formal means to represent both. We restrict decisions to be decisions between two mutually excluding actions. Consequently, the effect of a decision is a 1-bit-information which we imagine to flow on so-called information flow lines. If we accept the fact that in a universe nothing can be gained or lost, which then is also true for information, the information flow lines are closed. But normally we are not interested in a whole universe. We rather deal with systems as parts of a universe, and the border lines or interfaces between a system and its environment. So information flow lines are either closed within the system or they are open and lead through the system from border to border line (fig. 2.2).

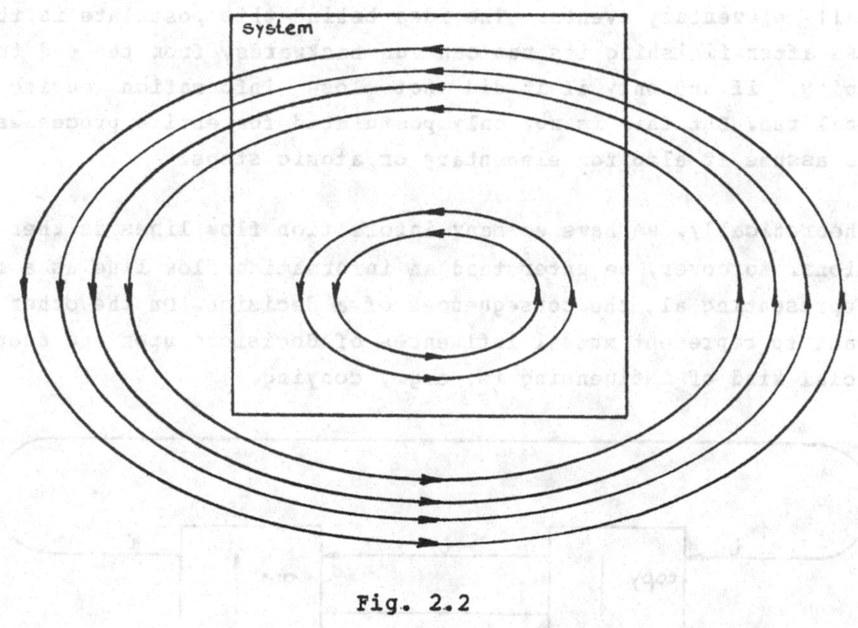

Fig. 2.2

The open flow lines begin where we do not know or do not regard the reasons for a decision - at some interface (source of information). Likewise they end at some other interface, thus representing the fact that we do not know or do not regard further consequences (sink of information). In fig. 2.3 we see the diagram of information flow lines benonging to the CE-system shown in fig. 2.1.

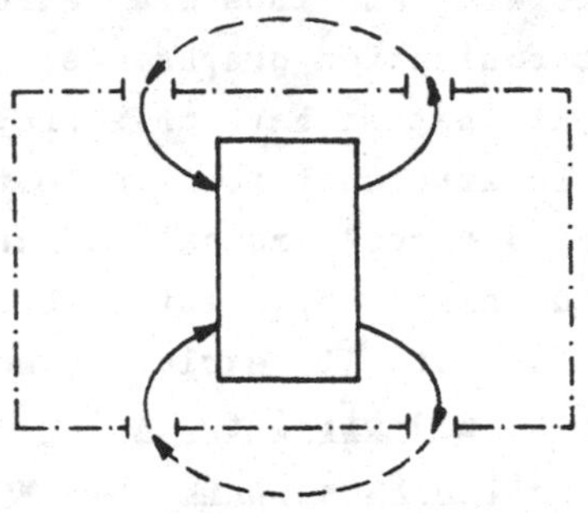

Fig. 2.3

By postulating that information flow lines are closed within the universe we have obtained that no information can be lost (or gained) on a large scale. But we do not want to lose information at all. Therefore we postulate in addition the time reversal invariance of information flow on a microscopic level, i.e. time reversal invariance for all elementary events. The idea behind this postulate is that a process after finishing its run can run backwards, from the end to the beginning, if and only if it did not lose information during its original run. But this is not only postulated for entire processes. We rather assume it also for elementary or atomic steps.

Theoretically, we have as many information flow lines as there are decisions. Moreover, we unterstand an information flow line as a means for representing all the consequences of a decision. On the other hand we want to represent mutual influences of decisions upon one another. A special kind of influencing is, e.g., copying.

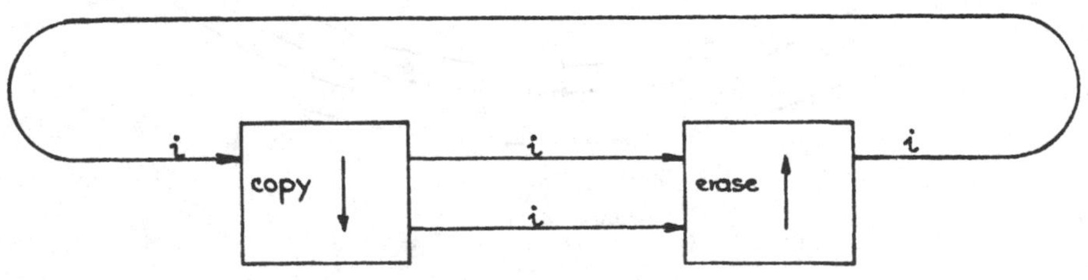

Fig. 2.4

If we would represent copying and erasing like in fig. 2.4 we would not be able to distinguish clearly between both information flow lines, i.e. we have two 'identical' information flow lines which both carry the consequences of one and the same decision. We therefore give up the idea of splitting and joining information flow lines and introduce a flow of constant values, a special case of the so-called <u>enlogy</u>, in addition to the flow of variable information values. So, for the example of fig. 2.4 we get the representation of fig. 2.5. The enlogy in this example can be unterstood as clean paper, magnetic tape, etc.

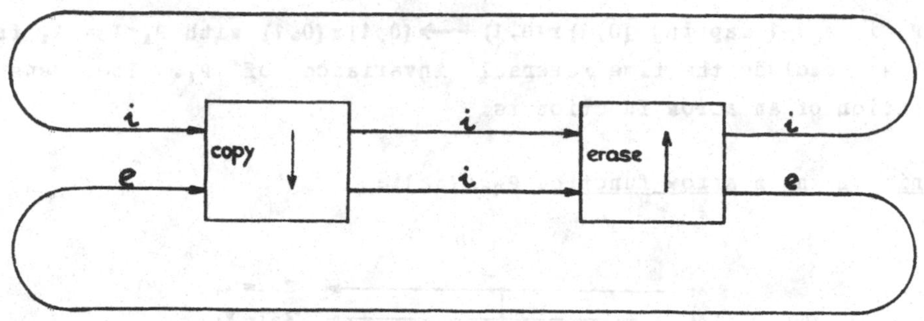

Fig. 2.5

We now come to formalizing the 'links' between information flow lines which shall be used to represent the mutual influences.

Let us consider two decisions α and β which are connected in the following way: the effects c of α are only dependent on the causes a of α, but the effects d of β are dependent on the causes b of β <u>and</u> on the decision α - and consequently on the causos a of α (fig. 2.6).

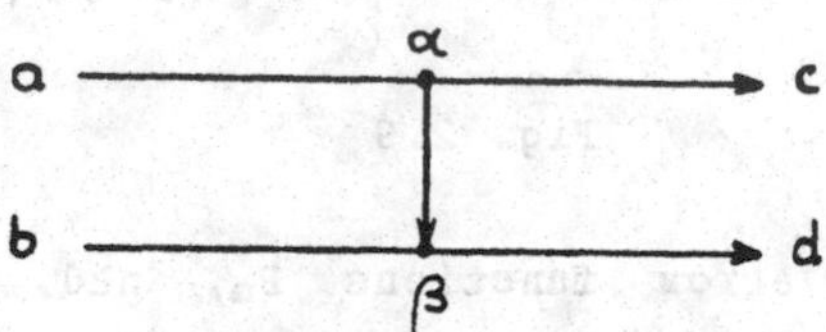

Fig. 2.6

More precisely, we use the fact that bits are representable by boolean variables and define:

<u>Definition</u>: <u>1-st arrow function P_1</u>

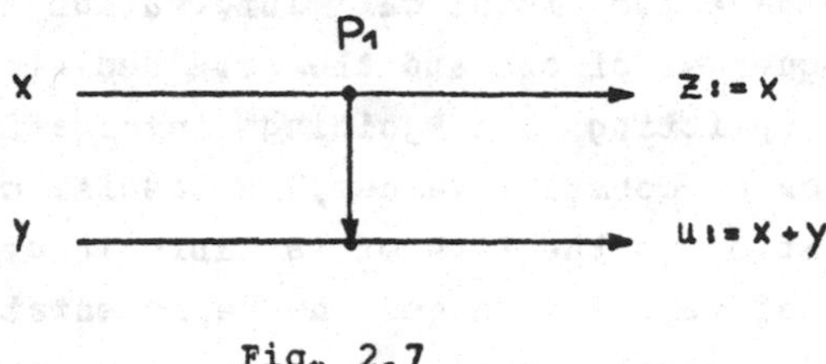

Fig. 2.7

where u,x,y,z are boolean variables and + is the sum modulo 2.

P_1 is a 1-1-mapping $\{0,1\}\times\{0,1\}\longrightarrow\{0,1\}\times\{0,1\}$ with $P_1^{-1} = P_1$ from which we conclude the time reversal invariance of P_1. The general definition of an arrow function is:

<u>Definition</u>: <u>n-th arrow function</u> P_n, $(n\geq 1)$:

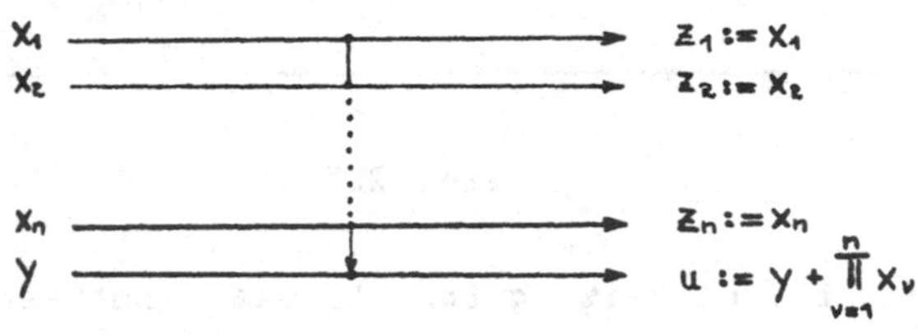

Fig. 2.8

<u>0-th arrow function</u> P_0:

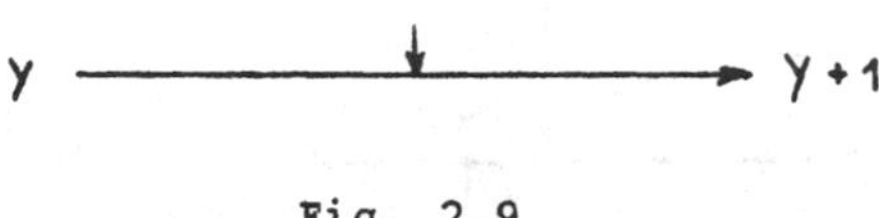

Fig. 2.9

<u>Proposition</u>: (1) All arrow functions P_n, $n\geq 0$, are bijective with $P_n^{-1} = P_n$

(2) All arrow functions P_n, $n>2$, can be build from P_0, P_1, P_2.

(3) All functions $f: 2^n \longrightarrow 2^m$ -embedded in bijections $2^p \longrightarrow 2^p$ -can be represented by arrow functions whereby a number of inputs might be constant (enlogy!)

The following construction shows how to build P_{n+1} by P_2 and P_n:

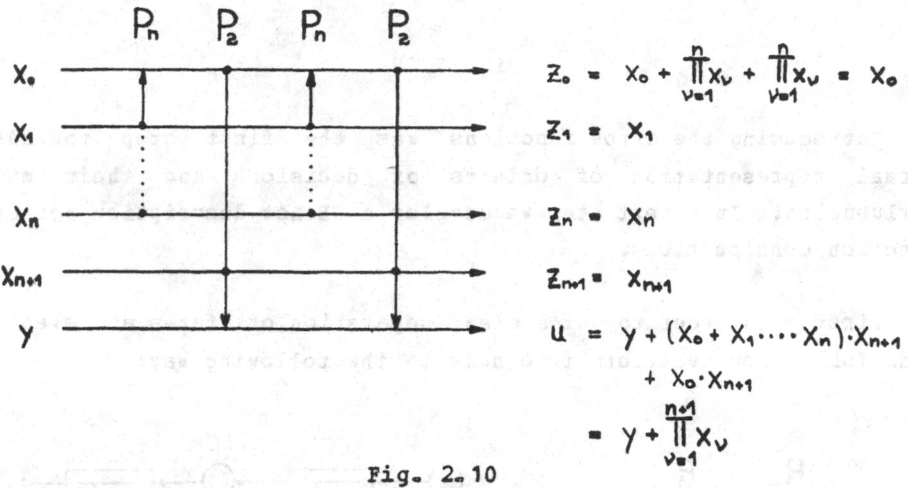

Fig. 2.10

Next we show how to express the conditional exchange function Q (Quine) by arrow functions:

$$Q(a,x,b) := a+x\bullet a+x\bullet b = \begin{cases} a, \text{ if } x=0 \\ b, \text{ if } x=1 \end{cases}$$

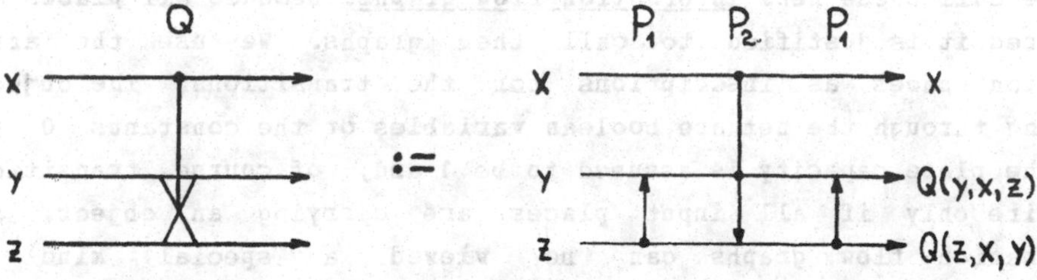

Fig. 2.11

Similarly, one can express P_2 by Q and P_1:

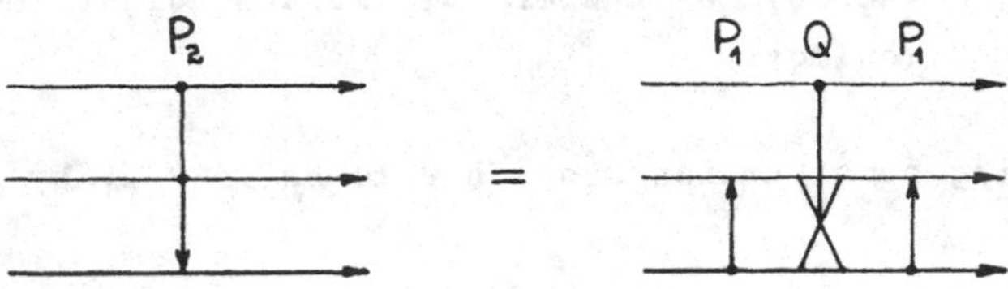

Fig. 2.12

Introducing the arrow functions was the first step towards a formal representation of effects of decisions and their mutual influencing. In a next step we develop a CE-net description for arrow function constructions.

First, in order to get a clear separation of states and events we transform arrow functions into nets in the following way:

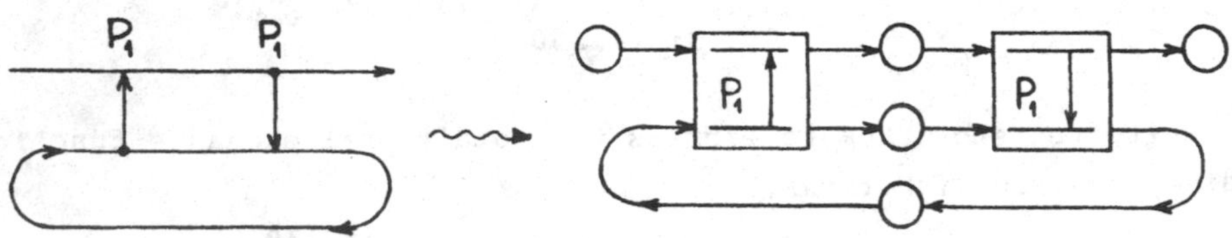

Fig. 2.13

We call these nets <u>information flow graphs</u>. Because all places are unshared it is justified to call them graphs. We use the arrow function names as inscriptions for the transitions. The objects flowing through the net are boolean variables or the constants 0 and 1. The place capacity is assumed to be 1 and, of course, transitions may fire only if all input places are carrying an object. So, information flow graphs can be viewed a special kind of predicate/transition-nets which we shall introduce in chapter 4.

2.3. CE-System Representation of Information Flow Graphs

Now it would be interesting to see how the transitions in information flow graphs are internally organized. The internal structure would be sufficiently clear if we had a condition/event-net representation of all transitions. Because of the above proposition it is enough to know the structure of P_0, P_1, and P_2 or Q.

To start with, the internal structure of P_1 is shown in fig. 2.14(b).

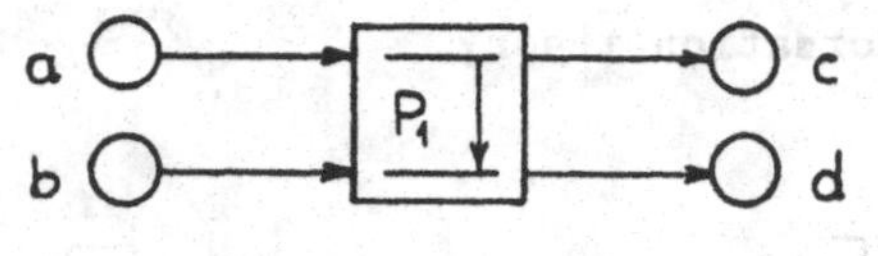

(a)

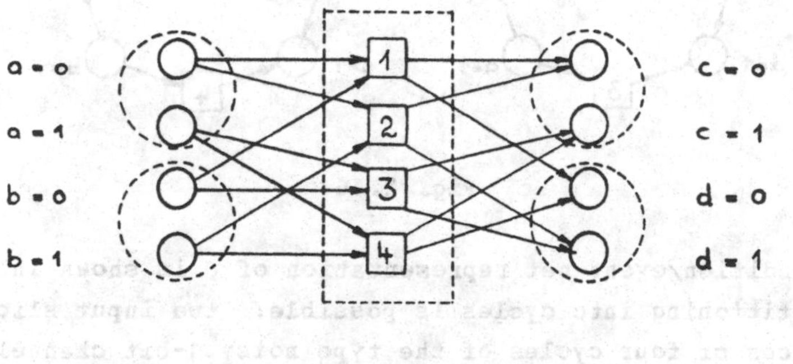

(b)

Fig. 2.14

There are two ways to partition the net of fig. 2.14(b) into cycles. In fig. 2.15 a partition into two cycles of different type is shown which we call <u>input-slice</u> and <u>output-slice</u>. On the other hand, in fig. 2.16 a partition into two cycles of the same type is shown.

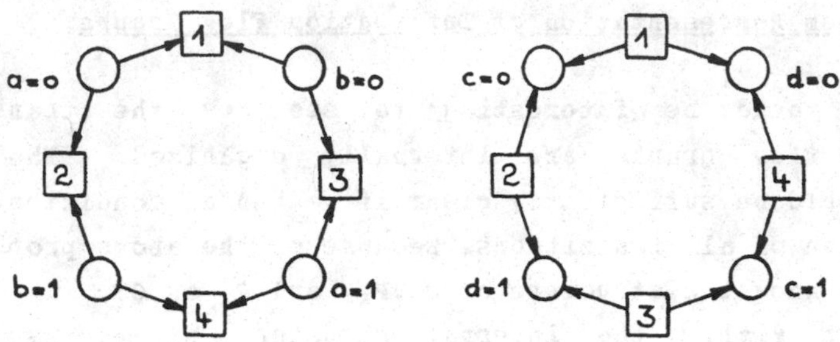

Fig. 2.15

This type can be regarded as a net representation of the <u>noisy 1-bit channel</u> in information theory.

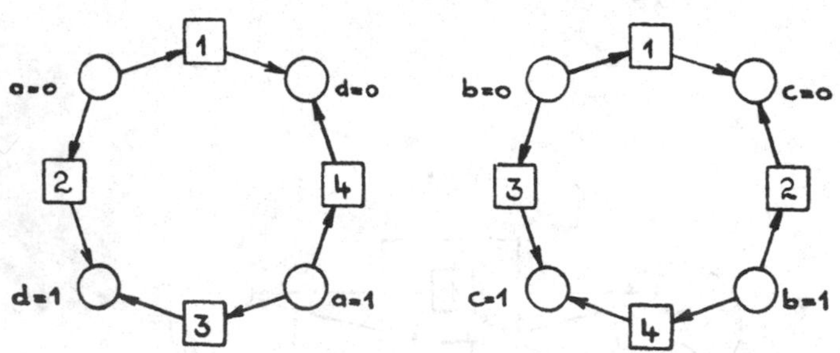

Fig. 2.16

The condition/event-net representation of Q is shown in fig. 2.17. Again partitioning into cycles is possible: two input slices and two output slices or four cycles of the type noisy 1-bit channel.

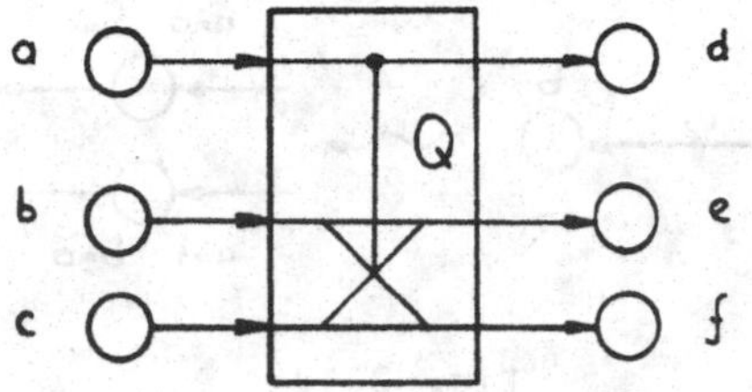

(a)

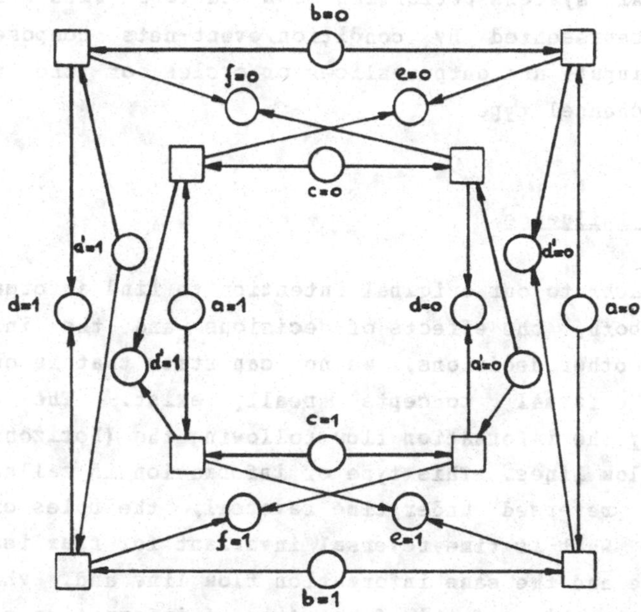

(b)

Fig. 2.17

This net representation of Q requires an enlogy of 1 bit. Together with place a=0 (a=1) place a'=0 (a'=1) has to be marked.
The representation of P_0 consists simply of a 'consistent naming' of places (fig. 2.18). Even in the information flow graph we do not need a transition.

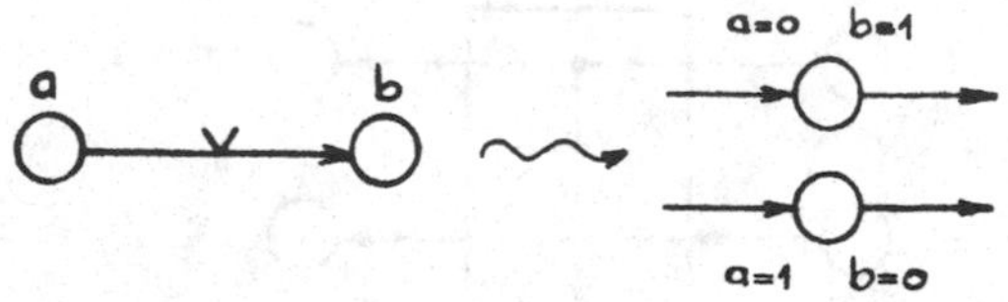

Fig. 2.18

The result of this rather technical part of the section can be summarized in the following proposition:

Proposition: All systems performing computations with bits can be represented by condition/event-nets composed of either input- and output-slices or cycles of the noisy 1-bit channel type.

2.4. Flux and Influence

Coming back to our original intention to find a formal means for representing both, the effects of decisions and the influences of decisions on other decisions, we now can state that in our model two corresponding formal concepts really exist. The effects are represented by the information flow following the (horizontally drawn) information flow lines. This type of information is called flux. Its direction is reversed under time reversal, the roles of source and sink as well. What is time reversal invariant for flux is its being bound to one and the same information flow line and, what is nearly the same, that nothing of this first type of information can be lost.
On the other hand a second type of information flow exists which represents the influences of decisions on decisions and which therefore is called influence. In the diagrams the influence is following the (vertically drawn) arrows of the arrow functions. There are important differences between flux and influence. The influence of a decision is in general not bound to one line. It can branch out and thus be influencing a big part of the system. The most surprising difference, however, is that the direction of an influence is time reversal invariant. That means for the flux of a decision that independently of its running forward or backward the direction of influences caused by it is the same in either case. That shall be

demonstrated by means of P_1 as a conclusion of this section:

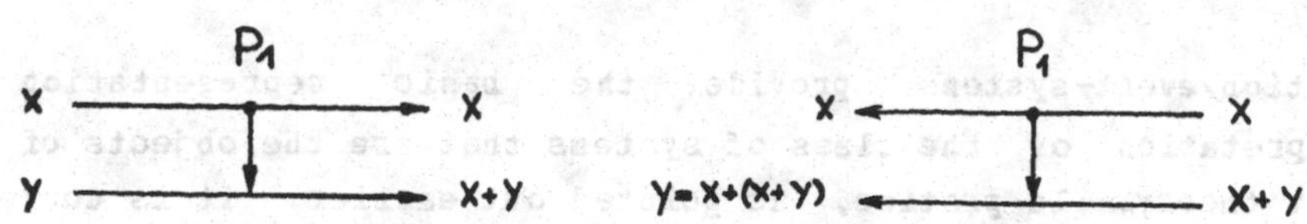

Fig. 2.19

In both directions is the upper flux not influenced whereas the lower flux is. So, in both cases the upper flux is influencing the lower one.

3. BIPOLAR SYNCHRONIZATION SYSTEMS

3.0. Introduction

Condition/event-systems provide the basic representation and interpretation of the class of systems that are the objects of study in net theory. In pratice, as pointed out earlier, it is convenient and indeed necessary to develop higher level representations of systems. In this chapter and the next one we will study two such representations. The model presented here is called *bipolar synchronization systems*.

We have formulated this model in order to isolate and study an important organizational principle which is often - implicitly or explicitly - employed in the construction and use of complex information processing systems. This principle consists of recognizing that the *absence* of effects, signals and entities can be frequently used together with the presence of effects, signals and entities to achieve the desired coordination among a group of concurrently acting agents. Consequently, we will, in our model, *explicitly* represent the *executions* of the actions that are committed due to the outcome of a decision *and* the *non-executions* of the actions that are omitted due to the outcome of a decision. In fact, we will go one step further and demand that in our systems, the executions of the actions that are commissioned by a decision be synchronized with the non-executions of the actions that are omitted (because of the decision), before this decision is permitted to be made again. Since ours is a first and preliminary attempt in this direction, we have carried out our study for a class of systems which exhibit a rather restricted form of decision-making capability and concurrency in their behaviour.

The organization of this chapter is as follows. In the next section, we introduce the basic aspects of bipolar synchronization systems through the aid of a simple illustrative example. The two sections that follow develop the required terminology which then leads to the formulation of the model. Section 3.4 reports the major results we have at present concerning bipolar synchronization systems. In the final section we exhibit a basic interpretation of the model in terms of CE-systems.

3.1. An Informal View of the Model

A bipolar synchronization system consists of a finite strongly connected directed graph together with a token distribution over the arcs to reflect the (distributed) system state. Token distributions are transformed by node firings. We distinguish between two kinds of nodes called v-nodes and &-nodes. We will also use two types of tokens called h-tokens and l-tokens. A v-node will exhibit decision-making capability. A &-node will have the capability to initiate and terminate concurrently executable actions. A h-token passing through an arc will model the execution of the action associated with that arc. On the other hand, an l-token passing through an arc will model the omission of the action associated with that arc. Now, with this in mind, we shall consider the simple 'structured' program shown in fig. 3.1.

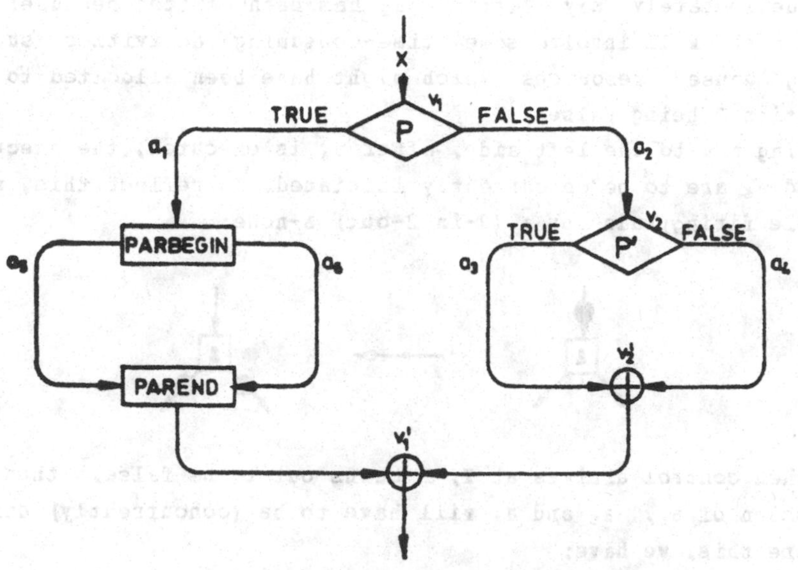

Fig. 3.1.

When control reaches th point "X", the predicate P will be tested. If P is true (false) the action a_1 will be executed (omitted) and 'concurrently' the action a_2 will be omitted (executed). To reflect this we have the following firing rule for a (1-in 2-out) v-node:

The darkened token is a h-token (execute signal) and the plain token is a l-token (omit signal). Assume that when control arrives at X, P is found to be true. Then all the actions associated with the right branch are to be omitted. This means that 'after' a_2 has been omitted, a_3 and a_4 should be omitted and this can be done concurrently. To model this, we have the firing rule:

We deliberately say "after" a_2 has been omitted because: This omission might well involve some time-consuming activities such as returning unused resources which might have been allocated to a_2 in anticipation P being false.

Turning now to the left side, after a_1 is executed, the executions of a_5 and a_6 are to be concurrently initiated. To reflect this, we use a suitable firing rule for a (1-in 2-out) &-node:

If when control arrives at X, P turns out to be false, then after the omission of a_1, a_5 and a_6 will have to be (concurrently) omitted. To capture this, we have:

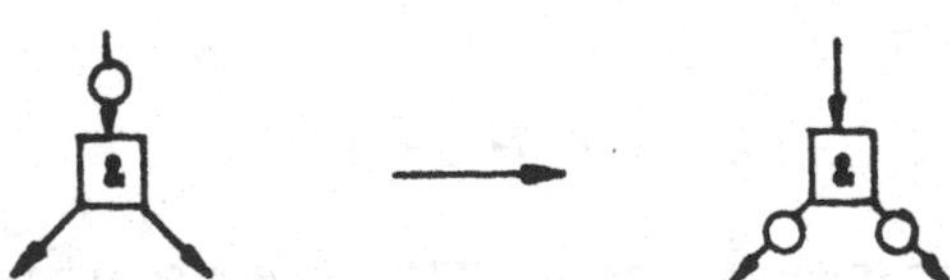

Starting from the beginning, if P is false, then after a_2 is executed, either a_3 will be executed and a_4 omitted or vice versa. The node v_2' may be viewed as essentially synchronizing the execution of a_3 with the non-execution of a_4 or vice versa before passing the control on to v_1'. Consequently, we have the firing rule for a (2-in 1-out) ∇-node:

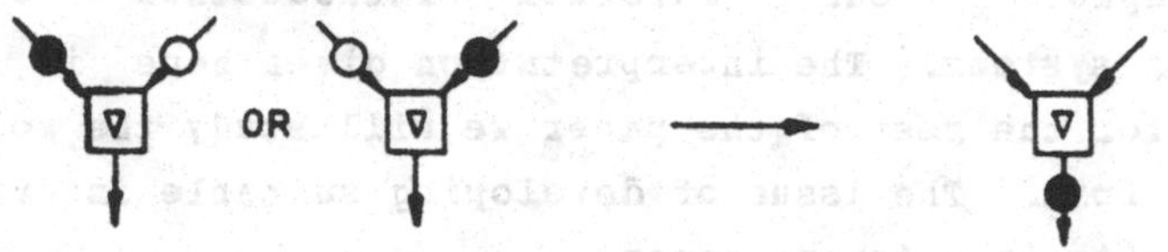

A similar argument for the case where P is true yields:

The corresponding firing rules for a &-node, by considering the PAREND statement, are:

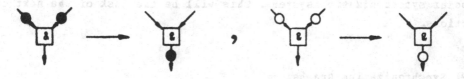

Now, if the node v_2' at its input side ever senses that <u>both</u> a_3 and a_4 have been concurrently executed then this reflects a "bad" and unintended flow of control. (We assume that there are no exit and entry points of control other than the ones shown in fig. 1). To model this we have:

<u>Dead lock</u>

Turning to the PAREND statement and arguing in a related fashion, we derive:

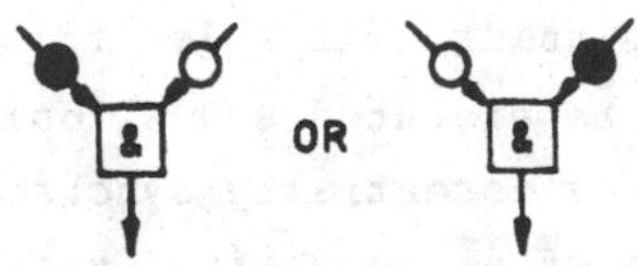

Dead lock

This completes our informal introduction to bipolar synchronization systems. The interpretation given here is a rather loose one and for the rest of the paper we will study the model in its uninterpreted form. The issue of developing suitable interpretations will be dealt with in a future paper.

We are now ready to present some formal material. As mentioned earlier, a bipolar synchronization system is a finite directed strongly connected graph together with a marking of the arcs where we distinguish between two kinds of nodes and two types of tokens. A directed graph with just one kind of nodes and one type of tokens is called a synchronization graph (also known as marked graph). Since the theory of synchronization graphs is well-understood [13,6,27], we will start with a restricted class of synchronization graphs called live and safe synchronization graphs. We will then extend the notion of a live and safe synchronization graph along two directions to obtain bipolar synchronization systems. This will be the task of the next two sections.

3.2. Synchronization Graphs

A synchronization graph is basically a finite directed graph together with a variable marking of its arcs. For our purposes, it is necessary to work with directed graphs which have multiple arcs between a pair of nodes as also self-loops. Hence, in this paper:

Definition: A directed graph is a quadruple
$G = (V,A;Q,Z)$ where:

1) V is a finite set of nodes.
2) A is a finite set of arcs. $(V \cap A = \emptyset)$
3) $Q: A \to V$ and $Z: A \to V$ are the source function and target function respectively.

Let $G = (V,A;Q,Z)$ be a directed graph. Then a marking of G is a function $M:A \to N$. $M(a)$ tells the number of 'tokens' on the arc a.

Definition: A synchronization graph is a quintuple $MG = (V,A;Q,Z,M)$ where:

1) $G = (V,A;Q,Z)$ is a directed graph.
2) M is a marking of G called the initial marking.

In diagrams, the elements of V will be drawn as boxes. If $a \in A$, $Q(a)=v_1$ and $Z(a)=v_2$ then there will be a directed arc from v_1 to v_2 labelled a. If $M(a)=k$ then we will indicate this by placing k tokens on the arc a. An example of a synchronization graph is shown in fig. 3.2.

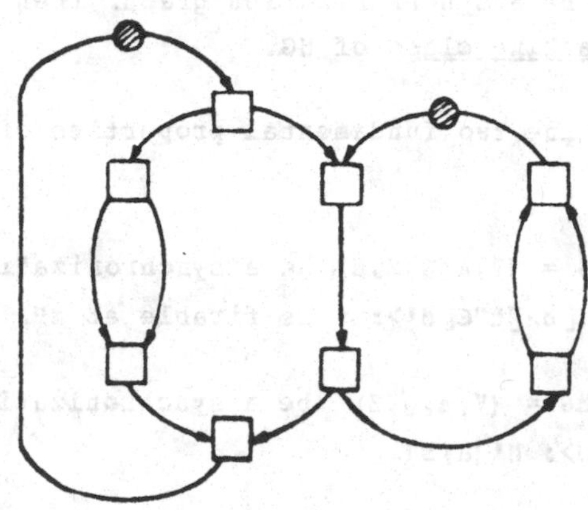

Fig. 3.2

The initial marking of a synchronization graph can be transformed into a new marking by a node firing. In stating this rule as also in many other parts of this section we shall make use of the following notation:

Let $G = (V,A;Q,Z)$ be a directed graph and $v \in V$. Then,

$I(v) = \{a \in A \mid Z(a)=v\}$ (The set of input arcs of v)

$O(v) = \{a \in A \mid Q(a)=v\}$ (The set of output arcs of v).

Now let $G = (V,A;Q,Z)$ be a directed graph and M be a marking of G. Let $v \in V$. Then v is firable at M if:

$\forall a \in I(v): M(a)>0$.

When v fires a new marking M' of G is reached where, for all $a \in A$,

$$M'(a) = \begin{cases} M(a)-1, & \text{if } a\in I(v)-O(v) \\ M(a)+1, & \text{if } a\in O(v)-I(v) \\ M(a), & \text{otherwise.} \end{cases}$$

We will denote this one-step transformation of M into M' by $M[\!\!\to M'$. The set of all markings of G that can be reached from M through node firings is called the forward marking class of M. Formally,

<u>Definition</u>: Let G = (V,A;Q,Z) be a directed graph and M a marking of G. Then the <u>forward marking class defined by</u> M is denoted as [M> and is the smallest set of markings of G given by:

1) $M\in[M>$
2) if $M'\in[M>$ and $M'[\!\!\to M''$ then $M''\in[M>$.

Let MG = (V,A;Q,Z,M) be a synchronization graph. Then we will say that [M> is the <u>forward marking class</u> of MG.

We can now define two fundamental properties of synchronization graphs.

<u>Definition</u>: Let MG = (V,A;Q,Z,M) be a synchronization graph. MG is <u>live</u> if: $\forall v\in V\forall M'\in[M>\exists M''\in[M'>$: v is firable at M".

<u>Definition</u>: Let MG = (V,A;Q,Z) be a synchronization graph. MG is <u>safe</u> if: $\forall a\in A\forall M'\in[M>: M'(a)\leq 1$.

The synchronization graph shown in fig. 3.2 is live and safe. Live and safe synchronization graphs can be elegantly characterized as shown in [6,13]. Before citing these results, we shall develop some more graph-theoretic terminology. Let G = (V,A;Q,Z) be a directed graph and let $\Pi = a_1,a_2,\dots,a_n$ be a sequence of arcs of G. Let $Q(a_1)=v$ and $Z(a_n)=v'$. Then Π is a <u>directed path</u> of <u>length n</u> (from v to v') if for $1\leq i<n$, $Z(a_i)=Q(a_{i+1})$. Let Π be a directed path in G. Then Π is an <u>elementary circuit</u> of G if:

1) $Q(a_1)=Z(a_n)$
2) For $1\leq i\leq j\leq n$, $Z(a_j)=Q(a_i)$ implies i=1 and j=n.

A <u>basic circuit</u> is an elementary circuit of a synchronization graph which carries just one token. To be precise, let $\Pi = a_1,a_2,\dots,a_n$ be an elementary circuit of (V,A;Q,Z) where MG = (V,A;Q,Z,M) is a synchronization graph. Then $M(\Pi)$ is the <u>token load</u> of Π and is given by: $M(\Pi) = M(a_1)+M(a_2)+\dots+M(a_n)$.

If Π is an elementary circuit and $M(\Pi)=1$ then Π is said to be a basic circuit. Basic circuits will play an important role in the development of section 3.4. To return to this section, a well-known result concerning live and safe synchronization graphs states:

Theorem 3.1: (see [6,13]) Let $MG = (V,A;Q,Z,M)$ be a synchronization graph. Then MG is live and safe iff

1) For every circuit Π of $(V,A;Q,Z)$, $M(\Pi)>0$.

2) Every arc is contained in a basic circuit of MG.

We conclude this section with the introduction of a more convenient formalism for dealing with (live and) safe synchronization graphs. Let $MG = (V,A;Q,Z,M)$ be a safe synchronization graph and $M\in[M\rangle$. Since for all $a\in A$, $M'(a)=0$ or $M'(a)=1$, we can view M' as a subset of arcs. In other words, $M' = \{a\in A \mid M'(a)=1\}$.

The firing rule then becomes: v is firable of M' if $I(v) \subseteq M'$. When v fires the new marking M'' that is obtained is given by $(M'-I(v)) \cup O(v)$ and so on. In this paper we shall deal only with live and safe synchronization graphs. Hence, from now we shall use this formalism for dealing with our synchronization graphs.

3.3. The Model

We will formulate the model in three steps. To start with:

Definition: A bipolar graph (bp-graph) is a 5-tuple $BP = (V_\nabla, V_\&, A;Q,Z)$ where:

1) $V_\nabla \cup V_\& \neq \emptyset$ and $V_\nabla \cap V_\& = \emptyset$

2) $(V_\nabla \cup V_\&, A;Q,Z)$ is a directed graph.

V_∇ is the set of ∇-nodes and $V_\&$ is the set of &-nodes.

A marking of BP is an ordered pair of arcs (M_H,M_L) such that:

1) $M_H, M_L \subseteq A$ and $M_H \cap M_L = \emptyset$.

2) $(V_\nabla \cup V_\&, A;Q,Z,M_H \cup M_L)$ is a live and safe synchronization graph.

If $a\in M_H$ (M_L) we will say that a carries a h-token (l-token) under (M_H,M_L). In diagrams we will indicate this by placing a darkened (plain) token on a. An example of a bp-graph together with a marking is shown in fig. 3.3.

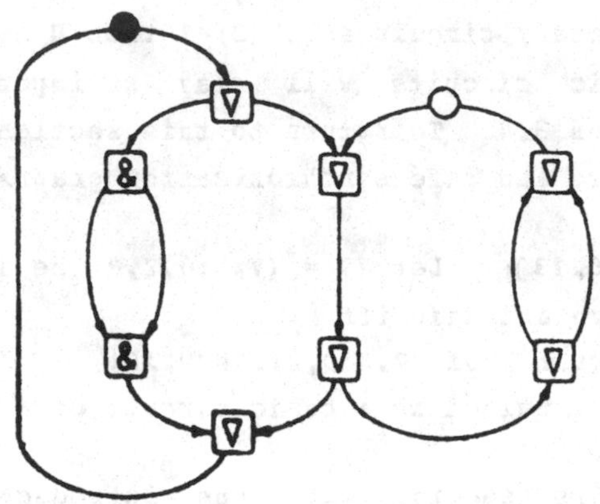

Fig. 3.3

A marking of a bp-graph can be transformed into a new marking through node firings. We will now state the rules for node firings. These rules are the natural extensions of the firing rules which were informally introduced in section 3.1.

Let BP = $(V_\nabla, V_\& ;A;Q,Z)$ be a bp-graph and (M_H, M_L) a marking of BP. The material that follows, unless stated otherwise, is developed w.r.t. this bp-graph and the marking (M_H, M_L).

Let v be a ∇-node of BP. Then v is _firable_ at (M_H, M_L) if:

1) $I(v) \subseteq M_H \cup M_L$
2) $|I(v) \cap M_H| \leq 1$.

When v _fires_ a new marking (M', M'') is reached which is given by,

1) $M_H' \cup M_L' = ((M_H \cup M_L) - I(v)) \cup O(v)$
2) $|M_H' \cap O(v)| = |M_H \cap I(v)|$.

Roughly speaking, one token is removed from each input arc of v and one token is added to each output arc of v. Some output arc of v will carry a h-token (and the remaining output arcs of v l-tokens) iff some input arc of v carries a h-token under (M_H, M_L). That (M_H', M_L') is indeed a marking of BP can be shown easily using the theory of synchronization graphs.

Let u be a &-node of BP. u is _firable_ at (M_H, M_L) if:

1) $I(u) \subseteq M_H \cup M_L$
2) $I(u) \subseteq M_H$ or $I(u) \subseteq M_L$.

When u fires, a new marking (M_H', M_L') is reached which is given by:

1) $M_H' \cup M_L' = ((M_H \cup M_L) - I(u)) \cup O(u)$.

2) $O(u) \subseteq M_H'$ (M_L') iff $I(u) \subseteq M_H$ (M_L).

If (M_H, M_L) can be transformed to (M_H', M_L') through a node firing we will indicate this as $(M_H, M_L) \mapsto (M_H', M_L')$.

If the second part of the conditions imposed on the firability of a node is violated we will say that the node is in dead lock. Specifically, let v be a ∇-node of BP. Then v is in <u>dead lock</u> at (M_H, M_L) if $|I(v) \cap M_H| > 1$. Let u be a &-node of BP. Then u is in <u>dead lock</u> at (M_H, M_L) if $I(u) \cap M_H \neq \emptyset$ <u>and</u> $I(u) \cap M_L \neq \emptyset$. A node which is in dead lock can never fire again. This is a firing rule convention that we shall adopt.

We can now define two sets of reachable markings associated with a marking of a bp-graph. In doing so, as also through the remaining part of this material, we will adopt a convenient notation for dealing with markings. If (M_H, M_L) is a marking of BP we will often write this as simply M and (M_H', M_L') as M' etc. Only when necessary we will explicitly indicate the partitioning of the arcs into those that carry a h-token (M_H) and those that carry a l-token (M_L) under M.

<u>Definition</u>: Let BP = $(V_\nabla, V_\&, A; Q, Z)$ be a bp-graph and M a marking of BP. Then the <u>forward marking class</u> of BP <u>defined by</u> M is denoted as [M> and is the smallest set of markings of BP given by:

1) $M \in [M>$

2) If $M' \in [M>$ and $M' \mapsto M''$ then $M'' \in [M>$.

<u>Definition</u>: Let BP = $(V_\nabla, V_\&, A; Q, Z)$ be a bp-graph and M a marking of BP. Then the <u>full marking class</u> of BP <u>defined by</u> M is denoted as [M] and is the smallest set of markings of BP given by:

1) $M \in [M]$

2) If $M' \in [M]$ and $M' \mapsto M''$ then $M'' \in [M]$

3) If $M' \in [M]$ and $M'' \mapsto M'$ then $M'' \in [M]$.

We are now prepared to define our system model called bipolar synchronization system (bp-system). Basically, a bp-system is a bp-graph together with a full marking class.

<u>Definition</u>: A <u>bipolar synchronization system</u> is a 6-tuple S = (V ,V ,A;Q,Z,[M]) where:

1) BP = $(V_\nabla, V_\&, A; Q, Z)$ is a bp-graph

2) $M = (M_H, M_L)$ is a marking of BP

3) [M] is the full marking class of BP defined by M.

In diagrams, we will indicate the underlying BP and a representative member of [M]. Fig. 3.3 may now be viewed as an example of a bp-system.

We conclude this section by formulating the notion of good behaviour.

<u>Defintion</u>: Let $S = (V_\nabla, V_\&, A; Q, Z, [M])$ be a bp-system. S is <u>well-behaved</u> if:

$\forall a \in A \; \forall M' \in [M] \; \exists M'' \in [M'\rangle : a \in M''$.

Intuitively, in a well-behaved system, independent of the 'initial marking', we can execute the action associated with any arc, as often as desired. It is easy to show:

<u>Proposition</u>: Let $S = (V_\nabla, V_\&, A; Q, Z, [M])$ be a well-behaved bp-system. Then $\forall w \in V_\nabla \cup V_\& \; \forall M' \in [M]$: w is <u>not</u> in dead lock at M'.

This once again follows from the properties of a live and safe synchronization graph and our firing rules.

3.4. <u>Synthesis Techniques</u>

In this section we present the major results that we have to date regarding bp-systems. In developing these results our main aim has been to look for techniques for systematically constructing well-behaved systems. Due to lack of space, we state here the results without proof. Detailed proofs will appear in a forthcoming paper. Our approach to attacking the synthesis problem is 'top-down'. We start with some simple 'seed' systems. These systems are then repeatedly refined to generate more complex systems. The seed systems called elementary systems are essentially of two types.

<u>Definition</u>: A <u>∇-elementary</u> system is a bp-system of the form $S = (V_\nabla, \emptyset, A; Q, Z, [M])$ where:

1) $|V_\nabla| = 1$.
2) $|M_H| = 1$.

In other words, there is a single ∨-node, say v. All arcs are self-looping on v ($Q(a)=Z(a)=v$). Exactly one arc carries a h-token and the remaining arcs carry one l-token each (Recall that the underlying marked graph is required to be live and safe). A ∨-elementary system is shown in fig. 3.4.a.

<u>Definition</u>: A <u>&-elementary</u> system is a bp-system of the form $S = (\emptyset, V_{\&}, A; Q, Z, [M])$ where:

1) $|V_{\&}|=1$.
2) $M_H=A$.

There is a single &-node, say u. All arcs are self-looping on u and each of them carries a h-token. In fig. 3.4.a if we change the inscription to read & and turn the l-token into a h-token then we will obtain a &-elementary system.

An <u>elementary bp-system</u> is a bp-system which is either a ∨-elementary system or a &-elementary system. Clearly, all elementary systems are well-behaved.

We shall now present two refinement rules using which an interesting subclass of well-behaved bp-systems can be constructed. The first rule consists of introducing a new node on an existing arc. The new node can be either a ∨-node or a &-node. Since there is little chance of this rule being misunderstood, we shall show it only graphically.

<u>Rule-1</u> (<u>Arc refinement</u> rule):

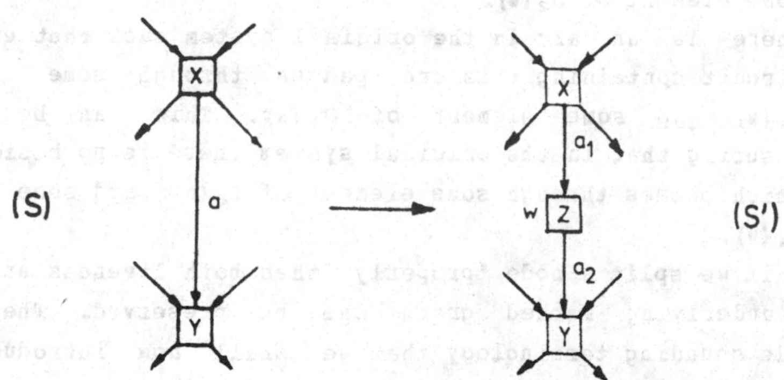

The arc a is replaced by a_1 and a_2. A new node w is introduced. ($X, Y, Z \in \{\vee, \&\}$)

Let M be the representative marking chosen to indicate the full marking class of S. Then we obtain M', the representative marking of

S' as follows: If $a \in M_H$ (M_L) then $a_2 \in M_H'$ (M_L'). In either case a_1 is left unmarked. We will say that S' is an arc-refinement of S. It can be easily shown that if S is a bp-system then S' is also a bp-system.

The second rule consists of splitting a node into two nodes of the same type and introducing an arbitrary number of parallel arcs between the new pair of nodes. Graphically, what we have in mind would look as shown below:

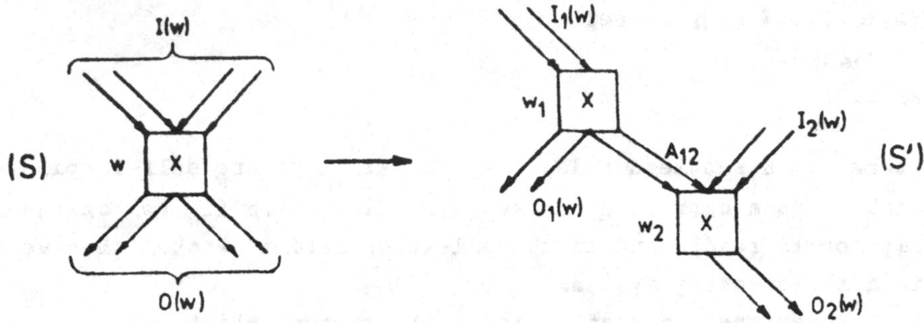

w is replaced by w_1 and w_2. If w is a ∨-node (&-node) then w_1 and w_2 are chosen to be ∨-nodes (&-nodes). A_{12} is the new set of arcs introduced. $I(w)=I_1(w) \cup I_2(w)$ and $O(w)=O_1(w) \cup O_2(w)$. This node splitting will not disturb the liveness property of the underlying marked graph. But in general safety will not be preserved. The underlying marked graph of the new system can fail to be safe in two ways:

1) One (and hence all) of the new arcs that we have introduced does not lie on a basic circuit. This can be avoided by ensuring that in the original system there is at least one basic circuit which passes through some element of $I_1(w)$ and some element of $O_2(w)$.
2) There is an arc in the original system such that every basic circuit containing this arc passes through some element of $I_2(w)$ and some element of $O_1(w)$. This can be avoided by ensuring that in the original system there is no basic circuit which passes through some element of $I_2(w)$ and some element of $O_1(w)$.

Thus if we split a node 'properly' then both liveness and safeness of the underlying marked graph can be preserved. The somewhat formidable sounding terminology that we shall now introduce merely formalizes these simple considerations.

Let S = (BP,[M]) be a bp-system and w be a node of S. Then $R(w) \subseteq I(w) \times O(w)$ is the binary relation defined as:

$(x,y) \in R(w)$ iff there is a basic circuit (of the underlying marked graph of S) passing through x and y.

Let S, w and R(w) be defined as stated. Now a splitting of w is a pair of partitions $\pi = (\sigma,\tau)$, where $\sigma = \{I_1(w), I_2(w)\}$ is a two block partition of I(w) and $\tau = \{O_1(w), O_2(w)\}$ is a two block partition of O(w). In other words,

$$I_1(w) \cup I_2(w) = I(w),\ O_1(w) \cup O_2(w) = O(w),\ I_1(w) \cap I_2(w) = \emptyset = O_1(w) \cap O_2(w).$$

We will denote this partition pair $\pi (=(\sigma,\tau))$ as:

$$\pi : (I(w), O(w)) \rightarrow (I_1(w), O_1(w)), (I_2(w), O_2(w)).$$

Now π is called a proper splitting just in case,

1) $R(w) \cap (I_1(w) \times O_2(w)) \neq \emptyset$.
2) $R(w) \cap (I_2(w) \times O_1(w)) = \emptyset$.

It is easy to show that a proper splitting of a node in a live and safe marked graph always yields a new live and safe marked graph. Keeping this in mind, we can now state the second refinement rule:

Rule-2 (Node refinement rule): Let $S = (V_\nabla, V_\&, A; Q, Z, [M])$ be a bp-system, w a node of S and

$$\pi : (I(w), O(w)) \rightarrow (I_1(w), O_1(w)), (I_2(w), O_2(w))$$

a proper splitting of w. Let $w_1, w_2 \notin V_\nabla \cup V_\& (\cup A)$, $A_{12} \neq \emptyset$ and $A_{12} \cap (A \cup V_\nabla \cup V_\&) = \emptyset$. Then the (π, A_{12})-refinement of S is the bp-system $S' = (V'_\nabla, V'_\&, A'; Q', Z', [M'])$ where:

1) $V' = \begin{cases} V - \{w\} \cup \{w_1, w_2\}, & \text{if } w \in V \\ V, & \text{otherwise.} \end{cases}$

2) $V' = \begin{cases} V - \{w\} \cup \{w_1, w_2\}, & \text{if } w \in V \\ V, & \text{otherwise.} \end{cases}$

3) $A' = A \cup A_{12}$.

4) $\forall a' \in A': Q'(a') = \begin{cases} w_1, & \text{if } a' \in O_1(w) \cup A_{12} \\ w_2, & \text{if } a' \in O_2(w) \\ Q(a'), & \text{otherwise.} \end{cases}$

5) $\forall a' \in A': Z'(a') = \begin{cases} w_1, & \text{if } a' \in I_1(w) \\ w_2, & \text{if } a' \in I_2(w) \cup A_{12} \\ Z(a'), & \text{otherwise.} \end{cases}$

6) $M_H' = M_H$ and $M_L' = M_L$.

If the details concerning π and A_{12} are not important - as will always be the case - we will simply say that S' is a node-refinement of S.

Using these two rules, we can construct an interesting class of bp-systems called well-structured systems.

Definition: The class of well-structured bp-systems is denoted as WS and is given by:

1) If S is an elementary system then S∈WS.
2) If S'∈WS and S" is an arc-refinement of S' then S"∈WS.
3) If S'∈WS and S" is a node-refinement of S' then S"∈WS.
4) No other bp-system is in WS.

The system shown in fig. 3.3 is well-structured. The means for constructing it, starting from an elementary system and using Rule-1 and Rule-2 is shown in fig 3.4.a through 3.4.e.

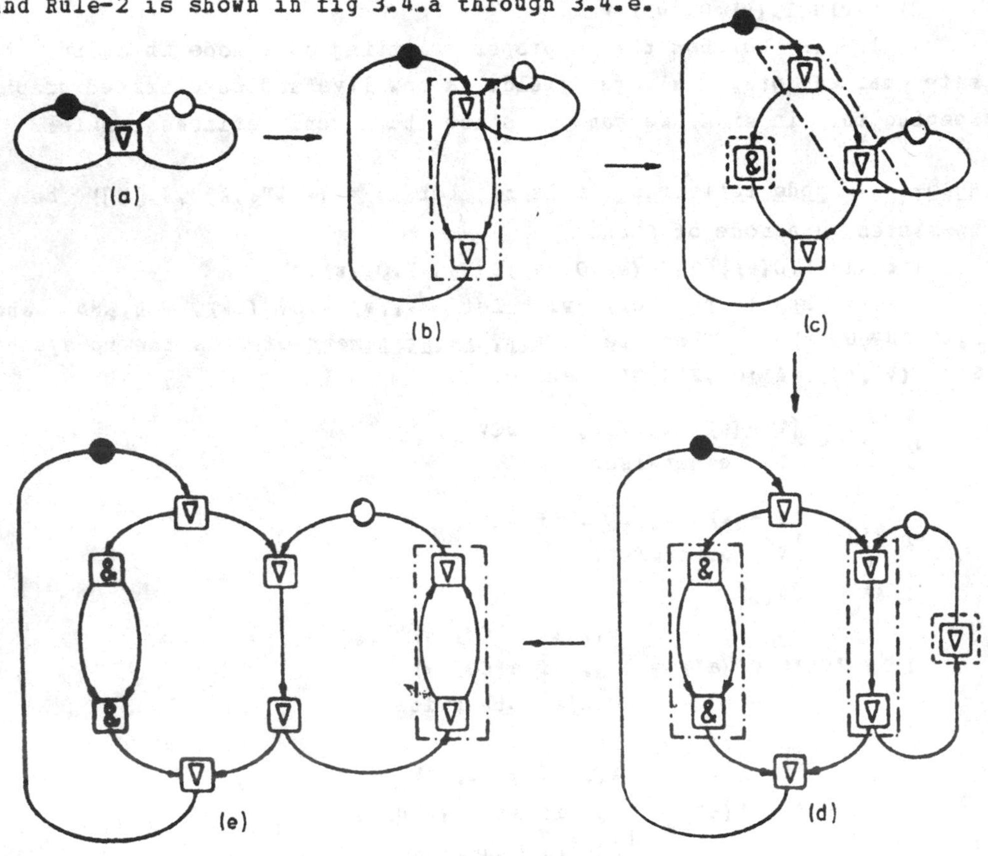

Fig. 3.4

The first result concerning this class of systems is:

Theorem 3.2: Every well-structured bp-system is also well-behaved.

As might be expected, the converse is unfortunately not true. The system shown in fig. 3.5 is well-behaved but is not well-structured.

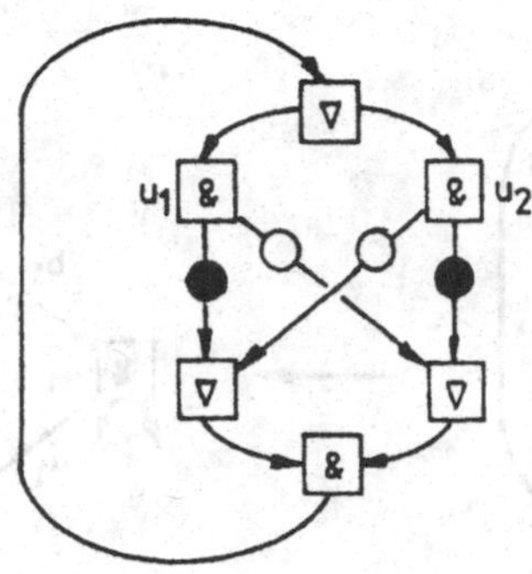

Fig. 3.5

This may not be obvious but it turns out that well-structured systems have a pleasing behavioural property using which we can at once certify that the system shown in fig. 3.5 is not well-structured. This behavioral property can be stated as:

<u>Definition</u>: Let $S = (V_\nabla, V_\& A; Q, Z, [M])$ be a bp-system and S^{-1} be the reverse bp-system, $S^{-1} = (V_\nabla, V_\&, A; Q', Z', [M])$ where $Q' = Z$ and $Z' = Q$. Then S is <u>strongly well-behaved</u> if both S and S^{-1} are well-behaved.

Thus a strongly well-behaved bp-system is well-behaved in both forward and reverse directions. Well-structured bp-systems have this nice behavioral property. In fact we can say more.

<u>Theorem</u> 3.3: A bp-system is well-structured if, and only if, it is strongly well-behaved.

Now for the system shown in fig. 3.5, if we reverse the direction of all the arrows then it is easy to see that in the reverse system, at the marking shown, the nodes u_1 and u_2 are in dead-lock. Since the reverse system is not well-behaved, we can conclude, due to theorem 3.3 that the system shown in fig. 3.5 is not well-structured.

We shall now formulate two additional transformation rules using which we can construct well-behaved systems which are not necessarily well-structured.

The first rule states that the transformation shown below is permissable:

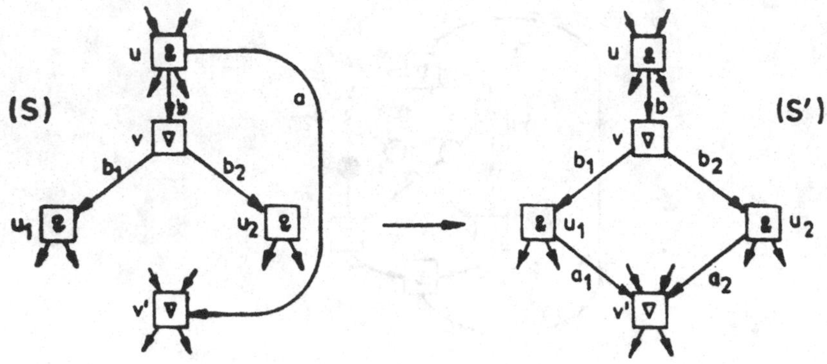

Formally:

<u>Rule-3</u> (<u>∇-diamond</u> rule): Let $S = (V_\nabla, V_\&, A; Q, Z, [M])$ be a bp-system such that:

1) v and v' are ∇-nodes of S.
2) u, u_1 and u_2 are &-nodes of S.
3) There are arcs b, b_1 and b_2 such that $I(v)=\{b\}$, $O(v)=\{b_1,b_2\}$, $Q(b)=u$, $Z(b_1)=u_1$ and $Z(b_2)=u_2$.
4) There is an arc a such that $Q(a)=u$ and $Z(a)=v'$.
5) None of the above mentioned arcs are marked under M.

Then a <u>∇-diamond</u> transformation of S is the bp-system $S' = (V_\nabla, V_\&, A'; Q', Z', [M])$ where:

1) $A' = A-\{a\} \cup \{a_1,a_2\}$ where $a_1,a_2 \notin A$.

2) $\forall a' \in A'$: $Q'(a') = \begin{cases} u_1, & \text{if } a'=a_1 \\ u_2, & \text{if } a'=a_2 \\ Q(a'), & \text{otherwise.} \end{cases}$

3) $\forall a' \in A'$: $Z'(a') = \begin{cases} v', & \text{if } a' \in \{a_1,a_2\} \\ Z(a'), & \text{otherwise.} \end{cases}$

The arc a is removed and two new arcs a_1 and a_2 are introduced so that v, v', u_1, u_2 form a diamond shape through b_1, b_2, a_1, a_2. Our requirement that all the arcs involved in the transformation be token-free might appear troublesome. However, since we will be applying the rule to only well-behaved bp-systems, a suitable marking at which the rule becomes applicable can be obtained by a limited amount of node firings. We will return to this issue towards the end of this section. For now, we shall give a second transformation rule. This rule is the reverse-dual of the ∇-diamond rule in that we obtain it by interchanging ∇- and &-nodes and reversing the direction of all arcs. Pictorially, the rule states:

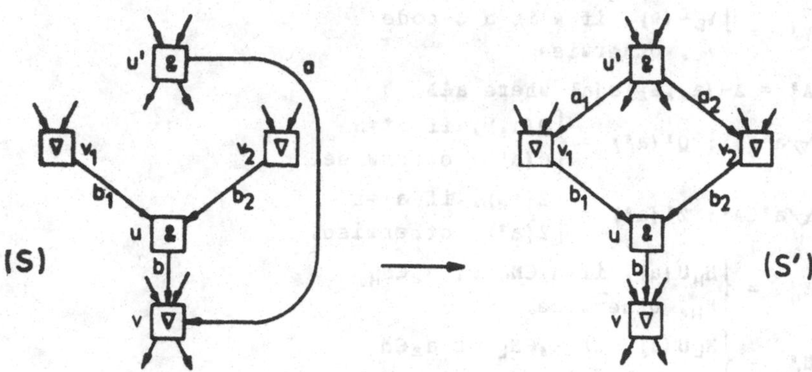

Rule-4 (&-diamond rule): Let $S = (V_\nabla, V_\&, A; Q, Z, [M])$ be a bp-system such that:

1) u and u' are &-nodes of S.
2) v, v_1 and v_2 are ∇-nodes of S.
3) There are arcs b, b_1 and b_2 such that $O(u)=b$, $I(u)=\{b_1,b_2\}$, $Z(b)=v$, $Q(b_1)=v_1$ and $Q(b_2)=v_2$.
4) There is an arc a such that $Z(a)=v$ and $Q(a)=u'$.
5) None of the arcs mentioned above is marked under M.

Then a &-diamond transformation of S is the bp-system $S' = (V\ ,V\ ,A';Q',Z',[M])$ where:

1) $A' = A-\{a\}\cup\{a_1,a_2\}$ where $a_1,a_2 \notin A$.

2) $\forall a' \in A'$: $Q'(a') = \begin{cases} u', & \text{if } a \in \{a_1,a_2\} \\ Q(a'), & \text{otherwise.} \end{cases}$

3) $\forall a' \in A'$: $Z'(a') = \begin{cases} v_1, & \text{if } a'=a_1 \\ v_2, & \text{if } a'=a_2 \\ Z(a'), & \text{otherwise.} \end{cases}$

The diamond-transformation rules have been stated w.r.t a 1-in 2-out ∇-node(v) and a 2-in 1-out &-node(u). To generate as large a class of well-behaved systems as possible, we will need to generalize this rule. Instead, we will introduce two reduction rules which when combined with the two diamond rules provide the same amount of expressive power. The first rule is the 'reverse' of the arc-refinement rule.

Rule-5: Let $S = (V_\nabla, V_\&, A; Q, Z, [M])$ be a bp-system, $a_1,a_2 \in A$ and w a node such that $Z(a_1)=Q(a_2)=w$ and $I(w)=\{a_1\}$ and $O(w)=\{a_2\}$. Then the bp-system $S' = (V_\nabla^1, V_\&^1, A';Q',Z',[M'])$ is an arc-reduction of S where:

1) $V'_\nabla = \begin{cases} V_\nabla - \{w\}, \text{ if } w \text{ is a } \nabla\text{-node} \\ V_\nabla, \text{ otherwise.} \end{cases}$

2) $V'_\& = \begin{cases} V_\& - \{w\}, \text{ if } w \text{ is a } \&\text{-node} \\ V_\&, \text{ otherwise.} \end{cases}$

3) $A' = A - \{a_1, a_2\} \cup \{a\}$ where $a \notin A$.

4) $\forall a' \in A'$: $Q'(a') = \begin{cases} Q(a_1), \text{ if } a'=a \\ Q(a'), \text{ otherwise.} \end{cases}$

5) $\forall a' \in A'$: $Z'(a') = \begin{cases} Z(a_2), \text{ if } a'=a \\ Z(a'), \text{ otherwise.} \end{cases}$

6) $M'_H = \begin{cases} M_H \cup \{a\}, \text{ if } a_1 \in M_H \text{ or } a_2 \in M_H \\ M_H, \text{ otherwise.} \end{cases}$

7) $M'_L = \begin{cases} M_L \cup \{a\}, \text{ if } a_1 \in M_L \text{ or } a_2 \in M_L \\ M_L, \text{ otherwise.} \end{cases}$

The next rule is in some sense the reverse of our node-refinement rule.

Rule-6: Let $S = (V_\nabla, V_\&, A; Q, Z, [M]$ be a bp-system, w_1 and w_2 two nodes of the same type and $A_1 \subseteq A$ such that:

1) $\forall a \in A_1$: $Q(a)=w_1$ and $Z(a)=w_2$.
2) $\forall a \in A_1$: a is not marked under M.
3) Under M, the only token-free directed paths from w_1 to w_2 are those (of length 1) provided by the arcs in A_1.

Then the bp-system $S' = (V', V', A'; Q', Z', [M'])$ is a node-reduction of S where:

1) $V'_\nabla = \begin{cases} V_\nabla - \{w_1, w_2\} \cup \{w\}, \text{ if } w_1 \text{ and } w_2 \text{ are } \nabla\text{-nodes } (w \notin V_\nabla \cup V_\&) \\ V_\nabla, \text{ otherwise.} \end{cases}$

2) $V' = \begin{cases} V_\& - \{w_1, w_2\} \cup \{w\}, \text{ if } w_1 \text{ and } w_2 \text{ are } \&\text{-nodes } (w \notin V_\nabla \cup V_\&) \\ V_\&, \text{ otherwise.} \end{cases}$

3) $A' = A - A_1$.

4) $\forall a' \in A'$: $Q'(a') = \begin{cases} w, \text{ if } a' \in O(w_1) \cup O(w_2) \\ Q(a'), \text{ otherwise.} \end{cases}$

$Z'(a') = \begin{cases} w, \text{ if } a' \in I(w_1) \cup I(w_2) \\ Z(a'), \text{ otherwise.} \end{cases}$

5) $M'=M$ and $M'=M$.

Thus a pair of nodes w_1, w_2 is collapsed into a single node w and the bundle of arcs directed from w_1 to w_2 is deleted. The condition that the two nodes be of the same type is crucial. Now using these additional rules we can generate a new class of systems called well-formed systems.

<u>Definition</u>: The class of <u>well-formed</u> bp-systems is denoted as WF and is given by:

1) If S is an elementary system then S∈WF.
2) If S∈WF and S' is an arc refinement of S then S'∈WF.
3) If S∈WF and S' is a node refinement of S then S'∈WF.
4) If S∈WF and S' is a ∨-diamond transformation of S then S'∈WF.
5) If S∈WF and S' is a &-diamond transformation of S then S'∈WF.
6) If S∈WF and S' is an arc-reduction of S then S'∈WF.
7) If S∈WF and S' is a node reduction of S then S'∈WF.
8) No other bp-system is in WF.

It is easy to show that well-formed systems are also well-behaved. But surprisingly enough, the two diamand rules provide all the (additional) expressive power we need. This is our main result:

<u>Theorem</u> 3.4: A bp-system is well-behaved iff it is well-formed.

Thus using the six rules we construct only well-behaved systems and we can construct <u>all</u> of them.

Now, in the synthesis of a system, we have to choose a suitable marking in the marking class before applying some of our rules. Such a suitable marking can be arrived at by systematically firing the required number of nodes, so as to obtain, a specific token-free set of arcs. In carrying out these node firings if decisions have to be made, they can be made in an arbitrary fashion. The marking class of the system we are trying to design will remain unaffected. This is brought out by the following result.

<u>Theorem</u> 3.5: Let $S = (BP,[M])$ be a well-behaved system and $M',M'' \in [M]$. Then $[M'\rangle \cap [M''\rangle \neq \emptyset$.

A well-behaved system has the Church-Rosser property (w.r.t. forward reachability). There is a <u>unique</u> part of the full marking class which is strongly connected w.r.t. forward firings of the nodes. And the well-behaved system will 'eventually' get into this portion of the full marking class regardless of the starting point and regardless of the outcomes of the decisions made in the initial phase of the behaviour.

3.5. Basic Representation of BP-Systems

In this section we will briefly sketch the means for obtaining the basic representation of a bp-system in terms of a CE-system. We shall do this in an informal fashion. The more formally inclined reader should consult the latter chapter on net morphisms to see how one would go about obtaining the basic interpretation of a bp-system through the aid of net morphisms.

Let S be a bp-system and CE(S) be a CE-system which is supposed to provide a basic representation of S. To get at CE(S) we need to derive a CE-net together with a class of cases (of this CE-net) which is closed under full reachability. We obtain the conditions of CE(S) from the arcs of S. Specifically, for each arc a of S, there will be a pair of conditions a_H and a_L in CE(S). Let M be a representative marking of the full marking class of S. Then we obtain a representative case c of the full case class of CE(S) in the natural way. If a carries a h-token under M then $a_H \in c$. If a carries a l-token under M then $a_L \in c$. Otherwise neither a_H nor a_L is in c. In graphical terms:

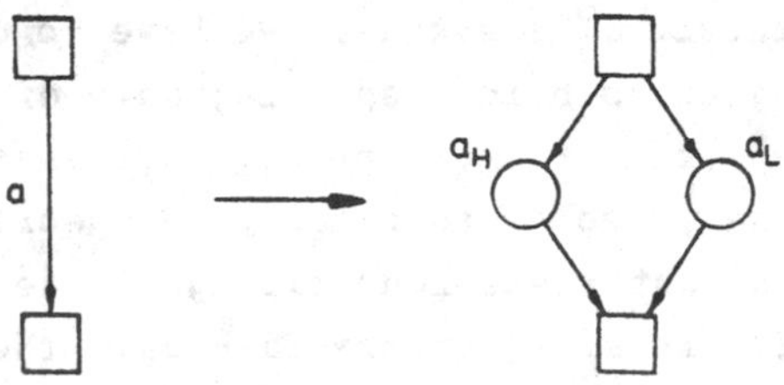

The events of CE(S) are obtained by 'blowing-up' the nodes of S into a number of events. First consider a 2-in 2-out v-node v with $I(v)=\{a,b\}$ and $O(v)=\{f,g\}$. Then v is blown up into five events and these are connected to the conditions corresponding to I(v) and O(v) as shown below:

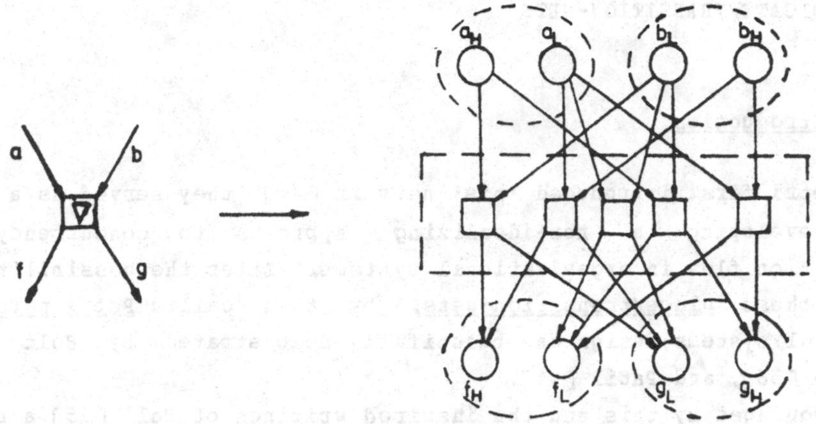

In the case of a 2-in 2-out &-node the corresponding condition-event structure is simpler.

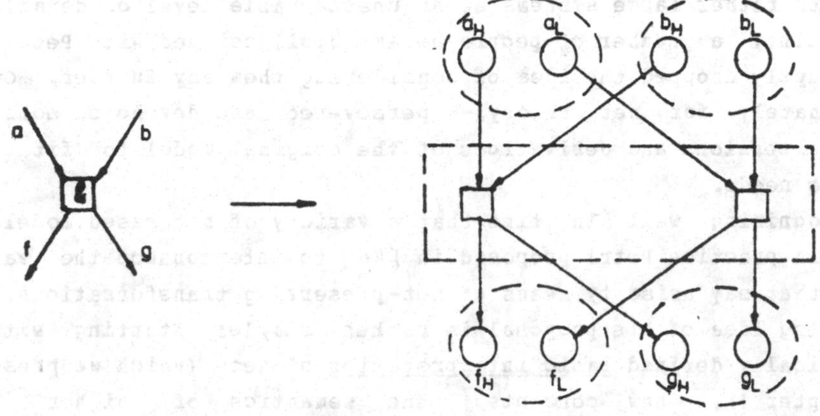

The alert reader will have noticed that what we have sketched here is, strictly speaking, a means for obtaining a (safe) place/transition-system representation of a BP-system. Some of the generated transitions may be 'dead' due to possible dead locks in our bp-system S. But this is not a serious problem. The special role of dead transitions for CE-systems will be studied in Chapter 5.

Now, given a bp-system S, if we just want to 'follow' the flow of h-tokens, then there is a second set of transformation rules using which we can derive a free-choice net FC(S) corresponding to S. Free-choice nets are a subclass of transition nets which have received a good deal attention in the literature (see [21]). We can show that S is well-behaved iff FC(S) is live and safe and satisfies a certain decomposition condition. We will not go into this any further here.

4. PREDICATE/TRANSITION-NETS

4.0. Introduction

When Petri first introduced 'his' nets in [44], they served as a basis for developing a non-idealizing approach to concurrency and information flow in organizational systems. Later the possibility of using these place/transition-nets, by then called Petri nets, in practical systems design was beautifully demonstrated by Holt [26], Shapiro [56], and Patil [41].

Encouraged by this and the inspired writings of Holt [25] a number of attempts were made to put Petri nets to the same kind of use, but in more ambitious settings. Here, the user of Petri nets was quickly and rudely brought up to face the fact that he was being forced to deal with rather large systems at an unacceptable level of detail. At this point, a number of people became disillusioned with Petri nets and promptly dropped the idea of considering them any further. Others - fortunately for net theory - persevered and developed some very useful extensions and derivations of the original model to fit their specific needs.

Recognizing well in time that a variety of net based models are needed in practice Petri proposed in [46] to interconnect the various models that may arise by means of net-preserving transformations. The underlying idea of his proposal is rather simple: Starting with an axiomatically defined basic interpretation of nets (which we presented in chapter 1), new concepts, the semantics of higher level interpretations are deduced by completion and abstraction until the level of practical systems organization is reached.

The formal aspects of this programme - whose practical difficulties are in no way underestimated - are treated in chapter 8 where we present the category of net morphisms. In this chapter, we present a second example of a higher-level net interpretation which is based upon the basic interpretation in a strictly formal way. While we took, in the preceding chapter, advantage of a higher level representation of a restricted class of 'ordinary' Petri nets, we go in this chapter to the other extreme: We add to the modelling power and complexity of Petri nets a new dimension, namely the notion of individuals and their changing properties and relations.

We shall see that this step is comparable - quantitatively and qualitatively - to that of going from propositional logic to first order predicate logic. This similarity is not at all accidental. Indeed, once the relationship between logic and net theory is established through the vehicle of enlogic structure (and we do so in chapter 6), the extension proposed in this chapter will be seen to be perfectly natural.

The text we present here is a slightly modified version of a paper which appeared in quite a different context [19].

4.1. First-Order Schemes of Place/Transition-Nets

In the basic interpretation of nets, the condition/event-net model of dynamic systems (CE-nets), the circles (places) represent conditions which in some cases hold and in others don't. A current case of a modelled system is represented by marking exactly those conditions which hold in this case. The boxes (transitions) represent events; each occurrence of an event is an elementary and indivisible change in condition holdings: the 'preconditions' of the event cease to hold, the 'postconditions' begin to hold.

In fig. 4.1, a section of a CE-net is shown which contains two events each having two preconditions and one postcondition. In the case represented by the marking, the upper event may occur since its preconditions hold (may cease to hold) and its postcondition doesn't (may begin to hold).

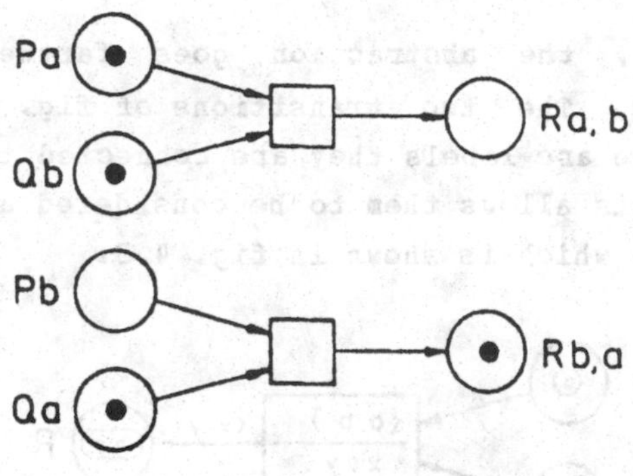

Fig. 4.1

Conditions of a CE-net may be viewed as atomic propositions with changing truthvalues. In fig. 4.1, the conditions are named by instances of predicates P, Q, and R, formed by means of individual symbols a, b. In the case represented in fig. 4.1, individual a has the property P, a and b have the property Q, and b is in relation R to a. By an occurrence of the 'enabled' upper event, a looses property P, b looses property Q, and a gets into relation R to b. Thus, P and Q are *variable* properties and R is a *variable* relation; P, Q, and R, are predicates with changing extensions.

In fig. 4.2, the properties P and Q and the relation R themselves are represented by places. In order to represent the same case as in fig. 4.1, they are marked by their corresponding extensions: place P carries the set {a}, Q carries {a,b}, and R carries {<b,a>}. The two events of fig. 4.1 are specified in fig. 4.2 by means of individual symbols labelling the arcs. In this way, fig. 4.2 represents exactly the same section of a condition/event-systems as fig. 4.1. The size of the net has been reduced by introducing *condition schemes* (predicates); this is compensated by more complex inscriptions to the net: (tuples of) individual symbols marking the places and labelling the arcs.

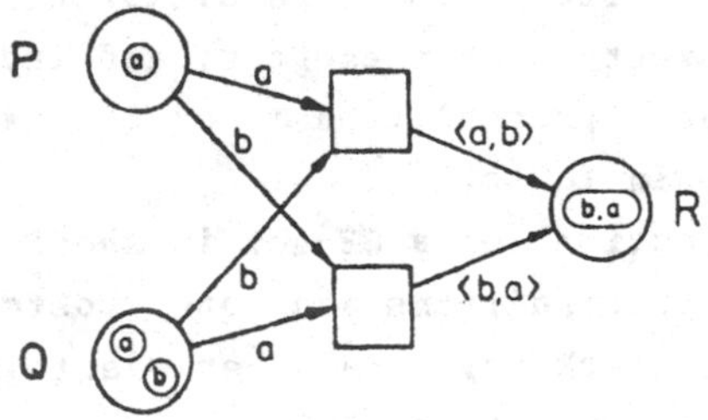

Fig. 4.2

In a next step, the abstraction goes farther by introducing *transition schemes*. The two transitions of fig. 4.2 are 'similar', i.e. except for the arc labels they are connected to the same places in the same way. This allows them to be considered as two instances of a transition scheme which is shown in fig. 4.3.

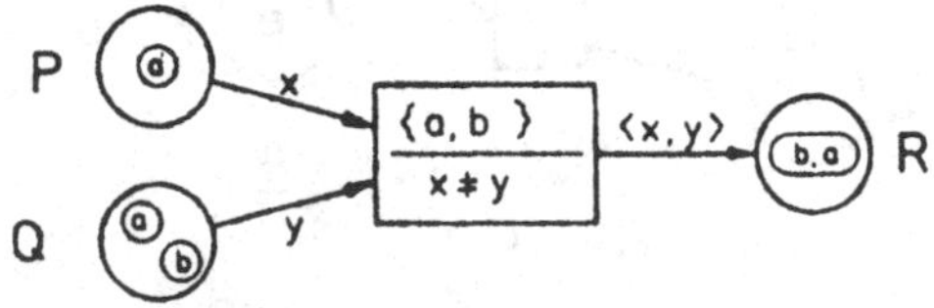

Fig. 4.3

Here the arc labels are tuples of individual *variables*. An instance of the transition scheme is generated by means of consistent substitution of variables by individual symbols. In order to denote the set of valid instances, the list of corresponding value assignments could be inscripted into the box; in our case, for example: $(x,y) \leftarrow (a,b),(b,a)$. Instead we have chosen a logical formula which, when interpreted within the given range $\{a,b\}$, is true exactly for those assignments belonging to the valid instances. This, in general, yields much more a concise representation.

The schematic representation of 'ordinary' Petri nets (PT-nets) for which we have seen a very simple example shall now be completed. Our aim is to create a new type of Petri net model which combines the preciseness of modelling by nets with the power of both first-order predicate logic and linear algebra. Of course these 'generalized' Petri nets shall include the ordinary ones as special cases. The main additions to the elements of fig.3 will be the following:

1. The range of the variables is assumed to be the same for all transitions, a given set of individuals U. U may be structured by functions and relations, named by certain operators (including individual symbols as no-argument operators) and predicate symbols. Then any logical formula using variables, equality, and the operators and predicates associated with U may be inscribed on a transition.
2. The arcs are labelled by formal sums (polynomials) of tuples of variables if the transition is connected to a place by 'multiple' arcs.
3. The places may carry more than one copy of an 'item' (tuple of individual symbols) up to a 'capacity' K.

In this way we get the following

<u>Definition</u>: A <u>predicate/transition-net</u> <u>(PrT-net)</u> consists of the following constituents:

1. A <u>directed net</u> (S,T;F) where
   - S is the set of predicates ('first-order' places) ◯,
   - T is the set of ('first-order') transitions □,
   - $F :\subseteq S\times T \cup T\times S$ is the set of arcs ⟶.
2. A structured set $U = (U; op_1,\ldots,op_m; P_1,\ldots,P_n)$ with operators op_i and predicates P_i.
3. A labelling of arcs assigning to all elements of F a formal sum of n-tuples of variables where n is the 'arity' of the predicate connected to the arc. The zero-tuple indicating a no-argument predicate (an ordinary place) is denoted by the special symbol $\emptyset$.

Examples:

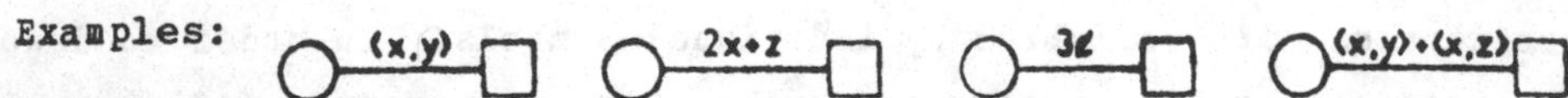

4. An inscription on transitions assigning to some elements of T a logical formula built from equality, operators and predicates given with U; variables occurring free in a transition have to occur at an adjacent arc.
Examples:

5. A <u>marking</u> of predicates of S with n-tuples of individuals (items).
Examples:

6. A natural number K which is a universal bound for the number of copies of the same item which may occur at a single place (K may be called <u>place capacity</u>).
7. The <u>transition rule</u> "⁓" which expresses the common interpretation of predicate/transition-nets:
Each element of T represents a class of possible changes of markings (ordinary transitions). Such an <u>indivisible</u> change consists of removing (○—□) and adding (□—○) copies of items from/to places according to the schemes expressed by the arc labels. It <u>may</u> occur whenever, for an assignment of individuals to the variables which satisfies the formula inscripted to the transition, all input places carry enough copies of proper items and for no output place the capacity K is exceeded by adding the respective copies of items.
Example: For a structure ({a,b,c}; < := alphabetical ordering) and K = 3, two of the nine instances of the following transition are enabled under the marking shown on the left side. Due to conflict, however, at most one will occur. For the assignment (x,y,z) ← (a,b,c) the resulting marking is shown on the right side.

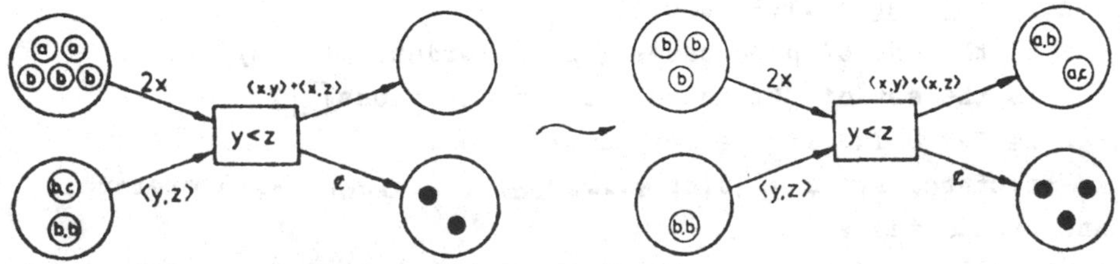

Since we are going to demonstrate the use of PrT-nets rather extensively in the next sections, we mention here only some notational conventions and special cases:

1. If no individuals appear in the net, i.e. all places are no-argument predicates, we get ordinary Petri nets (PT-nets).
2. If additionally $K = 1$ we get CE-nets.
3. If there are individuals but $K = 1$, we have first-order predicate schemes of CE-nets.
4. If the set of individuals is unstructured - except for the individual symbols - these symbols may be called <u>colours</u> of tokens as in the Coulored Petri net model of [53,54].
5. If a formula at a box has the form $v = t \wedge \ldots$ where v is a variable and t a term, all occurrences of v in and around the transition may be replaced by copies of t .

   Example:

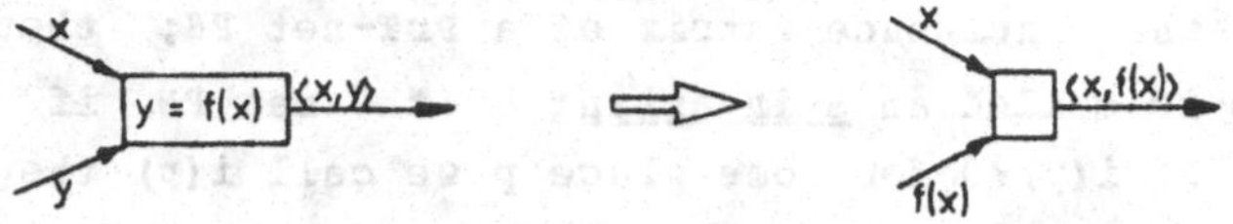

6. Formal sums of items may be also used for denoting the marking of places. They may, and will, be treated as integer polynomials in several variables.

We shall see that integer polynomials in items play the same role in our model as integers play in ordinary Petri nets. In fact, the transfer of the linear-algebraic techniques for Petri nets to predicate/transition-nets is based exactly upon this 'extension' of the integers. Therefore we introduce here a minimum of notation needed in the next sections. The formal apparatus of polynomial rings over commutative rings may be found in any book on algebra, e.g. [23].

1. An integer polynomial in n variables $p \equiv p(v_1,\ldots,v_n)$ is a sum $\Sigma\, p_{k_1\cdots k_n} \bullet v_1^{k_1} \bullet \ldots \bullet v_n^{k_n} | k_1 \geq 0, \ldots, k_n \geq 0$ where each $p_{k_1\cdots k_n}$ is an integer called the <u>coefficient</u> of the 'object' $v_1^{k_1} \bullet \ldots \bullet v_n^{k_n}$.
2. In our case, the variables are the items, i.e. tuples of individual names. The empty item $\emptyset$ is the unit element of the ring (the 0th power of any item). The integers are identified with polynomials of degree 0 (in $\emptyset$ only).
3. For two polynomials $p=p(v_1,\ldots,v_n)$ and $q=q(v_1,\ldots,v_n)$ we write $p \leq q$ iff $p_{k_1\cdots k_n} \leq q_{k_1\cdots k_n}$ for all $k_i \geq 0$.
4. For a polynomial $p=p(v_1,\ldots,v_n)$ we denote by $|p|$ the <u>(unit) value</u> (sum of coefficients) $p(1,\ldots,1)$.
5. For a vector (matrix) of polynomials, its value is defined as the vector (matrix) of the values of its elements.

   If C and D are matrices of polynomials then $|C \bullet D| = |C| \bullet |D|$. In the same way, if x and y are vectors in polynomials then $|x * y| = |x| * |y|$ for the inner product.

6. To a set of items we assign its <u>characteristic</u> polynomial by means of an operator π: $\pi(X) := \Sigma x | x \in X$.
7. The <u>incidence matrix</u> of a pure $(F \cap F^{-1} = \emptyset)$ predicate/transition-net is a mapping C from S T into integer polynomials such that

$$C(s,t) := \begin{cases} -l \mid l \text{ is the label of } (s,t) \in F \\ l \mid l \text{ is the label of } (t,s) \in F \\ 0 \mid \text{otherwise} \end{cases}$$

4.2 Invariant Assertions and Linear Algebra

Let C be the incidence matrix of a PrT-net PN; then a vector i of polynomials is called an <u>S-invariant</u> of the net PN if $C^T \cdot i = 0$ (cf. [30,32,18]. If $i(p) \neq 0$ for some place p we call i(p) the <u>weight</u> of p in i, and i an S-invariant <u>through</u> p.

The unit value |C| of C is the incidence matrix of an ordinary Petri net |PN|, the <u>(unit) value of PN</u>. Because of

$$|C^T \cdot i| = 0 \implies |C|^T \cdot |i| = 0$$

we see that the value of an S-invariant is an S-invariant of the value (of the net).

In place/transition-nets we take advantage of equations of the following kind:

(*) $\quad i^T \cdot M = i^T \cdot M_0$, for an S-invariant i and all $M \in [M_0]$

which states that the inner product of an S-invariant with the elements of one marking class is an invariant quantity. The unknowns of (*) are the elements of M because i and M_0 consists of integer constants. The normal application of (*) is to assume values for some elements of M and then to try to solve (*). If (*) is not solvable, then we know for sure that no marking $M \in [M_0]$ exists for which the assumption holds. On the other hand, every solution of (*) shows that there exist markings for which the assumption is satisfied. Moreover, our knowledge about such markings has grown.

The interpretation of (*) for predicate/transition-nets is more complicated. As any PrT-net can be regarded as a scheme of 'layers of ordinary PT-nets', the corresponding incidence matrix and the S-invariants also must be regarded as schemes. So i in (*) is not a constant vector. M_0, however, because representing a fixed initial marking is constant. If we again make some assumptions about M, and if these assumptions are consistent with $[M_0]$, then we have implicitely determined the net-layers in which the change from M_0 to M can take place at all. What we need now are the instances of i which belong to these layers. In other words, we have to substitute the variables in i by constants such that we get S-invariants belonging to the layers under consideration. We find this substitution by solving (*). Moreover, solving (*) yields more knowledge about M under the assumption mentioned above. In case the assumption is contradictory to $[M_0]$ the equation (*) is not solvable.

By means of the example of fig. 4.4 we will show that S-invariants are a powerful yet easy to handle instrument for finding invariant assertions about a system.

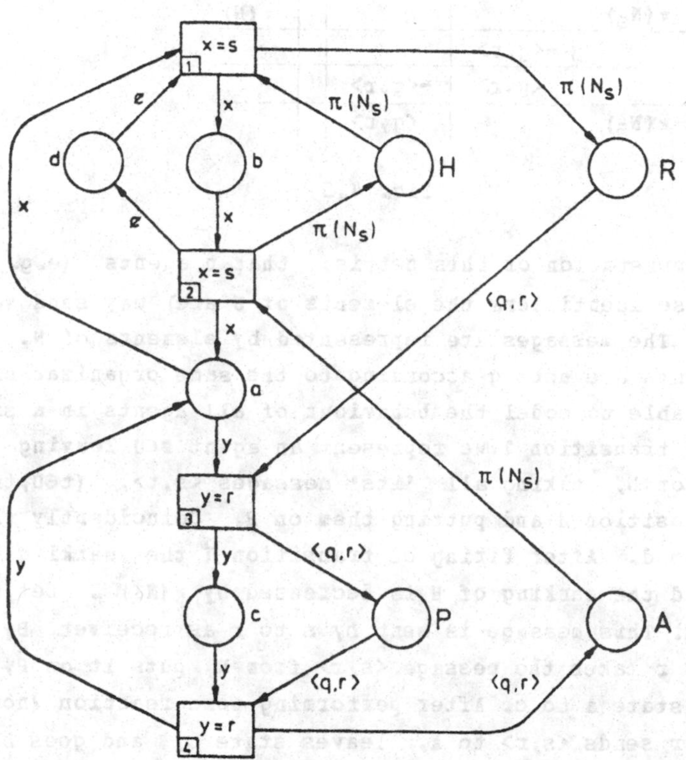

Fig. 4.4

The initial marking is M_0, where

$M_0(a) = \pi(U)$, for a finite set U with n elements;

$M_0(d) = \not{c}$;

$M_0(H) = \pi(N)$, for $N := (U\times U)-id$, and $N_s := N\cap(\{s\}\times U)$;

$M_0(p) = 0$ for all other places p.

Fig. 4.5 shows the incidence matrix of the net in fig. 4.4 together with the corresponding vector representation of M_0.

	x = s 1	x = s 2	y = r 3	y = r 4	M_0
a	-x	x	-y	y	$\pi(U)$
b	x	-x			
c			y	-y	
d	$-\not{c}$	$\not{c}$			$\not{c}$
H	$-\pi(N_s)$	$\pi(N_s)$			$\pi(N)$
R	$\pi(N_s)$		-<g,r>		
P			<g,r>	-<g,r>	
A		$-\pi(N_s)$		<g,r>	

Fig. 4.5

Our interpretation of this net is, that n agents (e.g. database managers whose identifiers the elements of U are) may send messages to each other. The messages are represented by elements of N. We assume that all agents are acting according to the same organization scheme. So we are able to model the behaviour of all agents in a single net. By firing of transition 1 we represent an agent $s\in U$ leaving its idle position a for b, taking all 'its' messages <s,t>, $(t\in U, t\neq s)$, from their homeposition H and putting them on R. Coincidently the token $\not{c}$ is taken from d. After firing of transition 1 the marking of R is increased and the marking of H is decreased by $\pi(N_s)$. Let <s,r> be a message on R. This message is sent by s to r as receiver. By firing of transition 3 r takes the message <s,r> from R, puts it on P, and goes itself from state a to c. After performing some reaction (not modelled in the net) r sends <s,r> to A, leaves state c, and goes back to the idle state a by firing of transition 4. If all the receivers $t\neq s$ have reacted like r all requests <s,t>, $(t\in U, t\neq s)$, can be taken from A back to H by s which by this changes itself from b to the idle state a putting a token $\not{c}$ back to d. All this occurs in one indivisible action by firing of transition 2.

In this description of the dynamic behaviour of the model we have traced the flow of markers which do not change their 'identity', i.e. the tuple of individual symbols carried by them. But, besides this 'natural' flow, there are others to be observed where markers change their identity. For example, repeated firing of transitions 1 and 2 yields an alternating change between a token (trivial marker) ϕ on d and some $s \in U$ on b (see S-invariant i3 below). It should be noticed that in this flow the identity of the marker is changed 'in' the transitions and not on the places.

In order to find such flows and study their significance for deriving behavioral properties of the system we look for S-invariants. For sake of simplicity we transform the incidence matrix in fig. 4.5 by renaming some variables according to the formulas assigned to the transitions. The result is shown in fig. 4.6; it is the basis for calculating seven S-invariants the vector representations of which are also shown in fig. 4.6.

	1	2	3	4	i1	i2	i3	i4	i5	i6	i7
a	-s	s	-r	r	1						
b	s	-s			1		ϕ				$\pi(N_S)$
c			r	-r	1			<q,r>	<q,r>•ϕ		
d	-ϕ	ϕ					s		r•$\pi(N_S)$	-$\pi(N_S)$	
H	-$\pi(N_S)$	$\pi(N_S)$				1				ϕ	s
R	$\pi(N_S)$		-<q,r>			1			r•ϕ		
P			<q,r>	-<q,r>		1		-r			
A		-$\pi(N_S)$		<q,r>		1			r•ϕ		

Fig. 4.6

Applying the equation (*) to the S-invariants i1,...,i7 we get the following (schemes of) invariant assertions, i.e. statements which hold for all follower markings of M_0:

(*') $i^T \bullet M$ = <u>constant</u> = $i^T \bullet M_0$

(1) $M(a)+M(b)+M(c) = \pi(U)$

This equation shows that always (under every marking) <u>all</u> agents are in some state. Using the values we get

(1') $|M(a)|+|M(b)|+|M(c)| = |\pi(U)| = n$

(2) $M(H)+M(R)+M(P)+M(A) = \pi(N)$

Similarly, all messages are always somewhere.

(3) $\not c \bullet M(b)+s\bullet M(d) = s\bullet \not c$

Here we see very clearly that the S-invariants indicate the "metamorphosis" of markers. Consequences of the equation are

(3') $M(b)=0 \iff M(d)=\not c$, $M(d)=0 \iff \exists s:M(b)=s$

(4) $\langle q,r\rangle \bullet M(c)-r\bullet M(P) = 0$

Consequently,

(4') $M(c)=0 \iff M(P)=0$, $\forall r: [M(c)=r \iff \exists q:M(P)=\langle q,r\rangle]$

And for the values:

(4") $|M(c)|-|M(P)| = 0$

(5) $\not c\bullet\langle q,r\rangle\bullet M(c)+r\bullet\pi(N_S)\bullet M(d)+r\bullet\not c\bullet(M(R)+M(A)) = r\bullet\not c\bullet\pi(N_S)$

The corresponding equation for the values is interesting, too:

(5') $|M(c)|+(n-1)|M(d)|+|M(R)|+|M(A)| = n-1$

(6) $-\pi(N_S)\bullet M(d)+\not c\bullet M(H) = -\pi(N_S)\bullet\not c+\not c\bullet\pi(N)$

Consequently,

(6') $M(d)=0 \iff \exists s:M(H) = \pi(N)-\pi(N_S)$, $M(d)=\not c \iff M(H)=\pi(N)$

(7) $\pi(N_S)\bullet M(b)+s\bullet M(H) = s\bullet\pi(N)$

(7') $M(b)=0 \iff M(H)=\pi(N)$, $\forall s: [M(b)=s \iff M(H)=\pi(N)-\pi(N_S)]$

These few examples show that S-invariants are a (conceptually) very simple means for finding invariant assertions. Of course one never needs 'all' S-invariants; normally one only looks for S-invariants through special places, which means adding corresponding restrictions (equations or inequalities) to the defining linear equation system.

4.3. An Example: The Analysis of a Distributed Data Base

Fig. 4.7 shows the PrT-net model of the organization scheme of a duplicate database system. It is G. Milne's modification [36] of a model by C.A. Ellis [9]. There exists another approach for verifying a scheme for organizing duplicate databases by Shapiro and Thiagarajan [57] which is quite different from ours even though it is also based on the Petri net theory.

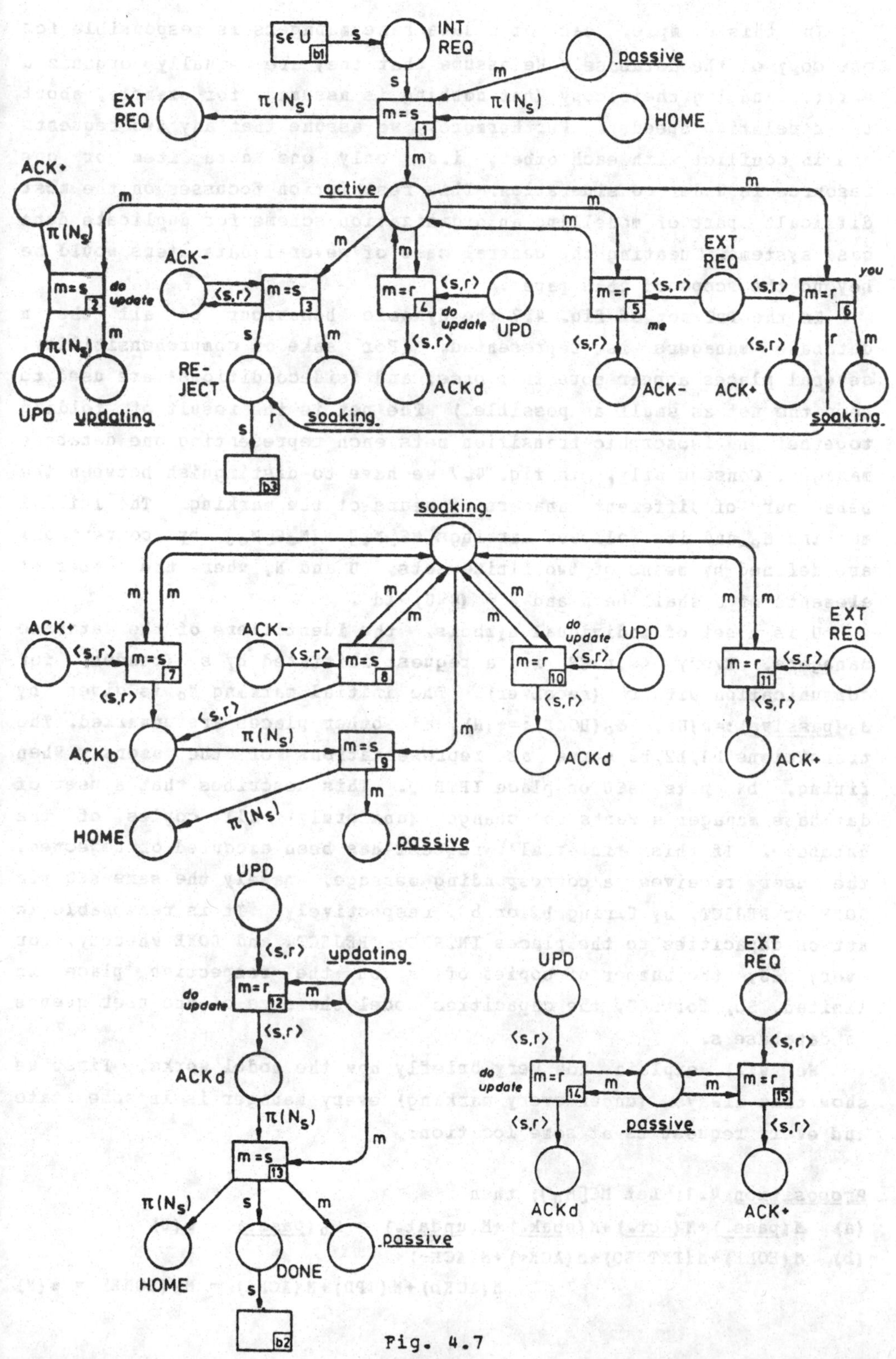
s∈U
b1
s
INT REQ
passive
m
π(N_s)
EXT REQ
m=s
1
HOME
ACK+
active
ACK-
⟨s,r⟩
m=s
2
do update
m=s
3
m=r
4
do update
UPD
EXT REQ
m=r
5
me
m=r
6
you
UPD
updating
RE-JECT
soaking
ACKd
ACK-
ACK+
soaking
r
b3
soaking
ACK+
m=s
7
ACK-
m=s
8
do update
UPD
m=r
10
EXT REQ
m=r
11
ACKb
m=s
9
ACKd
ACK+
HOME
passive
UPD
updating
m=r
12
do update
ACKd
m=s
13
UPD
EXT REQ
m=r
14
do update
m=r
15
passive
ACKd
ACK+
HOME
DONE
passive
b2

Fig. 4.7

In this example, each of n data base managers is responsible for one copy of the database. We assume that they are equally organized w.r.t. managing their copy (but nothing is assumed, for example, about their relative speeds). Furthermore, we assume that any two requests are in conflict with each other, i.e. only one data item or one resource is under consideration. This restriction focusses on the most difficult part of modelling an organization scheme for duplicate data base systems. Treating the general case of several data items would be beyond the scope of this paper.

In the PrT-net of fig. 4.7 the dynamic behaviour of all the n database managers is represented. (For sake of comprehensibility, several places appear more than once; and 'sideconditions' are used to keep the net as small as possible.) The net is the result of folding together n isomorphic transition nets each representing one database manager. Consequently, in fig. 4.7 we have to distinguish between the behaviour of different managers by means of the marking. The initial marking M_0 and its follower markings $M \in [M_0]$ ($M_0 \in [M_0]$ by convention) are defined by means of two finite sets, U and N, where the number of elements of U shall be n and $N = (U \times U) - id$.

U is a set of individual symbols, the identifiers of the database managers. Every $\langle s,r \rangle \in N$ is a request initiated by s (sender) for communication with r (receiver). The initial marking M_0 is given by $M_0(\underline{passive}) := \pi(U)$, $M_0(HOME) := \pi(N)$, all other places are unmarked. The transitions b1,b2,b3 serve as representations of the users. When firing, b1 puts $s \in U$ on place INTREQ. This describes that a user of database manager s wants to change (uniformly) all copies of the database. If this 'internal' request has been executed or rejected, the user receives a corresponding message, namely the same $s \in U$ via DONE or REJECT, by firing b2 or b3, respectively. It is reasonable to attach capacities to the places INTREQ, REJECT, and DONE whereby, for every $s \in U$, the number of copies of s on the respective place is limited. So, for $s \in U$, the capacities model the size of the user queues in database s.

We will explain now very briefly how the model works. First we show that always (under every marking) every manager is in some state and every request is at some location:

<u>Proposition</u> 4.1: Let $M \in [M_0]$; then

(a) $M(\underline{pass.}) + M(\underline{act.}) + M(\underline{soak.}) + M(\underline{updat.}) = M_0(\underline{pass.}) = \pi(U)$

(b) $M(HOME) + M(EXTREQ) + M(ACK+) + M(ACK-) +$
$M(ACKb) + M(UPD) + M(ACKd) = M_0(HOME) = \pi(N)$

Proof: There exist two S-invariants I1 and I2 (analogous to i1 and i2 of the previous section) with
I1(pass.)=I1(act.)=I1(soak.)=I1(updat.) = 1,
I1(p) = 0 for all other places p.
I2(HOME)=I2(EXTREQ)=I2(ACK+)=I2(ACK-)=I2(ACKb)= I2(ACKd)=I2(UPD) = 1
I2(q) = 0 for all other places q.
(a) and (b) are evaluations of (*) for I1 and I2. □

To trace an internal request for a manager k we start with the firing of transition 1. By doing so k goes from state passive to active and its requests <k,i>, (i∈U,i≠k), are put on EXTREQ, which means that they are sent to all other managers i, i≠k, as external requests. Then two possibilities are conceivable:
(1) k gets a positive acknowledgement from all the other managers. Then the corresponding marking M' enables transition 2: $k \le M'(\text{active}) \wedge \pi(N_k) \le M'(\text{ACK+})$. By firing of transition 2 k goes from active to updating and for every i∈(U-{k}) the request <k,i> is again sent to i, but now as an update request; furthermore we assume that k performs the update in database k. In database i≠k the corresponding update is performed by firing of transition 14, 4, 10 or 12, depending on manager i's current state. After all managers have performed this update as requested by k, the requests <k,i>, (i∈U,i≠k), are collected on place ACKd. So transition 13 is enabled and by its firing k changes back to passive and the requests are put back to HOME. Moreover, one copy of k is put on DONE as an acknowledgement for the user that 'its' update is performed in all copies of the database.
(2) In case one manager, say j≠k, is unable or unwilling to perform k's request as soon as possible, he sends a negative acknowledgement back to k; i.e. it fires transition 5 for m=r=j putting <s,r>=<k,j> from EXTREQ to ACK-. Now for k on active transition 3 is enabled. By firing it k goes from active to soaking and its user gets a negative acknowledgement in form of a copy of k on REJECT. In state soaking k collects all requests on ACKb by firing transition 8 and/or transition 7 (repeatedly). Then, by firing of transition 9, it goes back to passive and the requests <k,i>, (i∈U,i≠k), are put back to their homeposition HOME.

The rest of the model shall be described from the receivers point or view. In case a manager j is in state passive or soaking and receives an external request <k,j> on EXTREQ, it grants by firing transition 15 or 11. In case j is in state active there is a conflict between j and k. Firing transition 5 means not granting k's request by putting <k,j> on ACK- as a negative acknowledgement; firing transition 6 means for j abandoning its request in favour of k by changing to soaking, putting <k,j> on ACK+, and a copy of j on REJECT to inform the user. If j is in state updating it does not take notice of external request <k,j> on EXTREQ until being back in state passive. In any state, however, j has to notice an update request <k,j> from k on UPD, to perform the update requested by k, and to put <k,j> on ACKd as an update acknowledgement for k.

We are now prepared to formulate some results about the model. To start with, we state a result about a synchronization of a manager k and the requests <k,i>, $(i \in U, i \neq k)$, initiated by k:

Proposition 4.2: Let $M \in [M_0]$; then

$k \leq M(\text{passive}) \iff \#(N_k) \leq M(HOME)$

$k \leq M(\text{active}) + M(\text{soaking}) \iff \#(N_k) \leq M(EXTREQ) + M(ACK+) + M(ACK-) + M(ACKb)$

$k \leq M(\text{updating}) \iff \#(N_k) \leq M(UPD) + M(ACKd)$

Before we prove this, we interpret it by dividing the places of $I1 \cup I2$ into three "request regions": no request region (NR), external request region (ER), update request region (UP).

$NR \cap I1 := \{\text{passive}\}$, $NR \cap I2 := \{HOME\}$

$ER \cap I1 := \{\text{active}, \text{soaking}\}$, $ER \cap I2 := \{EXTREQ, ACK+, ACK-, ACKb\}$

$UR \cap I1 := \{\text{updating}\}$, $UR \cap I2 := \{UPD, ACKd\}$

(Here we have identified the S-invariants I1, I2 with the sets of places they pass through.)

Proposition 4.2 then states that a manager k is in one of these request regions if, and only if, all its requests <k,i>, $(i \in U, i \neq k)$, are in the same region.

Proof: The stated property holds for M_0 (trivial). The property is also inductive since it is preserved by transitions 1,2,9, and 13, which are the only changes from one region into another. □

For applying the organizational scheme it is important to know wether it is deadlockfree and consistent.

Theorem 4.3 (liveness): Under any marking $M \in [M_0]$ there exists an enabled transition.

Proof: First let us mention that this statement is non-trivial in the case of finite capacities for INTREQ (for every $k \in U$).

Because of proposition 4.1 every manager is always in one of four states. Let k be a given manager, and $M \in [M_0]$:

(1) $k \leq M$(passive) ==> $\pi(N_k) \leq M$(HOME) because of proposition 4.2.
Notice now that there is for every $s \in U$ a positive capacity for INTREQ:
$k \leq M$(INTREQ) ==> transition 1 is enabled
$k \leq M$(INTREQ) ==> transition b1 is enabled.

(2) $k \leq M$(active) ==> $\pi(N_k) \leq M$(EXTREQ)+M(ACK+)+M(ACK-)+M(ACKb) because of proposition 4.2.

(2.1) $\neg\exists j$: $\langle k,j\rangle \leq M$(ACKb) because putting $\langle k,j\rangle$ on ACKb is only possible for $k \leq M$(soaking).

(2.2) $\pi(N_k) \leq M$(ACK+)+M(ACK-);
$\pi(N_k) \leq M$(ACK+) ==> transition 2 is enabled,
$\exists j$: $\langle k,j\rangle \leq M$(ACK-) ==> transition 3 is enabled.

(2.3) $\exists j$: $\langle k,j\rangle \leq M$(EXTREQ);
$j \leq M$(pass.)+M(act.)+M(soak.) ==> one of transitions 15,5,6,11 is enabled;
$j \leq M$(updat.) see (4) below.

(3) $k \leq M$(soaking) ==> $\pi(N_k) \leq M$(ACK+)+M(ACK-)+M(ACKb)+M(EXTREQ)

(3.1) $\pi(N_k) \leq M$(ACKb) ==> transition 9 is enabled,

(3.2) $\exists j$: $\langle k,j\rangle \leq M$(ACK+)+M(ACK-) ==> transition 7 or 8 is enabled.

(3.3) $\exists j$: $\langle k,j\rangle \leq M$(EXTREQ) see (2.3) above.

(4) $k \leq M$(updating) ==> $\pi(N_k) \leq M$(UPD)+M(ACKd)

(4.1) $\pi(N_k) \leq M$(ACKd) ==> transition 13 is enabled,

(4.2) $\exists j$: $\langle k,j\rangle \leq M$(UPD) ==> one of the transitions 14,4,10,12 is enabled for j (because of propos. 4.1 applied to j). □

Consistency means for the model under consideration that after every complete update the n copies of the database are identical. Under the assumption that the model is consistent for the initial marking M_0, the next theorem guarantees consistency:

<u>Theorem</u> 4.4 (consistency): For any $M \in [M_0]$ and $k \in U$:

$$k \leq M(\text{updating}) \implies i \not\leq M(\text{updating}),\ (i \in U, i \neq k)$$

<u>Proof</u>: Let $k \leq M$(updating) and $\langle i,k\rangle \leq M$(EXTREQ); then $\langle i,k\rangle$ cannot leave EXTREQ for ACK+ because transition 6 is not enabled. So it is impossible to bring both k and i to place updating. □

As a consequence of theorem 4.4 transition 12 turns out to be useless for the model in its present form. Transition 12 would, however, be necessary if the model would be refined by adding further resources, thus granting concurrent updating.

We will finish our analysis of the scheme with some critical remarks using a catalogue of properties of a 'good' solution given by Ellis [9]. The model is *homogeneous* (all managers have essentially identical control programs), *speed independent*, *deadlockfree*, *consistent*, *functional* (in applications there are no restrictions concerning data and functions).

The model is, however, not free from *critical blocking*. Even for two managers this can be shown easily. Let U:={a,b}, N={<a,b>,<b,a>}. In case both have sent an external request to each other the current marking is M where M(*active*)=a+b, M(EXTREQ)=<a,b>+<b,a>. So we observe a double activation for transitions 5 and 6. If transition 5 fires twice, for the follower marking M' M'(*active*)=a+b, M'(ACK-)=<a,b>+<b,a> holds. No updating can be performed before at least one manager has been back in *passive*. If under M transition 6 fires twice for the follower marking M" M"(*soaking*)=a+b holds. Again, no updating can be performed before a or b has been back to passive. Because this double firing of transition 5 or 6 can be repeated without any intermediate updating, the possibility of critical blocking has to be taken into account. But this drawback can be eliminated by adding mechanisms guaranteeing fair schedules. According to theorem 4.3 deadlock freeness is guaranteed for any resolution of conflicts between competing requests.

As a major drawback the lack of *partial operability* (cf. [9]) has to be viewed. Let, again for two managers, M(*active*)=a+b, M(EXTREQ) = <a,b>+<b,a>. Now we assume b abandoning its request in favour of a by firing transition 6. Then the current marking is M"' where M"'(*active*)=a, M"'(*soaking*)=b, M"'(ACK+)=<a,b>, M"'(EXTREQ)=<b,a>. If now a is unable or unwilling to send <b,a> back to b, i.e. firing transition 5 putting <b,a> on ACK-, b starves. In case of a crash of manager a the system dies - a violation of partial operability.

5. NET COMPLETIONS OF CE-SYSTEMS

5.0. Introduction

In chapter 2 we studied the completion of a CE-system w.r.t. information flow. In this chapter we introduce two other types of completions called T-completion and S-completion. The T-completion of a CE-system will enable us to establish a simple and yet effective path of accessing the tools and techniques of 'static' logic via net theory. The S-completion of a CE-system will be used to derive a metric for our systems.

5.1 T-completion of a CE-system

We start with two defintions.

Definition : Let $N = (S,T;F)$ be a net. N is T-complete if:
$\forall S_1, S_2 \subseteq S$ such that $S_1 \cup S_2 \neq \emptyset$:
$\exists t \in T$ such that $\bullet t = S_1$ and $t \bullet = S_2$.

Thus in a T-complete net, every 'conceivable' T-element (T-element expressible in terms of S) is a member of T. Given a net $N = (S,T;F)$ which is not T-complete we can systematically add the missing T-elements to obtain a T-complete net. This new net is then referred to as the T-completion of the original net. Formally:

Definition : Let $N = (S,T;F)$ be a net. Then the T-completion of N is the net $N' = (S,T',F')$ where:

1) $T' = T \cup \Delta T$ where
$\Delta T = \mathcal{P}(S) \times \mathcal{P}(S) - (\{(\bullet t, t\bullet) \mid t \in T\} \cup \{(\emptyset,\emptyset)\})$

2) $F' = F \cup \Delta F$ where
$\Delta F = \bigcup\{(S_1 \; \{(S_1,S_2)\}\} \cup \{(S_1,S_2)\} \; S_2) \mid (S_1,S_2) \in \Delta T$

We note that, if $(S_1,S_2) \in T'-T$,then $\bullet(S_1,S_2) = S_1$ and $(S_1,S_2)\bullet = S_2$. A net (fig. 5.1.a) and its T-completion (fig. 5.1.b) are shown in fig. 5.1.

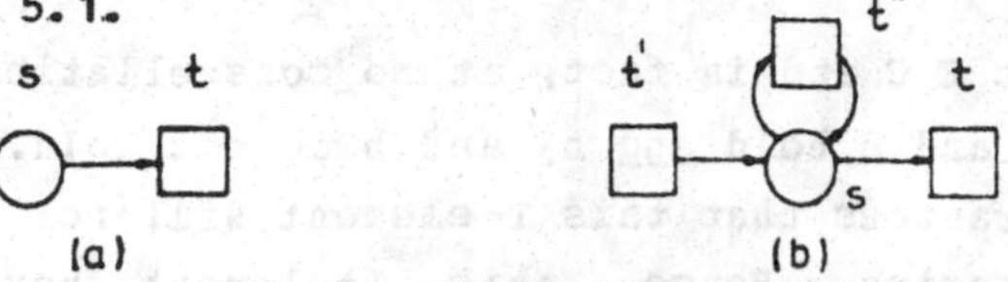

Fig. 5.1

We shall start with a CE-system $\Sigma = (B,E;F,C)$ and obtain the T-completion of $N(\Sigma)$, say $N' = (B,T';F')$. Using our knowledge of C, we can systematically classify the elements of T" (the T-elements of the T-completion of $N(\Sigma)$) to be one of three types: <u>process extensions</u>, <u>violations</u> and <u>facts</u>.

To this end, let $\Sigma = (B,E;F,C)$ be a CE-system and let $D = K-C(K=\mathcal{P}(B))$. D is the set of all constellations which are not cases of Σ. Let $N' = (B,T';F')$ be the T-completion of $N(\Sigma)$. Using C and D, we can classify the elements of T' as follows: Let $t \in T'$.

1) $t \in CC$: Iff $\exists\, c_1, c_2 \in C$ such that $c_1 - c_2 = \bullet t$ and $c_2 - c_1 = t\bullet$

2) $t \in CD$: Iff $\exists\, c \in C$ and $d \in D$ such that $c - d = \bullet t$ and $d - c = t\bullet$

3) $t \in DC$: Iff $\exists\, d \in D$ and $c \in C$ such that $d - c = \bullet t$ and $c - d = t\bullet$

4) $t \in DD$: Iff $\exists\, d_1, d_2 \in D$ such that $d_1 - d_2 = \bullet t$ and $d_2 - d_1 = t\bullet$

In general, an element of T' might appear in none or some (or all) of the four subsets (of T') CC, CD, DC and DD. Consequently, T' can be divided into 16 disjoint sets. We shall now briefly look at some of the more interesting groupings of these 16 subsets of T'.

The subset CC of transitional forms correspond almost exactly to the <u>extensions of processes</u> that can run on Σ. (Thus, in our view, a process is that which transforms a case into a case.) We say "almost" because the extensions of the cyclic processes whose initial and final cases are idential will not appear in CC. We will have more to say about processes in the section 5.3 where we will have to define them formally.

We shall now consider an impure T-element $t \in T'$: $(\bullet t \cap t\bullet \neq \emptyset)$. Since , for any two sets X,Y, $(X-Y) \cap (Y-X) = \emptyset$, t can not be a member of any of the subsets CC, CD, DC and DD. For the sake of concreteness assume that $\bullet t = \{b_1, b\}$ and $t\bullet = \{b, b_2\}$ as indicated:

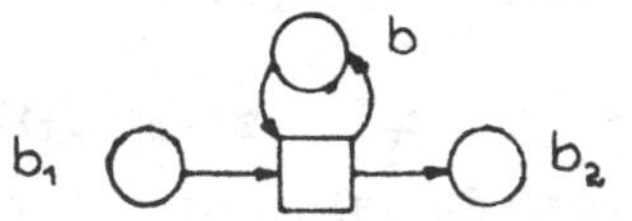

b
b_1
b_2

At no case $c \in C$ and in fact, at no constellation $k \in K$, can it be true that b_1 and b hold <u>and</u> b_2 and b do not hold. In other words, the impurity guarantees that this T-element will not have concession at any configuration. Hence, this T-element may be viewed as a representation of the logically true statement (tautology): At every configuration $k \in K$ either b holds or b does not hold. Thus the transitional forms in T'-(CCUCDUDCUDD) represent tautologies regarding the conditions of Σ.

Next we turn our attention to the set CD-CC. The elements in this set do possess concession. But they are neither events nor processes because the occurance of a T-element in CD-CC will lead to a constellation which is not in C. Hence these transitional forms are called violations. At present, we know very little about the structure of violations (see [60]).

We now come to the most interesting subclass, namely, (DCUDD) - (CCUCD). Firstly, the T-elements in this set are pure. Secondly, they do not have concession at any case. Hence they are the pure dead transitions of Σ. Now consider one T-element in (DCUDD) - (CCUCD) of the form:

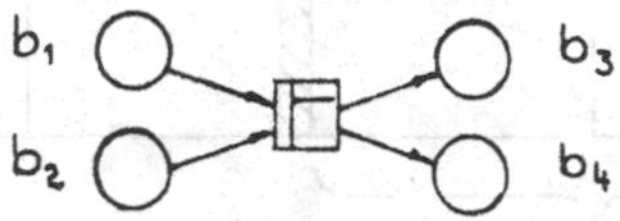

b_1, b_2, b_3 and b_4 are conditions in Σ. They hold at some cases and do not hold at other cases. Hence in the behaviour of Σ, a statement of the form "condition b_3 holds" has a changing truth value. The truth-values of a set of such statemants concerning the conditions of Σ, will in general, change dynamically and concurrently. Yet, because the T-element shown above is in (DDUDC) - (CCUCD), we can assert: At all cases in C, b_1 does not hold or b_2 does not hold or b_3 holds or b_4 holds. Thus this transitional form represents an invariant assertion concerning four boolean variables (conditions) whose truth-values change ynamically. Consequently, this T-element is called a fact of Σ.

Given a set of facts of Σ, we can derive other facts using an expansion rule and a resolution rule. These rules are easy to state and handle in their graphical form. It is also known (see [59]) that these two rules together provide the full power of propositional calculus for dealing with the facts of a CE-system.

The various interesting subclasses defined by CC, CD, DC, DD have been collected together and shown in fig. 5.2. This is the enlogic structure of the given CE-system.

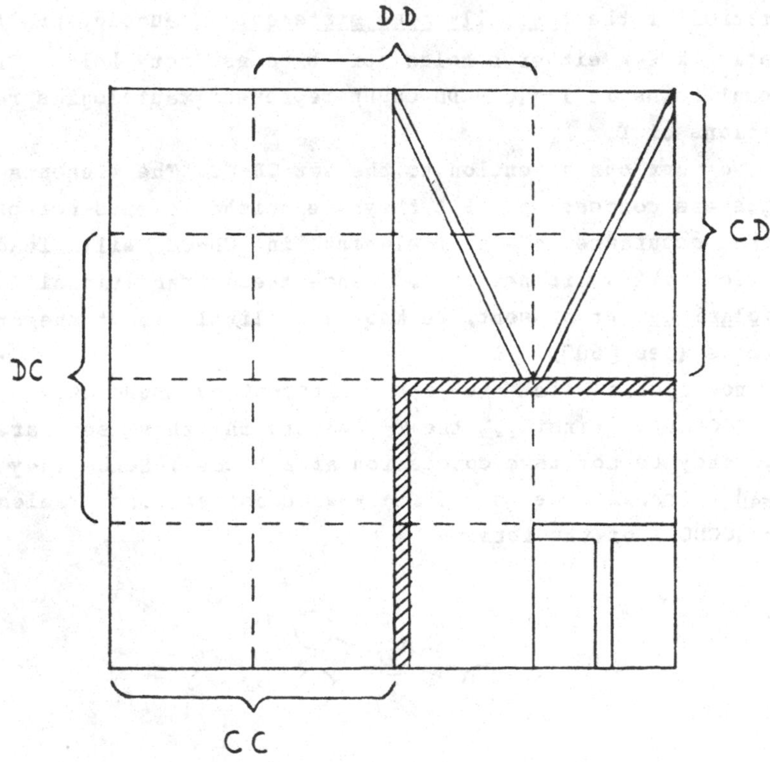

Fig. 5.2

Before we conclude this section a few remarks are in order. Firstly, the idea of T-completion is more of a conceptual tool than a practical tool of analysis. It completes our language for dealing with CE-systems as far as expressions involving the conditions are concerned. Secondly, once C is given, our transition rule and the extensionality principle more or less forces us to interpret the various elements of the T-completion in the manner outlined. Finally, knowing that there is a formal and natural basis for the notions of facts, processes and violations, we can from now on use these notions confidently and precisely to enrich the descriptive power of the net language at all possible levels. For example, at the basic level, we can use the representation shown in fig. 5.4 to (equivalently) represent the CE-system of fig. 5.3.

There is one box structure representing a fact and the other boxes are meant to be events. It is the task of the implementations to ensure that the boxes representing events can occur at least once and the box represening the fact never occurs. A detailed study of translating a mixed specification (fig. 5.4) into a pure (implementable) specification (fig. 5.3) at higher levels has been carried out in [18]: Also, in the next chapter the reader will find some additional information concerning the use of facts in net theory.

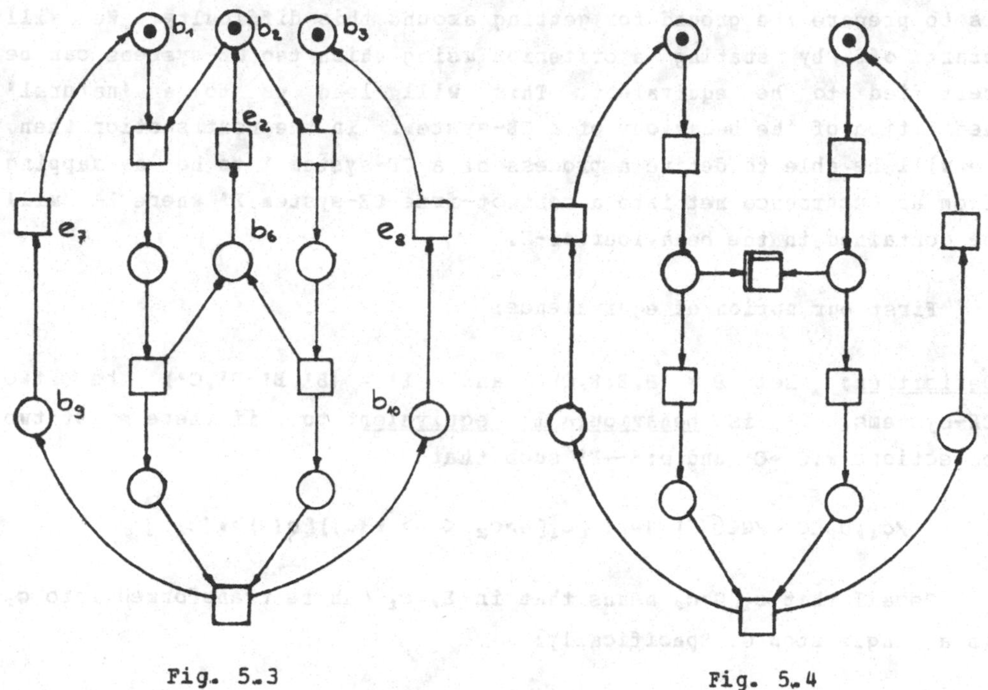

Fig. 5.3

Fig. 5.4

5.2. Equivalence and Behaviour of CE-systems

Our purpose next is to work out an interpretation for the S-elements obtained through the S-completion of a CE-system. For doing this, we will have to formalize the notion of a process (of a CE-system and devise a means for counting the number of occurrences of an event w.r.t. a given process).

We would like to view a process as a mapping from an occurrence net into a CE-system. (An occurrence net is, roughly speeking, an acyclic CE-system in which for every condition b $|{\bullet}b|, |b{\bullet}| \leq 1$.) There are two major reasons for taking this approach. Firstly, we hope to, in our future work relate the CE-system formalism to that of K-dense non-sequential processes (occurrence nets) which can be obtained from the axiomatic foundations of general net theory (see the contributions of C.A. Petri on concurrency in this volume). Secondly, we would like to have CE-systems and their processes coexist within the same category of nets (consult chapter 8 for amplification).

There is however, an accompanying snag with this view of a process. Namely, if a CE-system Σ has contact, then our approach will not yield all the interesting processes of Σ. The task of this section is to prepare the ground for getting around this difficulty. We will start off by stating a criterion using which two CE-systems can be certified to be equivalent. This will lead us to a 'natural' definition of the behaviour of a CE-system. In the next section then, we will be able to define a process of a CE-system Σ to be a mapping from an occurrence net into a contact-free CE-system Σ' where Σ' will be contained in the behaviour of Σ.

First our notion of equivalence:

<u>Definition</u>: Let $\Sigma = (B,E;F,C)$ and $\Sigma' = (B',E';F',C')$ be two CE-systems. Σ' is <u>behaviourally equivalent</u> to Σ if there exist two bijections $\pi: C \to C'$ and $\varrho: E \to E'$ such that:

$$\forall c_1, c_2 \in C \;\forall G \in \mathcal{P}(E) - \{\emptyset\}: [c_1[G>c_2 \iff \pi(c_1)[\varrho(G)>\pi(c_2)]$$

Recall that $c_1[G>c_2$ means that in Σ, c_1 can be transformed into c_2 in a single step G. Specifically:

1) $G \neq \emptyset$ and $G \subseteq E$
2) $\forall e \in G : {}^\bullet e \subseteq c_1$ and $e^\bullet \cap c_1 = \emptyset$
3) $\forall e_1, e_2 \in G: {}^\bullet e_1 \cap {}^\bullet e_2 = \emptyset = e_1{}^\bullet \cap e_2{}^\bullet$
4) $c_2 = (c_1 - \bigcup \{{}^\bullet e \mid e \in G\}) \cup \bigcup \{e^\bullet \mid e \in G\}$

Thus Σ' is equivalent to Σ just in case the steps in Σ' are isomorphic images of the steps in Σ. It is readily verified that this definition of behavioural equivalence is an equivalence relation. Hence it can be used to partition the class of CE-systems into eauivalence classes. This means, that we can put down the following - perhaps trite but nevertheless 'safe' - definition of behaviour.

<u>Definition</u>: Let Σ be a CE-system. Then the <u>behaviour</u> of Σ is denoted as $BH(\Sigma)$ and is given by:

$$BH(\Sigma) = \{\Sigma' \mid \Sigma \text{ and } \Sigma' \text{ are equivalent CE-systems}\}.$$

We will use the remaining portion of this section to show that for every CE-system Σ, there exists a contact-free CE-system Σ' in $BH(\Sigma)$.

To this end we start with:

__Definition__: Let $\Sigma = (B,E;F,C)$ be a CE-system. Let $b,\bar{b} \in B$. Then $\bar{b}$ is said to be the __complement__ of b if $\bullet b = \bar{b}\bullet$ and $b\bullet = \bullet\bar{b}$.

Since the underlying net (B,E;F) is required to be simple, we can indeed talk about __the__ complement of a condition. We also note that if $\bar{b}$ is the complement of b then b is the complement of $\bar{b}$. Next we can state:

__Proposition__ 5.1: Let $\Sigma = (B,E;F,C)$ be a CE-system. Let $b,\bar{b} \in B$ such that $\bar{b}$ is the complement of b. Then, $\forall c \in C$: $b \in c$ iff $\bar{b} \notin c$

__Proof__: Follows easily from our definition of concession and the fact that C is required to be an equivalence class of the full reachability relation $(R_1 \cup R_1^{-1})^*$ (see chapter 1).

Using this proposition we can show that if in a CE-system every condition is accompanied by its complement then it is a contact-free CE-system. To start with we recall that:

Let $\Sigma = (B,E;F,C)$ be a CE-system. Then Σ is __contact-free__ if, $\forall c \in C$ and $\forall e \in E$:

1) $\bullet e \subseteq c \Longrightarrow e\bullet \cap c = \emptyset$
2) $e\bullet \subseteq c \Longrightarrow \bullet e \cap c = \emptyset$.

__Theorem__ 5.2: Let $\Sigma = (B,E;F,C)$ be a CE-system such that: $\forall b \in B$ $\exists \bar{b} \in B$ such that $\bar{b}$ is the complement of b. Then Σ is contact-free.

__Proof__: Let $c \in C$ and $e \in E$ sucht that:

__Case 1__: $\bullet e \subseteq c$ and $e\bullet \cap c \neq \emptyset$

Let $b \in e\bullet \cap c$. Then $\bar{b} \in \bullet e$ and, by proof of 5.1, $\bar{b} \notin c$ where $\bar{b}$ is the complement of b. But this contradicts $\bullet e \subseteq c$.

__Case 2__: $e\bullet \subseteq c$ and $\bullet e \cap c \neq \emptyset$.

Let $b \in \bullet e \cap c$. Then for $\bar{b}$, the complement of b, we have $\bar{b} \in e\bullet$ and by proof 5.1, $\bar{b} \notin c$. But this contradicts $e\bullet \subseteq c$.

Starting from a CE-system $\Sigma = (B,E;F,C)$, we can 'add' some new conditions to Σ to obtain a CE-system Σ' such that:

In Σ' every condition is accompanied by its complement. To formalize this idea we have:

__Definition:__ Let $\Sigma = (B,E;F,C)$ be a CE-system. Then the __S-complementation__ of Σ is the quadruple $\Sigma' = (B',E;F',C')$ where:

1) $B' = B \cup \Delta B$ where
   $\Delta B = \{(b\bullet, \bullet b) \mid b \in B\} - \{(\bullet b, b\bullet) \mid b \in B\}$
2) $F' = F \cup \Delta F$ where
   $\Delta F = \bigcup (S_1 \times \{(S_1, S2)\} \cup \{(S_1, S_2)\} \times S_2) \mid (S_1, S_2) \in \Delta T$
3) $C' = \{c \cup \bar{c} \mid c \in C\}$ where $\forall c \in C : \bar{c} = \{b \mid b \in \Delta B \text{ and } \bar{b} \in c\}$

It is easy to see that Σ' is indeed a CE-system. In fact, by construction, it satisfies the hypothesis of theorem 5.2 and hence is contact-free. We can now state:

__Theorem__ 5.3: Let $\Sigma = (B,E;F,C)$ be a CE-system and $\Sigma' = (B',E;F',C')$ its S-complementation. Then Σ' is equivalent to Σ.

__Proof__: Keeping in mind the notation introduced in our previous definition, choose $\pi: C \to C'$ with $\pi(c) = c \cup \bar{c}$, and $\rho: E \to E$ to be the identity function. Clearly π and ρ are bijections. We claim without proof that for all $e \in E$:

1) $\bullet e(\text{in } \Sigma') = \bullet e(\text{in } \Sigma) \cup \{\bar{b} \mid \bar{b} \in \Delta B \text{ and } b \in e\bullet(\text{in } \Sigma)\}$
2) $e\bullet(\text{in } \Sigma') = e\bullet(\text{in } \Sigma) \cup \{\bar{b} \mid \bar{b} \in \Delta B \text{ and } b \in \bullet e(\text{in } \Sigma)\}$

Using these two facts and proposition 5.1, it is a matter of detail to verify that, if $c_1, c_2 \in C$ and $\emptyset \neq G \subseteq E$,

$$c_1[G>c_2 \iff \pi(c_1)[\rho(G)>\pi(c_2)$$

__Corollary__ 5.4: Let Σ be a CE-system. Then there is a $\Sigma' \in BH(\Sigma)$ such that Σ' is contact-free.
__Proof__: Follows at once from theorems 5.2 and 5.3

5.3. The Processes of a CE-System

As mentioned earlier, we shall view a process of a CE-system Σ to be a mapping from an occurrence net into Σ. To get around the problem of contact, we will in fact view a process of Σ to be a mapping from an occurrence net into __some__ $\Sigma' \in BH(\Sigma)$ where Σ' is contact-free. Accordingly, we shall first develop some terminology concerning occurrence nets.

Definition: Let $N = (B,E;F)$ be a net. Then N is an occurrence net if:
1) $F^+ \cap id = \emptyset$ (N is acyclic: $(x,y) \in F^+ \implies (y,x) \notin F^+$)
2) $\forall b \in S$: $|{}^\bullet b|$, $|b^\bullet| \leq 1$.

Let $N = (B,E;F)$ be an occurrence net. F^+ defines a strict partial order over the elements of N because N is acyclic. We will use the symbol $<$ to denote this partial order. To be specific, $x < y$ iff $(x,y) \in F^+$. Next we need the notion of a slice.

It is a maximal set of 'unordered' S-elements. Formally:

Definition : Let $N = (B,E;F)$ be an occurrence net; and $c \subseteq B$. Then c is a slice of N if:
1) $\forall b_1, b_2 \in c$: not($b_1 < b_2$ or $b_2 < b_1$)
2) $\forall b \in B-c \; \exists b' \in c : b < b'$ or $b' < b$

The set of slices of an occurrence net will be denoted as SL. Now the relation $<$ can be extended to SL as follows: Let $c, c' \in SL$. Then $c \sqsubseteq c'$ if:
$\forall b \in c \; \exists b' \in c' : b < b'$ or $b = b'$

It is easy to show that under this ordering $(SL, \sqsubseteq)$ is a complete lattice. We are now prepared to give our definitions of a process. In doing so and in the discussion that follows, the CE-system under consideration, unless otherwise stated, is assumed to be contact-free.

Defintion: Let $N = (B_1, E_1; F_1)$ be an occurrence net and $\Sigma = (B_2, E_2; F_2, C)$ be a CE-sysem. Then a mapping $pr: B_1 \cup E_1 \rightarrow B_2 \cup E_2$ is called a process of Σ relative to N if it meets the following conditions:
1) $\forall (x,y) \in F_1$: $(pr(x), pr(y)) \in F_2$
2) $pr(B_1) \subseteq B_2$ and $pr(E_1) \subseteq E_2$

   (1 and 2 together mean that pr is a folding)
3) $\forall c' \in SL$(of N) $\exists c'' \in C$: $pr[c'] \subseteq c''$

   (Every slice of N is mapped onto a portion of a case of Σ).
4) $\forall b_1, b_2 \in B_1$: $pr(b_1) = pr(b_2) \implies (b_1 < b_2$ or $b_2 < b_1)$

   (Two occurrences of the same conditions lie on a line).
5) $\forall e \in E_1 \; \forall e' \in E_2$: $pr(e) = e' \iff [pr({}^\bullet e) = {}^\bullet e'$ and $pr(e^\bullet) = e'^\bullet]$

   (Two process events correspond to the same system event iff they effect the same changes in Σ).

We will frequently label the elements of B_1 and E_1 with their images in B_2 and E_2 respectively, as specified by pr. This is the scheme that we have already followed in chapter 1. Moreover, we will almost always refer to the labelled net N itself as a process of Σ, instead of exhibiting the process morphism pr from N into the net of Σ. This should cause no confusion and will simplify our presentation.

The crucial idea that we are trying to capture is the number of times an event occurs in a process of Σ. As already pointed out in section 1, in our view, a process of Σ is that which changes a case into case.

To bring this view into our formalism, let $N = (B_1, E_1; F_1)$ be an occurrence net, $\Sigma = (B_2, E_2; F_2, C)$ a CE-system and pr a process of Σ relative to N. pr and SL (the slices of N) can be used to identify a subset of C as follows:

$$pr(SL) = \{ c'' \in C \mid \exists\ c' \in SL \text{ such that } pr(c') \subseteq c'' \} .$$

Given N, pr and Σ, we choose two distinguished cases in $pr(SL)$, say c_0'' and c_f'' as the <u>initial</u> and <u>final</u> cases of pr. pr is viewed as transforming c_0'' into c_f''. Not every pair of elements of $pr(SL)$ can be chosen to be the initial and final cases of pr. The choice is guided by a pair of elements $c_0', c_f' \in SL$ which map into c_0'' and c_f'' respectively.

<u>Defintion</u>: Let $N = (B_1, E_1; F_1)$ be an occurrence net, $\Sigma = (B_2, E_2; F_2, C)$ a CE-system and pr a process of Σ relative to N. Then the <u>initial</u> and <u>final cases</u> of pr are denoted as c_0'' and c_f'' and are two elements of $pr(SL)$ for which:

There exist $c_0', c_f' \in SL$ such that,

1) $pr(c_0') \subseteq c_0''$ and $pr(c_f') \subseteq c_f''$.
2) $c_0' \sqcup c_f' = \sqcup SL$, the greatest element of $(SL, \sqsubseteq)$
3) $c_0' \sqcap c_f' = \sqcap SL$, the least element of $(SL, \sqsubseteq)$.

$\sqcup$ and $\sqcap$ are the standard lattice operation on the complete lattice $(SL, \sqsubseteq)$. It will often be the case that $c_0' \sqsubseteq c_f'$ but we do not demand it. We do not demand it, because we would not like to rule out <u>skew processes</u>. A skew process is a process for which, assuming the notations already mentioned, $c_0' \not\sqsubseteq c_f'$. For example, a skew process of the system shown in fig. 5.3 can be drawn as:

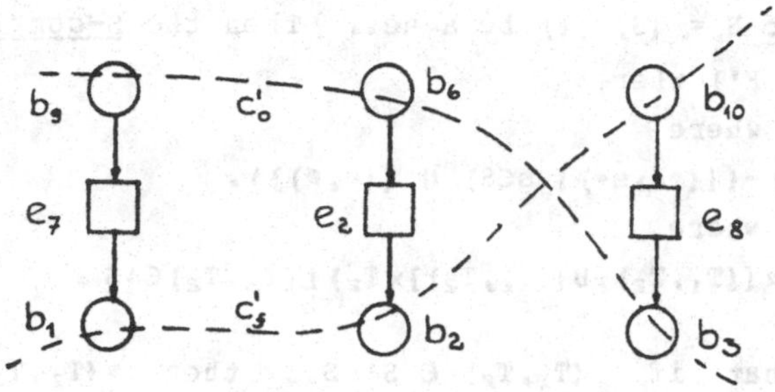

We can now state the means for counting the number of occurrences of an event in a process.

<u>Defintion</u> : Let $N = (B_1, E_1; F_1)$ be an occurrence net, $\Sigma = (B_2, E_2; F_2, C)$ a CE-system and pr a process of Σ relative to N. Let c_0', c_f' $(\in SL)$ be the pre-images of the initial and final case of pr as already defined. Finally, let $e \in E_2$. Then,

$$\#(e|pr) = \begin{cases} |\{e' \in E_1 | pr(e') = e\}|, & \text{if } \exists b' \in c_0' \; \exists e' \in pr^{-1}(e): b' < e' \\ -|\{e' \in E_1 | pr(e') = e\}|, & \text{if } \exists b' \in c_0' \; \exists e' \in pr^{-1}(e): e' < b' \\ 0, & \text{otherwise.} \end{cases}$$

If $pr(e') = pr(e'') = e$, then $e' < e''$ or $e'' < e'$. In fact e' and e'' lie on a line. Moreover, c_0' and c_f' are maximal sets of pairwise concurrent elements. Finally, $<$ is a transitive relation. Using these facts, we can easily show that $\#(e|pr)$ is indeed well-defined. For example for the skew process sk shown above,
$\#(e_7|sk) = 1$ and $\#(e_8|sk) = -1$.
This notation is extended to sets of events in the obvious way.

We are now ready to turn to our original task: To classify the S-elements obtained through S-completion of a CE-system.

5.4. <u>S-Completion of a CE-System</u>

As in the case of T-completion, we start with two definitons.

<u>Defintion</u> : Let $N = (S, T; F)$ be a net. N is <u>S-complete</u> if $\forall T_1, T_2 \subseteq T$, such that $T_1 \cup T_2 \neq \emptyset$:
$\exists s \in S$ such that $\bullet s = T_1$ and $s \bullet = T_2$.

<u>Defintion</u> : Let $N = (S,T;F)$ be a net. Then the <u>S-completion</u> of N the net $N' = (S',T;F')$ where:

1) $S' = S \cup \Delta S$ where
   $\Delta S = \mathcal{P}(T) \times \mathcal{P}(T) - (\{(\bullet s, s\bullet) \mid s \in S\} \cup \{(\emptyset,\emptyset)\})$.
2) $F' = F \cup \Delta F$ where
   $\Delta F = \bigcup (T_1 \times \{(T_1,T_2)\} \cup \{(T_1,T_2)\} \times T_2) \mid (T_1,T_2) \in \Delta S$

We note that if $(T_1,T_2) \in S'-S$, then $\bullet(T_1,T_2) = T_1$ and $(T_1,T_2)\bullet = T_2$. The notion of a process can be used to define a distance funcion over the S-elements of the S-completion of a CE-system as follows.

<u>Definition</u> : Let $\Sigma = (B,E;F,C)$ be a CE-system and $N' = (S',E;F')$ the S-completion of $(B,E;F)$. Let $\Sigma' \in BH(\Sigma)$ such that Σ' has the same set of events as Σ and is contact-free. Then $\sigma : S' \to \mathbb{N} \cup \{\omega\}$ is the <u>synchronic distance function</u> of Σ and is given by:

$$\sigma(s) = \begin{cases} \text{Max}\{\Vert \#(\bullet s \mid pr) - \#(s\bullet \mid pr) \Vert \mid pr \text{ is a process of } \Sigma\}, & \text{if defined} \\ \omega, & \text{otherwise.} \end{cases}$$

Here $\Vert i-j \Vert$ denotes the absolute value of $i-j$ where i and j are integers. It is essential, for our intended interpretation that σ be completely determined by Σ alone. In other words, it is necessary to show that σ is independent of the choice of $\Sigma' \in BH(\Sigma)$. The proof of this fact is straightforward though somewhat tedious. (Hence we will leave it as an exercise to the reader !)

Going back to the definition under consideration, $\sigma(s)$ is a measure of the synchronic distance between $\bullet s$ and $s\bullet$. Hence we will frequently write $\sigma(E_1,E_2)$ with $E_1,E_2 \subseteq E$ instead of $\sigma(s)$. σ is called a distance function because it has the following properties:

Let $E_1,E_2,E_3 \subseteq E$.

1) $\sigma(E_1,E_2) = 0 \iff E_1 = E_2$
2) $\sigma(E_1,E_2) = \sigma(E_2,E_1)$ (symmetry)
3) $\sigma(E_1,E_3) \leq \sigma(E_1,E_2) + \sigma(E_2,E_3)$ (triangular inequality)

Thus σ defines an <u>integer metric</u> over $\mathcal{P}(E)$. Let $\Sigma = (B,E;F,C)$ be a CE-system and $N' = (S',E;F')$ the S-completion of $(B,E;F)$. Using σ, we can collect together the S-elements of N into equivalence classes, where for $s_1,s_2 \in S$, $s_1 \sim s_2$ iff $\sigma(s_1) = \sigma(s_2)$. S together with this equivalence relation is called the <u>synchronic structure</u> of Σ. Among these equivalence classes two of the important ones are:

1) The set of S-elements $S^1 \subseteq S'$ where $\forall s \in S^1$: <u>$\sigma(s)=1$</u>. For example B (the conditions of Σ) will be a subset of S^1. Let $s \in S^1$. Then this element represents the fact that in <u>any</u> process of Σ, event occurrences in $\bullet s$ must strictly <u>alternate</u> with event occurrences in $s\bullet$.

2) The set of S-elements $S^2 \subseteq S'$ where, $\forall s \in S^2$, <u>$\sigma(s)=2$</u>. Let $s \in S^2$, $\bullet s = E_1$ and $s\bullet = E_2$. Then $\sigma(s) = 2$ denotes the fact that in some process, some event in E_1 and some other event in E_2 can occur <u>concurrently</u>. On the other hand if two events e_1 and e_2 can occur concurrently in some process, $\sigma(s) \geq 2$ where $\bullet s = \{e_1\}$ and $s\bullet = \{e_2\}$. This however is true only because we have carefully brought the notion of a skew-process into the theory. To bring out this subtle but important point consider the CE-system shown below:

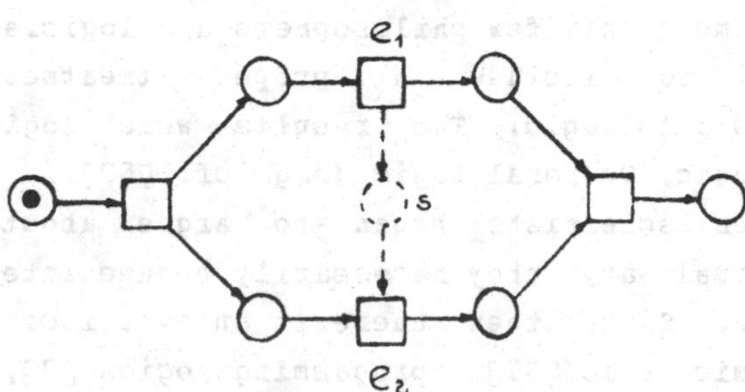

If we consider only 'normal processes', we will conclude that $\sigma(s) = 1$, where $\bullet s = \{e_1\}$ and $s\bullet = \{e_2\}$. But then e_1 and e_2 are most certainly not alternating. Moreover, suppose we 'add' the S-element shown in dotted lines and view the new net as a place-transition system, which has the same behaviour as the original CE-system. In this system, we can verify through observation that the capacity of the place s is 2. (It should be initially marked because otherwise e_1 must occur before e_2. If it is initially marked, then it can acquire an additional token because otherwise e_2 must occur before e_1.)

As in the case of T-completion, the idea of S-completion is a very useful conceptual tool. In chapter 7 , we will discuss some of higher-level applications of this concept.

6. NETS AND LOGIC

6.0. Introduction

The laws of formal logic allow to derive new knowledge from given knowledge in a strictly formal process. "Formal" here means that the rules controlling that process depend only on the form in which a piece of knowledge is expressed, and not on its meaning.

A statement S follows logically from a statement P if there is no world conceivable in which P is true and S is false. In classical, 'static' logic, the worlds under consideration do not change: For a given world, a statement S may hold or not hold, or it may be impossible to find out whether it holds or not. But it does not happen that the truthvalue of the statement S changes, in a given world, while being considered.

For some time, only few philosophers and logicians were looking for ways how to include a proper treatment of changing states-of-affairs into logic. The results were logics like Modal Logic, Deontic Logic, Temporal Logic (e.g. cf. [52]).

When computer scientists began to argue about properties of programs in a formal way, they necessarily became interested in the logic of change. Since then there is an ever increasing number of logics: Algorithmic logic [37], progamming logics [7], dynamic logic [39], propositional modal, temporal logics of programs [12,22,51], process logic [40].

All these approaches restrict system behaviour to sequences of changes. Either they consider only sequential programs or they reduce 'parallelism' to arbitrary interleaving in time. The purpose of this chapter is to indicate several connections between net theory of (nonsequential) processes and systems and logic. We wish to indicate how logic can be applied in those contexts where temporally and causally independent changes occur, as e.g. in computer systems with components widely distributed in space.

The reader might get the impression that net theory is just the result of adding to logic an appropriate notion of change. This, however, would not reflect the historical truth; rather, the basic notions of net theory are chosen in such a way that logic finds its place in it in a natural way.

6.1. Nets and Propositional Logic

In the basic interpretation of net theory, a dynamic system Σ is modelled as a system of conditions and events, $\Sigma = (B,E;F,C)$. The conditions can be viewed as atomic propositions about the system with changing truthvalues; in some cases of the system they hold, in some they don't. The events are repeatable elementary changes of the truthvalues of some conditions. A single occurrence of an event consists of changing the truthvalues of its pre-conditions from true to false and the values of its post-conditions from false to true. Therefore an event possesses concession (a chance to occur) in a given case $c \in C$ iff each of its preconditions and none of its post-conditions holds in c (formally: is a member of c).

Let us now consider an arbitrary proposition p which is built from conditions of Σ by means of the connectives of propositional logic ($\neg, \wedge, \vee, ==>, <==>$). In each case, p is either true or false; but this truthvalue may change with the occurrence of events, it does not hold for the 'world' Σ. If, however, p is always true, i.e. holds in all cases of Σ, we call p a valid assertion about Σ and write $\Box_{\Sigma} p$, or just $\Box p$. We shall see that this notion is much closer related to the notion of change than we might expect.

Theorem 6.1: Consider the following transitional form t which shall represent a conceivable elementary change of conditions in Σ. Then the following statements about Σ are equivalent:

(1) In no case of Σ, t has concession (t is 'dead' in Σ).

(2) In all cases of Σ, the proposition $(\neg a \vee \neg b \vee c \vee d \vee e)$ is true.

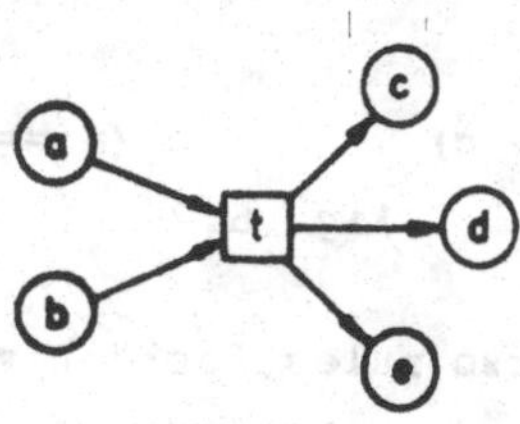

Fig. 6.1

Thus, dead transitional forms of Σ represent valid assertions about Σ. Within the enlogic structure of Σ which classifies all its transitional forms, they are called facts for they represent statements which are factually true; pictorially, they are represented by the symbol ◫ [48].

This result demonstrates that the static aspects of dynamic systems are an integral part of net theory. It is an immediate consequence of the choice of basic notions made by net theory. And there is only little more needed in order to integrate propositional logic into the theory of condition/event-systems on the basis of a <u>net calculus of propositional logic</u> .

From theorem 6.1 we can conclude that every valid assertion which is logically equivalent to a single disjunctive term (a set of atoms and negated atoms connected by <u>or</u>) can be represented by a fact. And since every propositional formula possesses an equivalent <u>conjunctive normal form</u> which consists of a set of disjunctive terms connected by <u>and</u>, we get the following

<u>Theorem</u> 6.2: Every valid assertion about a condition/event-system Σ can be equivalently represented by a set of facts of Σ.

<u>Corrolary</u>: The tautologies in conditions of Σ are exactly those (trivial) assertions which are represented by impure transitional forms.

Two simple examples are shown in fig. 6.2.

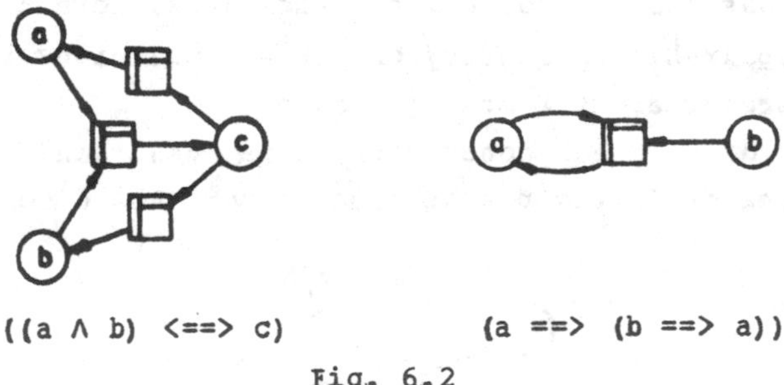

((a ∧ b) <==> c) (a ==> (b ==> a))

Fig. 6.2

<u>Theorem</u> 6.3: There are two rules for deriving facts from given facts which together constitute a consistent and complete (net) calculus of propositional logic:

(1) <u>Expansion</u> : Let t be a fact of Σ and t' a transitional form in conditions of Σ with $\bullet t \subseteq \bullet t'$ and $t\bullet \subseteq t'\bullet$. Then t' is a fact of Σ, too.

Example :

(2) Resolution : Let t_1, t_2 be facts of Σ which are connected by a 'bridge' $b \in t_1{\bullet} \cap {\bullet}t_2$, and let t' be the result of merging t_1 and t_2 along b : ${\bullet}t' = {\bullet}t_1 \cup ({\bullet}t_2 - b)$ and $t'{\bullet} = (t_1{\bullet} - b) \cup t_2{\bullet}$. Then t' is a fact of Σ.

Example:

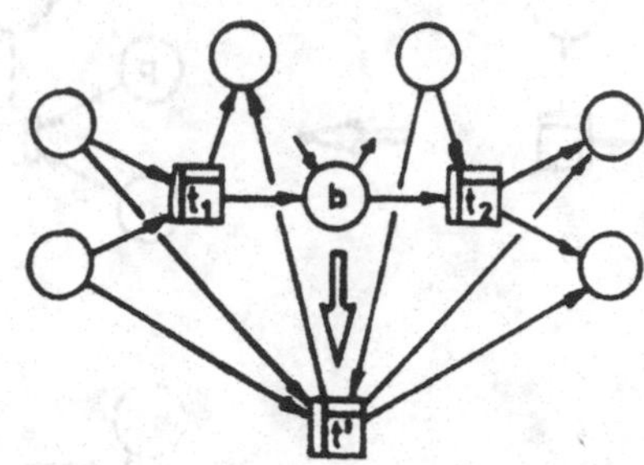

Lemma 6.4: Let p be a valid assertion about Σ and q any proposition in conditions of Σ. Then q follows logically from p iff the assumption that $(p \wedge \neg q)$ is a valid assertion can be refused by means of deriving from its fact representation the 'inconsistent fact', an isolated ⊟, by means of resolution only.

The following transformation rules allow to generate the fact representation (conjunctive normal form) of an arbitrary propositional formula p.

1. One starts with the 'signed' formula ⊟→(p) .

2. As long as there is an S-element with a composite inscription, one of the following transformations can be applied reducing the length of one inscription. (Since all propositional connectives can be expressed in terms of $\neg$ and $\wedge$, we leave it to the reader to complete the list). The dottet lines denote the connections of the T-element to the unaffected context.

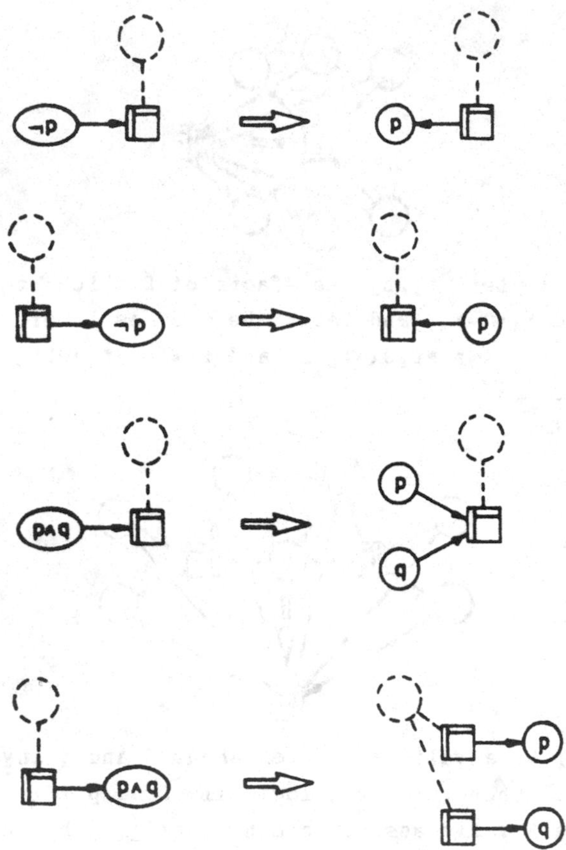

3. When eventually all inscriptions are atomic, all S-elements with the same inscription are mapped onto the corresponding condition.

As an exercise, derive the representations shown in fig. 6.2.

6.2. The Logic of Place/Transition-Systems

Since dead transitional forms of CE-systems lead to a net calculus of propositional logic, it is natural to ask what we can express by dead transitional forms in place/transition-systems.

Let $PN = (S,T;F,K,W,M_0)$ be a PT-net: $N = (S,T;F)$ is a net of places S, transitions T, and arcs F; $K:S\to\mathbb{N}\cup\{\omega\}$ assigns to each place its token capacity, and $M_0:S\to\mathbb{N}\cup\{\omega\}$ its initial token count. $W:F\to\mathbb{N}$ assigns to each arc its multiplicity.

A transition t has concession (may fire) in a given marking M, iff all its input places carry enough tokens: $s\in{\bullet}t \implies M(s)\geq W(s,t)$, and no output place carries too many tokens: $s \in t^\bullet \Longrightarrow M(s) \leq K(s)-W(t,s)$. If we now treat places just as integer variables to which the markings assign their 'current' value, then for the transitional form t shown in fig. 6.3 the following two statements about the PT-system PN are equivalent:

(1) In no marking of the marking class of PN, t has concession: t is dead in PN.

(2) In all markings, the following proposition holds:
$a_1<v_1 \vee \ldots \vee a_m<v_m \vee b_1>K(b_1)-w_1 \vee \ldots \vee b_n>K(b_n)-w_n$

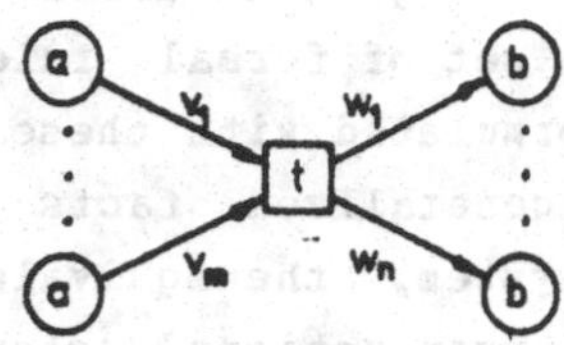

Fig. 6.3

Thus, dead transitional forms of a PT-system PN represent valid assertions about PN, formulated in terms of the changing values of the integer variables $s \in S$.

The expressive power of dead transitions is stated in the following

<u>Theorem</u> 6.5: If PN is finite and all places have finite capacities, then every valid assertion about (the marking class of) PN can be represented by a set of dead transitional forms.

The net representation of valid assertions becomes extremely succinct if we use additional S-elements which are to be inscribed with arbitrary integer-valued expressions built from the places (integer variables) of PN.

We assume, for sake of simplicity, that all places of PN have the same finite capacity which we denote again by K. Then for arbitrary integer valued expressions in places, $X_1,\ldots,X_m$ and $Y_1,\ldots,Y_n$, and arbitrary integers $v_1,\ldots,v_m$ and $w_1,\ldots,w_n$, the 'generalized fact' in fig. 6.4 represents the assertion

$X_1<v_1 \vee \ldots \vee X_m<v_m \vee Y_1>K-w_1 \vee \ldots \vee Y_n>K-w_n$

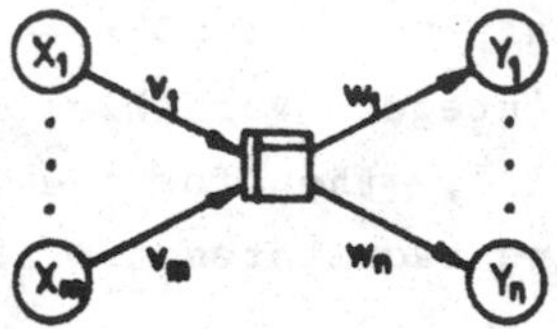

Fig. 6.4

We now define a class of expressions in places which we call just <u>quantities</u> of PT-nets. These quantities provide a simple yet extremely powerful means for formulating valid assertions about PT-nets. They have been chosen because a set of formal rules allows to transform each 'generalized fact' formulated with these quantities into a net of elementary facts. When generalized facts are used for <u>specifying</u> properties of a designed system, the equivalent elementary facts can be translated into an organizational scheme which guarantees their validity. For more details, see [18].

<u>Definition</u>: Let S be the set of places of a PT-net PN with uniform capacity K. Then a <u>quantity</u> is an expression in places built by means of linear integer combination and forming the maximum, minimum and complement relative to K:

(1) A place $s \in S$ is a quantity;

(2) If X, Y are quantities and $z \in Z$ is an integer, then $X + Y$, $X - Y$, $z \cdot X$ are quantities;

(3) If X,Y are quantities, then $X \sqcap Y$, $X \sqcup Y$ and X' are quantities where $X \sqcap Y := \min\{X,Y\}$, $X \sqcup Y := \max\{X,Y\}$, $X' := K-X$

Note that for K=1 the boolean lattice operation $\sqcap$, $\sqcup$ and ' become the propositional connectives $\vee$,$\wedge$ and $\neg$ as for conditions.

Two examples shall demonstrate the use of quantities for a succinct representation of valid assertions about PT-nets:

$a \sqcap b < 1$ (Mutual Exclusion of a and b)

Fig. 6.5

2a-b = 0 with K = 2 (Simple S-invariant)

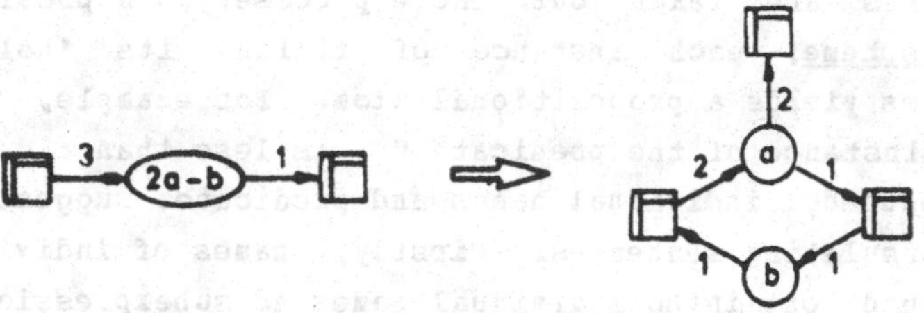

Fig 6.6

6.3. Nets and First-Order Predicate Logic

There are, at this point, two possible ways to establish the relationship between net theory and first-order predicate logic (FOL).

If we just continue with the technique of the foregoing sections, we have to show that there is a transition net model of dynamic systems whose dead transitios constitute a basis for a net calculus of FOL. And if our terminology is not totally misleading, this net model should be the predicate/transition-nets introduced in chapter 4.

If we wish, however, to follow the historical development of the matter, we have to extend the net calculus of PL to FOL independently of the existence of PrT-nets, as it was done in [20,59]. The PrT-nets then are an example of applying a principle which may play an important role in the future development of general net theory: A new level of net interpretation is introduced in parallel to rising the level in a different branch of learning to which, on a lower level, a close conceptual and formal relationship with net theory has already been established.

For this section we choose the second alternative and indicate very briefly how net representation can be extended from PL to FOL. In doing so we do not demand that the reader ignores the existence of PrT-nets. He may well look at the nets representing first-order sentences as belonging to the PrT-net model where they represent valid assertions. He may even wonder why PrT-nets have not been invented immediately with the net calculus of FOL.

Predicate logic begins when we talk about _individuals_, their _properties_ and their _relations_. While in PL the propositional atoms are really atomic without internal structure, just being carriers of truth values, they may contain, in predicate logic, _names_ as subexpressions designating individuals. And, loosely speaking, a predicate is what is left from a propositional atom when all individual names are taken out. More precisely, a predicate is a propositional scheme; each instance of filling its 'holes' with individual names yields a propositional atom. For example, "1 is less than 3" is an instance of the predicate " . is less than : ".

Once introduced, individual names and predicates suggest two more devices for formulating sentences. Firstly, names of individuals may again be compound containing individual names as subexpressions. Thus, individuals may be designated 'indirectly' by means of naming schemes, normally called functions or operations. For example, "the sum of 2 and 3" is an instance of the naming scheme "the sum of . and : "; it designates the individual 5.

Secondly, indefinite individual names - variables - may be used in connection with two quantifiers "for all" and "there exists some". Thus one is able to build sentences like, for example, "For all x there is some y and some z such that x is less than the sum of y and z". Here, by convention, the quantifiers run over a set of individuals, often called the universe (of discourse), which is presumed to be given and fixed.

Since logic is concerned with the form of sentences rather than their use for communication, the laws of predicate logic are studied on the basis of some strictly formal language, e.g. such that the sentence above would be written as "$(\forall x)(\exists y)(\exists z) Lx,s(y,z)$". In practice, elements of both strictly formal and more natural ways of expressing knowledge are combined for formulating first-order sentences.

The basis for incorporating these sentences of 'static' logic into net models of dynamic systems is the following simple transformation of propositional facts whose conditions are instances of predicates:

All instances of the same predicate are folded onto an S-element representing that predicate. The identity of the instances is preserved by inscribing the lists of individual names on the corresponding arcs. Fig. 6.7 shows an example.

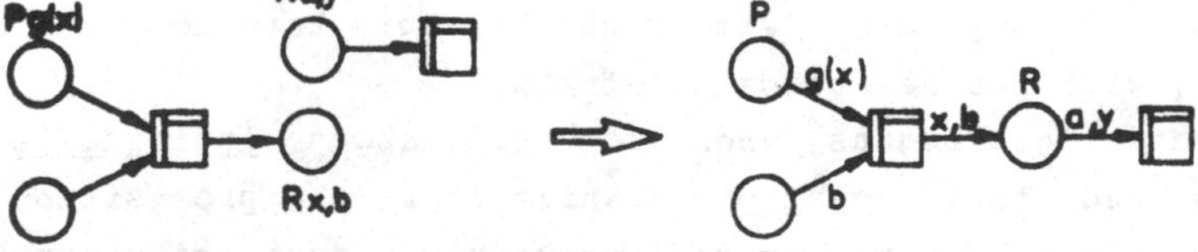

Pg(x) Ra,y Rx,b Qb ⇨ P g(x) x,b R a,y b Q

Fig 6.7

The question now is how to represent real first-order-sentences, i.e. those containing quantifiers and variables. In order to answer this we have to refer to a well-known result of FOL (see e.g. [5]).

Each first-order sentence can be transformed into a logically equivalent sentence in which a quantifier-free formula ('matrix') is preceded by a list of quantifiers binding all variables occurring in the matrix. The matrix can be transformed into its conjunctive normal form, the disjunctive subformulas of which are called <u>clauses</u>. The result is called the <u>prenex normal form</u> of the first-order sentence.

For example, the characterization of a strict partial order $<$: $\neg\exists x{:}x<x \wedge \forall x,y,z{:}[x<y \wedge y<z \Longrightarrow x<z]$, possesses the prenex normal form $\forall u \forall x \forall y \forall z{:}[\neg u<u \wedge (\neg x<y \vee \neg y<z \vee x<z)]$. It can be easily represented by a net similar to that in fig. 6.8 if we declare that, <u>seperately for each box</u>, <u>all individual variables occurring at the adjacent arcs are universally bound</u>.

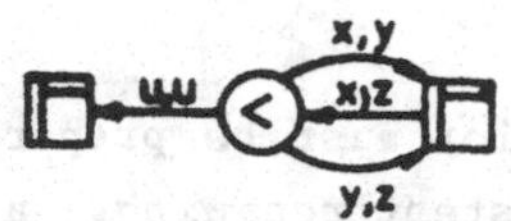

Fig. 6.8

Existential quantifiers, however, cannot be handled in this way. Consider, for example, the sentence $\forall x \forall y{:}[x\neq y \Longrightarrow \exists z{:}(x<z \wedge z<y)]$ expressing the density of $<$. It possesses the prenex normal form $\forall x \forall y \exists z{:}[(x=y \vee x<z) \wedge (x=y \vee z<y)]$. How can we guarantee that in all cases, the two occurrences of the variable z in the two clauses $(x=y \vee x<y)$ and $(x=y \vee z<y)$ designate the same individual which has to be chosen dependent on the choice of the 'independent' variables x and y ?

If the sentence is true for a given $<$, then it must be possible to construct a <u>(Skolem-)function</u> which assigns to each pair of individuals x,y exactly one of the one or more z whose existence is stated. If, for example, our universe is the set of rational numbers, then $(x+y)/2$ would do. From a strictly formal point of view, the existential prefix $\forall x \forall y \exists z$ is equivalent to the existence of such a two-argument function $\hat{z}(.,:)$ in the universe. The number of arguments is, of course, the number of preceding universal quantifiers. Thus, the sentence above is <u>logically</u> equivalent to the sentence $\forall x \forall y{:}[(x=y \vee x<\hat{z}(x,y)) \wedge (x=y \vee \hat{z}(x,y)<y)]$ which is represented by the net in fig. 6.9 .

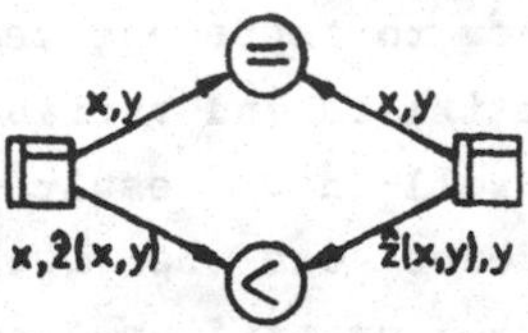

Fig. 6.9

By this 'Skolemization' we get for every first-order sentence an equivalent net representation, and by that the basis for a net calculus of FOL by generalizing the expansion and the resolution rule, and introducing a substitution ('re-naming') rule.

By <u>expansion</u>, a connection to an arbitrary predicate may be added to a given box.

The <u>resolution</u> rule is applicable at all 'bridges' whose two arcs are inscribed identically.

In most cases, resolution must be prepared by <u>unifying</u> the two lists by means of consistent renaming, according to the following rule:

<u>Substitution</u> : Let $v_1,\ldots,v_n$ be individual variables occurring at a given fact, and let $t_1,\ldots,t_n$ be arbitrary individual expressions. If, simultaneously for all i, all occurrences of v_i are replaced by t_i, then the result represents a logical consequence of the given fact; it is a fact, too.

Applying unification and resolution to the net of fig 6.7 leads to the following derivation shown in fig. 6.10:

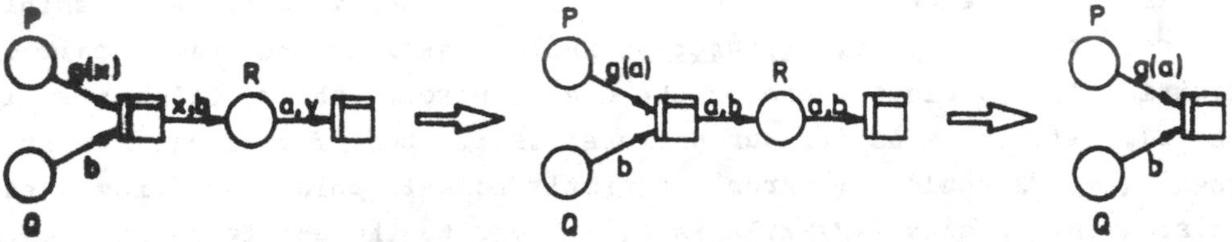

Fig 6.10

So much on the relationship between nets and first-order predicate logic. For more details, the reader is referred to [8,59]. We wish to conclude this section with a remark on the dead transitional forms, i.e. the facts, of predicate/transition-nets.

In the PrT-net model we have carefully to distinguish between those predicates which are fixed and associated with the set of individuals, and those predicates expressing variable properties and relations whose extensions (markings) are subject to change in the modelled system. The variable predicates are the places of the PrT-net while the constant predicates only appear in formulas inscribed in the transitions (as places, they would be isolated).

The situation becomes different, however, if we add facts to the representation of a given system. The inscìptions in dead transitions which we have not encountered in this section can be replaced by additional net structure including places with constant marking.

For example, the diagrams (a) and (b) in fig. 6.11 represent the same valid assertion $\forall x \forall y:[x<y \Longrightarrow [Px \wedge Qy \Longrightarrow Rx,y]]$. In (c) the property of < being a strict partial order (fig. 6.8) is added.

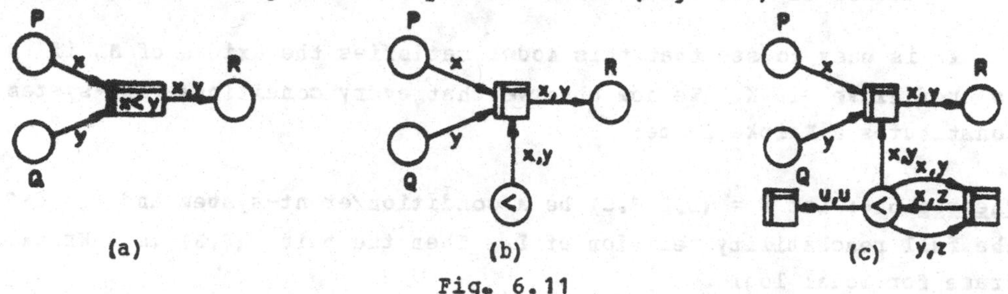

Fig. 6.11

6.4. Nets and Modal Logic

The classical approach to the treatment of changing states-of- affairs in logic is extending propositional logic (PL) to modal logic (ML) by including modal prefixes "It is possible that ..." and "It is necessary that ...". Thus the sentences of ML are built from atomic propositions by means of the connectives of PL $(\neg, \wedge, \vee, \Longrightarrow, \Longleftrightarrow)$ and two unary operators Δ (possibility) and $\Box$ (necessity).

The laws of ML in addition to PL are such that, for example,

(1) $p \Longrightarrow \Delta p$

(2) $\Delta(p \vee q) \Longleftrightarrow (\Delta p \vee \Delta q)$

(3) $\neg\Delta(p \wedge \neg p)$

(4) $\Box p \Longleftrightarrow \neg\Delta\neg p$

(5) $\Box p \Longrightarrow \Delta p$

are theorems of ML, but

(6) $\Delta p \Longrightarrow p$

is not. This can be achieved by choosing (1) - (4) to be axioms.

A derived notion which is typical for ML is that of <u>entailment</u> (strict implication):

(7) (p =>> q) :<==> □(p ==> q)

A way of interpreting the sentences of ML has been shown by Kripke [29]. Let K be a set of <u>constellations</u> (possible 'worlds') and R ⊆ K×K be a relation expressing which worlds may change into which other worlds; then F = (K,R) is called a <u>frame</u>. The statement that a proposition p holds then must include a reference to a particular world k∈K for which p holds.

(1) -p holds in k iff p does not hold in k

(2) (p∨q) holds in k iff p holds in k or q holds in k

(3) ◇p holds in k iff p holds for some k' with k R k'

(4) □p holds in k iff p holds for all k' with k R k'

It is easy to see that this model satisfies the axioms of ML if R is reflexive in K. We now observe that every condition/event-system constitutes a Kripke frame:

<u>Theorem</u> 6.6: Let Σ = (B,E;F,C) be a condition/event-system and R = C×C the full reachability relation of Σ. Then the pair (C,R) is a Kripke frame for modal logic.

<u>Corrolary</u>: A proposition p is a valid assertion about Σ iff □p holds in (some, and therefor every, case of) Σ. And for all conditions b ∈ B, (◇b ∧ ◇¬b) holds in Σ; conditions are <u>contingent</u>.

Thus, the case/noncase cut in the power set of the conditions of a system Σ which distinguishes between what can be the case in Σ and what can't, is the <u>modal</u> cut. And the notion <u>fact</u> within the enlogic structure of a system corresponds to modal necessity.

In many applied contexts, the modal cut in systems is only the basis for further classification of cases. For example, the cases (possible constellations) may be divided into desirable ('good') and non-desirable ('bad'), or into permitted and forbidden ones. The logic which deals with propositions possibly prefixed by "It is permitted that ..." or "It is obligatory that ..." is called <u>deontic logic</u> (DL).

The sentences of DL are formed from atomic propositions by means of the connectives of modal logic and the <u>deontic</u> prefixes ! (obligation) and @ (permission). The laws of DL, in addition to those of ML, are such that, for example,

(1) !p <==> ¬@¬p

(2) @p ∨ @¬p

(3) !p ==> @p

(4) !p ==> Δp

are theorems, but

(5) @p ==> p

(6) p ==> @p

(7) Δp ==> @p

are not. This can be achieved by taking (1), (2), and

(8) @(p∨q) <==> @p∨@q

to be axioms.

Deontic logic can be derived from modal logic by means of a deontic constant (nullary operator) * which is to be interpreted as a given set of 'bad' or 'forbidden' constellations [1]. * holds in constellation k iff k is 'bad'. If not all possible constellations are bad, i.e. if * satisfies the axiom

(9) Δ¬*

then the following definitions satisfy the axioms of DL:

(10) @p :<==> Δ(p∧¬*)

(11) !p :<==> (¬p =>> *) [□(¬p ==> *)]

Thus, in terms of CE-systems, modal logic reflects the cut between cases and non-cases, and deontic logic a cut between 'good' and 'bad' cases. Of course, we could continue in this line by making an ever finer classification of the cases. For example, the full spectrum from 'perfect' to 'disastrous' might be the basis for explicating the notion 'graceful degradation' as used in connection with 'fault tolerance' of hardware. The following diagram gives an interpretation of four such classes for a simple control system:

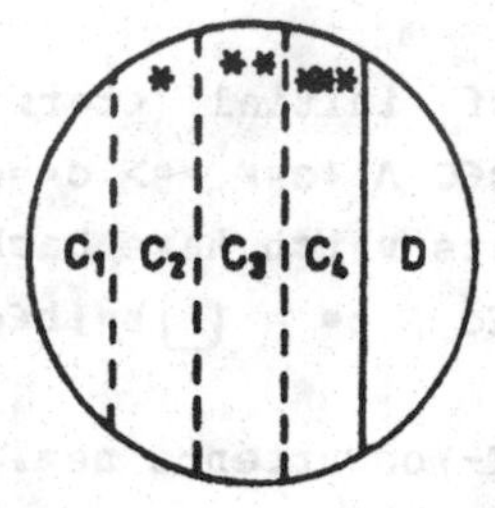

$C = C_1 \cup C_2 \cup C_3 \cup C_4$: possible

C_1: desired

C_2: to be corrected (result of deviation)

C_3: to be repaired (result of malfunction)

C_4: to be replaced (result of destruction)

D : impossible (by laws of physics)

$K = C \cup D = \mathcal{P}(B)$: conceivable

Fig. 6.12

6.5. Nets and Temporal Logic

Adding to propositional logic the modal operator Δ ("It is possible, that ...") is one way of dealing with changing states-of-affairs in logic. It leads to modal logic (ML), and we have seen how close this is related to the theory of condition/event-systems. Another approach which more directly attacks the notion of 'change in time' is that of adding a temporal operator like "first-then" or "and next" [62] to propositional logic.

If p and q are propositions, then (p/q) shall be a proposition of *temporal logic* (TL) to be read as "First p, then q". Note that we do not say "First p *and* then q" since for us it is not at all clear whether / is a relative of $\wedge$ or not.

The worlds for which the propositions of TL shall make sense (i.e. shall either hold or not hold, in a meaningful way), are again condition/event-systems. However, for conditions a and b, the truthvalue of the proposition "first a, then b" cannot be determined if a and b may occur repeatedly. To which of the occurrences of a and b does the proposition refer?

For that reason we shall deal in TL with *repetition-free* CE-systems (comparable to straight-line or single-assignment programs). For practical purposes, a certain subclass of repetition-free CE-systems is of particular interest; its elements are called, for reasons which become obvious from their definition, *transfers* (e.g. QUINE-transfer):

Definition: A safe condition/event-system $\Sigma = (N,C)$ is called *repetition-free* iff there is no process in Σ in which an element of N occurs more than once:

(1) process $p:N' \to (N,C) \implies$ subnet inj. $p:N' \to N$

Σ is called a *transfer* iff, additionally,

(2) N is finite and connected, and

(3) the initial <terminal> cases of Σ consist of initial <terminal> conditions only: $c \in C \wedge {\uparrow}c=\emptyset \implies {\bullet}c=\emptyset$ and $c \in C \wedge {\downarrow}c=\emptyset \implies c{\bullet}=\emptyset$ (Where ${\uparrow}c$ < ${\downarrow}c$ > denotes the set of events which have backward <forward> concession in c, and ${\bullet}c = \bigcup \{{\bullet}b \mid b \in c\}$, $c{\bullet} = \bigcup \{b{\bullet} \mid b \in c\}$.)

Our first example is the following marked (T-)occurrence net.

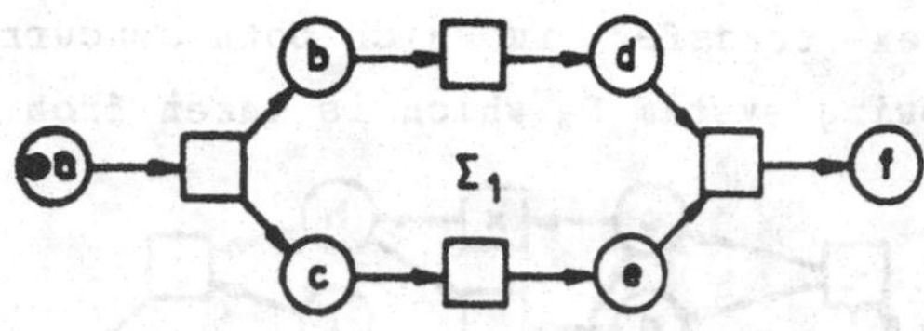

Fig. 6.13

It is no problem to verify that, for example, the proposition $(b \Longrightarrow (c \vee e))$ is a valid assertion about Σ_1, i.e. holds in all cases of Σ_1. Another valid assertion is $[a \vee ((b \vee d) \wedge (c \vee e)) \vee f]$. In both assertions, the or-connectives are due to the change of conditions in the course of a process. Consequently, we may read them more precisely as "first - or then - ", provided we arrange the operands in proper order.

This observation can be further generalized: First, as long as our systems are conflict-free, all essential instances of logical or are due to the change of conditions. And second, if two conditions a and b occur one after another, the proposition "a and b" cannot hold in any case.

Therefore we now add to the language of PL a temporal connective / which is defined as "first - or then - ". Then the two examples of valid assertions about Σ_1 become $(b \Longrightarrow (c/e))$ and $[a/((b/d) \wedge (c/e))/f]$, and in this way reflect very precisely the temporal order in Σ_1.

Our next example of a 'world' of TL is the following system Σ_2 which is essentially the dual of Σ_1:

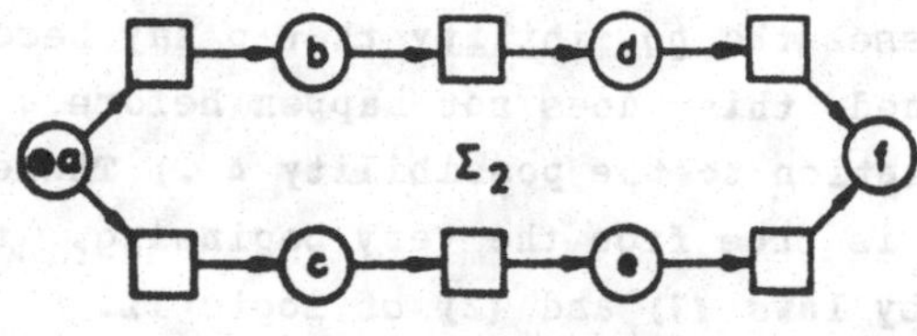

Fig. 6.14

Here, a conflict has to be decided in the initial case yielding two alternative processes in Σ_2. As a consequence, a second kind of or occurs which shall be denoted by the symbol $\triangledown$. Then the invariant assertion $[a \vee b \vee c \vee d \vee e \vee f]$ reads more precisely as $[a/((b/d) \triangledown (c/e))/f]$.

A more complex transfer in which both concurrency and conflict arise is the following system Σ_3 which is taken from [14].

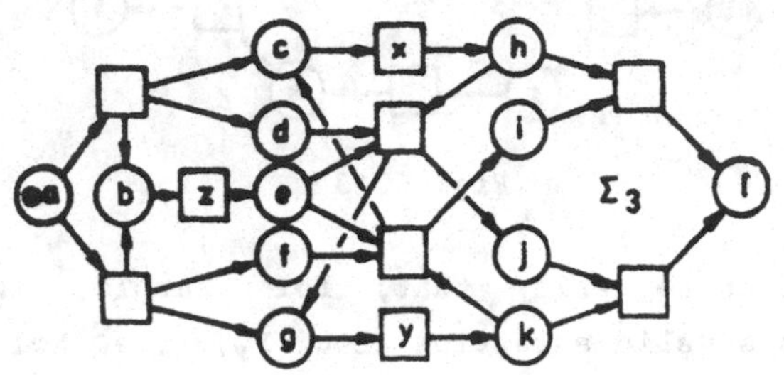

Fig. 6.15

This example shows that repetition-free CE-systems are not necessarily cycle-free. Valid assertions about Σ_3 are, for example, $[c \Longrightarrow ((d \wedge e) \triangledown i)]$ and $[(b/e) \Longrightarrow [((c/h) \wedge e) \triangledown ((g/k) \wedge f)]]$.

Now, after having some intuitive understanding of the temporal connective / in our TL, we should formalize this understanding by means of stating at least some of the laws ruling TL. As in PL and ML, $(p \Longrightarrow q)$ shall be a theorem of TL iff assertion p implies assertion q, i.e. q holds for all those 'worlds' (repetition-free CE-systems) for which p holds. Then the main two axioms for TL are the following:

(1) $p \Longrightarrow (p/q)$

(2) $q \Longrightarrow (p/q)$

These postulates may still be hard to accept; they seem counter-intuitive. However, one should realize that the "or" in "First p or then q" expresses the <u>possibility</u> that p may become false during a process, provided this does not happen before q has become true. (Note the close relation to the possibility Δ .) Therefor, if p never becomes false or q is true from the very beginning, then (p/q) holds 'trivially', i.e. by laws (1) and (2) of logic TL.

We distinguish in TL between two kinds of 'or' of different strength. The weaker one is expressed more precisely by means of / , while the stronger one is denoted by $\triangledown$. Given a set of cases C, the difference between / and $\triangledown$ is the one between "In all cases of C, p or q" and "In all cases of C p, or in all cases of C q".

Thus the main axioms of TL can be combined in

(3) $(p \triangledown q) \Longrightarrow (p/q)$

The complete list of axioms of TL would include laws of associativity, distributivity, and so on. It can be found in [15]. We just show the lattice diagram of logical consequence $\models$ for all propositions formed from two atomic propositions (conditions) a and b by means of $\wedge$, $\triangledown$, and /. There are ten equivalence classes (with respect to $\models$) of such propositions, each represented by a shortest one. Tautologies are represented by the constant $\top$ ("true") and contradictions by the constant $\bot$ ("false").

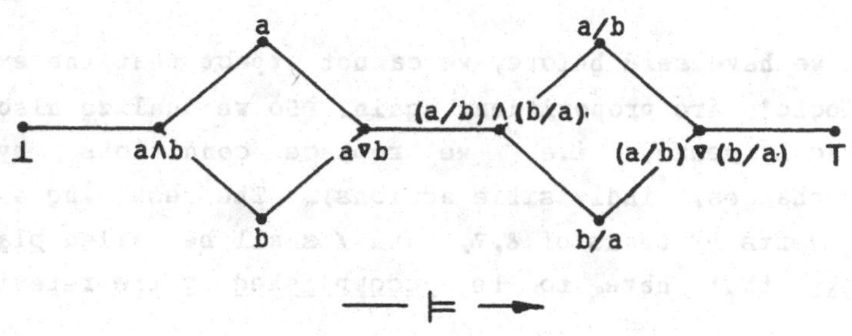

Fig. 6.16

As an exercise, give an example which demonstrates that a||b := (a/b)$\wedge$(b/a) and a$\triangledown$b are not equivalent.

The duality principle of lattice theory (the reverse of a lattice is a lattice, too) suggests to dualize TL and to look for an interpretation. Let us denote the dual of $\models$ by $\supset$, its 'and' (meet) by &, its 'or' (join) by $\triangledown$, and the additional operator "first - then" again by /. Then the dual of an implication of TL p $\models$ q is a statement d(p) $\supset$ d(q) where d(p$\wedge$q) := (p$\triangledown$q), d(p$\triangledown$q) := (p&q), d(p/q) := (p/q).

The main laws of TL then become

(1') (p/q) $\supset$ p

(2') (p/q) $\supset$ q

or, equivalently,

(3') (p/q) $\supset$ (p&q)

which shows that the temporal connective / of the dual of TL is a <u>stronger</u> relative of <u>and</u>, "first - <u>and</u> then - ".

The dual of the diagram in fig. 6.16 is the following one:

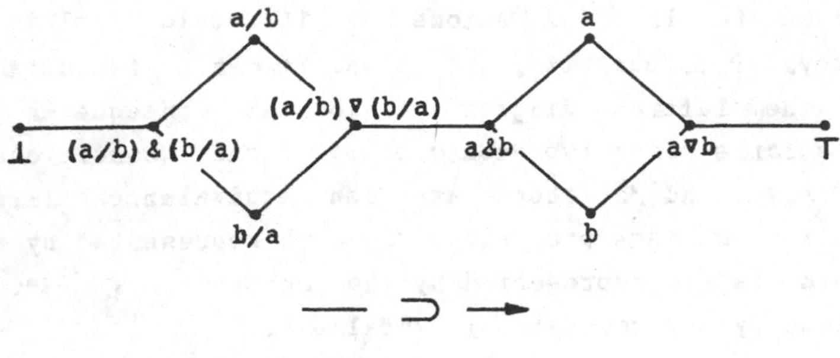

Fig. 6.17

By what we have said before, we cannot expect that the expressions of this 'logic' are propositions again. So we dualize also in the net-theoretical sense, i.e. we replace conditions by events (elementary changes, indivisible actions). The resulting expressions built from events by means of &, ∇, and / shall be called plans. They denote tasks that have to be accomplished by the repetition-free systems.

More precisely, the lattice and net theoretic dual of logical implication in TL is interpreted in the following way:

p ⊃ q :<==> Every execution of the plan p accomplishes the task denoted by the plan q.

Then e.g. [((x&z)/y) ∇ ((y&z)/x)] ⊃ (x&y&z) is a theorem about accomplishment.

Given a plan p, the set of all plans which are equivalent to p with respect to accomplishment expresses the task denoted by p. It can be modelled by a transfer in a standard way. For example, the transfer Σ_3 in fig. 6.15 represents the task [((x&z)/y) ∇ ((y&z)/x)]. The unnamed events represent its 'organizational overhead'.

The dual of TL is the theory ('logic') of accomplishment, the lowest conceptual level of a logic of action and decision which may be the begin of an envisaged Formal Pragmatics. Originally, it was not developed in the way presented here. Rather, it was found independently when studying an algebra of communication forms, a simple language for 'protocols' at interfaces between components of condition/event-systems and their environments [44]. A more detailed study of the laws of accomplishment can be found in [15,17].

7. SYNCHRONY THEORY

7.0. Introduction

In this chapter, we shall take a more detailed look at the notion of synchronic distance. Recall that this measure was introduced in chapter 5 using the S-completion of a condition/event-system. We shall be interested here in viewing synchronic structures as a specification and analyzing tool. Consequently we first have to extend the basic notions. We then give a detailed example in support of our contention that synchronic structures can indeed be used for obtaining succinct and precise descriptions of system performance. In the last section we show by examples that there are interesting relationships between synchrony theory and the calculus of relative frequencies.

7.1. The Weighted Synchronic Distance

Whenever we analyse or build systems consisting of several components we observe that the individual capabilities of the system components have to be restricted for the benefit of the entire system. Being restricted in some sense normally means for a component that it is depending on other components. So it is quite conceivable that a measure for mutual dependencies of system components would be an important means for analyzing and specifying systems.

It will be shown in the sequel that the <u>synchronic distance</u> and its extension, the <u>weighted synchronic distance</u> , are useful means for measuring dependencies between event-like components. More precisely, they are measures for dependencies caused by event synchronizations and belong so to the important invariants characterizing systems behaviour.

Before introducing the synchronic distance as a concept within the place/transition-nets it has to be mentioned that the notion of process, so far defined only for condition/event-systems, can be generalized for place/transition-system in the obvious way.

<u>Definition</u>: Let $PN = (S,T;F,K,W,M_0)$ be a place/transition-system, let PR be the set of all processes (including non-sequential ones), let $a,b\subseteq T$ be two sets of transitions; then the <u>synchronic distance</u> $\sigma(a,b)$

between a and b is defined as

$$\sigma(a,b) := \max_{p \in PR} (|\#(a|p) - \#(b|p)|),$$

where $\#(a|p)$ and $\#(b|p)$ indicate how often during p a transition of a and b, resp., fires.

a and b are called synchronous with distance $\sigma(a,b)$. If $\sigma(a,b) = \infty$ we call a and b asynchronous.

$\sigma(a,b) = 1$ means that transitions of a and transitions of b fire alternatingly.

Example: a = {u}, b = {v} (fig. 7.1)

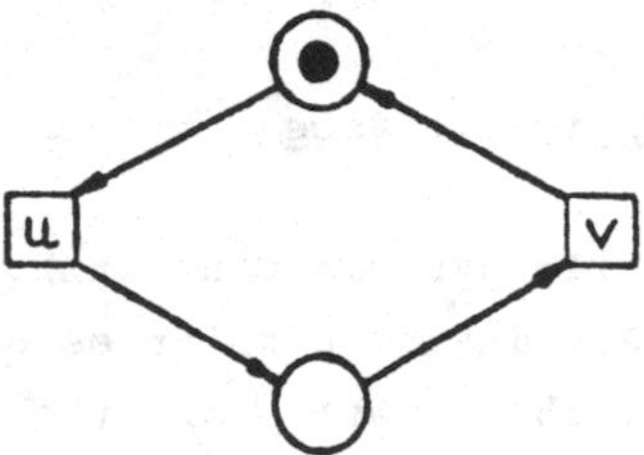

Fig. 7.1

(unless otherwise stated we attach an unbounded capacity to all places)

$\sigma(a,b) = 2$ means that after maximally two transition firings in a (in b) a transition of b (of a) has to fire.

Example: a = {u}, b = {v} (fig. 7.2)

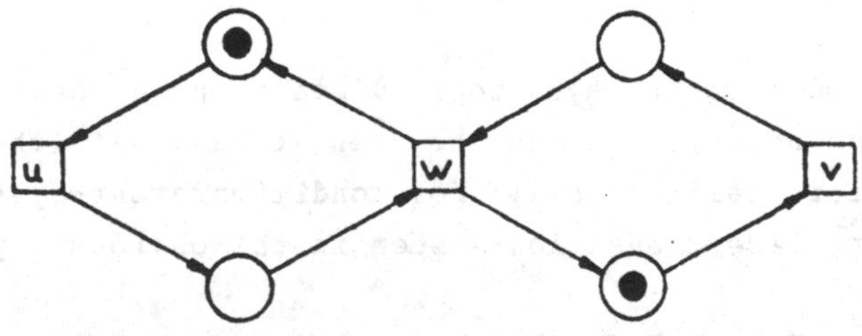

Fig. 7.2

After firing of v the process $p = \langle u,w,u \rangle$ is possible with $\#(a|p) = 2$, $\#(b|p) = 0$, $\sigma(a,b) = 2$

Modelling two 'synchronized' events u and v by $\sigma(\{u\},\{v\}) = 0$ is not correct in general, because coincident means 'at the same time for all conceivable observers'. Normally we cannot guarantee that one of both events does not precede the other one a little. If u precedes v 'at some time' and v precedes u 'at the next time' we observe two successive occurrences of v not being separated by an occurrence of u. So we have to use $\sigma(\{u\},\{v\}) = 2$ which might be surprising.

For the next example (fig. 7.3) we find

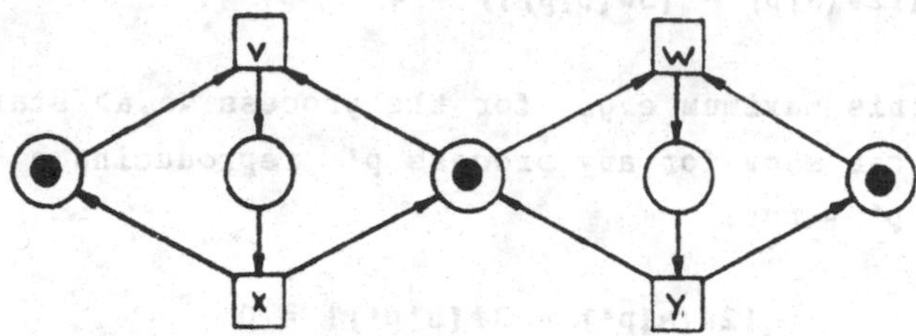

Fig. 7.3

$$\sigma(\{v\},\{w\}) = \sigma(\{v\},\{y\}) = \sigma(\{x\},\{w\}) = \sigma(\{x\},\{y\}) = \infty$$
$$\sigma(\{v\},\{x\}) = \sigma(\{w\},\{y\}) = 1$$
$$\sigma(\{v,w\},\{x,y\}) = 1$$

Obviously this system is fully described by the above values of σ. On the other hand there are good reasons for generalizing the concept of synchronic distance. In the following example (fig. 7.4) we regard the initial marking $M_0(x) = 4$, $M_0(y) = 0$.

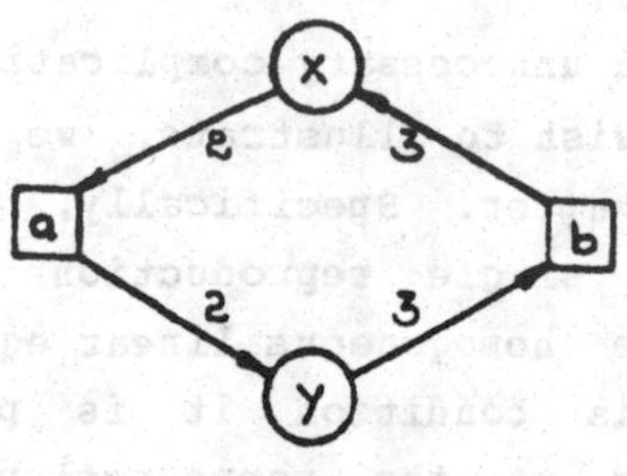

Fig. 7.4

The process $r = \langle a,a,b,a,b \rangle \in PR$ reproduces M_0. Here a occurs once more than b. So, in the n-fold repetition $r^n \in PR$ of r, a has n occurrences more than b:

$|\#(a|r^n) - \#(b|r^n)| = n$

(in the formulas we now use a instead of {a})

Consequently $\sigma(a,b) = \max_{p \in PR} (|\#(a|p) - \#(b|p)|)$ is not finite.

But a and b are undoubtedly dependent. So we have to look for a measure that describes this dependency adequately. If we attach 'suitable' weights to $\#(a|p)$ and $\#(b|p)$, such that the absolute difference equals zero for every reproducing process, we get a finite measure. For the net of fig. 7.4 under marking M_0 we find

$$\max_{p \in PR} (|2\#(a|p) - (3\#(b|p)|) = 4$$

and we obtain this maximum e.g. for the process <a,a> starting at M_0. Moreover, one can show for any process p' reproducing a marking of $[M_0\rangle$ (e.g. for $p' = r^n$):

$$|2\#(a|p') - 3\#(b|p')| = 0$$

This yields: $\min_{p \in PR} (|2\#(a|p) - 3\#(b|p)|) = 0$

What we need next is a method for calculating suitable weights.

<u>Definition</u>: Let C be the incidence matrix of a place/transition-net; then we call the solutions $t \neq 0$ of $C \cdot t = 0$ the <u>T-invariants</u> of the net.

If a T-invariant is non-negativ, minimal and integer we call it a <u>reproduction component</u>.

In order to avoid unnecessary complications which might obscure the main ideas that we wish to illustrate, we shall use a restricted class of nets in this chapter. Specifically, we shall consider those nets which have just a single reproduction component (the linear solution space of the homogeneous linear equation system above has dimension 1). Under this condition it is particularly simple to understand the meaning of the reproduction component: Let M be a marking of a place/transition-net with incidence matrix C and reproduction component r and let M be reproduced by a process p then:

$$M + C \cdot t\langle p\rangle = M$$

Here the T-vector t<p> indicates for every transition how often it occurs in p. Since t<p>≠0 is a non-negative integer solution of $C \cdot t = 0$ we know that $t\langle p\rangle = l \cdot r$ ($l \in \mathbb{N}$) holds. So the vector of firing counts of every process reproducing a marking M is a multiple of r.

__Definition__: Let PN = $(S,T;F,K,W,M_0)$ be a place/transition-system and let PR be the set of all processes. Let r be the reproduction component of the underlying net. Let a,b be two transitions and let d be the greatest common divisor (GCD) of r(a) and r(b); then the __weighted synchronic distance__ s(a,b) between a and b is defined as

$$s(a,b) := \frac{1}{d} \cdot \max_{p \in PR} (|r(b) \cdot \#(a|p) - r(a) \cdot \#(b|p)|)$$

In contrast to the definition of the synchronic distance the weighted synchronic distance is only defined between transitions. Of course, it is possible to extend this definition to sets of transitions, too. We have chosen the simpler version because it is sufficient for the purpose of this chapter and in order to keep the representation as simple as possible.

To get some deeper insight we use a very simple place/transition-net (fig. 7.5), a so called __regulation circuit__.

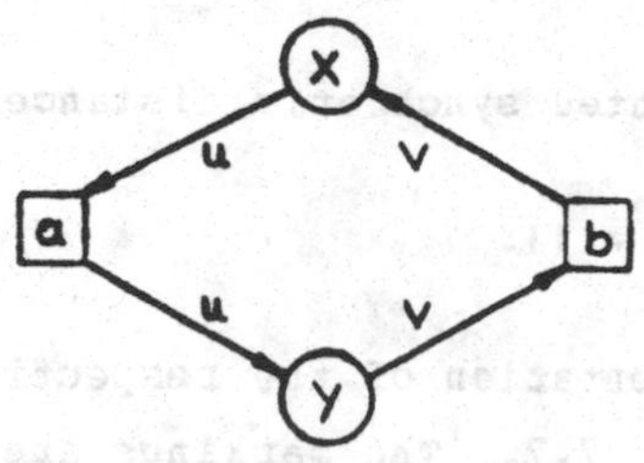

Regulation circuit R Fig. 7.5

The incidence matrix of R is C =

	a	b
x	-u	v
y	u	-v

So the reproduction component is $r = \frac{1}{d} \cdot \begin{pmatrix} v \\ u \end{pmatrix}$

where d is GCD of u and v.

Let g and k be two natural numbers with $g \geq k$. Let M_0 be a live marking of R with $M_0(x) = g - k$, $M_0(y) = k$;

then $s(a,b) = \frac{1}{d} \cdot \max_{p \in PR} (|u \cdot \#(a|p) - v \cdot \#(b|p)|)$

$$= \left[\frac{g-k}{d}\right] + \left[\frac{k}{d}\right]$$

where $[q] := \max\{n \in N \mid n \leq q\}$ (M_0 is live iff $g \geq u+v-1$) .

This maximum is obtained by all processes transforming the markings

$$\begin{pmatrix} \max_{M \in [M_0>} M(x) \\ g - \max_{M \in [M_0>} M(x) \end{pmatrix}, \begin{pmatrix} g - \max_{M \in [M_0>} M(y) \\ \max_{M \in [M_0>} M(y) \end{pmatrix} \in [M_0> \text{ into each other}$$

In case R is 'standardized' (d=1): $s(a,b) = M(x)+M(y) = g$.

For u = 2, v = 3 (see fig. 7.4) we now regard R under two different markings:

M : $M(x) = 3$, $M(y) = 1$ and

M': $M'(x) = 5$, $M'(y) = 6$.

The corresponding weighted synchronic distances are

$s(a,b) = 4$ and $s'(a,b) = 11$.

A graphical representation of the respective process behaviour is shown in fig. 7.6 and 7.7. The markings are represented by the grid points in an area bounded by two parallel straight lines and the axes. The origin in fig. 7.6 corresponds to M, the origin in fig. 7.7 corresponds to M'. The slope of the boundary lines is $tg(\alpha) = 2/3$. Two markings are equal iff the corresponding grid points are situated on one line with slope 2/3. The extremal markings (all tokens on x or on y) are thus represented by the grid points on the boundary lines.

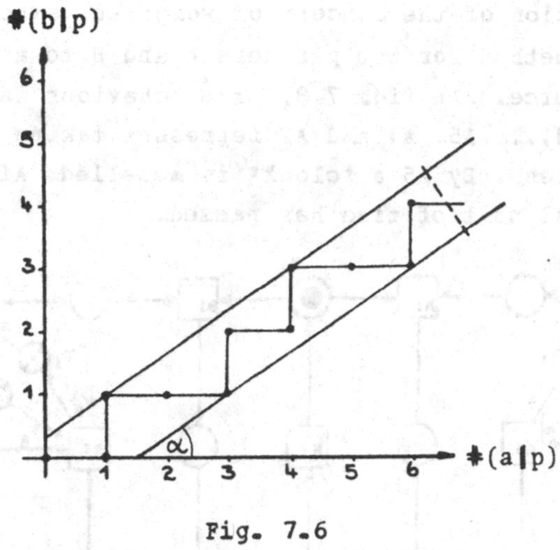

Fig. 7.6

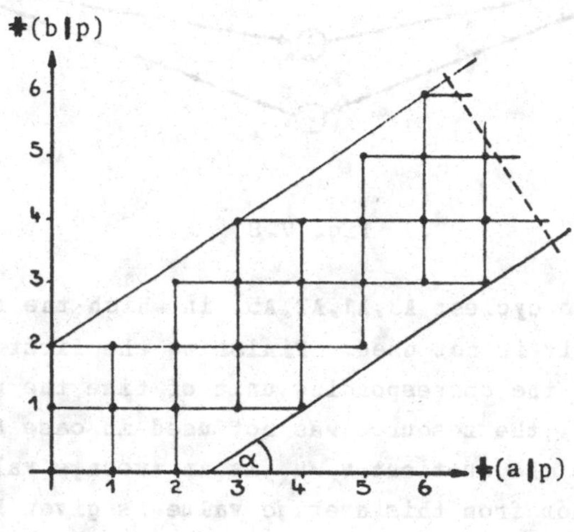

Fig. 7.7

Other initial markings with 4 resp. 11 tokens would lead to a translation of the boundary lines without changing their distance. The greater this distance is the greater is the 'degree of freedom' for the processes, that is to say, the more it is possible for a process to deviate from the rate 2/3 for the firing counts of b and a, resp. So <u>the weighted synchronic distance is a measure for this degree of freedom</u>. The distance between the boundary lines shown in fig. 7.6 is the smallest one possible for a live marking; i.e. decreasing s(a,b) below 4 leads to dead markings.

As an application of the concept of weighted synchronic distance we shall show a method for two partners A and B to achieve 'fairness' in sharing a resource. In fig. 7.8, A's behaviour is represented by the transitions A1,....,A5. A1 and A2 represent taking the resource and giving it back, resp. By A5 a 'clock' is modelled. After every firing of A5 an individual unit of time has passed.

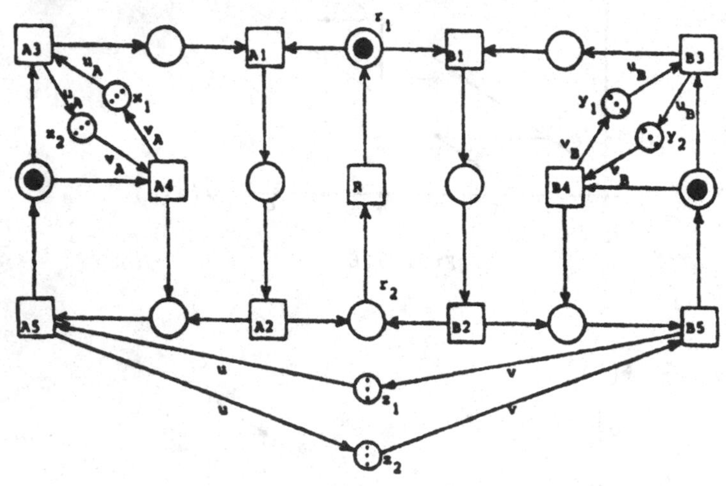

Fig. 7.8

We observe two cycles: A3,A1,A2,A5, in which the resource is used, and A4,A5, where it is not used. Finishing the first one by firing of A5 means that in the corresponding unit of time the resource has been used. Similarly, the resource was not used in case A5 terminates the second cycle. So the quotient v_A/u_A is an average value for the usage rate. The deviation from this average value is given by s(A3,A4). (For initial marking M and u_A,v_A respectively prime we get
s(A3,A4) = $M(x_1)+M(x_2)$; see above)

Thus A can express his interests by (u_A,v_A, s(A3,A4), $M(x_1)$).
$M(x_1)$ is given in order to characterize the initial state.

Likewise B's interests are given by (u_B,v_B, s(B3,B4), $M(y_1)$).

After evaluating the interests of both partners we now have to compare them. This is achieved by comparing the clocks, or more precisely, the units of time. Again, we use the concept of weighted synchronic distance and represent this comparison by the quadruple

$$(u, v, s(A5,B5), M(z_1)).$$

Now we have a framework for a contract between A and B because we can calculate s(A1,B1) on the basis of our intermediate results. For simplicity we assume that

$(u_A + v_A)\cdot u\cdot v_B$ and $v_A\cdot v\cdot(u_B + v_B)$ are respectively prime:

$$s_0 = s(A1,B1) = \max_{p\in PR}(|(u_A + v_A)\cdot u\cdot v_B\cdot\#(A1|p) - v_A\cdot v(u_B + v_B)\cdot\#(B1|p)|)$$

$$= u\cdot v_B\cdot(s(A3,A4) + v_A)$$
$$+ v\cdot v_A\cdot(s(B3,B4) + v_B)$$
$$+ v_A\cdot v_B\cdot s(A5,B5)$$

Details of this calculation can be found in [31].

If both partners are satisfied with this weighted synchronic distance between their respective usages of the resource they can fix the regulation as a quadruple

$$((u_A + v_A)\cdot u\cdot v_B,\ v_A\cdot v\cdot(u_B + v_B),\ s_0, M).$$

If not, they only can decrease the weighted synchronic distance between A1 and B1 because increasing is not possible without changing the interests. In case they agree on decreasing, the net of fig. 7.8 has to be completed by the regulation circuit of fig. 7.9

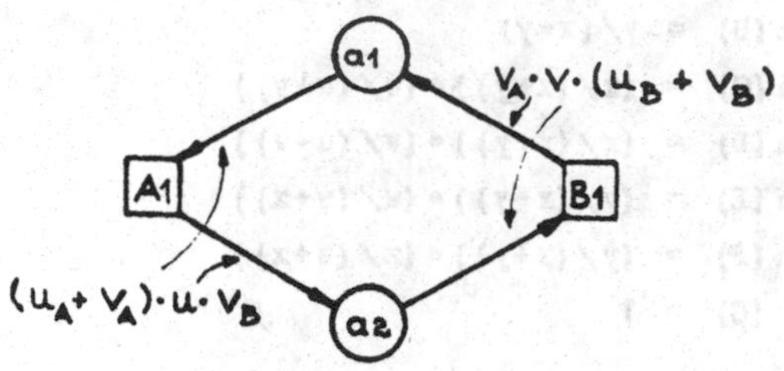

Fig. 7.9

then the partners fix their contract in the following form

$((u_A + v_A)\bullet u\bullet v_B,\ v_A\bullet v(u_B + v_B), M(a_1) + M(a_2), M(a_1))$

where $M(a_1) + M(a_2) < s_0$ is the new weighted synchronic distance between A1 and B1.

The arbitration mechanism shown here is neither deterministic nor probabilistic but <u>well-defined</u>. It can be extended, in a straightforward way, to represent one partners reaction to the other one's being unable or unwilling to use the resource according to the contract.

7.2. Synchrony Theory and Relative Frequencies

As already mentioned, the synchronic distance is a measure for the dependency between events. So the question arises, whether there is a relationship between this notion of dependency in synchronic theory and the probabilistic notion of dependency. We shall show now by means of examples that indeed there is such a relationship and apply then the underlying idea to compute the weights $(u_A + v_A)\bullet u\bullet v_B$ and $v_A\bullet v\bullet(u_B + v_B)$ of the example above in an effective way.

To start with we solve for the place/transition-net of fig. 7.10 the equation system

$$K\bullet h = 0 \quad (K \text{ incidence matrix})$$
$$h(G) = 1$$

The solution is
$$h(A) = x/(x+y)$$
$$h(B) = y/(x+y)$$
$$h(C) = (x/(x+y))\bullet(u/(u+v))$$
$$h(D) = (x/(x+y))\bullet(v/(u+v))$$
$$h(E) = (y/(x+y))\bullet(w/(w+z))$$
$$h(F) = (y/(x+y))\bullet(z/(w+z))$$
$$h(G) = 1$$

h is a T-invariant but no reproduction component because it is not integer. Note that h is the vector of <u>relative frequencies</u>.

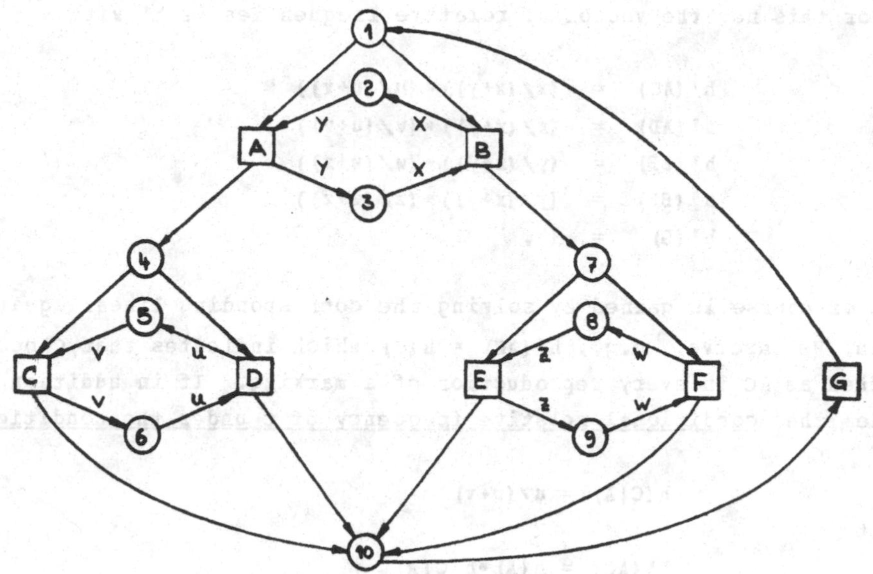

Fig. 7.10

A further observation in the net of fig. 7.10 are the causal dependencies between A and C, A and D, B and E, B and F. Now, in order to get a bridge to the calculus of relative frequencies, we need the 'joint' events AC, AD, BE, and BF.

Therefore, in the net of fig. 7.11 the events A and C, A and D, B and E, B and F are combined to indivisible events.

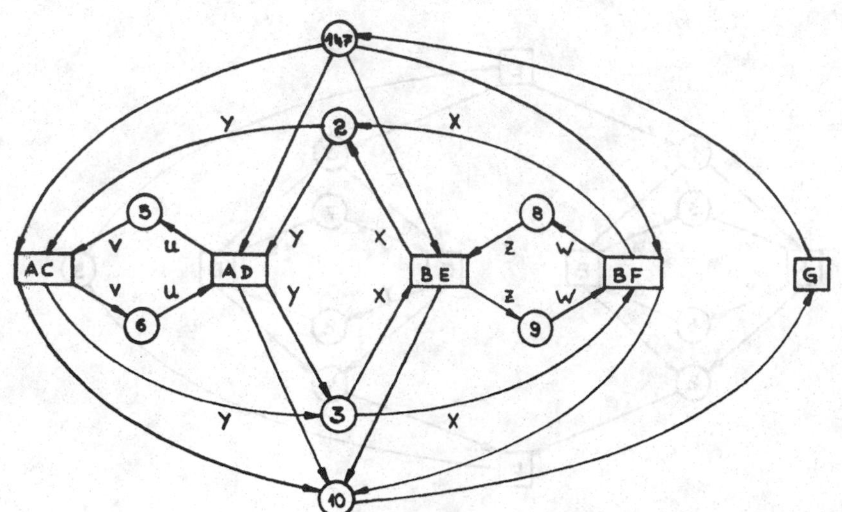

Fig. 7.11

For this net the vector of relative frequencies is h' with

$$h'(AC) = (x/(x+y))\cdot(u/(u+v))$$
$$h'(AD) = (x/(x+y))\cdot(v/(u+v))$$
$$h'(BE) = (y/(x+y))\cdot(w/(w+z))$$
$$h'(BF) = (y/(x+y))\cdot(z/(w+z))$$
$$h'(G) = 1\ ,$$

which of course is gained by solving the corresponding linear equation system. We observe, e.g., $h'(AC) = h(C)$ which indicates that C occurs as often as AC in every reproduction of a marking. If in addition we define the <u>conditional relative frequency of C under the condition A</u> as

$$h(C|A) := u/(u+v)$$

we get

$$h'(AC) = h(A)\cdot h(C|A),$$

which is the well-known frequency formula for dependent events representing the causal dependency of C on A.

In fig. 7.12 we observe causal independencies between A and C, A and D, B and C, B and D, because of the possibility of concurrent occurrence.

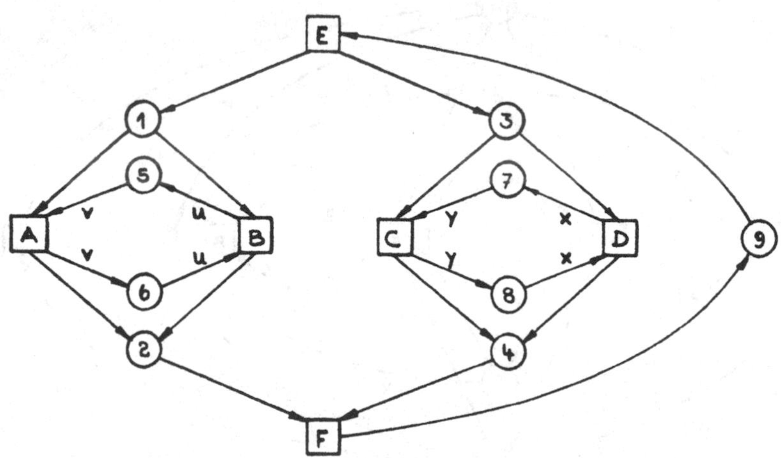

Fig. 7.12

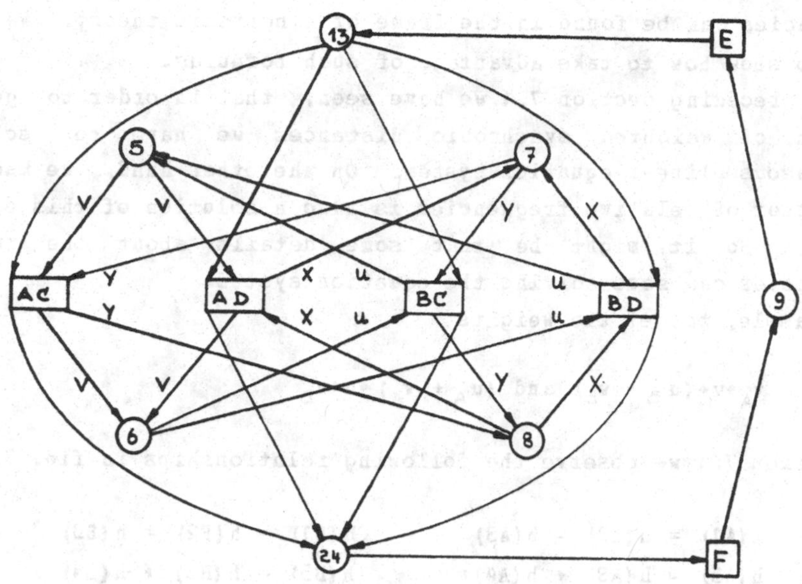

Fig. 7.13

Again we combine these pairs of events to single ones (fig. 7.13) and find the following relative frequencies:

$h(A) = u/(u+v)$	$h'(AC) = (u/(u+v)) \cdot (x/(x+y))$
$h(B) = v/(u+v)$	$h'(AD) = (u/(u+v)) \cdot (y/(x+y))$
$h(C) = x/(x+y)$	$h'(BC) = (v/(u+v)) \cdot (x/(x+y))$
$h(D) = y/(x+y)$	$h'(BD) = (v/(u+v)) \cdot (y/(x+y))$
$h(E) = h(F) = 1$	$h'(E) = h'(F) = 1$

This yields:

$$h'(AC) = h(A) \cdot h(C),$$

the well-known formula for independent events representing the causal independency, that is to say the concurrency, of A and C.

Even though we have only regarded examples, what we have found is a significant consistency between the synchronic and probabilistic notion of dependency. We easily could supplement this considerations by showing that further well known formulas concerning relative

frequencies can be found in the frame of synchronic theory. We rather want to show how to take advantage of such formulas.
In the preceding section 7.1 we have seen, that in order to get the weights of weighted synchronic distances we have to solve a homogeneous linear equation system. On the other hand, we know that the vector of relative frequencies is also a solution of this equation system. So it might be that some details about the relative frequencies can save solving the equation system.
For example, to get the weights

$$v_A \cdot v \cdot (u_B + v_B) \text{ and } (u_A + v_A) \cdot u \cdot v_B$$

of section 7.1 we observe the following relationships in fig. 7.8:

$$h(A1) = h(A2) = h(A3) \qquad h(B1) = h(B2) = h(B3)$$
$$h(A5) = h(A3) + h(A4) \qquad h(B5) = h(B3) + h(B4)$$
$$h(A3)/h(A4) = v_A/u_A \qquad h(B3)/h(B4) = v_B/u_B$$
$$h(A5)/h(B5) = v/u.$$

This yields:

$$h(A1)/h(B1) = (h(A1)/h(A5)) \cdot (h(A5)/h(B5)) \cdot (h(B5)/h(B1))$$
$$= (h(A3)/(h(A3)+h(A4))) \cdot (h(A5)/h(B5)) \cdot ((h(B3)+h(B4))/h(B3))$$
$$= (1/(1 + u_A/v_A)) \cdot (v/u) \cdot (1 + u_B/v_B)$$
$$= (v_A/(u_A + v_A)) \cdot (v/u) \cdot ((u_B + v_B)/v_B)$$
$$= v_A \cdot v \cdot (u_B + v_B)/(u_A + v_A) \cdot u \cdot v_B$$

This example shows that we may regard the theory of relative frequencies, which is a combinatorial part of probability theory, also as a part of synchrony theory. Moreover, the solution of the fairness example is a combinatorial one - in contrast to probabilistic approaches. So we may regard synchrony theory as a basis of a combinatorial approach for description and measurement of system performance.

8. THE CATEGORY OF NETS

8.0. Introduction (Why categories?)

If nets are to be a useful tool for representing systems on more than one logical level, then it must be possible to perform operations on nets like refinement, contraction, extension, completion, division, restriction, etc. such that the results are nets again. Furthermore, more complex transformations which system representations may undergo in the course of analysis or design must be expressible as compounds of some simpler, basic ones.

Let us call such a single step of transformation leading from one net N_1 to another net N_2 a morphism (by which, at this point, we only wish to indicate that the transformations shall depend on, or respect, the structure of nets). If we name the morphism f, we call N_1 the source and N_2 the target of f and write $f:N_1 \to N_2$ in texts, or $N_1 \xrightarrow{f} N_2$ in diagrams like

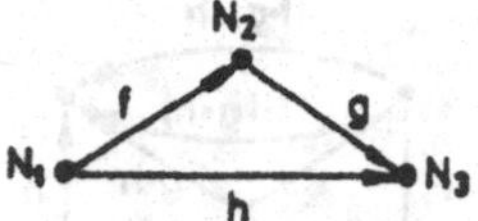

Although we would be free, in principle, to choose an arbitrary set of such morphisms and call it the set of net morphisms, we should try to be as economical as possible. That means that the set of net morphisms should be just comprehensive enough to express all interesting relations between nets by means of morphism diagrams.

The notion of a category (cf. [34], e.g.) can help us to choose the right set of morphisms. This is because, loosely speaking, a category is a collection of (structured) objects and (structure respecting) morphisms which satisfies certain postulates.

The most important principle for obtaining succinct descriptions of a set of morphisms is that of composition : Anytime there are two morphisms f and g such that the target of f is the source of g, it makes sense to talk about their composite f followed by g which shall be denoted by f•g, or just fg. (Note that we prefer the diagram oriented 'path-notation' f•g to the function oriented reversed notation g•f read as "g after f".)

We now postulate that in the set of net morphisms f•g denotes again a morphism, the image of f and g under the (partial) operation of composition: The morphism f•g "is defined" iff the target of f and the source of g are identical. This is pictured by the following diagram in which the existence of the dotted arrow is implied by the existence of the solid ones:

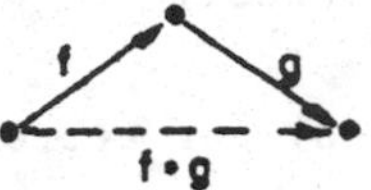

Next we demand that in a chain of more than two morphisms the final result of composition shall not depend on the order in which composition is performed: Composition is associative, the following statements are to be equivalent:

- fg and gh are defined;
- f(gh) is defined;
- (fg)h is defined;
- f(gh) and (fg)h are defined and equal.

Pictorially this may be represented by the statement that the following diagram is commutative:

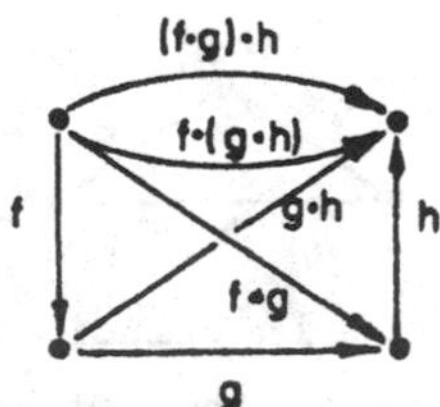

A diagram is commutative when, for each pair of its vertices N_1 and N_2, any two paths of equally directed arrows leading from N_1 to N_2 yield, by composition of labels, equal arrows from N_1 to N_2.

That there exist morphisms at all, can be guaranteed by a seemingly rather technical postulate. Namely for each net N at least the idendity morphism $1_N: N \rightarrow N$ exists such that for any two morphisms $f: N_1 \rightarrow N$ and $g: N \rightarrow N_2$: $f \bullet 1_N = f$ and $1_N \bullet g = g$. This may be represented pictorially by the statement that the following diagram is commutative:

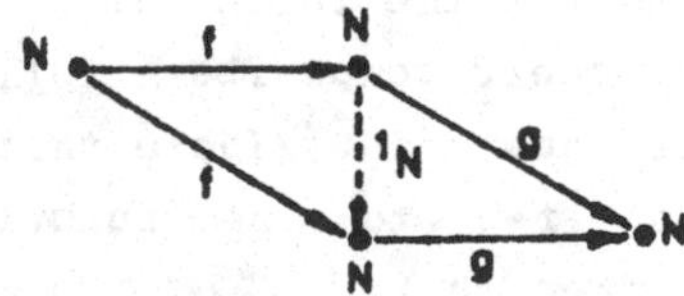

A collection of objects and morphisms as described so far is called a category. The postulates we have stated are collected together in the following

<u>Definition</u>: A tuple C = (O,M;dm,cd,I,•) is called a <u>category</u> iff it satisfies the following postulates:

(1) The tuple (O,M;dm,cd) is a directed graph; O is the set of vertices called the <u>objects</u> of C, M is the set of arrows called the <u>morphisms</u> of C, and dm,cd are functions from M into O assigning to each morphism its <u>source</u> and <u>target</u>, respectively.

(2) I is a function from O into M assigning to each object a its <u>identity</u> morphism denoted by 1_a.

(3) • is a function from the set of <u>composable</u> pairs of morphisms, $\{f,g \mid cd(f)=dm(g)\}$ into M.

(4) The functions dm,cd,I,• are interrelated in the following way:
- $dm(1_a) = cd(1_a) = a$
- $dm(f \bullet g) = dm(f)$ and $cd(f \bullet g) = cd(g)$
- $1_{dm(f)} \bullet f = f \bullet 1_{cd(f)} = f$
- $f \bullet (g \bullet h) = (f \bullet g) \bullet h$

Thus we are now looking for a proper <u>category of nets</u> which is the formal model of the 'system' of systems representations which nets and net transformations shall constitute.

8.1. <u>The Structure of Nets</u> (What are the objects?)

Before we are able to give a formal definition of the notion 'net morphism' which respects the structure of nets, we must study in little more detail what this structure is. Or, in other words, before we specify the morphisms of the category of nets, we must specify its objects. The reason for this being a matter of concern at all is the existence of several different, yet equally useful and structurally equivalent, forms in which nets may appear. And this place here seems most appropriate for trying a systematic approach to the different forms and their comparison.

Since we have already encountered the form N = (S,T;F) we start with this and use it as the common reference form:

<u>Definition</u>: Let S and T be two sets and F a binary relation in S∪T. The triple N=(S,T;F) is called a (<u>directed</u>) <u>net</u> - in STF-form - iff

(1) $S \cap T = \emptyset$

(2) $S \cup T \neq \emptyset$

(3) $F \subseteq S \times T \cup T \times S$

(4) $dom(F) \cup cod(F) = S \cup T$

<u>Defintion</u>: Let $N = (S,T;F)$ be a net in STF-form. Thenwe call

(1) $X := S \cup T$ the set of (S- or T-) elements of N;

(2) F the <u>flow</u> relation of N;

(3) $P := (F \cup F^{-1}) \cap (S \times T)$ the <u>adjacency</u> relation of N;

(4) $Z := F \cap (S \times T)$ the <u>target</u> relation of N;

(5) $Q := F^{-1} \cap (S \times T)$ the <u>source</u> relation of N;

(6) $\Pi := \{A \subseteq X \mid a \in A \wedge xPa \Longrightarrow x \in A\}$ the <u>topology</u> of N.

There are several ways to build from these derived notions equivalent forms of nets. They allow different approaches to the notion net for which we give three examples.

The purpose of the first alternative, $N = (X;P,F)$ is to work with only one carrier set and to get the distinction between S- and T-elements from the adjacency relation P. The advantage of such homogeneous forms will become clear in connection with the notion of a morphism.

<u>Definition</u>: Let X be a set and P,F binary relations in X. The triple $N = (X;P,F)$ is called a net in <u>XPF-form</u> iff

(1) $X \neq \emptyset$

(2) $dom(P) \cap cod(P) = \emptyset$

(3) $dom(P) \cup cod(P) = X$

(4) $(F \cup F^{-1}) \cap (dom(P) \times cod(P)) = P$

<u>Proposition</u>: A triple $N = (X;P,F)$ is a net in XPF-form iff the triple (S,T;F) with

(1) $S = dom(P)$

(2) $T = cod(P)$

is a net.

The second alternative, $N = (X;Z,Q)$ introduces the 'orientation' of the 'undirected' net (X;P) by distinguishing two kinds of adjacency: $P \rightarrow Z \cup Q$. Its heterogeneous STZQ-form $N = (S,T;Z,Q)$ was historically the first in which nets appeared. It shows nets as generalized directed graphs (graph = two sets + two functions; net = two sets + two relations).

<u>Definition</u>: Let X be a set and Z,Q binary relations in X. The triple $N = (X;Z,Q)$ is called a net in <u>XZQ-form</u> iff

(1) $X \neq \emptyset$

(2) $dom(Z \cup Q) \cap cod(Z \cup Q) = \emptyset$

(3) $dom(Z \cup Q) \cup cod(Z \cup Q) = X$

<u>Proposition</u>: $N=(X;Z,Q)$ is a net in XZQ-form iff the triple $(S,T;F)$ with

(1) $S = dom(Z\cup Q)$

(2) $T = cod(Z\cup Q)$

(3) $F = Z\cup Q^{-1}$

is a net.

Finally, the third alternative, $N = (X;\Pi,F)$ puts the stress on the very close relationship of nets to topological spaces. The justification for calling Π a topology will be given a little later. Its importance for net theory becomes obvious when looking at the corresponding net morphisms.

<u>Definition</u>: Let X be a set, Π a set of subsets of X, and F a binary relation in X. The triple $N = (X;\Pi,F)$ is called a net in XΠF-form iff

(1) $X \neq \emptyset$

(2) $\forall x\in X:[\dot{x}\in\Pi \vee (X-\dot{x})\in\Pi]$ $\qquad (\dot{x} := \{x\})$

(3) $\neg\exists x\in X:[\dot{x}\in\Pi \wedge (X-\dot{x})\in\Pi]$

(4) $A\in\Pi \iff A\subseteq X \wedge [y\in A \wedge (X-\dot{y})\in\Pi \wedge x(F\cup F^{-1})y \implies x\in A]$

(5) $(X-A)\in\Pi \iff [x\in A \wedge x\in\Pi \wedge x(F\cup F^{-1})y \implies y\in A]$

<u>Proposition</u>: A triple $N = (X;\Pi,F)$ is a net in XΠF-form iff the triple $(S,T;F)$ with

(1) $S = \{x|x\in\Pi\}$

(2) $T = \{y|(X-\dot{y})\in\Pi\}$

is a net.

There are cases in which one does not distinguish between a given net and its 'Gestalt' as represented by the mere diagram of the net which does not tell which element of the net is represented by which element of the diagram. We call this Gestalt of a net $N = (X;P,F)$ also the <u>abstract net</u> belonging to the <u>(concrete)</u> net N. For example, ○→□ shows the Gestalt of all concrete nets consisting of two elements and one arc leading from the S-element to the T-element.

The Gestalt of a net exhibits exactly all <u>structural</u> properties of N, i.e. those properties which are independent of the identity of its elements. Formally, it can be defined as the class of all nets which are <u>isomorphic</u> to N where two nets N and N' are isomorphic iff there exists an <u>homomorphism</u> from N into N', i.e. a mapping $h:X\to X'$ with $h[P] \subseteq P'$ and $h[F] \subseteq F'$, such that h^{-1} is a homomorphism from N' into N.

Since we don't want to give preference to any of the forms in which concrete nets may appear to us, one may think of a net as an 8-tuple (or h-tuple - 'h' for horrible) $N = (X;S,T,P,\Pi,Z,Q,F)$ with the corresponding properties. We prefer, however, to consider for any of the forms the remaining forms as being derived, or implicitly given.

Two constituents of the structure of nets, namely the P-relation and the Π-subsets, are worth some more investigation.

<u>Definition</u>: Let X be a set and P a binary relation in X. The pair $U = (X;P)$ is called an <u>undirected net</u> iff

(1) $X \neq \emptyset$

(2) $dom(P) \cap cod(P) = \emptyset$

(3) $dom(P) \cup cod(P) = X$

<u>Proposition</u>: If $N = (X;P,F)$ is a net, then $(X;P)$ is an undirected net, namely the associated undirected net of N which, pictorially, is the result of omitting arrowheads.

<u>Definition</u>: Let $R = (X;\Pi)$ be a topological space, i.e. let X be a set and Π a set of subsets of X (the <u>open</u> subsets of X) such that

(1) $X = \bigcup \Pi$

(2) $\Sigma \subseteq \Pi \implies \bigcup \Sigma \in \Pi$

(3) $A,B \in \Pi \implies A \cap B \in \Pi$

Then R is called a <u>Petri space</u>, and Π a <u>net topology</u> of X, iff

(1') $X = \bigcup \Pi \neq \emptyset$

(3') $\emptyset \neq \Sigma \subseteq \Pi \implies \bigcap \Sigma \in \Pi$ (R is <u>elementary</u>)

(4) $\forall x \in X: [\dot{x} \in \Pi \vee (X-\dot{x}) \in \Pi]$ (R is "$T_{1/2}$")

(5) $\neg \exists x \in X: [\dot{x} \in \Pi \wedge (X-\dot{x}) \in \Pi]$ (R has no isolated points)

The notion of a Petri space is the result of structurally 'balancing' the notion of a topological space. In Petri spaces there is no structural difference between "open" and "closed": The axiom (3') is equivalent to demanding that the set of sets which are closed under Π also forms a topology of X and thus gives rise to a powerful <u>duality</u> principle for <u>elementary</u> spaces. (4) demands that each singleton of X is open or closed ((5): no singleton is both open and closed), and thus (4) weakens the separation axiom T_1 which demands that all singletons are closed. On the other hand, (4) implies the separation axiom T_0. Thus it may be called the separation axiom $T_{1/2}$.

__Theorem__ 8.1: If $N = (X;\Pi,F)$ is a net, then $(X;\Pi)$ is a Petri space and Π is called __the topology__ of N.

__Corrolary__: A set $A \subseteq X$ of elements of N is open in the topology of N (i.e. $A \in \Pi$) iff its surface in N consists of S-elements only; especially every subset of S is open. Dually: A set $A \subseteq X$ is closed under Π (i.e. $X-A \in \Pi$) iff its surface in N consists of T-elements only; especially every subset of T is closed.

The next theorem shows that not only $(X;P,F)$ and $(X;\Pi,F)$ are equivalent forms of nets but also $(X;P)$ and $(X;\Pi)$ are equivalent forms of the topological structure of nets:

__Theorem__ 8.2: If $U = (X;P)$ is an undirected net, then $(X;\Pi)$ with $\Pi = \{A \subseteq X \mid y \in A \wedge xPy \Longrightarrow x \in A\}$ is a Petri space. Conversely, if $R = (X;\Pi)$ is a Petri space, then $(X;P)$ with $P = \{x,y \mid x \neq y \wedge y \text{ \underline{at} } x\}$ is an undirected net, where a point x is said to be __at__ a point y iff it belongs to the closure of the singleton $\dot{y}$:

$x \text{ \underline{at} } y \;:\Longleftrightarrow\; \forall A \in \Pi : [x \in A \Longrightarrow y \in A]$

Furthermore, each transformation is the inverse of the other. Thus the notions "undirected net" and "Petri space" are structurally equivalent.

Consequently we may characterize a net as an elementary $T_{1/2}$-space without isolated points together with an orientation of its at-relation. (For more details concerning net topologies refer to [11].)

The diagram in fig. 8.1 summarizes the contents of this section. It shows a small segment of the net representation of mathematical knowledge as introduced in [16]. Each S-element ◯ represents a whole 'domain' of mathematical objects, the set-theoretic models of a certain axiomatic specification. The T-elements ☐ 'produce' new objects from given ones according to the inscribed specifications. The ultimate source for all objects is a given universe of sets. The arcs are labelled by naming schemes ('procedure parameters'). If at a domain, an outgoing arc is unlabelled then it carries, by convention, the same naming scheme as the incoming arcs of that domain.

If in this diagram, two domains are connected by a closed directed path, their specifications are structurally equivalent.

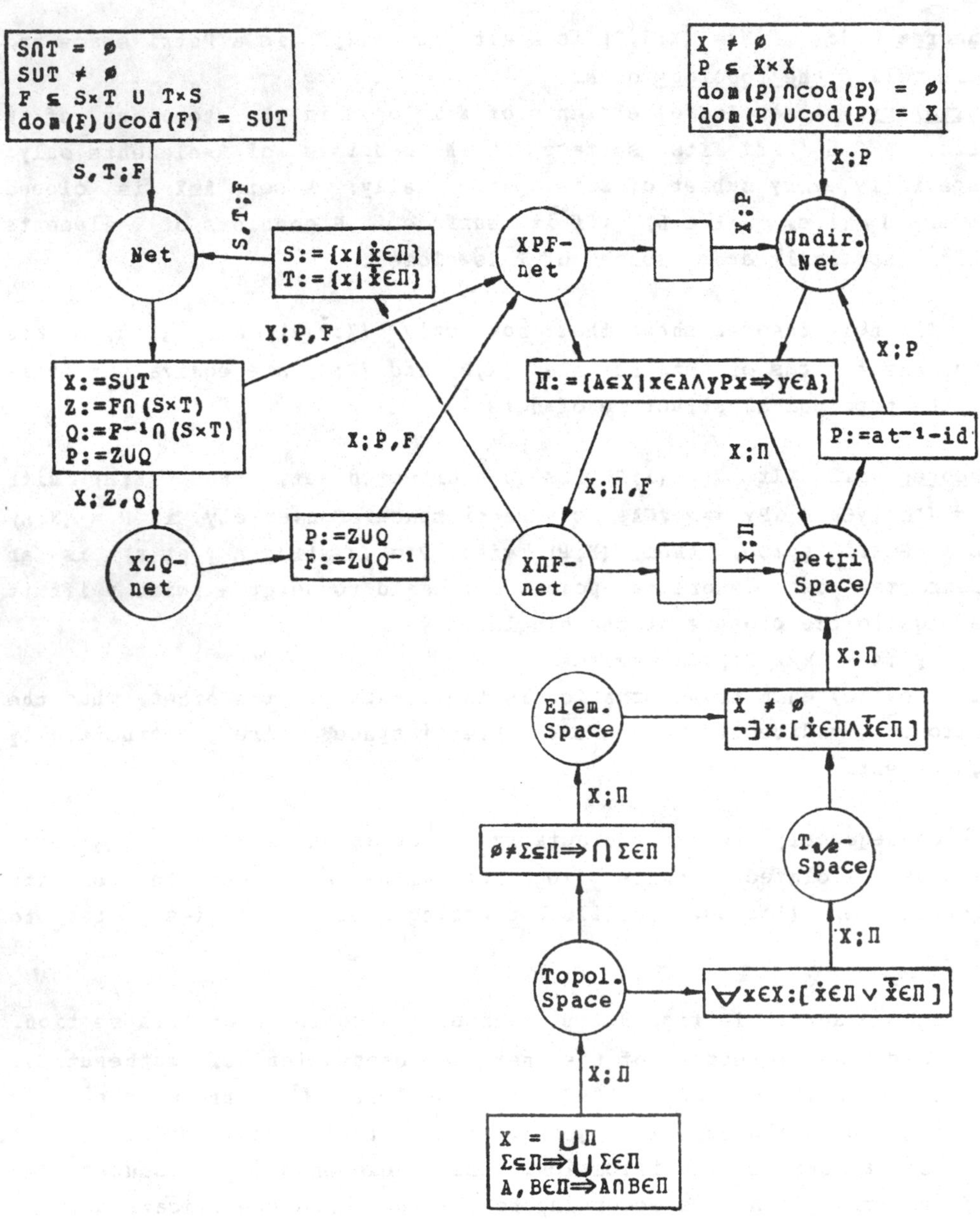

S∩T = ∅
S∪T ≠ ∅
F ⊆ S×T ∪ T×S
dom(F)∪cod(F) = S∪T
S,T;F
Net
S,T;F
S:={x | ẋ∈Π}
T:={x | x̄∈Π}
XPF-net
X;P
Undir. Net
X;P
X ≠ ∅
P ⊆ X×X
dom(P)∩cod(P) = ∅
dom(P)∪cod(P) = X
X;P,F
X:=S∪T
Z:=F∩(S×T)
Q:=F⁻¹∩(S×T)
P:=Z∪Q
Π:={A⊆X | x∈A∧yPx⇒y∈A}
X;P
P:=at⁻¹-id
X;P,F
X;Π
X;Z,Q
X;Π,F
XZQ-net
P:=Z∪Q
F:=Z∪Q⁻¹
XΠF-net
X;Π
Petri Space
X;Π
Elem. Space
X ≠ ∅
¬∃x:[ẋ∈Π∧x̄∈Π]
X;Π
∅≠Σ⊆Π⇒⋂Σ∈Π
T½-Space
X;Π
Topol. Space
∀x∈X:[ẋ∈Π∨x̄∈Π]
X;Π
X = ⋃Π
Σ⊆Π⇒⋃Σ∈Π
A,B∈Π⇒A∩B∈Π

Fig. 8.1

8.2. Net Morphisms (Respecting the structure of nets)

Now, after having some understanding of the structure of nets, we give without further justification a formal definition of net morphisms [46]. Whether it yields the desired, or expected, properties of the category of nets shall be discussed afterwards.

Definition: Let N_1 and N_2 be nets and $f:X_1 \to X_2$ be a mapping of the set of elements of N_1 into the set of elements of N_2. The triple (N_1,N_2,f) is called a net morphism if it respects P and F, i.e. preserves P ∪ id and F ∪ id.

(1) $f[P_1] \subseteq P_2 \cup id$

(2) $f[F_1] \subseteq F_2 \cup id$

In this case, we also write $f:N_1 \to N_2$ provided that it is clear from the context whether f denotes the morphism or the mapping.

Theorem 8.3: Nets and net morphisms form a category, the category of nets, which is denoted by NET.

Pictorially, the properties of respecting P and F are expressed by the following diagrams in which again dotted elements are implied by the solid part.

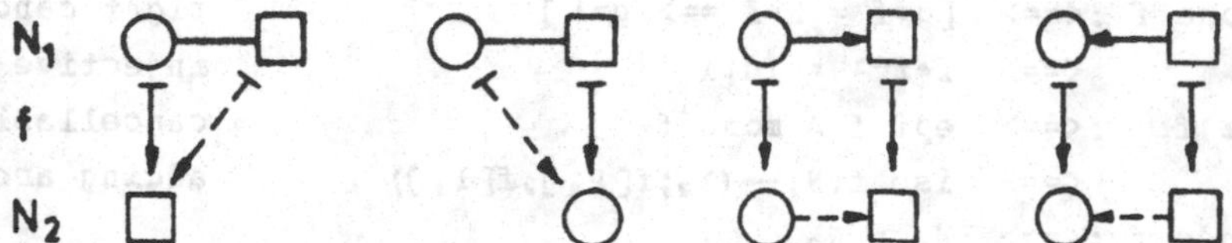

It should be noticed that net morphisms are not necessarily net homomorphisms, yet include them as a special, and important, case. Net homomorphisms - which preserve, rather than only respect, P and F - are called foldings. For example, processes are foldings which map an occurrence net into a condition/event-net.

The difference between net morphisms and net homomorphisms becomes especially clear when we express net morphisms in ΠF-form. The weaker "respecting P" rather than the stronger "preserving P" is equivalent to being continuous with respect to the topological structure of nets.

Theorem 8.4: $f:N_1 \to N_2$ is a net morphism iff f is continous and respects F:

(1) $A \in \Pi_2 \Longrightarrow f^{-1}[A] \in \Pi_1$

(2) $f[F_1] \subseteq F_2 \cup id$

An *invertible* morphism, i.e. a morphism $f:N_1 \to N_2$ for which a morphism $g:N_2 \to N_1$ exists such that $f \circ g = 1_{N_1}$ and $g \circ f = 1_{N_2}$, is also called an *isomorphism*, and of course two nets are isomorphic (possess the same Gestalt) if they are connected by an isomorphism. A morphism $f:N_1 \to N_2$ which shows that the Gestalt of N_1 is a subnet of the Gestalt of N_2 is called a *subnet injection*. (Recall that N' is a subnet of N iff $X' \subseteq X$ and $P'=P|X'$, $F'=F|X'$.

If the image of N_1, $f[N_1] = (f[X_1];f[P_1],f[F_1])$ is a subnet of N_2 (which means that each arc in N_2 connecting two images of elements has a pre-image in N_1), the morphism f is called *F-strict* ; and if the image of N_1 is a net at all, f is called a *proper* morphism.

Next we give a list of properties of morphisms which may be met at some point in general net theory. Among them are some which are defined for categories in general - like, for example, isomorphisms -. For them, the usual definition may be followed by an equivalent formulation for the net morphisms:

Definition: Let $f:N_1 \to N_2$ be a net morphism.

I: General properties

(1)	epi f	:<==>	$[f \circ g = f \circ h \Rightarrow g = h]$	left cancellable
		<==>	$f[X_1] = X_2$	surjective
(2)	mono f	:<==>	$[g \circ f = h \circ f \Rightarrow g=h]$	right cancellable
		<==>	$f \circ f^{-1} = id \mid X$	injective
(3)	bi f	:<==>	epi f $\wedge$ mono f	cancellable
		<==>	iso $f:N_1 \to (X_2;f[P_1],f[F_1])$	adding arcs
(4)	endo f	:<==>	$N_1 = N_2$	
(5)	iso f	:<==>	$\exists g:N_2 \to N_1:[f \circ g=1_{N_1} \wedge g \circ f=1_{N_2}]$	invertible
		<==>	morphism $f^{-1}:N_2 \to N_1$	
(6)	auto f	:<==>	endo f $\wedge$ iso f	

II: Depending on P, but not on F:

(7)	proper f	:<==>	Net $(f[X_1];f[P_1],f[F_1])$	image of N_1 is a net
(8)	prendo f	:<==>	proper f $\wedge$ endo f	
(9)	P-strict f	:<==>	$f[P_1] = (P_2 \cup id) \mid f[X_1]$	P in image is induced by f
(10)	SS f	:<==>	$f[S_1] \subseteq S_2$	
(11)	TT f	:<==>	$f[T_1] \subseteq T_2$	
(12)	folding f	:<==>	$f[P_1] \subseteq P_2$ $[\Leftrightarrow f[F_1] \subseteq F_2]$	homomorphism
(13)	open f	:<==>	$A \in \Pi_1 \Rightarrow f[A] \in \Pi_2$	
(14)	closed f	:<==>	$(X_1 - A) \in \Pi_1 \Rightarrow (X_2 - f[A]) \in \Pi_2$	

III: Depending on F:

(15) F-strict f :<==> $f[F_1] = (F_2 \cup id) | f[X_1]$ F in image is induced by f

(16) subnet inj. f:<==> mono f ∧ F-strict f

(17) quotient f :<==> epi f ∧ F-strict f as for quotient topology

IV: Special operations on nets

(18) S-/T-/(X-)simplification f :<==> quotient f onto largest possible S-/T-/(X-)simple net

S-/T-/(X-)simple N :<==> $\forall x,y \in$ S/T/X$:[\bullet x = \bullet y \wedge x\bullet = y\bullet \Longrightarrow x = y]]$

(19) S-/T-/(X-)complementation f :<==> subnet inj. f into smallest possible S-/T-/(X-)complemented net

S-/T-/(X-)complemented N :<==> $\forall x \in$ S/T/X $\exists y \in X:[\bullet x = \bullet y \wedge x\bullet = y\bullet]$

(20) S-/T-completion f :<==> subnet inj. f into smallest S-/T-complete net

S-/T-complete N :<==> $\forall A,B \subseteq$ T/S$:[A \cup B \neq \emptyset \Longrightarrow \exists x \in$ S/T$:[\bullet x = A \wedge x\bullet = B]]$

No net can be both S-complete and T-complete (Cantor's theorem about the cardinality of powersets).

V: The basic morphism for interpreted nets

(21) process f :<==> open folding f ∧ OccNet N_1 ∧

$$\exists C_1, C_2:[\text{CESys }(N_2,C_2) \wedge C_1 \subseteq \text{Kens}(F_1^+ \cup F_1^-) \cap \mathcal{P}(S_1) \wedge \forall c \in C_1 \exists c' \in C_2: f[c] \subseteq c' \wedge \forall c \in C_1 \forall x,y \in c:[x \neq y \Longrightarrow f(x) \neq f(y)]\ ]$$

OccNet N :<==> Net N ∧ $F^+ \cap id | X = \emptyset \wedge \forall s \in S[\,|\bullet s| \leq 1 \wedge |s\bullet| \leq 1]$

CESys (N,C) :<==> Net N ∧ N=(B,E;F) ∧ simple N ∧ $C \subseteq \mathcal{P}(B)$ ∧

$$\forall e \in E \exists c \in C:[\bullet e \subseteq c \wedge e\bullet \cap c = \emptyset] \wedge$$

Ken(C,"full reachability")

Example: (See symbol of Advanced Course on G.N.T.)

The logical structure of this list is depicted by the following diagram in fig. 8.2. The extension on top of net morphisms anticipates the subsequent sections.

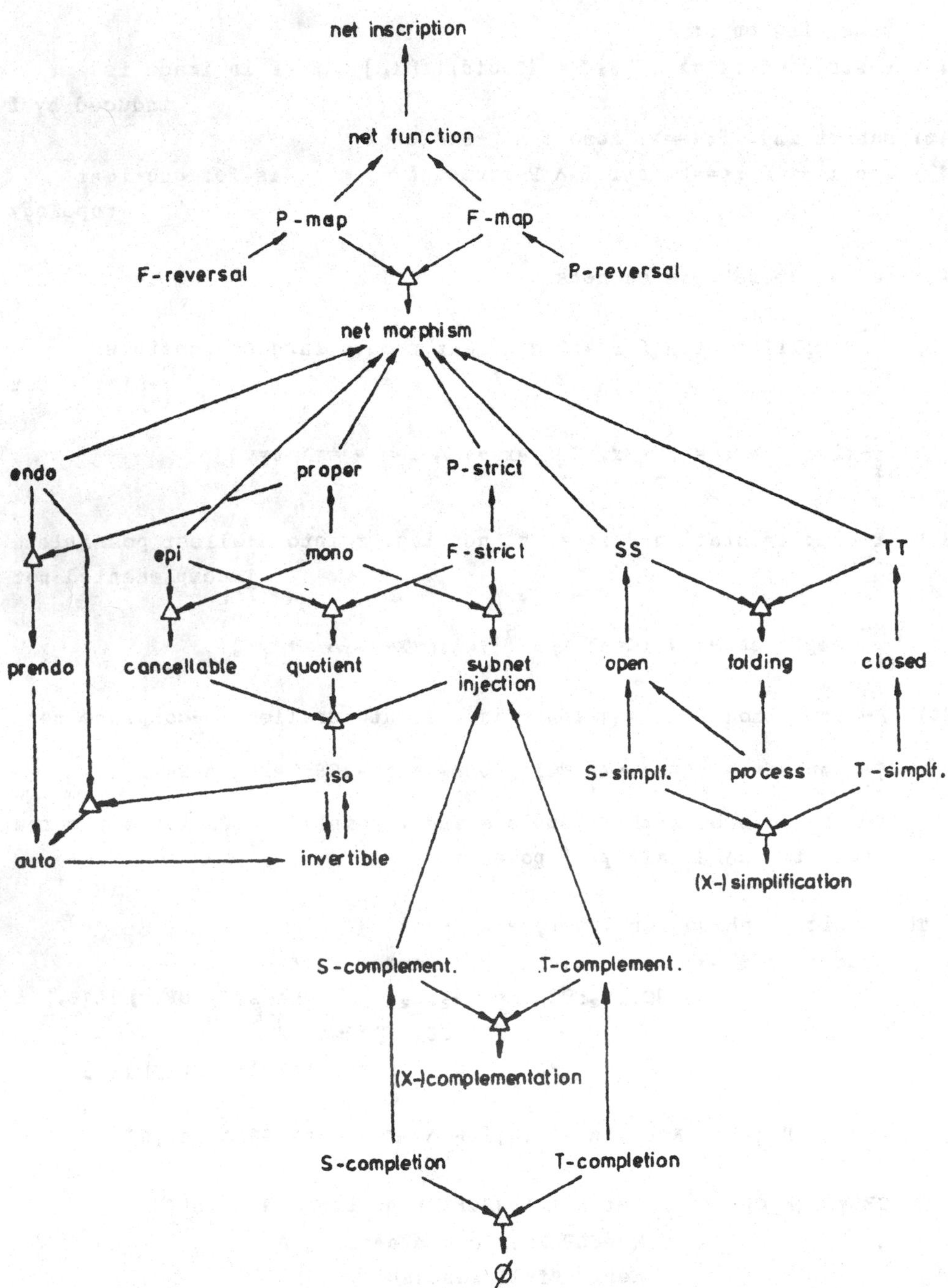
net inscription
net function
P-map
F-map
F-reversal
P-reversal
net morphism
endo
proper
P-strict
epi
mono
F-strict
SS
TT
prendo
cancellable
quotient
subnet injection
open
folding
closed
iso
S-simplf.
process
T-simplf.
auto
invertible
(X-) simplification
S-complement.
T-complement.
(X-)complementation
S-completion
T-completion
Ø
PETRI '79

Fig. 8.2

8.3. Some Functors (Limitations for net morphisms)

So far we have seen that net morphisms are a very natural and powerful vehicle for expressing a great variety of tranformations, or operations, performable on nets. Yet there are, of course, also limitations implied by the chosen definition. In fact, most of the transformations of systems descriptions occurring in the course of systems organisation cannot be expressed by a single net morphism. This shall give us now the opportunity to show the power of the category of nets being just more than only a collection of morphisms.

The first consequence of the definition of net morphisms which might be viewed as a shortcoming is the asymmetry of source and target of a morphism. Except for isomorphisms, the reverse of the mapping f in a net morphism $f:N_1 \to N_2$ does not constitute a net morphism $f^{-1}:N_2 \to N_1$. Thus if, for example, N_2 is the result of contracting N_1, then the opposite refinement of N_2 into N_1 is not a net morphism.

However, the reversal of all arrows of a category, i.e. telling the target first and the source second, is an operation on categories in general, yielding for each category its opposite. Thus, the opposite of the category NET, denoted by NET^{op}, has the same objects as NET, and its morphisms are all triples (N_2, N_1, f^{-1}) such that (N_1, N_2, f) is a morphism of NET.

Pictorially, we may freely move forward and backward along the arrows in a morphism diagram as long as we indicate the directions of our moves properly. Thus, in general, formal relations between nets are represented by more or less complex morphism diagrams rather than by a single morphism.

The main tool for dealing with categories as a whole are mappings between categories called functors. If C_1 and C_2 are categories, then a functor $H:C_1 \to C_2$ maps the objects of C_1 into the objects of C_2 and the morphisms of C_1 into the morphisms of C_2 in a way which is consistent with composition and identities: $H(1_a) = 1_{H(a)}$ and $H(f \circ g) = H(f) \circ H(g)$.

For example, assigning to each net $N = (X;P,F)$ its topological space $R = (X;\Pi)$ induces a (forgetful) functor $FOm:NET \to TOP$ from the category of nets into the category TOP whose objects are all topological spaces and whose morphisms are all continous mappings from one space into another. The image of NET under this F-omission is a full subcategory of TOP, denoted by NTOP. Its objects are the Petri spaces and its morphisms all continous mappings between them. All properties of net morphisms which do not depend on F (groups I and II of the property list of section 2) are carried over onto NTOP by the functor FOm.

There are two rather important transformations of nets which also cannot be expressed by morphisms: <u>dualization</u> of nets (<u>P-reversal</u> , interchanging open and closed) and <u>reversal</u> of nets (<u>F-reversal</u>):

PRev: $(S,T;F) \mapsto (T,S;F) =: (S,T;F)^d$
FRev: $(S,T;F) \mapsto (S,T;F^{-1}) =: (S,T;F)^{-1}$

Yet these transformations are again so general that they apply to the category NET as a whole rather than to individual nets only. They define two self-inverse functors of NET onto itself.

Both P-reversal and F-reversal of a net N are <u>net functions</u> in the sense that they map the elements and arcs of N into elements and arcs, respectively, of another net. If we call such a net function a <u>P-map</u> iff it respects P, and an <u>F-map</u> if it respects F, then a net morphism is characterized by being both a P-map and an F-map.

Since we have expressed already F-omission, F-reversal, and P-reversal by means of functors, we may also ask what <u>P-omission</u> might be. Pictorially, P-omission means distinguishing no longer between ◯-nodes and □-nodes; the result then is a <u>directed graph</u> with X being the set of nodes and F the set of arrows.

Formally, a directed graph is a quadruple $G = (V,A;i,t)$ where V is the set of vertices disjoint from A, the set of arrows, and $i,t:A \to V$ are two functions assigning to each arrow its initial and terminal end point, respectively. Observe that every directed graph $G = (V,A;i,t)$ without isolated vertices is a special net in STZQ-form, $(V,A;t,i)$; conversely, every net $(S,T;Z,Q)$ with $Z,Q:S \to T$ being functions is a directed graph $(T,S;Q,Z)$. Pictorially:

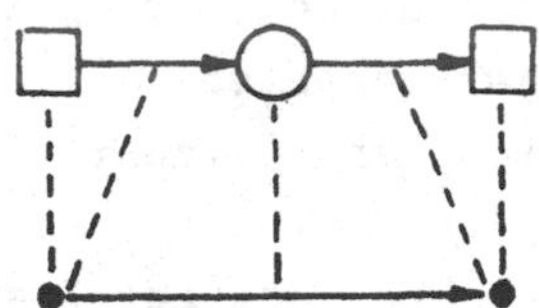

A graph morphism $m:G_1 \to G_2$ from a directed graph G_1 to a directed graph G_2 is a mapping of $V_1 \cup A_1$ into $V_2 \cup A_2$ which is consistent with the i- and t-functions: $\forall x \in V_1 \cup A_1$: $m \circ ({}^{i_1}_{t_1} \cup id|V_1)(x) = ({}^{i_2}_{t_2} \cup id|V_2) \circ m(x)$. The corresponding category of directed graphs is denoted by GRPH.

P-omission now is a forgetful functor POm:NET→GRAPH. It assigns to each net $N = (X;P,F)$ the graph of the relation F,

$POm(N) := (X, F; \{x,y\to x \mid xFy\}, \{x,y\to y \mid xFy\})$, and to each net morphism $f: N_1 \to N_2$ the corresponding graph morphism $POm(f): POm(N_1) \to POm(N_2)$ with $POm(f) := f \cup \{x,y\to f(x),f(y) \mid xFy \wedge f(x) \neq f(y)\} \cup \{x,y\to t \mid xFy \wedge f(x)=f(y)=z\}$. (The specialist will observe, that POm is the <u>adjoint</u> of viewing directed graphs without isolated vertices as special nets.)

8.4. <u>The Context</u> (What to do with morphisms and functors?)

We have concentrated, so far, on the nets themselves and the way of expressing formal relationships between them, but we should make clear that nets - although interesting mathematical objects - do not exist for their own sake. Rather, nets almost always appear in connection with some interpretation, in most cases that of representing a dynamical system.

In this setting, the purpose of the language of categories, and especially of the category of nets, is to serve as the main formal tool for expressing relationships between nets and their interpretations.

While the naked net diagram represents a certain decomposition of the system into components, all kinds of inscriptions to the elements of the diagram may be used to express the knowledge needed for understanding the system on the logical level chosen in connection with the decomposition. Such inscriptions may be, for example: additional graphical symbols or devices, texts in a natural language, (normally enriched by technical terms typical for a certain branch of learning), expressions of a strictly formal language, or diagrams in a graphical language, developed in some technical area.

Formally, any mapping which assigns elements of a given set ('language') L to a net N and its constituents may be viewed as an <u>inscription</u> of N. Then, for example, net morphisms themselves are net inscriptions: A morphism $f: N_1 \to N_2$ inscribes N_2 on N_1: the set $(\{N_1\} \cup S_1 \cup T_1 \cup F_1)$ is mapped into $L = (\{N_2\} \cup S_2 \cup T_2 \cup F_2)$ such that N_2 is assigned to N_1, elements of $S_2 \cup T_2$ are assigned to the elements of $S_1 \cup T_1$, and elements of $S_2 \cup T_2 \cup F_2$ are assigned to the elements of F_1.

This course material is full of inscribed nets. In fact, only occurence nets are not inscribed - as long as they are not mapped into a condition/event-system in order to model a process of that system. Thus net theory is essentially the <u>theory of net inscriptions</u>, concerned with their syntax, their semantics, and above all, their pragmatics.

Net theory itself provides the basic interpretation of nets, the net model of condition/event-systems, which reflects and explicates an understanding of processes and systems on the basis of the notions of concurrency and information flow . However, this is not meant to be the logical level of dealing with problems of systems organization in practice. On the contrary, it is the main goal of net theory to make the use of nets 'open ended'. Any kind of interpretation or usage of nets shall be supported as long as it helps to increase the knowledge about systems, or to improve the methods of systems organization.

The graphical language of nets provides a powerful tool already in the stages of symbolic treatment of processes and systems in which knowledge, intensions, purposes, interests, constraints, etc. are still expressed in a rather informal way.

Few, simple principles for using net inscriptions in connection with a choice of a certain initial interpretation of the functional units and (like channel and agency, role and activity, product type and production facility, place and transition, variable and change, condition and event) allow nets to be used also by non-specialists in a precise way which may be called preformal rather than informal. The purpose of all the net formalism then is to provide the theorems, methods, instruments, and experience, needed for a formal treatment of preformal systems specifications.

We may presume that in most cases inscribed nets model condition/event-systems, yet on a logical level which is not that of the most detailed, basic interpretation of nets. Then several tasks can be envisaged for net theory whose accomplishment may enlarge both the body of knowledge available in net theory and the supply of 'interesting problems'.

For example, a highly specialized language developed in some area shall be used in connection with nets. The purpose could be to make results of net theory accessible in that area, or to make knowledge or techniques of that area applicable to net models, or to use the net language as a common basis for comparing or integrating different approaches for solving similar problems.

Another situation is that for a certain class of problems an appropriate language has to be developed on the basis of net knowledge. This already led to a great number of Petri net derivatives or net-based models and design tools, e.g. the evaluation nets [38] or GRAFCET [2].

Finally, there is some hope that by the preformal use of nets exact methods can be introduced into branches of learning which are concerned with systems of ever growing complexity without any support of formal tools. (See e.g. [35].)

Since the Advanced Course presents quite a few of examples, we show in this section only a toy example of what we may call net semantics. It solves a very simple problem of the first category mentioned above: integrate an existing formal language, namely that of regular expressions, into net theory by giving to it a net semantics which is consistent with its semantics outside net theory.

Our purpose is to state the rules for constructing a class of morphism diagrams. Each diagram contains in one place a net inscribed by an regular expression and at another place a place/transition-net with the same meaning. The whole procedure is divided into a sequence of steps which we shall sketch very briefly:

1. The purpose of the language of regular expressions is to specify the behaviour of simple sequential agencies of a system in terms of a finite set of elementary actions identified by their names $\{a_1,\ldots,a_n\}$. An agency receives its execute (control) signal via a single input channel and delivers it, upon termination, via a single output channel which is different from the input channel. The presence of the execute signal on a channel is represented by putting a token onto the corresponding ○-symbol. (Thus the preformal channel/agency interpretation reduces to a simple place/transition-model.)

2. If the expression is the name of an action, the marker is transported from the input to the output channel by exactly one performance of the denoted action.

3. Three operators are provided to build more complex expressions from the atomic ones. If X and Y are regular expressions, then (X/Y) is read "first X and then Y" and expresses sequential composition, (X∨Y) is read "X or Y" and expresses choice, and X* is read "a finite number of X'es in sequence" and expresses iteration.

The constant ⊤ denotes a 'NOP', i.e. a mere transport of the execute signal, without performing any of the named actions. The constant ⊥ denotes the impossibility of performing any task at all.

4. By means of componentwise refinement, the interior of an agency with non-elementary behavior is developed. This formal process is controlled by the syntactical structure of the inscriptions.

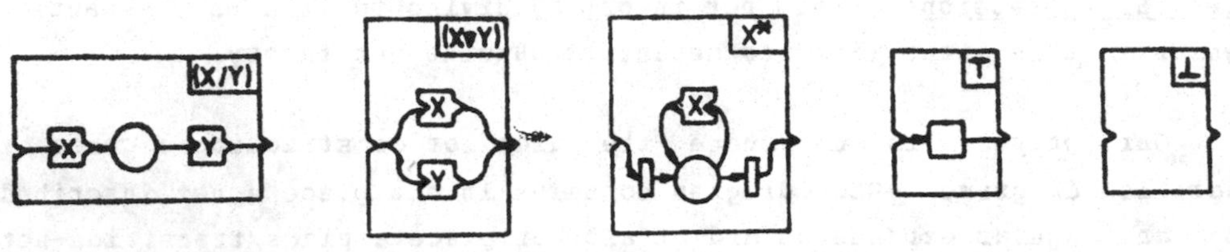

Example:

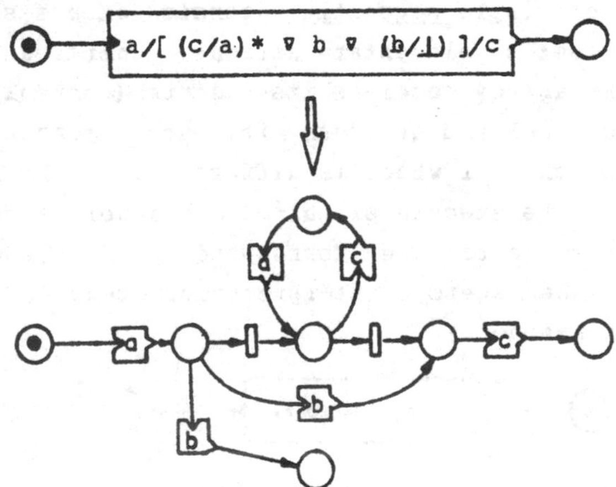

5. Finally, all occurrences of the same action are collected and combined to constitute this action.

Example:

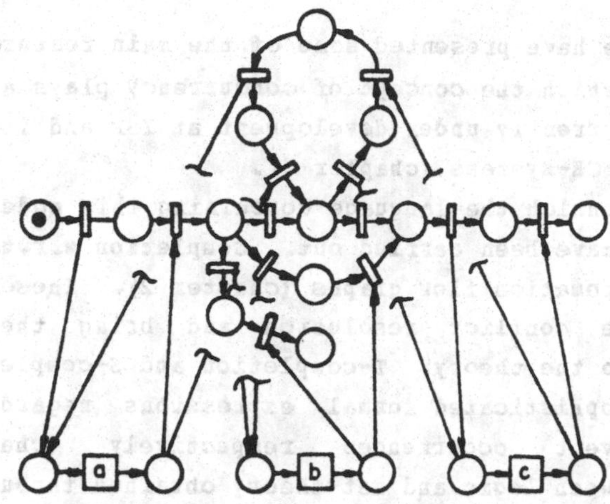

6. To show the consistency of this net semantics of regular expressions with their usual interpretation means to show that the set of all sequences of action occurrences leading from the initial to the final state is isomorphic to the set of character strings generated by the regular expression. We leave that to the reader as an exercise.

9. SUMMARY

In this paper, we have presented some of the main features of a theory of systems in which the concept of concurrency plays a central role. This theory is currently under development at ISF and is founded upon the model called CE-systems (chapter 1).

In order to enrich the language concerning this model, three types of completions have been carried out. Completion w.r.t. information flow leads to infomation flow graphs (chapter 2). These graphs enable us to explicate conflict resolution and bring the notion of information into the theory. T-completion and S-completion enable us to derive more sophisticated formal expressions regarding condition holdings and event occurrences respectively (chapter 5). The relationship between logic and net theory obtained through the enlogic structure can be further exploited in a number of different ways (chapter 6). Similarly, once we have the concept of synchronic distance, we can generalize this idea and apply it more directly to the study of systems (chapter 7).

From the point of view of applications, it is important to develop a family of net based models. We have exhibited two such models that we have formulated and studied (chapter 3 and 4). Elsewhere in the course material, the reader will find many other net based models. The question as to what is meant by a family of net based models is sufficiently important to deserve a precise formulation. This we have done by presenting the category of nets (chapter 8).

In presenting all this material we have tried our best to focus upon those formal aspects which in our opinion, are more relevant from the point of view of practice. Finally, writing this paper has been, for us, a valuable educational experience. We hope that reading the paper will turn out to be, for at least a few, a similar experience.

Acknowledgements: Our present and improved version of the process definition (in chapter 5) has been considerably influenced by the critical observations of Antoni Mazurkiewicz. We have also profited from our discussions with Gordon Plotkin, Matthew Hennessy and Grzegorz Rozenberg. We gratefully acknowledge the timely help provided by Monika Kammer in preparing the manuscript. We also sincerely thank our collegues from ISF, Helga Genrich, Athanassios Kappos, and Eva Pless for their help, patience and encouragement.

References

1. Anderson, A.R.: The Formal Analysis of Normative Systems. In The Logic of Action and Decision, ed. Rescher, N., Pittsburgh : The University of Pittsburgh Press, 1967
2. Blanchard, M.: Le GRAFCET pour une Representation Normalisee de Cahier des Charges d'un Automatisme Logique. Automatique et Informatique Industrielle, No. 61, pp. 27-32 + No. 62 , pp. 36-40 (1977)
3. Best, E.: A Theorem on the Characteristics of Non-Sequential Processes. Computing Laboratory Technical Report No. 116, University of Newcastle-upon-Tyne (1977)
4. Chaney, T.J.; Ornstien, S.M.; Littlefield, W.M.: Beware the Synchronizer. COMPCON-72, IEEE Computer Society Conference, pp. 12-14, 1972
5. Chang, C.; Lee, R.: Symbolic Logic and Mechanical Theorem Proving. New York, London : Academic Press, 1973
6. Commoner, F.; Holt, A.W.: Even, S.; Pnueli, A.: Marked Directed Graphs. J. Computer and System Sc. 5 , 511-523 (1971)
7. Constable, R.L.: On the Theory of Programming Logics. Proc. ACM STOC 9 , pp. 269-285 (1977)
8. Darlington, J.L.: A Net Based Theorem Proving Procedure for Program Verification and Synthesis. In Proc. of the 4th Workshop on Artificial Intelligence, Bad Honnef. Institut für Informatik, Universität Bonn, 1979
9. Ellis, C.A.: Consistency and Correctness of Duplicate Database Systems. Proc. of the 6th Symposium on Operating System Principles, Purdue University, Nov. 1977, ACM Operating Systems Review Vol. 11 , Nr. 5, 1977
10. van Emde Boas, P.: The Connection Between Modal Logic and Algorithmic Logics. In Mathematical Foundations of Computer Science, ed. Winkowski, J., Lecture Notes in Computer Science 64, pp. 1-15, Berlin, Heidelberg, New York : Springer, 1978
11. Fernandez, C.: Net Topology I, II. ISF-Reports 75.09, 76.02, St.Augustin : Gesellschaft für Mathematik und Datenverarbeitung, 1975, 1976
12. Fischer, M.J.; Ladner, R.E.: Propositional Modal Logic of Programs. Proc. ACM STOC 9 , pp. 286-294, 1977

13. Genrich, H.J.; Lautenbach, K.: Synchronisationsgraphen. Acta Informatica 2 , 143-161 (1973)

14. Genrich, H.J.: Extended Simple Regular Expressions. In Mathematical Foundations of Computer Science, ed. Becvar, J., Lecture Notes in Computer Science 32, pp. 231-237, Berlin, Heidelberg, New York : Springer, 1975

15. Genrich, H.J.: Ein systemtheoretischer Beitrag zur Handlungslogik. ISF-Report 75.03, St.Augustin : Gesellschaft für Mathematik und Datenverarbeitung, 1975

16. Genrich, H.J.: The Petri Net Representation of Mathematical Knowledge. ISF-Report 76.05, St.Augustin : Gesellschaft für Mathematik und Datenverarbeitung, 1976

17. Genrich, H.J.: Ein Kalkül des Planens und Handelns. In Ansätze zur Organisationstheorie rechnergestützter Informationssysteme, ed. Petri, C.A., Berichte der Gesellschaft für Mathematik und Datenverarbeitung 111, pp.77-92, München, Wien : R. Oldenbourg 1979

18. Genrich, H.J.; Lautenbach, K.: Facts in Place/Transition-Nets. In Mathematical Foundations of Computer Science, ed. Winkowski, J., Lecture Notes in Computer Science 64, pp. 213-231, Berlin, Heidelberg, New York : Springer, 1978

19. Genrich, H.J.; Lautenbach, K.: The Analysis of Dristibuted Systems by Means of Predicate/Transition-Nets. In Semantics of Concurrent Computation, ed. Kahn, G., Lecture Notes in Computer Science 70, pp. 123-146, Berlin, Heidelberg, New York : Springer, 1979

20. Genrich, H.J.; Thieler-Mevissen, G.: The Calculus of Facts. In Mathematical Foundations of Computer Science, ed. Mazurkiewicz, A., Lecture Notes in Computer Science 45, pp. 588-595, Berlin, Heidelberg, New York : Springer, 1976

21. Hack, M.: Analysis of Production Schemata by Petri Nets. MIT-Project MAC, TR-94 (1972)

22. Harel, D.; Meyer, A; Pratt, V.R.: Computability and Completeness in Logics of Programs. Proc, ACM STOC 9 , pp. 261-268 (1977)

23. Herstein, I.N.: Topics in Algebra, 2nd Edition. Lexington, Toronto : Xerox College Publishing, 1975

24. Holt, A.W.: Net Models of Organizational Systems, in Theory and Practice. In Ansätze zur Organisationstheorie rechnergestützter Informationssysteme, ed. Petri, C.A., Berichte der Gesellschaft für Mathematik und Datenverarbeitung 111, pp.39-62, München, Wien : R. Oldenbourg, 1979

25. Holt, A.W.; Commoner, F.: Events and Conditions. Report of the Project MAC Conference on Concurrent Systems and Parallel Computation, pp. 3-52, 1970

26. Holt, A.W. et al.: Information System Theory Project : Final Report. Princeton, N.J. : Applied Data Research Inc., RADC-TR-68-305, NTIS AD 676972, 1968

27. Jump, J.R.; Thiagarajan, P.S.: On the Equivalence of Asynchronous Control Structures. SIAM Journal on Computing, 2, No.2, 67-87 (1973)

28. Kahn, G.; Plotkin, G.D.: Domains Concrets. IRIA Rapport de Recherche No. 336, Le Chesnay: IRIA, 1978

29. Kripke, S.: Semantical Considerations on Modal Logic. Acta Philosophica Fennica 16 , pp. 83-94 (1963)

30. Lautenbach, K.: Exakte Bedingungen der Lebendigkeit für eine Klasse von Petri-Netzen. Berichte der GMD 82, St.Augustin : Gesellschaft für Mathematik und Datenverarbeitung Bonn, 1973

31. Lautenbach, K.: Ein kombinatorischer Ansatz zur Beschreibung und Erreichung von Fairness in Scheduling-Problemen. In Applied Computer Science 8, ed. Mühlbacher, J., München, Wien : Verlag Carl Hanser, 1977

32. Lautenbach, K.; Schmid, H.A.: Use of Nets for Proving Correctness of Concurrent Process Systems. Proceedings of IFIP Congress 74, North Holland Publ. Comp., 1974

33. Lautenbach, K; Wedde, H.: Generating Control Mechanisms by Restrictions. In Mathematical Foundations of Computer Science, ed. Mazurkiewicz, A, Lecture Notes in Computer Science 45, pp. 416-422, Berlin, Heidelberg, New York : Springer, 1976

34. Mac Lane, S.: Categories for the Working Mathematician. New York, Heidelberg, Berlin: Springer, 1971

35. Meldman, J.: A Petri-Net Representation of Civil Procedure. IDEA : The Journal of Law and Technology, 19 , no. 2, pp. 123-148 (1978).

36. Milne, G.J.: Modelling Distributed Database Protocolls by Synchronisation Processes (Draft Version, Nov. 1978), Department of Computer Science, Edinburgh University

37. Mirkowska, G.: Algorithmic Logic and its Application in the Theory of Programs. Fundamenta Informaticae 1 , pp: 1-17, 147-165 (1977)

38. Nutt, G.J.: The Formulation and Application of Evaluation Nets. Thesis, Computer Science Group, University of Washington, Seattle (1972)

39. Parikh, R.: The Completeness of Propositional Dynamic Logic. In Mathematical Foundations of Computer Science, ed. Winkowski, J., Lecture Notes in Computer Science 64, pp. 403-415, Berlin, Heidelberg, New York : Springer, 1978

40. Parikh, R.: A Decidability Result for a Second Order Process Logic. MIT/LCS/TM-112, Cambridge, Mas.: MIT Laboratory for Computer Science, 1978

41. Patil, S.S.: Coordination of Asynchronous Events. MIT, Project MAC, Technical Report 72, Cambridge, Mass., 1970

42. Patil, S.S.: Synchronizers and Arbiters. Computation Structures Group Memo 91, Project MAC , M.I.T., Cambridge, Mass., 1972

43. Petri, C.A.: Fundamentals of a Theory of Asynchronous Information Flow. In Proceedings of IFIP Congress 62, North-Holland Publ.Comp., Amsterdam

44. Petri, C.A.: Kommunikation mit Automaten. Bonn : Institut für Instrumentelle Mathematik, Schriften des IIM Nr. 2, 1962

45. Petri, C.A.: Grundsätzliches zur Beschreibung diskreter Pozesse. 3. Colloquium über Automathentheorie, Basel : Birkhäuser Verlag, 1967

46. Petri, C.A.: Concepts of Net Theory. Mathematical Foundations of Computer Science, Math. Institute of the Slovak Ac. of Sciences, 1973

47. Petri, C.A.: Non-Sequential Processes. ISF-Report 77.05, St.Augustin : Gesellschaft für Mathematik und Datenverarbeitung, 1975

48. Petri, C.A.: Interpretations of Net Theory. ISF-Report 75.07, St.Augustin : Gesellschaft für Mathematik und Datenverarbeitung, 1975

49. Petri, C.A.: General Net Theory. Computing System Design : Proceedings of the Joint IBM University of Newcastle upon Tyne Seminar, Sept. 1976 / Shaw, B. (Ed.), University of Newcastle upon Tyne (1977)

50. Petri, C.A.: Concurrency as a Basis for System Thinking. ISF-Report 78.06, St. Augustin : Gesellschaft für Mathematik und Datenverarbeitung, 1978

51. Pnueli, A.: The Temporal Logic of Programs. Proc. IEEE FOCS 18, pp.46-57 (1977)

52. Rescher, N. (ed.): The Logic of Action and Decision. Pittsburgh : The University of Pittsburgh Press, 1967

53. Schiffers, M.: Behandlung eines Synchronisationsproblems mit gefärbten Petri-Netzen. Universität Bonn, Diplomarbeit (1977)

54. Schiffers, M; Wedde, H.: Analyzing Program Solutions of Coordination Problems by CP-nets. Mathematical Foundations of Computer Science 1978 / Winkowski, J. (Ed.), Berlin, Heidelberg, New York : Springer Verlag (1978)

55. Shapiro, R.M.: Towards a Design Methodology for Information Systems. In Ansätze zur Organisationstheorie rechnergestützter Informationssysteme, ed. Petri, C.A., Berichte der Gesellschaft für Mathematik und Datenverarbeitung 111, pp.107-118, München, Wien : R. Oldenbourg 1979

56. Shapiro, R.M.; Saint, H.: The Representation of Algorithms. Applied Data Research, Inc., Final Techn. Report RADC-TR-69-313, Vol. 2, NTIS AD 697026, New York, 1969

57. Shapiro, R.M.; Thiagarajan, P.S.: On the Maitenance of Distributed Copies of a Database. St.Augustin : Gesellschaft für Mathematik und Datenverarbeitung Bonn, Interner Bericht ISF-78-04 (1978)

58. Thiagarajan, PS.; Genrich, H.J.: Assignment Systems - A Model for Asynchronous Computations. ISF-Report 76.10, St.Augustin : Gesellschaft für Mathematik und Datenverarbeitung, 1976

59. Thieler-Mevissen, G.: The Petri Net Calculus of Predicate Logic. ISF-Report 76.09, St.Augustin : Gesellschaft für Mathematik und Datenverarbeitung, 1976

60. Thieler-Mevissen, G.: Die Struktur der Violations eines Systems. ISF-Report 78.01, St. Augustin : Gesellschaft für Mathematik und Datenverarbeitung, 1978

61. Wedde, H.: Lose Kopplung von Systemkomponenten. Bericht der GMD 96, St.Augustin : Gesellschaft für Mathematik und Datenverarbeitung, 1975

62. von Wright, G.H.: And Next. Acta Philosophica Fennica 18, pp.293-304, Helsinki 1965

FORMAL PROPERTIES OF PLACE/TRANSITION NETS

M. Jantzen and R. Valk

University of Hamburg

Abstract

Definitions and theorems fundamental for the study of general Petri nets or place/transition nets are presented. The results give properties of marking graphs, provide insight into the computational complexity of several decision procedures, show the intimate relation of reachability sets to Presburger formulas, and deal with state-machine composition and the deadlock-trap property.

Contents list

Introduction

The aim of this work is neither to give an overview of the historical development of the theory of Petri nets nor to be a complete list of all results, which have been obtained so far. We tried to select some topics, which are in a certain sense basic and representative, and which give insight in the types of problems that arise when working with place/transition nets or with concurrent systems in general.

In the definitions we tried to be coherent to the other work in these proceedings and to unify a lot of different notions, as for instance the different firing rules. The static notion of a place/transition net is opposed to its dynamical behaviour by investigating marking- and coverability-graphs and description methods for reachability sets. Properties of the net structure, like state-machine composition and deadlock-trap property are used to derive behavioural properties as liveness. Furthermore we selected some complexity results as a warning to care for the computational efficiency of net algorithms. We felt that an understanding of the problems and methods involved with all of these results would be impossible without proofs or even sketches of proofs.

1. Basic Properties of Net Behaviour

We first provide the notion of place/transition-nets (PT-nets for short) together with the relevant technical definitions. PT-nets can be considered as a generalization of the basic concept of condition/event-systems in that each S-element of the PT-net is a place which may contain more than one token, i.e. is a counter. In modelling real systems it may be convenient to have predefined capacities or bounds for the places which should never be exceeded. This is reflected in two distinct transition rules. The weak transition rule is commonly used when dealing with PT-nets without capacities (see [16,17,36] and many others). The strict transition rule is the proper generalization of the transition rule usually used for condition/event-systems (see [37]).

Let $\mathbb{N} := \{0,1,\dots\}$ be the set of non-negative integers and $\mathbb{Z}$ be the set of all integers. For notational convenience we add a new element to $\mathbb{Z}$ which satisfies the following properties:
$\omega + z := z + \omega := \omega + \omega := \omega - \omega := \omega$ for all $z \in \mathbb{Z}$. $0 \cdot \omega := \omega \cdot 0 := 0$. $\omega \cdot n := n \cdot \omega := \omega$ for all $n \in \{\omega, 1, \dots\}$. $z \leq \omega$ for all $z \in \mathbb{Z}$.
Let $\mathbb{N}_\omega := \mathbb{N} \cup \{\omega\}$ and $\mathbb{Z}_\omega := \mathbb{Z} \cup \{\omega\}$.

For any two matrices or column-vectors x,y over $\mathbb{Z}_\omega$ the relations and operations $x+y$, $x-y$, $x=y$, $x \leq y$, $\max(x,y)$, $\min(x,y)$ are understood componentwise. In contrast to these definitions let $x < y$ iff $x \leq y$ and $x \neq y$. By $\binom{x}{y}$ we denote the column-vector composed by x and y.

In general, mappings $f: M_1 \times \dots \times M_n \longrightarrow \mathbb{Z}_\omega$ are identified with $(|M_1|, \dots, |M_n|)$-matrices over $\mathbb{Z}_\omega$ if the domain is finite and a fixed ordering of the elements of the sets M_i can be assumed. So, if f and g are mappings into $\mathbb{Z}_\omega$ then $f \leq g$ is equivalent to $f(x) \leq g(x)$ for each $x \in \mathrm{dom}(f) \cap \mathrm{dom}(g)$.

A triple $(S,T;F)$ is called a directed net iff $S \cap T = \emptyset$, $S \cup T \neq \emptyset$, $F \subseteq S \times T \cup T \times S$, $\mathrm{dom}(F) \cup \mathrm{cod}(F) = S \cup T$. Thus a net is a bipartite, directed graph. The elements of S (resp. T) are called S-elements (resp. T-elements). A directed net is called pure iff $(x,y) \in F$ implies $(y,x) \notin F$. For $x \in S \cup T$ we write ${}^\bullet x := \{y \mid (y,x) \in F\}$ and similar $x^\bullet := \{y \mid (x,y) \in F\}$.

A tuple $(S,T;F,K,W,M_o)$ is called <u>place/transition-net</u> or <u>PT-net</u> iff it satisfies the following properties (1) to (4):

(1) (S,T;F) is a directed net. The elements of S are called <u>places</u> and carry a variable number of tokens. The elements of T are called <u>transitions</u> and represent elementary changes of the distribution of tokens over the places. If not explicitly stated, S and T are finite sets with cardinality $|S|$ and $|T|$.

(2) $K:S \longrightarrow \mathbb{N}_\omega$ assigns to each place its, possibly unlimited, token <u>capacity</u>. If $K(s) = \omega$ for each $s \in S$ then K may be omitted.

(3) $W:F \longrightarrow \mathbb{N}$ assigns to each arc its <u>multiplicity</u>. If $W(x)=1$ for each $x \in F$ then W may be omitted.

(4) The <u>initial marking</u> $M_o:S \longrightarrow \mathbb{N}$ has to satisfy the capacity constraints, i.e. $M_o \leq K$.

For a given PT-net the $(|S|,|T|)$-matrices $W_Z:S \times T \longrightarrow \mathbb{N}$ and $W_Q:S \times T \longrightarrow \mathbb{N}$ are defined by

$$W_Z(s,t) := \begin{cases} W(s,t) & \text{if } (s,t) \in Z := F \cap S \times T. \\ 0 & \text{otherwise.} \end{cases}$$

$$W_Q(s,t) := \begin{cases} W(t,s) & \text{if } (s,t) \in Q := F^{-1} \cap S \times T. \\ 0 & \text{otherwise.} \end{cases}$$

The <u>incidence matrix</u> C of the - not necessarily pure - net is then define by $C := W_Q - W_Z$.

The <u>strict transition rule</u> is defined for <u>markings</u> $M,M':S \longrightarrow \mathbb{N}_\omega$ and sets $U \subseteq T$, $U \neq \emptyset$, of concurrently firable transitions by the use of a 'one-step' relation $[U\rangle$.

$$M\,[U\rangle\,M' :\Longleftrightarrow \quad M \geq W_Z \cdot u \ \wedge \ M' = M + C \cdot u \ \wedge \ M' \leq K \ \wedge$$
$$\forall t_1,t_2 \in U : t_1 \neq t_2 \Longrightarrow ({}^\bullet t_1 \cup t_1^\bullet) \cap ({}^\bullet t_2 \cup t_2^\bullet) = \emptyset .$$

$u \in \mathbb{N}^{|T|}$ as a column-vector represents the <u>characteristic function</u> $u:T \longrightarrow \{0,1\}$, $u(t) :=$ <u>if</u> $t \in U$ <u>then</u> 1 <u>else</u> 0 <u>fi</u>.

Let $M[\to\rangle M' :\Longleftrightarrow \exists U \subseteq T : M[U\rangle M'$. Let $[\Rightarrow\rangle$ denote the reflexive, transitive closure of the relation $[\to\rangle$. We also write $M[\lambda\rangle M$, and if $M[U_1\rangle M_1$, $M_1[U_2\rangle M_2$, ... , $M_{n-1}[U_n\rangle M_n$ holds we write $M[U_1,\dots,U_n\rangle M_n$. If the sets $U_i = \{t_i\}$ contain only one element we may omit the brackets and write $M[t_1t_2\cdots t_n\rangle M_n$ for short. The word $t_1t_2\cdots t_n \in T^*$ is then called a <u>firing sequence</u> which leads M into M_n.

The <u>weak transition rule</u> is defined similar by the use of the one-step relation $(U\rangle$, where $U \subseteq T$, $U \neq \emptyset$, is a set of concurrently firable transitions. $M(U\rangle M' \;:\Longleftrightarrow\; M \geq W_Z \cdot u \wedge M' = M + C \cdot u$.

Let $M(\text{-}\rangle M' \;:\Longleftrightarrow\; \exists U \subseteq T : M(U\rangle M'$, and let $(=\rangle$ denote the reflexive, transitive closure of the relation $(\text{-}\rangle$. Again we use the obvious notations $M(U_1,U_2,\ldots,U_n\rangle M'$, $M(\lambda\rangle M$, and $M(t_1t_2\ldots t_n\rangle M'$.

For all $w \in T^*$ we write $M[w\rangle \;:\Longleftrightarrow\; \exists M' : M[w\rangle M'$ and we write $M(w\rangle \;:\Longleftrightarrow\; \exists M' : M(w\rangle M'$. So $M[t\rangle$ (resp. $M(t\rangle$) denotes the fact that the transition t is <u>enabled</u> at the marking M under the strict (resp.weak) transition rule.

Note that for arbitrary capacity $M[\text{-}\rangle M'$ implies $M(\text{-}\rangle M'$ but the converse is not true, even if the capacities are unbounded. (see the example below). If the underlying net has unbounded capacities then $M[w\rangle M'$ is equivalent to $M(w\rangle M'$ for each $w \in T^*$.

If $M(U_1,\ldots,U_n\rangle M'$ then $M' = M + C \cdot \sum_{i=1}^{n} u_i$, where each u_i is the characteristic vector of the set U_i , $1 \leq i \leq n$. If each set U_i contains exactly one element t_i , then by our notation $M(w\rangle M'$ for some $w \in T^*$ and the equation above may be written as $M' = M + C \cdot Pk(w)$, where $Pk: T^* \longrightarrow \mathbb{N}^{|T|}$ is the Parikh mapping defined by:

$$Pk(w) := \begin{pmatrix} \#t_1(w) \\ \vdots \\ \#t_T(w) \end{pmatrix}$$. In this case T is supposed to be the ordered set $\{t_1,t_2,\ldots,t_{|T|}\}$ and $\#t_i(w)$ is the number of occurences of the symbol t_i in the word $w \in T^*$.

<u>Example</u>

Consider the net $N = (S,T;F,K,W)$ which is shown in figure 1.1. The capacity K is there expressed by writing $s_i/K(s_i)$ as a label on the place $s_i \in S := \{s_1,s_2,s_3\}$

<u>Figure 1.1</u>

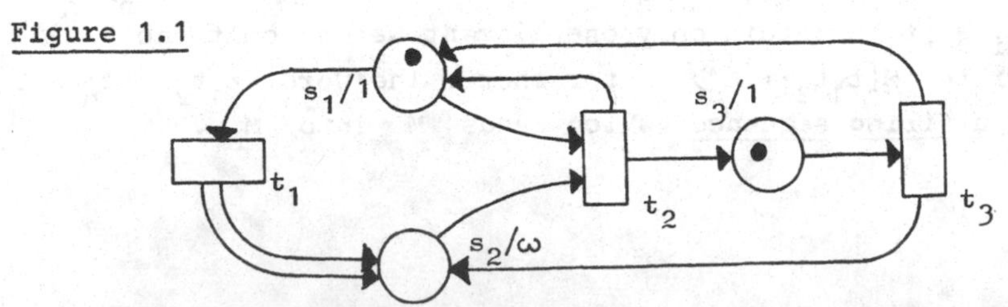

If we define M by $M(s_1) = 1$, $M(s_2) := 0$, $M(s_3) := 1$ and M' by $M'(s_1) := 1$, $M'(s_2) := 3$, $M'(s_3) := 0$ then we obtain $M(\{t_1,t_3\}\rangle M'$, $M(t_3t_1\rangle M'$, and $M[t_1t_3\rangle M'$ but neither $M[t_3t_1\rangle M'$ nor $M[\{t_1,t_3\}\rangle M'$. The matrices W_Z, W_Q, and C are given by:

$$W_Z = \begin{pmatrix} 1 & 1 & 0 \\ 0 & 1 & 0 \\ 0 & 0 & 1 \end{pmatrix}, \quad W_Q = \begin{pmatrix} 0 & 1 & 1 \\ 2 & 0 & 1 \\ 0 & 1 & 0 \end{pmatrix}, \text{ and } \quad C = \begin{pmatrix} -1 & 0 & 1 \\ 2 & -1 & 1 \\ 0 & 1 & -1 \end{pmatrix}.$$

If $w \in \{t_1t_3t_2\}^*$ then $Pk(w) = \begin{pmatrix} k \\ k \\ k \end{pmatrix}$ for some $k \in \mathbb{N}$, and $M(w\rangle M''$ is true for $M'' = M + C \cdot \begin{pmatrix} k \\ k \\ k \end{pmatrix} = \begin{pmatrix} 1 \\ 0 \\ 1 \end{pmatrix} + \begin{pmatrix} 0 \\ k \\ 0 \end{pmatrix} \cdot 2 = \begin{pmatrix} 1 \\ 2 \cdot k \\ 1 \end{pmatrix}$.

Now classes of forward reachable markings are defined by: $[M\rangle := \{M' \mid M[=\rangle M'\}$ and $(M\rangle := \{M' \mid M(=\rangle M'\}$. The full marking classes of a marking M are defined by: $[M] := \{M' \mid M \underset{s}{\sim} M'\}$ and $(M) := \{M' \mid M \underset{w}{\sim} M'$, where $\underset{s}{\sim}$ (resp. $\underset{w}{\sim}$) is the transitive and symmetric closure of the relation $[=\rangle$ (resp. $(=\rangle$). Again $[M]$ equals (M) if the capacities of the underlying PT-net are all unbounded. The set $(M_o\rangle$ is often called the reachability set of a PT-net with initial marking M_o.

It is sometimes useful to represent the elementary changes of markings by a so-called marking graph. This graph is a directed, labelled graph, the nodes of which are the reachable markings $M \in [M_o\rangle$ (resp. $M \in (M_o\rangle$), and the arcs are labelled by the transitions which cause the marking changes under the relation $[t\rangle$ (resp. $(t\rangle$).

Let $N = (S,T;F,K,W,M_o)$ be a given PT-net. The strict marking graph of N is given by the triple $G = (Z,E,T)$, where $Z = [M_o\rangle \subseteq \mathbb{N}^{|S|}$ is the set of nodes, $E \subseteq Z \times T \times Z$ is the set of directed, labelled arcs: $E := \{(z,t,z') \mid z,z' \in [M_o\rangle, z[t\rangle z'\}$. The weak marking graph is defined similar, except that we define the arcs by $E := \{(z,t,z') \mid z,z' \in (M_o\rangle, z(t\rangle z'\}$.

It is obvious that marking graphs can be infinite if the net has unbounded capacities or if the weak transition rule is used to define the arcs. Since the relations $[t\rangle$ and $(t\rangle$, $t \in T$, do not reflect the concurrently firing transitions one could as well define a so-called large marking graph, where the arcs are labelled by sets of transitions, so that $E := \{(z,U,z') \mid z,z' \in [M_o\rangle, z[U\rangle z'\}$ represents the one-step changes within the net. We do not want to use this kind of a large marking graph in the sequel.

Example

Let $N = (S,T;F,K,M_o)$ be the PT-net of figure 1.2, then figure 1.3 shows a small part of its infinite weak marking graph, and figure 1.4 shows its strict marking graph, where $K(s) := 1$ for all $s \in S$ and M_o is the marking drawn in figure 1.2.

Figure 1.2

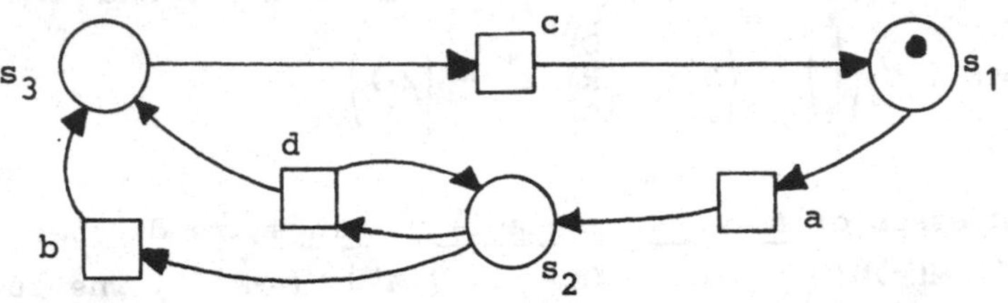

In order to simplify the notation we may represent a marking $M \in \mathbb{N}$ by the word $s_1^{x_1} \cdots s_r^{x_r} \in \{s_1,\dots,s_r\}^*$, where $r := |S|$ and $x_i :=$ M(s s_i^1 will be written as s_i and s_i^0 will be omitted.

Figure 1.3

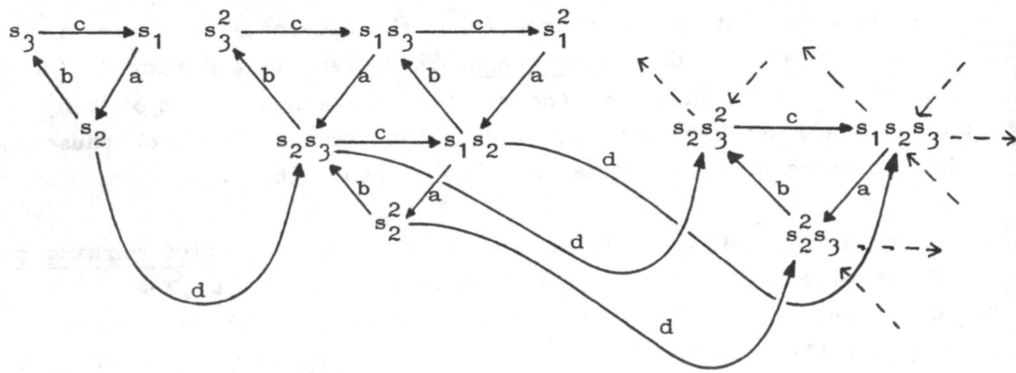

Figure 1.4

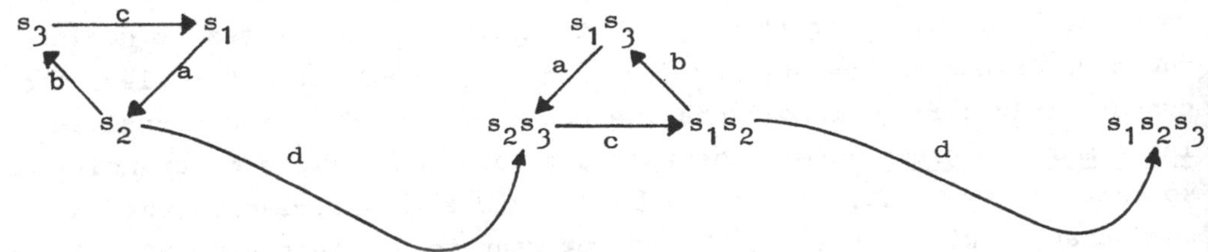

Sometimes, especially if the marking graph is finite, it is helpful to know the structure of the marking graph as long as the markings do not exceed a certain bound. If the reachable markings exceed this bound it would then be interesting to know whether those markings exceed any bound. A place $s \in S$ is called <u>bounded</u> iff $\exists n \in \mathbb{N}\ \forall M \in [M_o\rangle : M(s) \leq n$. A set $S' \subseteq S$ of places is <u>simultaneously unbounded</u> iff $\forall n \in \mathbb{N}\ \exists M \in [M_o\rangle\ \forall s \in S' : M(s) \geq n$. These questions give raise to the definition of a finite - not necessarily unique - coverability graph. Since the weak transition rule is a special case of the strict transition rule we present a construction which yields some coverability graph with respect to the strict transition rule.

<u>Construction 1.1</u>

step 1 : Let $N = (S,T;F,K,W,M_o)$ be a PT-net. Gr will be a directed, labelled graph. Let initially Gr be a graph with no arc and M_o as its only node.

step 2 : Choose some node M of Gr and some transition $t \in T$, such that the pair (M,t) has not been considered in previous steps, and t is enabled at M under the weak transition rule. If no such pair exists, then stop.

step 3 : Now $M(t\rangle M'$ holds for some $M' \in \mathbb{N}_\omega^{|S|}$. If M' is a node already contained in Gr, then add the new arc (M,t,M') to Gr and return to step 2. Otherwise do step 4.

step 4 : Let $P(M') := \left\{ M'' \;\middle|\; \begin{array}{l} M'' \leq M' \text{ and } M'' \text{ is a} \\ \text{predecessor of } M \text{ in Gr} \end{array} \right\} \cup \{M'\}$

Let $\widetilde{M} := M' + \omega \cdot \sum_{M'' \in P(M')} (M' - M'')$.

step 5 : If $\widetilde{M} \leq K$ then add $(M,t,\widetilde{M})$ as a new arc to Gr and add $\widetilde{M}$ as a new node to Gr if $\widetilde{M}$ is not contained in Gr.
Return to step 2.

Figure 1.5 shows some fairly small coverability graph of the PT-net from figure 1.2, where now all the capacities are unbounded. The labels of the arcs are indexed to describe the order in which they have been constructed.

It is easy to see that for each firing sequence $w \in T^*$ of a PT-net N which starts at M_o, there exists a path in the coverability graph which spells out the word w. Thus, considered as a finite automaton, the coverability graph describes a regular set $R \supseteq \{w \mid M_o(w\rangle\} =: L(N)$. The set L(N) itself need not be regular, but it is decidable whether it is regular or not. (see [41])

Figure 1.5

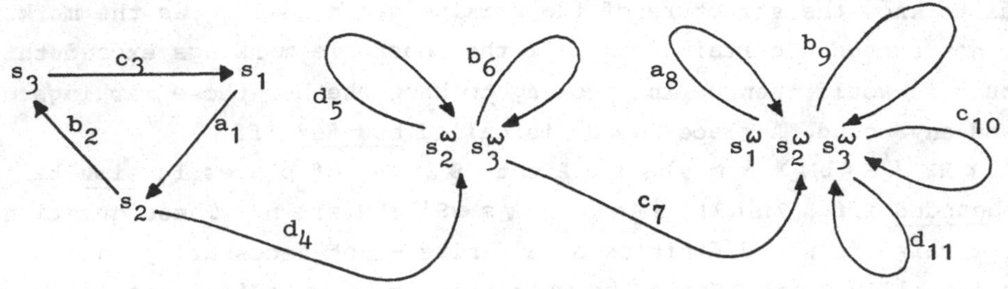

Theorem 1.1

Each coverability graph as defined by construction 1.1 is finite. A set of places $S' \subseteq S$ is simultaneously unbounded iff there exists a node M in the coverability graph such that $M(s) = \omega$ for all $s \in S'$.

Proof

Let M be some node in Gr and $t \in T$ such that $M(t\rangle M'$ holds and M' is a new node not contained in Gr. If $P(M') = \{M'\}$ then $\widetilde{M} = M'$ and $\widetilde{M}$ is inserted into Gr by step 5 iff $\widetilde{M} \leqslant K$.
If $P(M') = \{M', M_1, \ldots, M_k\}$ for some $k \geqslant 1$, then there are firing sequences $w_i \in T^+$ such that $M_i(w_i\rangle M'$. Since $M_i \leqslant M'$, each firing sequence w_i can also be applied to M', in each case yielding some marking $M_i' \geqslant M'$. Now each w_i can be applied to M' any number of times. Thus $M'(w_1^n w_2^n \ldots w_k^n\rangle M_n$ holds for each $n \in \mathbb{N}$, showing that - under the weak transition rule - all those coordinates of M_n for which $M' - M_i$ is non-zero simultaneously can exceed any bound. Now in step 4 $\widetilde{M}$ is defined in such a way that all these coordinates are equal to ω and the new node $\widetilde{M}$ is then inserted into Gr iff $\widetilde{M} \leqslant K$.
Since any set of incomparable vectors from $\mathbb{N}_\omega^{|S|}$ is finite one concludes that the construction terminates and produces a finite graph Gr such that a set of places S' is simultaneously unbounded if there exists a node M in Gr with $M(s) = \omega$ for all $s \in S'$.
Conversely it is not hard to see that if a place is unbounded there must exist a node M in Gr such that $M(s) = \omega$.

qed

The original tree-based construction is known as the coverability tree and can be found in [24] . As a corollary we obtain

Theorem 1.2

For any given finite PT-net $N = (S,T;F,K,W,M_o)$ and each marking $M \in \mathbb{N}^{|S|}$ it is decidable whether:

(a) there exists a reachable marking $M' \in [M_o\rangle$ such that $M' \geqslant M$, i.e. M' covers M.

(b) a set $S' \subseteq S$ is simultaneously unbounded.

(c) the weak transition rule coincides with the strict transition rule, i.e. $(M_o\rangle = [M_o\rangle$.

The following theorem relates directed, labelled graphs with nodes from the set $\mathbb{N}^r$ to marking graphs of finite PT-nets.

Theorem 1.3

A directed, labelled graph $G = (Z,E,T)$ is the strict marking graph of some PT-net $N = (S,T;F,K,W,M_o)$ iff the following conditions hold:

(1) $Z \subseteq \mathbb{N}^{|S|}$ is the set of nodes and $\forall z \in Z : z \leqslant K$.

(2) $(z,t,z') \in E \wedge (z,t,z'') \in E \Longrightarrow z' = z''$.

(3) $\forall t \in T \ \exists k_t \in \mathbb{Z}^{|S|} : \left[(z,t,z') \in E \Longrightarrow z - z' = k_t\right]$.

(4) $\forall t \in T \ \forall z \in Z : \left[m_t \leqslant z \Longleftrightarrow \exists z' \in Z : (z,t,z') \in E\right]$, where $m_t := \min\{x \mid x,y \in Z, (x,t,y) \in E\}$.

(5) $M_o \in Z$ is a predecessor of each $z \in Z$.

Proof

If G is the strict marking graph of some PT-net N then it is not hard to verify properties (1) to (5). Conversely, suppose $G = (Z,E,T)$ is some directed labelled graph which satisfies (1) to (5). The following construction defines a PT-net $N = (S,T;F,K,W,M_o)$ which has G as its strict marking graph:

$S := \{s_1,\ldots,s_r\}$, where $Z \subseteq \mathbb{N}^r$.

$F \cap S \times T := \{(s,t) \mid t \in T, s \in S, m_t(s) \neq 0\}$.

$W((s,t)) := m_t(s)$ for all $t \in T$ and $s \in S$.

$F \cap T \times S := \{(t,s) \mid t \in T, s \in S, m_t(s) - k_t(s) \neq 0\}$.

$W((t,s)) := m_t(s) - k_t(s)$ for all $t \in T$ and $s \in S$.

For a more detailed proof see [26].

qed

If the nodes of a directed graph are not from the set $\mathbb{N}^r$ then it is not easy to see whether the graph is isomorphic to a strict marking graph of some PT-net or not. The next theorem states that this question is decidable under certain weak restrictions.

Theorem 1.4

It is decidable whether a given finite, connected, directed , and labelled graph $G = (Z,E,T)$ is isomorphic to the strict marking graph of some PT-net $N = (S,T;F,K,M_o)$ without multiple arcs.

Proof

Enumerate all possible bijections $f:Z \longrightarrow \{0,1,\ldots,|E|\}^k$, where $k := 4^{|T|}$. Then use theorem 1.3 to prove whether the graph $f(G)$, which is obtained from G by replacing each node $z \in Z$ by $f(z)$, is the strict marking graph of some PT-net without multiple arcs. If there is no PT-net for any of the graphs $f(G)$ then there does not exist a PT-net at all. The formal proof can be found in [26] , where it has been shown that if there exists a PT-net with a finite, connected weak marking graph G then there exists a PT-net $N = (S,T;F,K,M_o)$ such that $|S| \leqslant 4^{|T|}$, $K(s) \leqslant |E|$ for all $s \in S$, and its strict marking graph is equal to its weak marking graph, and is moreover isomorphic to G.

qed

It is obviously decidable whether a given marking M is forward reachable within a given PT-net, if its marking graph is finite. The general problem is known as the reachability problem : "is $M \in (M_o\rangle$ for a given PT-net and a given marking M ?" .

There are quite a number of problems which are equivalent to the reachability problem. So far none of them has trustworthy been proved to be decidable, unless it is a common conjecture that the reachbility problem is indeed decidable.

Sometimes we wish to know whether a given local configuration of a concurrent system may occur regardless of the state of the rest of the system, hence it is only necessary to know whether a given submarking can be reached from the initial marking or whether there exists a reachable marking which does not exceed a predefined capacity. We will see that all these questions are equivalent to the reachability problem. For completeness and later use we prove the following result which should be compared with theorem 1.2.(a).

Theorem 1.5

If the reachability problem is decidable, then for each $M \in \mathbb{N}_\omega^{|S|}$ and each PT-net $N = (S,T;F,W,M_o)$ it is decidable whether there exists a marking $M' \in (M_o\rangle$ which is covered by M, i.e. $M' \leqslant M$.

Proof

Construct a new PT-net $\overline{N} := (S,\overline{T};\overline{F},\overline{W},M_o)$ by defining
$\overline{T} := T \cup \{\overline{t}_1,\ldots,\overline{t}_{|S|}\}$, $\overline{F} := F \cup \{(s_i,\overline{t}_i) \mid s_i \in S\ ,\ M(s_i) = \omega\}$.
$\overline{W}((x,y))$:= if $(x,y) \in F$ then $W((x,y))$ else 1 fi .

Thus for each place $s_i \in S$, where $M(s_i) = \omega$ there exists a transition $\overline{t}_i$ which subtracts tokens from s_i . Now some $M' \leqslant M$ is reachable in N iff some $M'' \in L(M)$ is reachable in $\overline{N}$, where
$L(M) := \{\overline{M} \mid$ if $M(s_i) = \omega$ then $\overline{M}(s_i) = 0$ else $\overline{M}(s_i) \leqslant M(s_i)$ fi $\}$
is a finite set.

qed

Another important concept for studying the behaviour of PT-nets is that of liveness. In a given PT-net $N = (S,T;F,K,W,M_o)$ a transition $t \in T$ is called live at a marking M iff $\forall M' \in (M\rangle\ \exists M'' \in (M'\rangle : M''(t\rangle$. Thus a transition t is not live iff there exists a marking $M' \in (M\rangle$ such that no marking in $(M'\rangle$ enables t . The marking M' is then called t-dead , and alternatively t is called dead at M'. A marking M is called dead iff M is t-dead for every transition $t \in T$. The total PT-net N is called live iff each transition is live at the initial marking M_o.

We will show that the liveness problem : "is t live at a given marking M ?" is equivalent to the reachability problem. Our proof is a slightly modificated version of the proof in [16]. Though the proof is lengthy, it nicely demonstrates the different techniques that are often used in proving results about PT-nets. First we show that reachability reduces to liveness.

Theorem 1.6

If liveness is decidable for a transition of a given PT-net, then reachability is decidable for any given marking M.

Proof

To solve the problem whether a given marking M is reachable within a given PT-net N we construct a new PT-net N' by adding two new places s'_1, s'_2 and the new transitions a,b,c, and t'_i , $1 \leqslant i \leqslant |S|$ as is indicated by figure 1.6 below. The place s'_1 self-loops on every transition $t_i \in T$ and initially has one token. Each transition t'_i self-loops on the corresponding place s_i and adds a token to s'_2 . The transition a self-loops on s'_1 and adds a token to s'_2 . Transition b subtracts exactly $M(s_i)$ tokens from place s_i and also subtracts the token from s_1'. Finally transition c subtracs a token from s_2'. No other arcs are added to the PT-net N. The places of the old net N are initially marked by M_o.

Figure 1.6

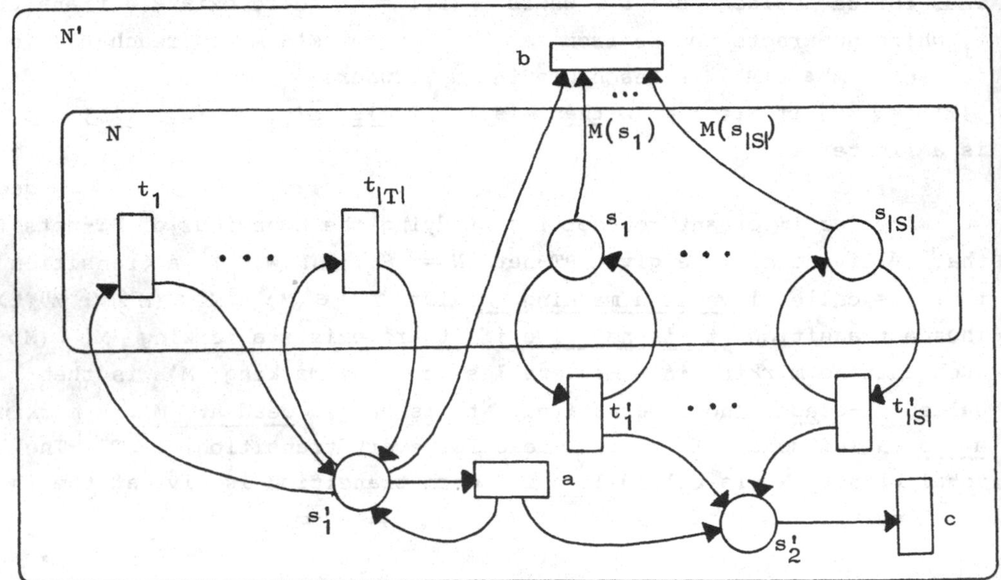

As long as s_1' has the token N' behaves like N on the places s_i and in addition may add any finite number of tokens to s_2'. Now if M is reachable in N then transition b may fire once and a marking is reached, where s_2' is the only place containing a finite number of tokens. Thus c is not live. If M is not reachable in N then either b will never be enabled, the token at s_1' will stay there for ever, transition a may fire at any time, and therefore transition c is live or there exists some $M' > M$ such that b is enabled. But if b then fires at least one place s_k, $1 \leq k \leq |S|$, has one or more tokens which will never disappear since the transitions t_i of N are never enabled again. Now the transition t_k' is enabled at every reachable marking, which shows that also in this case c is live. Thus the transition c is live at the initial marking of N' iff M is not reachable in N.

qed

In order to reduce the liveness problem to the submarking reachability problem, which by theorem 1.5 has been reduced to the reachability problem, we study t-dead markings in more detail. The following definition is consistent with the definition given before and generalizes it to arbitrary vectors from $\mathbb{N}_\omega^n$.

A marking $M \in \mathbb{N}_\omega^n$ is <u>t-dead</u> iff no reachable marking $M' \in (M\rangle$ enables t. Recall that the transition rule has been defined also for vectors from $\mathbb{N}_\omega^n$. Two useful facts about t-dead markings shall be pointed out.

<u>Theorem 1.7</u>

(a) For any given $M \in \mathbb{N}_\omega^n$ and any PT-net N it is decidable whether M is a t-dead marking.

(b) If $M \in \mathbb{N}_\omega^n$ is a t-dead marking then each $M' \leq M$ is a t-dead marking too.

<u>Proof</u>

(a) According to construction 1.1 design some coverability graph Gr for N which has M as its initial node. Now M is t-dead iff Gr does not contain an arc labelled by t. (b) If $M' \leq M$ is not t-dead then there exists $w \in T^*$ such that $M'(wt\rangle$ holds. Then also $M(wt\rangle$ is true, contradicting the assumption that M is t-dead.

<u>qed</u>

We now construct a <u>maximal set of t-dead markings</u> and fix the underlying net for the rest of this section. Let $n := |S|$.

$D_t := \{ M \in \mathbb{N}_\omega^n \mid M \text{ is t-dead and } M' > M \text{ implies } M' \text{ not t-dead} \}$.

D_t can be called maximal, since any t-dead marking $M \in \mathbb{N}_\omega^n$ is covered by some $M' \in D_t$.

<u>Theorem 1.8</u>

The set D_t is finite for each transition t and can be constructed effectively.

<u>Proof</u>

Since D_t is a set of incomparable vectors from $\mathbb{N}_\omega^n$ with respect to the partial order $\leq$ it must be finite. Now let $L_t \subseteq \{0,\omega\}^n$ such that

$$L_t := \left\{ M \in \{0,\omega\}^n \;\middle|\; \begin{array}{l} M \text{ is t-dead and } M' > M \text{ for } M' \in \{0,\omega\}^n \\ \text{implies that } M' \text{ is not t-dead} \end{array} \right\}.$$

Clearly L_t is a finite set of incomparable t-dead vectors and it can be constructed effectively since by theorem 1.7 (a) it is decidable whether some $M \in \{0, \omega\}^n$ is t-dead or not. Moreover, changing any zero coordinate of some $M \in L_t$ into ω gives a new marking which is not t-dead. Thus for any $M \in L_t$ there exists some vector $V(M) \in \mathbb{N}^n$ such that $M + V(M)$ is still t-dead but any vector $M' > M + V(M)$ is not t-dead. These vectors $V(M)$ will be found by successively testing vectors $M + V$, $M \in L_t$, $V \in \mathbb{N}^n$ for t-deadness. Since $D_t = \{M + V(M) \mid M \in L_t\}$ the proof is finished.

qed

Theorem 1.9

The reachability problem is decidable iff the liveness problem for single transitions is decidable.

Proof

Let N be a fixed PT-net and suppose there exists some $M \in (M_o\rangle$ and some $M' \in D_t$ such that $M \leq M'$. Then obviously M is t-dead and t is not live at M_o. Conversely, if t is not live then there exists some t-dead marking $M \in (M_o\rangle$ which - like any t-dead marking - is covered by some marking $M' \in D_t$. Thus t is not live iff $\exists M' \in D_t \ \exists M \in (M_o\rangle : M \leq M'$. Since D_t is finite and can be construct effectively this is decidable if the reachability problem is decidable, as has been shown in theorem 1.5. That reachability reduces to liveness has already been shown by theorem 1.6.

qed

2. Complexity of Basic Problems

The following section deals with the computational complexity of decision procedures for various questions about PT-nets. As we will see, most of even the decidable problems are very hard to solve and this may be seen as a warning to those who intend to construct algorithms which base upon these decision procedures.

Within this context a very useful concept due to Rabin and Hack [18] is that of a weak Petri net computer which we will define as follows.

A PT-net $N_f := (S,T;F,W)$ with r distinguished input places (usually denoted by in_i, $1 \leq i \leq r$), one extra output place (out), one extra start place (on), one extra stop place (off), and possibly a finite number of internal places (s_i, $i \in \mathbb{N}$) is called a weak Petri net computer for the function $f: \mathbb{N}^r \longrightarrow \mathbb{N}$ iff there exists for each vector $x \in \mathbb{N}^r$ with components x_1 to x_r a proper initialization $M_x \in \mathbb{N}^{|S|}$ such that (1) to (5) holds:

(1) $M_x(on) = 1$ and $M_x(in_i) = x_i$ for $1 \leq i \leq r$.

(2) $M_x(out) = M_x(off) = M_x(s_i) = 0$ for all internal places s_i.

(3) $\forall M \in (M_x\rangle,\ M \neq M_x : M(on) = 0 \ \wedge\ 0 \leq M(off) \leq 1 \ \wedge\ M(out) \leq f(x_1,..,x_r)$

(4) $\forall M \in (M_x\rangle\ \forall t \in T : M(t\rangle \Longrightarrow M(off) = 0$.

(5) $\forall 0 \leq k \leq f(x_1,...,x_r)\ \ \exists M \in (M_x\rangle : M(out) = k \ \wedge\ M(off) = 1$.

The following figures provide examples of weak Petri net computers for the functions $add: \mathbb{N}^2 \longrightarrow \mathbb{N}$, $add(x_1,x_2) := x_1+x_2$, (figure 2.1), $f: \mathbb{N} \longrightarrow \mathbb{N}$, $f(x_1) := a \cdot x_1 + b$, $a,b \in \mathbb{N}$, (figure 2.2), and $mul: \mathbb{N} \longrightarrow \mathbb{N}$, $mul(x_1,x_2) := x_1 \cdot x_2$, (figure 2.3).

Figure 2.1

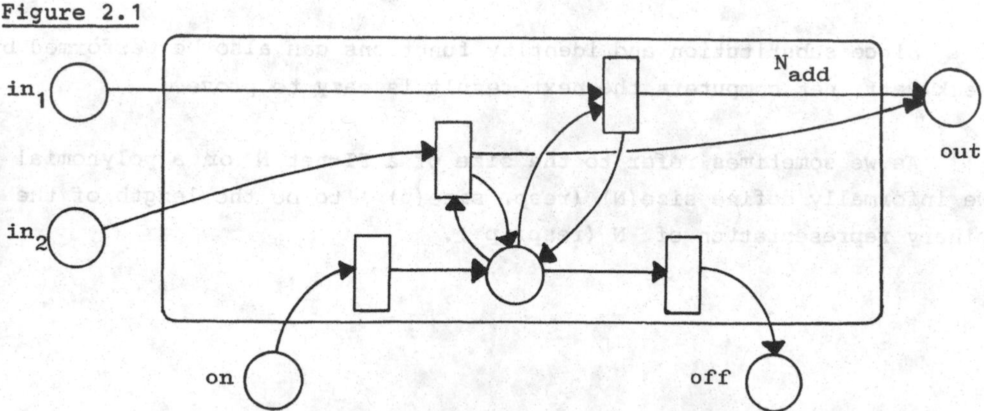

Figure 2.2

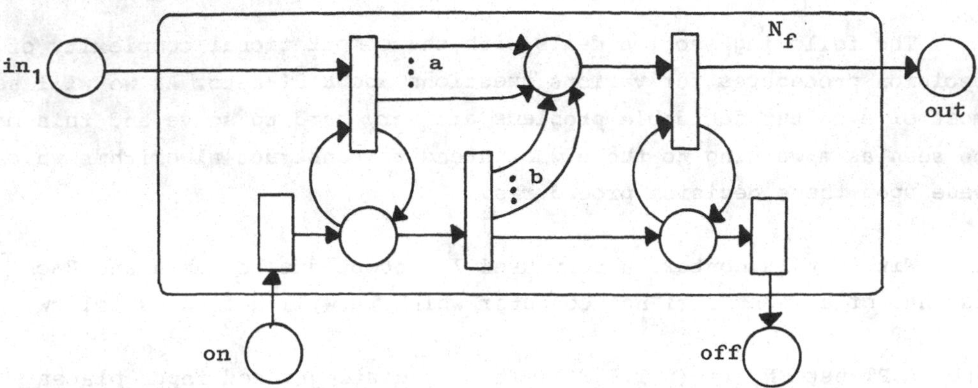

Figure 2.3

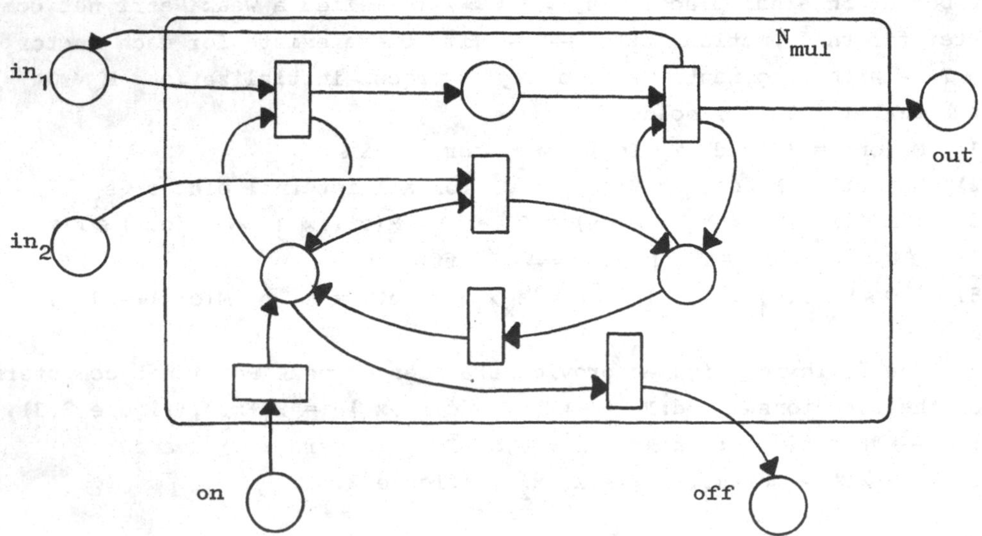

Since substitution and identity functions can also be performed by weak Petri net computers the next result is easy to prove.

As we sometimes refer to the size of a PT-net N or a polynomial p we informally define size(N) (resp. size(p)) to be the length of the binary representation of N (resp. p).

Theorem 2.1

Polynomials $p:\mathbb{N}^r \longrightarrow \mathbb{N}$ with non-negative integer coefficients are weakly computable by Petri nets of size $O(\text{size}(p))$.

We omit a detailed proof and refer to figure 2.4. The PT-net shown there weakly computes $g(x_1,\dots,x_r) := c\cdot x_1\cdot \dots \cdot x_r$, where the subnets are those from figure 2.2 and figure 2.3. Moreover, it can be changed such that it weakly computes g correctly even if all the internal places are forced to be bounded by $\max(c,x_i)$. Thus it is possible to construct a weak Petri net computer for an arbitrary polynomial p, where each internal place is bounded by $\max(x_i,c(p))$, $c(p)$ beeing the greatest coefficient of p.

Figure 2.4

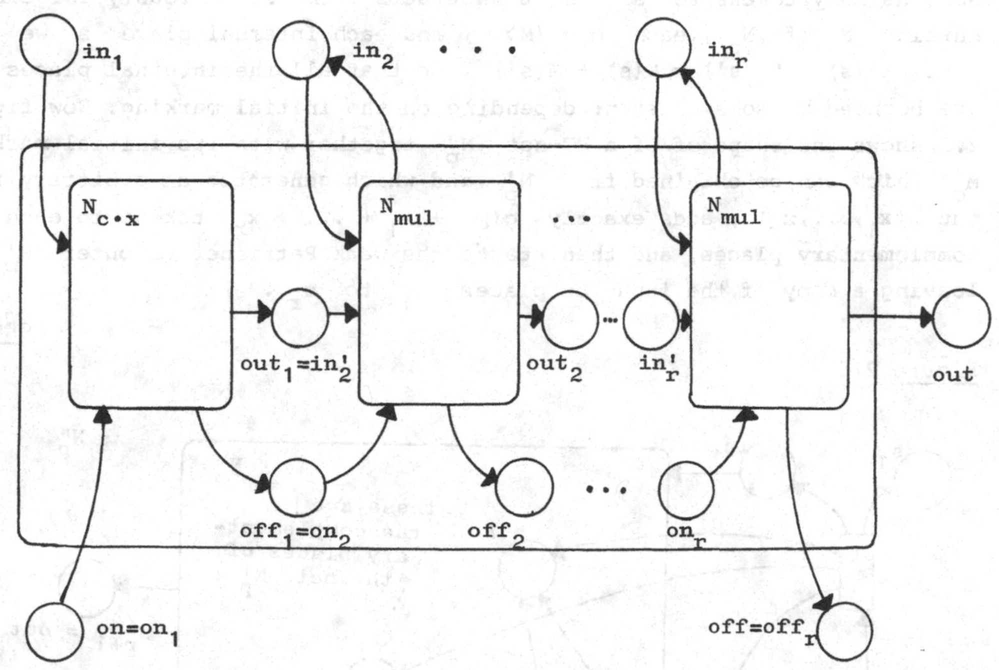

If for a polynomial p we define the graph of p $G(p)$ by $G(p) := \{ (x_1,\dots,x_r,y) \mid 0 \leq y \leq p(x_1,\dots,x_r) \text{ , } x_i \in \mathbb{N} \}$ then the above remark could be stated as follows.

Theorem 2.2

For each polynomial p with non-negative integer coefficients there exists a PT-net $N = (S,T;F,W,M_o)$ such that $G(p) = pr((M_o\rangle)$ where $pr: \mathbb{N}^{|S|} \longrightarrow \mathbb{N}^{r+1}$ is the projection onto the first $r+1$ coordinates. In addition each place $s_i \in S$, except for $i = r+1$, is bounded by $c(p) + x_1 + \ldots + x_r$.

Proof

Let N_p be a weak Petri net computer for the polynomial p which is not yet initalized and each internal place of which could be bounded by $\max(x_i, c(p))$. We then construct a new PT-net N_p' by adding complemantary places s' for each of the internal places $s \in S$ of the net N_p in such a way that each input transition of s subtracts as many tokens from s' as it adds to s, and each output transition of s adds as many tokens to s' as it subtracts from s. Obviously for each marking M of N_p', each $M' \in (M\rangle$, and each internal place s we have $M'(s) + M'(s') = M(s) + M(s')$, so that all the internal places are bounded by some constant depending on the initial marking. Now figure 2.5 shows the shape of of a PT-net N_p'' together with its initial marking M_o which can be obtained from N_p' and which generates an arbitrary input $(x_1,\ldots,x_r)$, adds exactly $c(p) + x_1 + \ldots + x_r$ tokens to each complementary places, and then starts the weak Petri net computer N_p' leaving a copy of the input on places s_1 to s_r.

qed

Figure 2.5

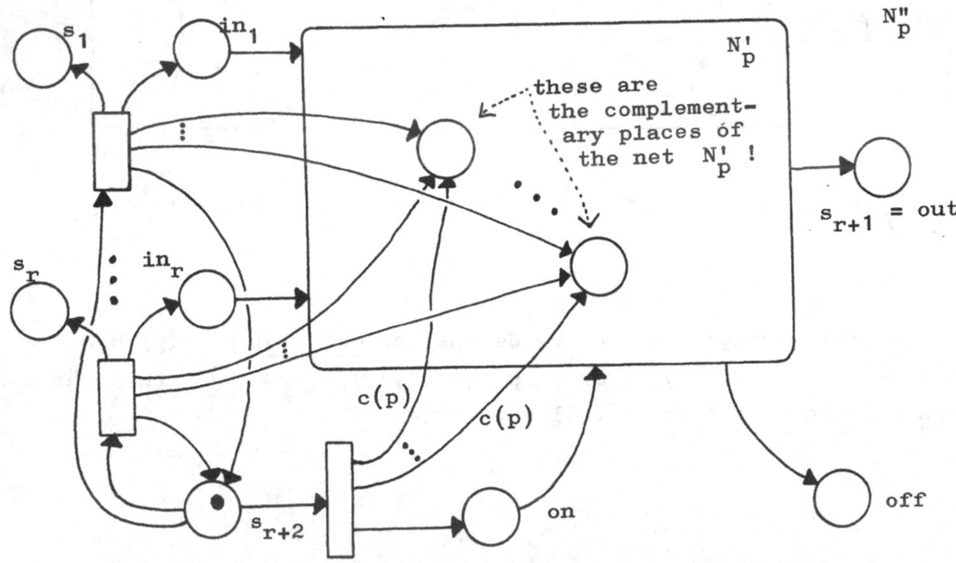

The following undecidability result is a consequence of the undecidability of Hilbert's tenth problem and will later on be reduced to the inclusion problem for reachability sets of PT-nets, thus showing the latter to be undecidable too.

Theorem 2.3

For arbitrary polynomials $p,q: \mathbb{N}^r \longrightarrow \mathbb{N}$ with non-negative integer coefficients it is undecidable whether $G(p) \subseteq G(q)$.

The proof can be found in [18,33]. Now we can prove an undecidability result about PT-nets.

Theorem 2.4

For given PT-nets $N = (S,T;F,W,M_o)$ and $\overline{N} = (\overline{S},\overline{T};\overline{F},\overline{W},\overline{M}_o)$ with the same number of places it is undecidable whether $(M_o\rangle \subseteq (\overline{M}_o\rangle$, a fixed bijection between the sets of places beeing assumed.

Proof

We will indicate how to construct for any two polynomials p and q with non-negative integer coefficients two PT-nets N_p and N_q such that $G(p) \subseteq G(q)$ iff $(M_{op}\rangle \subseteq (M_{oq}\rangle$. Then theorem 2.3 applies immediately.

Let N_p'' and N_q'' be PT-nets as constructed in the proof of theorem 2.2 , where in addition the arcs of multiplicity $c(p)$ respectively $c(q)$ in both nets are replaced by arcs of multiplicity $\max(c(p),c(q))$, and some unmarked places are added to level the number of places in both nets. Now figure 2.6 shows how one can modify these PT-nets to obtain the desired PT-nets N_p and N_q , their initial markings M_{op} and M_{oq} , and the bijection between the places.

qed

As Hack [18] reported, theorem 2.4 has been proved by Rabin (1966, unpublished) by reducing the undecidable problem of finding integer roots for exponential equations to the inclusion problem of vector addition systems. The following theorem is stronger than theorem 2.4 and is due to Hack [18] .

Theorem 2.5

The equality problem for reachability sets of PT-nets is undecidable.

Figure 2.6

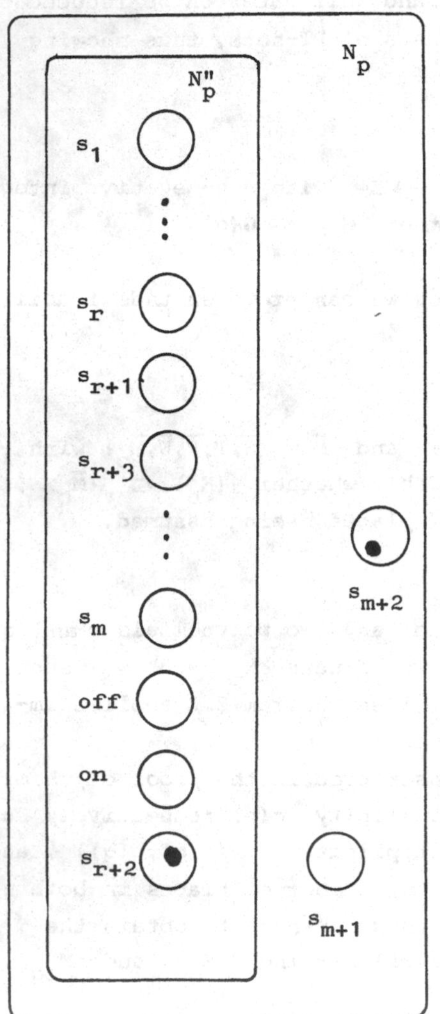

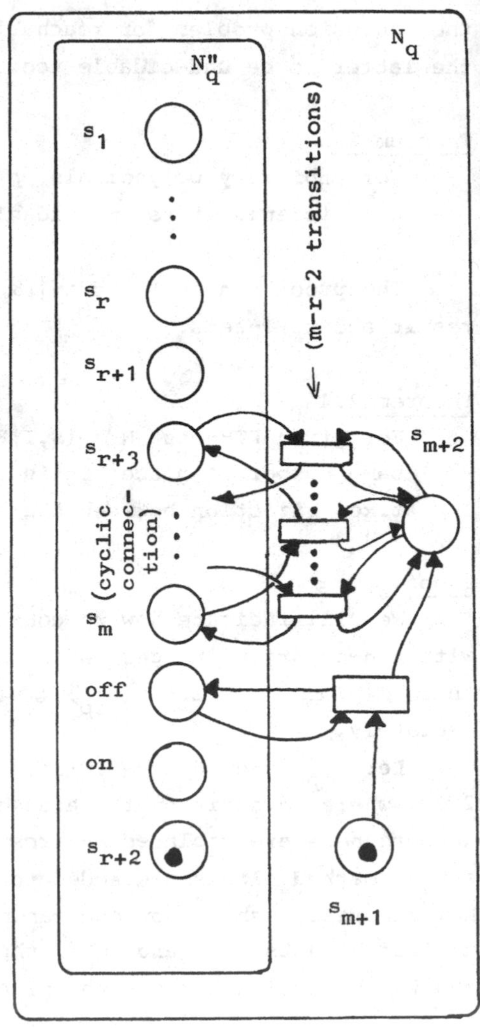

As we have seen that polynomials are weakly computable by Petri nets the question arises whether there are even more complicated functions which can be weakly computed by Petri nets. Let for example

$A_o(x) := 2\cdot x + 1$, $A_{n+1}(x+1) := A_n(A_{n+1}(x))$, $A_{n+1}(0) := A_n(0)$,

then the function $A(n) := A_n(2)$ majorizes the primitive recursive functions and as we shall see $A_n : \mathbb{N} \longrightarrow \mathbb{N}$ is weakly computable by a Petri net of size proportional to n.

If - in order to construct a small weak Petri net computer for A_n - we want to use a weak Petri net computer iteratively several times, then it would be nice to restart the net merily by transferring the token from thestop place back to the start place and putting a new input on the input places. Unfortunately this is not possible for arbitrary weak Petri net computers as can be seen by the net from figure 2.3.

Therefore we say that a weak Petri net computer for a function $f:\mathbb{N} \longrightarrow \mathbb{N}$ and with the set of places S has the <u>iteration property</u> iff $\forall M,M' \in \mathbb{N}^{|S|}: (M(on) = M'(off) = 1 \wedge M(off) = M'(on) = 0 \wedge M' \in (M\rangle) \Longrightarrow (\sum_{s \in S} M'(s) \leq f(\sum_{s \in S} M(s)))$.

It can be shown that if $f:\mathbb{N} \longrightarrow \mathbb{N}$ is a strictly increasing function , i.e. $f(n+1) > f(n)$, and if N_f is a weak Petri net computer for f which has the iteration property, then the net N_g as defined by figure 2.7 is a weak Petri net computer which also has the iteration property and weakly computes $g:\mathbb{N} \longrightarrow \mathbb{N}$, where g is defined by $g(n+1) := f(g(n))$, $g(0) := f(0)$. Thus $g(n)$ is the n-th iteration of f applied to $f(0)$ and is strictly increasing. See [34] for details.

<u>Figure 2.7</u>

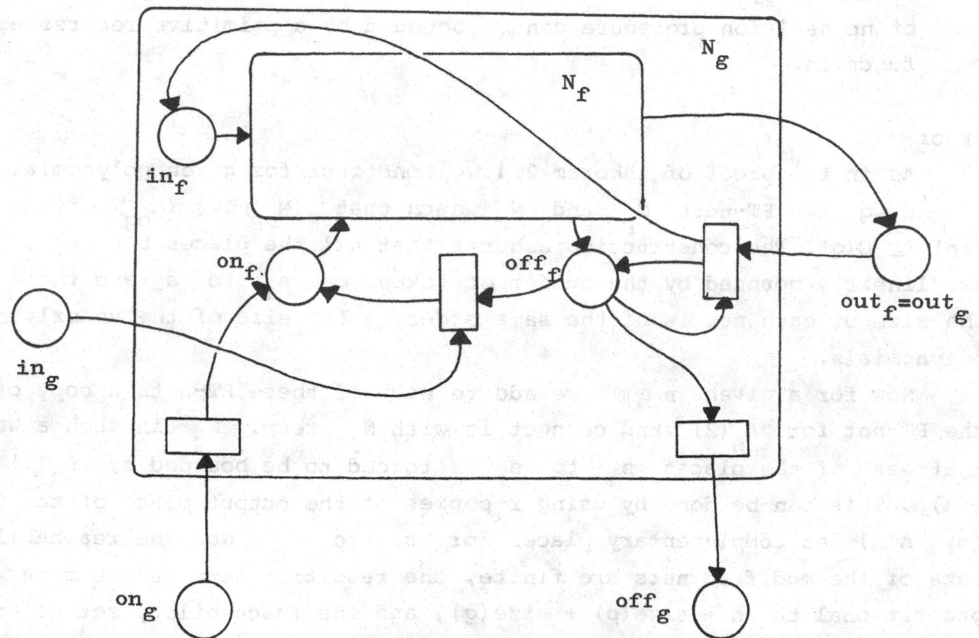

Theorem 2.6

For each $n \in \mathbb{N}$ there exists a weak Petri net computer for the function $A_n : \mathbb{N} \longrightarrow \mathbb{N}$, the size of which is proportional to n, and its reachability set $(M_o\rangle$ is finite for any proper initialization.

Proof

Apply the construction indicated by figure 2.7 n-times starting wi[th] the weak Petri net computer for $A_o(x) := 2 \cdot x + 1$ which can be derive[d] from figure 2.3.

qed

As a consequence of theorem 2.6 we see that the space and time complexity of the construction 1.1 for the coverability graph is not primitive recursive as a function of the size of the PT-net.

Obviously the containment problem and the equality problem for finite reachability sets is decidable by the brute force algorithm, so it is natural to ask for a better algorithm. The following result shows that there does not exist any fast algorithm for this problem.

Theorem 2.7

The containment problem and the equality problem for finite reachability sets of PT-nets is decidable, but the complexity of no decision procedure can be bounded by a primitive recursive function.

Proof

As in the proof of theorem 2.4 we construct for given polynomials p and q two PT-nets N_p and N_q such that $(M_{op}\rangle \subseteq (M_{oq}\rangle$ iff $G(p) \subseteq G(q)$. The construction ashures that all the places but s_{r+1} are linearly bounded by the number of tokens on s_1 to s_r and that the size of each net is of the same order as the size of the underlying polynomials.

Now for a given $n \in \mathbb{N}$ we add to each of these PT-nets a copy of the PT-net for $A_n(2)$ and connect it with N_p resp. N_q in such a way that each of the places s_1 to s_r is forced to be bounded by $A_n(2) = A(n)$. This can be done by using r-copies of the output place of the ne[t] for $A(n)$ as complementary places for s_1 to s_r. Now the reachabili[ty] sets of the modified nets are finite, the resulting nets have a size proportional to $n + \text{size}(p) + \text{size}(q)$, and the reachability set of one net is contained in the reachability set of the other net iff

$\forall x \in \{0,1,\dots,A(n)\}^r : p(x) \leq q(x)$. As in the proof for theorem 2.3 one can show that a given polynomial $f: \mathbb{N}^r \longrightarrow \mathbb{N}$ has a solution for $f(x) = 0$ with $0 \leq x \leq (A(n))^r$ iff the above inequality holds. Thus any fast decision procedure for the containment problem of finite reachability sets would yield a fast decision procedure for the existence of zeroes of a polynomial bounded by A(n). This latter problem has been shown by Adleman/Manders [1] not to be decidable within primitive recursive time and space.

This completes the proof as regards the containment problem. Since Hack's reduction of the general inclusion problem to the equality problem for reachability sets preserves finiteness and can be performed in short time, the complexity of the equality problem for finite reachability sets is at least as hard as the containment problem.

<u>qed</u>

A detailed version of the proof for theorem 2.7 can be found in Mayr [34] . The paper of Cardoza/Lipton/Meyer [5] only gives a sketch of a proof not using the essential concept of the iteration property for weak Petri net computers in order to define the n-th iterative of a function.

Up to now we presented problems which are certainly intractable. The next results come up with decidable problems which are practically intractable even though the complexity decreased considerably. It is known that the reachability problem for reversible Petri nets is decidable, since forward marking classes of reversible PT-nets are semilinear sets. See section 3 for definitions and further results.

<u>Theorem 2.8</u>

The reachability problem for reversible Petri nets is complete in exponential space, i.e. it can be decided within exponential space and each problem which is decidable within this space bound can be reduced to it using only logarithmic space.

For the proof see [5] . In [31] it is shown that reachability for arbitrary nets at best is decidable within exponential space, a result which immediately follows from theorem 2.8. The proof from [31] also gives a lower bound for the <u>boundedness problem</u>, which is to determine if a given PT-net has a finite reachability set.

Theorem 2.9

There is a constant c such that the boundedness problem for arbitrary PT-nets N cannot be decided in space $2^{c\cdot\sqrt{size(N)}}$.

For the proof see [31] and a remark in [38] . Since Lipton did not present an exponential space algorithm to decide boundedness , and since construction 1.1 is not primitive recursive, the next result of Rackoff [38] is important.

Theorem 2.10

There is a constant $d>0$ such that the boundedness problem for arbitrary PT-nets N can be decided within space $2^{d\cdot size(N)\cdot \log(size(N))}$

Unfortunately, even more restricted problems which are known to be decidable are practically intractable as can be seen by results from [23

Theorem 2.11

The following problems are complete for polynomial space:

(a) To decide for a given PT-net and a fixed $k \in \mathbb{N}$ whether each place of the net is bounded by k .

(b) To decide the reachability problem for a given PT-net which is known to be k-bounded for a given $k \in \mathbb{N}$.

(c) To decide the reachability problem for a given PT-net, where the number of input places of each transition equals the number of its output places.

Theorem 2.12

The non-liveness problem for free choice nets and problem (c) from theorem 2.11 are both complete for nondeterministic polynomial time

(For the definition of liveness see section 1, for that of a free choice net see section 4).

As a consequence of the preceeding results we conclude that for practical use it is either necessary to restrict oneself to very simple classes of Petri nets, or one should not expect to find computational simple algorithms which automatically solve problems similar to those discussed in this section.

3. Marking Classes and Presburger Formulas

For the analysis of a net a description of the marking class can be desirable and helpfull. In this chapter marking classes of place/transition nets are described by formulas comming from logic and linear algebra.

A Presburger formula is a first order formula over the integers whose only atomic formulas are of the form x+y=z and $x \leq y$. If $p(x_1,..,x_n)$ is a Presburger formula with free variables $x_1,...,x_n$ then $V_p := \{(a_1,...,a_n) \in \mathbb{Z}^n \mid p(a_1,...,a_n) \text{ is true}\}$ is the vector set of p.

If for example x=0 is a short notation for x+x=x and x=1 stands for $\exists x=0 \wedge \exists y : (y=0 \wedge \forall z : (y \leq z \Rightarrow x \leq z))$, then $p(x_1,x_2,x_3) := (x_1=1 \wedge \exists x : (x_2 \geq x \wedge x=x_3+x_3 \wedge \exists z : (z=0 \wedge x \geq z)))$ is a Presburger formula with vector set $V_p = \{ (a_1,a_2,a_3) \in \mathbb{Z}^3 \mid a_1=1 \wedge a_2 \geq 2 \cdot a_3 \geq 0 \}$

A set $A \subseteq \mathbb{N}^k$ is said to be linear, if there are elements $v_o,v_1,...,v_m \in \mathbb{N}^k$ such that $A = \{ v_o+k_1 \cdot v_1+...+k_m \cdot v_m \mid k_1,...,k_m \in \mathbb{N} \}$. A is said to be semilinear, if A is a finite union of linear sets. It has been shown by Ginsburg and Spanier [11] , that a set is semilinear if and only if it is the vector set of a Presburger formula.

Unfortunately not all nets have semilinear forward marking classes. For instance there is a (free-choice) net having a forward marking class with the set $\{(n,m) \in \mathbb{N}^2 \mid n \leq 2^m+1 \}$ as a projection in the first two components (figure 3.1).

Figure 3.1

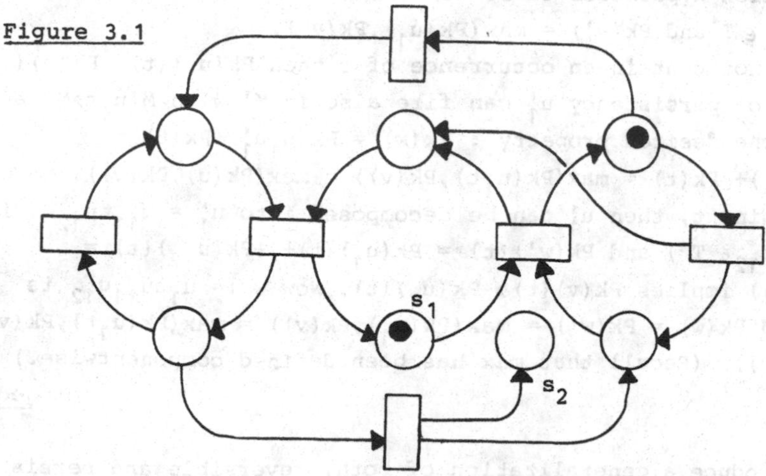

Therefore we consider certain subclasses of nets. For a concurrent system the property that from any state the initial state is reatainable may be a reasonable requirement for wellformedness. A net having this property will be called reversible. As in section 2 all nets in this section are place/transition -nets $N = (S,T;F,W,M_o)$ with unbounded capacities (see section 1). Such a net N will be called reversible if $M_o \in (M\rangle$ for all reachable markings $M \in (M_o\rangle$.

A net is called persistent, if an enabled transition can loose its concession only by its own firing. Formally N is persistent if for all $t_1, t_2 \in T$, $t_1 \neq t_2$ and all reachable markings $M \in (M_o\rangle$, $M(t_1\rangle$ and $M(t_2\rangle$ imply $M(t_1 t_2\rangle$. In the case of condition/event nets persistency implies conflict freeness. Persistency has been introduced by Karp and Miller [24] as a property of parallel program schemata. Liveness is shown to be decidable for persistent nets in [25] , where also the following property is given.

Lemma 3.1

If transition sequences $u,v \in T^*$ are firable in a marking M of a persistent net, then a sequence $w \in T^*$ is firable in M with Pk(w) = max(Pk(u) , Pk(v)). Moreover, there is such a w with w = uu' for some $u' \in T^*$.

Proof

The lemma will be shown by induction on the length lg(u) of the sequence u. If lg(u)=0 take w := v. If lg(u) > 0 then $u = u_1 t$ for some $t \in T$, $u_1 \in T^*$. By induction hypothesis there is $w' \in T^*$ such that $M(w'\rangle$ and $w' = u_1 u_1'$ for some $u_1' \in T^*$ and $Pk(w') = max(Pk(u_1),Pk(v))$.

If u_1' does not contain an occurrence of t then $Pk(u_1)(t) \geq Pk(v)(t)$. By the property of persistency u_1' can fire also in M' with $M(u_1 t\rangle M'$ and $w := u_1 t u_1'$ has the desired property : $Pk(w) = Pk(u_1 u_1')+Pk(t) = max(Pk(u_1),Pk(v))+ Pk(t) = max(Pk(u_1 t),Pk(v)) = max(Pk(u),Pk(v))$.

If u_1' contains t, then u_1' can be decomposed into $u_1' = u_{11} t u_{12}$ (with $u_{11} \in (T-\{t\})^*$, $u_{12} \in T^*$) and $Pk(w')(t) = Pk(u_1)(t)+1+Pk(u_{12})(t) = max(Pk(u_1),Pk(v))$ implies $Pk(v)(t) > Pk(u_1)(t)$. Now $w := u_1 t u_{11} u_{12}$ is firable in M and $Pk(w) = Pk(w') = max(Pk(u_1),Pk(v)) = max(Pk(u_1 t),Pk(v)) = max(Pk(u),Pk(v))$. (Recall that max has been defined componentwise.)

qed

We now introduce a generalization of both, reversible and persisten nets. A net $N = (S,T;F,W,M_o)$ is called persistently-reversible, if there is a subset $\hat{T} \subseteq T$ such that $(M_o\rangle = \{M' \mid \exists\, w \in \hat{T}^* \;\exists\, v_1, v_2 \in T^* \exists M \in \mathbb{N}^{|S|} : M_o(w\rangle M(v_1\rangle M'(v_2\rangle M\}$ and if $\hat{T} \neq \emptyset$ the subnet $\hat{N} = (S,\hat{T};\hat{F},\hat{W},M_o)$, $\hat{F} = F \cap (S \times \hat{T} \cup \hat{T} \times S)$, $\hat{W}(x,y) = W(x,y)$ is persistent.

The unbounded, free-choice net in figure 3.2 is persistently-reversible ($\hat{T} = \{t_1,t_4\}$), but neither persistent nor reversible.

Figure 3.2

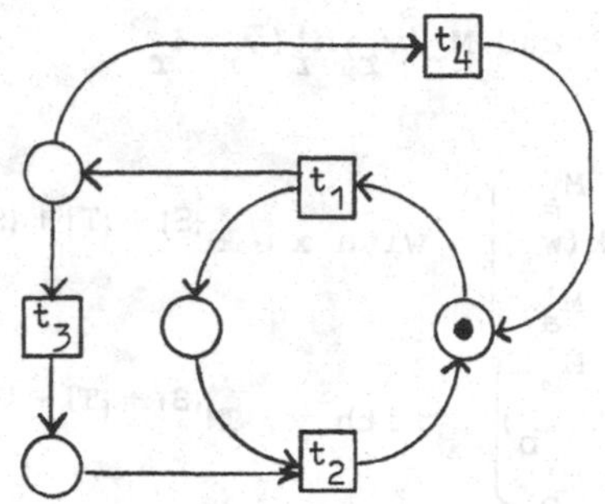

Informally speaking, the marking graph of an persistently-reversible net can be decomposed into a collection of strongly connected components which are reachable by firings of the persistent subnet.

To prepare the main result of this section, we define the notion of a slice as a technical tool. A subset $R \subseteq \mathbb{N}^k$ is called a slice if $r+x+y \in R$ holds for all $x,y \in \mathbb{N}^k$ with r, $r+x$, $r+y \in R$. As a result of Eilenberg and Schützenberger [8] slices are semilinear sets. Moreover every semilinear set is the projection of a slice [21].

Theorem 3.2

The set of forward reachable markings in a persistently-reversible net is semilinear and therefore a vector set of a Presburger formula.

Proof

Let be N and $\hat{N}$ as in the definition before. Then for all transitions $t \in \hat{T}$ the columns $\begin{bmatrix} C(s_1,t) \\ \vdots \\ C(s_S,t) \end{bmatrix}$ of the incidence matrices of N and $\hat{N}$ are identical. The same holds for the matrices W_Q. Therefore we can consider firings of $t \in \hat{T}$ in $\hat{N}$ as firings of N as well.

Since slices and projections of slices are semilinear, for the proof of the theorem it is sufficient to show that the following set $R \subseteq \mathbb{N}^{|S|+|T|+|S|}$ is a slice :

$$R := \left\{ \begin{pmatrix} M \\ Pk(w) \\ M' \end{pmatrix} \;\middle|\; M, M' \in \mathbb{N}^{|S|} \wedge w \in \hat{T}^* \wedge \exists\, v, \bar{v} \in T^* : M_o(w{>}M(v{>}M'(\bar{v}{>}M \right\}$$

To do this let

$$r := \begin{pmatrix} M_r \\ Pk(w_r) \\ M'_r \end{pmatrix} \in R \quad \text{and } M_r(v_r{>}M'_r(\bar{v}_r{>}M_r$$

$$a := r + x := \begin{pmatrix} M_a \\ Pk(w_a) \\ M'_a \end{pmatrix} \quad \text{with } x \in \mathbb{N}^{|S|+|T|+|S|} \text{ and } M_a(v_a{>}M'_a(\bar{v}_a{>}M_a$$

$$b := r + y := \begin{pmatrix} M_b \\ Pk(w_b) \\ M'_b \end{pmatrix} \quad \text{with } y \in \mathbb{N}^{|S|+|T|+|S|} \text{ and } M_b(v_b{>}M'_b(\bar{v}_b{>}M_b$$

We have to show that $c := r + x + y = \begin{pmatrix} M_c \\ Pk(w_c) \\ M'_c \end{pmatrix} \in R$.

From $M_o(w_r{>}$, $M_o(w_a{>}$ and lemma 3.1 we know that there is $w \in \hat{T}^*$ such that $M_o(w{>}M'$ and $w = w_r v_{ra}$ (for some $v_{ra} \in \hat{T}^*$) and $Pk(w) = \max(Pk(w_r), Pk(w_a))$. $r \leq a$ implies $Pk(w_r) \leq Pk(w_a)$, hence $Pk(w) = Pk(w_a)$ and $M_o(w_r{>}M_r(v_{ra}{>}M_a$ i.e. :

(1) $\exists\, v_{ra} \in \hat{T}^* : M_r(v_{ra}{>}M_a \;\wedge\; Pk(v_{ra}) = Pk(w_a) - Pk(w_r)$

Substituting a by b we obtain by the same arguments :

(2) $\exists\, v_{rb} \in \hat{T}^* : M_r(v_{rb}{>}M_b \;\wedge\; Pk(v_{rb}) = Pk(w_b) - Pk(w_r)$

Since $c = r + x + y = a + b - r$ we have

(3) $M_c = M_a + M_b - M_r = M_r + C\cdot Pk(v_{ra}) + C\cdot Pk(v_{rb})$

By $a \geq r$ (and therefore $M_a \geq M_r$) we obtain :

(4) $M_r(v_{ra}{>}M_a(v_{rb}{>}M_c$ and $C\cdot Pk(v_{ra}) \in \mathbb{N}^{|S|+|T|+|S|}$

and by $b \geq r$ (and therefore $M_b \geq M_r$) also :

(5) $M_r(v_{rb}{>}M_b(v_{ra}{>}M_c$ and $C\cdot Pk(v_{rb}) \in \mathbb{N}^{|S|+|T|+|S|}$.

Thus choosing $w_c := v_{ra}v_{rb} \in \hat{T}^*$ we obtain the first part of c, namely $M_o(w_r{>}M_r(w_c{>}M_c$.

It is now left to show that for $M'_c = M'_a + M'_b - M'_r$:

(6) $\exists\, v_c \in T^* : M_c(v_c\rangle M'_c$ and

(7) $\exists\, \bar{v}_c \in T^* : M'_c(\bar{v}_c\rangle M_c$

To prove (6) we define $v_c := v_b \bar{v}_r v_a$. Since $M_c \geq M_b$ and $M_b(v_b\rangle M'_b(\bar{v}_b\rangle M_b$ there is a marking M' such that

(8) $M_c(v_b\rangle M'(\bar{v}_b\rangle M_c$ and

$$(9)\begin{cases} M' = M_c + C\cdot Pk(v_b) \underset{(\text{by } (3))}{=} M_r + C\cdot Pk(v_{rb}) + C\cdot Pk(v_{ra}) + C\cdot Pk(v_b) \\ \underset{(\bar{2})}{=} M_b + C\cdot Pk(v_b) + C\cdot Pk(v_{ra}) = M'_b + C\cdot Pk(v_{ra}) \underset{(\bar{4})}{\geq} M'_b \geq M'_r \end{cases}$$

Now by the definition of $r \in R$: $M'_r(\bar{v}_r\rangle M_r(v_r\rangle M'_r$ and $M' \geq M'_r$ in (9) we obtain :

(10) $M'(\bar{v}_r\rangle M''(v_r\rangle M'$ for some marking M'' and

$$(11)\begin{cases} M'' = M' + C\cdot Pk(\bar{v}_r) \underset{(\bar{9})}{=} M'_b + C\cdot Pk(v_{ra}) + C\cdot Pk(\bar{v}_r) \underset{(9)}{\geq} \\ M'_r + C\cdot Pk(v_{ra}) + C\cdot Pk(\bar{v}_r) = M_r + C\cdot Pk(v_{ra}) = M_a \end{cases}$$

Together with $M_a(v_a\rangle M'_a(\bar{v}_a\rangle M_a$ inequality (11) gives

(12) $M''(v_a\rangle M'''(\bar{v}_a\rangle M''$ for some marking M''' and

$$(13)\begin{cases} M''' = M'' + C\cdot Pk(v_a) \underset{(\bar{11})}{=} M' + C\cdot Pk(\bar{v}_r) + C\cdot Pk(v_a) \underset{(\bar{9})}{=} \\ M_r + C\cdot Pk(v_{rb}) + C\cdot Pk(v_{ra}) + c\cdot Pk(v_b) + C\cdot Pk(\bar{v}_r) + C\cdot Pk(v_a) = \\ (M_r + C\cdot Pk(v_{ra}) + C\cdot Pk(v_a)) + (C\cdot Pk(v_{rb}) + C\cdot Pk(v_b)) + C\cdot Pk(\bar{v}_r) = \\ = M'_a + (M'_b - M_r) + (M_r - M'_r) \\ = M'_c \end{cases}$$

This proves (6). Finally to show (7) we define $\bar{v}_c := \bar{v}_a v_r \bar{v}_b$ and obtain by (12),(10) and (8) : $M'_c \underset{(\bar{13})}{=} M'''$ and $M'''(\bar{v}_a\rangle M''(v_r\rangle M'(\bar{v}_b\rangle M_c$.

qed

From this theorem we now formulate the following special cases.

Corollary 3.3

If $N = (S,T;F,W,M_o)$ is a persistent net, then

a) the set of forward reachable markings $(M_o\rangle$ is semilinear, and

b) the set of all firing sequences of N has a semilinear Parikh-image, i.e. $\{Pk(w) \in \mathbb{N}^{|T|} \mid M_o(w\rangle\}$ is semilinear.

Proof

Part a) follows from the theorem, since N is persistently-reversible (take $\hat{T} := T$). Part b) follows from the proof of the theorem, since the set is a projection of the semilinear set R.

qed

The result of corollary 3.3.a) has been proved first in [28] in a direct way, which is more complicated since slices are not used, and wh: did not give the result of 3.3.b). Both proofs do not give an effective procedure to compute the semilinear set.

Corollary 3.4

a) The full marking class of a net N is semilinear.

b) The forward marking class of a reversible net N is semilinear.

Proof

Part b) follows from the theorem, since a reversible net is persis- tently-reversible (Take $\hat{T} = \emptyset$, then $\hat{T}^* = \{\lambda\}$). Now part a) follows fror part b), since for any net $N = (S,T;F,W,M_o)$ a second net $N' = (S',T';F',$ $W',M_o')$ can be constructed with $[M_o] = (M_o'\rangle$. This can be done by adding t each transition $t \in T$ a number of new transitions which simulate a rever firing of t.

qed

Whereas part a) of corollary 3.4 is known from the theory of commu tative semigroups [4,8,21] , part b) has been recently published in [2] The proof given in [2] is much more complicated and does not use slices On the other hand it is shown in addition, that reversibility is a deci- dable property of nets.

The next theorem not only provides a further class of nets to have a semilinear reachability set, but also gives a characterisation of semi linear sets by nets. Let a place s of a net $N = (S,T;F,W,M_o)$ be reversa bounded if there exists a constant $k \in \mathbb{N}$, such that for every possible firing sequence $w \in T^*$, $M_o(w\rangle$, the place s alternately increases and decreases by at most k times.

Theorem 3.5

A set $L \subseteq \mathbb{N}^n$ is semilinear iff there exists a net $N = (S,T;F,W,M_o)$ and a vector $y \in \mathbb{N}^{|S|-n}$ such that $L = \{ x \in \mathbb{N}^n \mid \begin{bmatrix} x \\ y \end{bmatrix} \in (M_o\rangle \}$ and each place $s \in S$ is either bounded or reversal-bounded.

Proof

Let Rev be the class of languages accepted by reversal-bounded mult counter-machines in real time. By a result of Baker and Book [3] Rev equals the least intersection-closed trio $\mathcal{M}_\cap(a^nb^n)$ generated by the language $\{ a^nb^n \mid n \geq 0 \}$.

It is easy to see that for each net $(S,T;F,W,M_o)$, each place of which is either bounded or reversal bounded, the language $L' := \{ Pk(w) \mid M_o(w\rangle \}$ is a member of this family. Moreover Latteux [29] has shown that Pk(L) is a semilinear set for every $L \in \mathcal{M}_\cap(a^nb^n)$. This shows that Pk(L') is a semilinear set.

The equation $(M_o\rangle = \{ C \cdot Pk(w) + M_o \mid M_o(w\rangle \}$, which is valid for any net with incidence matrix C, shows that the set $(M_o\rangle$ is semilinear, if the underlying net has only bounded and reversal-bounded places. Note, that in general a set $K := \{ C \cdot a + b \mid a \in S \}$ need not be semilinear if C is an arbitrary integer matrix, $b \in \mathbb{N}^r$ is fixed and S is a semilinear set. But it can be shown that $K \cap \mathbb{N}^r$ is always semilinear.

Now for a fixed vector y the set $L = \{ x \in \mathbb{N}^n \mid \binom{x}{y} \in (M_o\rangle \}$ is a projection of the intersection of semilinear sets $L = (M_o\rangle \cap \{ \binom{x}{y} \mid x \in \mathbb{N}^n \}$ and therefore semilinear too. This gives a simpler proof for the if-part, which is also a result of Ibarra [20] . Moreover it has been shown that the entire set of reachable markings $(M_o\rangle$ is semilinear.

To show that each semilinear set $L \subseteq \mathbb{N}^n$ can be generated by some net with bounded and reversal bounded places, we use a result of Liu and Weiner [32] , which states that each semilinear set is the finite intersection of stratified semilinear sets L_i, which are of either form :

$$L_i = \{ x \in \mathbb{N}^n \mid \ c_i \cdot x = 0 \} \qquad \text{or}$$

$$L_i = \{ x \in \mathbb{N}^n \mid \frac{a_i + c_i \cdot x}{b_i} \in \mathbb{N} \}$$

where $a_i, b_i \in \mathbb{Z}$ and $c_i \in \mathbb{Z}^n$ are fixed for each L_i.

It is not difficult (but tedious) to construct nets $N_i = (S_i, T_i; F_i, W_i, M_{oi})$ with bounded and reversal bounded places only, and vectors $y_i \in \mathbb{N}^{|S_i| - n}$ such that $L_i = \{ x \in \mathbb{N}^n \mid \binom{x}{y_i} \in (M_{oi}\rangle \}$. The usual construction for intersection then yields the desired net for L. This result has also been claimed in [13] .

<u>qed</u>

At the end of this section on semilinear sets let us mention, that the problem to decide whether a given marking belongs to a semilinear set is NP-complete [39] . The procedure in [2] to construct a semilinear set from a reversible net is based on the coverability graph and we therefore conject that it is at least exponential.

But our study of semilinear sets was not motivated by the goal to find automatic procedures, but more to show this interconnection of net theory and Presburger logic. For instance, this can be very usefull for valididation and documentation of net based concurrent systems.

4. Synthesis by State Machines and the Deadlock Trap Property

In many applications concurrent systems are built up by synchronization of sequential processes. Thus, it is not surprising that already the early papers of Petri pursue the idea of composition of nets by subnets, which are models of sequential systems. In this section we investigate some structural properties that guarantee liveness of such interconnections. These structural properties are closely related to the so-called deadlock-trap property, which is also a necessary and sufficient condition for liveness of some classes of nets.

A state-machine net is a net-representation of the model of a finite automaton or finite sequential machine. If such a state-machine net contains one token only, no concurrent behaviour is possible and we have a formal model for representation of sequential processes. We also define the dual notion of a synchronization graph.

First recall that for a directed net $N = (S,T;F)$ and a set $Y \subseteq X := S \cup T$ of elements the sets $^{\bullet}Y := \{ x \in X \mid \exists y \in Y : (x,y) \in F \}$ and $Y^{\bullet} := \{ x \in X \mid \exists y \in Y : (y,x) \in F \}$ denote the set of input elements and output elements of Y, respectively. For $Y = \{y\}$ we also write $^{\bullet}y$ and $y^{\bullet}$.

N is called a <u>state-machine net</u> (<u>SM-net</u>) if $\forall t \in T : |^{\bullet}t| = |t^{\bullet}| = 1$. N is called a <u>synchronization graph</u> (<u>SG-net</u>) if $\forall s \in S : |^{\bullet}s| = |s^{\bullet}| = 1$. A net is said to be <u>strongly-connected</u>, if the graph of N is strongly connected (i.e. $\forall x,x' \in X : x \neq x' \Rightarrow$ there is a directed path from x to x'). A strongly-connected SM-net is also called a <u>SCSM-net</u>.

In order to say that a net is composed by SM-nets, we use the notion of a covering by closed subnets. A directed net $\hat{N} = (\hat{S},\hat{T};\hat{F})$ is a <u>subnet</u> if $\hat{S} \subseteq S$, $\hat{T} \subseteq T$ and $\hat{F} = F \cap (\hat{S} \times \hat{T} \cup \hat{T} \times \hat{S})$. It is a <u>closed subnet</u> if in addition $\hat{T} = {}^{\bullet}\hat{S} \cup \hat{S}^{\bullet}$ (i.e. $\hat{S} \cup \hat{T}$ is a closed subset of $S \cup T$). A closed subnet is uniqely defined by its set of places S , therefore $\hat{N}$ is also denoted by $\langle \hat{S} \rangle$. If the closed subnet is a SM-net (SCSM-net), it is called a <u>SM-component</u> (<u>SCSM-component</u>).

A collection $N_i = (S_i,N_i;F_i)$, $i \in I := \{1,\dots,n\}$ of nets is a <u>covering</u> of $N = (S,T;F)$, if $S = \bigcup_{i \in I} S_i$, $T = \bigcup_{i \in I} T_i$ and $F = \bigcup_{i \in I} F_i$.

If all nets N_i are SM-components (SCSM-components), then the collectic is a <u>SM-covering</u> (<u>SCSM-covering</u>) of N, and N is said to be <u>SM-coverat</u> (<u>SCSM-coverable</u>). A SCSM-coverable net is also called a <u>state-machine decomposable net</u> (<u>SMD-net</u>).

If not mentioned explicitly in the rest of this section all nets ar supposed to be place/transition-nets $N = (S,T;F,M_o)$ with infinite capacities ($\forall s \in S : K(s) = \omega$) and trivial multiplicities of arcs ($\forall f \in$ $W(f) = 1$). Furthermore we assume that they are connected graphs and tha every transition has an input place. All the definitions made above holc also for P/T-nets (with respect to the underlying directed net (S,T;F)). Note that by assuming all nets to be connected all SMD-nets are strongly connected.

In this section we are mainly interested in the property of livenes of nets (cf. section 1). It should be clear that a SM-net containing a least one token is live iff it is strongly connected.

Both nets N_1 and N_2 in figure 4.1 are SCSM-nets and therefore live for every marking M_o which is different from the null-vector.Now suppose that these nets represent two sequential processes, which have identical events t_1, t_6 and t_7 and the common condition s_7. Then the composed syst is represented by the net N_3 in figure 4.2 (from [14]), where these transitions and places are identified. $\{N_1,N_2\}$ is a SCSM-covering of N_3 and N_3 is therefore a SMD-net. Let be M_{o1}, M_{o2}, M_{o3} initial markings for N_1, N_2, N_3, respectively, with one token in s_7. We now compare the behaviour of N_3 with the expected behaviour of the composition of N_1 and N_2. For $M_{o1}(t_1t_2t_6t_1\rangle$ in N_1 and $M_{o2}(t_1t_4t_6t_1\rangle$ in N_2 in the composed net N we expect

(1) $\qquad M_{o3}(t_1t_2t_4t_6t_1\rangle$.

In fact, this is true for N_3. But for $M_{o1}(t_1t_2t_6t_1\rangle$ and $M_{o2}(t_1t_5t_7t_1$

(2) $\qquad M_{o3}(t_1t_2t_5t_6t_7t_1\rangle$

does not hold in N_3. Moreover N_3 has no live initial marking.This shows that liveness of the SCSM-components does not imply liveness of the composed net. Therefore another property must be required.

An <u>allocation</u> of a directed net N = (S,T;F) is a function al : T→• such that $al(t) \in {}^\bullet t$ for all $t \in T$. A subnet $\hat{N} = (\hat{S},\hat{T};\hat{F})$ and a subset $\hat{S} \subseteq S$ are said to <u>agree with al</u>, if $al(t) \in \hat{S}$ for all $t \in \hat{S}^\bullet$. A SMD-net N is called a <u>state-machine-allocatable net</u> (<u>SMA-net</u>), if for every

Figure 4.1

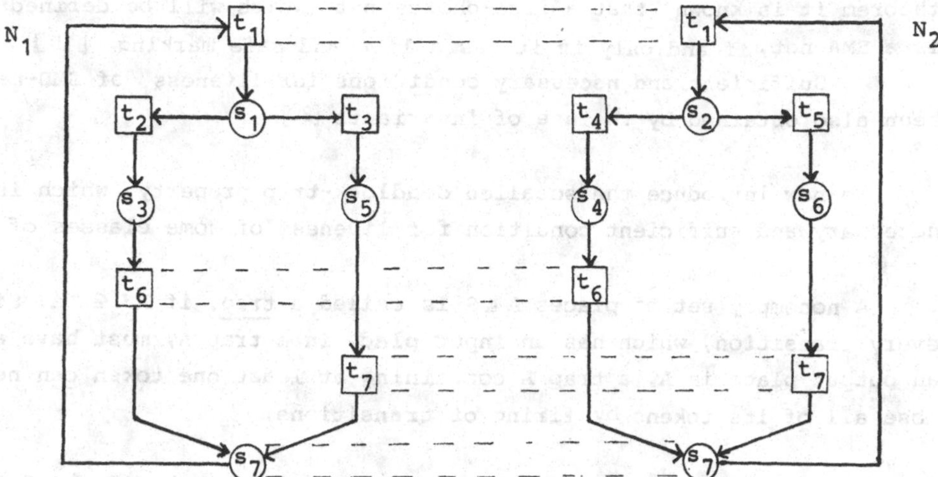

Figure 4.2

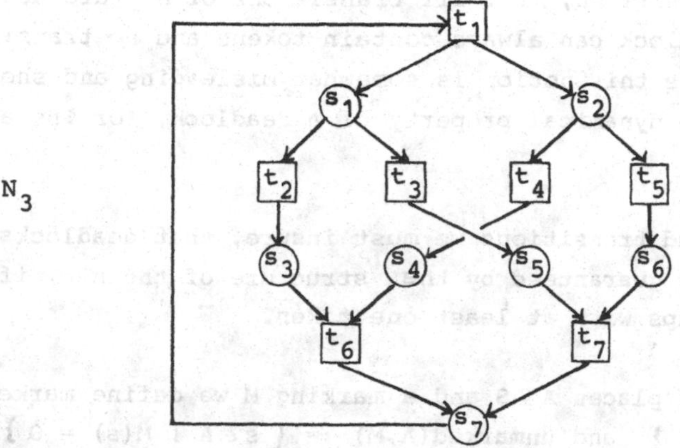

allocation al at least one SCSM-component agrees with al.

For the net N_3 in figure 4.2 only for transitions t_6 and t_7 a non-trivial choice of an allocation is possible. If $al_1(t_6) = s_3$ and $al(t_7) = s_5$, the net N_1 in figure 4.1 agrees with al_1, but there is no SCSM-component that agrees with al_2 where $al_2(t_6) = s_3$ and $al_2(t_7) = s_6$. Therefore N_3 is not a SMA-net. Note, that in some sense al_1 and al_2 are related to the firings (1) and (2), respectively.

Theorem 4.1 [14]

If $N = (S,T;F,M_o)$ is a SMA-net, such that every SCSM-component contains a token, then N is live.

The proof of this theorem will be given later. In addition to the theorem it is known, that a free-choice net (which will be defined later) is a SMA-net, if and only if it has a live and safe marking [15].

Sufficient and necessary conditions for liveness of SMD-nets have been also obtained by the use of invariants [30].

We now introduce the socalled deadlock-trap property, which is a necessary and sufficient condition for liveness of some classes of nets.

A nonempty set of places $A \subseteq S$ is called a trap, if $A^\bullet \subseteq {}^\bullet A$. Since every transition, which has an input place in a trap A, must have also an output place in A, a trap A containing at least one token can never lose all of its tokens by firing of transitions.

A nonempty set of places $A \subseteq S$ is called a deadlock, if ${}^\bullet A \subseteq A^\bullet$. A deadlock A having lost all its tokens can never obtain a token again by firing of transitions, i.e. all transitions of $A^\bullet$ are dead. On the other hand a deadlock can always contain tokens and no transition must be dead. Therefore this notion is somewhat misleading and should not be confused with the dynamical property of a deadlock, for instance a dead marking.

To avoid dead transitions we must insure, that deadlocks never become unmarked. This is guaranteed by the structure of the net, if the deadlocks contain traps with at least one token.

For a set of places $A \subseteq S$ and a marking M we define marked(A,M) := $\{ s \in A \mid M(s) > 0 \}$ and unmarked(A,M) := $\{ s \in A \mid M(s) = 0 \}$. A is said to be marked (unmarked) in M, if marked(A,M) $\neq \emptyset$ (marked(A,M) $= \emptyset$). If M is not mentioned, we suppose $M = M_o$.

A net $N = (S,T;F,M_o)$ has the deadlock-trap property (dt-property) if every deadlock of N contains a trap, which is marked in M_o.

Theorem 4.2

A net having the dt-property has no reachable dead marking.

Proof

By the dt-property every deadlock D in N is marked in every $M \in (M_o\rangle$. Now suppose that N has a dead marking $M \in (M_o\rangle$. Then D := unmarked(S,M) is a deadlock. In fact, $D \neq \emptyset$, and since every $t \in {}^\bullet D$ is dead, also $t \in D^\bullet$.

D is unmarked in contradiction to the assumption.

qed

Since not every net having the dt-property is live (figure 4.3), we must restrict our attention to appropriate subclasses.

Figure 4.3

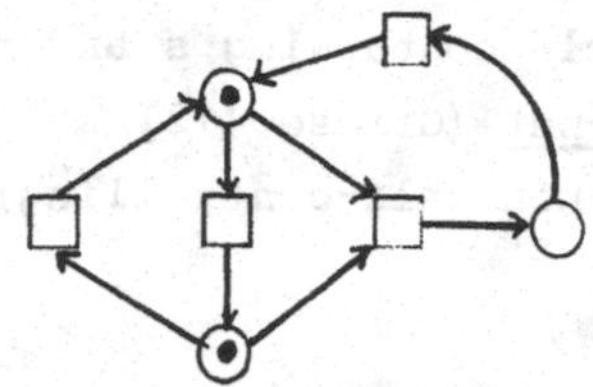

A net N is a free-choice net (FC-net) (Hack [15]), if $\forall s \in S$ $\forall t \in T : s \in {}^{\bullet}t \Rightarrow s^{\bullet} = \{t\} \vee {}^{\bullet}t = \{s\}$.

Remark : The original definition of free-choice nets is more general (Commoner [7]) : $\forall s_1, s_2 \in S : s_1^{\bullet} \cap s_2^{\bullet} \neq \emptyset \Rightarrow s_1^{\bullet} = s_2^{\bullet}$. Following [14] nets having this property are called extended free-choice nets (EFC-nets).

A place s is called a conflict-place, if it has more than one output transition. In a free-choice net these output transitions are either all firable or none of them is firable. To give some examples, the nets in figures 3.1 and 3.2 are live FC-nets. For a FC-net the dt-property is necessary and sufficient for liveness, but for many simple synchronisation problems this class is too restrictive (e.g. two sequential processes with a common critical region, synchronized by a simple "semaphore" place are not representable by a FC-net). Therefore we consider the following extensions of free-choice nets.

For transitions $t_1, t_2 \in T$, and $w \in T^*$ the relation $t_1 \xrightarrow{w} t_2 :\Longleftrightarrow$ $\forall M \in \mathbb{N}^{|S|} : (M(t_1 > \Rightarrow M(wt_2>)$ is the extended choice relation. N is called CNI-net (Memmi [35] , from French : "graphe à choix non imposé", i.e. non-forced choice net), if $\forall t_1 \in T \; \forall t_2 \in ({}^{\bullet}t_1)^{\bullet} \; \exists w \in T^*: t_1 \xrightarrow{w} t_2$ $\wedge$ if $s \in {}^{\bullet}t_1 - {}^{\bullet}t_2$ then $C \cdot Pk(w)(s) \leq 0$ else $C \cdot Pk(w)(s) = W_Z(s,t_2) - W_Z(s,t_1)$.

Every FC-net (and every EFC-net) is also a CNI-net (take $w = \lambda$). If an output transition of a conflict-place s in a CNI-net has concession, then no output transition of s is dead.

In a net N a sequence $x_o, x_1, \ldots, x_n$ ($x_i \in X = S \cup T$, $n \geq 1$) with $(x_i, x_{i+1}) \in F$ ($0 \leq i < n$) is called a <u>simple path</u> from x_o to x_n, if $x_i \neq x_j$ for $i \neq j$. The sequence is a <u>cycle</u> if $x_o = x_n$ and a <u>simple cycle</u> if in addition $x_i \neq x_j$ for $0 \leq i < j < n$. Now a conflict-place s is called <u>self-controlling</u>, if there is an output transition $t_1 \in s^\bullet$ such that

a) there is a simple path from s through t_1 to a $t_2 \in s^\bullet - \{t_1\}$ and

b) there is a cycle containing s and t_1.

A net N is called <u>NSK-net</u> (Griese [12] , from German : "nicht selbst kontrollierend", i.e. non self-controlling), if no conflict-place of N is self-controlling.

Every FC-net is a NSK-net. By a self-controlling conflict-place it can be prohibited that a deadlock becomes unmarked without using the dt-property. By excluding self-controlling conflict-places the dt-property becomes necessary for liveness. For a more detailed discussion of this see [12] .

Testing the FC-property for a net requires linear time with respect to the size of the net. A procedure to test the CNI-property is in general at least as hard as the coverability problem (i.e. at least exponential, see section 2), whereas the NSK-property has a significant lower complexity. But each of these concepts can be used as a tool in verification proofs of liveness for particular nets.

Another more direct extension of FC-nets (also with linear complexity) is due to Holt [19] . A net N is <u>extended simple</u> (<u>ES-net</u>), if $\forall s_1, s_2 \in S : s_1^\bullet \cap s_2^\bullet \neq \emptyset \Rightarrow (s_1^\bullet \subseteq s_2^\bullet \vee s_2^\bullet \subseteq s_1^\bullet)$.

The dt-property is necessary and sufficient for liveness in the case of FC-nets [15] , CNI-nets [35] and NSK-nets [12] and also sufficient for ES-nets [19] . In the following we give a new and unified proof for the sufficiency, which is derived from a proof by Krieg [27] for the case of FC-nets.

For any marking M of a net $N = (S,T;F,M_o)$ we define $dead_M := \{ t \in T \mid t \text{ is dead in } M \}$. Since $M(\to M'$ implies $dead_M \subseteq dead_{M'}$, the markings of $MAX := \{ M \in (M_o\rangle \mid \forall M' \in (M\rangle : dead_{M'} = dead_M \}$ are maximal with respect to this property. Note, that for $M \in MAX$ all transitions $t \in T - dead_M$ are live in M.

Lemma 4.3

If $N = (S,T;F,M_o)$ is a FC-, CNI-, NSK-, ES- or SMA-net and $M \in$ MAXMAX, then $\forall t \in dead_M \ \exists s \in {}^\bullet t \ \forall M' \in (M\rangle : M'(s) = 0$.

The proof of this lemma will be given in an appendix to this section.

Theorem 4.4 [15,35,12,19]

If N is a FC-, CNI-, or NSK-net, then the dt-property is necessary and sufficient for liveness. It is sufficient for ES-nets.

Proof

We only prove the sufficiency of the property and refer to the literature for the necessity. Suppose that the net is not live. Then at least one transition is dead in a reachable marking, and MAX contains at least least one marking M, such that $D := dead_M$ is not empty. We show that $A := \{ s \in {}^\bullet D \mid \forall M' \in (M\rangle : M'(s) = 0 \}$ is an unmarked deadlock. Therfore N cannot have the dt-property.

By lemma 4.3 A is nonempty. Every $t \in {}^\bullet A$ must be dead, i.e. ${}^\bullet A \subseteq D$. By the same lemma for every $t \in D$ there is $s \in {}^\bullet t$ such that $M'(s) = 0$ for all $M' \in (M\rangle$, i.e. $s \in A$ and $D \subseteq A^\bullet$.

qed

Proof of theorem 4.1

Let N be a SMA-net, such that every SCSM-component contains a token. Suppose that N is not live. Then as in the preceeding proof it follows from lemma 4.3, that there is a deadlock D, which is unmarked in some reachable marking M.

We now define a sequence of sets of places $Q_o, Q_1, \ldots,$ by $Q_o := D$ and $Q_{i+1} := \bigcup \{ \hat{S} \mid \langle \hat{S} \rangle$ is a SCSM-component and $\hat{S}^\bullet \cap Q_i^\bullet \neq \emptyset \}$. Since the net is strongly connected and SMD, there is a $o \leq k$ such that $Q_o \subsetneq Q_1 \subsetneq \ldots \subsetneq Q_k = S$. The inclusions hold, since all $\langle Q_i \rangle$ ($o < i \leq k$) are SMD-nets. All Q_i are deadlocks.

We now inductively define an allocation al, that agrees with every Q_i. If $t \in Q_o^\bullet$ let $al(t) \in Q_o$. If al(t) is already defined for all $t \in Q_i^\bullet$ and Q_{i+1} is the union of places of SCSM-components $\langle \bar{S}_1 \rangle, \ldots, \langle \bar{S}_r \rangle$ with $\bar{S}_i^\bullet \cap Q_i^\bullet \neq \emptyset$ (by definition), then let $al(t) \in \bar{S}_1$ for all $t \in \bar{S}_1^\bullet - Q_i^\bullet$ and $al(t) \in \bar{S}_{j+1}$ for $t \in \bar{S}_{j+1}^\bullet - (\bar{S}_j^\bullet \cup \ldots \cup \bar{S}_1^\bullet \cup Q_i^\bullet)$ $(1 \leq j < r)$.

Now it will be shown, that for every SCSM-component $\langle B \rangle$, that agrees with al, and all $0 \leq i < k$: $B \subseteq Q_{i+1} \Rightarrow B \subseteq Q_1$. Assume $B \subseteq Q_{i+1}$ and let be $\langle \bar{S}_j \rangle$ the first SCSM-component with $\bar{S}_j^\bullet \cap B^\bullet \neq \emptyset$ in the definition of al before. For every $t \in \bar{S}_j^\bullet \cap B^\bullet$ we have a) $al(t) \in \bar{S}_j$ by the definitio of $\bar{S}_j$ and al, b) $al(t) \in B$ since B agrees with al and c) $^\bullet t = \{ al(t) \}$ by a) and b) and since $\bar{S}_j$, B are SCSM-components. From a),b),c) it follows $t \in \bar{S}_j^\bullet \cap B^\bullet \Rightarrow {}^\bullet t \subseteq \bar{S}_j \cap B$ and therefore $S_j = B$. To prove $B \subseteq Q_i$ let be $s_o \in B$ and $t \in \bar{S}_j^\bullet \cap Q_i^\bullet = B^\bullet \cap Q_i^\bullet$. Since B is a SCSM-component, there is a path $s_o, t_o, \ldots, s_{n-1}, t_{n-1}, s_n, t_n = t$. $al(t) \in Q_i$ by the definition of al, $al(t) \in B$ since B agrees with al, hence ${}^\bullet al(t) \subseteq {}^\bullet Q_i \subseteq Q_i^\bullet$, ${}^\bullet al(t) \subseteq {}^\bullet B \subseteq B^\bullet$ (Q_i,B are deadlocks) and consequently $t_{n-1} \in Q_i^\bullet \cap B^\bullet$. Continuing in this way we obtain $t_o \in Q_i^\bullet \cap B^\bullet$ and $s_o \in B$.

By this we have shown, that any SCSM-component <B>, that agrees wit al, must be contained in Q_k, $Q_{k-1}, \ldots$ and finally in $Q_o = D$. But D is empty and cannot contain a token, in contradiction to the assumption.

qed

This proof is similar to a proof in [15] , but avoids transformatio of SMA-nets into FC-nets as in [14] .

We have already mentionned, that a SM-net is live iff it is marked and strongly connected. This result could be also derived as a corollar of theorem 4.4. There is a similar corollary for the dual case of SG-ne This corollary was one of the first nontrivial results on liveness in t theory of Petri nets.

<u>Corollary 4.5</u> [6,9,10]

A SG-net N is live if and only if every cycle contains at least on token.

<u>Proof</u>

A deadlock is minimal, if it contains no other deadlocks. In a SG-net a set $A \subseteq S$ is a minimal deadlock iff it is the set of places of a simple cycle.

If N is live, and since N is a FC-net, by theorem 4.4 the dt-prope holds. The set of places of every cycle is a deadlock and therefore mark Conversely, suppose that every cycle contains at least one token. Then every deadlock contains a minimal deadlock, which is a simple cycle, an therefore a marked trap. By theorem 4.4 the net is live.

qed

In this section we were interested in SMD-nets and the deadlock-trap property. Using both properties together results on nets, that are live and safe, can be derived : a CNI-net $N = (S,T;F,M_o)$ is live and safe iff it has the dt-property and has a SCSM-covering, where each component contains exactly one token [15,35] . (N is <u>safe</u> if $M(s) \leq 1$ for all $M \in (M_o\rangle$ and $s \in S$.)

A summary of the results of this section is given by a net-representation in [22] . In the following we give examples of nets from [40] , which have combinations of the following 12 properties :

SCSM (SCSM-net), SM (SM-net), SCMG (strongly connected MG-net), MG (MG-net), FC (FC-net), EFC (EFC-net), SMA (SMA-net), SMD (SMD-net), SMDR (SMDR-net : SMD-net where every minimal closed subnet is a SCSM-component), LSP (has a live, safe and persistent initial marking M_o (which is indicated)), LS (has a live and safe M_o), LB (has a live and bounded M_o). From 2^{12} combinations of these properties only the following 26 cases are possible :

SCSM	SM	SCMG	MG	FC	EFC	SMA	SMD	SMDR	LSP	LS	LB	
-	-	-	-	-	-	-	-	-	-	-	-	1
-	-	-	-	-	+	-	-	-	-	-	-	2
-	-	-	-	+	+	-	-	-	-	-	-	3
-	+	-	-	+	+	-	-	-	-	-	-	4
-	-	-	+	+	+	-	-	-	-	-	-	5
-	-	-	-	-	-	-	+	-	-	-	-	6
-	-	-	-	-	-	-	+	+	-	-	-	7
-	-	-	-	-	+	-	+	-	-	-	-	8
-	-	-	-	-	+	-	+	+	-	-	-	9
-	-	-	-	+	+	-	+	-	-	-	-	10
-	-	-	-	+	+	-	+	+	-	-	-	11
-	-	-	-	-	-	-	-	-	-	-	+	12
-	-	-	-	-	-	-	+	-	-	-	+	13
-	-	-	-	-	-	-	+	+	-	-	+	14
-	-	-	-	-	-	-	-	-	-	+	+	15
-	-	-	-	-	-	-	+	-	-	+	+	16
-	-	-	-	-	-	-	+	+	-	+	+	17
-	-	-	-	-	+	-	+	+	-	+	+	18
-	-	-	-	-	-	+	+	+	-	+	+	19
-	-	-	-	+	+	+	+	+	-	+	+	20
+	+	-	-	+	+	+	+	+	-	+	+	21
-	-	-	-	-	-	-	-	-	+	+	+	22
-	-	-	-	-	-	-	+	-	+	+	+	23
-	-	-	-	-	-	-	+	+	+	+	+	24
-	-	+	+	+	+	+	+	+	+	+	+	25
+	+	+	+	+	+	+	+	+	+	+	+	26

In figure 4.4 26 nets are given, which have exactly these properties properties.

Figure 4.4

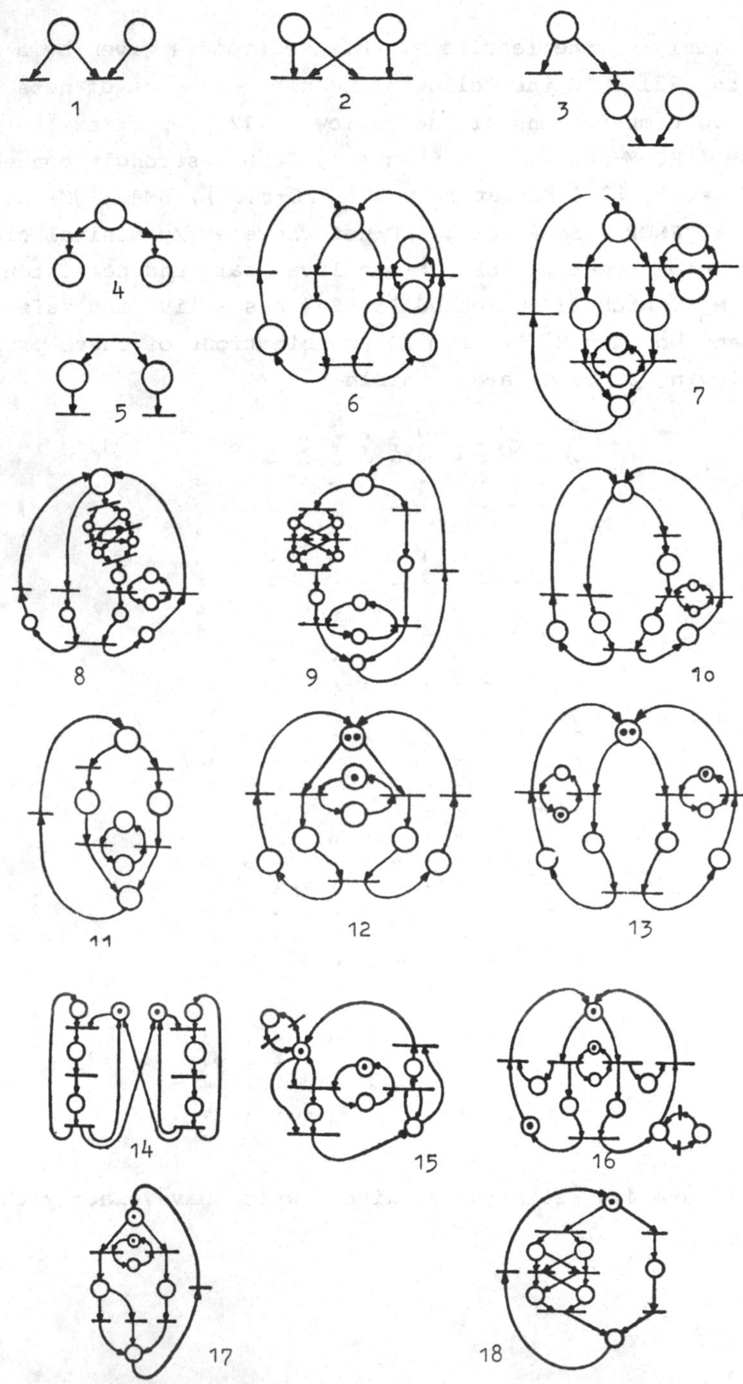

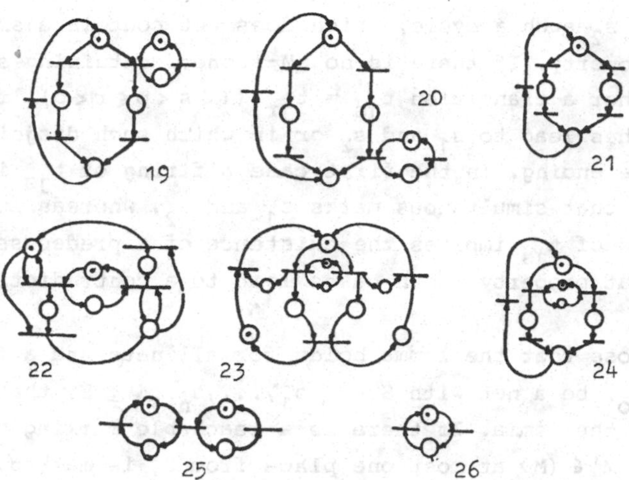

Appendix

Before proceeding to the proof of lemma 4.3, we give a new lemma holding for arbitrary nets. (Note that this lemma can be interpreted as a necessary condition for the holding of a particular "fact".)

Lemma 4.6

Let be $S_1 = \{s_1,\dots,s_n\}$, $(n \geq 2)$ a set of places of a net $N = (S,T;F,M_o)$, all of which have a live input transition $t_{ji} \in {}^{\bullet}s_i$. (the t_{ji} are not necessarily distinct). If there is no reachable marking $M \in (M_o>$, that marks all s_i $(1 \leq i \leq n)$ simultaneously, then N has a SCSM-subnet $\bar{N}$ containing at least two places of S_1.

Proof

To prove the lemma by induction on n, we first suppose n = 2. Since t_{i1} and t_{i2} are live, but s_1, s_2 cannot be marked simultaneously, we have $t_{i1} \neq t_{i2}$. s_1 can be marked in some $M \in (M_o>$. Now suppose that there is no path in the net, leading from s_1 to s_2. Then, since t_{i2} is live, there is a firing sequence starting in M, that marks s_2 without removing the tokens from s_1. This is in contradiction to the assumption of the lemma. Therefore there is a path from s_1 to s_2. By the same argument also a path from s_2 to s_1 exists and by the liveness of t_{i1} and t_{i2} all transitions of at least one such cycle are live.

Now it is left to prove, that at least one such cycle through s_1 and s_2 is a SM-subnet. Let be $s_{j1},t_{j1},\dots,s_{jp},t_{jp},\dots,s_{jq}$ with $s_{j1} = s_{jq} =$

s_1 and $s_{jp} = s_2$ such a cycle, which does not contain a smaller cycle with that property. If there is no SM-subnet containing s_1 and s_2, then there is either a transition $t_{js} = t_{jr}$ $(1 \leq s < p \leq r < q)$, from which eith disjoint pathes lead to s_1 and s_2 or in which such disjoint pathes fro s_1 and s_2 are ending. In the first case a firing of t_{js} implies a follower marking that simultanous marks s_1 and s_2, whereas in the second case a firing of t_{js} implies the existence of a predecessor marking $M \in (M_o\rangle$ with that property. Both cases lead to a contradiction to the assumption.

Now suppose that the lemma holds for all nets and a fixed $n \geq 2$. Let $N = (S,T;F,M_o)$ be a net with $S_1 = \{s_1,\ldots,s_{n+1}\} \subseteq S$, that satisfies the condition of the lemma. If there is a reachable marking $M \in (M_o\rangle$, such that for all $M' \in (M\rangle$ at most one place from S_1 is marked, then the indu tion hypothesis can be applied to $N = (S,T;F,M)$ with $S_1' = \{s_1,\ldots,s_n\}$. If this case does not hold, then for every $M \in (M_o\rangle$ pairs(M) $\neq 0$, where pairs(M) $:= \{(s_i,s_j) \mid i \neq j \wedge \exists M' \in (M\rangle : (M'(s_i) > 0 \wedge M'(s_j) > 0)$
Since $M_2 \in (M_1\rangle$ implies pairs$(M_2) \subseteq$ pairs(M_1) and pairs(M) is nonempty for every $M \in (M_o\rangle$, there is a particular pair (s,s'), $s \neq s'$ and a marking $M \in (M_o\rangle$ with $\forall M' \in (M\rangle \; \exists M'' \in (M'\rangle : (M''(s) > 0 \wedge M''(s') > ($
We now transform the net N into a net $N' = (S \cup \{s_o\}, T \cup \{t_o,\bar{t}_o\}; F', M)$ with new elements $s_o, t_o, \bar{t}_o$ and $F' := F \cup \{(s,t_o),(s',t_o),(t_o,s_o),(s_o,\bar{t}_o),(\bar{t}_o,s),(\bar{t}_o,s')\}$.

By the definition of M the new transition t_o is live in M. A markin with tokens in all places of S_1 is reachable in N iff a marking with tokens in all places of $S_2 := (S_1 - \{s,s'\}) \cup \{s_o\}$ is reachable in N'. By induction hypothesis at least two places of S_2 are contained in a SCSM-subnet of N'. But then also two places of S_1 must be contained in SCSM-subnet of N.

<u>qed</u>

<u>Proof of lemma 4.3</u>

Let be $D := dead_M$ and assume the contrary :

(I) $\quad \exists t_1 \in D \; \forall s \in {}^{\bullet}t_1 \; \exists M' \in (M\rangle : M'(s) > 0$

Transition t_1 would not be dead in M', if $|{}^{\bullet}t_1| \leq 1$. Therefore we assume $|{}^{\bullet}t_1| \geq 2$.

Now let be $S_1 := \{s_i \in {}^{\bullet}t_1 \mid s_i$ has a live input transition $t_{ji}\}$. By (I) every place $s \in {}^{\bullet}t_1 - S_1$ must be marked in M and remains marked in all $M' \in (M\rangle$ (if not it would have a live input transition). Therefore in the following we forget the places of ${}^{\bullet}t_1 - S_1$.

Since $t_1 \in D$ is dead in no marking $M' \in (M\rangle$ all places of S_1 can be marked. Applying lemma 4.6 to the net M, where all $t \in D$ are deleted, we obtain a SCSM-subnet $N' = (S',T';F',M)$ and $s_1,s_2 \in S' \cap {}^{\bullet}t_1$. Since the transitions $t \in T' = T - D$ are not dead, by the definition of M they are all live in M (in the net N).

Let be $t_1 \in {}^{\bullet}s_1$, $t_1' \in s_1^{\bullet}$, $t_2 \in {}^{\bullet}s_2$, $t_2' \in s_2^{\bullet}$ transitions of T'.

a) for FC- and CNI-nets :

Since $\{t_1',t_1\} \subseteq s_1^{\bullet}$, $t_1' \neq t_1$ (since $t_1 \in D$, $t_1' \in T-D$), $s_2 \in {}^{\bullet}t_1$, $s_2 \neq s_1$ N cannot be a FC-net. Transition $t_1' \in s_1^{\bullet}$ is firable in some $M' \in (M\rangle$, but not $t_1 \in s_1^{\bullet}$. Therefore N cannot be a CNI-net.

b) for NSK-nets :

There is a simple path from s_1 through t_1' and s_2 to t_1 and a cycle containing s_1 and t_1'. Therefore N cannot be a NSK-net.

c) for ES-nets :

$t_1 \in s_1^{\bullet} \cap s_2^{\bullet}$, but since N' is a SM-net $t_1' \notin s_2^{\bullet}$, $t_2' \notin s_1^{\bullet}$. Therefore N cannot be a ES-net.

d) for SMA-nets :

Define $Q_0 := S'$ and inductively Q_{i+1} from Q_i and also the allocation al as in the proof of theorem 4.1. Let be $\langle B\rangle$ a SCSM-component, that agrees with al. Then by the proof of theorem 4.1 : $B \subseteq Q_1$. In a similar way we can conclude $S' \subseteq B$. Therefore every SCSM-component, that agrees with al, contains the input places s_1 and s_2 of t_1, which is impossible by the definition of a SCSM-component. Therfore N cannot be a SMA-net.

qed

References

1. Adleman,L.,Manders,K. : Computational Complexity of Decision Procedures for Polynomials. in:Conf.Proceedings of the 16-th IEEE Annual Symp. on Foundat. of Computer Sci.,pp 169-177,(1975).

2. Araki,T.,Kasami,T. : Decidable Problems on the Strong Connectivity of Petri Net Reachability Sets. Theoret.Comp. Sci., 4, pp 99-119, (1977).

3. Baker,B.S.,Book,R.V. : Reversal-Bounded Multipushdown Machines. Journ. Comp. Syst. Sci., 8, pp 315-332,(1974).

4. Biryukov,A.P. : Some Algorithmic Problems for Finitely Defined Commutative Semigroups. Siberian Mathematics Journ., 8, pp 384-391, (1967).

5. Cardoza,E.,Lipton,R.,Meyer,A.R. : Exponential Space Complete Problems for Petri Nets and Commutative Semigroups. in: Conf. Proc. of 8-th Annual ACM Symp. on Theory of Computing, pp 50-54, (1976).

6. Commoner,F.,Holt,A.W., Even,S.,Pnueli,A. : Marked Directed Graphs. Journ. Comp. Syst. Sci., 5, pp 511-523, (1971).

7. Commoner,F. : Deadlocks in Petri Nets. Wakefield, Mass., Applied Data Research, Report CA-7206-2311, (1972).

8. Eilenberg,S.,Schützenberger,M.P. : Rational Sets in Commutative Monoids. Journ. of Algebra, 13, pp 173-191, (1969).

9. Genrich,H.J. : Einfache nicht-sequentielle Prozesse. GMD Bonn, ISF Bericht Nr. 37, (1971).

10. Genrich,H.J.,Lautenbach,K. : Synchronisationsgraphen. Acta Informatica, 2, pp 143-161, (1973).

11. Ginsburg,S.,Spanier,E.H. : Semigroups, Presburger Formulas, and Languages. Pacific Journ. Math., 16, pp 285-296, (1966).

12. Griese,W. : Lebendigkeit in NSK-Petrinetzen. Techn. Univ. München, TUM-INFO-7906, (1979).

13. Gurari,E.M.,Ibarra,O.H. : An NP-Complete Number-Theoretic Problem. Journ. ACM, 26, pp 567-581, (1979).

14. Hack,M. : Extended State-Machine Allocatable Nets, an Extension of Free Choice Petri Net Results. Cambridge, Mass., MIT, Project MAC, CSG-Memo 78-1, (1974).

15. Hack,M. : Analysis of Production Schemata by Petri Nets. Cambridge, Mass., MIT, Project MAC, MAC TR-94, (1972). Corrections to MAC TR-94 Comp. Struct. Note 17, (1974).

16. Hack,M. : The Recursive Equivalence of the Reachability Problem and the Liveness Problem for Petri Nets and Vector Addition Systems. in: Conf. Proc. of the 15-th Annual IEEE Symp. on Switching and Automata Theory, pp 156-164, (1974).

17. Hack,M. : Petri Net Languages. Cambridge, Mass., MIT, Project MAC, Comp. Struct. Group Memo 124, (1975).

18. Hack,M. : The Equality Problem for Vector Addition Systems is Undecidable. Theoretical Comp. Sci., 2, pp 77-95, (1976).

19. Holt,A.W. : Final Report for the Project 'Development of the Theoretical Foundations for Description and Analysis of Discrete Information Systems'. Wakefield, Mass., Applied Data Res., Report CADD-7405-2011, (1974).

20. Ibarra,O.H. : Reversal-Bounded Multicounter Machines and Their Decision Problems. Journ. ACM, 25, pp 116-133, (1978).

21. Jaffe,J.M. : Semilinear Sets and Applications. Cambridge, Mass., MIT, Lab. for Comp. Sci., MIT/LCS/TR-183, (1977).

22. Jantzen,M. : Structured Representation of Knowledge by Nets as an Aid for Teaching and Research. in these Proceedings.

23. Jones,N.D.,Landweber,L.H.,Lien,Y.E. : Complexity of Some Problems in Petri nets. Theoretical Comp. Sci., 4, pp 277-299, (1977).

24. Karp,R.M.,Miller,R.E. : Parallel Program Schemata. Journ. Comp. Syst. Sci., 3, pp 147-195, (1969).

25. Keller,R.M. : A Fundamental Theorem of Asynchronous Parallel Computation. in: Parallel Processing, Lecture Notes in Computer Sci., 24, pp 102-112, Berlin: Springer, (1975).

26. Krieg,B. : Petrinetze und Zustandsgraphen. Univ. Hamburg, Fachbereich Informatik, Bericht Nr. IFI-HH-B-29/77, (1977).

27. Krieg,B. : Petrinetze. Univ. Hamburg, Fachbereich Informatik, unpublished lecture notes, (1979).

28. Landweber,L.H.,Robertson,E.L. : Properties of Conflict Free and Persistent Petri Nets. Journ. ACM, 25, pp 352-364, (1978).

29. Latteux,M. : Cônes Rationnels Commutativement Clos. R.A.I.R.O., Informatique théorique, 11, pp 29-51, (1977).

30. Lautenbach,K.,Schmid,H.A. : Use of Petri Nets for Proving Correctness of Concurrent Process Systems. in: Information Processing 74, pp 187-191, North-Holland Publ. Comp., (1974).

31. Lipton,R.J. : The Reachability Problem Requires Exponential Space. Yale Univ., Dept. of Comp. Sci., Research Report #62, (1976).

32. Liu,L.,Weiner,P. : A Characterization of Semilinear Sets. Journ. Comp. Syst. Sci., 4, pp 299-307, (1970).

33. Matiyasevič,Y. : Enumerable Sets are Diophantine. (Russian), Dokl. Akad. Nauk, SSSR, 191, pp 279-282, (1970). Translation in: Soviet Math. Doklady, 12, pp 249-254, (1971).

34. Mayr,E.W. : The Complexity of the Finite Containment Problem for Petri Nets. Cambridge, Mass., MIT, Lab. for Comp. Sci., MIT/LCS/TR-181, (1977).

35. Memmi,G. : Fuites dans les Réseaux de Petri. R.A.I.R.O., Informatique Theorique, 12, pp 125-144, (1978).

36. Peterson,J.L. : Computation Sequence Sets. Journ. Comp. Syst. Sci., 13, pp 1-24, (1976).

37. Petri,C.A. : Interpretations of Net Theory. GMD Bonn, Interner Bericht Nr. ISF-75-07, (1975).

38. Rackoff,C. : The Covering and Boundedness Problems for Vector Addition Systems. Theoretical Comp. Sci., 6, pp 223-231, (1978).

39. Thiet-Dung Huynh : On the Complexity of Semilinear Sets. Saarbrücken Univ. des Saarlandes, Fachbereich Angewandte Mathematik und Informatik, Bericht Nr. A 79/16, (1979).

40. Ullrich,G. : Der Entwurf von Steuerstrukturen für parallele Abläufe mit Hilfe von Petrinetzen. Univ. Hamburg, Fachbereich Informatik, Bericht Nr. IFI-HH-B-36/77, (1977).

41. Valk,R.,Vidal-Naquet,G. : On the Rationality of Petri Net Languages. Lecture Notes in Comp. Sci., 48, pp 319-328, (1977).

LINEAR ALGEBRA IN NET THEORY

by

G. MEMMI

ECA-Automation (Paris)

and

G. ROUCAIROL

LITP, Institut de Programmation - Université Paris VI

INTRODUCTION

Various physical phenomena are characterized by some conservation and stability principles which are also found in Net Theory. Basically, for place-transition nets, these principles are related to the reproducibility of a set of events (or firing of transitions) and the conservation of a weighted sum of tokens over the evolution of the markings of a net. These facts, which may also be viewed as particular instances of invariant assertions about the behaviour of a system, can be conveniently determined using Integer Linear Algebra as first pointed out in [LA 73]. This technique, which allows one to find properties of a net depending only on its structure and valuable for all its initial states, have been shown useful either in analyzing and proving correctness of concurrent systems or in evaluating their performance [GEL 80]. [LAS 74], [MU 77], [RA 74], [SI 80].

In the first part of the paper (section 2) we define structural properties of a net related respectively to its boundedness and the reproducibility of firing of its transitions. For each of these properties we give an algebraïc characterization which on the one hand points out their duality aspects and on the other hand allows a synthesis of their interaction into a same net from which necessary conditions for liveness are deduced (section 3).

In the last part of the paper (section 4) we show that structural properties of a net can be found only by looking at a limited number of its components (so-called minimal). This result provides a tool which may be used either in order to find local properties of concurrent system or in order to derive global properties from the assembling of subsystems. As an application, we define an upper bound of the marking of a place as well as another necessary condition for livaness.

1. BASIC DEFINITIONS AND NOTATIONS

In this paper we shall consider a place-transition net as a 5-tuples $N = (S,T\ ;\ F,K,W)$ with an infinite capacity of places $(K : S \to \{\omega\})$. The converse of N is a net $N^- = (S,T\ ;\ F^{-1}, K, W^-)$ such that $\forall\ (y,x) \in F^{-1}\ W^-(y,x) = W(x,y)$. A marked net is a net N together with an initial marking M_o and it is denoted (N,M_o).

The firing of a transition t, enabled under a marking M and leading to a marking M' is denoted $M(t>M'$. This notation is naturally extended over any sequence of firings of transitions. Let v be a firing sequence, the characteristic vector of v, denoted $\bar{v}$, is a vector of integers indexed by the set of transitions, whose each component represents the number of occurrences of the corresponding transition in v.

Let v be a firing sequence from a marking M towards a marking $M'(M(v>M')$, then it can be easily deduced from the firing rule that M and M' satisfy the fundamental equation :

$$\boxed{M' = M + C\,\bar{v}} \quad (*)$$

where C is the incident matrix of the net (for a definition of C, see reference [JAV 80] in this volume). This equation is the basic object with which we could apply linear algebra techniques, in the sequel. But let us remark that dealing with such an equation any information is lost about the order of transitions in v.

2. STRUCTURAL PROPERTIES OF NETS AND THEIR ALGEBRAIC CHARACTERIZATION

We characterize structural properties of a net related respectively to boundedness and reproducibility of firing of transitions. Then we come up to the notions of S-or T-invariant which are representative of some principles of stability and conservation. (All the proofs of the results presented here in are not given but they are extensively described in [ME 78]).

2.1. Properties related to boundedness

2.1.1. *Definitions*

- A net N is strongly bounded iff for any initial marking, the marked net is bounded
- A net N is intrinsically strongly bounded (i.s.b) iff any net, obtained from N by reversing the direction of all the edges incident to any subset of T, is strongly bounded.

Remark. Reversing the direction of the edges incident to a transition t implies a change of the sign of the elements of the column corresponding to t in C .

2.1.2. Algebraic characterization

Notation

If x and y are two vectors with n components,
$x = (x_i)_{i=1,\ldots,n}$; $y = (y_i)_{i=1,\ldots,n}$.
We write $x \gneq y$ iff $x \geq y$ and $x \neq y$
$x > y$ iff for all i in $[1,n]$ $x_i > y_i$

Let N be a net.

Theorem 1. The following propositions are equivalent
(1) N is strongly bounded *(2)* $\nexists g \geq 0\ Cg \gneq 0$ *(3)* $\exists f > 0\ f^T C \leq 0$

Sketch of proof

The equivalence between *(2)* and *(3)* may be derived from Farkas' lemma [HU 69] (see appendix).

(1) → (2) : Suppose there exists $g \geq 0$ such that $Cg \gneq 0$, then there exist two markings M,M', and a firing sequence v such that $\bar{v} = g$ and $M(v{>}M' = M + Cg$. (take as the marking $M(p)$ of any place p an integer greater or equal to $\sum_{t \in p^{\bullet}} g_t\ W(p,t)$). Hence $M' \gneq M$. Therefore N is not bounded.

(3) → (1) : Let M_0 be an initial marking of N . Let $M \in (M_0>$ and $g \in \mathbb{N}^{|T|}$ such that $M = M_0 + Cg$. Consider the scalar product $f^T.M = f^T.M_0 + (f^T C).g$, we deduce then from *(3)* : for all place $p \in S, M(p) \leq \frac{f^T.M_0}{f(p)}$, therefore N is bounded.
(Remark that this result gives an upper bound for the marking of every place) □

By similar considerations we obtain

Theorem 2. The following propositions are equivalent
(1) N is i.s.b *(2)* $\nexists g\ Cg \gneq 0$ *(3)* $\exists f > 0,\ f^T C = 0$

Theorem 3. The following propositions are equivalent
(1) N^- is strongly bounded *(2)* $\nexists g \geq 0,\ Cg \lneq 0$ *(3)* $\exists f > 0,\ f^T C \geq 0$

2.2. Properties related to reproducibility of firing of transitions

2.2.1. Definitions

- a net N is strongly non-finishing (s.n.f) iff there exist an initial marking M_0 and a firing sequence v from M_0 such that every transition occurs infinitely often in v.

<u>Remark</u>. If N is live for some initial marking, then N is s.n.f.

- a net N is <u>intrinsically strongly non-finishing</u> (i.s.n.f) iff any net, obtained from N by reversing the direction of all the edges incident to any subset of S, is s.n.f.

<u>Remark</u>. Reversing the direction of the edges incident to a place p implies a change of the sign of the elements of the row corresponding to p in C.

2.2.2. *Algebraic characterization*

Theorem 4. The following propositions are equivalent
(1) N is s.n.f *(2)* $\exists\, g > 0\ Cg \geq 0$ *(3)* $\nexists\, f \geq 0\ f^T C \lneq 0$

Theorem 5. The following propositions are equivalent
(1) N is i.s.n.f *(2)* $\exists\, g > 0\ \ Cg = 0$ *(3)* $f\ \ f^T C \not\gtrless 0$.

Theorem 6. The following propositions are equivalent.
(1) N^- is s.n.f *(2)* $\exists\, g > 0\ \ Cg \leq 0$ *(3)* $\exists\, f > 0\ \ f^T C \not\gtrless 0$

2.3. S and T-invariants

Définitions

- a vector $x \in \mathbb{N}^{|S|}$ (resp. $\mathbb{N}^{|T|}$) is called an <u>S-invariant</u> (resp. a <u>T-invariant</u>) iff $x^T \cdot C = 0$ (resp. $Cx = 0$)
- the set of places (resp. of transitions) whose corresponding components in x are <u>strictly positive</u> is called the <u>support</u> of x and is denoted by $\|x\|$.
- an <u>S-invariant net</u> (resp. an <u>T-invariant net</u>) is a net whose set of places (resp. of transitions) is the support of an S-invariant (resp. an T-invariant).

The existence of an S-invariant or an T-invariant means that the Kirchoff's law is satisfied respectively either for the transitions or the places of a net. Moreover we can deduce easily from equation *(*)* two fundamental properties of the behaviour of a net which justify-a posteriori- the name of invariant.

Property 1

- x is an S-invariant iff for any initial marking M_0, for any marking $M \in (M_0>$ $x^T M = x^T M_0$
- x is an T-invariant iff there exist a firing sequence v and a marking M such that $M(v>M$ and $\bar{v} = x$.

Remark. If x is either an T-or an S-invariant, then $^{\bullet}\|x\| = \|x\|^{\bullet}$ (if x is an S-invariant, this implies $\|x\|$ is both a siphon (a dead lock) and a trap [CO 72], [BES 75]).
From theorems 2 and 5 we deduce immediately :

Property 2.

A net is an S-invariant net (resp. an T-invariant net) iff it is intrinsically strongly bounded (resp. i.s.n.f)

The notion of invariant has been shown very useful for proving assertions about the behaviour of a system. For some applications of this notion the reader my refer to [GLT 80] section 4 and 7, and [SIF 80] in this volume.

3. CORRELATION OF STRUCTURAL PROPERTIES

A straightforward application of the algebraic interpretation theorems we have obtained in the preceding section, leads to the following result which synthetizes several sparse results [LAS 74], [LI 76], [SI 78].

First of all we split our propositions into two groups :

Group 1

(a) N is strongly bounded $(\exists f > 0,\ f^TC \leq 0)$
(b) N^- is strongly bounded $(\exists f > 0,\ f^TC \geq 0)$
(a,b) N is a S-invariant net $(\exists f > 0,\ f^TC = 0)$

Group 2 (dual)

(a) N^- is s.n.f $(\exists g > 0,\ Cg \leq 0)$
(b) N is s.n.f $(\exists g > 0,\ Cg \geq 0)$
(a,b) N is a T-invariant net $(\exists g > 0,\ Cg = 0)$

Theorem 7.

If one proposition of group *1(a)* and one proposition of group *2(b)* are true, <u>or</u>, one proposition of group *1(b)* and one proposition of group *2(a)* are also true then all the propositions of the two groups are true and it also may be shown that the graph of N is strongly connected.
From this result and the preceding ones we derive corollaries which give necessary conditions for a net to be either live or live and bounded.

Corollary 1.

If N is bounded and if there exists an initial marking M_0 such that the marked net (N,M_0) is live, then N is both a T-invariant net and a S-invariant net.

Corollary 2.

If there exists $f \geq 0$, $f^T C \lneq 0$ then

(1) there does not exist an initial marking M_0 such that (N,M_0) is live.

(2) N is not a T-invariant net.

Corollary 3.

If there exists $f \geq 0$, $f^T C \gneq 0$ then

(1) if there exists an initial marking M_0, such that (N,M_0) is live, then (N,M_0) is not bounded

(2) N is not a T-invariant net.

Corollary 4.

If there exists $g \geq 0$ $Cg \lneq 0$ then

(1) if N is strongly bounded, then it does not exist a marking M_0, such that (N,M_0) is live.

(2) N is not a S-invariant net

Corollary 5.

If there exists $g \geq 0$ $Cg \gneq 0$ then

(1) N is not strongly bounded

(2) N is not a S-invariant net

4. DECOMPOSITION OF INVARIANTS AND APPLICATIONS

We define a set of generators for the invariants of a net.
Obviously a set of generators is given by the set of minimal invariants for the usual partial ordering $\geq$ on vectors. But we are going to introduce a smaller set of generators.

Definition

Let x be either a S-invariant or a T-invariant, $\|x\|$ is minimal iff it does not contain another support of invariant but itself and the empty-set.

One must point out that the support of a minimal invariant is not necessarily minimal.

Example

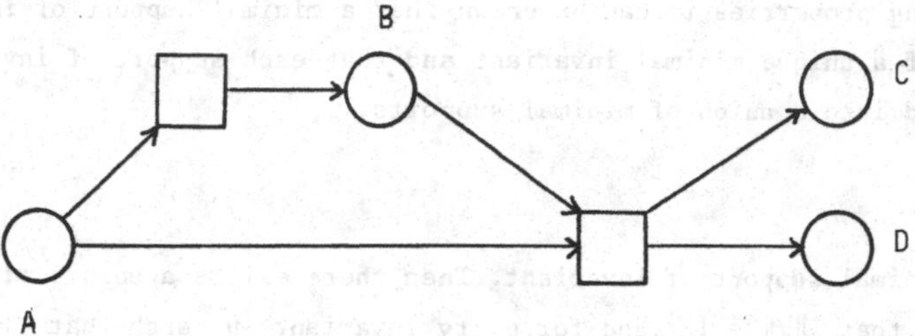

There are two minimal supports of S-invariants : {A,B,C} and {A,B,D} . The corresponding minimal invariants are respectively $(1,1,2,0)^T$, $(1,1,0,2)^T$. But the support of the minimal invariant $(1,1,1,1)^T$ is {A,B,C,D} .

Remark.

The set of places (resp. of transitions) of a strongly-connected state machine (resp. marked graph) is a minimal support of an S-invariant (resp. an T-invariant).

4.1. Basic properties of invariants

Property 3.

Let x,y be two invariants (of the same kind) and $(k,l) \in \mathbb{N}^2$

- $kx + ly$ is an invariant
- if $x-y$ has no negative component it is an invariant
- $\|x + y\| = \|x\| \cup \|y\|$

Property 4.

Let I_0 and I_1 be two supports of invariants with $I_1 \subsetneq I_0$

Then there exists another support of invariant I_2 such that $I_0 = I_1 \cup I_2$ and $I_2 \subsetneq I_0$

(with $I_0 = \|x\|$, $I_1 = \|y\|$, one can find $k = \prod_{i \in I_1} y(i)$ and $l = \min_{j \in I_0} (x(j) \prod_{i \in I_1 - \{j\}} y(i))$ such that $kx - ly$ is an invariant and $\|kx - ly\| = I_2$) .

4.2. Decomposition theorems

From the preceding properties it can be shown that a minimal support of invariant is the support of a unique minimal invariant and that each support of invariant may be decomposed into a union of minimal supports.

Theorem 8.

Let I_0 be a minimal support of invariant. Then there exists a unique minimal invariant x such that $\|x\| = I_0$ and for every invariant y such that $\|y\| = I_0$ there exists an integer h such that $y = hx$.

Sketch of proof

Let x be a minimal invariant such that $\|x\| = I_0$ (obviously such a x exists) and let y such that $\|y\| = I_0$. As in property 4 we can find k and l such that $ky - lx$ is an invariant and $\|ky - lx\| \subseteq I_0$. But I_0 is minimal thus $ky = lx$. x is minimal, hence $l > k$ therefore x is unique. Consider now the euclidian division $l = h\,k + r$ with $0 \leq r < k$; so $k(y - hx) = rx$. If $r \neq 0$ then $y - hx \leq x$ which contradicts x being minimal. Therefore $y = hx$ (Q.E.D)

Theorem 9.

Let I_0 be the support of an invariant and $I_1, \ldots, I_m$ be the minimal supports contained in I_0 then :

- $I_0 = \bigcup_{i=1,m} I_i$
- for every invariant y such that $\|y\| = I_0$, $y = \sum_{i=1,m} \lambda_i x_i$ where $\forall i \in [1,m]\ \lambda_i \in \mathbb{Q}^+$ and x_i is an invariant whose support is I_i .

  (The proof is by induction on I_0 using property 4 and a reasoning similar to the preceding proof).

4.3. Applications of the decomposition theorems for S-invariants

We deduce from the preceding decomposition results an upper bound of the marking of a place and a necessary for liveness.

Theorem 10.

Let p be a place of a support of an S-invariant in a net N, $I_1, \ldots I_m$ the minimal supports containing p, $x_1, \ldots, x_m$ the minimal S invariants associated with the preceding supports and M_0 an initial marking of N . Then for any reachable marking M, $M(p)$ is finite and

$$M(p) \leq \min_{y \in Y} \left[\frac{M_0^T \cdot y}{y(p)} \right] = \min_{i=1,\ldots,m} \left[\frac{M_0^T \cdot x_i}{x_i(p)} \right]$$

where Y is the set of S-invariants whose supports contain p.

(This theorem means that an upper bound of the marking of p may be known only by considering the minimal supports containing p).

Theorem 11.

Let (N, M_0) be a live marked net. Then for every minimal S-invariant x such that $\|x\|$ is minimal we have :

$$M_0^T \cdot x \geq \max_{t \in T} \left[\sum_{p \in S} x(p) \cdot W(p,t)\right]$$

5. EXAMPLE

Consider the following net

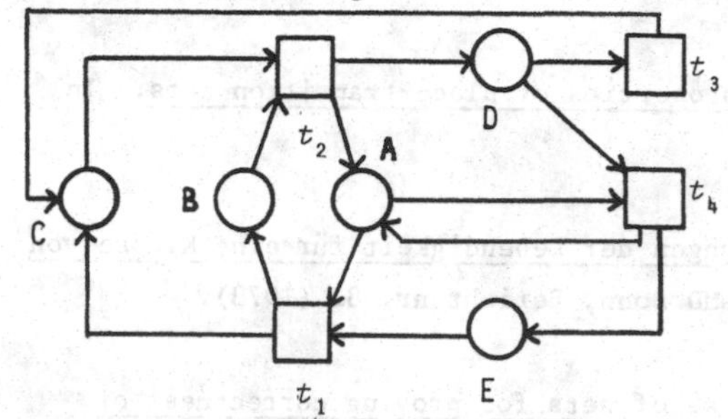

For this net there are two minimal supports of S-invariants :
$\|(1,1,0,0,0)^T\| = \{A,B\}$,
$\|(0,0,1,1,1)^T\| = \{C,D,E\}$.
Applying theorem 10 for the initial marking $M_0 = (1,1,1,5,3)^T$, we get
$M(A) \leq 2$, $M(B) \leq 2$, $M(C) \leq 9$,
$M(D) \leq 9$, $M(E) \leq 9$.

Consider now the following vector $f = (0,1,0,1,1)^T$, we have $f^T C = (0,0,-1,0)^T \leq 0$.
Then from corollary 2, we know that N is not live for any initial marking and N is not a T-invariant.

BIBLIOGRPHY

[BES75] E. Best, H. Schmid. Systems of open paths in Petrinets. Proc. of the Symp. ou M.F.C.S. 75. Lect. Notes in Comp. Sc. n° 32. Springer Verlag ed. 1975.

[CO72] F. Commoner. Deadlocks in Petri nets. CA-7206-2311, Applied Data Research, Wakefield, Mass., June 1972.

[HU69] T.C. HU. Integer Programming and networks flows. Addison Wesley reading. Mass. 1969.

[GLT80] H.G. Genrich, K. Lautenbach, P.S. Thiagarajan. An overview of net theory. In this volume.

[HA72] M. Hack. Analysis of production schemata by Petri nets. M.S. Thesis, MAC TR 94, MIT Cambridge Mass. sept. 1972.

[JAV80] M. Jantzen, R. Valk. Formal properties of place-transition nets. In this volume.

[LA73] K. Lautenbach. Exakte Bedingungen der Lebendigkeit für eine Klasse von Petri-Netzen. St. Augustin, GMD Bonn, Bericht nr. 82 (1973).

[LAS74] K. Lautenbach, H.A. Schmid. Use of nets for proving correctness of concurrent systems. Proc. IFIP Congress 74. North-Holland Publ. Comp. (1974).

[LI76] Y.E. Lien. Termination properties of generalized Petri-nets. S.I.A.M. j. Comp., June 1976, Vol. 5, n°2, pages 251-265.
- A note on transition systems. J. inf. Sciences 1976, vol.10, n°4, p. 347-362.

[ME77] G. Memmi. Semiflows and invariants. Applications in Petri nets theory. Journées d'étude sur les réseaux de Petri. A.F.C.E.T. Institut de Programmation. Paris mars 1977.

[ME78] G. Memmi. -Application of the semiflow to the boundedness and liveness problems in the Petri-nets theory. Proc. of the Conf. on Information Sciences and Systems. Johns Hopkins University. Baltimore Maryland. march 1978.

- Fuites et semi-flots dans les Réseaux de Petri. Thèse de Docteur-Ingénieur. Institut de Programmation. Université Paris 6. Dec. 1978.

[ME79] G. Memmi. Notion de dualité et de symétrie dans les réseaux de Petri. Proc. of the Symp. on Semantics of concurrent computations. Evian July 1979. Lect. Notes in Comp. Sciences n°70. Springer-Verlag ed.

[MU77] T. Murata. State equations, controllability, maximal matchings of Petri nets. IEEE Trans. Autom. and Control. Vol AC-22 n°3, June 1977, pp. 412-416.

[RA74] G. Ramchandani. Analysis of asynchronous concurrent systems by timed Petri-nets. Ph. D thesis. MAC-TR-120. Cambridge Mass. Feb. 1974.

[SI78] J. Sifakis. Structural properties of Petri-nets. Proc. of M.F.C.S. 78 Lect. Notes in Comp. Sciences. Springer Verlag ed. 1978.

[SI80] J. Sifakis. Use of Petri-nets for performance evaluation. In this volume.

Appendix

Theorem (Farkas, Camion, Abadie)

One and only one of the two following systems has a solution :

$$S_1 : Ax \geq b$$

$$S_2 : \begin{cases} u \geq 0 \\ u^T A = 0 \\ u^T b > 0 \end{cases}$$

(Elements of A, u, b, x belong to $\mathbb{Z}$)

Corollary

One and only one of the two systems has a solution :

$$S_1 : \begin{cases} Ax \geq b \\ x \geq 0 \end{cases} \qquad S_2 : \begin{cases} u \geq 0 \\ u^T A \leq 0 \\ u^T b > 0 \end{cases}$$

ATOMICITY OF ACTIVITIES

by

E. Best

Computing Laboratory
University of Newcastle upon Tyne
England

Abstract

Using structured occurrence graphs, we present an operational characterisation of the atomicity of activities. Broadly, activities are defined to occur atomically if they do not interleave with each other. We discuss our characterisation and use it as a starting point for the discussion of implementation issues and the problem of incorporating atomic actions into a concurrent programming language. We finally examine the use of structured occurrence graphs in connection with techniques for error recovery in decentralised systems.

Contents

Introduction

To date, software faults are likely to be present in every major computer system. The fact that it may be an extremely demanding task to write a correct program has helped to instil in the "scientific community" grevious doubts as to whether it is at all possible to produce programs which are both large and correct. [DEM79], for example, have gone to the point of suggesting that the notion of correctness is a priori void for large programs.

In these notes we refrain from explicitly refuting the arguments brought forward in [DEM79]. Rather, without trying to belittle the theoretical and practical difficulties of proving the correctness of programs, we take it as our starting point that there is not any fundamental obstacle in the way of program validation; as far as provability in general is concerned, no distinction can be made between a small program and a large program. This we take to be true for software as such, i.e. irrespective of any particular hardware implementation. (In the opinion of the author it is quite possible to go one step further by stating that the property of being provable is a characteristic property of software).

Usually the validation of a program, say S, involves a theorem of the form

{P} S {Q}

which means that whenever S is executed in an initial state satisfying the assertion P then the assertion Q holds upon termination of S (if at all S terminates).

For example, for the program

```
S1        do x<y --> y := y-x
          [] y<x --> x := x-y
          od
```

one can prove that {P1} S1 {Q1} with

P1: x = X and y = Y are natural numbers (X and Y are constants)

Q1: x = y = gcd(X,Y).

For the benefit of readers not conversant with guarded commands (the programming language of [DIJ76] which we use in these notes) we include a brief description. The repetitive clause

<u>do</u> B1 --> S1 [] ... [] Bn --> Sn <u>od</u>,

where the Bi are boolean expressions and the Si are statements, is executed by repeatedly selecting one of the true Bi and executing the corresponding Si, while not all Bi are false. Thus, for example, <u>do</u> B --> S <u>od</u> is equivalent to <u>while</u> B <u>do</u> S. The alternative clause

<u>if</u> B1 --> S1 [] ... [] Bn --> Sn <u>fi</u>

is executed by selecting a true Bi and executing Si just once; if no true Bi can be found then the execution is aborted. Thus, for example, <u>if</u> B --> S1 [] <u>not</u> B --> S2 <u>fi</u> is equivalent to <u>if</u> B <u>then</u> S1 <u>else</u> S2.

The proof that S1 computes the greatest common divisor of x and y can be derived from the working of the components of S1 (i.e., comparison, subtraction, assignment and repetitive clause) which is assumed to be known. In order that such a derivation be formally possible it is imperative that there be a formal understanding of all components, i.e. that there be a formal semantics. The reader is referred to [DIJ76] for the formal semantics of guarded commands.

Let us assume that the behaviour of a given program, say S, has been proved to be

{P} S {Q}.

Given an initial state satisfying P then for a final state to actually satisfy Q the essential requirement is that the <u>only</u> way of changing the state is through actions of S.

This requirement, however, is jeopardised in the presence of concurrency. (In a particular implementation it may also be violated by hardware failures, but we ignore this case). For suppose that parallel to S there is a program S' with the (proved) behaviour

{P'} S' {Q'}

where P' and Q' refer to the same state space as P and Q. Then due to possible interleaving of S and S' the overall behaviour cannot in general be deduced from the two individual behaviours {P} S {Q} and {P'} S' {Q'}.

Let us consider a particular example. The effect of the program

```
S2        (x,y) := (y,x)
```

is to interchange the values of x and y. (We have used the "concurrent assignment statement" whose semantics require x and y first to be read and then to be changed). Formally, {P2} S2 {Q2} with

P2: x = X and y = Y are natural numbers

Q2: x = Y and y = X.

Let us now consider the composite system

S1 || S2,

where we use the operator || to express parallel operation.

Nothing that has been said so far prevents the possibility of, say, S1 detecting a state in which $0 < x < y$, then S2 interchanging the values of x and y and finally S1 subtracting x from y. As can easily be appreciated, a negative value would thus be assigned to y.

In other words the overall behaviour of the composite system S1 || S2 cannot be deduced from the two individual behaviours {P1} S1 {Q1} and {P2} S2 {Q2}. The reason is that the latter describe only the <u>overall</u> behaviour of S1 and S2, not their detailed behaviour. Thus in a concurrent environment care must be taken to ensure that an operation in fact <u>does</u> have the overall effect it can be formally proved to have by considering its components only.

We take such care by introducing <u>atomic actions</u>. We enclose the two pieces of program in angle brackets:

```
S1'       <do x < y --> y := y-x
           [] y < x --> x := x-y
           od>

S2'       <(x,y) := (y,x)>
```

and postulate that the two components of the new composite system

S1' || S2'

"don't interleave". All executions of S1' and S2' occur as if "atomically" or "instantaneously". We use the angle bracket notation out of convenience and because it has already been widely propagated (see, for example, [DLM78], [DIJ78] and [VLS79]).

Thus in the new composite system S1' || S2' no negative values will be computed (assuming, of course, that x and y are positive initially). In fact the overall effect of S1' || S2' is the same as the overall effect of S1. This can now be deduced from the two formulas {P1} S1 {Q1} and {P2} S2 {Q2}, using the property of the gcd of being a symmetric function.

What exactly does it mean that the two actions "don't interleave", or "occur atomically"? This is the question to be answered in the present notes. In its answer the occurrence net model defined in [GES80] proves to be of use. (Actually we use occurrence graphs, but throughout these notes we make little distinction between the two. Their precise correlation is given in section 1). To the knowledge of the author, occurrence nets have first been studied in [HOL68], and their suitability for the characterisation of atomicity has first been stipulated in [MER77]. The present notes in fact immediately originate from [MER77].

The idea behind our precise characterisation of atomicity is really quite simple. We exclude occurrences of the type described above, whereby part of S1 occurs, then (part of) S2 and then again part of S1. However, it turns out that the simplicity of the idea is elusive. We need a surprisingly elaborate argument to capture its formal essence. We have found that structured occurrence graphs (or some equivalent formalism) are the appropriate mathematical framework in which that argument can be made. We define structured occurrence graphs in section 1 and present the argument (i.e. our characterisation of atomicity) in section 2.

The fact that structured occurrence graphs are natural for our characterisation of atomicity makes a curious contrast with the empirical observation that in most application programs (to date at least) one level of atomicity is sufficient. [DLM78], for example, go so far as to disallow the nesting of atomic actions. We remark to this that our characterisation of atomicity is an operational one, that is, we consider as our basic formal object not a program but a single computation arising from a program.

Before we go into the details of our formalism let us summarise our motivation. We assume that a piece of program, say S, can be proved to have a certain overall behaviour. The specification of S as an atomic action means that S is guaranteed to behave accordingly, even in the presence of possible interferences by other programs. Thus the characteristic property of an atomic action is that it can, once and for all, be described by its overall behaviour, and it is this property which makes atomic actions attractive for the purposes of program verification, particularly in the case of concurrent programs.

For example, it is possible to prove that S2 has the same overall behaviour as the following program:

```
x := x-y; y := x+y; x := y-x .
```

However, unless the two programs are specified to be atomic actions, they may behave differently in a concurrent environment.

It follows as a natural objective to design concurrent programming languages so that they support atomic actions. One of the intended contributions of these notes is to provide a formally satisfactory basis for such a design.

We introduce our formalism by considering Dijkstra's process synchronisation primitives P and V which are by now traditional examples of actions with an implicit atomicity requirement (see [DIJ68], page 68). Let us re-examine what this means in the case of V. If applied to a semaphore variable s, the action V effects an "instantaneous increase of the value of s by 1". Thus V(s) is equivalent to <s:=s+1> with an integer variable s.

Assume that a single V consists of two subactions, one reading the value of s followed by one overwriting the value of s with the value of s+1. We use a graphical representation in which the two subactions are represented by boxes and their precedence relation by an arrow:

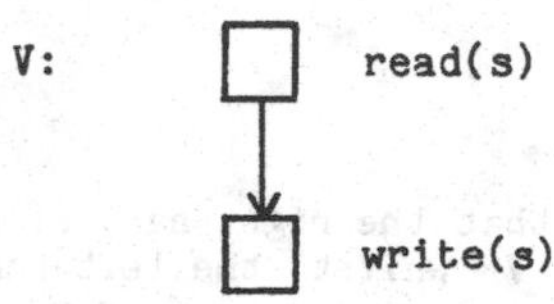

Figure 1

Each actual execution of V(s) follows this pattern and can therefore be described by such a graph. We say that an occurrence of V(s) consists of an event of reading s followed by an event of overwriting s.

More generally, a directed graph whose vertices and edges are interpreted as events and precedence relations between events, respectively, is called an occurrence graph.

Let us now consider the parallel command

S3 V(s) || V(s)

in more detail. Since the two V operations access the same variable concurrently and since the result of, say, two concurrent writes to a single variable need not be defined, an assumption has to be made about such accesses. We introduce the rule that any two accesses to a common variable must be sequenced unless both are reads.

This rule is one of the most commonplace assumptions in the whole of concurrent programming, and we mention it explicitly because we use it in all of our examples and because we believe that it has to be critically reviewed. It is discussed at the end of section 2.

A computation in which the two actions of S3 "interleave" is described by the following occurrence graph:

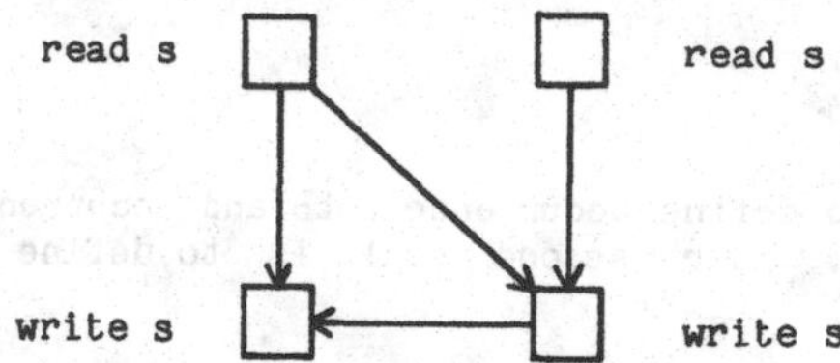

Figure 2

As a result of this computation, s is only incremented by 1 instead of, as it should be, by 2. Thus computations such as this one are meant to be excluded by the atomicity requirement of V. We say that atomicity is violated by this computation.

We extend our graphical tool to represent not only events and their relations but also atomicity requirements of actions. We represent the atomicity of V by collapsing the parts of the graph which correspond to V according to the following rule:

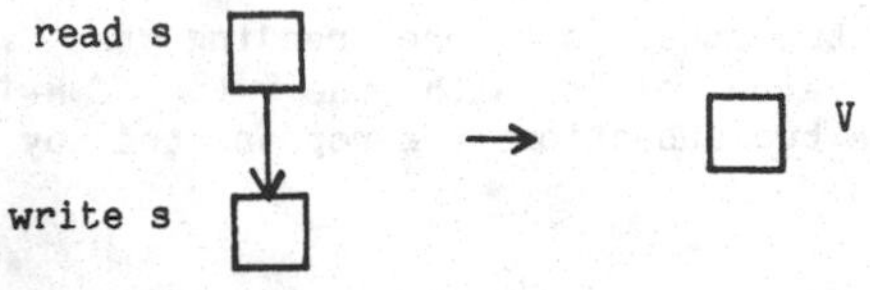

Figure 3

The interpretation of this rule is this, that the right hand side of Figure 3 gives an "atomic", or "abstract", view of V whilst the left hand side gives a more "detailed" view of V. The former describes an occurrence of V as a single event, the latter describing it as an activity comprising two sub-events.

If we describe both occurrences of V in Figure 2 as single events then we obtain:

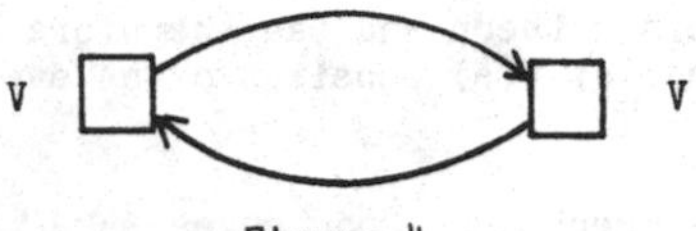

Figure 4

This directed cycle signifies that neither of the two occurrences can be identified as having occurred "before" the other. But nor are the two occurrences concurrent in the sense of being fully independent. Rather, they interleave. We define the presence of such cycles to be indicative of a violation of atomicity.

The graph shown in Figure 4 gives a more abstract view of the computation described in detail in Figure 2. The former arises from the latter through the collapsing rule shown in Figure 3. The collapsing, in turn, arises from the atomicity requirement of V.

In general, we consider a single computation which is described at various levels of detail by a collection of occurrence graphs. We assume that there is a detailed description, called the basic graph, and that all other graphs arise from the basic graph through the collapsing rule, as dictated by the atomicity specifications. Thus we are led to consider structured occurrence graphs as our tool for representing events, their interrelation and atomicity specifications.

1 Structured Occurrence Graphs

Our first goal in this section is to define occurrence nets and ocurrence graphs and to clarify their relationship. Our second goal is to define structured occurrence graphs.

For the general definition of a net see [GES80]. An occurrence net is a net (B,E;F) where B is the set of conditions, E the set of events and F the flow relation, which satisfies two properties:

- it is acyclic, and
- each condition has at most one input event and at most one output event.

As usual, conditions are represented by circles, events by boxes and the flow relation by arrows. An example of an occurrence net is shown in Figure 5:

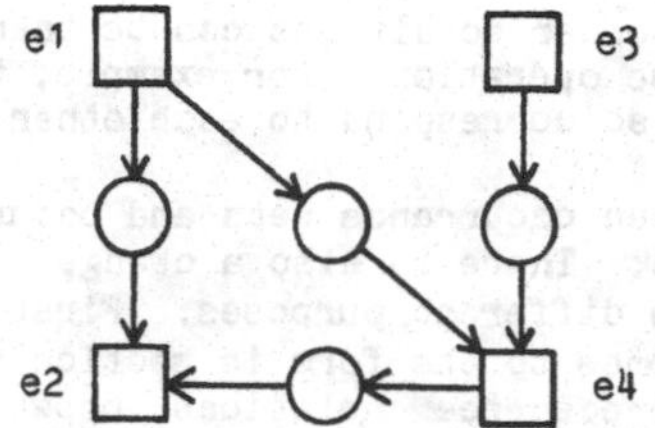

Figure 5

An occurrence graph is a directed graph whose vertices are interpreted as events and whose edges are interpreted as precedence relations between events. We allow occurrence graphs to be cyclic. For example, Figure 4 shows a cyclic occurrence graph while Figure 6 shows an acyclic occurrence graph:

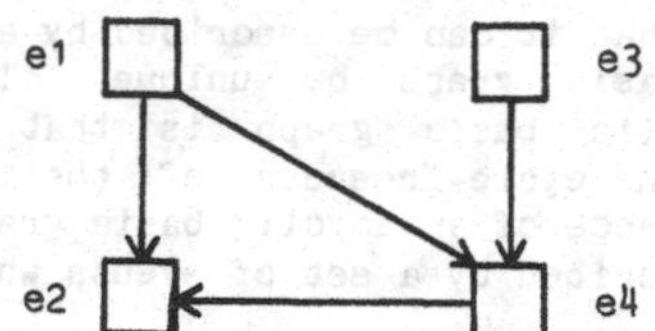

Figure 6

If e and e' are events of an occurrence graph then we write e < e' and say that e precedes e' (alternatively, that e' succeeds, or follows, e) if there is a directed path from e to e'. We say that e immediately precedes e' (or that e' immediately follows e) if a directed edge, but no longer path, leads from e to e'. Thus in Figure 6, e1 immediately precedes e4; also, e1 precedes, but does not immediately precede, e2. The notions of immediate predecessor and successor always make sense for the (finite) graphs considered in these notes. The general conditions for them to make sense are discussed in [BES80a].

In general, a pair e,e' of events stands in one of the following four relations:

(i) Neither e < e' nor e' < e; in this case, e and e' are said to be concurrent or independent (for example, e1 and e3 are concurrent in Figure 6).

(ii) e < e' but not e' < e; e is said to strictly precede e' (for example, e1 strictly precedes e2 in Figure 6).

(iii) e' < e but not e < e'; e is said to strictly follow e'.

(iv) Both e < e' and e' < e; in this case there is a cycle between e and e', and e and e' are said to interleave.

Occurrence graphs, as they have been defined above, correspond to occurrence nets as follows. Each acyclic occurrence graph can be transformed into an occurrence net if each edge

of the graph is replaced by a condition

Conversely, each occurrence net without border conditions can be transformed into an acyclic occurrence graph by the inverse operation. For example, the net shown in Figure 5 and the graph shown in Figure 6 so correspond to each other.

Thus the chief formal distinction between occurrence nets and occurrence graphs is that the latter are allowed to be cyclic. There is also a change of emphasis. The conditions of an occurrence net serve two different purposes. Firstly, they serve to model "local states"; this aspect comes to the fore in section 4 of the present notes. Secondly, they serve to define precedence relations between events, and sections 1-3 are exclusively concerned with this aspect. For this reason it is convenient to use occurrence graphs. We now turn to structured occurrence graphs.

We consider a computation generated by a program making use of atomic actions. We assume that this computation can be described by an occurrence graph to such a degree of detail that no two events of the graph interleave. We call such a graph a basic graph. For example, we regard the graph shown in Figure 2 as a basic graph of an execution of S3.

Thus, firstly we assume that the computation can be described at all by an occurrence graph. Secondly we assume that it can be described by an acyclic basic graph. We do not postulate that the basic graph be unique. The reason for postulating the existence of an acyclic basic graph is that in our view the "basicness" of an event is expressed by the cycle-freeness of the environment of this event. By postulating the existence of an acyclic basic graph we therefore postulate that the computation can be described by a set of events which are basic without further justification.

Occurrences of atomic actions correspond to subgraphs. For example, in

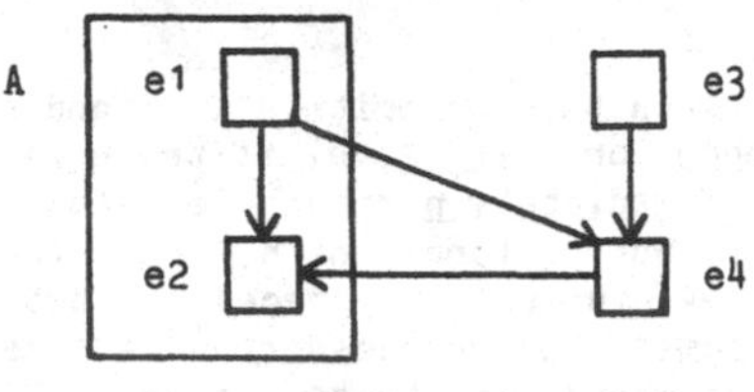

Figure 7

A is the subgraph corresponding to an occurrence of V(s). Atomicity specifications are represented by collapsing the subgraphs which correspond to occurences of atomic actions. As an example, if we collapse the subgraph A of the graph shown in Figure 7, we obtain the following new graph:

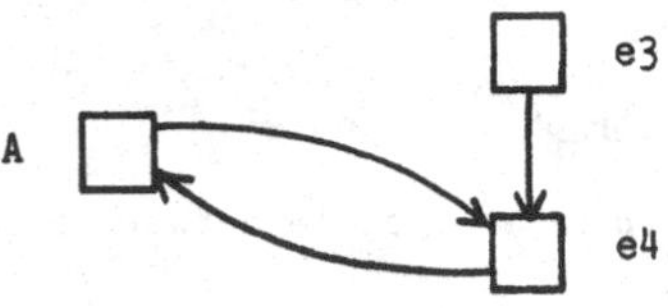

Figure 8

We now define in general what we mean by "collapsing a subgraph". Let an arbitrary occurrence graph be given. A subgraph generated by a subset of events is defined as that subset of events together with all edges which have both endpoints in the subset. Thus, in Figure 7, A is the subgraph generated by the set {e1,e2} of events.

For a subgraph A we can identify three sets of events:

- The set ^{o}A of immediate predecessors of A (= {e4} in Figure 7)
- The set $\mathring{A}$ of events generating A, or sub-events of A (= {e1,e2} in Figure 7)
- The set A^{o} of immediate successors of A (= {e4} in Figure 7).

A subgraph A of an occurrence graph can be <u>collapsed</u> by replacing the whole subgraph by a single vertex, or box, labelled A, and connecting ^{o}A to A and A to A^{o}, thus transforming the original graph into a new graph. <u>Opening</u> A is the inverse operation. For example , of the graphs shown in Figures 7 and 8, the latter is derived from the former by collapsing A, and the former from the latter by opening A.

A is viewed as an <u>extended activity</u> in the original graph and as a single event, or an <u>atomic activity</u>, in the new graph.

In addition we obey the following convention: if A contains a cycle in the original graph then a loop is appended to A in the new graph. (This is not much more than a formal nicety with the purpose of making theorems 1 and 2 true; an example will be found later in Figure 11).

<u>Theorem 1</u>: If some sub-event of A is in a cycle (in the original graph) then A is also in a cycle (in the new graph).

<u>Proof</u>: If the entire cycle is contained in A then, by the convention just introduced, a loop is appended to A. If the cycle is contained only partly in A then the collapsing of A cannot make it disappear.

This completes our definition of the collapsing rule. There may be many occurrences of atomic actions in a single computation. We now consider the computation as a whole.

As already mentioned, we assume the computation to be described in detail by an acyclic basic graph. Less detailed descriptions arise as new graphs are obtained through the collapsing rule. It is natural that (possibly large) activities, when seen as single events, are allowed to be the sub-events of (even larger) activities. However, their very nature prohibits atomic activities to partially overlap. Hence we assume that the collapsing rule defines a well-nested structure on the basic graph.

We also assume that there is one largest activity of which all others are sub-activities, namely the entire computation seen as a single event. In other words, we assume the existence of a most abstract occurrence graph consisting of a single box containing the entire basic graph.

In summary, we consider a well-nested structure, or "box structure", imposed on the basic graph. Our example, which has already been considered in parts, is shown in full in the next Figure:

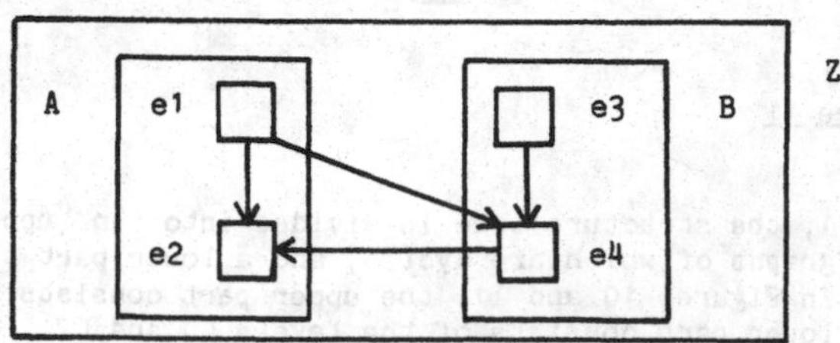

Figure 9

The box structure imposed on the basic graph can be characterised by a structure tree whose leaves are the basic events and whose root is the most abstract event (i.e. the entire computation seen as a single event, such as "Z" in Figure 9). Each "horizontal cut" through the tree identifies a level of abstraction. Corresponding to Figure 9 we have the following tree and five levels of abstraction, L0-L4:

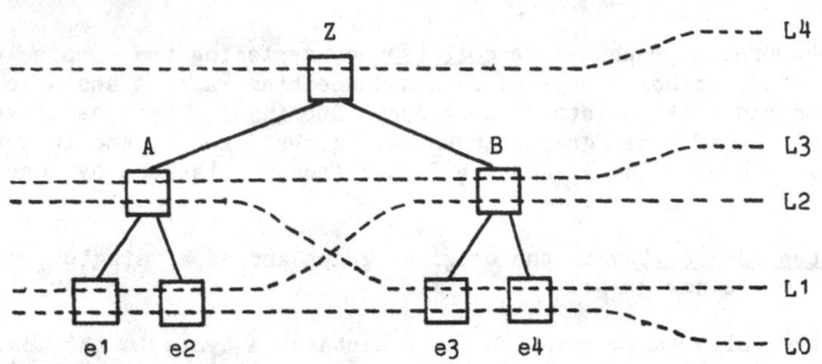

Figure 10

Of the five levels, L0 is the most detailed level and L4 is the most abstract level. For each level, an occurrence graph is defined. While the basic graph, that is the graph belonging to L0, is by definition acyclic, other level graphs may contain cycles. All level graphs are determined by the basic graph and the collapsing rule. For our example we have:

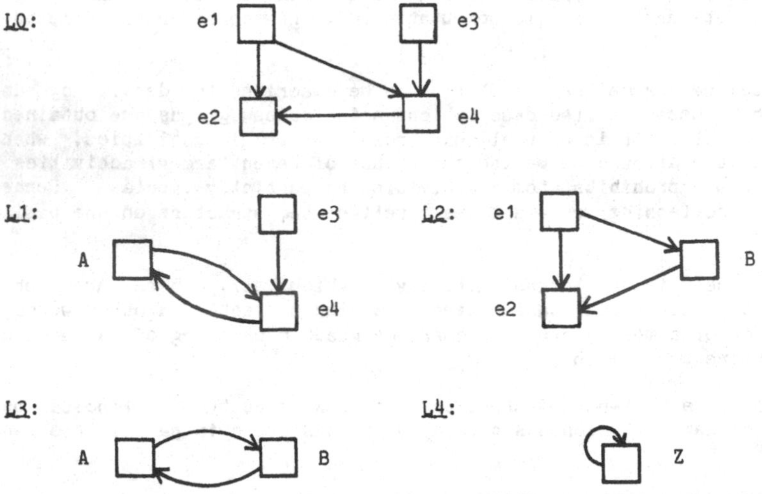

Figure 11

As a consequence of theorem 1, the structure tree is divided into an upper part (possibly empty) the level graphs of which are cyclic, and a lower part the level graphs of which are acyclic. In Figures 10 and 11, the upper part consists of the levels L1, L3 and L4, and the lower part consists of the levels L0 and L2. This remark completes our definition of structured occurrence graphs.

2 The Atomicity Criterion

Let us assume a program to be given which uses atomic actions. Let us further assume a structured occurrence graph to describe a particular execution of this program. The basic graph describes a set of primitive occurrences and their precedence relations, while the structure imposed on the basic graph describes the atomicity specifications. Our goal in this section is first to state and then to discuss the atomicity criterion.

We take the view that the "basicness" of the events of the basic graph is characterised by the fact that the latter is acyclic. We extend this view to all levels of abstraction by defining the structured graph (and the computation described by it) to violate atomicity if and only if it contains a cyclic level graph. Alternatively, a computation is defined to satisfy atomicity if all levels of abstraction (not just the basic level) describe a partial ordering of events. For example, the computation described in Figures 9-11 fails to satisfy atomicity, in accordance with our exploratory examination following Figure 2.

Thus the characteristic property of atomic actions is that they lead to partial orderings of events on all levels of abstraction. The absence of cycles, as required by the atomicity criterion, is tantamount to the absence of activity interleaving as defined in (iv) of section 1. Naturally, activity interleaving pertains not to activities in isolation but to the way in which activities are related to each other. This is the reason why the atomicity criterion specifies a property of a computation as a whole, not of a single activity.

However, we can also localise those activities which actually "cause atomicity to be violated". To this end, we define recursively what it means for an activity to occur atomically, as follows:

(A1) Basic events occur atomically.

(A2) An activity occurs atomically if
  (a) all of its sub-activities occur atomically, and
  (b) whenever it is in a cycle then opening it does not break the cycle.

Formally, the atomicity criterion and the definition (A1)-(A2) are interrelated as follows:

Theorem 2: (i) Each cycle contains at least one box which does not occur atomically.

(ii) If a box is not in a cycle then it occurs atomically.

Proof: (i) If all of the boxes of a cycle are opened completely then the cycle disappears due to the cycle-freeness of the basic graph; hence, by (A2), one of the boxes of the cycle does not occur atomically.

(ii) If a box is not in a cycle then, by theorem 1, neither are its sub-boxes, nor its sub-sub-boxes, etc; hence it occurs atomically.

Corollary: A computation satisfies atomicity if and only if all activities occur atomically.

We discuss (A1)-(A2) by considering the computation described in Figure 11 in detail. At L0, the event e4 (strictly) follows e1 and (strictly) precedes e2. Both e1 and e2, however, are part of a single activity, namely A. We say that the event e4 interferes with the activity A. This is also expressed by the fact that when A is described atomically, i.e. by a single event at L1, it is in a cycle which can be broken by opening it. Thus, (A2b) is violated and A does not occur atomically.

Thus, our definition characterises atomic occurrences by this property, that neither they nor their sub-activities are interfered with by other events in the way described in the last paragraph. Z, for example, does not occur atomically since A is a sub-activity of Z. B, on the other hand, is not interfered with by other events: even though it is in a cycle at L3, opening it does not break the cycle. Hence B occurs atomically.

In general, according to our definition, the atomic occurrence of an acticity depends on its environment (i.e. on the absence of interferences by other events). We refer to this by calling the atomicity criterion *context-dependent*. The reader should be aware of the following symmetric example which is slightly more subtle than the example which has been discussed so far. Consider the following program:

S4 <x:=0; y:=0> || <y:=1; x:=1>

and the following atomicity-violating execution of S4:

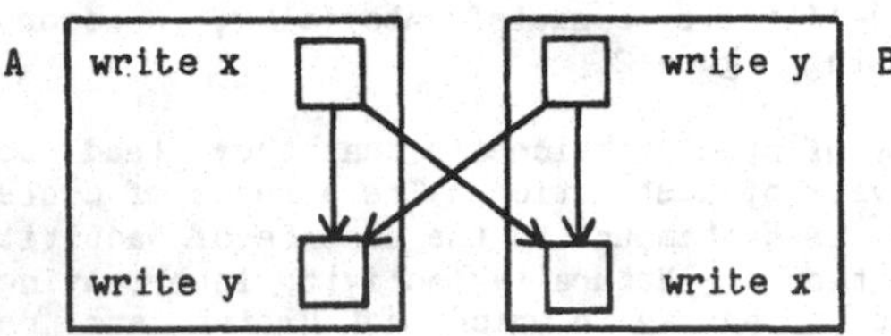

Figure 12

The graph shown in Figure 12 violates atomicity but this cannot be realised by just considering the possible interferences of the basic events with other activities. Indeed, no basic event interferes with A; neither does a basic event interfere with B. Rather, the *event B* interferes with A (i.e. it occurs after part of A and before another part of A); similarly, the *event A* interferes with the activity B. (Note that the graph shown in Figure 12 does *not* describe an atomicity-violating execution of the program

S4' <x:=0; y:=0> || (y:=1; x:=1)).

Thus, whether A occurs atomically, depends, not merely on the relationship between A and its environment, but also on the fact that B is seen atomically; and vice versa. We refer to this by calling the atomicity criterion *structure-dependent*. We have been forced to define structured occurrence graphs in the way we have done in section 1 in order to characterise atomicity correctly in cases such as described in Figure 12.

This ends our discussion of (A1)-(A2). There is also the possibility for an activity to "occur atomically" by virtue of its internal structure rather than by virtue of non-interference from outside. By "internal structure" of an activity we mean the way in which its sub-activities are arranged. We call such activities *contractions* and define them recursively as follows:

(C1) Basic events are contractions.

(C2) An activity A is a contraction if
- (a) all its sub-activities are contractions, and
- (b) for each pair of events a1,a2 such that $a1 \in {}^{\circ}A$ and $a2 \in A^{\circ}$ there is a path leading from a1 through $\hat{A}$ to a2.

(This definition may appear slightly unclear in that the sets ${}^{\circ}A$ and A° are defined only with respect to a level of abstraction; it can readily be seen, however, that if (C2b) is true on one level then it holds on all levels, and hence we are justified in neglecting the dependency on levels).

Formally, the definitions (C1)-(C2) and (A1)-(A2) are interrelated as follows:

<u>Theorem 3</u>: (i) Contractions occur atomically.

(ii) Unless A is a contraction, an atomic activity can be defined such that A does not occur atomically.

<u>Proof</u>: (i) (C2b) implies (A2b).

(ii) Suppose that A is not a contraction and that A violates (C2b) (if A satisfies (C2b) then we can make the same argument for some sub-box, or sub-sub-box, of A). Then there are $a1 \in {}^{\circ}A$ and $a2 \in A^{\circ}$ such that no path leads from a1 through $\mathring{A}$ to a2. The activity sub-graph generated by {a1,a2} leads, if seen atomically, to a cycle that can be broken by opening A.

Again we discuss (C1)-(C2) by considering Figure 11. The sub-event e4 of B, for example, follows ${}^{\circ}B$ and precedes B° (be it L2 where ${}^{\circ}B = \{e1\}$, $B^{\circ} = \{e2\}$, or L3 where ${}^{\circ}B = B^{\circ} = \{A\}$). This means that B is a contraction. Collapsing B can be thought of as contracting B into e4 - hence the admittedly not very satisfactory term.

In general, any contraction can be thought of as containing a "moment" which comes after all of its preceding events but before all of its succeeding events. Collapsing such an activity can be thought of as contracting it into this "moment". Consider again Figure 11. As we have seen, B is a contraction; A, however, is not a contraction: there is no path from e4 ($\in {}^{\circ}A$ at L1) across e1 or e2 ($\in \mathring{A}$) back to e4 ($\in A^{\circ}$ at L1).

In general, in order to detect whether or not a given activity A occurs atomically, we have to consider cycles which may extend far beyond the boundaries of A. Whether A is a contraction can however be determined from the consideration of the internal structure of A alone; and theorem 3(i) tells us that if so, then A occurs atomically. Conversely, theorem 3(ii) states, not that all non-contractions occur non-atomically, but that it is impossible to determine, from the internal structure of a non-contraction, whether or not it occurs atomically.

This ends our discussion of (C1)-(C2). To be of use, our characterisation of atomicity requires two addenda. Firstly, given an ordinary programming language supporting atomic actions, how can the structured graphs describing the executions of a program actually be derived? And secondly, given that it is possible to derive the graphs, how can it be ensured that they satisfy atomicity (i.e. how can atomicity be implemented)? In the remainder of this section we discuss the first question while a discussion of the second question is deferred to section 3. We shall be led to the main conclusion that care is needed in formalising the semantics of a language which supports atomic actions.

In our examples we use a very simple programming language which allows concurrent access to common variables. For such accesses we have introduced a sequencing rule (see the paragraphs following Figure 1) and we have used this rule in the determination of the basic graph (cf. the two basic graphs shown in Figures 2 and 12). We claim that this rule is in fact not appropriate for the derivation of the basic graph.

The deficiency we have in mind is that the phrases "reading a variable" and "overwriting a variable" lack the required precision. The difference between, say, "reading the least significant bit of a variable" and "reading the most significant bit of a variable" disappears in these phrases.

To be more specific, consider the following example:

S5 <x := 2*y <u>mod</u> 2 + x <u>mod</u> 2> || <y := 2*x <u>mod</u> 2 + y <u>mod</u> 2> .

According to our rule, the basic graph

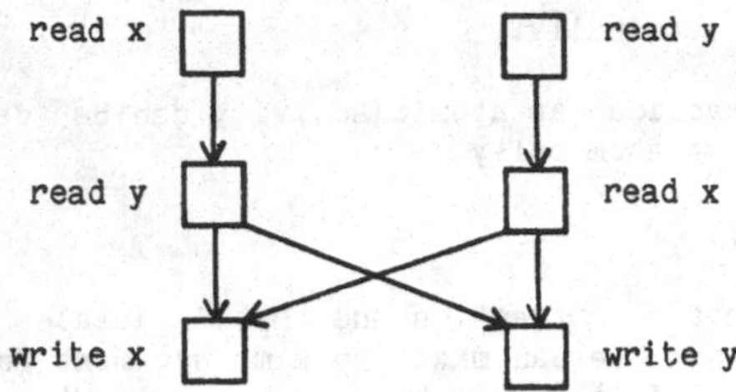

Figure 13

appears to describe an atomicity-violating execution of S5. But this is in fact not true. Rather, the interleaving shown in Figure 13 never leads to an unintended result, irrespective of the initial values of x and y.

Let us examine S5 a little closer. We can think of the two variables x and y to be composed of bits, and we claim that S5, in effect, reads only the least significant bits of x and y, and overwrites only the rest of x and y. In other words, if x0 denotes the least significant bit of x and xr the rest (i.e. x = 2*xr + x0), and similarly, y = 2*yr + y0, then S5 is only a fancy way of writing

S5' <xr := y0> || <yr := x0>

In S5', but not in S5, the actual independence of the two actions is evident.

We interpret this example as follows. Presumably for good reasons, the programmer has found it necessary to distinguish between x and y. Let us for the sake of simplicity assume that x and y encompass the entire state space; the state vector is then v = (x,y). We can say that v is "programmer-structured" into x and y, or that v = (x,y) is the virtual structure of the state vector. On the other hand, the operations contained in S5 inflict a different structure upon v, namely its partitioning into a set of four variables xr, x0, yr and y0. We could say that v is "command-structured" in this latter way, or that v = (xr,x0,yr,y0) is the actual structure of the state vector.

Because the actual structure indicates the actual manner in which variables are accessed, this structuring, rather than the more arbitrary virtual structure imposed by the programmer, ought to be the basis for the determination of the basic graph. The virtual structure indicates how actions appear to depend on each other while the actual structure determines the real dependencies between actions.

In order to determine the real dependencies it seems that in the last instance we have to decompose all variables into their constituent bits and all actions into constituent actions which are so "small" that no confusion is possible about their real dependencies. This opens up an entire programme for research: to investigate the interplay between variables and actions on all possible levels of abstraction, starting with the state vector (regarded as a single variable) and state transformations (regarded as atomic actions), via "ordinary" variables and atomic actions down to the level of bits (regarded as variables) and operations on bits (regarded as basic atomic actions).

Clearly such an across-the-board investigation runs into the problems of exploding complexity. It will therefore be necessary to subject the possible forms of the interplay between variables and actions to severe restrictions in the form of a set of axioms. It is quite conceivable that this eventually leads to an axiomatic basis for a concurrent programming language analogous to the axiomatic basis for a sequential language described in [DIJ76].

All of this has been mentioned for the sake of completeness, in order to show the limitations of our operational characterisation of atomicity. Fortunately we did not have to take these complications into account at an earlier stage; we could just assume the basic graph to describe the actual dependencies between basic events. We emphasise, however, that the operational characterisation of atomicity given in this section does not automatically lead to (but is an essential precondition for) the axiomatic incorporation of atomic actions into a programming language.

3 Implementation of Atomicity

It is a well known mathematical fact that each finite partial ordering can be extended to a total, or linear, ordering. We call such an extension a "serialisation". Since by our assumption the basic graph is acyclic it can be serialised, i.e. the basic events can be arranged in a linear ordering. We can strengthen this result in the following theorem:

Theorem 4: A structured occurrence graph satisfies atomicity if and only if the basic graph can be serialised such that all level graphs describe a linear ordering of events.

Proof: Assume that a given structured occurrence graph violates atomicity. Then there is a cyclic level graph the events of which can clearly not be serialised.

Conversely, assume that a given structured occurrence graph satisfies atomicity. We serialise the basic events by processing the structure tree in the following way: starting with the outermost box (i.e. the root of the tree) we open all boxes and arrange their sub-boxes in a linear order (which is possible by assumption); this process stops when all basic events (i.e. the leaves of the tree) have been serialised. Eventually all level graphs describe a total ordering.

Because of theorem 4 one may be tempted to believe that atomicity can always be implemented by "serial execution" (compare, for example, [DIJ78]: "atomic actions ... can be implemented by ensuring between their executions mutual exclusion in time"). This is however an illusion, as the following example shows:

S6 <V(s1);P(s2)> || <V(s2);P(s1)> ,

where two semaphore variables s1 and s2 are used, both of which we assume to be initialised to 0. The P operation is defined in [DIJ68] as "decreasing the value of its argument semaphore by 1 as soon as the resulting value would be non-negative".

Thus, before either action of S6 can finish it has to wait for the other one to start. All "executions" of S6 thus follow the pattern of Figure 12, and in other words, S6 is not implementable at all. This is not unlike a deadlock situation, and in fact one would expect a proper implementation to deadlock. (Note however that S6 can be implemented if at least one of the semaphores is initialised to 1, and also that

S6' <V(s1);P(s2)> || (V(s2);P(s1))

can be implemented.)

Thus our first observation is that the problem of implementing atomicity is related to the problem of avoiding deadlocks. There seem to be two systematic ways of dealing with programs of the kind of S6: either we could try to prohibit them by suitably restricting the semantic power of the programming language, or we could postulate them to be equivalent to a special invalid command, say the "abort" command.

The second possiblity would be similar in spirit to the course taken in [DIJ76] where non-terminating loops are also semantically equated to "abort". The author is however not satisfied with such an equivalence, for two reasons. Firstly, it seems possible and reasonable (see [BES80b]) to interpret the "abort" command of [DIJ76] operationally as abolishing the state space in which it is executed. This makes it decidedly inequivalent to either infinite loops or programs of the type of S6. Secondly, S6 is just a trivial program exposing a pattern which might in other programs be deeply hidden. Proving the absence of this pattern might not be easy, especially as it may extend over an arbitrary number of concurrent actions. Hence equating such patterns with "abort" is liable to distract the programmer's attention away from the obligation of proving their absence.

Let us therefore in the remainder of this section settle for an attempt to prohibit the pattern exposed in S6. We first remark that the "wait" command which is implicit in the P operation is not the cause of the trouble. As remarked rightly in [LOM77], infinite looping can be regarded as an instance of the same problem. We can in fact immediately "translate" S6 into the following unimplementable program which uses "busy waiting" on two integer variables x and y (initialised to 0):

S7 <x:=1; <u>do</u> y≠1 --> skip <u>od</u>> || <y:=1; <u>do</u> x≠1 --> skip <u>od</u>> .

The trouble with S6 and S7 is the interlacing of the two concurrent actions whereby the successful termination of the one is made dependent on the progress of the other. We attempt to analyse what has to be done in order to prohibit such an interlacing. Let us for the remainder of this section concentrate on a program, say S, containing a number of, say N, concurrent atomic actions:

S <action 1> || <action 2> || ... || <action N> .

Suppose that S is about to be executed. We say that an action of S can <u>pass</u> if it can start occurring and, if so, is guaranteed to terminate, independently of any other action. We say that S satisfies the condition (R1) if at least <u>one</u> of the N actions can pass.

As an example, reconsider S6 with s1=1, s2=0 initially:

S6 <V(s1);P(s2)> || <V(s2);P(s1)>

In this case the first action cannot pass but the second action can. Hence (if s1=1, s2=0 initially) S6 satisfies (R1). (If s1=s2=0 initially then S6 does <u>not</u> satisfy (R1)).

Suppose that S satisfies (R1) and that it is about to be executed. Then it is possible to select an action which can pass, execute it without touching the others, and obtain a new program which is similar to S except that it consists of N-1 rather than of N actions. If the new program again satisfies (R1) then another action can be chosen for execution, and in this way eventually the whole program can be executed. It can immediately be appreciated that this is the minimal condition for the implementability of S.

An actual implementation of this can hardly be expected to know in advance which action is the one to be excuted first. It may therefore have to try and err, for example by trying to execute the actions in some order and backtracking if an action cannot be executed (this poses some special problems in the case of infinite looping). It seems therefore that a serial algorithm with backtracking is the appropriate general implementation of programs for which (R1) but no stronger property is known to hold.

The requirement that in S <u>all</u> atomic actions can pass is a stronger condition than (R1). We define S to satisfy (R2) in this case. For example, S6 satisfies (R2) only if both s1 and s2 are initially positive. A good example of a system satisfying (R2) is a database system in which the typical transaction accesses a set of data. reads and/or changes them and releases them on termination.

A program satisfying (R2) can be implemented without trial-and-error. The N actions of S can simply be executed in some arbitrary order. It seems, therefore, that a serial algorithm without backtracking (i.e. the "serial execution" referred to at the beginning of this section) is the appropriate general implementation of programs for which (R2) but no stronger property is known to hold.

It is possible to summarise our discussion so far under the aspect of a trade-off between the two desiderata: "ease of implementation" and "power of programming language". If the latter is unrestricted then we have seen that an implementation may be unattainable. If the latter is restricted by (R1) or (R2) then the former corresponds to the strategies of "serial implementation with backtracking" and "serial implementation without backtracking", respectively.

The other end of the scale is the case in which the implementation of atomicity is trivial. This is true for sequential programs which always terminate. (There is no point in specifying a sequential program to be atomic, in a sequential environment).

It is also possible to view the "two-phase protocol" of [EGL76] under this aspect. Suppose that a set of variables is given and suppose the N actions of S to be simple sequential programs (called <u>transactions</u>) containing four types of primitive commands: reads, writes, locks and unlocks. Suppose further that each action locks the variables it reads or overwrites before accessing them and unlocks them afterwards. The semantics of the lock and unlock commands is that they prevent a variable to be locked concurrently by two actions.

A transaction is defined to be <u>two-phase</u> [EGL76] if it does not contain a lock command following an unlock command (intuitively, all the variables used in the transaction are first locked and then unlocked). We define such actions to satisfy the condition (R3).

All occurrences of two-phase transactions are contractions, so by theorem 3(i) atomicity is always satisfied. In other words: in order to ensure the atomicity of actions satisfying (R3) it is only necessary to implement correctly the actions of locking and unlocking. This can be done by a decentralised mechanism: each variable has at its disposal a local "scheduler" which ensures the correct locking of that variable. (Deadlocks are possible).

We can summarise our trade-off scheme as follows:

power of programming language	ease of implementation
unrestricted	impossible
(R1)	sequential with backtracking
(R2)	sequential without backtracking
(R3)	decentralised
sequential	trivial

The author feels unable at present to comment any further on the implementation question; indeed he feels uneasy about this whole approach. One worry about the scheme outlined above is that whichever implementation strategy is chosen, the potential concurrency which may be present in a given program is not taken into account.

As we have seen at the end of section 2, the potential concurrency of a program (the actual independence of actions) depends on the overlapping of variables in the actual structure. Thus we might expect an analysis of the kind which has been advocated at the end of section 2 to solve the "implementation problem" as well. Perhaps it is better to view the implementation of each individual program to be a separate problem, rather than to look for a general implementation strategy.

4 Error Recovery in Decentralised Systems

In this section we consider systems which provide, in addition to their normal functions, a measure of fault tolerance. The idea is to enable the system to function properly, or tolerably, even in the presence of faults. We confine ourselves to a technique known as backward error recovery which frequently is a part of an overall strategy of fault tolerance [RLT78].

The question how backward error recovery could be implemented in a decentralised system, say in a computer network, has led the authors of [MER77] to consider occurrence graphs as a suitable formalism. Their idea has been to describe the activity of a decentralised system by an occurrence graph and backward error recovery by what might be called a recovery structuring of this graph. Our goal in this section is to outline, illustrate and slightly generalise the work of [MER77]. For more details the reader is referred to [MER77], [MER78] and [BER78].

[RLT78] characterise backward error recovery as involving the "backing up of one or more processes of a system to a previous state which it is hoped is error-free". This presupposes that some states which are hoped to be error-free have previously been saved. We call such states restorable states.

In the simplest case we consider a sequential system in which on occasions the current state is made restorable (i.e. saved). If at some later point an error is detected then backward error recovery is initiated and the system is reset to a restorable state. How an error can actually be detected and what happens after backing up are questions falling outside the scope of concern of this section.

It might be interesting though to note that the recovery block scheme described in [RAN75] accomodates error recovery in a structured way. The states on entry of a recovery block are automatically made restorable, and upon exit from a recovery block a programmer-supplied acceptance test is evaluated to check the validity of the results computed within the recovery block. If the results are found to be invalid then backward error recovery is initiated and the recovery block prescribes an "alternative algorithm" to be executed when error recovery is completed.

Using the occurrence net model we can describe a sample system of this kind as follows:

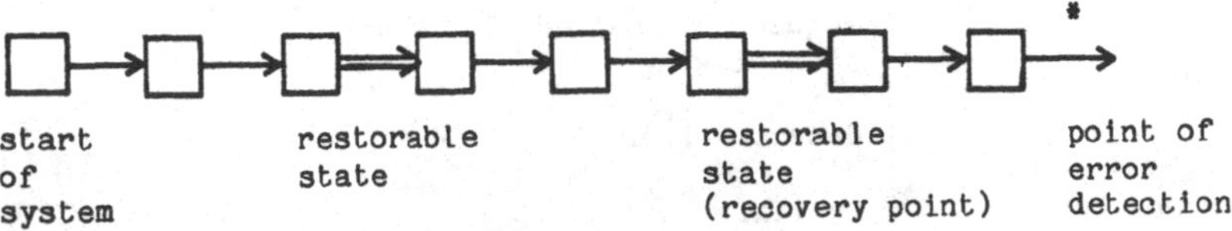

Figure 14

In the graph shown in Figure 14 we have used double arrows to describe restorable states; we call such double arrows restorable conditions (in accordance with the correspondence between arrows and conditions mentioned in section 1). The graph describes a sequential activity which, it is assumed, has progressed to a certain point indicated by the "dangling" arrow, i.e. the condition not having an output event. We call such a condition an active condition.

Suppose that an error has just been detected, represented in the graph by an asterisk. Backward error recovery ensues and causes the system to be reset to a restorable state. We assume that for reasons of efficiency the system is reset to the most recent restorable state which we call the recovery point (the assumption being that all of the activity prior to the recovery point is correct but that all of the activity after the recovery point is suspect in the sense that it may be erroneous).

We can describe the total effect of the backward error recovery mechanism as follows:

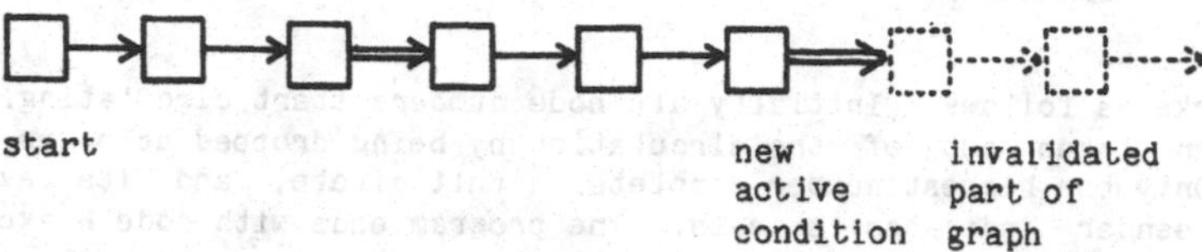

Figure 15

The recovery point is made to be the new active condition from which new activity can spring. The part of the old activity invalidated by this is represented by dotted lines in Figure 15. We call the two invalidated events of the graph a unit of recovery for the simple reason that one of them is invalidated as a consequence of the other being invalidated.

We now turn to the more general case of a decentralised system. In order to illustrate the sorts of problems introduced by this generality we take an example from [CHR79]. We consider a circular arrangement of N nodes (numbered from 1 to N) in which nodes can receive messages from their right hand neighbours and pass messages to their left hand neighbours (otherwise nodes are assumed to be independent). To be explicit, we consider four nodes with four one-frame buffers between them:

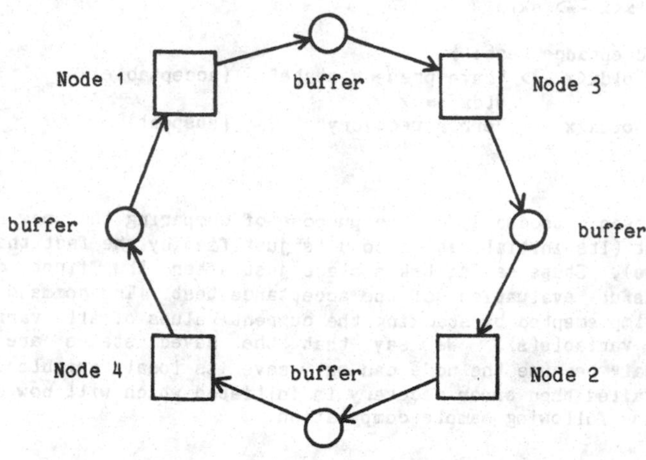

Figure 16

We are requested to write an algorithm enabling an individual node, say numbered i, to determine whether it is the one with the maximal number, i.e. whether i=N. In the solution of [CHR79], node i observes the following algorithm:

```
S8.     !i;
        do true --> ?x;                          {x is a local variable}
                    if x>i --> !x
                    [] x=i --> "success"
                    [] x<i --> skip
                    fi
        od.
```

We use in S8 a dialect of guarded commands and CSP [HOA78] as follows. Nodes may put a message into their output buffer by means of !<message> and receive a message from their input buffer by means of ?<message>. Sending and receiving are delayed until the buffers are empty or full, respectively (we do not make the more stringent assumption that has apparently be made in [HOA78], that sending and receiving are coincident).

The program works as follows. Initially all node numbers start circulating. Node numbers are then taken out of the circulation by being dropped at nodes with a higher number. Only the highest number completes a full circle, and its eventual return to the sender indicates success. The program ends with node N executing "success" and all other nodes waiting for more input.

There is a natural way of incorporating an acceptance test. In normal operation node numbers circulate such that the sequence of numbers received by a node is strictly increasing. This condition can be checked, for example by comparing the two values of x just before and just after the input command ?x. For the sake of illustration we have chosen to contort the program slightly by inserting this test after the alternative command (instead of, as would be more sensible, just after the input command), such that there is the possibility of a wrong value being passed on to another node before it is detected:

```
S8'     oldx := 0;
        !i;
        "save present state";
        do true --> ?x;
                    if x>i --> !x
                    [] x=i --> "success"
                    [] x<i --> skip
                    fi;
                    {acceptance test: }
                    if oldx<x --> "save present state";   {acceptable}
                                  oldx := x
                    [] oldx≥x --> "error recovery"        {suspect}
                    fi
        od.
```

The variable oldx has been introduced for the purpose of comparing the new input with the previous input (its initialisation to 0 is justified by the fact that all node numbers are positive). State saving takes place just after the first output and after each successful evaluation of the acceptance test. The command "save present state" could be implemented by stacking the current values of all variables including the control variable(s). We say that the saved states are local restorable states - "local" because the node can only save its local variables. If the acceptance test is failed then error recovery is initiated which will now be illustrated in detail by the following sample computation:

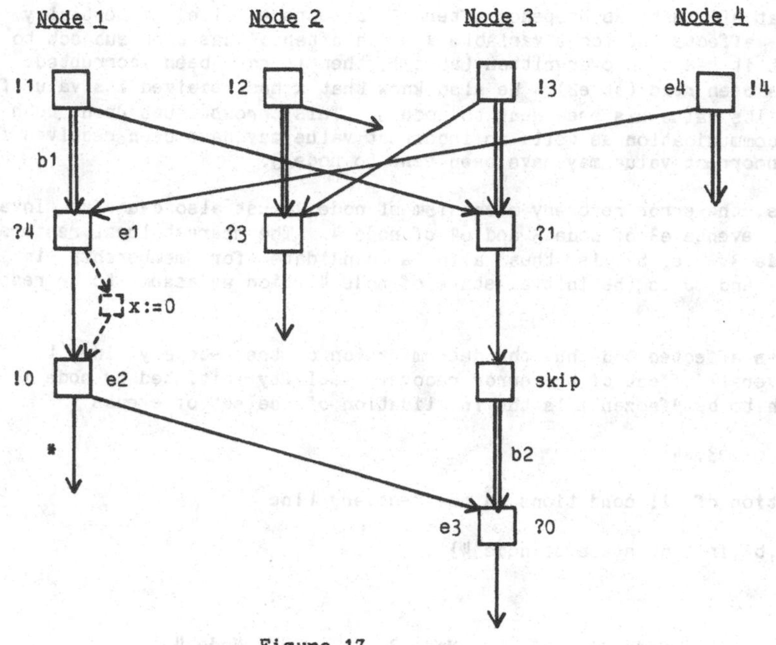

Figure 17

In the occurrence graph shown in Figure 17 the four sequential activities represented by the vertical arrows correspond to the individual activities of the four nodes. Squares correspond to what we choose to consider as basic events. The non-vertical arrows represent the inter-node communication delays. The local restorable states are represented by double arrows, and we also have four vertical active conditions representing the points of progress of the four nodes, and another active condition representing the fact that node 2 has deposited a message for node 4 which the latter has not yet received.

Suppose that just before node 1 sends its second message to node 3 (cf. the event e2 in Figure 17) the value of x gets lost which is indicated by an event "x:=0" in Figure 17. Node 1 can detect this error, though only after the wrong value has already been passed to node 3.

We assume that as a result of the detection of this error the normal progress of node 1 is halted and error recovery activity is initiated. Our aim is now to examine the overall effect which the error recovery algorithm is intended to have; we deal later with the question of how this effect can be achieved. In analogy to the sequential case we would like to determine a recovery point, i.e. an assumedly correct state to which the activity can be backed up in a safe way. Due to the decentralised nature of the system it is likely that this recovery point comprises a whole set of local restorable states, and we therefore give it the name of a recovery line.

Note that, in our example, while node 1 is engaged in error recovery activity, other nodes may be unaware of the fact that an error has been detected and may still be in normal progress; alternatively, they may themselves be engaged in their own error recovery. We take however no account of these complications for the moment and consider all activity to be "frozen" in the state shown in Figure 17.

We proceed to determine the recovery line. First of all we see that the nearest local restorable state of node 1 is the one labelled b1; the condition b1 is therefore a first candidate for belonging to the recovery line.

This means that all that has happened after b1 is suspect, i.e. potentially erroneous. This affects the local variable x which after b1 has been subject to the following: first it has been overwritten (at e1), then it has been corrupted, and finally it has been read (at e2). We also know that x has received its value from node 4 and that its value has been sent to node 3. This throws doubt upon both of these acts of communication as well: an incorrect value may have been received from node 4 and an incorrect value may have been sent to node 3.

In other words, the error recovery mechanism of node 1 must also cause an invalidation of the events e3 of node 3 and e4 of node 4. The nearest local restorable condition of node 3, i.e. b2, is thus also a candidate for membership in the recovery line, and so is the initial state of node 4 which we assume to be restorable by default.

Nothing else is affected and thus the determination of the recovery line is completed. The overall effect of the error recovery activity initiated by node 1 (assuming the graph to be "frozen") is the invalidation of the set of events

A = {e1,e2,e3,e4}

and the restoration of all conditions on the recovery line

R = {b1,b2,initial state of node 4} :

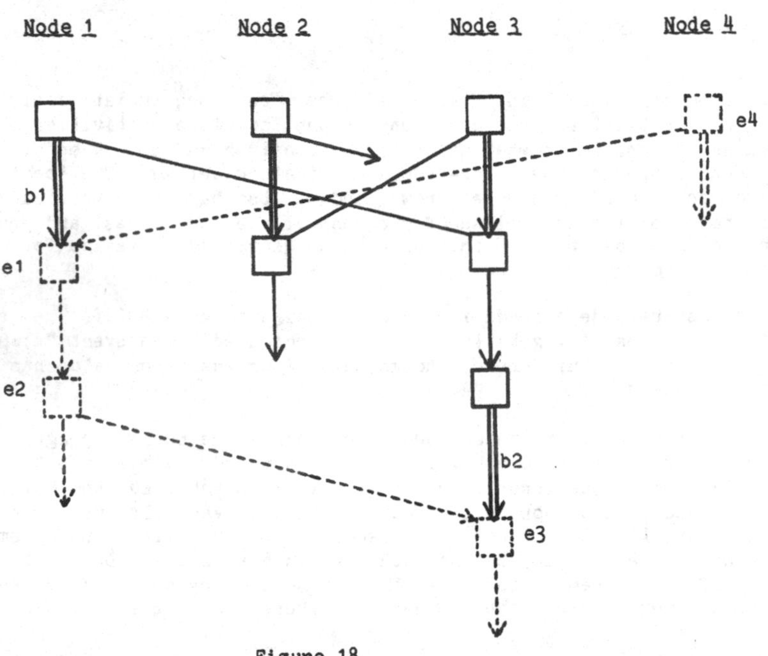

Figure 18

In analogy with the sequential case discussed earlier we call the set A of events a <u>unit of recovery</u>. The set A has this characteristic property of a unit of recovery, that an invalidation of any member of A entails the invalidation of all members of A, and that it is a maximal set with this property.

Using the occurrence graph model it is possible to give an alternative and more formal definition of the notion of a unit of recovery. We give a simple version of this definition which however exhibits the idea and suffices for the purposes of our example. The general definition can be found in [BER78]. Let an occurrence graph be given which is endowed with restorable and active conditions. We define the "units of recovery" to be those sets of events which can be collapsed together into a single box by exhaustively applying the rule

(where it is essential that the condition on the left hand side is not restorable).

It is easy to see that the exhaustive application of this rule to the graph shown in Figure 17 causes all of e1-e4 to be collapsed into a single event. In fact as an end result we obtain the following new graph:

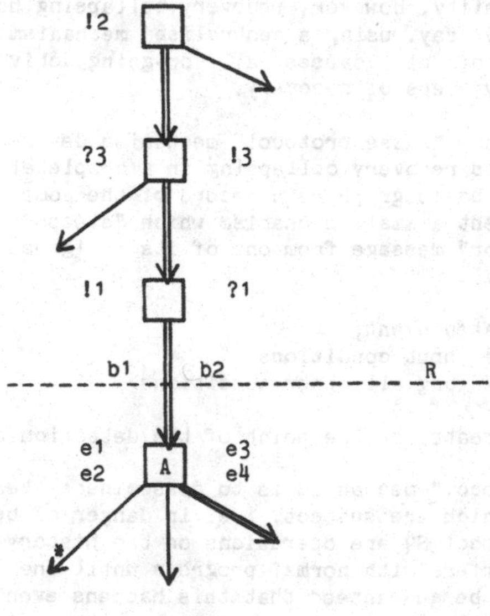

Figure 19

We call this graph the <u>recovery collapsed graph</u> associated with the basic graph shown in Figure 17. The two graphs describe the same computation but the second is a more appropriate description of the effect which the error recovery algorithm is intended to have. In fact, the activity "find the recovery line" is described as an atomic activity in the recovery collapsed graph. The recovery lines can be read off as the set of input conditions of the respective boxes in the recovery collapsed graph.

We have here the case that a structure is imposed on the graph, not directly through the programmer's atomicity specifications, but indirectly through the distribution of restorable and active conditions. (Note that we have made no assumption about the nature of this distribution; the programmer is allowed to insert state saving whenever it is deemed necessary). The structure tree associated with our example computation is shown in the following Figure:

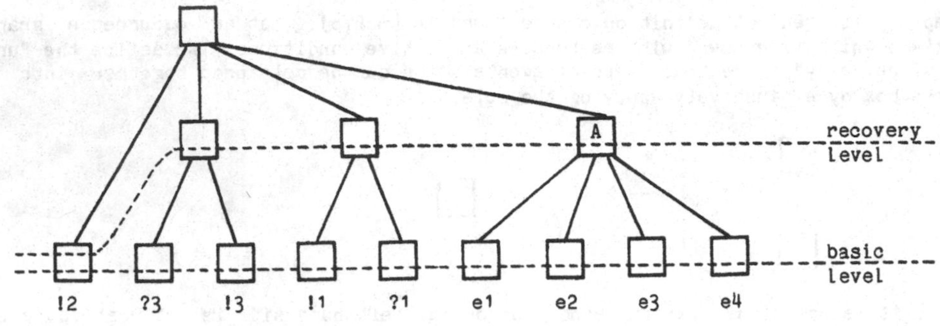

Figure 20

In the recovery collapsed graph the activity "find the recovery line" is described as an atomic activity. In reality, however, recovery collapsing has to be implemented. We could implement it by, say, using a centralised mechanism which whenever an error is detected, first of all causes all on-going activity to halt and thereafter performs the necessary steps of recovery.

Instead, however, we describe the "chase protocol" mechanism devised by the authors of [MER77] which implements recovery collapsing in a completely decentralised manner. The idea is to keep the basic graph as a record of the computational history and to associate with each event a small mechanism which "sleeps" until it is woken up by the receipt of an "error" message from one of its neighbours. Then the mechanism performs the following:

```
S9        <invalidate the associated event;
           restore all restorable input conditions;
           send "error" messages along all other conditions>
```

"Error" messages are initially created at the point of the detection of an error.

The effect of this "chase protocol" mechanism is to disseminate "error" messages through all parts of the graph which are suspect, i.e. in danger of being erroneous. The operations of the chase protocol S9 are operations on the history of the computation and do not therefore interfere with normal progress until the latter is halted through invalidation (it must be guaranteed that this happens eventually for normal progress which is affected by the error; by what means this can be guaranteed does not interest us here - it could be a priority or an interrupt scheme).

It is therefore quite safe for a decentralised system to be engaged in this form of recovery collapsing at one or more locations and simultaneously in normal progress at other locations. [MER77] and [MER78] contain a formal proof of the fact that the chase protocol mechanism is independent of normal activity even to such a degree that local states, once restored, may safely give rise to new activity, even though error recovery may not yet be completed and may in fact subsequently invalidate this new activity.

Chase protocols can be characterised as performing recovery collapsing at the latest possible point in time (namely when necessitated by the occurrence of an error) and in a decentralised fashion. It is quite conceivable that recovery collapsing takes place at other times and in other ways. In particular, the programmer can aid the task of recovery collapsing by inserting state saving commands in a disciplined way, but this possibility is not considered any further in these notes. (If the programmer is allowed complete freedom in choosing when to perform state saving, as we have assumed throughout this section, then it may so happen that certain restorable states are useless. For a characterisation of such states, see [BER78]).

Many other questions arise. For example, how are restorable conditions determined? That is, given a set of global variables, what subset of these has to be stored to give a "local restorable state"? Are there in some sense "minimal" subsets of this kind? A second question is the following. If a decentralised arrangement is given (say the one shown in Figure 16), then an actual implementation of error recovery would be greatly aided by having at its disposal the "reverse" arrangement (for example, as shown in Figure 17, error recovery has to invalidate the event e4 of node 4, which could easily be done if node 1 could directly send a message to node 4). To what extent is this true in general? The treatment of these questions is beyond the scope of this section.

Conclusion

We have used the occurrence net model in two different ways. Mainly we have used it as a conceptual tool but in section 4 we have also alluded to the possibility of it being useful as a practical tool whereby the computational history of a decentralised system could be kept in store and processed in a decentralised way. Time will tell whether this is actually feasible; suffice it to mention that a project is underway in Newcastle with the aim of investigating a possible implementation of the "chase protocol" mechanisms.

As a conceptual tool, the occurrence net model has helped us to cast certain intuitions about atomic actions in a precise form. A particular benefit has been the clarification of the relationship between the notions of "atomic occurrence", "contraction" and "serialisability" by relating them to one fundamental notion, namely the notion of a partial ordering of events.

The concept of an atomic action is considered by the author to match in significance the concept of a variable, both theoretically and concerning their use in a programming language. Variables and atomic actions can be considered dual to each other in the sense of indicating the "units of information" and "units of change" respectively.

Both concepts are simple but elusive (witness the brief discussion at the end of section 2 which calls for a major reappraisal of the role of variables). The author believes that this elusiveness stems from the fact that these two concepts can only be fully understood in their relationship. A programmer may imagine to have complete freedom in the choice of variables, but in fact this choice is determined by the actions that are to be carried out on these variables. Conversely, it may appear that there is freedom to choose one's units of change arbitrarily; but in a concurrent environment this is not necessarily so.

Thus the study of the structure of actions must be complemented by the study of the structure of variables, and both must be combined to the study of their interplay. The present notes contain less than half the work necessary towards this goal, but the author hopes that they can be used as a basis for further work.

Acknowledgements

The author remains grateful for having been influenced by the fruitful ideas of Philip Merlin. He also thankfully acknowledges the great debt he owes to Pete Lee, Brian Randell and Santosh Shrivastava who in many ways contributed substantyally to these notes, not least by interfering with the author's activity by pointing out countless mistakes, small and great. (Any remaining deficiencies are of course the author's responsibility).

This research has been carried out with the support of the Science Research Council of Great Britain.

References

[BER78] Best, E. and Randell, B.: A Formal Model of Atomicity in Asynchronous Systems. TR/130, Computing Laboratory, University of Newcastle upon Tyne, December 1978 (submitted for publication).

[BES80a] Best, E.: The Relative Strength of K-Density. In this volume.

[BES80b] Best, E.: Notes on Predicate Transformers and Concurrent Programs. TR/145, Computing Laboratory, University of Newcastle upon Tyne, to appear in January 1980.

[CHR79] Chang, E. and Roberts, R.: An Improved Algorithm for Decentralised Extrema-Finding in Circular Configurations of Processes. CACM 22/5, May 1979, pp. 281-283.

[DEM79] DeMillo, R., Lipton, R. and Perlis, A.: Social Processes and the Verification of Computer Programs. CACM 22/5, May 1979.

[DIJ68] Dijkstra, E.W.: Co-operating Sequential Processes. In: Programming Languages (ed. F. Genuys), Academic Press, London and New York, 1968.

[DIJ76] Dijkstra, E.W.: A Discipline of Programming. Prentice Hall, 1976.

[DIJ78] Dijkstra, E.W.: Finding the Correctness Proof of a Concurrent Program. Proc. of the Koninklijke Nederlandse Akademie van Wetenschappen, Amsterdam, Series A, Volume 81(2), June 1978.

[DLM78] Dijkstra, E.W., Lamport, L., Martin, A.J., Scholten, C.S. and Steffens, E.F.M.: On-the-Fly Garbage Collection: An Exercise in Co-operation. CACM 21/11, November 1978, pp. 966-975.

[EGL76] Eswaran, R., Gray, J., Lorie, R. and Traiger, I.: On the Notions of Consistency and Predicate Locks. CACM 19/11, November 1976, pp. 624-633.

[GES80] Genrich, H.J. and Stankiewicz-Wiechno, E.: A Dictionary of Some Basic Notions of Net Theory. In this volume.

[HOA78] Hoare, C.A.R.: Communicating Sequential Processes. CACM 21/8, August 1978, pp. 666-677.

[LOM77] Lomet, D.: Process Structuring, Synchronisation and Recovery Using Atomic Actions. Proc. of the ACM Conference on Language Design for Reliable Software, Sigplan Notices 12/3, March 1977, pp. 128-137.

[MER77] Merlin, P. and Randell, B.: Consistent State Restoration in Distributed Systems. TR/113, Computing Laboratory, University of Newcastle upon Tyne, September 1977 (submitted for publication).

[MER78] Merlin, P. and Randell, B.: State Restoration in Distributed Systems. In: FTCS-8, IEEE Toulouse, June 1978, pp. 129-134.

[RAN75] Randell, B.: System Structure for Software Fault Tolerance. IEEE Transactions on Software Engineering, SE-1, 2, June 1975, pp. 220-232.

[RLT78] Randell, B., Lee, P.A. and Treleaven, P.C.: Reliable Computing Systems. In: Lecture Notes in Computer Science, Vol. 60, Springer Verlag Berlin 1978.

[VLS79] Van Lamsweerde, A. and Sintzoff, M.: Formal Derivation of Strongly Correct Concurrent Programs. Acta Informatica 12, 1979, pp. 1-31.

CONCURRENCY

C.A. Petri
GMD Bonn

Abstract

A relation of concurrency can be defined in every occurrence net and every synchronization graph. In some instances, the occurrence net resp. the synchronization graph can be recomputed from the concurrency relation. It has been found that nets which can be constructed from a concurrency relation play an important role in applications. Concurrency structures which define uniquely an occurrence net or an condition-event-system are called "ropes". The properties of binary relations producing ropes are considered to be - all or in part - candidates for axioms of "coexistence", with concurrency as one special instance. -

Two elements x, y of an occurrence net $(S,T;F)$, $x,y \in S \cup T = X$ [1] are said to be concurrent iff there is no directed causal chain between them :

$$x \text{ co } y \;:\Longleftrightarrow\; (x,y) \notin F^+ \;\wedge\; (y,x) \notin F^+$$

i.e. $$\text{co} := X \times X - (F^+ \cup (F^+)^{-1})$$

Writing $x < y$ for $(x,y) \in F^+$, and $y > x \;:\Leftrightarrow\; x < y$, we have

$$\text{co} = \overline{< \cup >}$$

Since $<$ is a strict partial ordering of X , we have

(1) $\quad id|X \subseteq \text{co} \qquad$ co is reflexive

(2) $\quad \text{co} = \text{co}^{-1} \qquad$ co is symmetric

(3) $\quad \text{co} = \widehat{\text{co}} \qquad$ co is a similarity relation

Note that $\widehat{\text{co}} := \text{co} \cup \text{co}^{-1} \cup id|X$, so that $(1) \wedge (2) \Longleftrightarrow (3)$.
(Please refer to the Dictionary [1] when in doubt about notations or definitions. It is part of these proceedings.

We shall always have

$$x \text{ co } x$$

$$x \text{ co } y \Longrightarrow y \text{ co } x$$

but <u>not necessarily $x \text{ co } y \wedge y \text{ co } z \Longrightarrow x \text{ co } z$</u> .

The disorder relation $co = \overline{< \cup >}$ is not necessarily transitive since the irreflexive and transitive order relation $<$ is only partial. Therefore, co is not an equivalence relation. Although we would like to speak of equivalence classes of co , which would then be fully ordered and would correspond to the idea of an objective state-of-affai at time t , we have to be content with less. We look for those subsets of X which are as large as possible and within which co is transitive. These subsets of X will not necessarily be disjoint, and will be called the Kens of co . For any relation $R \subseteq X \times X$, let

$$\mathrm{Ken}(A,R) :\Leftrightarrow \bigwedge x,y \in A : x \hat{R} y \wedge \bigwedge x \in X-A \bigvee y \in A : x \overline{\hat{R}} y$$
$$\mathrm{Kens}(R) := \{ A \mid \mathrm{Ken}(A,R) \}$$

The rest of this paper will closely follow [2]. Definitions :

$$li := \overline{co} \cup id \mid X$$

$x\ li\ y \Leftrightarrow x F^* y \vee y F^* x$ means „x and y lie on a line" :

$\mathbb{L}$:= Kens(li)		the set of lines
$\mathbb{C}$:= Kens(co)		the set of cuts
C := $\mathbb{C} \cap \mathcal{P}(S)$		the set of cases

Cases are those cuts which consist of S-elements only. They will be usable in our context after S has been defined in terms of co . We demand

(4) $$co = \left\{ (x,y) \mid \bigvee c \in \mathbb{C} : x \in c \wedge y \in c \right\}$$

which is trivial for finite X . Now it does not matter whether we take co or $\mathbb{C}$ as our only primitive concept. $\mathbb{C}$ and co can be defined in terms of each other. Of course,

$$X = dom(co) = cod(co) = dom(li) = cod(li)$$
$$co \cap li = id \mid X$$

Def.: $(X,<)$ is called a natural order iff

$$SPO(X,<) \quad \wedge \quad < \neq \emptyset \quad \wedge$$
$$\left\{ R \mid SPO(X,R) \wedge R \cup R^{-1} = < \cup > \right\} = \{ <, > \}$$

(X,co) is called a natural disorder if (not "iff") there is a natural order (X,<) and $co = \overline{< \cup >}$

with SPO = strict partial order :

$$SPO(X,<) :\Leftrightarrow id \mid X \cap < = \emptyset \qquad \text{(irreflexive } <)$$
$$\wedge <^2 \subseteq < \qquad \text{(transitive } <)$$
$$\wedge < \subseteq X \times X \qquad (< \text{ a relation in X})$$

We can now state our main requirement for ropes :

(5) <u>(X,co) is a natural disorder</u>

For full ("linear") orders FO(X,<) , defined by

$$FO(X,<) \;:\Leftrightarrow\; SPO(X,<) \;\wedge\; (< \cup > \cup\, id \mid X) \;=\; X \times X$$

we have $\quad co \;=\; id \mid X$.

Full orders are natural iff $|X| = 2$.

Remarks : (5) implies (1), (2), (3) and many of the following numbered formulas. These formulas shall be given mainly to make local aspects of the global postulate (5) more clearly visible. It should be clear that a natural disorder can serve to define a directed order only up to its direction : (X,<) belongs to the same disorder as (X,>). Inverting the direction of order will leave all axioms, and all theorems up to the level of condition-event-systems unaffected; the phenomenon of <u>influence</u> (on the level of information flow nets) will be the first instance in net theory where direction does matter.

In the same spirit, we have not fully defined natural disorders; we have used "if" instead of "iff". Many applications indicate that the important <u>invariant</u> basic order-producing relation is not binary and directed, but quaternary and undirected; it is the <u>separation relation</u> of four different points on a line. Example : summer and winter separate spring and fall on a cyclic line :

$$\Big\{\{\text{summer, winter}\}\;,\;\{\text{spring, fall}\}\Big\} \in \text{Sep}$$

Note that the explication of an element of a separation relation does not even require brackets such as are used in denoting an ordered pair. Separation relations are well known from projective geometry. They can be used to define <u>cyclic</u> as well as cycle-free partial orderings, also natural ones. The reader may do so as an exercise after studying the final example of this paper, and may thus complete the definition of "natural disorder".

Once a direction is given for one pair of non-concurrent points in a natural ordering, it is uniquely defined for all such pairs. This holds for cycle-free as well as for cyclic natural orders. <u>Direction is a one-bit convention.</u>

Next we shall indicate our <u>scope of concern</u>, which we limit to the <u>interior</u> of process domains on the one hand, and to structures of more than two elements on the other hand :

(6) $\quad |X| > 2$

In the <u>interior</u> of an occurrence net, each S-element has <u>exactly</u>

one beginning and one end; if a T-element had only one immediate predecessor and successor, it could not belong to a natural order. We sharpen this requirement to represent the idea that a T-element stands for an <u>interaction</u> between entities whose history is given by lines (their world-lines, in the terminology of relativity). Therefore, at least two lines must <u>intersect</u> in each T-element :

$$x \in S \longrightarrow |{}^{\bullet}x| = |x^{\bullet}| = 1$$
$$x \in T \longrightarrow |{}^{\bullet}x| \geqslant 2 \text{ and } |x^{\bullet}| \geqslant 2$$

We use this to formulate the type of <u>density</u> required for ropes. Ordinary density of a relation $<$ is defined by

(§): $\bigwedge x,y \in X : \bigvee z \in X : x < y \Rightarrow x < z \wedge z < y$

i.e. $< \subseteq <^2$

or, with the "immediate predecessor" relation $\lessdot := < - <^2$:

$$\lessdot = \emptyset$$

We weaken (§) to (§§):

(§§): $\bigwedge x,y \in \underline{T} \; \bigvee z \in X : \ldots$ <u>and</u> $\bigwedge x,y \in \underline{S} \; \bigvee z \in X : \ldots$

This is what is meant by <u>N-density</u> : we demand the existence of an element z <u>between</u> x and y only if x and y are on a line in an <u>N-shaped</u> diagram :

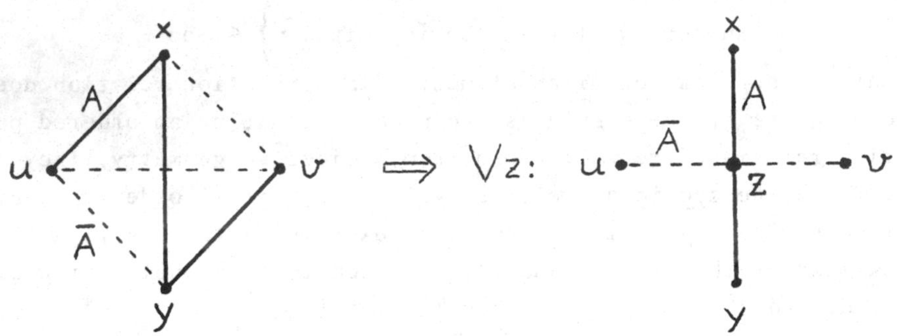

formally, with $A := \hat{R} := R \cup R^{-1} \cup id$:

Ndense (R) : $\Longleftrightarrow$

$$\bigwedge xyuv \bigvee z : uAxAyAv \wedge x\bar{A}v\bar{A}u\bar{A}y \Longrightarrow xAzAy \wedge u\bar{A}z\bar{A}v$$

(7) Ndense (co)

If co is Ndense, so is $\overline{co}$, li , $\overline{li}$, $<$ and $>$.

N-density does not imply density, and vice versa (!).

N-density is a necessary, but not sufficient requirement when we demand that "<u>every cut</u> through a rope <u>cuts every line</u>" :

$$c \in \mathbb{C} \wedge l \in \mathbb{L} \implies c \cap l \neq \emptyset$$

We define this property for any relation $R \subseteq X \times X$:

$$\text{Kdense}(R) \ :\Leftrightarrow \bigwedge a,b : \text{Ken}(a,R) \wedge \text{Ken}(b,\bar{\hat{R}}) \implies |a \cap b| = 1$$

(8) Kdense (co)

If co is Kdense, so is $\overline{\text{co}}$, li , $\overline{\text{li}}$, $<$ and $>$.
K-density implies N-density : (8) $\Longrightarrow$ (7).
N-density is the "local" part of the "global" K-density.
The following postulates refer (more directly than (7) and (8)) to a symmetry between co and li = $\overline{\text{co}} \cup \text{id} \mid X$:

(9) $\text{co}^* = \text{li}^*$

(10) $\text{co}^* = X \times X$

(11) $\text{li}^* = X \times X$

By the definition of li = $\overline{\text{co}} \cup \text{id} \mid X$, (9) implies (10) and (11).
From (1) - (9) it follows that co is not transitive :

$$\underline{\text{co}^2 - \text{co} \neq \emptyset}$$

We can sum up (9) - (11) in the statement

(12) $\text{co}^* = \overline{\text{co}}^*$: <u>co is "coherent"</u>

We now want to express that co (resp. $\mathbb{C}$) is the only basic relation from which we construct; items which cannot be distinguished in terms of co and li are regarded as identical. With
$\text{Co}(x) := \{y \mid x \text{ co } y\}$ and $\text{Li}(x) := \{y \mid x \text{ li } y\}$, we write

(13) $\text{Co}(x) = \text{Co}(y) \iff \text{Li}(x) = \text{Li}(y)$

(14) $\text{Co}(x) = \text{Co}(y) \implies x = y$ (co is <u>reduced</u>)

(15) $\text{Li}(x) = \text{Li}(y) \implies x = y$ (li is <u>reduced</u>)

Again, (13) implies the more easily understandable (14) and (15).
"Co(x) = Co(y)" is clearly an equivalence relation $\widetilde{\text{co}}$ in X :

$$\widetilde{\text{co}} = \overline{\text{co}\ \overline{\text{co}} \cup \overline{\text{co}}\ \text{co}}$$

If (14) is not valid in some given (X,co) , we have just to "reduce" X to $X/\widetilde{\text{co}}$ and to reduce co correspondingly. (14) enforces the absence of subnets N_1 :

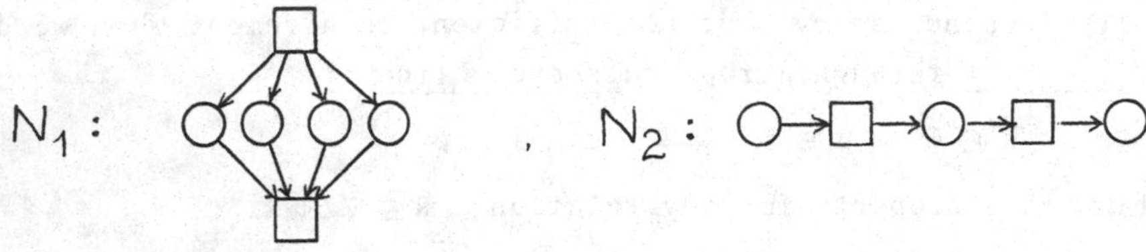

and (15) the absence of open subnets N_2 .

The relation P is given for any net (S,T;F) by

$$P = (F \cup F^{-1}) \cap (S \times T)$$

We can define P in terms of co thus :

$$x \; P \; y \; :\Leftrightarrow \; Li(x) \subseteq Li(y) \wedge x \neq y$$

i.e. $P = \overline{co} - \overline{co}\;\overline{li}$, equivalently.

It is plausible to define, in view of (13) (14) (15), a relation D :

$$x \; D \; y \; :\Leftrightarrow \; Co(x) \subseteq Co(y) \wedge x \neq y$$

i.e. $D = \overline{li} - \overline{li}\;\overline{co}$.

With respect to occurrence nets, we can indicate the meaning of P and D shortly thus :

x P y means "x is <u>changed by</u> y"
x D y means "x is <u>a detail of</u> y" or in other words : when we know x is occurring then we know that y is also occurring (concurrently).

Our postulates about P and D are :

(16) $P^2 = D^2$

(17) $P^2 = \emptyset$ (there are no "changes of changes")

(18) $D^2 = \emptyset$ (there are no "details of details")

Again, (16) is equivalent to (17) $\wedge$ (18). We define

$$S := dom(P)$$
$$T := cod(P)$$

and find that $cod(D) \subseteq S$:

all non-details are S elements . They turn out to be precisely those S-elements which do not contribute to $<\!|\,T$, the partial order of <u>event</u>-occurrences.

(19) $(P \cup P^{-1})^* = X \times X$

(20) $(D \cup D^{-1})^* = X \times X$

Postulate (19) is plainly required if the resulting order is to be natural and <u>combinatorial</u>; i.e. for occurrence nets

$$F = \lessdot = < - <^2 \qquad \text{and} \qquad < = (\lessdot)^+$$

$<$ is nowhere dense (but everywhere Kdense and Ndense).
(20) is the symmetric counterpart of (19)

Finally, we mention two consequences of (1) - (20) as separate postulates, because it may be that the global postulate (5), (X,co) is a natural disorder, cannot be verified in some application. The essence of (5) is expressed locally by (21), (22).
With $p(x)$, the "proximity" of $x \in X$, defined by

$$p(x) := \left\{ y \mid x\ P\ y \vee y\ P\ x \right\}, \qquad \text{we demand}$$

(21) $\bigwedge x : \quad co^2 \mid p(x) \subseteq co$ (co is <u>locally transitive</u>)

(22) $\bigwedge x : \quad \overline{co}^2 \mid p(x) \subseteq co$ ($\overline{co}$ is <u>locally orientable</u>)

A structure (X,co) with (1) - (22) is called a <u>rope</u>, and if the orderings produced by it are cycle-free, a <u>straight rope</u>.

<u>Theorem</u> : For every rope (X,co) there are precisely two nets (S,T;F) and $(S,T;F^{-1})$ with S and T as defined above, and with F <u>compatible with</u> co as indicated above (for straight ropes : $\overline{co} = F^+ \cup (F^+)^{-1}$). The structures (S,T;F,C) and (S,T,F^{-1},C) satisfy the axioms for condition-event-systems [1] with $C = \text{Kens}(co) \cap \mathcal{P}(S)$.

<u>Theorem</u> : Every <u>straight</u> rope is (X,co) of precisely two strict partial orderings $(X,<)$ and $(X,>)$; these possess <u>a generalized Dedekind continuity</u> : GDcont $(X,<)$ and GDcont $(X,>)$.

Remember that a <u>Dedekind cut</u> on a <u>full</u> order $(X,<)$ with $co = id \mid X$ is given by a subset A of X (with $\overline{A} := X - A$) :

$$\text{Dcut}(A) \iff \bigwedge x \in A, y \in \overline{A} : x < y \ \wedge\ A \neq \emptyset \quad \overline{A} \neq \emptyset$$

For the purpose of generalizing this concept, we do not follow convention, but define (equivalently for full orders) :

$$\text{Dcut}(A) :\iff \emptyset \subsetneqq A \subsetneqq X \ \wedge\ \bigwedge x \in A, y \in \overline{A} : \neg(x > y)$$

For Dedekind continuity, it is required that <u>either</u> A has a maximal element, <u>or</u> $\overline{A}$ has a minimal element for every Dcut A :

$$\text{Dcont}(X,<) :\iff \bigwedge A : \text{Dcut}(A) \longrightarrow \left| \text{Max}(A) \cup \text{Min}(\overline{A}) \right| = 1$$

where $\text{Max}(A) := \left\{ x \mid x \in A \wedge \bigwedge y \in A : \neg(x < y) \right\}$

Now a Dcut in a <u>partial</u> order may have many maximal elements,

$|Max(A)| \geqslant 1$. We introduce the notion of an <u>objectivly maximal</u> element an element which remains maximal for all Dcuts B which separate X in the "vicinity" of the element in the same way as Dcut A : Let Line(L) $:\Leftrightarrow L \in \mathbb{L}$; $\mathbb{L}$ = Kens(<) as above. We define

$$\mathrm{Obmax}(A) := \left\{ x \mid x \in \mathrm{Max}(A) \wedge \mathrm{Dcut}(A) \wedge \bigwedge B, L : \mathrm{Dcut}(B) \wedge \mathrm{Line}(L) \Longrightarrow \left(x \in \mathrm{Max}(B \cap L) \Longrightarrow x \in \mathrm{Max}(B)\right) \right\}$$

$$\mathrm{Obmin}(\bar{A}) := \left\{ x \mid x \in \mathrm{Min}(\bar{A}) \wedge \mathrm{Dcut}(A) \wedge \bigwedge B, L : \mathrm{Dcut}(B) \wedge \mathrm{Line}(L) \Longrightarrow \left(x \in \mathrm{Min}(\bar{B} \cap L) \Longrightarrow x \in \mathrm{Min}(\bar{B})\right) \right\}$$

$$c(A) := \mathrm{Obmax}(A) \cup \mathrm{Obmin}(\bar{A})$$

<u>GDcont</u>$(X,<)$ $:\Longleftrightarrow \mathrm{SPO}(X,<) \wedge < \neq \emptyset \wedge \bigwedge A, L : \mathrm{Dcut}(A) \wedge \mathrm{Line}\ L \Longrightarrow |L \cap c(A)| = 1$

<u>Theorem</u> : $\mathrm{Line}(X) \Longrightarrow (\mathrm{GDcont}(X,<) \Longleftrightarrow \mathrm{Dcont}(X,<))$
i.e. for full orders, Obmax reduces to Max and GDcont to Dcont.

<u>Theorem</u> : If $(X,<)$ is produced by a straight rope, then

$$\bigcup c(A) : A \subseteq X = S = \mathrm{dom}(\overline{co} - \overline{co\ li})$$

This explains our interest in <u>cases</u> $c \in C = \mathbb{C} \cap \mathcal{P}(S)$: they correspond formally to the real numbers on the line $\mathbb{R}$ in the $\mathrm{SPO}(\mathbb{R},<)$, where $co = id|\mathbb{R}$ and GDcont implies density; while in general, GDcont implies K- and N-density. -

<u>Example</u> : The smallest known rope is shown in Fig. 1b, the smallest known straight rope is infinite (but remember the remarks about scope of concern preceding postulate (6)); a finite section of it is shown in Fig. 1d. The relation co is represented by dotted lines, with the selfloops for $co \cap id$ omitted.
Fig. 1d can be <u>folded</u> onto Fig. 1b just as Fig. 1c is folded onto Fig. 1a. Fig. 1d can also be folded onto Fig. 2, but Fig. 2 does not represent a rope, because it does not satisfy postulate (8), the requirement of K-density.

Fig. 2 is the concurrency structure of a condition-event-system which is, in a certain sense, "too small". It is instructive to find that system and to describe its deficiencies a) formally, and b) in terms of some application.

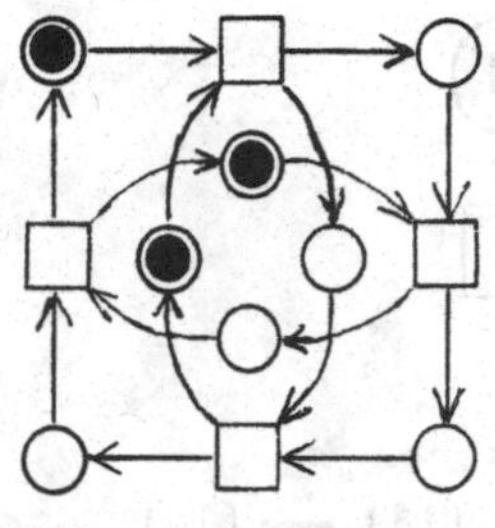

1a) A Condition-Event-System

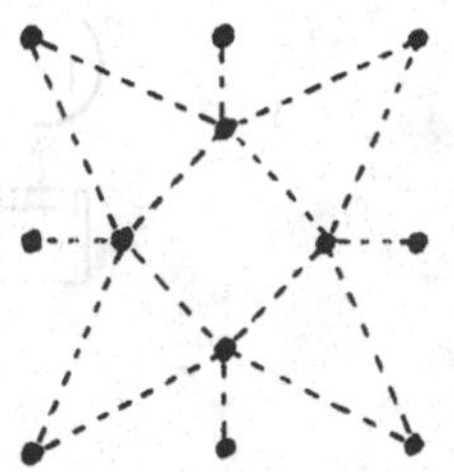

1b) The concurrency structure of the system 1a)

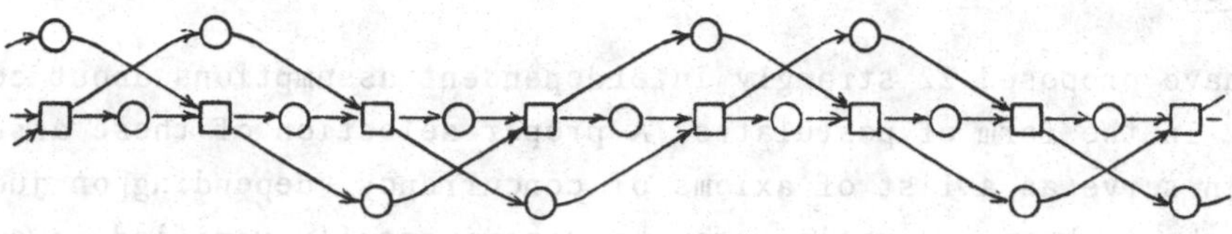

1c) Section of the cycle-free occurrence net of the system 1a)

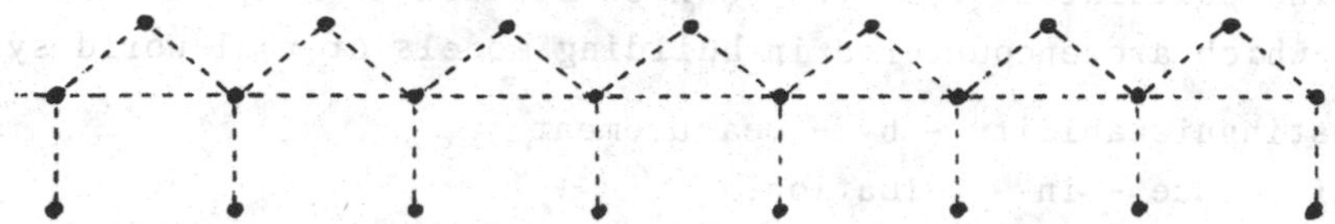

1d) The concurrency structure of 1c)

Fig. 1 : Examples of ropes and nets

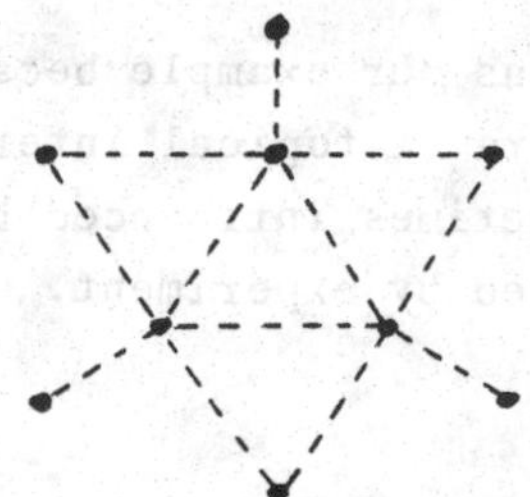

Fig. 2 : A concurrency structure which is not a rope

Exercises : Find a line and a cut in Fig. 2 which do not intersect. Verify (1) - (22) in Fig. 1b. Find an application of Fig. 1 and discuss (1) - (22) in terms of this application. Draw the net of postulates and interdependences, by expanding the diagram Fig. 3 :

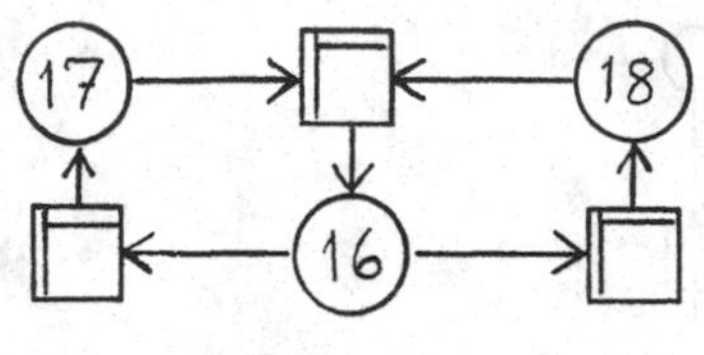

Fig. 3

i.e. (16) $\rightarrow$ (17); (16) $\rightarrow$ (18) ; (17) $\wedge$ (18) $\rightarrow$ (16)
which is the same as saying (16) $\leftrightarrow$ (17) $\wedge$ (18) .

Conclusion

We have proposed 22 strongly interdependent assumptions about concurrency in the form of postulates. A proper selection of these assumptions can serve as a list of axioms of concurrency, depending on judgement which of these assumptions can be experimentally verified in a given area of application (e.g. (10)) or express most nearly our ideas about how to master conceptually a given area of application (e.g. (5) or (8)). The postulates (1) - (22) can be applied to many similarity relations which are encountered in building models of real-world systems

- Indistinguishability - by - measurement
- Indifference - in - valuation,
  Indifference as to utility
- Disorder (in many areas)
- Causal independence
- Compatibility (symmetric part only)
- Concurrency

We have chosen concurrency as our example because distributed systems and "parallel" processing are of topical interest, and because activities in these areas are sometimes influenced by opinions about concurrency which can be refuted by experiment.

References

[1] Genrich, H.J. and Stankiewicz-Wiechno, E.: A Dictionary of some basic Notions of Net Theory. In these proceedings (1979)

[2] Petri, C.A.: Concurrency as a Basis of Systems Thinking. in: Proc. 5th Scandinavian Logic Symposium. Eds.: F.V.Jensen, B.H. Mayoh, K.K.Möller. Aalborg Universitetsforlag, 1979

THE RELATIVE STRENGTH OF K-DENSITY

by

E. Best

Computing Laboratory
University of Newcastle upon Tyne
England

Abstract

K-density is a property of occurrence nets which can be thought of as mathematical models of processes. We study K-density both formally, as compared with other axioms, and informally, as interpreted and compared with the properties of continuity and computability. We show that, in a certain sense, K-density is an axiom of discreteness.

Contents

Introduction

More than a decade has passed since the development of programming had reached a stage in which it appeared possible to cast the semantics of a given programming language in precise formal terms. No longer would programmers have to ponder over an ambiguous description, nor to speculate about the intentions of a compiler writer, in order to understand their own program. No longer would a program give two different results when executed on two different computers. Or so was the hope.

In these notes we are concerned with a theoretical questions of formal semantics. Let us briefly consider how we would go about in trying to formalise the meaning of a program. Because the variables of a program span a state space and because programs operate on sets of states, it is natural to consider the set of all sets of states and the set of functions on it. Within this framework we could start to do mathematics. Because of its vast generality, we would first of all expect to have to introduce a number of axioms. We are interested in such axioms which restrict the functions used to correspond to the programs whose semantics is to be described.

From a mathematical point of view one candidate for such an axiom soon suggests itself. The power set of the state space is not merely a set but rather a set on which quite a "nice" structure is imposed. With the operations of set union and set intersection it forms what is known as a "complete lattice", and in fact it even forms a so-called "boolean algebra". There is one very natural property which functions on complete lattices "ought to" satisfy, namely the property of continuity. This, in rough terms, may have been one of the motivations which led a school of mathematical semantics, represented by C. Strachey and D. Scott, to advocate and carry through the study of continuous functions on complete lattices.

An additional motivation may have been the fact that there is a vague connection between continuity and the property of computability. Continuity, in intuitive terms, says that the function of a limit (of a sequence) can be approached ("computed") by the function of that sequence. It seems that Scott and Strachey were well aware of, and keen on exploiting, that connection, as witnessed, for example, by statements such as the following: " ... the functions we use - and which are appropriate to computation theory - ... are continuous" [SCS71].

This vague connection notwithstanding, the continuity axiom figures rather as a mathematical nicety without real meaning in our discussion so far. It can only become meaningful if further meaning is assigned to the mathematical framework of powerset and functions. How can we make precise the intuitive correspondence between functions and programs? One possible answer to this question is given within the formalism of guarded commands (see [DIJ76]). Every guarded command program leads to a function, to be described in more detail below, called a predicate transformer. Amongst other things, all predicate transformers are continuous, and this continuity furthermore characterises a certain property of programs.

We examine this special significance of the continuity property a little closer. A guarded command program can abstractly be thought of as a function from ("initial") states to sets of ("final") states. A program may countenance "non-determinacy" in the sense that whenever it is started in an initial state then it ends up in any of the corresponding final states. The semantics of a program is given by its predicate transformer which maps sets of final states into sets of initial states (indicating, for a given set of final states, the largest set of initial states which guarantees termination of the program in one of the given final states).

Within the guarded command formalism as outlined above, the fact can be proved that the predicate transformer of a program uniquely characterises the program. In other words, we can describe a program either as a function from initial states to sets of final states, or, equivalently, by its predicate transformer. It turns out that the continuity of the latter characterises this property of the former, that it maps initial states only into finite sets of final states [WAN77]. Thus, when such a program is started then there is a bound on the number of possible outcomes. Bounded non-determinacy in this sense is the precise interpretation of continuity within the framework of the guarded command formalism.

The "programs" excluded by the continuity axiom are those which would be "able to make within a finite time a choice out of infinitely many possibilities" ([DIJ76], chapter 9). As an example, we examine the prototype of this sort of "programs". Suppose we are requested to write a program implementing the assignment Sx = "set x to any positive integer". We could try

```
S =   go_on := true;
      x := 1;
      do go_on --> x := x+1
      [] go-on --> go_on := false
      od.
```

The repetitive clause do-od means that a non-deterministically chosen one of the statements following the arrows "-->" can be repeated until the "guard" go_on is false. S differs from Sx in that it may fail to terminate (if the first guarded clause is always chosen), whilst Sx is implicitly assumed to terminate; and this is the only difference. As it turns out, the predicate transformer of S does not violate continuity, but the function corresponding to Sx does.

Much the same situation arises with the undecidable problem par excellence, namely the halting problem. Suppose we are requested to write a program Sh which decides, given an arbitrary program, whether or not the latter terminates. Note that Sh is thus implicitly assumed to terminate. The most general way of finding out is for Sh to start simulating the given program. If the latter halts then Sh halts as well with the result that "The Given Program Halts"; however, if the given program fails to terminate then the implicit requirement for Sh to terminate gives rise to a "non-continuous" situation similar to the one described in the last paragraph.

This comparison of Sx and Sh indicates a palatable connection between the properties of continuity and computability. The immediate question arises whether they coincide in some sense. This question has to be answered in the negative: continuity is strictly weaker than computability (for the general case see the discussion in [SCO76] and for the guarded command formalism see [BES80b]). In these notes we are interested in the similarity between the two properties more than in their difference.

In which sense are Sx and Sh similar? Both are "unimplementable" in the sense that a general implementation cannot be guaranteed to terminate and therefore necessarily violates the specifications. There is no such thing as a "terminating non-terminating process". The operational fact that a process either terminates or not appears therefore to be the essence of the similarity between Sx and Sh.

This operational characteristic, namely the absence of a "terminating non-terminating process", bears a strong resemblance to an axiom which has been introduced by Petri in [PET77] and which is called K-density. This at last leads us to the main theme of these notes: we wish to introduce and discuss in detail the axiom of K-density. For this discussion the vague connection between K-density, continuity and computability serves as no more than a motivation. We concentrate on K-density throughout sections 1-3 and do not take up the wider issue of that connection until section 4.

The point of departure of the present discussion has been the attempt to formalise the meaning of a program. Usually, a given program defines the pattern of a possible multitude of individual "happenings", or "processes"; this is referred to by calling a program an "executional abstraction". The reader can find the notion of an executional abstraction scrutinised in the first chapters of [DIJ76]. We now shift our attention from the program to the processes. K-density is in the first instance a property of a single process, not a property of a program.

There are many conceivable ways of mathematically modelling a process; there is however only one way known to the author of attempting to use first principles in the derivation of such a model, namely the one advocated by Petri in [PET80a] and [PET80b]. In this approach, processes are modelled by "occurrence nets" the precise definition of which is given in section 1 of the present notes and in [GES80].

K-density, then, is a property of an occurrence net. It can be defined very nicely and elegantly (see section 1). Even so, its strength and its significance are not self-evident. For instance, K-density is weak enough to render all finite occurrence nets K-dense, but this is a fact which requires a proof. It is with facts of this nature that sections 1-3 are concerned. We illuminate the strength of the axiom of K-density by comparing it with a number of related axioms.

In section 1 we shall define and characterise K-density by classifying the cases in which it is violated. In section 2 we consider a number of decreasingly powerful axioms, all of which have K-density as a consequence. In section 3, on the other hand, we consider a sequence of axioms all of which are weaker than K-density. In section 4 we consider the specific interpretation of occurrence nets as models of processes, and illustrate the significance of K-density and all the other axioms introduced in the previous sections.

1 Characterisation of K-Density

We consider nets N = (B,E;F) where

B is the set of *conditions*,
E is the set of *events* and
F is the *flow relation*.

See [GES80] for the general definition of a net. We assume that N satisfies the two properties of an occurrence net:

- each condition $b \in B$ has at most one predecessor ($|b\cdot| \leq 1$) and at most one successor ($|\cdot b| \leq 1$), and

- N is acyclic.

As a matter of convenience we abbreviate "occurrence net" to "net" throughout these notes. As an example, we consider the following net N0 which is taken from [BES80a]:

N0

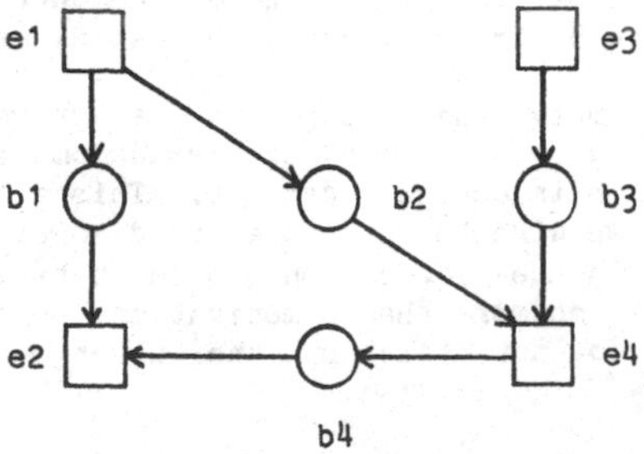

Figure 1

In contradistinction to [BES80a] where events are the only basic objects of study, we are here equally much concerned with conditions. We use the neutral term

"<u>element</u>" to refer to either an event or a condition, and we define

$$X := B \cup E$$

to be the set of all elements. Thus, for N0 we have

$$X = \{e1,e2,e3,e4,b1,b2,b3,b4\}.$$

We further define three relations, <, li and co, on the set of elements as follows:

$$x < y \quad :\Leftrightarrow \quad x\ F^{+}\ y$$
$$x\ \mathrm{li}\ y \quad :\Leftrightarrow \quad x < y \ \underline{or}\ x = y \ \underline{or}\ y < x$$
$$x\ \mathrm{co}\ y \quad :\Leftrightarrow \quad x = y \ \underline{or}\ \underline{not}\ x\ \mathrm{li}\ y.$$

Thus, an element x <u>precedes</u> an element y (x < y) if there is a directed F-chain of elements leading from x to y. Two elements x and y are <u>on a line</u> (x li y) if they are equal or if one of them precedes the other. Two elements are <u>concurrent</u> (x co y) if they are equal or if they are not on a line.

For example, in N0 we have b2 < e2, e1 li b4, b1 co b2, etc. Note that both li and co are symmetric and reflexive; neither needs to be transitive. By contrast, < is irreflexive and transitive. For a justification of the potential non-transitivity of co, see [PET80a].

We now extend the relations co and li. A subset of X in which any two elements are concurrent is called a <u>cut-set</u>; take, for example, {b1,b2,e3} in N0. Similarly, a subset any two elements of which are on a line is called a <u>line-set</u>; take, for example, {e1,e4,b4,e2}. If such sets are moreover <u>maximal</u> then they are called <u>cuts</u> and <u>lines</u>, respectively. In our example, {b1,b2,e3} is indeed a cut, but {e1,e4,b4,e2} is not a line because it is not maximal: b2 can be added to the set without destroying its property of being a line-set.

In the mathematical literature there is an abundance of similar definitions. To mention but one, lines and cuts are analogous to "maximal chains" and "maximal antichains", respectively, in a partial ordering. There is one difference, though: partial orderings are defined as structures (E,<), and chains and antichains are subsets of E. In other words, they contain only one type of element whereas lines and cuts contain two types of elements, namely events and conditions. This difference is important both formally, because events turn out to be the significant constituent elements of lines while conditions are the significant elements of cuts, and informally, because lines can be interpreted as "extended events" and cuts can be interpreted as "extended conditions" (see section 4).

If we are given a line-set then we can always find some line containing it, and the analogue is true for cut-sets. This proposition is obvious for finite nets but can be proved in general only by making use of the axiom of choice; we assume, therefore, that the latter holds. As examples, take the cut-set {b1,b2} which is contained in the cut C={b1,b2,e3} (and also in {b1,b2,b3}), and the line-set {e1,b4} which is contained in the line L={e1,b2,e4,b4,e2} (see Figure 2 overleaf).

In the net shown in Figure 2, C meets L in b2, or $b2 \in C \cap L$. It follows immediately from the definitions that the intersection of an arbitrary cut and an arbitrary line contains <u>at most</u> one element. Indeed, the existence of two distinct elements in that intersection is excluded by our definition of co. The K-density axiom requires that there also be <u>at least</u> one element in that intersection. More formally, a net is called <u>K-dense</u> if

$$|C \cap L| = 1$$

for all cuts C and lines L. The reader is encouraged to verify that N0 is K-dense.

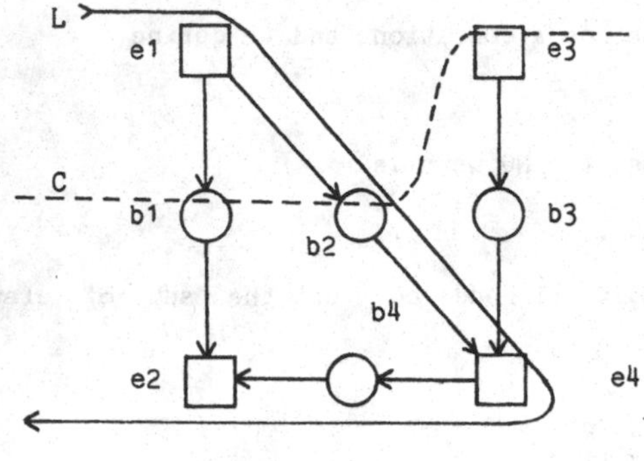

Figure 2

We now define the two simplest non-K-dense nets, N1 and N2:

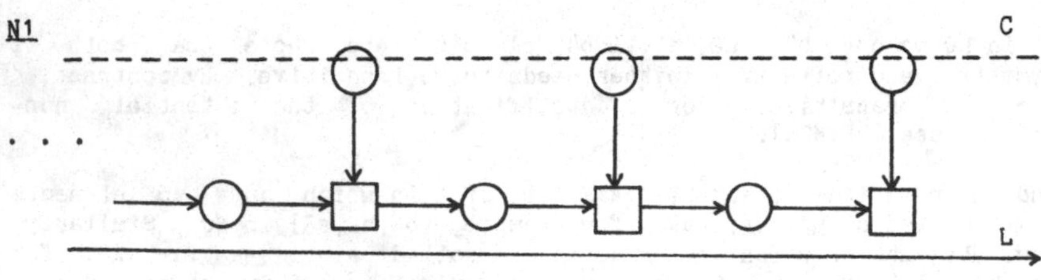

Figure 3

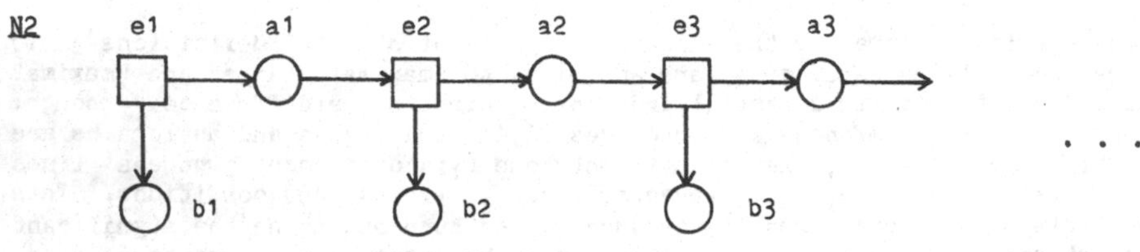

Figure 4

Both nets are infinite as indicated by the ellipses, and neither of them is K-dense. For N1, the disjoint cut C and line L are shown. N1 and N2 can be derived from each other by arrow-reversal. The cut and line corresponding to C and L in N2 are {b1,b2,b3,...} and {e1,a1,e2,a2,e3,...}, respectively.

Evidently there are arbitrarily many more complicated non-K-dense nets. There are, for example, nets containing infinite lines which consist only of events (see [PET77]). However, in a sense to be made precise now, nets violating the axiom of K-density contain N1 or N2, or both, as "causal components". We first define this notion and thereafter illustrate it by two examples.

For a net, say N', to be a causal component of an arbitrary net N, we require that the set of conditions and events of N' be embedded in the respective sets of N. We further require that the "precedes" relations <' and < agree in N' and N; by implication, the relations co',li' and co,li then also agree in N' and N. Thus, formally, N'=(B',E';F') is called a <u>causal component</u> of N=(B,E;F) - in signs: N' $\leq$ N - if

$B' \subseteq B$, $E' \subseteq E$ and $x <' y \iff x < y$ for all $x,y \in X'$.

N' may be a causal component of N without being a subnet of N (see [GES80] for the definition of a subnet); conversely, N' may be a subnet without being a causal component. We illustrate this difference with the help of two examples, N3 and N4:

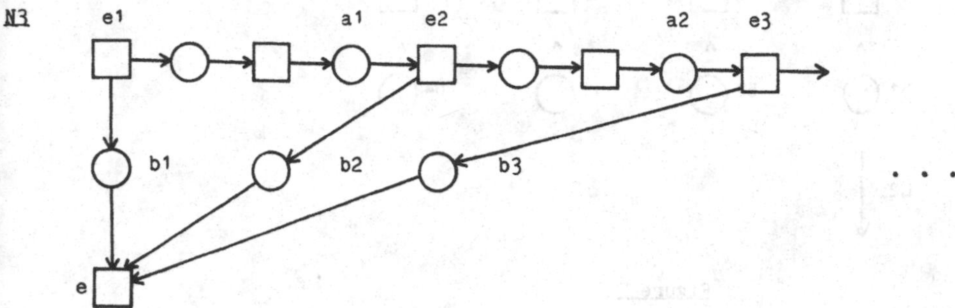

Figure 5

As suggested by the labelling, N2 is a causal component of N3. However, the arrow (e1,a1) of N2 is missing in N3; therefore, N2 is not a subnet of N3.

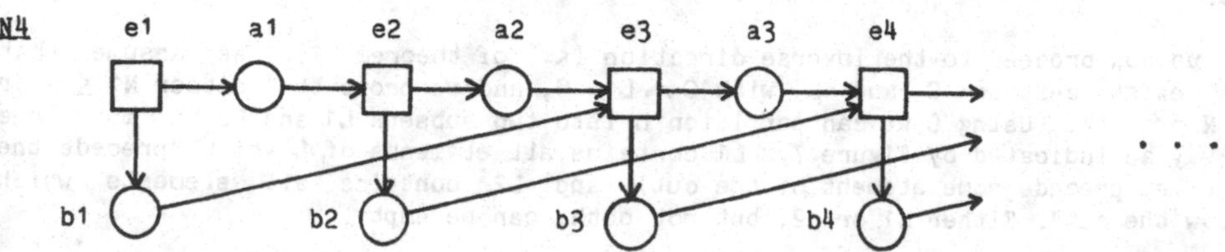

Figure 6

Again as indicated by the labelling, N2 is a subnet of N4. It is not, however, a causal component of N4 because, for example, b1 co e3 in N2 and b1 < e3 in N4.

We now give a characterisation of K-density:

Theorem 1   N is K-dense $\iff$ neither N1 $\leq$ N nor N2 $\leq$ N.

In words: if N is K-dense then neither N1 nor N2 are causal components of N (strictly speaking we ought to say: "... are isomporphic to a causal component of N", but we ignore this distinction). For example, N3 cannot therefore be K-dense. Conversely, if neither N1 nor N2 are causal components of N then N is K-dense. Thus, for example, N4 is K-dense.

We present an outline of the proof of theorem 1; for details the reader is referred to [BES77]. Let us first prove the direction ($\Rightarrow$). We assume that N2 $\leq$ N and show that N is not K-dense; the case in which N1 $\leq$ N can be treated symmetrically.

By assumption, e1,e2,e3 etc (see Figure 4) are events of N; what is more, e1 < e2 < e3 ... in N, ei < bi in N and also bi co bj in N. {e1,e2,e3,...} is thus a line-set in N, and {b1,b2,b3,...} is a cut-set in N. An earlier proposition allows us to pick a line L containing the set {e1,e2,e3,...}. We are now constructing a cut C which is disjoint with L. It can be shown that L splits into two subsets, L^1 and L2, according to the following pattern:

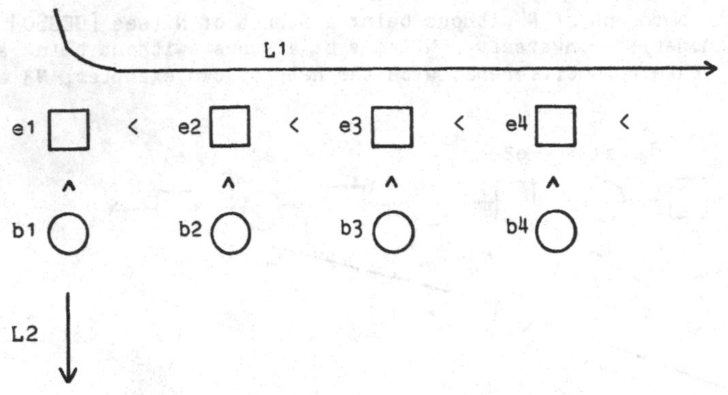

Figure 7

(where L2 is possibly empty).

None of the bi can belong to either L^1 or L2, indicating a "gap" between L^1 and L2. The cut C is to be placed in this gap. If L2 = Ø we can just simply define C such that it contains the cut-set $\{b^1, b2, b3, \ldots\}$; if however L2 ≠ Ø then the construction is somewhat more elaborate. In both cases we end up with a cut C situated, as it were, between L^1 and L2 such that $C \frown L = \emptyset$. Hence N is not K-dense.

Let us now proceed to the inverse direction (<=) of theorem 1. We assume that there exist certain C and L with $C \frown L = \emptyset$, and we prove that either $N^1 \leq N$ or $N2 \leq N$ or both. Using C we can partition L into two subsets L^1 and L2 in much the same way as indicated by Figure 7. L^1 contains all elements of L which "precede the cut" (i.e. precede some element of the cut) and L2 contains all elements which "follow the cut". Either L^1 or L2, but not both, can be empty.

Now L^1 either has or has not an element, say y^1, which is "nearest to the cut"; that is to say that all other elements y of L^1 are before y^1: $y < y^1$. Similarly, L2 either has or has not a nearest element to C, say y2; that is to say that all other elements y of L2 are after y2: $y2 < y$. In combination there are four possibilities which can be represented schematically as follows:

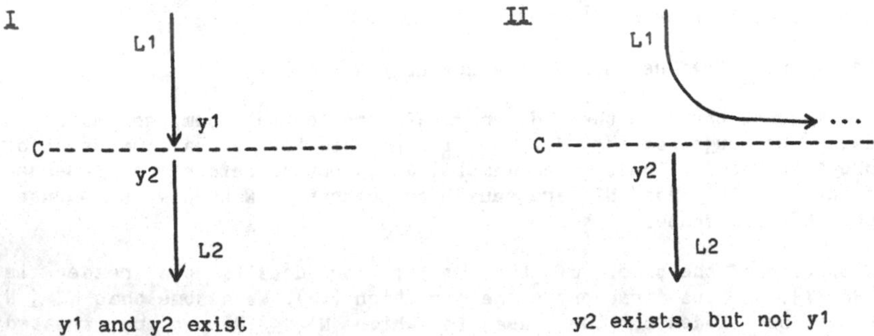

Figure 8

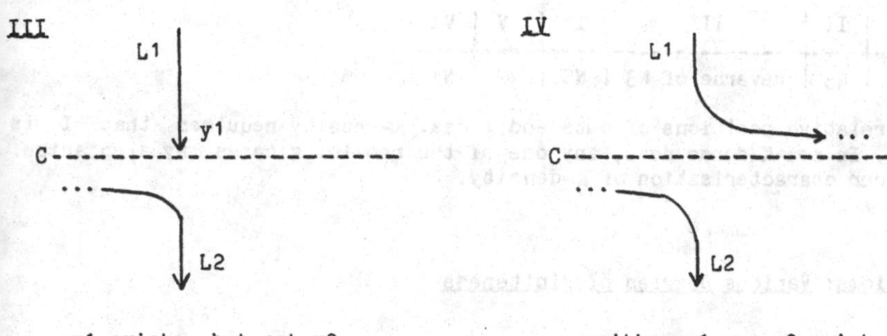

y1 exists, but not y2   neither y1 nor y2 exist

Figure 8 (continued)

One can show that in case I, i.e. if both L^1 and L2 have nearest elements, $C \frown L \neq \emptyset$. Hence our assumption excludes case I; that is, either L^1 or L2 or both fail to have nearest elements. The proof is completed by showing that if L^1 (or L2) fails to have nearest elements, then $N2 \leq N$ ($N^1 \leq N$, respectively).

If we include in our case distinction the special cases $L^1=\emptyset$ and $L2=\emptyset$ corresponding to IV:

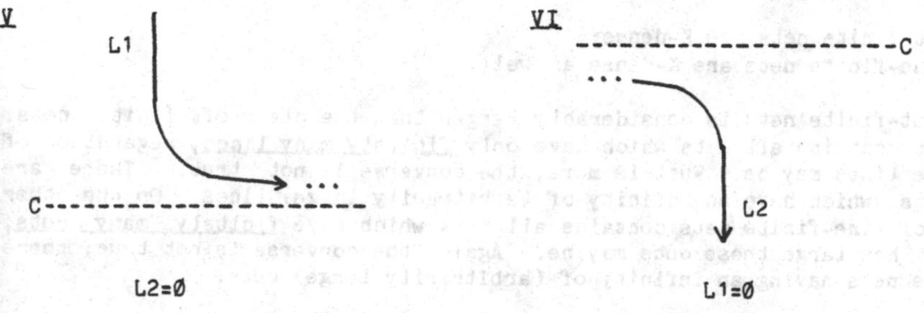

Figure 9

and if we define a net N5 as follows:

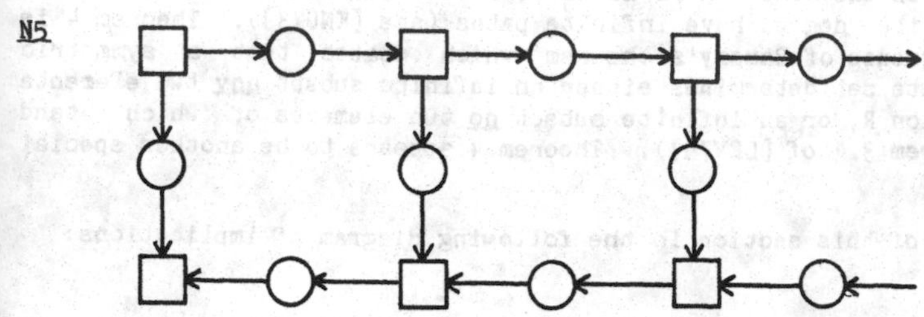

Figure 10

then we have the following correspondence:

case	I	II	III	IV	V	VI
net	N4	N3	reverse of N3	N5	N2	N1

As regards the relative positions of cuts and lines, K-density requires that I is always the case. In non-K-dense nets, any one of the remaining cases may also arise. This completes our characterisation of K-density.

2 Stronger Axioms: Various Degrees of Finiteness

Since N1 and N2 are both infinite, theorem 1 immediately implies the following result which has been alluded to in the introduction:

Theorem 2: Finite nets are K-dense.

This result has been proved in [HOL68] (however, the authors of [HOL68] did not then discuss K-density any further).

Theorem 2 can be strengthened considerably. Note that in N1 and N2 both the line and the cut contain an infinite number of elements. The proof of theorem 1 shows that nets having only finite cuts (or finite lines) cannot contain either N1 or N2 as causal components and must therefore by the same token be K-dense. We say that a net is cut-finite if it contains only finite cuts, and line-finite if it contains only finite lines. We have just seen:

Theorem 3: Cut-finite nets are K-dense;
line-finite nets are K-dense as well.

The set of cut-finite nets is considerably larger than the class of finite nets. For example, it contains all nets which have only finitely many lines, regardless of how large these lines may be. What is more, the converse is not true. There are cut-finite nets which have an infinity of (arbitrarily large) lines. On the other hand, the set of line-finite nets contains all nets which have finitely many cuts, regardless of how large these cuts may be. Again, the converse is not true: there are line-finite nets having an infinity of (arbitrarily large) cuts.

There is, however, no infinite net which is cut-finite and line-finite at the same time; that is,

Theorem 4: Nets which are both cut-finite
and line-finite are finite.

Theorem 4 can be proved in the same way as Koenig's infinity lemma which states that infinite trees of finite degree have infinite paths (see [KNU73]). Theorem 4 is also an immediate consequence of Ramsay's theorem which states that a symmetric relation R on an infinite set determines either an infinite subset any two elements of which stand in relation R, or an infinite subset no two elements of which stand in relation R (see theorem 3.1 of [LEV79]). Theorem 4 appears to be another special case of Ramsay's theorem.

We sum up the results of this section in the following diagram of implications:

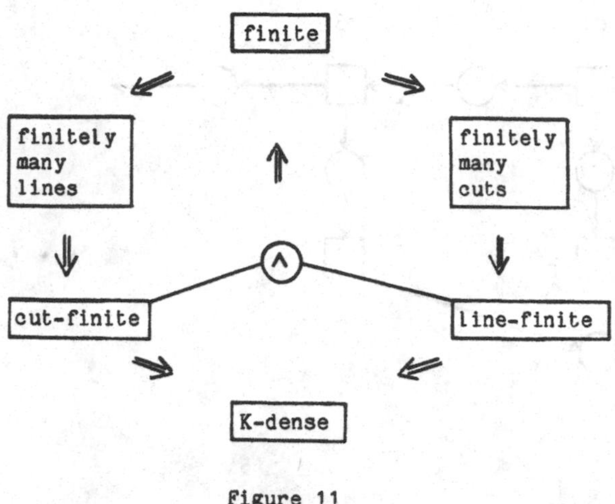

Figure 11

3 Weaker Axioms: Various Degrees of Discreteness

Figure 11 can be taken as the upper half of a diagram showing the position of K-density with respect to a set of related axioms. In this section we are concerned with the lower half of such a diagram, that is, we consider three axioms which are even weaker than K-density.

For the first axiom, E-discreteness, reconsider Figure 5. Note that in N3 there is an infinite chain of events from e1 to e; that is, we can write

$$e^1 < e2 < e3 < \ldots < e,$$

where the ellipsis is thought to stand for an ascending infinite chain of events. We call a net E-discrete if there is no infinite chain, be it ascending or descending, between any pair of events. Thus, N1, N2 and N4 are E-discrete but N3 and N5 are not.

For our second axiom, consider again N3. As far as the precedence relation < between events is concerned, condition b1 is redundant because the precedence of e1 with respect to e is equally well expressed by the path leading across a1, e2 and b2. Hence < would not suffer a change in the rest of the net if b1 and its adjacent arrows were eliminated. The same is true for b2, and in fact for any bi. On the other hand, we could not take all bi out of the net because this would disconnect e from its predecessors. We cannot, by eliminating redundant conditions, reduce N3 to a net without redundant conditions.

This is in contrast to, say, N4 in which all the bi can be eliminated, reducing the net to a straight chain not containing any redundant conditions. We call nets which are reducible in this way E-combinatorial, in analogy to a similar property described in [PET80b]. Thus N1, N2 and N4 are E-combinatorial while N3 and N5 are not.

For our third axiom, convergence-freeness, we compare N3 with the following net:

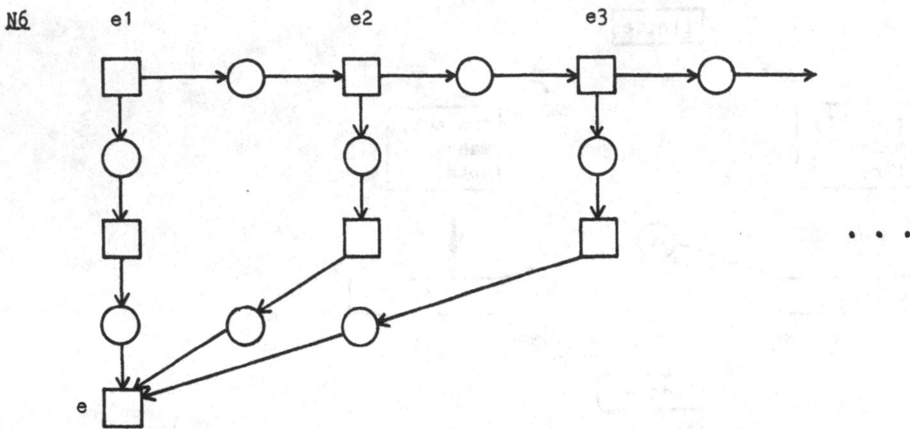

Figure 12

In N3, e can be called a "limit point" of the sequence e1,e2,e3,..., because the ei tend to come "arbitrarily close" to e with increasing i. This is not true in N6. Here, no matter how large i, the event ei is always separated from e by a distinct event not belonging to the sequence e1,e2, etc. In this case, e cannot reasonably be called a "limit point" of the sequence. We call a net convergence-free if it contains no limit points. Of the nets considered so far, only N3 is not convergence-free; note in particular that N5 is convergence-free although there are "bounded" infinite chains of events.

We obtain:

Theorem 5: K-dense nets are E-discrete;

Theorem 6: E-discrete nets are E-combinatorial;

Theorem 7: E-combinatorial nets are convergence-free.

Theorem 5 can be proved by showing that non-E-discrete nets fall under one of the cases II-IV of Figure 8, and vice versa. Thus while K-density excludes all of II-VI, E-discreteness excludes only II-IV. The interested reader is encouraged to convince himself or herself of the truth of theorems 6 and 7. Theorem 6 is discussed at length in [ORE62]. The reverse directions of the theorems do not hold. N1 is E-discrete but not K-dense; N6 is E-combinatorial but not E-discrete; finally, N5 is convergence-free but not E-combinatorial.

By way of summary, we can complement the diagram shown in Figure 11 as follows:

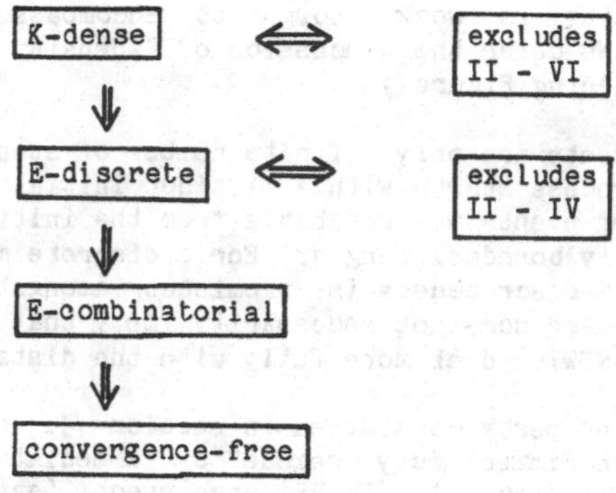

Figure 13

4 Interpretation

Our goal in this section is to explore the significance of all the properties introduced in the preceding sections. As indicated in the introduction, we think of an occurrence net as a mathematical model of a process. For the purposes of illustrating the axioms it is convenient and sufficient to imagine a process to be the activity, or task, performed by a set of sequential actors whose number may vary, and who may interact with each other. Lines then correspond to "sequential subprocesses" (such as the activity of a single actor) and cuts correspond to "global states" (say, consisting of the sum of the local states of the actors at a certain time). Let us now consider the axioms in turn, as they appear in the diagrams shown in Figures 11 and 13.

Finite nets describe finite processes. This means two things. Firstly, the "length" of the process is bounded, i.e. there is a finite lapse (of time) between the start and the end of the process. Secondly, the "width" of the process is bounded, i.e. there is an overall bound on the number of actors and interactions involved in the process.

Nets which have only finitely many lines correspond to processes involving an overall bounded set of actors and interactions (although the process may take an infinite time). On the other hand, nets having only finitely many cuts correspond to tasks which take a finite time (although the number of actors involved may be infinite).

Cut-finite nets describe processes whose global states are finite although not necessarily bounded. As an example, we can conceive of a process involving a finite set of actors whose combined effort it is to create, and add to the set, a new actor; in this process there is at any time a finite number of actors, but this number is overall unbounded. Similarly, line-finite nets describe processes whose sequential subtasks are finite but not necessarily bounded.

Theorem 4 can be interpreted as follows: if at any time there are only finitely many actors, and if each sequential subprocess terminates then the entire process terminates <u>and</u> involves only a finite overall number of actors. This result can therefore be helpful in proving the space and time finiteness of concurrent processes. This interpretation of theorem 4 is in fact a generalisation of the interpretation of Koenig's lemma in [KNU73].

According to Figure 11, K-density is weak enough to encompass all of the properties interpreted so far. We defer the discussion of K-density to the end of this section and proceed by considering Figure 13.

In an E-discrete net, any two events are only a finite number of steps apart. For example, if we assume that a process starts with a distinct initial event then E-discreteness asserts that all other events are reachable from the initial event by paths of finite (but not necessarily bounded) length. For a discrete model, this is a reasonable postulate; note that E-discreteness is prominent amongst the "laws" contained in [HEB78]. E-discreteness does not necessarily imply that cuts are also a finite number of steps apart. [NPW79] deal more fully with the distance of cuts.

Convergence-freeness, the third property considered in section 3, allows us to speak of the set of events which "immediately precede" or "immediately succeed" a given event. An example is shown in Figure 10. In N5, each event (save the first one) has an immediate predecessor, even though the net is not E-discrete. By contrast, no "immediate predecessor" can be defined of e in N3 (see Figure 5).

Provided the net is even E-combinatorial, it can be reduced to a net in which the only incoming arrows of a given event come from its immediate predecessors, and the only outgoing arrows lead to its immediate successors. Note that N6 (see Figure 12) is already reduced in this way, although it fails to be E-discrete. Note also that N5 cannot be reduced in this way even though it is convergence-free.

We needed the two properties discussed in the last two paragraphs in [BES80a] where we were led to define the sets of immediate predecessors and successors of an activity. It is useful to know that (according to Figure 13) these two properties are implied by K-density just as well as E-discreteness.

We now turn to the axiom of K-density. The original interpretation given to K-density in [PET77] is that it requires all global states to determine a unique local state of each subactivity. According to Figure 8, K-density precludes lines being partitionable into two entirely disconnected subsets L1 and L2 (where the cases V and VI of Figure 9 can be considered degenerate cases). In this sense, K-density requires sequential subactivities to be "continuous".

Let us finally consider the following non-K-dense net which is very similar to the one shown in Figure 5:

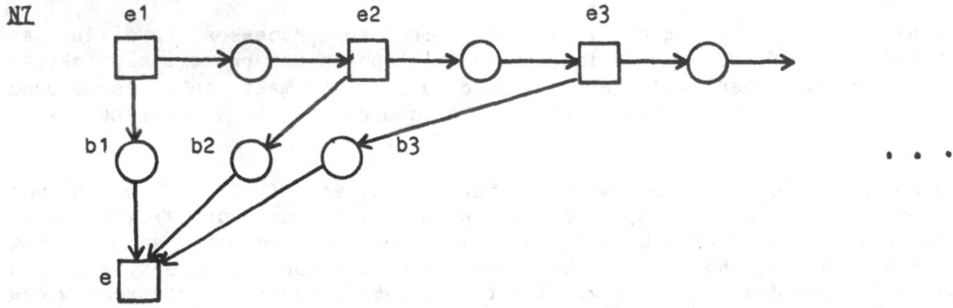

Figure 14

In N7 e is separated from its "history" e1,e2,e3,... by the "gap" {b1,b2,b3,...}. N7 models a process in which, as it were, e1,e2,e3 etc. occur and "then", miraculously, e occurs; the sequence of ei thus models a non-terminating sequential task which is brought to a halt by e. The net thus describes a "terminating non-terminating sequential process" - a glaring contradiction.

As we have argued in the introduction, the non-existence of a "terminating non-terminating process" is the underlying reason of the non-implementability of both Sx ("set x to any positive integer") and Sh ("solve the halting problem"): nets such as N7 do not describe real processes and have therefore to be excluded from consideration, for example by the adoption of K-density as an axiom. This both shows the connection of K-density to the properties of continuity (as defined in the introduction) and computability, and indicates its significance, namely to combine ease of formulation and attractiveness of interpretation with the power to exclude such unwanted structures as N7 (and, for that matter, also of N6 and N5).

Conclusion

The main aim of these notes has been to convey an understanding of K-density and to exhibit its relationship to other axioms. Our framework has been the occurrence net model of processes. A few general results should be stressed in conclusion.

It has turned out that occurrence nets are not per se "discrete" models of processes although this is suggested by their definition. Indeed, there are many possible "bridges between discrete and continuous models" [PET80a] of which K-density is but one. In this respect, the message of Figures 11 and 13 is that K-density, broadly speaking, strikes a certain balance between finiteness and continuity.

We further remark that the conceptual distinction between events and conditions is an important one. This distinction corresponds to the distinction li/co (sequential/concurrent) and also to the distinction between lines (sequential processes) and cuts (global states). Indeed, it is fundamental to the whole of general net theory.

The reader should be aware that [PET80b] attempts to derive the distinction between events and conditions from first principles. "Ropes" and the more general concurrency structures of [PET80b] should therefore not be confused with occurrence nets. For example, theorem 2 notwithstanding, the reader will find an example of a finite non-K-dense concurrency structure in [PET80b]. This is because "ropes" are allowed to be "cyclic", and only "acyclic ropes", or "straight ropes" as they are called in [PET80b] are, in effect, occurrence nets. However, straight ropes satisfy also a number of other properties which need not be satisfied by occurrence nets, for example the axiom of "coherence". A given occurrence net is therefore not necessarily also a straight rope. In summary, all results of the present notes hold for straight ropes as well and can be expected to hold in a stronger form because of the additional properties satisfied by straight ropes.

Let us finally return to a comparison between the axioms of K-density and continuity. We have seen in the introduction that the latter has a firm place and interpretation within the formalism of guarded commands, but that it does not coincide with the property of computability. In order to relate these three properties more precisely we would first have to draw up a common framework. Such an endeavour is beyond the scope of the present notes. The author is however of the opinion that it is possible to find such a common framework, despite the strongly "axiomatic" flavour of the continuity property of guarded command programs as opposed to the more "operational" flavour of the other two properties.

Acknowledgements

The author is indebted to M. Shields for discussions on the subject of these notes, and to G. Plotkin for pointing out the connection between theorem 4 and Ramsay's theorem.

References

[BES77] Best, E.: A Theorem on the Characteristics of Non-Sequential Processes. TR/116, Computing Laboratory, University of Newcastle upon Tyne, November 1977. Also to appear in Fundamenta Informaticae.

[BES80a] Best, E.: Atomicity of Activities. In this volume.

[BES80b] Best, E.: Notes on Predicate Transformers and Concurrent Programs. TR/145, Computing Laboratory, University of Newcastle upon Tyne, 1979 (to appear).

[DIJ76] Dijkstra, E.W.: A Discipline of Programming. Prentice Hall 1976.

[HEB78] Hewitt, C. and Baker, H.: Actors and Continuous Functionals. In: Formal Description of Programming Concepts (ed. E. Neuhold), North Holland 1978.

[HOL68] Holt, A.W. et al.: Final Report of the Project on Information Systems Theory. Applied Data Research ADR6606, and USAF - Rome Air Development Centre, RADC-TR-68-305, 1968.

[KNU73] Knuth, D.E.: The Art of Computer Programming, Vol.1: Fundamental Algorithms. Addison-Wesley Publishing Company, second edition 1973.

[LEV79] Levy, E.: Basic Set Theory. Springer Verlag, Berlin-Heidelberg-New York, 1979.

[NPW79] Nielsen, M., Plotkin, G. and Winskel, G.: Petri Nets, Event Structures and Domains. In: Semantics of Concurrent Computation, Lecture Notes in Computer Science 70, Springer Verlag, Berlin 1979.

[ORE62] Ore, O.: Theory of Graphs. American Mathematical Society, Colloquium Publications, Vol. XXXVIII, Rhode Island 1962.

[PET77] Petri, C.A.: Non-Sequential Processes. GMD-ISF Report ISF-77-05, Bonn, June 1977.

[PET80a] Petri, C.A.: Introduction to General Net Theory. In this volume.

[PET80b] Petri, C.A.: Concurrency. In this volume.

[SCS71] Scott, D. and Strachey, C.: Towards a Mathematical Semantics for Computer Languages. Oxford University Computing Laboratory, August 1971.

[SCO76] Scott, D.: Data Types as Lattices. SIAM Computing, Vol. 15, No. 3, September 1976, pp. 522 - 587.

[WAN77] Wand, M.: A Characterisation of Weakest Preconditions. JCSS 15, 1977, pp. 209-212.

REDUCTIONS OF NETS AND PARALLEL PROGRAMS

G. Berthelot
G. Roucairol
LITP, Institut de Programmation, Université Paris VI

R. Valk
Fachbereich Informatik, Universität Hamburg

Abstract

Reductions of concurrent systems reduce the degree of parallelism by introducing indivisible sequences of operations, which reduces the complexity of the system. If fundamental properties are preserved, this method simplifies analysis and verification. Reductions are given for transition systems, place/transition nets and parallel programs.

Introduction

In general the behaviour of concurrent systems has such a complexity, that universal methods for analysis, verification and documentation are impracticable. This is more precisely shown in [8] for place/transition nets. In particular cases by a reduction this complexity can be considerably decreased by transforming sequences of operations in some processes of the system into indivisible regions. This method has its analogon in the method of stepwise refinement in computer programs and in the notion of net morphisms in net theory.

In the first section reductions are defined for the very general formalism of transition systems, which allow applications to various models of concurrent systems. Preservation of some important properties by such reductions is shown. In the second section three particular reduction rules for place/transition nets are given. Since these rules are special cases of the reductions in the first section, all results already derived there, also apply to nets. Other reduction rules known in literature or arising in applications can be verified by the same method. In the last section reductions of some types of parallel programs with arbitrary semantics are introduced, again as an application of the results in the first section.

1. Reductions of transition systems

The marking graph of a place/transition net gives a description of the net behaviour. Whereas there are many different formal models of concurrent systems, their dynamical behaviour can be represented in a similar way by transition systems. A transition system can be seen as an abstraction of a marking graph in such a way, that the nodes are not necessarily markings but arbitrary states of the system. To point out this analogy, transition systems could called "transition graphs" as well.

$TS = (Q,T,(\,\rangle,Q_o)$ is a <u>transition system</u> [9,11] , if Q, T, $Q_o \subseteq Q$ and $(\,\rangle \subseteq Q \times T \times Q$ are sets. Q is the <u>set of states</u>, T the <u>set of transitions</u>, Q_o the <u>set of initial states</u>, and $(\,\rangle$ the <u>transition relation</u>. Instead of $(q,w,q') \in (\,\rangle$ we also write $q(w\rangle q'$. By the transitive closure and defining $q(\lambda\rangle q$ the transition relation is extended to $(\,\rangle \subseteq Q \times T^* \times Q$. For $q \in Q$, $w \in T^*$ let be $q(w\rangle$ if $\exists\, q' : q(w\rangle q'$ and we say that <u>w can fire in q</u>. Define $q(\,\rangle q'$ if $\exists\, w \in T^*$: $q(w\rangle q'$ and $(q\rangle := \{ q' \in Q \mid q(\,\rangle q' \}$ for all $q,q' \in Q$. $(Q_o\rangle := \bigcup_{q_o \in Q_o} (q_o\rangle$ is the <u>reachability set of TS</u> .

A transition $t \in T$ is <u>live in state q</u>, if $\forall q' \in (q\rangle \;\; \exists q'' \in (q'\rangle : q''(t\rangle$, a subset $\hat{T} \subseteq T$ is <u>live in a set $\hat{Q} \subseteq Q$</u>, if t is live in q for all $t \in \hat{T}$ and all $q \in \hat{Q}$. The transition system TS is <u>live</u>, if T is live in Q_o. A state q is <u>dead</u> if no transition can fire in q. TS is <u>determinate</u>, if $(Q_o\rangle$ contains at most one dead state. TS is <u>confluent</u>, if $\forall q,q',q'' \in (Q_o\rangle : q(\,\rangle q' \wedge q(\,\rangle q'' \Rightarrow \exists\, q''' \in Q : (\, q'(\,\rangle q''' \wedge q''(\,\rangle q''' \,)$. TS <u>has a home state</u> q if $\forall q' \in (Q_o\rangle :: q \in (q'\rangle$. TS <u>halts in a state q_f</u>, if $q_f \in (Q_o\rangle$ and q_f is dead. TS is <u>bounded</u>, if $(Q_o\rangle$ is finite. TS is <u>reversible</u>, if $q_o \in (q\rangle$ for all $q_o \in Q_o$ and $q \in (q_o\rangle$. TS is <u>non-halting</u>, if no reachable state is dead.

We now define reductions of transition systems. By a reduction sequences of several transitions are reduced to only one indivisible transition. This correspondence is described by two mappings m_1 and m_2.

A transition system $TS = (Q,T,(\,\rangle,Q_o)$ is said <u>to reduce</u> to $\widehat{TS} = (\hat{Q},\hat{T},(\!(\,\rangle\!\rangle,\hat{Q}_o)$ <u>with respect to (m_1,m_2,i)</u>, if

$m_1 : T \longrightarrow \mathcal{P}_o(\hat{T}) \cup \{\{\lambda\}\}$ and

$m_2 : \hat{T} \longrightarrow \mathcal{P}_o(T^+)$ are mappings,

$i : \hat{Q} \longrightarrow Q$ is an injection

and the following conditions (A1) - (A4) hold. Then $\widehat{TS}$ is also called a <u>reduction of TS</u>. To simplify the notation and since i is injective, we identify $\hat{Q}$ with $i(\hat{Q})$ and consider $\hat{Q}$ as a subset of Q. So, instead of $i(q) \in Q$ for $q \in \hat{Q}$ we simply write $q \in Q$.

(A1) a) $\forall q_o \in Q_o \;\; \exists \hat{q}_o \in \hat{Q}_o \; : \; q_o(\;\rangle \hat{q}_o$

b) $\forall \hat{q}_o \in \hat{Q}_o \;\; \exists q_o \in Q_o \; : \; q_o(\;\rangle \hat{q}_o$

(A2) $\forall q_o \in Q_o \; \forall q \in Q : \; q_o(\;\rangle q \implies \exists \hat{q}_o \in \hat{Q}_o \; \exists \hat{q} \in \hat{Q} \; : \; q(\;\rangle \hat{q} \; \wedge \; \hat{q}_o(\;\rangle\!\rangle \hat{q}$

(A3) $\forall \hat{q}, \hat{q}' \in (\hat{Q}_o\rangle\!\rangle \; \forall t \in \hat{T} \; : \; \hat{q}(t\rangle\!\rangle \hat{q}' \implies \exists w \in m_2(t) \; : \; \hat{q}(w\rangle \hat{q}'$

(A4) $\forall \hat{q}, \hat{q}' \in (\hat{Q}_o\rangle\!\rangle \; \forall x \in T^* : \; \hat{q}(x\rangle \hat{q}' \implies \exists w \in m_1(x) \; : \; \hat{q}(w\rangle\!\rangle \hat{q}'$

The reduction is <u>initial state preserving</u>, if (A1) is replaced by

(A1') $Q_o = \hat{Q}_o$ and <u>strict</u> if (A4) is replaced by

(A4') $\forall \hat{q}, \hat{q}' \in (\hat{Q}_o\rangle\!\rangle \; \forall x \in T^+ : \; \hat{q}(x\rangle \hat{q}' \implies \exists w \in m_1(x) \; : \hat{q}(w\rangle\!\rangle \hat{q}' \wedge w \neq \lambda$

In this definition we assume, that $\mathcal{P}_o(A) := \{ A' \mid A' \subseteq A \wedge A' \neq \emptyset \}$ and $T^+ := T^* - \{\lambda\}$. $(\hat{Q}_o\rangle\!\rangle$ is the reachability set in $\hat{TS}$ and m_1 and m_2 are extended to homomorphisms $m_1 : T^* \longrightarrow (\mathcal{P}_o(\hat{T}) \cup \{\{\lambda\}\})^*$ and $m_2 : \hat{T}^* \longrightarrow (\mathcal{P}_o(T^+))^*$. Note that $(\mathcal{P}_o(A))^*$ is a monoid with complex product as binary operation and unit $\{\lambda\}$.

<u>Remark</u> : By (A1) and (A3) also $(\hat{Q}_o\rangle\!\rangle \subseteq (Q_o\rangle$ holds (by our convention, the inclusion is understood modulo the injection i). By induction on the length of t, (A3) also holds for arbitrary $t \in \hat{T}^*$.

This definition extends the definition of a reduction of Kwong [11] , but nevertheless the following results from [11] remain valid.

<u>Theorem 1.1</u>

Let $\hat{TS}$ be a reduction of TS, which is supposed to be initial state preserving in b) and d) and strict in c) and d). Then

a) 1. TS has a home state iff $\hat{TS}$ has a home state.

2. If q_f is dead in TS and $\hat{TS}$, then TS halts in q_f iff $\hat{TS}$ halts in q_f.

b) 1. TS is confluent iff $\hat{TS}$ is confluent.

2. TS is reversible iff $\hat{TS}$ is reversible.

c) TS is non-halting iff $\hat{TS}$ is non-halting.

d) TS is determinate iff $\hat{TS}$ is determinate.

<u>Proof</u>

With the exception of b)2. all proofs are modified versions of proofs in [11] . If TS is reversible, $\hat{q} \in (q_o\rangle\!\rangle$, $q_o \in Q_o = \hat{Q}_o$ implies $\hat{q} \in (q_o\rangle$ (by (A3)) and $q_o \in (\hat{q}\rangle$. By (A4) $q_o \in (\hat{q}\rangle\!\rangle$ and $\hat{TS}$ is reversible. Conversely, if $\hat{TS}$ is reversible and $q \in (q_o\rangle$ then by (A2) $\exists \hat{q} \in \hat{Q} : q(\;\rangle \hat{q}$. Since $q_o \in Q_o = \hat{Q}_o$ by (A4) also $q_o(\;\rangle\!\rangle \hat{q}$ and $\hat{q}(\;\rangle\!\rangle q_o$. Finally by (A3) we obtain $q(\;\rangle \hat{q}(\;\rangle q_o$.

<u>qed</u>

We now introduce some additional properties of reductions to preseve liveness and boundedness.

With respect to m_1 we define $T_\lambda := \{ t \in T \mid m_1(t) = \{\lambda\}$, $T_o := T - T_\lambda$.
(m_1, m_2, i) are said to be consistent, if

(B1) $\bigcup_{t \in T} m_1(t) \supseteq \hat{T}$

(B2) $\forall q \in (\hat{Q}_o\rangle\rangle \ \forall t \in T : (\exists t_1 \in m_1(t) : q(t_1\rangle\rangle \Rightarrow \forall t_1 \in m_1(t) : q(t_1\rangle\rangle$

(B3) $\forall t \in T_o \ \ \forall w \in T^+ : w \in m_2(m_1(t)) \Longrightarrow w$ contains t .

(m_1, m_2, i) are strictly consistent, if in addition :

(B4) there is a mapping $f : T_\lambda \to T_o$ such that for all $t \in T_\lambda$:
$\forall q \in (Q_o\rangle \ : \ q(f(t) \rangle \Longrightarrow \exists q' \in (q\rangle \ : q'(t\rangle$.

TS boundedly reduces to $\widehat{TS}$, if :

(C) $(Q_o\rangle \cap \hat{Q}$ finite $\Longrightarrow (Q_o\rangle$ finite

Theorem 1.2

Assume that $TS = (Q, T, (\ \rangle, Q_o)$ reduces to $\widehat{TS} = (\hat{Q}, \hat{T}, (\ \rangle\rangle, \hat{Q}_o)$ with respect to (m_1, m_2, i).

a) If (m_1, m_2, i) are consistent, then T_o is live in Q_o iff $\widehat{TS}$ is live.

b) If (m_1, m_2, i) are strictly consistent, then TS is live iff $\widehat{TS}$ is live.

c) If TS boundedly reduces to $\widehat{TS}$, then TS is bounded iff $\widehat{TS}$ is bounded.

Proof

a) Suppose T_o as live and let be $t_1 \in \hat{T}$, $\hat{q}_1 \in (\hat{Q}_o\rangle\rangle$. We have to find a state q_5, reachable from q_1, such that t_1 can fire in q_5. By (B1) there is a $t \in T_o$ with $t_1 \in m_1(t) \neq \{\lambda\}$. By (A1) and (A3) $\hat{q}_1 \in (Q_o\rangle$ and since T_o is live, there are q_2, $q_3 \in Q$ and $x \in T^*$ with $\hat{q}_1(x\rangle q_2(t\rangle q_3$. By (A2) this sequence continues to $q_3(y\rangle \hat{q}_4$ where $\hat{q}_4 \in \hat{Q}$. Using (A4) we can find $w \in m_1(xty)$ with $\hat{q}_1(w\rangle\rangle \hat{q}_4$. $w \in m_1(x)m_1(t)m_1(y)$ decomposes into $w = w_1 w_2 w_3$, $w_1 \in m_1(x)$, $w_2 \in m_1(t)$. Let q_5 be a state with $\hat{q}_1(w_1\rangle\rangle q_5(w_2\rangle\rangle$. Now since (m_1, m_2, i) is consistent, from $q_5(w_2\rangle\rangle$ and $\{ w_2, t \} \subseteq m_1(t)$ by (B2) it follows $q_5(t_1\rangle\rangle$.

Conversely suppose that $\hat{T}$ is live in $\hat{Q}_o$. For $t \in T_o$, $q_1 \in (Q_o\rangle$ we have to find $q_4 \in (q_1\rangle$ where t can fire. By (A2) there is $\hat{q}_2 \in (\hat{Q}_2\rangle\rangle$ with $q_1(\ \rangle \hat{q}_2$. Let $t_1 \in m_1(t) \neq \{\lambda\}$ be a transition, which is live by assumption, i.e. there are states $\hat{q}_3, \hat{q}_4 \in \hat{Q}$ with $\hat{q}_2(\ \rangle\rangle \hat{q}_3(t_1\rangle\rangle \hat{q}_4$. By (A3) $\exists\ w \in m_2(t_1) : \hat{q}_3(w\rangle \hat{q}_4$. From $w \in m_2(t_1) \subseteq m_2(m_1(t))$ using (B3) we conclude $w = w_1 t w_2$ and $\hat{q}_3(w_1\rangle q_4(t\rangle$. Hence t is firable in a state q_4 which is reachable from q_1 and $\hat{q}_2$ (by (A3)).

b) To prove part b) of the theorem by a) it is sufficient to show, that T is live in TS if $T_o \subseteq T$ is live. If $q \in (Q_o\rangle$, $t \in T_\lambda$ then since T_o is live, there is $q_1 \in (q\rangle$ with $q_1(\ f(t) \rangle$ and by (B4) $\exists\ q_2 \in (q_1\rangle : q_2(t\rangle$.

c) If $(Q_o\rangle$ is finite, also $(Q_o\rangle\rangle \subseteq (Q_o\rangle$ is finite (cf. remark before theorem 1.1). Conversely, if $(\hat{Q}_o\rangle\rangle$ is finite, also $(Q_o\rangle \cap \hat{Q} \subseteq (\hat{Q}_o\rangle\rangle$ is finite. Since TS boundedly reduces to $\widehat{TS}$, also $(Q_o\rangle$ is finite.

qed

In the next section these results will be applied to reductions of nets.

2. Reductions of place/transition nets

In this section all nets are place/transition nets $N = (S,T;F,W,\underline{M}_o)$ with unbounded capacities. $\underline{M}_o$ is a finite set of initial markings. This extension from the ordinary assumption of one initial marking is a consequence of the results of this section. We adopt all definitions in [8] for $|\underline{M}_o| = 1$. By the extension the class of forward reachable markings becomes $(\underline{M}_o\rangle := \bigcup_{M \in \underline{M}_o} (M\rangle$. In the definition of the marking- and coverability-graph all initial markings must be taken as initial nodes. N is live (bounded, reversible), if N is live, (bounded, reversible) for all $M \in \underline{M}_o$. The next property of nets comes from modelling of terminating programs. But first recall, that a place $s \in S$ can be considered as a characteristic vector $s \in \{0,1\}^{|S|}$, for which we also write $\bar{s}$. If N has a unique place s_f without output transitions, N is said proper terminating in s_f, if N is bounded and $\forall M \in \underline{M}_o : \bar{s}_f \in (M\rangle$. The net is confluent, if $\forall M,M',M'' \in (\underline{M}_o\rangle : M(\rangle M' \wedge M(\rangle M'' \Rightarrow \exists M''' : (M'(\rangle M''' \wedge M''(\rangle M''')$. Now, since the marking graph of N is a transition system, as an immediate consequence we obtain the following theorem.

Theorem 2.1

Let $N = (S,T;F,W,\underline{M}_o)$ be a net with marking graph $TS = (\mathbb{N}^{|S|},T,(\ \rangle,\underline{M}_o)$, written as transition system TS. Then N has no reachable dead marking, is proper terminating in s_f, live, bounded, confluent and reversible, iff TS is non-halting, bounded and halts in $\bar{s}_f$, live, bounded, confluent and reversible, respectively.

We now define three reductions of nets, given by Berthelot [2], which have been shown to be usefull in proving correctness of concrete concurrent systems. In that reductions the indivisible compositions of two operations or transitions is expressed in terms of a substitution by a new transition. A place connecting these transitions is transformed into an isolated place, which could be deleted. For formal reasons only, we allow isolated places, which could be deleted. Two other reduction rules are then introduced to allow further such substitutions.

Recall that for a net $N = (S,T;F,W,\underline{M}_o)$ and a transition $t \in T$ the vector $W_Z(t) := \begin{pmatrix} W_Z(s_1,t) \\ \vdots \\ W_Z(s_S,t) \end{pmatrix} \in \mathbb{N}^{|S|}$ is the t-column of the matrix W_Z (see [8]) and describes the (weighted) set of input places of t. In the same way we define $W_Q(t)$ for the output places. They are called <u>input</u> and <u>output vector of t</u>. $C := W_Q - W_Z$ is the incidence matrix of N (see [8]) .

<u>A basic composition rule : the substitution R1</u> :

A place $s \in S$ is said to be <u>substituable</u> iff there exist an integer $m > 0$ and two subsets $T_H, T_F \subseteq T$ of transitions, such that :

(R1a) $\quad \forall f \in T_F : W_Z(f) = m \cdot \bar{s} \wedge s \notin f^\bullet \wedge f^\bullet \neq \emptyset$

(R1b) $\quad \forall h \in T_H : s \notin {}^\bullet h \wedge \exists k_h > 0 : W_Q(s,h) = m \cdot k_h$

(R1c) $\quad \forall t \notin T_H \cup T_F : s \notin {}^\bullet t \cup t^\bullet$.

Remark : These conditions imply, that when a transition $h \in T_H$ has fired, every transition in T_F has concession (which later on will imply property (B4)), but only a finite number of them can fire in sequence (which later on will imply property (C)).

For any $h \in T_H$ let be :

(R1d) $\quad Sub(h,s,T_F) := \{ W_Q(h) - k_h \cdot m \cdot \bar{s} + \sum_{f \in T_F} n_f \cdot W_Q(f) \mid \sum_{f \in T_F} n_f = k_h \}$

This set of vectors describes the effect of substituting the output place s of h by some combination of the output places of T_F (more precisely, the output vectors of the new transitions). Then composition of the transition h with elements of T_F is defined in the following way :

(R1e) For each $h \in T_H$ introduce a new set $R1(h,T_F) = \{t_1,\ldots,t_r\}$ with $r = |Sub(h,s,T_F)|$. Each of these new transitions has $W_Z(h)$ as input vector and as output vector a distinct element of Sub(h,s,T_F). Remove all transitions of T_H and T_F . s becomes an isolated place.

(R1f) Replace the initial marking set $\underline{M}_o$ by
$R1(\underline{M}_o) := \{ M - q_M \cdot m \cdot \bar{s} + \sum_{f \in T_F} n_f \cdot W_Q(f) \mid \sum_{f \in T_F} n_f = q_M \text{ and } M \in \underline{M}_o \}$,

where q_M is the integral quotient $q_M := M(s)$ <u>div</u> m .

(R1g) Define $\hat{T} := (T - (T_H \cup T_F)) \cup \bigcup_{h \in T_H} R1(h,T_F)$ and

and $m_1 : T \longrightarrow \mathcal{P}_o(\hat{T}) \cup \{\{\lambda\}\}$ by $m_1(t) := \begin{cases} R1(h,T_F) & \text{if } t \in T_H \\ \{\lambda\} & \text{if } t \in T_F \\ \{t\} & \text{otherwise} \end{cases}$

and $m_2 : \hat{T} \rightarrow \mathcal{P}_o(T^+)$ by $m_2(t) := \begin{cases} \{hw \mid w \in T_F^+ \wedge lg(w)=k_h\} & \text{if } t \in R1(h,T_F) \\ \{t\} & \text{otherwise} \end{cases}$

and $i : (R1(\underline{M}_o)\rangle \longrightarrow (\underline{M}_o\rangle$ by $i(M) := M$.

Note that in the particular case of $|Sub(h,s,T_F)| = 1$ for all $h \in H$, reduction rule R1 defines a net epimorphism.

As the example in figure 1 shows, this rule is much simpler than the formalism suggests. In this example we have for instance $T_H = \{h_1,h_2\}$, $T_F = \{f_1,f_2\}$ $R1(h_1,T_F) = m_1(h_1) = \{t_1,t_2,t_3\}$, $m_1(f_1) = \{\lambda\}$, $m_2(t_1) = \{h_1 f_1 f_1\}$. Only one resulting initial marking is indicated.

Figure 1

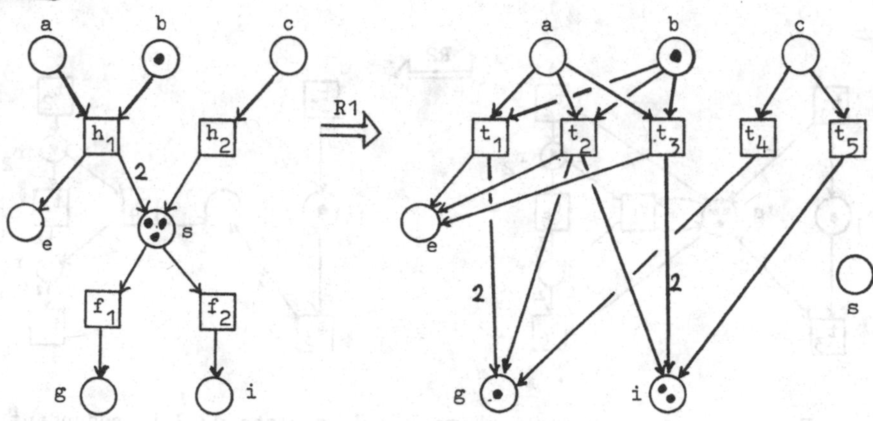

Simplification of a redundant place (R2) :

A place $s \in S$ is called redundant in regard to a subset $R \subseteq S$ of places, if for all reachable markings $M \in (\underline{M}_o\rangle$ the integer $M(s)$ is greater or equal to a linear combination of $\{ M(s) \mid s \in R \}$. In other words, the place s does not contribute firing conditions to the ones defined by R. Formally, a place is redundant, if there is a mapping $V : R \cup \{s\} \longrightarrow \mathbb{N}^+$ such that

(R2a) $\forall\ M \in \underline{M}_o \ \exists\ b_M \in \mathbb{N} \ : \ V(s)\cdot M(s) - \sum_{r \in R} V(r)\cdot M(r) = b_M$

(R2b) $\forall\ t \in T \ : \ V(s)\cdot W_Z(s,t) - \sum_{r \in R} V(r)\cdot W_Z(r,t) \leq \min\{ b_M \mid M \in \underline{M}_o \}$

(R2c) $\forall\ t \in T \ \exists\ c_t \in \mathbb{N} \ : \ V(s)\cdot C(s,t) - \sum_{r \in R} V(r)\cdot C(r,t) = c_t$

Remark : If N is live and bounded, then $c_t = 0$ for all $t \in T$.

(R2d) Let all places and transitions unchanged, but redefine $W_Z(t)$ and $W_Q(t)$ for each transition by $W'_Z(t) := W_Z(t) - W_Z(s,t)\cdot\bar{s}$ and $W'_Q(t) := W_Q(t) - W_Q(s,t)\cdot\bar{s} + c_t\cdot\bar{s}$

(R2e) Replace $\underline{M}_o$ by $\underline{M}'_o := \{ M - M(s)\cdot\bar{s} + [V(s)\cdot M(s) - \sum_{r \in R} V(r)\cdot M(r)]\cdot\bar{s} \mid M \in \underline{M}_o \}$

(R2f) Define $m_1 : T \longrightarrow \mathcal{P}_o(T) \cup \{\{\lambda\}\}$ by $m_1(t) := \{t\}$
and $m_2 : T \longrightarrow \mathcal{P}_o(T^+)$ by $m_2(t) := \{t\}$
and $i : (\underline{M}'_o\rangle \longrightarrow (\underline{M}_o\rangle$
by $i(M) := M - M(s)\cdot\bar{s} + \frac{1}{V(s)} \cdot [M(s) + \sum_{r \in R} V(r)\cdot M(r)]\cdot\bar{s}$

In the example of figure 2 the set R is R = $\{r_1,r_2,r_3\}$ and $(V(r_1),V(r_2), V(r_3),V(s)) = (4,2,1,2)$ and $(c_{t_1},\dots,c_{t_6}) = (0,0,2,1,0,0)$. Only one new initia marking is indicated.

Remark : In the initial net the firing sequence $t_2t_2t_4t_4t_6$ leaves one token in s. Since we cannot have $W'_Q(s,t_4) = 1/2$, we have $W'_Q(s,t_4) = 1$ in the reduced n But then in order to preserve S-invariance, we must have $W'_Q(s,t_3) = 2$, althoug the sequence t_1t_3 leaves only one token in s.

Figure 2

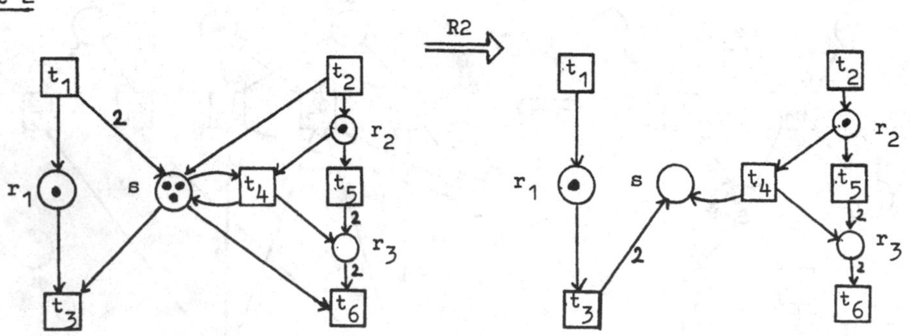

Remark : For the particular case, where R = ∅ a place $s \in S$ is redundant if $\forall t \in T\ \forall M \in \underline{M}_o$: $M(s) \geq W_Z(s,t)$ and $\forall t \in T\ \exists c_t \in \mathbb{N} : C(s,t) = c_t$. An example is given in figure 3.

Figure 3

Removing identity transitions and similar transitions (R3)

(R3a) A transition t is an identity transition, if $W_Z(t) = W_Q(t)$. It can b removed if $R_t := \{t' \in T \mid W_Q(t') \geq W_Z(t) \wedge t' \neq t\} \neq \emptyset$

Define $m_1(t_1) := \begin{cases} \{\lambda\} & \text{if } t_1 = t \\ \{t_1\} & \text{otherwise} \end{cases}$ $\quad m_2(t_1) := \begin{cases} t_2t^* & \text{if } t_2 \in R_t \\ \{t_1\} & \text{otherwise} \end{cases}$

(R3b) Transitions t_1 and t_2 are similar, if $W_Z(t_1) = W_Z(t_2)$ and $W_Q(t_1) =$ $W_Q(t_1) = W_Q(t_2)$. In this case t_1 can be removed. Define

$m_1(t) := \begin{cases} \{t_2\} & \text{if } t = t_1 \\ \{t\} & \text{otherwise} \end{cases}$ $\quad m_2(t) := \begin{cases} \{t_2\} & \text{if } t = t_1 \\ \{t\} & \text{otherwise} \end{cases}$

In both cases define $\underline{M}'_o := \underline{M}_o$ and i as the identity mapping on $\langle \underline{M}'_o \rangle$

A net $\hat{N}$ is called a reduction of a net N, if $\hat{N}$ is constructed by one of the reduction rules R1, R2 or R3. If (R3a) is not used, the reduction is called <u>strict</u>. The reduction is <u>initial marking preserving</u> if $\underline{M}_o = \{ i(M) \mid M \in \underline{M}'_o \}$.

<u>Theorem 2.2</u>

Let $N = (S,T;F,W,\underline{M}_o)$ and $\hat{N} = (S,\hat{T};\hat{F},\hat{W},\hat{\underline{M}}_o)$ be nets with transition systems (i.e. marking graphs) $TS = (\mathbb{N}^{|S|},T,(>,\underline{M}_o)$ and $\widehat{TS} = (\mathbb{N}^{|S|},\hat{T},(\gg,\hat{\underline{M}}_o)$, respectively. If $\hat{N}$ is a reduction of N, then TS boundedly reduces to $\widehat{TS}$ with respect to (m_1,m_2,i), where (m_1,m_2,i) are defined as in (R1g), (R2f), (R3a) or (R3b). (m_1,m_2,i) are strictly consistent. If the reduction of N to $\hat{N}$ is initial marking preserving or strict, then the reduction of TS to $\widehat{TS}$ is initial state preserving or strict, respectively.

This theorem follows from the proofs in [2]. As a corollary of theorems 1.1, 1.2 and 2.2 we then obtain :

<u>Theorem 2.3</u>

Let the net $\hat{N}$ be a reduction of a net N, which is supposed to be initial marking preserving in b) and strict in c).

a) N is live, bounded, proper terminating in s_f and has a home state iff $\hat{N}$ is live, bounded, proper terminating in s_f and has a home state, resp.
b) N is confluent and reversible iff $\hat{N}$ is confluent and reversible, resp.
c) No reachable marking is dead for N iff no reachable marking is dead for $\hat{N}$.

Furthermore, if N is S-invariant (for definition see [13]), then also $\hat{N}$ is S-invariant. The inverse statement is also true, if when applying R2 all integers c_t are zero [2]. The application of the three reduction rules in any order leads generally to different irreducible nets, but this is not the case, if the initial net is live and bounded. All derived irreducible nets are then isomorphic. Moreover state-machine nets and synchronization graphs (marked graphs) can be completely reduced [2].

For illustration, we give a nontrivial example of a reduction from [2] in figure 4, which is a net representation of the following semaphore program :

```
P :     var  Mutex = 1, Pl = 3, Po = 0 : semaphore ;
cobegin "producer1"   //   "producer2"   //   "consumer"
        t1 : produce       u1 : produce       v1 : P(Po)
        t2 : P(Mutex)      u2 : P(Mutex)      v2 : take up
        t3 : P(Pl)         u3 : P(Pl)         v3 : V(Pl)
        t4 : put down      u4 : put down      goto v1
        t5 : V(Po)         u5 : V(Po)
        t6 : V(Mutex)      u6 : V(Mutex)
        goto t1            goto u1
coend.
```

Figure 4

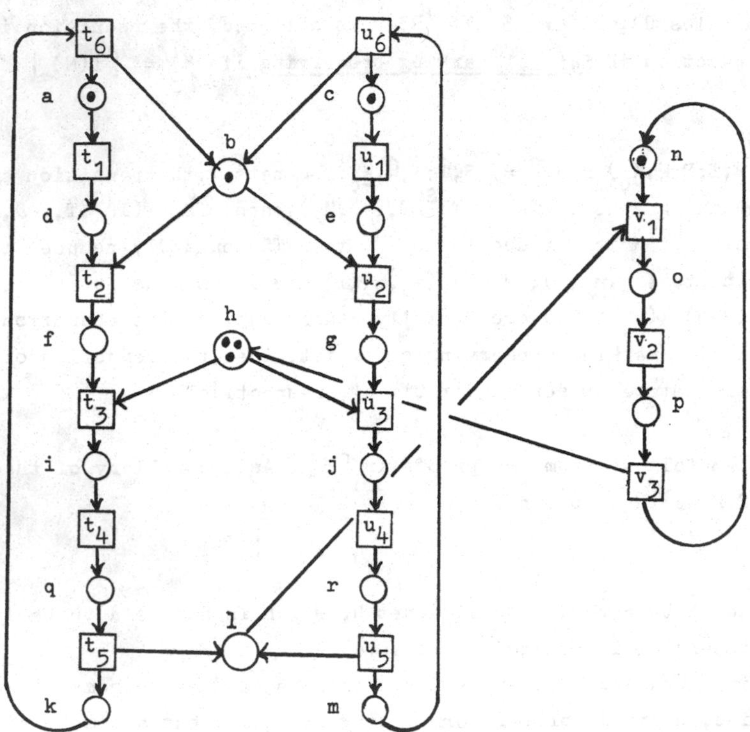

By reduction steps R1 (with s=a), R1 (s=c), R1 (s=i), R1 (s=j), R1 (s=p), R1 (s=o), R1 (s=q), R1 (s=r), R2 (s=d, R = {b,g,m} , V(d) = V(b) = V(g) = V(m) = 1), R2 (s=e, R = { b,f,k }), R1 (s=k), R1 (s=m), R2 (s=n, R = ∅), R1 (s=l), R2 (s=h, R = ∅), R1 (s=f), R1 (s=g), R3b, we obtain the net : ☐⇄⊙ (where all isolated places are omitted). The reduction is initial marking preserving and strict. Since the reduced net is trivially live, bounded, confluent, reversible and has no reachable dead marking by theorem 2.3 also the original net has these properties.

3. Reductions of parallel programs

In this section we show how reductions can be applied to parallel programs having arbitrary control and assignment statements. By a parallel program we understand a tupel $P = (V,M,\mathcal{A},Act,\mathcal{Z}_0)$, where $V = \{v_1,\ldots,v_n\}$ is a set of variables, which have values in a domain $M = M_1 \times \ldots \times M_n$ of memory states, a set of statements $\mathcal{A}$, a map Act and a set of initial states $\mathcal{Z}_0$. $\mathcal{Z}^t := M \times \mathcal{P}(\mathcal{A})$ is the total set of states. If $\alpha = (x,A) \in \mathcal{Z}^t$, then x is the memory state and A the control state or ready set of statements and we write A = ready(α). Act : $\mathcal{Z}^t \longrightarrow \mathcal{P}(\mathcal{A})$ gives for a state $\alpha = (x,A)$ a subset $Act(x,A) \subseteq A$ of active instructions, which can be executed. With each statement $a \in \mathcal{A}$ two mappings M_a and R_a are given, which describe an execution of a : $M_a : M \longrightarrow M$ gives the change of memory and $R_a : \mathcal{Z}^t \longrightarrow \mathcal{P}(\mathcal{A})$ with $\forall (x,A) \in \mathcal{Z}^t : A - \{a\} \subseteq R_a(x,A)$ the new control state. The statements in $Act(x,A) \subseteq A$ are the active statements, whereas statements in $A - Act(x,A)$ are said to be blocked. A statement $a \in \mathcal{A}$ is executable in a state $\alpha = (x,A)$ and produces a new state $\alpha' = (x',A')$ (formally $\alpha(a>\alpha')$, if $a \in Act(\alpha)$ and $x' = M_a(x)$ and $A' = R_a(\alpha)$. By the transitive closure this relation is extended for execution sequences $w \in \mathcal{A}^*$ and the set of states reachable by execution sequences from $\mathcal{Z}_0$ is the reachability set $\mathcal{Z}^r \subseteq \mathcal{Z}^t$ of P. A map Par : $\mathcal{A} \longrightarrow \mathcal{P}(\mathcal{A})$, defined by $Par(a) := \{ b \in \mathcal{A} - \{a\} \mid \exists \alpha \in \mathcal{Z}^r : \{a,b\} \subseteq Ready(\alpha) \}$ gives the statements which are (potentially) parallel with a.

Basic for the treatment of reduction is the notion of a mover [12] . A statement $a \in \mathcal{A}$ is called right (left) active mover, if $\beta(ab>\gamma$ implies $\beta(ba>\delta$ ($\beta(ba>\gamma$ imlpies $\beta(ab>\delta$) and right (left) value mover, if $\beta(ab>\gamma$ and $\beta(ba>\delta$ imply $\gamma=\delta$ ($\beta(ba>\gamma$ and $\beta(ab>\delta$ imply $\gamma=\delta$) for all $\alpha,\beta,\gamma,\delta \in \mathcal{Z}^r$, $a \in \mathcal{A}$ and $b \in Ready(\beta)$. If both properties hold a is a right (left) value-actve mover (RVA-mover (LVA-mover)).

Properties of movers are investigated in [10] . It should be clear, that parallel programs uniquely coresponds to transition systems. In [10] a general reduction theorem for parallel programs is given, which uniquely coresponds to the reduction of transition systems given in section 1. We do not discuss this general result, but give an application of that theorem to derive reductions from the (static) program listing itself. This is a generalization of a result in [12] to parallel programs.

The parallelism of the program is expressed by a statement cobegin P_1 // P_2 // ... // P_n coend. By this statement the subprograms P_1, ... , P_n are executed in parallel. By a jump from a statement b to a statement c we mean a goto statement or a conditional statement, by which the control can be transfered from b to c.

<u>Theorem 3.1</u> [10]

Let be P a program

P : <u>begin</u> w_o ; <u>cobegin</u> w_1 ; a_o ; a_1 ; ... ; a_n ; w_2 // w_3 // ... // w_n <u>coend</u> ; w_{n+1} <u>end</u>.

where all w_i are arbitrary sequences of statements not containing <u>cobegin</u> or <u>coend</u>, and where $R := \{a_o, a_1, \ldots, a_n\}$ has the following properties:

(1) no a_i $(1 \leq i \leq n)$ can be blocked in some reachable state.

(2) there is a $k \in \{0, \ldots, n\}$, such that $a_o, \ldots, a_{k-1}$ are RVA-movers and $a_{k+1}, \ldots, a_n$ are LVA-movers.

(3) none of the statements $a_1, \ldots, a_n$ can be reached by a jump from outside of R and a_o cannot be reached by a jump from R.

(4) inside of R no jumps from $\{a_k, \ldots, a_n\}$ to $\{a_1, \ldots, a_k\}$ are possible, where k is the k from (2).

If the statements in R are substituted by one indivisible statement a_R, we obtain a reduced program P/R. Then the transition system TS of P reduces to the transition system $\widehat{TS}$ of P/R with respect to a triple (m_1, m_2, i) of mappings. The reduction is strict and initial state preserving and (m_1, m_2, i) are consistent.

By this theorem the results of theorems 1.1 and 1.2 can be applied again. All definitions made for transition systems hold also for parallel programs if interpreted as transition systems.

<u>Theorem 3.2</u> [10]

Let P/R be the reduction of the parallel program P in theorem 3.1 and q_f a dead state of P and P/R. Then P has a home state, halts in q_f, is confluent, reversible, non-halting and determinate iff P/R has a home state, halts in q_f, is confluent, reversible, non halting and determinate, respectively. Furthermore P/R is live iff T_o is live in P.

We now give an example how verification of a parallel program can be simplified by reduction. The following program is again a producer/consumer situation, where an array A is copied to B using a bounded buffer of length n, to which two processes have concurrently acess.

```
P : const m,n : integer;
    var   i=j=1 : integer; full=0, empty=n : semaphore;
          buffer : array(o..n-1)of item; A, B : array(o..m)of item;
          x, y : item;
cobegin a1: if i>m then goto aend;  //  b1: if j>m then goto bend;
        a2: P(empty);                   b2: P(full);
        a3: x := A(i);                  b3: y := buffer(j mod n);
        a4: buffer(i mod n) := x;       b4: V(empty);
        a5: V(full);                    b5: B(j) := y;
        a6: i := i+1;                   b6: j := j+1;
        a7: goto a1;                    b7: goto b1;
        aend: skip;                     bend: skip;
coend.
```

Applying theorem 3.1 twice by substituting $R_1 := \{a2,\ldots,a7\}$ by the indivisible statement produce := [a2;a3;a4;a5;a6;a7] and $R_2 := \{b2,\ldots,b7\}$ by the indivisible statement consume := [b2;b3;b4;b5;b6;b7] we obtain the reduced program $P' := (P/R_1)/R_2$:

```
P' : declarations
cobegin a1: if i>m then goto aend; // b1: if j>m then goto bend;
         a8: produce;                  b8: consume;
         aend: skip;                   bend: skip;
coend.
```

This program P' is simpler in its concurrent behaviour and we obtain the following simplified invariant I, holding true for all reachable states of P' :

$$I := i>0 \land j>0 \land n-(i-j) = \text{empty} \land i-j = \text{full} \land$$
$$\text{buffer}(k \ \underline{\text{mod}} \ n) = A(k) \text{ for } k=j..i-1 \land B(k) = A(k) \text{ for } k=1..j-1$$

It is not hard to show, that I is an invariant for P'. Obviously, the state q_f, where both processes have terminated, is dead in P and P'. From the invariant I it follows, that the reduced program P' is determinate and halts in q_f with B = A. By theorem 3.2 also the original program P is determinate and halts in q_f with B = A. This proves that P is deadlock-free and partial correct.

Note that I is not an invariant for P. Such an invariant for P would be more complicated. Also this proof is shorter and easier to find than the corresponding proof of Owicki and Gries [14] .

References

1. Berthelot,G.,Roucairol,G. : Reduction of Petri Nets. in : Proc. of the Symp. on MFCS 76, Lect. Notes in Computer Sci. 45, pp 202-209, Springer Berlin, (1976).

2. Berthelot,G. : Verification de réseaux de Petri. Thèse de 3° cycle, Inst: tut de Programmation, Univ. Paris 6, (1978).

3. Berthelot,G. : Preuves de non-blocage de programmes parallèles par reduc- tion de réseaux de Petri. in : Proc. of the 1st European Conference on Parallel and Distributed Processing, J.C.Syre ed.,CEPADUES publ., (1979)

4. Byrn,W.H. : Sequential Processes, Deadlocks, and Semaphore Primitives. TR7-75, Havard Univ., Cambridge, Mass., (1975).

5. Cotronis,J.Y.,Lauer,P.E. : Verification of Concurrent Systems of Process in : Proc. of the International Computing Symposium 1977, Liège ; (1977).

6. Dadda,L. : The Synthesis of Petri Nets for Controlling Purposes and the Reduction of their Complexity. in : Proc. of the EUROMICRO Conf. North-Holland pub., (1976).

7. Gostelow,K.,Cerf,V.G.,Estrin,G.,Volansky,S., : Proper Termination of Flo of Control in Programs involving Concurrent Processes. SIGPLAN Notices 7,11,72 (1972).

8. Jantzen,M.,Valk,R. : Formal Properties of Place Transition Nets. in : these Proceedings.

9. Keller,R.M. : A Fundamental Theorem of Asynchronous Parallel Computation. in : Parallel Processing, Lecture Notes in Computer Sci., 24, pp 102-112, Springer, Berlin, (1975).

10. Kowalk,W.,Valk,R. : On Reductions of Parallel Programs. in : Automata, Languages and Programming, Lecture Notes in Computer Sci. 71, pp 356-369, Springer, Berlin, (1979).

11. Kwong,Y.S. : On Reduction of Asynchronous Systems. , Theor. Computer Sci. 5, pp 25-50, (1977).

12. Lipton, R.J. : Reduction : A Method of Proving Properties of Parallel Programs, Comm.ACM 18, pp 717-721, (1975).

13. Memmi,G.,Roucairol,G. : Linear Algebra in Net Theory. in : these Procee-dings.

14. Owicki,S., Gries,P. : An Axiomatic Proof Technique for Parallel Programs Acta Informatica 6, pp319-340, (1976).

ADEQUACY OF PATH PROGRAMS

by

E. Best

Computing Laboratory
University of Newcastle upon Tyne
England

Abstract

Syntax and semantics of a subset of the path notation are introduced. Then a property of path programs called adequacy is defined; roughly, programs are adequate if there is no partial deadlock. Finally, two results are presented concerning adequacy. The first result solves the adequacy problem for a certain subclass of programs, and the second result characterises the problem in terms of PT-nets for another subclass. An overview of the results on adequacy which have been obtained so far is also given. Even so, this is intended to serve as an introductory text.

Contents

Introduction

Path expressions [CAH74] have been introduced as a linguistic construct enabling the programmer to express a variety of synchronisation constraints. Meanwhile, the notation as well as the theory of path expressions have experienced a development. The purpose of these notes is to give a status report on these developments, as far as they pertain to the theory of path expressions, and in particular to the relationship between path expressions and PT-nets. Also, these notes are intended to be readable as an introductory text; more detailed accounts of the theory can be found in [LSB79] and other references.

Path expressions have been developed more fully, and given a semantics in terms of nets, in [LAC75], where paths have been combined with processes into a "higher level" notation. We now refer to this as the basic notation. The basic notation has been provided with macro facilities intended to ease the writing of large chunks of text. The full notation (basic and macro) is called COSY (COncurrent SYstem notation) and is described in [LTS79]. COSY is not portrayed in detail in the present notes; readers wishing to inform themselves more fully are referred to [LTS79] which also includes a number of programming examples.

Given those aims, it is both convenient and sufficient to restrict our framework to a subset of the basic notation, to be introduced in section 1.1. Sentences of this subset are called "path programs" or just "programs". The syntax defined in section 1.1 coincides with what has been termed "basic path notation" in [LBS78]. We are primarily interested in a property of the behaviour of programs, called adequacy. Adequacy of a program, defined formally in section 1.2, asserts that no operation of that program is ever prevented from occurring. Intuitively, adequacy corresponds to the absence of partial deadlocks, and formally, to the liveness of PT-nets as defined in [GES80].

It is particularly interesting to decide, just from looking at the program text (as opposed to running it), whether or not it is adequate. Since unfortunately the program text tends to conceal that property to a great degree, it is necessary to obtain results on adequacy. Such results can have varying nature, in fact we can make a rough distinction between three types of results:

(a) We could search for subclasses of programs which do have the pleasant property that they reveal their adequacy syntactically - that is, that we can decide on adequacy by examining the program text more or less closely. A result of this nature is described in section 2.1. Perhaps the most interesting lesson from this result is the insight that the goal of obtaining purely syntactic adequacy criteria is only nearly attainable, even for programs of relatively modest complexity. Even the "purest" syntactic criterion can be interpreted as stating a bound for the run-time which is required to check adequacy dynamically.

(b) Having identified such pleasant subclasses, we can look for larger classes the programs of which are in some way or another reducible to those of the pleasant classes, such that adequacy properties remain untouched. More generally, we are looking for adequacy-preserving transformations of path programs. A wealth of results of this nature is contained in [LSB78] and [SHI79], and we parenthetically illustrate two simple ones in section 2.1.

(c) We can use the formal semantics of programs to transform the adequacy problem into a problem concerning the liveness of PT-nets. Since liveness has been studied in detail for some time (see also [JAV80] and [MER80]), we can entertain the hope that a problem of the former kind can be solved by transforming it into an already solved problem of the latter kind; or, alternatively, that we can show the difficulty of an adequacy problem by reducing it to a problem the difficulty of which is well-known. A result of this nature, which the author believes to be new, is described in section 2.2. It is one out of a total of four results which establish a clear-cut correspondence between subclasses of programs and subclasses of nets. An overview of these correspondences is given in the conclusion.

1 Basic Path Notation

1.1 Syntax and Classification of Programs

The following six production rules define our notation:

S1	program	::=	begin path$^+$ process* end
S2	path	::=	path sequence end
S3	process	::=	process sequence end
S4	sequence	::=	sequence;orelement / orelement
S5	orelement	::=	orelement,element / element
S6	element	::=	operation / (sequence)

Underlined words, the comma, the semicolon and the parentheses in S6 are terminal symbols. Non-underlined words indicate non-terminal symbols. "*" and "+" indicate zero or more (one or more, respectively) repetitions of the preceding non-terminal, and "/" indicates syntactic alternatives. The non-terminal "operation" stands for a set of operationnames which are identifiers of the programmer's choosing. We use identifiers as terminals and assume that identical names denote the same operation.

The idea of this notation is that programmers can specify a set of processes (rule S3) such that each process groups together some operations by concatenation (rule S4) or non-deterministic choice (rule S5). Processes are assumed independent of each other unless the contrary is specified by means of a path or a set of paths. The exact semantics of bringing processes and paths together in a program is given in section 1.2.

S1 - S6 describe a subset of the notation introduced in [LAC75], which in turn is a subset of COSY [LTS79]. The reasons why we restrict ourselves to this subset are convenience and the fact that the additional features of the full notation do not contribute significantly to the behavioural complexity of programs (rather, they are intended to reduce their textual complexity). Indeed, it is easy to show (see, for example, [LBS78]) that the class of programs defined here corresponds behaviourally to the entire class of safe PT-nets, as do all the programs written in COSY.

In the sequel we consider various strings derivable from all or part of S1 - S6. The general form of such a string is

PROG = begin P Q end,

where P denotes the set of paths and Q the set of processes. In general, P and Q will be of the form

P = P1 ... Pn
Q = Q1 ... Qm,

respectively, where all Pi ($1 \leq i \leq n$) are derivable from S2, S4-S6, and all Qj ($1 \leq j \leq m$) are derivable from S3-S6. We allow Q but not P to be empty (rule S1) because the case of a set of independent processes is of little interest.

Interesting subclasses of programs can be defined if S5 is replaced by

S5' orelement ::= operation.

This prevents the use of the comma.

Other interesting subclasses can be defined if the following restriction is imposed:

R1 No operationname may occur repeatedly within an individual path or an individual process.

For example, the following program:

```
PROG1  =  begin path a;b;a;a;b end
                path c;a;c end
                path c;c;b;c end
          end
```

does not use the comma (i.e. can be derived even if S5 is replaced by S5'). On the other hand, it violates R1 because, for example, the operationname "a" occurs repeatedly within the first path.

In the paragraphs labelled (i)-(v) below we introduce a classification of programs based on the terminology of [LAC75]. This classification is chiefly used for establishing the correspondence between programs and nets. In (iv) and (v) we define two classes of programs which will be our sole interest in sections 1.2, 2.1 and 2.2. These two classes will also be defined separately by examples at the end of the present section. The reader has therefore the option of skipping (i)-(v) for the moment and coming back to the classification whenever the need arises.

(i) Terminal strings derivable from "path" by S2, S4-S6 are called "(individual) paths" or "R-paths" ("Repeat-paths"; this indicates that R1 may not be satisfied).

(ii) Terminal strings derivable from "process" by S3-S6 are called "(individual) processes" or "R-processes".

(iii) Terminal strings derivable from "program" by S1-S6 are called "(path) programs" or "GRGR-programs" (where the "G" stands for "General"). In this terminology, the first "GR" refers to the paths in the program, denoting the possibility of there being more than one ("G") R-paths; in the same way, the second "GR" refers to the processes. If Q is empty, i.e. if there are no processes, then we call the program a "GR-path". Thus, for example, PROG1 is a GR-path.

(iv) The replacement of S5 by S5' is indicated by appending the digit "0" in the appropriate place. Thus, programs using S5' instead of S5 and S6 are called "comma-free programs" or "GR0GR0-programs". Similarly, GR-paths using S5' are called "GR0-paths" or "comma-free paths", and R-paths using S5' are called "R0-paths".

(v) Finally, the holding of R1 is indicated by replacing the capital R (for "Repeat") by a capital E (for "Elementary"). Thus, R-paths (R-processes) for which R1 holds are called "E-paths" ("E-processes"); R0-paths (R0-processes) for which R1 holds are called "E0-paths" ("E0-processes"); GR-paths for which R1 holds are called "GE-paths"; GR0-paths for which R1 holds are called "GE0-paths"; finally, comma-free programs satisfying R1 are called "GE0GE0-programs".

In the main part of these notes we shall be interested in GR0-paths and in GE0GE0-programs. GR0-paths are programs containing only paths without commas.

Example of a GRO-path:

```
PROG2  =  begin path a;b;a;a;b end
                path c;a;c end
                path c;d;c;b;d;c;d end
                path c;e;d end
                path f;e;f;e end
          end.
```

GEOGEO-programs are programs without comma in which operationnames are not repeated within paths or processes.

Example of a GEOGEO-path:

```
PROG3  =  begin path a;b end
                path c;d end
                process a;b end
                process b;c end
                process d;c end
          end.
```

1.2 Semantics and Adequacy of Programs

In order to render this section as transparent as possible, we choose not to describe the complete semantics of the notation; for this, see [LSB79]. There are, in general, two ways of describing the meaning of programs, one in terms of nets and one in terms of firing sequences, of which the latter is perhaps more natural. The two methods are essentially compatible, that is, lead to essentially the same semantics. We use the firing sequence method to define the meaning of GRO-paths, and the net method to define the meaning of GEOGEO-programs. It involves some slight but no principal complications to define the semantics of the whole class of GRGR-programs, whether in terms of nets or in terms of firing sequences.

Semantics of GRO-paths

We consider programs of the form

```
PROG  =  begin  P1  ...  Pn  end
```

where each Pi is an RO-path. Our goal is to define the set of firing sequences of PROG.

Example:

```
PROG2  =  begin  P1 P2 P3 P4 P5  end

where   P1  =  path a;b;a;a;b end
        P2  =  path c;a;c end
        P3  =  path c;d;c;b;d;c;d end
        P4  =  path c;e;d end
        P5  =  path f;e;f;e end
```

We define the "cycle" of Pi, cyci, as the string obtained from Pi by omitting path - end and all semicolons; thus, cyc1 = abaab, cyc2 = cac, cyc3 = cdcbdcd, etc. We imagine that Pi is executed as follows: starting with the leftmost operation, the operations are executed one at a time from left to right, returning to the leftmost operation if the list is exhausted. Each string of operationnames obtainable in this way is called a firing sequence of Pi; in other words, the firing sequences of

Pi are the prefices of the infinite string (cyci)*. Thus, for example, ca and cac, but also the empty string and caccacc, are firing sequences of P2. In general, the semicolon denotes sequentialisation, and the pair path - end denotes repetition.

A string s is called a firing sequence of PROG if each projection of s onto a constituent path Pi is a firing sequence of Pi. The projection of s onto a path Pi, proj(Pi,s), is the string obtained from s by deleting all operationnames not contained in OPS(Pi). Thus, for example, s = cfedac is a firing sequence of PROG2. Proof:

proj(P1,s) = a = firing sequence of P1
proj(P2,s) = cac = firing sequence of P2,
etc.

On the other hand, s = cfedab fails to be a firing sequence of PROG2; its projection onto P3 is not a firing sequence of P3.

Thus, in effect, the individual paths of a GRO-path "synchronise" over common operationnames; operation b of P1, say, can be executed only when b of P3 is ready to be executed as well. The set of firing sequences thus defined constitutes, by definition, the semantics of a GRO-path. In the general case of characterising the behaviour of a program by means of firing sequences (see [SHI79] and [LSB79]), the definition of a "cycle" is more general than the one given here.

Semantics of GEOGEO-programs

We consider programs of the form

PROG = begin P1 ... Pn Q1 ... Qm end

where the Pi are EO-paths and the Qj are EO-processes. Our goal is to associate with PROG a marked PT-net.

Example:

PROG3 = begin P1 P2 Q1 Q2 Q3 end

where P1 = path a;b end
P2 = path c;d end
Q1 = process a;b end
Q2 = process b;c end
Q3 = process d;c end

We associate with each individual process a single cyclic marked net labelled with corresponding operationnames:

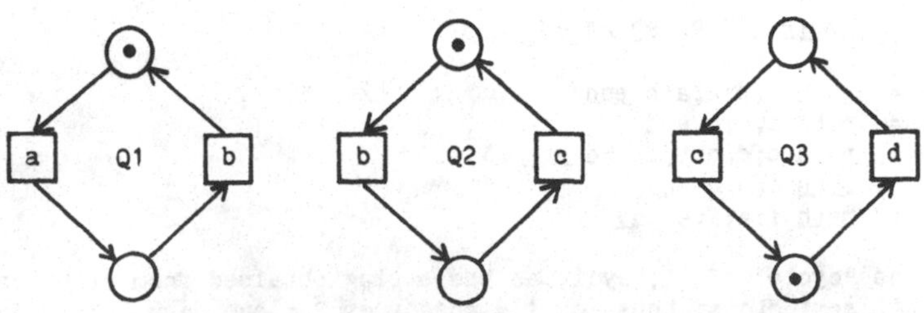

Figure 1

We assume that the firing of a transition labelled with an operationname is tantamount to an execution of that operation. Individually, the processes have therefore the same meaning as paths (sequentialisation and repetition). In combination, however, processes do not "synchronise", not even if there are common operationnames. The operation b, say, of the first net shown in Figure 1 could occur concurrently with its counterpart in the second net.

Any inter-process synchronisation is effected by the paths. As a consequence of the operation b being mentioned in a path (namely P1), any occurrences of b in Q1 and Q2 are mutually excluded. This, by definition, is the general semantic effect of bringing several processes and paths together in a single program. We thus arrive at the following final net:

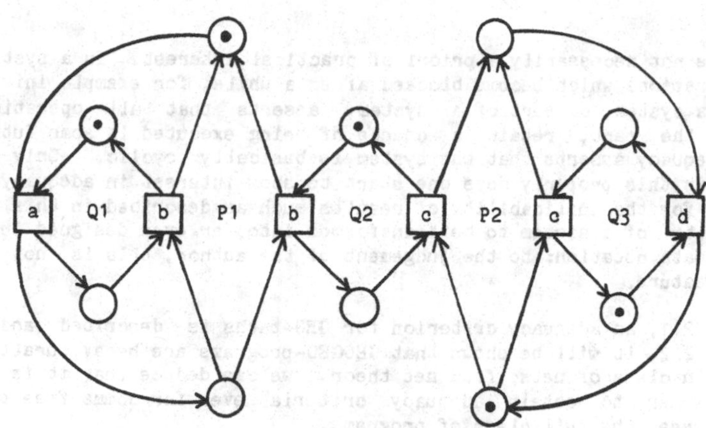

Figure 2

Note that all individual constraints are adhered to. For example, P1 requires a and b to occur cyclically in that order; P2 requires c and d to occur cyclically in that order; etc. Also, the mutual exclusion between processes is represented; for example, P1 specifies that only one of Q1 and Q2 is allowed to proceed with an execution of b in case both could do so. The net gives the complete behaviour of PROG3. Thus we see that Q1 can be repeated an unlimited number of times until Q2 is executed. Once operations b and c of Q2 have occurred, both Q1 and Q2 are and remain blocked, but Q3 can then be executed "forever".

It requires but a slight generalisation of this example to obtain the net for any arbitrary GEOGEO-program. The general rule is first to draw all the process nets and then to connect them appropriately by path nets. This rule can be generalised for GRGR-programs. It is compatible with the general firing sequence semantics but not quite with the old net semantics given in [LAC75] and [LBS78]; the latter introduce unlabelled transitions which are clumsy and hardly justifiable.

Adequacy

For a program to be adequate there must be no operation which is prevented from ever occurring again. PROG3 is not adequate because there are two operations, namely a and b, which may be prevented from occurring. PROG2, however, is adequate; the reader might like to convince himself or herself of this fact, or might prefer to wait until a proof is presented in section 2.1.

In firing sequence terms, adequacy is defined as follows: a program is called adequate if for each firing sequence x and for each operationname a, there is a continuation y such that xya is a firing sequence. In net terms: a program is adequate if for each successor marking M and operationname a, there is a successor marking L of M such that some transition labelled "a" is enabled under L.

In general, adequacy implies freedom from total deadlock. As our example PROG3 shows, the reverse is not necessarily true. "Freedom from partial deadlock" is a satisfactory description of adequacy. Adequacy corresponds to what has been termed liveness-5 in [LAU75], and to liveness in the sense of [GES80]. As witnessed in the sequence of papers [LAC75], [LBS78], [LSB78] and [LSB79], there has been rather a development before the present definition of adequacy has been arrived at.

2 Two Results Concerning Adequacy

Adequacy is not necessarily a priori of practical interest. In a system there may well be operations which become blocked after a while, for example initialisations. Adequacy of a system, or part of a system, asserts that all operations of the system, or the part, retain a chance of being executed in some future; roughly speaking, adequacy asserts that the system is basically cyclic. Only if one is interested in this property does one start to show interest in adequacy. A further precondition for the applicability of results such as described in this section is the capability of a system to be transformed into, or even designed in, a notation akin to the path notation; to the judgement of the author, this is not necessarily an obvious feature.

In section 2.1, an adequacy criterion for GRO-paths is described and discussed. In section 2.2, it will be shown that GEOGEO-programs are behaviourally equivalent with a certain class of nets; from net theory, we can deduce that it is an order of magnitude harder to obtain adequacy criteria even for comma-free programs, let alone, of course, the full class of programs.

2.1 Adequacy of GRO-Paths

An individual RO-path by itself is clearly adequate. Similarly, if in a GRO-program

PROG = <u>begin</u> P1 ... Pn <u>end</u>

the sets of operationnames of any two of its constituent RO-paths are disjoint then the whole program is adequate. Adequacy can therefore only be impeded if for a pair Pi and Pj ($i \neq j$):

$$OPS(Pi) \cap OPS(Pj) \neq \emptyset.$$

We can draw a graph of this relation, which we call the connectivity graph, or c-graph, of PROG. The Pi are the vertices of the graph, and two vertices are connected by an edge if they have at least one operationname in common. We label an edge with endpoints Pi and Pj with the set of operationnames they have in common. Thus, for PROG2 which encompasses the five RO-paths

P1 = <u>path</u> a;b;a;a;b <u>end</u>
P2 = <u>path</u> c;a;c <u>end</u>
P3 = <u>path</u> c;d;c;b;d;c;d <u>end</u>
P4 = <u>path</u> c;e;d <u>end</u>
P5 = <u>path</u> f;e;f;e <u>end</u>

we obtain:

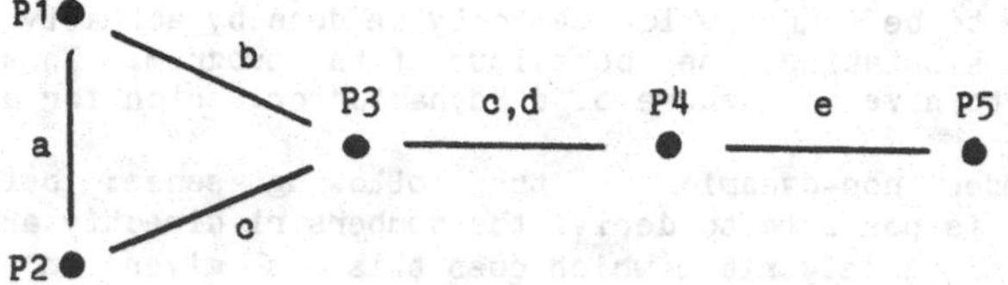

Figure 3

We call a GRO-path connected if its c-graph is connected. Without loss of generality, we shall only consider connected GRO-paths; if we have a disconnected one we can consider its connected components separately.

The adequacy criterion states that a connected GRO-path is adequate if and only if there is a non-empty firing sequence s which reproduces the initial state; formally:

Theorem 1 PROG is adequate <=> $\exists s \forall i$: proj(Pi,s) = $(\text{cyci})^{ri}$

(with some positive integers ri, $1 \leq i \leq n$, which can be chosen such that hcf(ri)=1).

Before interpreting this result, let us check it using an example. PROG1 has been defined in section 1.1 as follows:

```
        PROG1 = begin P1' P2' P3' end
where   P1'   = path a;b;a;a;b end
        P2'   = path c;a;c end
        P3'   = path c;c;b;c end.
```

We show that PROG1 is adequate. Define

s = cacbcaccabc.

By forming the projections of s onto all Pi':

```
proj(P1',s)  =  abaab
proj(P2',s)  =  caccaccac
proj(P3',s)  =  ccbcccbc
```

we see that with

(r1,r2,r3) = (1,3,2)

the condition of theorem 1 is satisfied. Hence PROG1 is adequate. Note that hcf(r1,r2,r3) = 1.

We now interpret this result. In its proof it turns out that, in general, once a part of a connected GRO-path is blocked, gradually all of the c-graph will become blocked and the system ends up in total deadlock. Thus, for connected GRO-paths, not only does adequacy imply freedom from total deadlock but also vice versa. There are two possibilities: either the program is not adequate and will sooner or later reach a state of total deadlock, or the program is adequate and will continually reproduce its initial state.

At first sight, theorem 1 does not have the form of a syntactic adequacy criterion that had been sought for in paragraph (a) of the introduction. In order to apply theorem 1, the string s has to be found, which can only be done by actually "firing" the operations, i.e. by simulating the behaviour of the program. Thus, on the contrary, the result seems to have the nature of a "dynamic" criterion for adequacy.

However, the result is indeed non-dynamic in the following sense: before the simulation takes place it is possible to derive the numbers ri directly and solely from the text of the program. An algorithm which does this is given in [LSB78]. The numbers ri give an upper bound on the simulation time necessary for deriving s. Given the knowledge of the ri, the theorem says that the number

r1*|cyc1| + r2*|cyc2| + ... + rn*|cycn|

(where |cyci| denotes the length of the string cyci) is an upper bound both for the length of a reproducing sequence and for the length of a deadlocking sequence. In case hcf(ri) = 1, the above number gives the exact length of a <u>shortest</u> reproducing sequence, if one exists (due to concurrency, there may exist several different reproducing sequences of equal length).

In summary, the result incorporates a mixture of syntactic (static) and dynamic arguments. In the opinion of the author this kind of "mixture" is unavoidable for such a result. Even the most commonplace "static" deadlock criterion, the cycle criterion for marked graphs (see [GEL73]), can be seen from a "dynamic" point of view: since marked graphs correspond to GEO-paths under the net semantics (see [LAC75]), theorem 1 reduces to the cycle criterion in the special case of GEO-paths. All ri are then equal to 1, and the algorithm of simulating the program to find a reproducing firing sequence s reduces to an algorithm for finding the cycles of the marked graph corresponding to the program.

It is possible to subject a GRO-path to a number of simplifications before theorem 1 is applied to it. We mention two such simplifications which preserve adequacy properties but may render the resulting path less complicated than the original one. Let a GRO-path and its c-graph be given.

<u>1. Simplification</u>:
Delete all operationnames not appearing in the c-graph. In PROG2, for example, f can be deleted because it does not appear in the c-graph of Figure 3; P5 then becomes <u>path</u> e;e <u>end</u>.

<u>2. Simplification</u>:
Find a vertex all of whose adjacent edges carry the same label (for example, a border vertex). Check whether the operationnames on those edges occur in the same order in the vertex and in all of its neighbouring vertices. If so, the vertex and its edges can be deleted; if not, the program is not adequate. Thus, in the example, vertex P5 and its adjacent edge disappears.

These simplifications can be repeated in arbitrary order until neither of them is applicable any longer. They preserve adequacy, that is, are results such as described in paragraph (b) of the introduction. Thus, as the reader might like to verify, it is possible to simplify PROG2 to obtain PROG1, which establishes the adequacy of PROG2 without the direct application of theorem 1. The reader is encouraged to prove directly that PROG2 is adequate.

Lastly, we mention that the numbers ri enable us to transform any adequate GRO-path into an adequate GEO-path. We replace each individual RO-path by an ri-multiple of itself and distinguish operationnames by a consistent numbering scheme; thus,

```
begin path a1;b1;a2;a3;b2 end
      path c1;a1;c2;c3;a2;c4;c5;a3;c6 end
      path c1;c2;b1;c3;c4;c5;b2;c6 end
end
```

is the GEO-path corresponding to PROG1. This construction does not work if the original GRO-path fails to be adequate, even though the ri are then also defined.

2.2 Equivalence of GEOGEO-Programs and Safe "Simple" Nets

In this section we consider comma-free programs. We show that nets corresponding to GEOGEO-programs, or GEOGEO-nets for short, are behaviourally equivalent to what has come to be called "simple" nets ([COM72] and [HAC72]). A PT-net is called "simple" if situations of the following type are ruled out:

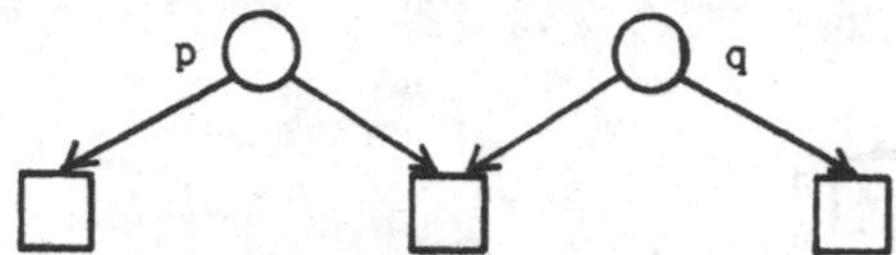

that is, if for no pair of places p,q the sets of output transitions partially overlap.

Formally, a net is called "simple" if for any pair p,q of places:

(i) $p^{\bullet} \cap q^{\bullet} = \emptyset$ or $|p^{\bullet}| = 1$ or $|q^{\bullet}| = 1$.

A net is called "extended simple" if

(ii) $p^{\bullet} \cap q^{\bullet} = \emptyset$ or $p^{\bullet} \subseteq q^{\bullet}$ or $q^{\bullet} \subseteq p^{\bullet}$.

Note that (i) implies (ii), in other words that every "simple" net is also "extended simple". Below we shall show that, conversely, an "extended simple" net can be transformed into a behaviourally equivalent "simple" net. The apostrophes are used for two reasons. Firstly, the class of "simple" nets must not be confused with the class of simple nets as defined in section 1 of [GES80]. Secondly, the terminology is deceptive because the study of "simple" nets is no simple matter. In particular, liveness criteria are known for a subclass, the class of free-choice nets (see [HAC72] and [JAV80]), but not for "simple" nets. There is evidence that the class of "simple" nets is an important one; it is roughly equal to the class of confusion-free nets (see the section on CE-nets in [GLT80]).

Note that the GEOGEO-net shown in Figure 2 is "simple". It follows from their construction that all GEOGEO-nets are "extended simple". We shall show below that, conversely, all safe "simple" nets can be transformed into behaviourally equivalent GEOGEO-nets. This establishes the essential behavioural equivalence of the three classes of GEOGEO-nets, safe "simple" nets and safe "extended simple" nets.

Theorem 2 "Extended simple" nets can be transformed into behaviourally equivalent "simple" nets.

The construction used in the proof of theorem 2 is fully described in [LSB78] and illustrated here with the following example:

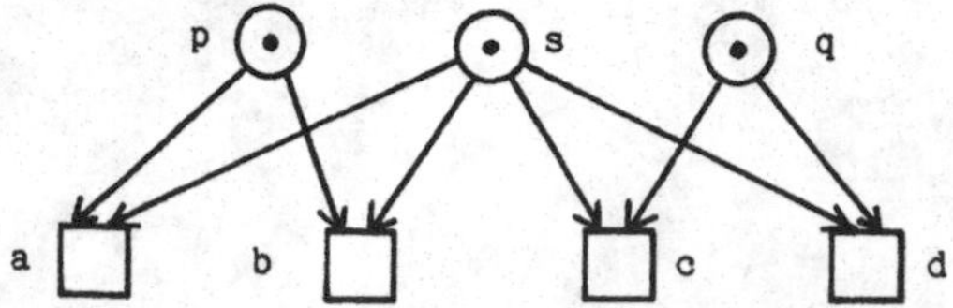

This net satisfies (ii) but not (i). We transform it into the following net in which the original marking is retained but two new places and four new transitions are added:

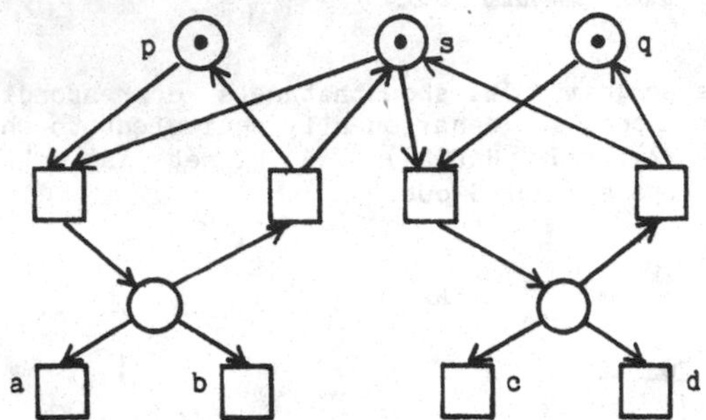

The second net is behaviourally equivalent with the first one and satisfies (i).

Theorem 3 Safe "simple" nets can be transformed into behaviourally equivalent GEOGEO-nets.

The proof of theorem 3 involves an elaborate construction which, again, is described in detail in [LSB78] and illustrated here with the following example:

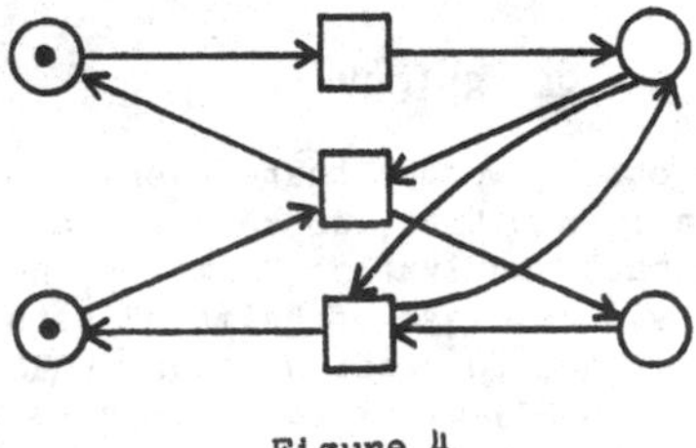

Figure 4

The net shown in Figure 4 is live, safe and "simple"; its initial marking, however, is not reproducible.

The net is first subjected to a number of elementary transformations which make it pure and decomposable into state machine components (for these definitions, see [GES80]). Safeness is a necessary precondition for the proper working of these transformations. Thereafter, some auxiliary transitions are introduced and all transitions are systematically labelled with operationnames. The final program then reads as follows:

```
PROG4  =  begin path a;b end path c;d;e;f end
                             path e;f;k;l end
                             path e;f;g;h end
                             path k;l;g;h end
                 process c;a;d end
                 process e;b;f end
                 process g;a;h end
                 process k;b;l end
          end.
```

The reader might find it entertaining to verify that, indeed, PROG4 is adequate but that its initial state is not reproducible.

PROG3 and PROG4 illustrate two characteristic differences between GEOGEO-programs and GRO-paths. For a (connected) GRO-path the following three properties are equivalent: adequacy, freedom from total deadlock, and the existence of a reproducing firing sequence. By contrast, PROG3 is globally deadlock-free but not adequate (compare Figure 2); and PROG4 is adequate but does not possess a reproducing firing sequence. These characteristic behavioural differences between the two classes indicate that the analysis of GEOGEO-programs is an order of magnitude harder than the analysis of GRO-paths. The discovery of exact adequacy criteria, or, for that matter, of exact bounds on the necessary simulation of GEOGEO-programs would be an achievement both in adequacy theory and in net the theory of nets.

Conclusion

More results on adequacy are described in [SHI79]. Most of them are of the type described in paragraph (b) of the introduction. Most notably, [SHI79] introduces a set of substitution rules which allow, among other things, a fairly large class of GR-paths to be transformed into behaviourally equivalent GRO-paths; this class is called the class of GR1-paths. For the benefit of readers wishing to have a coarse overview of the present state of the theory, we give a diagram showing essential inclusion relations between different classes of programs and nets.

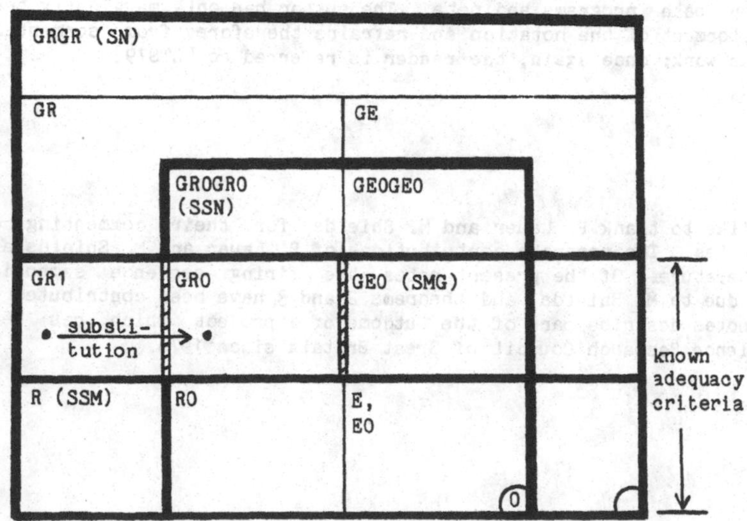

Legenda: SN - safe nets
SSN - safe "simple" nets
SMG - safe marked graphs
SSM - safe state machines
others - see (i)-(v) in section 1.1

The diagram is to be read as follows: the name of a class of programs is inscribed in the upper left hand corner of a rectangle representing that class; the corresponding lower right hand corner of the rectangle is marked "0" for classes whose name contains a "0", and it is the rightmost lower corner for all other classes. Inclusion of rectangles denotes syntactic inclusion of classes; thus, for example, every EO-path is also a GEO-path, but not every E-path is a GRO-path.

Bold lines delimit classes with essentially different behaviour. Thus, as mentioned in the concluding remarks of section 2.2, GR0-paths and GEOGEO-programs have essentially different behaviour. On the other hand, GE-paths and GRGR-programs are behaviourally equivalent; both classes, moreover, are essentially equivalent to the class of safe nets under the net semantics.

The boundary between GE0-paths and GR0-paths is shaded because GR0-paths are equivalent to GE0-paths only if they are adequate, as we have seen at the end of section 2.1. The boundary between GR1-paths and GR0-paths is shaded because of the inability of the author to judge about the behavioural differences between the two classes.

It can be hoped that this diagram is of use for the further extension of the results on adequacy. A general remark on the so-called "adequacy problem" or "liveness problem" may be in order. Many efforts have aimed at the discovery of "static liveness criteria" - that is, at finding purely static criteria for a dynamic property. To the mind of the author, a principal outcome not only of this article but of the present volume as a whole, is the insight that static and dynamic aspects cannot be separated entirely. Liveness results and adequacy results will always have to involve a mixture of static and dynamic arguments. In this spirit, the author would also venture to offer a precise definition of the "adequacy problem" as the problem of deriving from the program text only, exact (average) bounds on the length of the simulation that has to be carried out in order to check adequacy. Mutatis mutandis, this definition could be adopted for other problems as well.

This concludes a discussion of a few issues pertaining to adequacy and the relationship between path programs and nets. The author has only marginally been involved in the development of the notation and refrains therefore from commenting on this aspect of the work; once again, the reader is referred to [LTS79].

Acknowledgements

The author would like to thank P. Lauer and M. Shields for their commenting on drafts of these notes. The separate contributions of P. Lauer and M. Shields are evident from the literature. Of the present notes, the firing sequence semantics and theorem 1 are due to M. Shields, and theorems 2 and 3 have been contributed by the author. These notes describe part of the outcome of a project which has been sponsored by the Science Research Council of Great Britain since 1976.

References

[CAH74] Campbell, R.H. and Habermann, A.N.: The Specification of Process Synchronisation by Path Expressions. In: Lecture Notes in Computer Science 16, Springer Verlag, Berlin 1974.

[COM72] Commoner, F.: Deadlocks in Petri Nets. CA-7206/2311, Applied Data Research, Wakefield Massachussets, June 1972.

[GEL73] Genrich, H.J. and Lautenbach, K.: Synchronisationsgraphen. Acta informatica 2, 1973, pp. 143-161.

[GES80] Genrich, H.J. and Stankiewicz-Wiechno, E.: A Dictionary of Some Basic Notions of Net Theory. In this volume.

[GLT80] Genrich, H.J., Lautenbach, K. and Thjagarajan, P.S.: An Overview of Net Theory. In this volume.

[HAC72] Hack, M.H.T.: Analysis of Production Schemata by Petri Nets. TR-94, Project MAC, MIT, Boston, February 1972 (corrected June 1974).

[JAV80] Jantzen, M. and Valk, R.: Formal Properties of Place-Transition Nets. In this volume.

[LAC75] Lauer, P.E. and Campbell, R.H.: Formal Semantics for a Class of High-Level Primitives for Coordinating Concurrent Processes. Acta informatica 5, 1975, pp. 247-332.

[LAU75] Lautenbach,K.: Liveness in Petri Nets. GMD-ISF internal report, Bonn 1975.

[LBS78] Lauer, P.E., Best, E. and Shields, M.W.: On the Problem of Achieving Adequacy of Concurrent Programs. In: Formal Description of Programming Concepts (ed. E. Neuhold), North Holland 1978.

[LSB78] Lauer, P.E., Shields, M.W. and Best, E.: On the Design and Certification of Asynchronous Systems of Processes. Final Report, part II: Formal Theory of the Basic COSY Notation, ASM/45, Computing Laboratory, University of Newcastle upon Tyne, 1978 (also to appear as Technical Report).

[LSB79] Lauer, P.E., Shields, M.W. and Best, E.: Design and Analysis of Highly Parallel and Distributed Systems. To appear in: Lecture Notes in Computer Science, Springer Verlag, Berlin 1979.

[LTS79] Lauer, P.E., Torrigiani, P.R. and Shields, M.W.: COSY - a System Specification Language Based on Paths and Processes. Acta informatica 12, 1979, pp. 109-158.

[MER80] Memmi, G. and Roucairol, G.: Linear Algebra in Net Theory. In this volume.

[ROU80] Roucairol, G. and Valk, R.: Reductions of Nets and Parallel Programs. In this volume.

[SHI79] Shields, M.W.: Adequate Path Expressions. TR/142, University of Newcastle upon Tyne, 1979; also in: Proceedings of the International Symposium on Semantics of Concurrent Computation, in: Lecture Notes in Computer Science 70, Springer Verlag, Berlin 1970.

PERFORMANCE EVALUATION OF SYSTEMS USING NETS

J.SIFAKIS
Laboratoire IMAG
BP 53X
38041 GRENOBLE cédex
FRANCE

ABSTRACT

This paper presents a method for computing firing frequencies corresponding to steady state functionings of Timed Place-Transition Nets (TPTN). Two different models of TPTN's - the one with delays associated to its places and the other with delays associated to its transitions - are compared and proved to be equivalent. Given a TPTN it is provided a set of relations established between its initial marking, the firing frequences of its transitions and the delays associated to its places. Furthermore, for given initial marking and delays it is shown that maximal firing frequencies can be computed as solutions of a set of n linear equations, where n is the number of places of the TPTN. The presented results are illustrated by two applications.

I - INTRODUCTION

Performance evaluation methods allow to determine the limits of using a system (waiting times, throughputs) from the dynamic characteristics of its components (durations or execution probabilities of actions). Obviously, models of asynchronous systems such as PT-nets (PTN's) can not be directly used for performance studies since no assumption is made in these models about the duration of the actions or the instant of their initiation after they have been enabled. The use of asynchronous models for performance evaluation necessitates that they be augmented by introducing a time parameter providing a common frame for the expression and comparison of the speeds of their components.

Timed PT-nets (TPTN's) is the term denoting PTN's with temporal restrictions [1][2][3]. They have been used for studying time-dependent properties of systems modeled by PTN's. The litterature relative to the use of this model for performance evaluation is rather poor : C.Ramchandani gives in his PhD dissertation [1] a method for evaluating maximal firing frequences for sub-classes of TPTN's with constant delays associated to their transitions. The results presented in this paper generalize Ramchandani's results and have been published in detail in [2]. Finally, a more technical work on this domain is presented in [4] where the analysis of a system described by a TPTN is carried out on a state machine simulating it.

II - TIMED PLACE TRANSITION NETS

A <u>Timed Place-Transition Net (TPTN)</u> is a triplet $N_T=(N,T,\nu)$ where :

- $N=(S,T;F,K,W,M_0)$ is a Place-Transition Net (PTN)
- T is a totally ordered set by a relation $\geq$; we call <u>instants</u> the elements of T .
- ν is a mapping of SxT into T , called <u>time base</u> of N_T, such that $\forall(s,\tau_i)$ SxT , $\nu(s,\tau_i)\geq\tau_i$.

Representation : We represent a TPTN by associating to each place s of the corresponding PTN the mapping $\nu(s,\tau)$.

Simulation rules :

a/ A token in a TPTN may be in one of the two following states : <u>available</u> or <u>unavailable</u>. We associate to the initial marking M_0 an instant $\tau_0\in T$; at any instant τ the marking M of a TPTN is the sum of two markings M_a and M_u where M_a is the marking constituted of all the available tokens of M and M_u is the marking constituted of all the unavailable tokens of M.

b/ A transition is enabled by $M=M_a+M_u$ iff it is enabled by M_a in the corresponding PTN.

c/ The firing of an enabled transition t is defined exactly as for PTN's with the difference that only available tokens are moved from the input places of t. The transition firing "takes no time" ; if the firing of a transition is initiated at an instant τ then it is supposed to terminate at the same instant τ .

d/ If after the firing of a transition at the instant τ, an available token arrives a place s, this token becomes unavailable during the interval $]\tau,\nu(s,\tau)[$; then it becomes available.

Remark : According to the preceding rules, transition firings in a TPTN can occur only at instants of T .

Some authors (for example C.Ramchandani [1]) introduce TPTN's by associating the unavailability times to the transitions. It is possible to verify that the two models are equivalent.

A TPTN whose unavailability times are associated to the transitions is also a triplet $N'_T=(N',T,\nu')$ where $N'=(S',T';F',K',W',M'_0)$, T is a totally ordered set and $\nu':T'xT\to T$ such that $\forall(t,\tau_i)\in T'xT$, $\nu'(t,\tau_i)\geq\tau_i$. Its simulation rules can be resumed in the following manner :

The tokens of N'_T have two possible states : <u>reserved</u> or <u>non-reserved</u> ; only non-reserved tokens can be used in order to enable a transition. If a transition t is enabled then it can fire by reserving W'(s,t) non-reserved tokens at each input place $s\in{}^{\bullet}t$ during the interval $]\tau,\nu'(t,\tau)[$. The firing terminates at the instant $\nu'(t,\tau)$ by removing the reserved tokens from its input places and by putting W'(t,s) non-reserved tokens at each output place $s\in t^{\bullet}$. All the tokens are initially non-reserved.

It is possible to verify that being given N'_T one can find an equivalent TPTN N_T having its unavailability times associated to its places by effectuating the transformation illustrated in figure 1.

In this transformation every transition t of $N_{T'}$, is substituted by a sub-net constituted of two transitions t_b,t_e and a place s_t such that $\{t_b\}={}^{\bullet}s_t$ and $\{t_e\}=s_t^{\bullet}$. For every added place we put $\nu(s_t,\tau)=\nu'(t,\tau)$ and for the places s of the initial net $\nu(s,\tau)=\tau$, $\forall\tau\in T$.

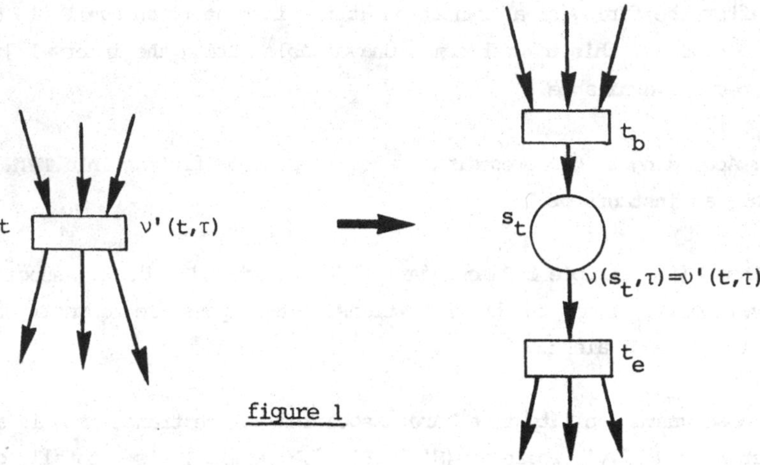

figure 1

Conversely, being given a TPTN, $N_T=(N,T,\nu)$ having its unavailability times associated to its places, it is possible to obtain an equivalent TPTN, $N_{T'}=(N',T,\nu')$ with $\nu':T\times T\to T$ by effectuating the transformation illustrated in figure 2.

In this transformation every place s of N_T is substituted by a sub-net constituted of two places s_b, s_e and a transition t_s such that $\{s_b\}={}^\bullet t_s$, $\{s_e\}=t_s^\bullet$.

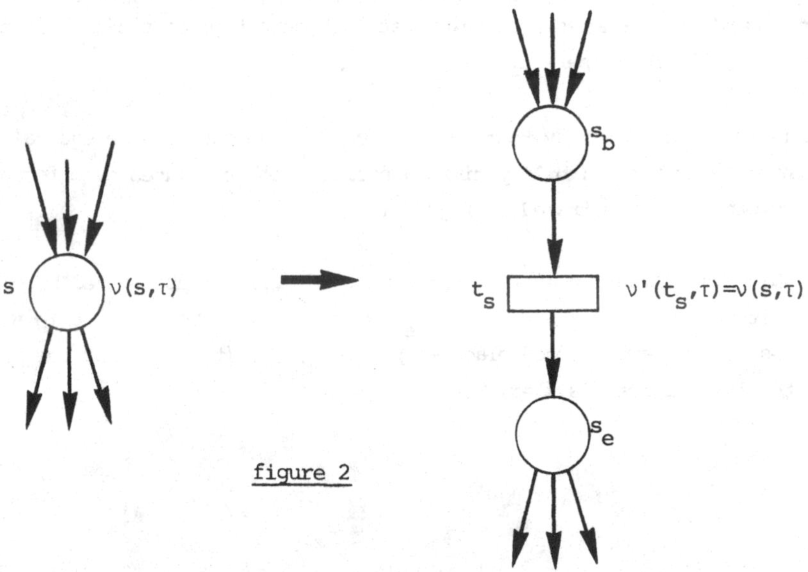

figure 2

To every added transition t_s we associate $\nu'(t_s,\tau)=\nu(s,\tau)$ and to all the transitions t of the initial net $\nu'(t,\tau)=\tau \quad \forall\tau\in T$. If M_0 is the initial marking of N_T, the initial marking M_0' of N_T' is such that : $\forall s$ place of N_T $M'_0(s_e) = M_0(s)$ and $M_0'(s_b)=0$.

The model studied in this paper is pure TPTN's such that $\forall s\in S$ $K(s)=\omega$, with constant unavailability times associated to their places. We take $T=\mathbb{R}$ and put for each place $s_i:\forall\tau\in T$ $\nu(s_i,\tau)-\tau=z_i$; i.e. a token is delayed in a place s_i by z_i time units where z_i is a real non negative number.

III - STEADY STATE FUNCTIONING OF A TIMED PT-NET

III.1. General case

Let $N_T=(N,\mathbb{R},\nu)$, $N=(S,T;F,K,W,M_0)$, $|T|=m$, $|S|=n$ be a TPTN . We define the matrices

$$C^+ = [c^+_{ij}]_{n\times m} \text{ with } c^+_{ij} = \begin{cases} W(t_j,s_i) & \text{if } (t_j,s_i)\in F \\ 0 \text{ if not} \end{cases}$$

$$C^- = [c^-_{ij}]_{n\times m} \text{ with } c^-_{ij} = \begin{cases} W(s_i,t_j) & \text{if } (s_i,t_j)\in F \\ 0 \text{ if not} \end{cases}$$

(the incidence matrix C is equal to $C=C^+-C^-$)

In order to study the functioning of N_T we introduce two temporal vector variables :

- $[M(\tau)]^T = [m_1(\tau),m_2(\tau),\dots,m_n(\tau)]$ representing the marking of the net at the instant τ .
- $[X(\tau)]^T = [x_1(\tau),x_2(\tau),\dots,x_m(\tau)]$ representing the firing vector at the instant τ .

The relation $M=M_0+CX$ can be written by using these temporal variables

$$M(\tau) = M(\tau_0)+CX(\tau)$$

If $\Delta\tau=\tau-\tau_0 \neq 0$ we have

$$\frac{\Delta M(\tau)}{\Delta\tau} = \frac{M(\tau)-M(\tau_0)}{\Delta\tau} = C\,\frac{X(\tau)}{\Delta\tau} = C\,I(\tau) \quad \text{where,}$$

. $\frac{\Delta M(\tau)}{\Delta\tau}$ is a vector representing the mean variation of the number of tokens in the interval $\Delta\tau$

. the i-th component of the vector $I(\tau)$ represents the mean firing frequence of the transition t_i during $\Delta\tau$.

The vector $I(\tau)$ is called <u>current vector</u> and obviously $\forall\tau\in\mathbb{R}\quad I(\tau)>0$.

We study the case where the firing frequences of the transitions are constant and the corresponding PTN N is bounded. Then, N has a periodic functioning and I is a solution of

$$CI = 0,\ I>0 \qquad (I)$$

Furthermore, the current vector I depends on the initial marking and the delays associated to the places.

Let $M(\tau_{k_1}),\ M(\tau_{k_2}),\ldots,M(\tau_{k_r})$ be the markings successively reached by a TPTN during the period of a periodic functioning and $\delta_1,\delta_2,\ldots,\delta_r$ their respective durations. Then the mean value $\overline{M}(\tau)$ of the vector variable $M(\tau)$ is equal to

$$\overline{M}(\tau) = \frac{\delta_1\ M(\tau_{k_1}) + \delta_2\ M(\tau_{k_2}) + \ldots + \delta_r\ M(\tau_{k_r})}{\delta_1 + \delta_2 + \ldots + \delta_r}$$

If J is an S-invariant of N then by multiplying by J^t the preceding relation we obtain

$$J^T\ \overline{M}(\tau) = J^T\ M(\tau_0) = J^T\ M_0$$

But the mean value $\overline{m}_j(\tau)$ of the variable $m_j(\tau)$ representing the number of tokens in a place s_j, must satisfy the inequality

$$\overline{m}_j(\tau) \geq z_j\ L_j^+\ I$$

where z_j is the delay associated to the place s_j, L_j^+ is the j-th row of the matrix C^+. The product L_j^+I represents the mean frequence of token arrivals at the place s_j and $z_jL_j^+I$ the mean number of the tokens of a place due to the (imposed) delay z_j.

Let Z the matrix of order n

$$Z = \begin{bmatrix} z_1 & 0 & 0 & \dots & 0 \\ 0 & z_2 & 0 & \dots & 0 \\ \cdot & & & & \\ \cdot & & & & \\ \cdot & & & & \\ \cdot & & & & \\ 0 & 0 & 0 & \dots & z_n \end{bmatrix}$$

The set of the inequalities $\{\overline{m_j}(\tau) \geq z_j \ \ L_j^+ I\}_{j=1}^n$ can be written in the form

$\overline{M}(\tau) \geq ZC^+I$

If J is an S-invariant of N we have

$J^T\overline{M}(\tau) = J^T M_0 \geq J^T ZC^+ I$ (II)

This inequality establishes a relation between the initial marking M_0, the delays associated to the places of a TPTN and the firing frequences of the transitions.

Let $\{J_1, J_2, \dots, J_q\}$ the set of S-invariants corresponding to the set of the elementary S-components of N. Then every inequality (II) can be expressed as the linear combination with non-negative coefficients of the set of the inequalities $\{J_k^T M_0 \geq J_k^T ZC^+ I\}_{k=1}^q$.

The relations

$CI = 0 \quad I > 0$ (I)

$\{J_k^T M_0 \geq J_k^T ZC^+ I\}_{k=1}^q$ (III)

describe the steady state behaviour of a TPTN. For every periodic functioning the current vector I satisfies these relations but the converse is not always true : a solution I_0 of (I) and (III) does not necessarily correspond to a feasible periodic functioning from M_0. This is due to the fact that the relation (III) takes into account only the imposed delays z_j. In fact the delay of a token in a place s_j is the sum of the delay z_j and of a variable "synchronization" delay due to the waiting of a token for other tokens to become available.

III.2. Functioning of a TPTN at is natural rate

Let I_0 be a current vector of a TPTN N_T. We say that I_0 corresponds to a functioning at natural rate of N_T if I_0 satisfies the equations

$$CI = 0 \qquad I>0 \qquad \text{(I)}$$
$$\{J_k^T M_0 = J_k^T ZC^+ I\}_{k=1}^q \qquad \text{(IV)}$$

where $\{J_k\}_{k=1}^q$ is a base of the space of the solutions of $C^T X=0$.

Functionings at natural rate correspond to functionings at maximal rate : the delays of the tokens in the places are exactly equal to their unavailability times z_j. Obviously, every solution of this system of equations is a maximal solution of (I) and (III) and consequently for every vector I corresponding to a feasible functioning there exists a solution I_0 of (I) and (IV) such that $I_0 \geq I$.

Proposition : There exists at most n linearly independent equations describing the functioning at natural rate of a TPTN with n places.

Proof : CI=0 contains ρ linearly independent equations where ρ is the rank of C and the dimension of the space of solutions of $C^T X=0$ is equal to $n-\rho$.

Example 1 : Let the TPTN of figure 3. We want to calculate the current vectors, (if there exists any), corresponding to functionings at natural rate. M_0 and Z are supposed given.

The elementary S-components of this TPTN are defined by the S-invariants :

$J_1^T = [11100]$, $J_2^T = [00011]$.

$J_1^T ZC^+ I = J_1^T M_0 \iff m_{01} + m_{02} + m_{03} = z_1(i_3+i_4) + z_2 i_2 + z_3 i_3$

$J_2^T ZC^+ I = J_2^T M_0 \iff m_{04} + m_{05} = z_4 i_2 + z_5 3i_1$

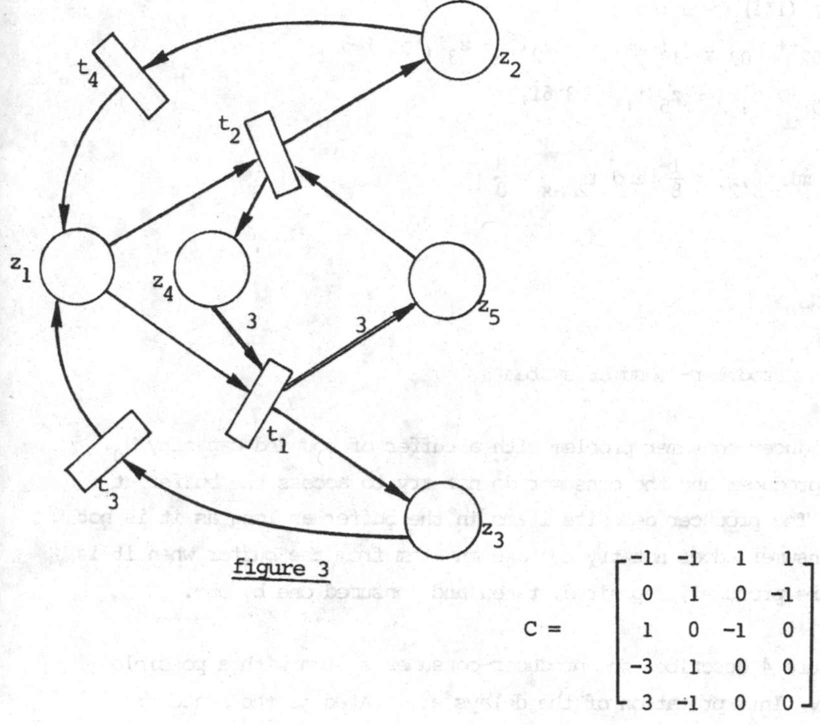

figure 3

$$C = \begin{bmatrix} -1 & -1 & 1 & 1 \\ 0 & 1 & 0 & -1 \\ 1 & 0 & -1 & 0 \\ -3 & 1 & 0 & 0 \\ 3 & -1 & 0 & 0 \end{bmatrix}$$

Solution of CI=0 : we find

$i_2 = i_4 = 3i_1,\ i_1 = i_3$

In order that a solution exists the following equation must be verified

$$\frac{m_{01} + m_{02} + m_{03}}{4z_1 + 3z_2 + z_3} = \frac{m_{04} + m_{05}}{3(z_4 + z_5)} \qquad (\alpha)$$

In this case

$$i_1 = \frac{m_{04} + m_{05}}{3(z_4 + z_5)}$$

Suppose that we have $z_1=z_2=z_3=z_4=z_5=1$ and $M_0^T=[10030]$. The equality (α) is not verified and consequently there is no possible functioning at natural rate.

The inequalities (III) give :

$$m_{01} + m_{02} + m_{03} \geq z_1(i_3+i_4) + z_2i_2 + z_3i_1 \Rightarrow 1 \geq 8i_1$$

$$m_{04} + m_{05} \geq z_4i_2 + z_53i_1 \Rightarrow 3 \geq 6i_1$$

Thus

$$i_{1max} = \min\{\frac{1}{8},\frac{1}{2}\} = \frac{1}{8} \text{ and } i_{2max} = \frac{3}{8}$$

IV - APPLICATIONS

Application 1 : Producer-Consumer system

Consider the producer-consumer problem with a buffer of bounded capacity N_0. We suppose the producer and the consumer do not try to access the buffer at the same time. The producer deposits items in the buffer as long as it is not full and the consumer does not try to take an item from the buffer when it is empty. Items are produced, deposited, taken and consumed one by one.

The TPTN of figure 4 describes the producer-consumer system with a possible initial marking. Interpretation of the delays associated to the places :

z_p : mean time of producing an item
z_d : mean time of depositing an item
z_t : mean time of taking an item
z_c : mean time of consuming an item.
z_s : mean time between two successive accesses to the buffer
z_a : mean waiting time of an item in the buffer.

We suppose that the z_i' s associated to the other places are equal to zero. The producer is allowed to deposit an item right after having produced one and he always finds the access to the buffer free. Also, the consumer is allowed to take an item right after having consumed one and he always finds the access to the buffer free.

By solving the equation CI=0 we find that the same current i must be assigned to all the transitions. Also, a cover by elementary S-components (state graphs in this case) is given in figure 5.

<u>Problem</u> : If we consider as initial marking this one given in figure 4 find the conditions for functioning at natural rate.

The inequality (II) applied for SG1, SG2, SG3, SG4 gives respectively :

$$i \le \frac{1}{z_p+z_d}\ ,\quad i \le \frac{1}{z_d+z_t+2z_s}\ ,\quad i \le \frac{1}{z_c+z_t}\ ,\quad i \le \frac{N_0}{z_d+z_t+z_a}$$

which gives :

$$i_{max} = \min\left\{\frac{1}{z_p+z_d}\ ,\ \frac{1}{z_d+z_t+2z_s}\ ,\ \frac{1}{z_c+z_t}\ ,\ \frac{N_0}{z_d+z_t+z_a}\right\}$$

Conditions for functioning at natural rate :

$$z_s = \frac{z_p-z_t}{2} = \frac{z_c-z_d}{2} \ge 0 \quad \text{and} \quad N_0-1 = \frac{z_a-2z_s}{z_p+z_d} = \frac{z_a-2z_s}{z_c+z_t} \ge 0$$

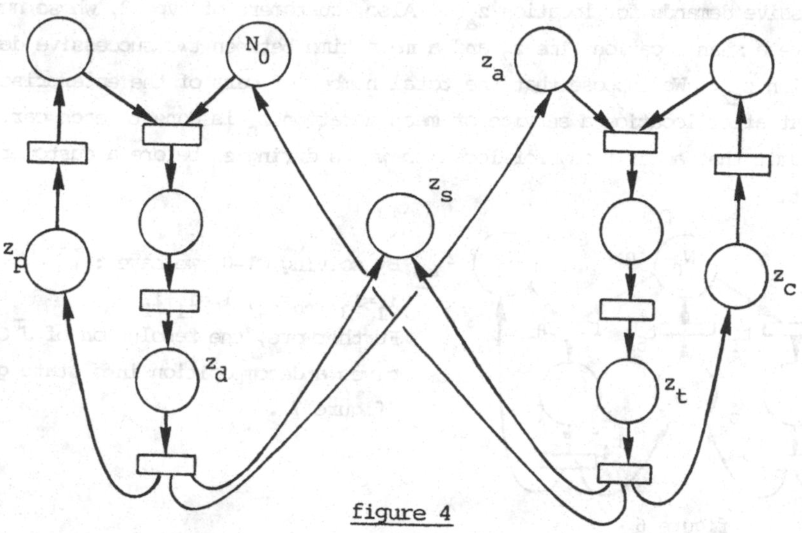

<u>figure 4</u>

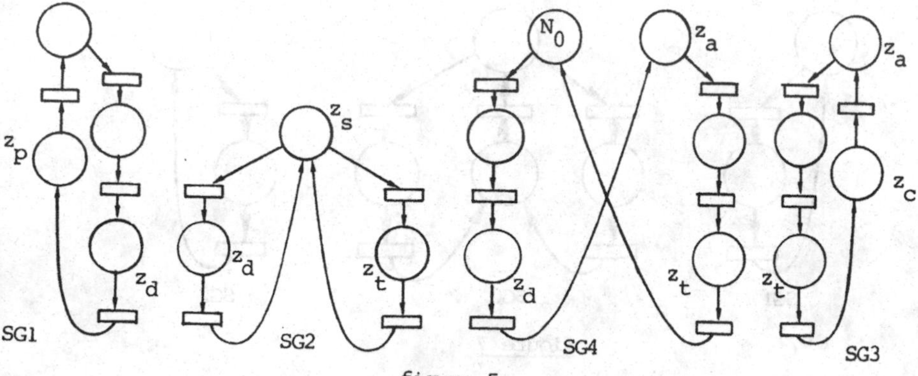

<u>figure 5</u>

Conclusion : The producer's and consumer's periods must be equal: $z = z_p+z_d = z_c+z$
Also, z_s, the mean time between two successive accesses, is given by :

$z_s = \frac{z_p-z_t}{2} = \frac{z_c-z_d}{2} \geq 0$. From $N_0-1 = \frac{z_a-2z_s}{z}$ we deduce that :

a/ for $z_a < 2z_s$, a functioning at natural rate is impossible,

b/ if $z_a=2z_s$, a minimum capacity $N_0=1$ is necessary,

c/ if $z_a > 2z_s$, a minimum capacity of $N_0 = 1 + \frac{z_a-2z_s}{z}$ is necessary.

Application 2 :

Let the TPTN of figure 6. One could imagine that it represents the functioning of an enterprise of car location having customers of two types. Customers of type 1, whose number is N_1, have a mean location time z_1 and a mean time between two successive demands for location z_{a1}. Also, customers of type 2, whose number is N_2, have a mean location time z_2 and a mean time between two successive demands for location z_{a2}. We suppose that the total number of cars of the enterprise is N_0 and that after location a service of mean duration z_s is done to each car. We finally admit that a car ready for location waits during z_0 before a customer demands it.

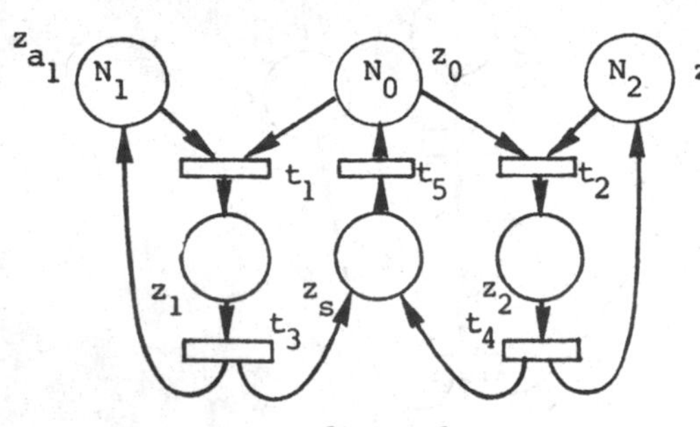

figure 6

By solving CI=0, we have :
$i_1=i_3$, $i_2=i_4$, $i_5=i_1+i_2$
Furthermore, the resolution of $J^T C=0$ gives a decomposition into state graphs (figure 7).

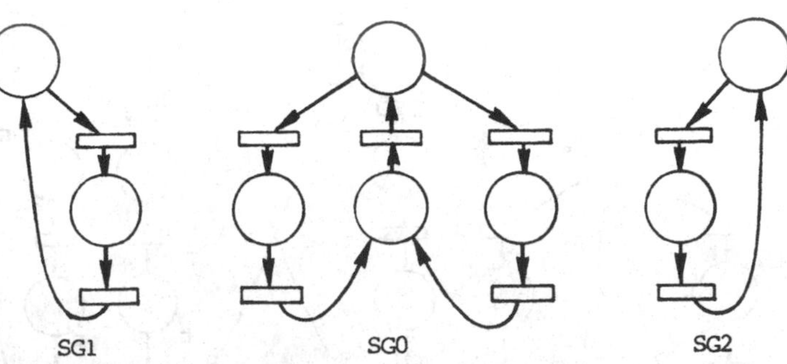

figure 7

Problem : If we know N_1 and N_2 as well as the delays associated to the places, determine N_0 such that a functioning at natural rate be possible.

The equations of charge conservation for SG1 and SG2 are respectively :

$$i_1 = \frac{N_1}{z_1+z_{a_1}} \qquad i_2 = \frac{N_2}{z_2+z_{a_2}}$$

For SG0, we have : $N_0 = (i_1+i_2)\ (z_0+z_s) + i_1z_1 + i_2z_2 \Rightarrow$

$$N_0 = \frac{N_1(z_0+z_1+z_s)}{z_{a_1}+z_1} + \frac{N_2(z_0+z_2+z_s)}{z_{a_2}+z_2}$$

N_0 is the minimum number of cars in order to satisfy the demands of the (N_1+N_2) customers.

REFERENCES

[1] RAMCHANDANI C. : Analysis of asynchronous concurrent systems by timed Petri nets. PhD thesis, M.I.T., september 1973.

[2] SIFAKIS J. : Use of Petri nets for performance evaluation . in Measuring Modelling and Evaluating Computer systems, eds H.Beilner and E.Gelenbe, pp. 75/93, North-Holland Publ.Co., 1977.

[3] MERLIN Ph.M. and FARBER D.J. : Recoverability of communication protocols, Implications of a theoretical study. IEEE Trans. on Comm., pp. 1036/1043, september 1976.

[4] HAN Y.M. : Performance evaluation of a digital system using a Petri net-like approach. Proc. National Electronics Conf., pp. 166/172, Chicago, 1978.

SURVEY OF FRENCH RESEARCH AND APPLICATIONS BASED ON PETRI NETS

C. André
LASSY : University of Nice

M. Diaz
LAAS, CNRS Toulouse

C. Girault
IP, University Paris VI

J. Sifakis
IMAG, University of Grenoble

INTRODUCTION

Models of control schemes based on place /transition nets are widely used by French research Laboratories and industrial groups for design, verification and implementation of process control systems as well as for studying properties of parallel programs and systems.

The theoretical researches developed particularly at the Univerisities of Grenoble and Paris, are related to decidability of net languages, Equi·valence of control schemes, semantics of programs, properties of sche-mes and performance evaluation. Other tools than PT-nets are often used, such as transition-systems [Sifakis 79], Karp and Miller auto-mata [Roucairol 78], unimodular modules [Memmi 78]; however a final return to the simple case of PT - nets is generally made to obtain less cumbersome or more precise results allowing pratical use. A popular trend is to search for new properties that depend only upon the struc-ture of the net and to use them in computer aided systems, thus avoi-ding the simulation of nets.

For operating systems and parallel programs, nets are mostly used to prove properties of synchronization algorithms,but they are also an underlying tool for designing distributed data bases, real time systems and data flow architectures.

For process control, PT-nets have been used in the last seven years particularly at LAAS, CERT and universities of Grenoble and Nice. To manage the increasing complexity of industrial control and their security requirements, laboratories and firms actively develop methodologies and computer aided tools for the design, verification and implementation of parallel systems [Berthomieu 79, Moalla 76, Michel 78]. Special hardware is often used, even designed, for easy asynchronous implementation [André 75 , David 78], but the trend is to use networks of microprocessors. A constant attention is put on detection and recovery of errors [Azema 77, Bellon 77, Marin 75, Sifakis 77] .

The classical decomposition of parrallel systems in a control schema SC, a data scheme SD and an interpretative schema SI is very convenient for focusing on control properties. SC is usually an extension of a PT-net such that the firing of transitions may depend upon some predicate on SD and may activate operators of SD; SD is a bipartite graph that describes the reading and writing of variables by operators, some of which are test operators; SI specifies the exact meaning of operators. There exist many different models allowing such decomposed descriptions their differences are based on the types of control schemes, on the duality between places and transitions, on the relations among the schemes on the form and domain of predicates, on the importance of the interpretative part, on the introduction of time considerations, and even on th constraints from the implementation technology or from the field of applications.

SEMANTICS OF PARALLEL SYSTEMS

Proofs of parallel systems

It is interesting to apply to PT-nets methods used for the statical analysis of parallel programs. This idea is exploited in [Sifakis 79]where it is given a general approach for verifying the properties of parallel systems. According to the approach, it is assumed that every system property can be defined a set of states, called target set, and a type of reachability. Nine different types of reachability are defined; by appropriately choosing the target set, a family of nine potentially different properties is generated. The main result is that the reachability types, and consequently system properties, can be characterized by simpl relations involving the set of the possible initial states and fixed points of given continuous predicate transformers depending on the targe set. It is finally shown that proving a given property amounts to computing iteratively greatest or least fixed points of continuous functions. These results have been applied to two models, called "Condition-Action" and "Invariant-Action" systems, which can be used for representing and studying PT-nets : a "Condition-Action" system acts as a set of guarded commands whereas an "Invariant-Action" system must keep true a characteristic predicate. Their application gives new verification methods for PT-nets and allows to establish some interesting connections between the methods and concepts used for programs and those used for nets. Furthermore, it is shown how some notions of net theory such as those of invariant and deadlock can be generalized and conversely how analysis methods applicable to PT-nets can be extended to other models.

Equivalence and transformations of parallel program schemata

This work is concerned with comparisons and transformations of parallel programs at a "syntactic level".i.e. without taking into account the meaning of the operations performed by a program schema as defined by Karp and Miller. In that formalism a program is represented as a tuple S = SC, SD where

. SD is a "data-flow schema" which describes the operators of the program and the variables that they use.

. SC is a "Control schema" defined as an automaton accepting words formed over an alphabet of events of beginning and end of operators; concurrency among operators is then represented by the possible interleaving of their beginnings and ends.

In this framework an equivalence between schemas may be defined by considering an equivalence between computations allowed by the control schemes -i.e- infinite words accepted by the control automaton and finite words accepted at a final state. The equivalence between computations which is considered is based upon the comparison of occurrences of operators which may transmit values from one to the other, in order to insure that the same values are computed in equivalent computations [Roucairol 74].

Example :
Let us consider the following computation :
$x = \bar{a}\,\underline{a}\,\bar{c}\,\bar{b}\,\underline{b}\,\underline{c}$ (where $\bar{a}$ means beginning of a and $\underline{a}$: end of a)
If the data flow schema is defined by :

(a) $Y := f_a (X)$, (b) $YY := f_b (Y)$, (c) $Z := f_c (Y)$
then there is a value transmission from the first occurrence of a to the first occurrence of b as well as to the first occurrence of c. Identical value transmissions exist in the following equivalent computation : $y = \bar{a}\ \underline{a}\ \bar{c}\ \underline{c}\ \bar{b}\ \underline{b}$ even in the case where operator b is such that $Y := f_b (Y)$.

This equivalence, which may be viewed as a direct extension of the equivalence introduced in the work of Keller, allows to compare schemes with different control-schemes and different amounts of variables. But its decidability reduces to the equivalence problem for multitape automata which is an open problem since ten years . Howewer for schemes with finite state control, equivalence of two schemes S and S' is decidable in the following cases:
let G (S) and G (s') be respectively the set of computations of S and S'

i) G (S) = G (S') .

ii) G (S)$\subseteq$G (S') and S' is conflict-free - i.e.S' does not contain concurrent execution of two operators sharing an output variable or a variable which is an output of one operator and an input of the other operator (this is in particular the case where the amount of concurrency in S is increased to obtain S').

iii) S and S' are compact - i.e. there is no operation in S and S' which is delayed after a test and which could be executed before.

If the equivalence is weakened in order to compare only finite computations, then it is also decidable in the case of equality or inclusion of the sets of finite computations. Considering only finite computations allows to compare schemes in which disjoint loops may be executed in a different order or concurrently. This weaker equivalence has been used in order to justify the transformation of structured sequential programs into parallel ones whose control schema is represented by a PT-net. With a proper labelling of transitions by symbols of beginning and end of operators, firing sequences of a net represent prefixes of computations For this kind of parallel programs conditions for renaming of variables have been pointed out.These conditions are defined directly on the structure of the control net, without requiring the knowledge of its case graph.

However in order to reach maximal parallelism, nets are not sufficient in the sense that it is not possible with counters to keep a track of an unbounded amount of history of a computation. But it is fondamental for instance to record order of decisions if tests are allowed to go faster than operations which are controlled by them. Hence, if we consider a generalization of the keller's notion of "queue realization", consisting in a net in which each place may coutain a tree of events instead of tokens. Then it has been shown that maximal parallelism may be reached [Roucairol 78].

The parallelism of an algorithm may be increased by considering its semantical properties instead of only its syntactical expression. As an example, the intricate parallelization of the polish-code generator in a compiler has been studied [Girault, Morcrette 77].

PROPERTIES OF NETS

Petri net languages

The description of Petri nets by their associated languages, sequences of firings of transitions and sequences of their labels, leads to the large class of nets for which the language is regular. For this class the reachability problem is easily solved [Valk, Vidal - Naquet 77]. It is shown that small nets have the same associated languages as very large finite automata [Valk, Vidal-Naquet 77]. Deterministic PT-nets for which at a given marking and for a given label at most one transition bearing this label is enabled, are investigated for application to the modelling of industrial processes.

Behaviour equivalence of nets

A new equivalence relation in PT-nets is defined [André 79-2]. A subset of transitions called a frontier is given. This behaviour of the net on the frontier is an homomorphic image of the firing sequence language of the net, but the mapping must satisfy the behaviour condition. Two nets with the same behaviour on the same frontier are said B-equivalent (behaviour-equivalent). The behaviour condition is such that the following property holds : for any firing sequence of a net, there exists a firing sequence on the B-equivalent net with the same trace on the common frontier; moreover for any subsequent sequence of the first net, there exists a subsequent sequence of the second one, with the same trace. An outcome, is that the B-equivalence preserves liveness properties and synchronic relations between transitions belonging to the frontier.

The main result concerns substitution : when a subnet is subtituted by an B-equivalence subnet, properties on the unmodified part of the net and on the frontier are preserved. By multiple substitutions, the analysis problem of a given net, can be decomposed into several analysis problems on nets for which the reachability sets are far smaller than the reachability set of the original net.

Reductions of nets

Successive reductions of a PT-net , provided that they preserve its properties, may be used to obtain a new net for which boundedness, live ness or proper termination are easily tested. Three types of reductions have been considered .R1: if a place is the only one input place of its output transitions, then this place together with all its input and out put transitions may be replaced by a set of new transitions, each one having the effect of the consecutive firings of one input transition an one or more output transitions. R2 : a redundant place for which the number of tokens depends linearly on those of other places may be suppressed. R3 : a transition that creates only a loop around a place may also be suppressed. It is stated upon which precise conditions these reductions can be achieved and preserve the properties of a net. The main and difficult result is that isomorphic irreducible nets can be ob tained independently of the order in which the reduction rules have bee applied (Church Rosser property). All state machines and event graphs can be completly reduced to a single transition. However rather simple nets cannot be reduced, thus new types of reductions are investigated [Berthelot 78, 79]. These reductions are now used at EDF (French organism for electricity supply) for simplification of large nets [Boussin 78]. Finally an unified framework for reduction of general transition systems, PT-nets are parallel programs is given in [Berthelot-Valk 79].

Structural properties of PT-nets

A great deal of interest is given to properties that rely only on the structure of a net and that can be studied just by looking into the properties of its incidence matrix. A net is structurally bounded if it is bounded for every initial marking and it is structurally live if there exists a marking for which it is live. It is shown that the verification of these properties is related to the type of solutions of equalities or inequalities involving the incidence matrix. It appears very often easier to decide that a net is bounded (resp. not live) for every marking rather than for a given marking [Memmi 77, Sifakis 78]. A systematization of the notions of duality and symmetry may thus be achieved [Memmi 79].

The theorems of Commoner and Hack are useful to check the liveness of free-choice nets from the relations among their traps and deadlocks. Sophisticated extensions of the notions of components without trap or without deadlock permit one to obtain, for any net, a necessary condition for the liveness of some of its transitions and a sufficient condition for the unboundedness of some of its places. Moreover the free choise definition has been extended from one step to firing sequences thus giving a greater class of nets for which the necessary and sufficient liveness condition of Commoner still holds [Memmi 78].

Performance evaluation

For timed nets with constant firing delays it is shown that the possible steady state can be described by a linear program in terms of their initial marking, firing frequencies and delays. The maximal frequencies may be computed by solving a system of linear equations [Sifakis 77, 79]. When probabilities are associated with non deterministic choices, a Markovian model gives the firing frequencies [Florin 78]; this generalizes the results given in the PhD thesis of Ramchandani. some application are the reliability-evaluations of a full duplex protocol or of the computer system for the Caracas tube [Florin,Lonc 79] .

OPERATING SYSTEMS

Models of synchronization

Nets have served to study busses, exchanges between processors and peripherals, and more complex protocols. Here, they are appreciated because they give a homogeneous description of both hardware equipment and software procedures [Azema 77, Vernel 77]. Several synchronization mechanisms including, of course semaphores and path expressions but also more complex ones such monitors, have been represented by PT-nets in order to compare them and to easily prove some of their properties [Vaudene 77, Girault 77]. Synchronization algorithms (such as strategies to solve readers and writers problems) have been designed.

Starting from simple solutions,transformations of the control scheme, refinements, displacements of computations from the interpretative scheme to the control scheme, give rise to complex solutions including priority rules and properties like fairness [Girault 77]. The management and coherence of multiple copies in distributed data bases have been expressed by using the evaluation nets of G. Nutt [Seguin 79].

Real time systems

Real time systems are a point of convergence between software an process control,this last aspect being presented below. When these systems are programmed on minicomputers, the parallelism is controlled by primitives of high level languages but PT-nets can be used at the design stage. For example, for a system of two redundant computers, the commutation of control from one to the other has been studied by means of PT-nets in order to avoid the loss and the duplication of messages [Natkin 79]. PT-nets have been used to describe the control of sets of synchronous automata,and then a high level language GAELIC has been designed based on nets extended for interruptions and abortions of tasks [Le Calvez 78].

MASC 16 (Modules for Alarm and Sequence Control) is a software package implemented on the series of Solar 16 minicomputers of SEMS Inc It is intended for systems ensuring the functions of watching and sequential control in a large variety of industrial applications. MASC 16 proposes the language MCL (Monitoring and Control Language) to describe automatic control systems in terms of GRAFCET. The description of an application is composed of two parts. One part is concerned with the actions (associated with places) varying from simple assignment command to the management of user tasks. The other part describes the logical conditions (associated with transitions) depending on system variables or on interface variables [Masc 79].

DESIGN METHODOLOGIES AND COMPUTER AIDED TOOLS

Complex applications require a methodology of design, based on a hierarchy of models introducing more and more considerations, supported by a computer aided system and, even, going down to the implementation. Here, the "operative part" formed by the data and interpretativ schemes (SD and SI) takes as much importance as the command part (SC) and needs compiling tools . For effective industrial applications there remain only a few complete methodologies that have been selected according to their convenience for design and validation, or to their computer aided system.

The L.A.A.S. methods and tools for design and validation of nets

The model that is used at the L.A.A.S. starts from the description of a parallel system by the tuple (SC, SD, SI). Here SC is a standard PT net. For association with SD, each transition t_i is "labelled" with a logical predicate $q(t_i)$ and a list $l(t_i)$ of operators. An enabled transition may fire only if the predicate is true and when it fires the operators of the list are actived. There are three types of modes in SD : the operators that execute operations on memory cells, the memory cells (some of which are input or output ones so that the outside world may read or write into them at any time), and the predicate cells that contain the evaluation of predicates. SI specifies operators, predicates and initializations [Valette 77] .

This decomposition is interesting because it allows three levels of validation in order to successively check the safeness and liveness of the standard net SC, the determinism of the system by considering SC and SD, and finally its semantic properties by means of classical assertions on SI. The complexity of the third level is nevertheless simplified by the correction of the structure granted by the first two levels [Valette 79] . For example, priority rules in synchronization mechanisms can be described by auxiliary variables and predicates. Only invariants on the net may thus prove the correctness of the mechanism before considering any priorities. An implementation by means of a monitor, as defined by J. Kessel, is directly obtained and the implementation proof appears as a straightforward consequence of the specification proof [Diaz 79] .

A methodology for the specification of distributed systems, based upon a Real Time Control Sytem model, is currently in use. This RTCS model is constituted of two descriptions, an informal one and a formal one. The informal part is a set of sentences written in natural language. This informal part is the starting point of the formal part of which it will appear as a comment. Writing the informal sentences is the designer's responsability, nevertheless he has to follow some guide-lines: he must define the needed control functions , the different levels and their interfaces, the specification of each subsystem. He has also to classify the objects of these subsystems inside one of six classes : external events, external actions, resources, control conditions, predicates, lower level functions. This classification is the basic starting point for deriving the formal part, i.e. the net SC and the labels SD. An object will appear as a place, a transition, a predicate according to the class in which it has been put [Ayache 79]. It must be also pointed out that the choice between what is expressed by the control and what is expressed by the data comes from the designer's specification. This methodology has been applied to the study of an electronic switching system. At the first level an interpreted net only describes the normal call from the point of view of a subscriber. Lower levels specify new services such as the conference among several subscribers or the holding (possibility to answer a call without departing from a first call) [Ayache 79].

To deal with such complex systems two complementary approaches have been developed. The first one, a top-down approach, splits the proof into smaller ones about subnets defined and verified by refinement : under some conditions the overall net is known to be correct without any more analysis [Valette 79]. The second one, a bottom up approach, constructs modules by merging sets of elementary actions and extracting only their external behaviour. Then these modules serve to construct upper ones. This has been applied to the design and verification of communication procedures [Azema 78] .

This methodology is supported, at every stage, by computer aided tools. An APL package allows classical analysis by scanning the forward marking class and using hardware simulation [Azema 76] . Another APL software, built around an integer linear program, gives all the invariants of a net. It also supports proofs about assertions that may be put in the form of linear relations [Berthomieu 79]. The algorithms related to the analysis of nets have been developed and constitute the body of a package allowing to deal with nets by using a graphic display Tektronix 4014 [Chezaviel 79] . This package firstly allows to draw and modify the nets, to store them in a library. Then it offers a lot of verification possibilities such as checking boundedness or liveness by enumeration of the reachable markings, by using reduction-rules or by looking for invariants. Furthermore, invariants can be obtained that constitute a base and also that support proofs about particular assertions. The 4014 graphic display is connected to a CII-Mitra 15 at the L.A.A.S. for the graphic handling. This Mitra 15 is connected from Toulouse to an I.B.M 370-168 in Paris, where all the analyses are done, because they generally require complex computations.

M.A.S., a tool for multilevel simulation of cooperating modules

M.A.S. is a tool for the functional multilevel simulation of systems conceived as the interconnection of cooperating modules. Each module is described independently at the desired level of detail and appropriate primitives permit to express the interconnections. The modules can be used in order to generate and study the behaviour of different configurations.

Each module description is composed of an operative part and a control part. The former is a set of operators (or procedures) acting upon the variables of the module ; the latter manages the activations of these operators and consists of a safe interpreted net. A module is simulated as follows. The arrival of a token at a place p_i activates a set of operators $\varphi(p_i)$ associated with this place ; this token is not available for enabling a further transition before the end of this activation. An activation holds until the time $\nu(p_i,\tau)$ computed at the time τ of its activation. The firing of an enabled transition t_k is synchronized by the occurrence of an associated external event $\mu(t_k)$ generated by the operative part and can also be conditionned by a predicate C (t_k) on the variables of the module. Hence this description takes into account the interaction of the control part with its environment materialized by the external events, the timing and the interpretation [Moalla 76]. The control is described in a non procedural sub language and the operators in an APL-like sub language [Zachariades 77] . The specification of M.A.S. has needed to make precise the behaviour of interpreted nets and to study their properties. It has been shown that the existing results on the characteristic properties of autonomous nets are only partially valid [Moalla 78].

M.A.S. is a tool for the verification by simulation of the properties of interpreted nets, for the functional validation of systems during their design and for the evaluation of their behaviour.

A methodology for secure design is proposed, based on three steps of formal transformations. First, the functional specifications are described by an interpreted net, thus allowing design errors in synchronization and parallelism to be detected by M.A.S. Then,the real time constraints are introduced and the net analysis shows whether or not they are respected for a given multiprocessor. Finally automatic implementation is obtained by a software interpretor on a microprocessor that is strictly equivalent to M.A.S. The use of the same model ensures a secure transition between these different design steps [Saucier 78 , Pilaud 78] .

The SINTRA CAD system

The SINTRA system is a set of packages for modeling,analysis, simulation, evaluation and implementation of real time systems elaborated by means of nets. The simulator has been defined with the collaboration of the M.A.S. team, therefore the model is also based on a set of interconnected modules of which the control part is a timed interpreted net. But, for concise description of complex industrial systems, inhibitor edges, valued edges, unsafe places, colored tokens and even further extensions are allowed.

The main package SIREP is composed of three parts. The graphical program offers an interactive graphical language for description and modification of nets, introduction of parameters, display of markings and of other informations. The driving program offers a set of commands to constitute files, modify nets, markings or predicates and introduce assertions to be verified. The simulation program gives the markings, interesting states, critical resources and traces. SIREP has now more than 12.000 Fortran instructions and uses a Tektronix 4015 for display [Chambon 79] . The other packages are IMPLA for automatic implementation of the control part on PLAs, IMPRO for the interpretation on a set of microprocessors MC 6800, and GEMO for parallelization of numerical repetitive instructions considering the limitations of particular host architectures [Michel 79, Gherbi 79] .

The GRAFCET normalization

The GRAFCET is the result of a normalization process originated from about 16 models that were employed for industrial design of automatic control devices. This model is derived from interpreted Petri nets, however there are several crucial differences between the two models. In GRAFCET the places are replaced by "steps" that may be "active" or not and that are associated with operations. Whereas the tokens are accumulated in a place, the activation of a step is a Boolean notion ; safeness is thus enforced but leads to confusions and control alone cannot describe the management of resources. Conversely whereas a token is indivisible and may be used for the firing of only one transition, the activation of the step may serve to the firing of all subsequent transitions and there is no notion of conflict. Moreover all such transitions must be simultaneously fired, losing the asynchronism in the control specification and requiring predicates to express exclusions and choices. In GRAFCET the predicates may depend not only on data but also on the activations of some steps and on the time elapsed since some of the last activations. In addition the actions may be conditioned by the activations of other steps [AFCET 78]. In conclusion, the loss of a separation between the control and the operative parts gives indeed more flexibility and opportunity for expression and simplification [Blanchard 79]; but as a counterpart it is nearly impossible to restrict the analysis of a system to the net alone [Valette 78]. The main goal of the model is to allow very quick and unambiguous specification for further design. This is the reason for which it is well accepted in industry and has motived hardware [David 78] and software [MASC 79] implementation tools. It is now taught in electronic university institutes of technology (I.U.T.) .

IMPLEMENTATION

Almost all implementations of nets on elementary hardware are concerned with safe nets where the conflicts have already been solved to ensure determinism. But, if high speed is not required, microprocessors may be used and the elimination of hardware limitations permits extensions of nets described in high level languages.

Hardware asynchronous implementation

Hardware implementations were the first to be used and methods have been provided for straightforward translation of safe nets into circuits.

The more elaborate method uses a specialized integrated circuit called CUSA (Universal Cell for Asynchronous Sequences) for each place. A CUSA is a module made of two gates with feedback and one delay carefully set to avoid hazards [SESCOSEM 75]. Any asynchronous machine can be built with CUSA starting from a flow graph. This method has been adapted to PT-nets using logical gates for each transition : an AND tests all input CUSAs plus external conditions ; when the transition fires the output CUSAs are set while the input CUSAs are reset [Mitrani 76]. The GRAFCET model being less strict than PT-nets, its synthesis is more constrained and needs a new adaptation [David 78].

A dual method takes standard RS cells for places and specialized circuits for their connection [Daclin 76] . Moreover a description language has been conceived for an optimization package [Courvoisier 74].

Implementation by PROMs and PLAs

An asynchronous implementation may be based on a hardware interpretation of state machines speeded up by tables stored in PROMs or RePROM In order to do so the nets must be decomposed into state machines synchronized by auxiliary events and conditions [André 75] . This method is now reconsidered for more elaborate components, the FPLAs ; using such components leads to simpler architectures.

FPLAs are LSI components on which Boolean functions, expressed by sums of products may be directly implemented. Here the graph of the reachable markings of a live and safe PT-net is considered as a finite state machine. Then these states are binary encoded and the firing rules are translated into Boolean functions using the current state cod and input signals to obtain the next state code and output commands [Kwan 77, Ayache 77, Michel 79]. Each cycle takes about 50 ns .

But the number of markings of a highly concurrent system may be prohibitive. In such a case a decomposition of the net itself into several state machines gives rise to a direct implementation on the same number of mutually synchronized PLAs. Introducing more information in each PLA allows to decrease their number. Instead of state machines, live and safe components are used for a generalized decomposition and are implemented according to the above method [Auguin 78]. This approach leads to incompletely defined Boolean functions using product terms instead o minterms. An original sub-optimal method of minimization of these Boolean functions gives a better use of each PLA. The whole method, decomposition and minimization, is programmed and constitutes an aid to design control systems. The program is written in FORTRAN IV on a 32 k 16 bits-words mini computer. It supplies the designer with the punched tapes needed to program PLAs.

Rather similar methods may be used with elaborate hardware such as programmable automata. On these automata PT-nets [Toulotte 78] as well as GRAFCET [Taconet 79] have been implemented by direct coding of a set boolean equations.

Software implementations

The need for flexible and quick implementations, the cost of complex hardware and of its maintenance, the increase in power and speed of microprocessors, and the use of microprocessors for the operative part of process control systems are the major reasons for which software systems are now widely spread to implement the control part. In particular when speed is desired the host architecture is built around a bit slice microprocessor controlling conventional ones for the operative part.

The Coleres system is built around a bit slice microprocessor INTEL 3001. A set of instructions is associated with each place, some of them for the structure of the net, the others for the interface with the operative part. The interpretation is synchronous with a delay of about 2.5 ms [Blanchard 77] . In another implementation, the net is programmed in an asynchronous logic array. Logical functions, operations concerning the data graph and the interpretation are treated by programs running on microprocessors with local memories [Courvoisier 78].

For applications such as signal processing, a PASCAL-like language : "LADSY" has been based on PT-nets with bounded capacities associated with each places [Arnaud 79] . These nets are equivalent to the generalized PT-nets but are more concise and are suitable to modelize synchronic relations between events [ANDRE 79] . The compiler generates a PT-net, with bounded capacities for the control part, and codes in an intermediate language for the operative part of the system. Analyses of the net are made to detect deadlock, unbounded resources, starvations ...

Simulation is needed to choose among implementation solutions and to take timing constraints into account. The actual control part can be implemented by a hardware interpreter of these nets, based on a bit slice microprocessor and designed to synchronize several microprocessors associated with the operative part [Taffazzoli 79] . Complete translation of the intermediate code for several target languages will achieve the automatization of the design.

The APRP system uses a microprocessor INTEL 8080. A high level language allows one to describe the external interface of the net (as in the M.A.S. model) and the actions associated with each place. It is possible to distinguish background actions that may be delayed as well as to associate auxiliary actions with the transitions [Silva 78] . The ARP system, developed at EDF, also runs on INTEL 8080 microprocessors. The main program simulates interpreted safe nets : delays and outputs are associated with places, while predicates are associated with transitions. Each transition takes from 1 to 3 ms with a 2 MHz INTEL 8080. A translator gives automatically the program of the net drawn on a graphic terminal. A third program written in Basic helps one to prove safeness and liveness by a reduction method. This provides a cheap, autonomous microcenter to develop nets [Tourres 76, Boussin 78] . Applications have been made to the modeling of cut-off stations.

FAULT TOLERANT SYSTEMS

One line test strategies

The M.A.S. system allows the description of the distribution of processes onto a set of processors. These processes are modelled as live and safe nets. An on-line test is made possible by introducing places t check the invariants of the system. For each place a dependancy graph between used and defined variables follows the propagation of errors. T determination of global dependency permits one to find optimal localization of rollback points [Bellon 77, 78] . At a higher level places ar associated with hardware modules of a system to be tested and transitic are used to follow the the information flow between modules. Generalize paths between source places (hardware input modules) and sink places (output modules) define partitions of the system. The intersection of a partitions gives subsets in which any simple failure can be localized.

Information capacities of edges serve to find good strategies for failure localization and to forecast their performances [Robach 77, Mili 78].

Redundant control

Some redundancy may be introduced in the implementation a net itself, in particular to check invariance of some weighted sums of tokens. Furthermore auxiliary places may be added to obtain more invariants [Marin 75]. A more general method is based on the notions of equivalence and realization for PT-nets. It is shown that there exist linear mappings G such that for every net having as incidence matrix C, the net having as incidence GC is a realization of the original net. An adequate choice of G gives distance properties to the markings of GC which thus can be verified using linear codes techniques. Two types of fault tolerant realizations are suggested. Furthermore, it is shown that when a PT-net remains bounded in case of errors, linear circuits may be used for error detection and correction [Sifakis 79].

The implementation of the software of a real time system is split into two distinct redundant parts : an "observer" implements a net based program which defines level functional specifications while a "worker" is composed of the set of processes which perform the intended tasks. The observer and the worker run in parallel, possibly on different hardware supports. At checkpoints the worker calls the observer to compare their respective control states and check that every computation sequence of the worker corresponds exactly to a valid firing sequence of the net. The response message of the observer may be used for recovery actions [Ayache 79].

ACKNOLEDGEMENTS

The authors whish to thank the French researchers and engineers working on Petri nets who have sent their contribution for this survey.

REFERENCES

ANDRE C. : Sur une méthode de conception assistée par ordinateur des systèmes logiques à évolutions simultanées. Thèse Doc. 3è cycle, Univ. de Nice, Juin 1975.

ANDRE C., ARMAND P., BOERI F. : Synchronic relations and applications in parallel computation. Digital Process, 1979.

ANDRE C., BOERI F., MARIN J. : Synthèse et réalisation des systèmes logiques à évolutions simultanées. Revue Rairo-Automatique, Vol.10, n° 4,pp.67-86.

ANDRE C., BOERI F. : The behaviour equivalence and its aplications in Petri nets analysis. Journées d'étude AFCET, Schémas de contrôle des systèmes informatiques et automatiques, Paris Sept. 1979.

ARMAND P. : Un langage de spécification de systèmes parallèles. Description de la synchronisation par des réseaux de Petri. Thèse de Doc. 3è cycle, Univ. de Nice Nov. 79.

AUGUIN M. : Conception des systèmes de commande à l'aide de réseaux logiques programmables. Thèse Doc. 3è cycle, Univ. de Nice, 1978.

AUGUIN M., BOERI F, ANDRE C. : New design using Plas and Petri nets. Meco'78 Measurement and Control International Symposium, Juin 1978, Athènes.

AYACHE J.M., LE DANOIS P. : Synthesis of logic systems with Pla's. Journées d'étude, Logique câblée ou logique programmée, Lausanne, Mars 1977, pp. 89-95.

AYACHE J.M., DIAZ M., VALETTE R. : A methodology for specifying in electronic switching systems. International Switching Symposium, ISS 79, Paris May 1979.

AYACHE J.M., AZEMA P., DIAZ M. : OBSERVER a concept for on line detection of control errors in concurrent systems. In IEEE, International Symposium on Fault Tolerant Computing, Madison, June 1979.

AZEMA P., DIAZ M., DOUCET J.E. : Multilevel description using Petri nets.Symposium on Computer hardware description languages, New York, Sept. 1975.

AZEMA P., VALETTE R., DIAZ M. : Petri nets as a common tool for design verification and hardware simulation. ACM-IEEE 13th Design Automation Conference, San Francisco, Palo Alto, June 1976.

AZEMA P., DIAZ M. : Test oriented interpreted Petri nets of concurrent systems. International Symp. on Fault-Tolerant Computing, Pittsburgh, June 21-23, New York 1976.

AZEMA P., DIAZ M. : Checking experiments for hardware and software concurrent systems. IEEE Fault Tolerant Computing Symposium, Los Angeles, June 1977 (short paper) and Internal Report, LAAS, Toulouse, December 1976.

AZEMA P., AYACHE J.M., BERTHOMIEU B. : Design and verification of communication procedures : a bottom up approach. 3rd Conference on software engineering, Atlanta, May 1978.

BELLON C., SAUCIER G. : On line test modeling in non redundant distributed systems. FTC7, Los Angeles, June 1977.

BELLON C. : Etude de la dégradation progressive dans les systèmes répartis. Thèse de 3è cycle, Grenoble Septembre 1977.

BELLON C., KUBIAK C., ROBACH Ch. : Modélisation des systèmes distribués en vue de la détection des pannes. Annales des Télécommunications, novembre-décembre 1978.

BERTHELOT G., ROUCAIROL G. : Reduction of Petri nets. Mathematical Foundation of Computer Science, Gdansk, Pologne, Sept. 1976. Lecture notes in Computer Science 45, Mazurkewicz Ed. Springer Verlag, Berlin, Heidelberg, New York, 1976, pp. 202-209.

BERTHELOT G. : Checking liveness of Petri nets. Proc. of the IMACS-AICA-GI Conference on Parallel Computers and Parallel Mathematics, March 1977, Feilmeier Ed. North Holland Publishing Company, 1977, pp. 217-220.

BERTHELOT G. : Verification des réseaux de Petri. Thèse Doc. 3è cycle, Université P et M. Curie, Paris, Janvier 1978.

BERTHELOT G. : Preuve de non blocage de programmes parallèles par réduction de réseaux de Petri. First European Conf. on Parallel and Distributed Processing, Toulouse May 1979.

BERTHELOT G., VALK R. : Reductions of nets and parallel programs. Advanced course on general net theory of processes and systems, Hamburg, Oct. 1979.

BERTHOMIEU B. : Analyse structurelle des réseaux de Petri, Méthodes et outils. Thèse Doc. Ingénieur, Univ. Paul Sabatier, Toulouse, Septembre 1979.

BLANCHARD M., CAVARROC J.C., GILLON J., THUILLIER G. : Conception modulaire d'automatismes séquentiels asynchrones. DERA-Télématique Electrique, Rapport DGRST 71.7.2912.01, Janvier 1976.

BLANCHARD M.,GILLON J. : Réalisations logiques programmées des réseaux de Petri. Journées d'étude, Logique câblée ou Logique programmée, Lausanne, mars 1977, pp. 51-57.

BLANCHARD M. : Le GRAFCET pour une représentation normalisée du cahier des charges d'un automatisme logique. Automatique et Informatique Industrielles, n° 61, pp. 27-32, n° 62, pp. 36-40, Novembre-Décembre 1977.

BLANCHARD M. : Automatismes logiques : GRAFCET ou réseaux de Petri. Le Nouvel Automatisme, Mai 1979, pp. 45-52.

BOUSSIN J. : Synthesis and analysis of logic automation systems. 7th Triennal World Congress, Helsinki, June 1978, Pergamon Press.

CASPI P., MILI A., ROBACH Ch. : An information measure on nets. IFAC Workshop on Information and Systems, Compiègne, Octobre 1977.

CHAMBON P. : Simulation de réseaux de Petri. 7ème Colloque sur le Traitement du Signa et ses Applications, Nice, Mai 1979.

CHEZALVIEL B., BERTHOMIEU B., BACHMAN S., DIAZ M. : Computer aided design and proof of parallel systems. Application to synchronization software. Internal Report, LAAS, Toulouse, Decembre 1978.

COURVOISIER M. : Etude des systèmes logiques de commande asynchrone à évolutions simultanées. Thèse Doc.ès-Sciences, Univ. Paul Sabatier, Toulouse, Février 1974.

COURVOISIER M. : Description et réalisation des systèmes de commande asynchrone à évolutions simultanées. Journée d'étude AFCET. Montpellier, 8 mars 1974.

COURVOISIER M., ESCOURROU A. : Description language and method of design of simultaneously evoluting asynchronous logic control systems. Congrès IFAC : Discrete Systems Riga, Septembre 1974.

COURVOISIER M. : Description et réalisation des systèmes de commande asynchrones à évolutions simultanées. RAIRO, Février 1975.

COURVOISIER M. : A parallel asynchronous architecture for control systems. Second Symposium IFAC : Discrete Systems, Dresde, Mars 1977.

COURVOISIER M., VALETTE R. : Description and realization of parallel systems. COMPCON Fall, 1977, Washington DC, pp. 167-172.

COURVOISIER M. : Realisation de systèmes logiques à évolutions simultanées par matric asynchrone. Electronics Letters, Vol.14 n° 4, Février 1978.

COURVOISIER M., GEFFROY J.C. : High security multicomputer based control station for a decentralized process control system. 5th Seminar Applied Aspects of the Automata Theory, Varna Bulgarie, Mai 1979.

DACLIN E., BLANCHARD M. : Synthèse des Systèmes logiques. Ed. Cepadues, Collection Sup-Aero, Décembre 1976.

DAVID R. : Synthèse à l'aide de CUSA d'un système séquentiel décrit par un GRAFCET Journées d'étude AFCET-SEE, Les Méthodes Modernes d'Etude et de Réalisation des Automatismes, Gif sur Yvette, 2-3 février 1978.

DAVID R., SILVA M. : Synthèse programmée des automatismes logiques décrits par réseau de Petri : Une méthode de mise en oeuvre sur microcalculateur. A paraître dans RAIRO-Automatisme, Vol. 13, n° 4, 1979.

DAVID R. : Modular design of asynchronous circuits defined by graphs. IEEE Trans. on Comp., Vol. C 26, n° 8, pp. 727-737, August 1977.

DEVY M., DIAZ M. : Multilevel specification and validation of the control in communication systems. First International Conference on Distributed Computing Systems, Huntsville Alabama, October 1-4, 1979.

DIAZ M., GEFFROY J.C., COURVOISIER M. : On-set realization of failsafe sequential machines. IEEE Trans, Comp., Vol. C-23, février 1974. pp. 133-138.

FLORIN G., NATKIN S. : Analyse des systèmes logiques et application à la tolérance aux pannes dans les réseaux de Petri. Journées AFCET, Réseaux de Petri, Nice,Déc.77.

FLORIN G., NATKIN S. : Evaluation des performances d'un protocole de communication à l'aide des réseaux de Petri et des processus stochastiques. Journées d'étude AFCET, Multiprocesseurs et Multiordinateurs en Temps Réel, Paris, Mai 1978.

FLORIN G., LONG P., NATKIN S. : An evaluation cad tool based on stochastic Petri nets. IFIP Working Conference on Fault Tolerant and Reliable Computing, Londres, Sept. 1979, to appear, North Holland.

FLORIN G. NATKIN S. : Quelques propriétés des réseaux de Petri Stochastiques. Journées d'étude AFCET, schémas de contrôle des systèmes informatiques et automatiques, Paris. Sept. 1979.

GHERBI B. : Conception de systèmes numériques à hautes performances. Thèse de Doc. 3è cycle, Université P. et M. Curie, Novembre 1979.

GIRAULT C., MORCRETTE M. :Syntactic analysis by specialized parallel operators. IMACS-GI Symposium on Parallel Computers - Parallel Mathematics, Munich, March 1977, Feilmeir Ed, North Holland Publishing Company, 1977.

GIRAULT C. : Réseaux de Petri et synchronisation de processus. Journées d'étude AFCET, Programmation globale des Synchronisations dans les applications en Temps Réel, Paris Nov. 1977, pp. 153-171.

KWAN C. : Utilisation des réseaux logiques programmables dans la conception de systèmes logiques. Thèse de Doc. 3è cycle, Université de Compiègne, 1976.

KWAN C., MICHEL C., LE BEUX P. : Logical systems using Plas and Petri nets. Programmable hardwired systems. Information Processing, Montreal, August 1977, IFIP, North Holland publishing Company, 1977.

LE CALVEZ F. : Définition d'un langage de description globale des applications en temps réel. Thèse de Doct. 3è cycle, Univ. P. et M. Curie, Paris, Janvier 1979.

LONC P. : Une nouvelle méthode d'étude de la sureté de fonctionnement. Application à l'étude du système informatique du métro de Caracas. Mémoire d'ingénieur, IEE-CNAM, Paris, Juillet 1979.

MARIN J. : Sur le test en ligne des machines séquentielles réalisées à partir de réseaux de Petri. Thèse Doct. 3è cycle, Univ. Nice, 1975.

MARIN J., ANDRE C., BOERI F. : Conception de systèmes séquentiels totalement autotestables à partir des réseaux de Petri. Revue RAIRO-Automatique, Vol.10, n° 11, 1976, pp. 23-40.

MASC 79: MASC 16, Modules for Alarm and Sequence Control. SEMS n° 1.164.705.000/3601, Grenoble, février 1979.

MEMMI G. : Semiflows and invariants, applications in Petri nets theory. Journées d'Etude AFCET, Réseaux de Petri, Mars 1977, Paris, pp. 145-150.

MEMMI G. : Applications of the semiflow notion to the boundedness and liveness problems in Petri net theory. Proc. of the 1978 Conference on Information Science and systems, Johns Hopkins University, Baltimore, USA.

MEMMI G. : Fuites de graphes à choix non imposé dans les réseaux de Petri. 3rd International Symp. on Programming, Paris, Avril 1978, B. Robinet Ed., Dunod Informat. Pub

MEMMI G. : Fuites dans les réseaux de Petri. RAIRO Inf. Théorique, Vol.12 n° 2, 1978.

MEMMI G. : Fuites et semi-flots dans les réseaux de Petri. Thèse de doct.Ingénieur, Université P. et M. Curie, Paris décembre 1978.

MEMMI G. : Notion de dualité dans les réseaux de Petri. International Symposium on Semantics of Concurrent Computation, Evian, July 1979, To appear in Lecture Notes in Comp. Science Springer Verlag Ed.

MEMMI G. ROUCAIROL G. : Linear algebra in net theory. Advanced Course on general net theory of processes and systems, Hamburg, Oct. 1979.

MICHEL C. : Ensemble d'outils pour la conception assistée par ordinateur de systèmes numériques à haute performance. 7ème Colloque sur le Traitement du Signal et ses Applications, Nice, Mai 1979.

MILI A. : Outils d'aide à la décision dans le test des systèmes logiques. Thèse Doct. 3è cycle, Université de Grenoble, juin 1978.

MITRANI E., TELLEZ-GIRON R., DAVID R. : Emploi des CUSA pour la synthèse directe de systèmes asynchrones définis par des graphes ou des réseaux de Petri. Colloque AFCET ADEPA, Automatismes Logiques, pp. 83-89, Paris, décembre 1976.

MOALLA M. : L'approche fonctionnelle dans la vérification des systèmes informatiques Proposition d'un ensemble de méthodologies. Thèse Doct.Ingénieur, ENSIMAG, Universit de Grenoble, Décembre 1976.

MOALLA M., SIFAKIS J., ZACHARIADES M. : Mas, un outil d'aide à la description et à la conception des automatismes logiques. Colloque ADEPA-AFCET, Automatismes Logiques. Recherches et Applications Industrielles, Paris, Décembre 1976.

MOALLA M. : PULOU J., SIFAKIS J. : Réseaux de Petri synchronisés. RAIRO Automatique, Vol. 12, n° 2, 1978, pp. 103-130.

MOALLA M., PULOU J., SIFAKIS J. : Synchronized Petri nets : a model for the description of non autonomous systems. Mathematical Foundations of Computer Science 1978, J. Winkowski Ed, Berlin Heidelberg, New York , Springer Verlag, 1978.

MOALLA M., SAUCIER G., SIFAKIS J., ZACHARIADES M. : A design tool for the multilevel description and simulation of systems of interconnected modules. 3rd Annual Sympos. on Computer. Architecture, Tampa, Florida,January 1979.

MOALLA M. SIFAKIS J., SILVA M. : A la recherche d'une méthodologie de conception sûre des automatismes logiques basée sur l'utilisation des réseaux de Petri. In Sûreté de Fonctionnement des Systèmes Informatiques, Monographie AFCET, to appear.

NATKIN S. : Quelques aspects de la sûreté de fonctionnement des systèmes informatiques. Mémoire d'Ingénieur, CNAM, Paris, Février 1979.

PILAUD D. SAUCIER G. : Conception de système temps réel à très haute sécurité sur microprocesseur. R.R. n° 130 ENSIMAG, Grenoble, Août 1978.

PRADIN B. : Un outil graphique interactif pour la vérification des systèmes à évolutions parallèles décrits par réseaux de Petri. Thèse de Doct.Ingénieur, Université Paul Sabatier, Toulouse, Décembre 1979.

RENALIER J. : Analyse et simulation en langage APL de systèmes de commande décrits par réseaux de Petri. Thèse Doct. 3è cycle, Univ. Paul Sabatier, Toulouse, Juin 1977.

ROBACH Ch., SAUCIER G.: System modelling and diagnosticability. COMPCON Spring 1977, Février 1977, San Francisco.

ROUCAIROL G. : Transformation de programmes séquentiels en programmes parallèles. Premier Colloque sur la Programmation, Paris, Avril 1974, Lecture Notes in Computer Science, n° 19, Springer Verlag Ed.

ROUCAIROL G. : Transformation of single assigment programs. 2nd Conference on Petri nets and related methods, M.I.T., July 1975.

ROUCAIROL G. : Parallelization of single assigment programs. IMACS-GI Symposium on Parallel Computers - Parallel Mathematics, Munich, march 1977, Feilmeier Ed. North Holland Publ. Company, 1977.

ROUCAIROL G. : Equivalences syntaxiques et transformations de programmes parallèles. Thèse Doct. ès Sciences, Univ. P. et M.Curie, Paris, Novembre 1978.

SAUCIER G. : Design methodology of high safety systems on microprocessor. Proc. of Euromicro Symposium, Munich, Octobre 1978.

SEGUIN J., SERGEANT G., P. WILMS : Un algorithme à consensus majoritaire pour le maintien de la cohérence d'informations dupliquées et réparties. Journées d'étude AFCET Bases de Données cohérentes. Paris, Mai 1979, Ed. Institut de programmation de Paris.

SIFAKIS J. : Etude du comportement permanent des réseaux de Petri temporisés. Journées d'étude AFCET Réseaux de Petri, Paris, Mars 1977, Ed. Institut de Programmation de Paris, 1977, pp. 165-184.

SIFAKIS J. : Use of Petri nets for performance evaluation. In Measuring, Modelling and Evaluating Computer Systems. North Holland Publ. Company, 1977, pp. 75-93.

SIFAKIS J. : Homomorphims of Petri nets. Applications to the realization of fault tolerant systems. R.R. 90, Lab. IMAG, Grenoble, Octobre 1977.

SIFAKIS J. : Structural properties of Petri nets. Mathematical Foundations of Computer Science 1978, J. Winkowski Ed., Berlin,Heidelberg, New York, Springer Verlag 1979, pp. 474-483.

SIFAKIS J. : Realization of fault-tolerant systems by coding Petri-nets. In Journal of Design Automation and fault-tolerant computing. Vol. III, n° 2, 1979.

SIFAKIS J. : Le contrôle des systèmes asynchrones. Concepts, propriétés, analyse statique. Thèse Doct. ès Sciences, Univ. de Grenoble, Juin 1979.

SIFAKIS J. : Use of Petri nets for performance evaluation. Advanced Course on general net theory of processes and systems, Hamburg, Oct. 1979.

SILVA M. : Tour d'horizon sur les automates programmables. Rapport interne LAG/INPG, n° 77-07, Grenoble, Mars 1977.

SILVA M. : Contribution à la synthèse programmée des automatismes logiques. Thèse Doct. Ingénieur, LAG, Grenoble, juin 1978.

TACONET B., CHOLLOT B. : Programmation du Grafcet sur automate programmable à langage logique, à relais ou booléen. Le nouvel Automatisme, n° 4, février 1979.

TAFAZZOLI M.E. : Réalisation d'un interprèteur matériel de réseaux de Petri à capacités, Application à la réalisation d'un système multiprocesseur. Thèse Doct. 3è cycle Université de Nice, Novembre 1979.

TOULOTTE J. : Réseaux de Petri et automates programmables. Automatisme, Tome 23, N° 6-7, juillet 1978.

TOURRES L. : Une méthode nouvelle d'étude des systèmes logiques et son application à la réalisation d'automatismes programmes. Revue Générale de l'Electricité, T. 85, n° 3, Mars 1976.

VALETTE R., PRAJOUX R. : A model for parallel control systems and communication systems. Conference on Information Science and Systems, The Johns Hopkins University, Baltimore, USA, April 1976.

VALETTE R. : Sur la description, l'analyse et la validation des systèmes de commande parallèle. Thèse Doct. ès-Sciences, Univ. Paul Sabatier, Toulouse, Novembre 1976.

VALETTE R., COURVOISIER M. : Recherche d'un modèle adapté aux systèmes de commande de processus à évolutions parallèles. RAIRO Automatique/Systems Analysis and Control, Vol. 11, n° 1, 1977, pp. 51-85.

VALETTE R. : An analysis oriented description of parallel systems allowing timing considerations. IFAC Symposium on discrete Systems, Dresden, March 1977.

VALETTE R. : Analysis of Petri nets by stepwise refinements. Journal of Computer and System Sciences, Vol. 18, n° 1, 1979.

VALETTE R., DIAZ M. : Top down formal specification and verification of parallel control systems. Digital Process, Volt. 4, n° 3, 1978.

VALETTE R. : Etude comparative de deux outils de représentation ; GRAFCET et réseau de Petri. Le Nouvel Automatisme, Décembre 1978, pp. 377-382.

VALETTE R., DIAZ M. : A methodology for easily provable implementation of synchronization mechanisms. First International Conf. on Parallel and Distributed Computing, Toulouse, February 1979, pp. 156-162.

VALK R., VIDAL-NAQUET G. : On the rationality of Petri net languages. Lecture Notes in Computer Science, Vol. 48, Berlin, Heidelberg, New York, Springer Verlag, 1977, pp. 319-328.

VAUDENE D., VIGNAT J.C. : Sémantique d'énoncé de synchronisation en termes de réseaux de Petri. Journées d'étude AFCET, Réseaux de Petri, Paris, Mars 1977, Ed. Institut de Programmation de Paris 1977, pp. 113-131.

VERNEL P. : Conception et réalisation d'un microcalculateur temps réel à grande sûreté de fonctionnement. Thèse Doct. ès-Sciences, Inst. Polytechn. de Lorraine, Nancy 77.

VIDAL-NAQUET G. : Méthodes pour les problèmes d'indécidabilité et de complexité pour les réseaux de Petri. Journées d'étude AFCET, Réseaux de Petri, Paris, Mars 1977, Mars 1977, Ed. Institut de Programmation de Paris 1977, pp. 137-144.

ZACHARIADES M. : Mas : Réalisation d'un langage d'aide à la description et à la conception des systèmes logiques. Thèse Doct. 3è cycle, Université de Grenoble, Sept. 77.

NETS IN MODELING AND SIMULATION

Jerre D. Noe*
Univ. of Washington, Seattle, Wa. 98195

Abstract

Place/Transition nets, or Petri Nets, have an appealing mix of simplicity and power for expressing essential interactions in concurrent systems. Yet, when one wishes to express the complexities of actual computing systems, and deal with performance questions typically asked about them, one needs further capabilities that are attuned to the application - a higher level modeling language.

This paper summarizes experience gained in the search for a suitably expressive graph modeling language, and presents a definition of a useful modeling method that has evolved and is adaptable to hierarchical views of large systems.

Table of Contents

*This work has been jointly supported by NSF Grants No. GJ-36273, MCS77-22819 and the University of Washington.

1. INTRODUCTION

Can nets be used to model computers under the control of operating systems in a way that provides insight to the systems' operations and quantitative analysis of pe formance? This was one of the motivating questions in a search by the author and cc leagues for a modeling method to handle large systems. A system is considered large if it is not possible for the details relevant to its operation to be kept in mind by one person. Thus, "large" refers not only to the intrinsic complexity of a syste but also the level of detail at which it is being considered. We are concerned ther with systems that imply modules and hierarchical levels of detail so that an observe can choose the required level for a portion of the system and still retail an understanding of its interaction with the remainder.

The results to date show that one can use net models to capture and convey a variety of levels of understanding of large systems, and nets can aid quantitative performance assessment, at least by simulation. Continuing work in relating the resulting modeling method to more fundamental nets (e.g. Place/Transition-Nets) seeks to make use of analytical tools developed at those underlying levels.

The following describes successive modifications of a modeling method; gives, in an appendix, a definition of the net modeling method (Pro-Nets) to which this evolution has led; makes observations on the shortcomings of the various approaches that have been used, and includes the author's current perception of the features that a comprehensive modeling method for large systems should have. The approach is experi mental since we have no way to derive an optimum modeling method. A brief chronicle of the investigations may be helpful to others who seek to model actual systems.

This work began by turning to Place/Transition Nets, called Petri Nets by Holt and his colleagues [2]. These nets were selected because they were capable of expre sing concurrency and synchronization found in multi-processing and multi-programming computer systems, and all the work described herein has stemmed from that initial choice.

2. FIRST EFFORTS

The initial attempt resulted in a model of the CDC 6400 that was done at a very non-detailed level. It showed the various queues where tasks were waiting for card readers, tape assignment, memory assignment, and the queues for successive interactions with central processor and disc. The model also displayed the interaction of tasks flowing through, along with the resources they acquired and returned while going through the system. In retrospect, it represented a very crude example but wa at least a start, and the exercise allowed a number of observations to be made about the modeling method [6].

2.1 Observations from the first experiment.

That first attempt showed a number of things:

a) Hierarchical description was not only desirable, it was essential because physical limitations made it impossible to draw any one net with maximum detail.

b) Two sorts of places, or locations, emerged in the nets -- one type that related to the status of tasks flowing through, and another type relating to the status of resources being assigned. This later generalized into means for associating data structures with each place.

c) There was a natural urge to identify particular tokens as they progressed through the net, and to associate elapsed time with various actions, since the system being modeled had specific jobs flowing through for which one was interested in characteristics such as "turnaround time", i.e., total time spent in the system.

d) It seemed natural to associate conflict resolution with a transition rather than with multiple arcs from a location, since transitions represent the actions in the net; one would expect decisions to be made there. When conflict is modeled by two arcs emanating from a place and going to separate transitions, the "decision maker" is then some underlying process, not shown in the model. Both methods of modeling conflict are useful, and this point is discussed further in a following section concerned with Pro-Nets.

e) A need for global variables emerged in this experiment (in spite of the inherent dangers of global variables). This became apparent in attempting to model tasks in a queue waiting for assignment of central memory. Each task may require a different amount of memory, and this is not easy to express in the structure of a net model. For example, one could develop detailed nets showing the assignment of the minimum quantum of memory, and arrange for assignment of varying numbers of these quanta, but this appeared to be a needlessly complicated approach. It seemed much easier to deal with a global variable representing the amount of memory available and to visualize a counter associated with the assigning transition that prevented assigning more than actually existed. It was not recognized until later that this was a form of abstraction and deserved more attention because of the general importance of abstraction in developing hierarchical models.

f) Another point became clear: the clarity of a model, i.e., the ease with which an observer could extract information from it, depended a great deal on the physical layout of the net. It proved to be very tedious to draw successive versions of the net as understanding developed, and this emphasized the importance of developing machine aids for that purpose.

2.2. Shortcomings of the first approach

A number of shortcomings of the modeling method, for this type of application, became obvious as a result of this initial attempt. No time duration was associated with transition firings, thus making it impossible to deal with quantitative measure such as throughput and turnaround time. There also was no formalized way to handle operations such as those on global variables, referenced above, nor was there any wa to formally relate successive models of the same subsystem at varying levels of detail; they were only related in a descriptive way. And finally, it was impossible to make use of analysis techniques developed by others who had been studying Petri Nets because during this experiment the primitives had been altered, e.g., providing transitions with exclusive OR inputs and outputs rather than purely AND logic.

3. THE SECOND EXPERIMENT: EVALUATION NETS

The next related work was done by a colleague, G.J. Nutt. As part of his doctoral thesis, he developed a net modeling method that took care of many of the shortcomings exposed by the previous example. The resulting nets were sufficiently different from Petri Nets that it was important to find a new name, in order to not spread confusion through the literature. Since his motivation at the time was to evolve a model to aid in simulation and evaluation of computer systems, he arrived at the name "Evaluation Nets" or "E-Nets". [13, 14].

3.1 Principal features of E-Nets:

Some important steps in the evolution of the modeling method were made by the definition and introduction of E-Nets.

a) Data structures were associated with the locations on the net. This gave the effect of data-bearing tokens flowing through, and gave an opportunity to provide input data to transitions and accept output data from them. The data structures could be null if uninterpreted nets were desired.

b) E-Nets provided transitions with associated procedures that could, when neede represent the specific actions taking place in a transition. This, of course still retained the ability of nets to express synchronization of conditions for the initiation of these actions. These transition procedures added the ability to operate on data attributes, and to assign time delay to the action The transition could make selections from a pair of inputs or could select on of a pair of outputs, and had resolution procedures associated with the transitions for precise specifications of these selections. Figure 1 shows the five primitives used and explains their actions.

The principal restrictions imposed by E-Nets were the following:

a) Firing began immediately upon enabling, and a second firing could not occur until the first had completed.

b) The input tokens remained in place during firing, then were picked up at the same instant output tokens were placed, at the end of the firing period;

c) Each location could have at most one arc in and one arc out;

d) Only five primitive transitions were provided;

e) There was a rigidly prescribed notation for expressing the procedures;

f) Safety was enforced by not allowing a transition to fire if any of its output places were occupied.

3.2 Observations on Evaluation Nets

E-Nets were used to model several example systems, including a more detailed model of the CDC 6400, under the Scope operating system, and the IBM System 360 under MFT. In use a number of limitations became evident:

a) The five primitives proved to be too restrictive. It was difficult to model structures with more than two inputs or two outputs per transition. Some larger structures were developed whose properties could be related to their implementations based on the five primitives, but still this proved to be too inflexible for general use [7].

b) The rigid notation for transition procedures proved to be rather limiting. There were times when one wished to use a variety of ways to express the actions or the procedures.

c) Requiring safety on all locations and preventing transition firings that would violate safety proved to be useful when dealing with primitive nets, but when attention began to be focused on abstractions of nets, this proved to be too restrictive.

d) The requirement for a single arc in and out of a location did not emerge as much of a modeling limitation because there were other more severe difficulties in developing abstractions of detailed nets. But later, as will be discussed in the next section, this proved to be an undesirable limitation.

4. THE THIRD EXPERIMENT: PRO-NETS

The experience gained in using E-Nets for modeling and through observing the effects of some of the inherent restrictions led to the next modification, termed Pro-Nets [9]. Again, the name was changed in order not to confuse the literature on the topic, and the term Pro-Net was suggested by the processors and processes that the nets are used to model. The formal definition of Pro-Nets has been further altered, based on modeling experience, and notation has been changed to make it more compatible with the series of lectures in this Advanced Course on General Net Theory. The current version is included in Appendix A and is useful for explaining some of the less obvious features, but the principal features will be described here and should suffice for this discussion.

4.1 Basic features:

The Pro-Net element is a T-element and is shown in Figure A-2, with its input and output S-elements; the allowable number of tokens on each place has an upper bound. Either conjunctive or disjunctive logic (or both) may be used on inputs and outputs with zero to a finite number of arcs of each type. This allows a wide variety of special cases of the basic element; it is best understood by examining its firing rules which are the same for Pro-Net Elements or Primitive Elements. These rules ar discussed here in terms of the notation of Figure A-1.

a) the T-element is enabled if all of the following hold:
   1) a token exists on each of the "AND" inputs in set $\{s_a\}$.
   2) a token exists on every S-element place in at least one of the subsets of the "selection" inputs in $\{s_b\}$ (denoted by small bars across the arcs; each spans a subset).
   3) the number of tokens on each of the "AND" outputs in set $\{s_c\}$ is less than the bound.
   4) the token count on each of the <u>selected</u> output subsets in $\{s_d\}$ is less tha the bound.
   5) state variables that have been declared to control initiation are found to have permissive values.
b) After enabling, the action of a Pro-Net-element will begin at a time t, such that $d_{min} \le t \le d_{max}$ where $0 \le d_{min} \le d_{max}$. This feature is adapted from the work of Merlin [5]. When action is initiated, it will endure for time τ, $\tau \ge 0$, and during that period, required input tokens will be marked "reserved
c) At the conclusion of action, a token will have been:
   1) removed from each S-element in $\{s_a\}$.
   2) removed from each S-element in the selected subset in $\{s_b\}$.
   3) added to each S-element in $\{s_c\}$.
   4) added to each S-element in the selected subset in $\{s_d\}$.

Tokens may be either simple, i.e., merely denoting by their presence that an S-element is marked, or they may be tokens with attributes, showing not only that a marking exists but also specifying data associated with that marking. Data may also be represented by variables that are local to the T-element or that are global, associated with the entire net.

Procedures associated with the T-element may select inputs, operate on data values, specify time delays and select outputs. The procedures may be specified in a language chosen by the modeler and they may be omitted if one is concerned only with the structure of the net and not its specific behavior. The paths selected through the T-elements with input/output choices are referred to as "T-Options".

Note that unlike E-Nets, Pro-Nets are defined such that multiple arcs are allowed to enter into or emerge from an S-element. This provides useful additional flexibility in describing conflicts at higher levels of abstraction. Conflicts between potential actions are commonly modeled in Petri Nets as shown in Figure 2(a).

When condition c holds it may be removed by the firing of either transition T1 or T2 but not both. This implies that the decision is made "off-stage" in some way not shown in the model, which is useful at some levels of representation. There are three desirable features of allowing such constructs:

a) There are times in the early development of a model in which one wishes to represent conflict, but the resolution methods have not yet been established.
b) There are other situations in which the conflicts are resolved by the structure in the remainder of the net, brought into effect through additional arcs into T1 and T2.
c) When exhaustive analysis is to be made of the net, considering all alternative paths (which is typical of much of the published works on analysis of Petri Nets), then this representation suffices.

Suppose, however, one wishes to explicitly include the arbiter that makes a decision. Where does one place the program segments that represent the decision process? They cannot be placed in the procedure describing transition T1 or in T2 because that would provide no correlation between their actions. Pro-Nets provide for modeling such decisions as shown in Figure 2(b), showing T1 and T2 as T-Options within one T-element. The T-element's priority procedure selects the appropriate input; this procedure, in addition to operating on data attributes of input tokens, may select the desired output.

Pro-Nets may be restricted to sub-classes for various purposes. For example, if we for a particular case elect not to use selector arcs into and out of a transition, allow bounds on places to become infinite, use no transition procedures, global variables, or token attributes, let the elapsed firing time (τ) be zero, and leave the firing delay bounds (d_{min}, d_{max}) unspecified, then we are left with normal Petri or Place/Transition Nets. If, in addition to the above restrictions, we used d_{min} and d_{max} as specified, the restricted Pro Nets would be equivalent to Merlin's Time-Petri-Nets.

4.2 The perception of time

The specifications of delay time associated with T-element firing requires some system-wide view of the treatment of time. The viewpoint adopted with Pro-Nets is as follows: A global read-only clock is assumed to exist; a local read-write clock exists in each T-element. The local clocks may or may not be running at the same speed and the inaccuracy implicit in their reading the global clock and resetting their local values may vary from one T-element to another due to transmission delay times or due to some perturbation in the mechanism. The local clocks therefore may or may not be synchronized with global time; they may be wrong for some period and then be updated by reading global time. However, local clocks can be used to distinguish between the relative arrival and departure time of tokens on input and output S-elements. This capability can be used for local synchronization among competi or cooperating inputs. Local clocks may also be used to estimate the action times r quired within the T-elements. These may later prove to be inaccurate in the view of some observer able to update more accurately from the global clock, but the times ca still serve as approximations. Local clocks could be updated upon initiation and a- gain at termination of firing (or more frequently if desired); this would provide a globally based measurement of elapsed time that would be independent of the local clock rate but would be affected by global reading uncertainties.

This view of time seems realistic and has many examples. To pick two, consider first the interaction of people: Insofar as we can perceive there is a global clock that we cannot reset. We make use of "accurate" read/write clocks that may be cryst or isotope controlled. We can also set our personal watches to these "secondary sta dards". Of course the time shown by our watches may be wrong and differ from the ti shown by others. If we attempt synchronizations that depend upon precise global tim ordering, we may fail. However, we can still perceive, locally, a sequence of event and can perceive "ties" and make rules for breaking them.

As a second example, consider the clock within a CDC 6400. Buried within it is an all-pervasive "clock-rate" that the system itself can read (and of course there are varying time delays to various parts of the system), but the system cannot chang it. This is used to operate a "micro-second clock". The operating system periodica ly looks at this clock -- typically a few times per millisecond -- and then updates "the millisecond clock" that is program accessible and is used for general system measurements that depend upon time. Note that the processors are handling synchronization problems based on their very local perception of time.

4.3 Pro-Net Application Examples

Pro-Nets have been used to develop several models and this has given some perspe tive on the method and let to some changes that are incorporated in the Appendix to this paper. Some of the previous E-Net models such as those for the CDC-6400 have been recast into Pro-Net form. Pro-Nets are directly applicable to quantitative models such as the simulation of the disk subsystem in [CRO 75]. An example of a descriptive model is included here and consists of excerpts from a technical report [10] that models the Logic Machine Mini-Computer (LM^2), which was designed and developed by Prof. T.H. Kehl [4].

This discussion will make no attempt to comprehensively explain the LM^2 and the reader is referred to the above reference for that purpose. The brief discussion here is limited to clarifying what is being modeled by the two Pro-Net examples shown in Figures 3 and 4. The general approach in the LM^2 architecture is to execute macro instructions by fetching micro-code for execution in the logic unit. With reference to Figure 3, start with an initial marking on the S-elements labelled

SUP STATE and PROG BEGIN. This denotes that the system has been returned to the supervisory state and a new program of macro instructions is ready to be executed. The reader can follow the example through with the aid of the following explanation of symbols.

CNSQ MICR	The control sequence macro routine
EXECUTE Z-JUMP	A T-element returning control to CNSQ due either to a program start or to conclusion of an interrupting activity such as direct memory access
I-REG	Instruction register
ROM LOOKUP	An action consisting of accessing a read only memory to convert from a macro instruction to a 50-bit control word that is to be decoded in three concurrent actions
INS/BR/T	Instruction branch table
H/W SWITCH	The action of switching internal circuits to place the arithmetic logic unit (ALU) in the proper configuration for the micro code that will be executed
DECODE	A micro instruction that determines what is to be done next. It results (elsewhere in the model) in acquiring a micro routine address.

Figure 4 shows more detail in memory access and the following terms are used.

PMAR	An instruction that places an address in the memory address register
MEM ADD REG	Memory address register
READ.ADV MACRO PC	An action that issues a memory access request and advances the macro program counter, which is modeled as a global variable
MEM-ACC	The memory access, which requires 325 nanoseconds
REWRITE	The remainder of the, 650 nanosecond memory cycle

Other portions of the model in the reference from which this example is extracted show the control processor executing a micro routine, executing a decode instruction, accessing a DMA branch table and a coroutine branch table. The general experience in applying the modeling method to the LM^2 was that it expressed control flow in a way that was very helpful in unravelling the very complex and intertwined reaction between hardware and software at the micro code level.

5. DESIRABLE ATTRIBUTES OF MODELING METHODS FOR LARGE SYSTEMS

Experience in applying these successive modeling methods to large systems (large in the sense defined above) has emphasized a number of properties to be desired in the choice of a modeling method. Some of these properties are at odds with each other, so any given modeling method will be forced to compromise, but recognition of the desired properties will aid in forming and evaluating any particular modeling scheme.

a) For complex systems, hierarchical modeling is essential.
Different levels of detail are appropriate when studying, or communicating, different properties of the overall system. Furthermore, when focusing on a substructure, one needs to suppress detail in the remainder of the system and treat it only through its links to the substructure being studied. Throughout these notes the terms "refinement" and "abstration" are used in the sense defined by [3]. The refinement displays greater detail; the abstraction lets the observer see only selected properties (e.g. input/output properties) of the system.

b) The same notation should be applicable to both abstrations and refinements.

c) The modeling method should allow easy progression from a rough, informal model to a more precisely defined model as understanding of the system grows. This is partially an application of hierarchical structure, but is also a statement that the syntax of the modeling method should not impose itself in such a rigid manner as to interfere with the real problem, i.e., understanding the system being modeled. These characteristics are needed both in the design of new systems and in modeling existing systems.

d) The model should serve for communication among human users and should be easily encodable to forms allowing machine manipulation.

e) The method should allow focus either on control alone or on control and data operations without drastically changing the general approach.

f) Viewing the graph model as an expression of the control structure -- and focusing, for the moment, on the subprocesses being controlled -- the modeler needs freedom to express the properties of these subprocesses in a variety of ways. The user, at various stages in model development, may wish to describe the subprocesses in natural language, or in a high or low level programming language, or as a hardware design. The user may also wish to describe a subprocess as a more detailed net model to display further structure (hierarchical modeling).

g) The user should not be required to map the model into radically different for for different purposes.
The modeling method should lend itself to study through analytic techniques where these are applicable, or to study through simulation techniques, or serve as a communication medium among humans or humans and machines.

h) For ease in use, the number of special modules and the number of syntactic an semantic rules should be minimized.

i) The method should allow the user to "trade off" between structural and behavioral refinement. The former shows specifications of internal control structure in greater detail; behavioral refinement, on the other hand, tells more about what the controlled subprocess does, but not necessarily more about its structure.

6. MACHINE AIDS TO MODELING

Experience in applying these nets to modeling of computer systems quickly demonstrated that numerous changes are required during the development of a model of any particular system. These changes typically arise from one of two sources: First, as one's understanding of the system grows (either during the design phase or during examination of an existing system), it is necessary to constantly revise and update the net model to reflect this understanding. Secondly, the comprehensibility of a net model to a human observer depends a great deal on its layout. The same set of S- and T-elements can appear totally confusing or quite coherent depending on how they have been arranged in relation to each other. This argues for development and use of machine aids, and during the period of experimentation with E-Nets, a graphical editor was developed that allowed the model designer to add, delete, and easily rearrange the net's elements and their labels. This proved to be an invaluable aid to what had been a very tedious operation. Figures 3 and 4 were prepared with this facility.

With a net editor, it became fairly simple to manipulate and store models consisting of nets with more than 500 symbols (S- or T-elements). An obvious next step was to use this stored structure for the rapid development of a simulation program. The uninterpreted net provided much of the control structure necessary for a simulation program. It was required then only to add the code representing the procedures in each of the T-elements in the network, these procedures expressing the time delays and the data operations. An experimental version of such a simulation facility was built and successfully tested. Such a facility would be a useful adjunct in an environment where the emphasis was on rapid development of simulation programs and frequent changes to the model. In an environment where the model was quite stable and the emphasis was on multiple executions, then more conventional approaches to simulation would be more efficient.

The net editor is described in the following references [8]. The simulator is described in [1]. These papers are also summarized in [11].

7. SUMMARY

This series of investigations was originally begun because of the great gap in existing ways to characterize large computer systems. At one extreme, one finds block diagrams which show the major elements and the interconnections that may exist between them, but give no clues about when or where these interconnections are used. At the other extreme, a computer system can be described by a comprehensive set of logic diagrams pertaining to the hardware, and complete listings (usually poorly do mented) of the code and microcode necessary to provide system operation. Nets appe ed attractive as a starting point in the search for a better modeling method, becau of their power to express concepts of concurrency and synchronization of events. T approach to working with Nets was rather different from that taken by most others i the field; rather than trying to extract some essential feature from real systems t could be expressed and studied in the context of a fixed modeling system, this appr instead attempted to adapt the modeling system to the problems being attacked. The is no way to derive directly an optimum modeling method, so one is driven to an exp mental approach, i.e., to pick a method with intuitively appealing features, test i improve upon it, and test again. The work, on one hand, has led this observer to a better understanding of what is needed for modeling at a variety of levels, and on the other hand, has produced some particular schemes that have been useful.

In retrospect, many of the driving forces in this evolution of method have rela to the problems of abstraction. Harking back to the extremes represented by the bl diagram and the complete listing and logic diagrams, one usually needs some mix of modeling levels that allows one to concentrate upon details in a given subsection while still maintaining grasp of the interaction between this subsection and the remainder of the system. This is an extremely important, but extremely difficult are in which to work. Some limited success in abstraction technique has been achieved with Pro-Nets, but the unsolved problems are many times greater than the solved ones More will be said on this later in [12].

REFERENCES

[1] Crowley, C.P. and Noe, J.D. "Interactive Graphical Simulation Using Modified Petri Nets", SIGSIM/NBS Symposium on the Simulation of Computer Systems, Boulde CO. Aug. 12-14, 1975.

[2] Holt, A.W., Commoner, F. "Events and Conditions", Record of the Project MAC Conference on Concurrent Systems and Parallel Computation, pp. 3-52, 1970.

[3] Horning, J.J., Randell, B. "Process Structuring", Computing Surveys, v. 5, No. 1 Mar. 73, pp. 5-30.

[4] Kehl, T.D., Moss, C., Dunkel, L. "LM^2 -- A logical machine mini-computer", IEEE Computer, Nov. 1975, pp. 12-22.

[5] Merlin, P.M., "A Study of the Recoverability of Computing Systems", Ph.D. Thesis Univ. of California, Irvine, CA. 1974.

[6] Noe, J.D., A Petri-Net Description of the CDC 6400, Proc. ACM Workshop on System Performance Evaluation, Harvard University, 1971, pp. 362-378.

[7] Noe, J.D. and Nutt, G.J. "Macro E-Nets for Representation of Parallel Systems", IEEE Transactions on Computers, vol. C-22, No. 8, Aug. 1973, pp. 718-727.

[8] Noe, J.D., Crowley, C.P., and Anderson, T.L. "The Design of an Interactive Graph cal Net Editor", Proc. CIPS-ACM, Pacific Regional Conf., May 1974, pp. 386-402. Also in Univ. of Washington Technical Report #74-07-30.

[9] Noe, J.D. "Pro-Nets: for Modeling Processes and Processors", Conf. on Petri Nets and Related Topics, MIT, July 1-3, 1975.

[10] Noe, J.D. and Kehl, T.H. "A Petri Net model of a modular micro-programmable computer (LM^2), TR#75-09-01, Computer Science Dept., Univ. of Washington, 22 pages.

[11] Noe, J.D. "Machine Aided Modeling, Using Modified Petri Nets", Proc. Conference: AFCET, Reseaux de Petri, l'Institut de Programmation de Paris 23, 24 March 1977. See also Séminaires IRIA, Modélisation et Evaluation des Systémes Informatiques, 1977, pp. 257-282.

[12] Noe, J.D. "Abstractions of Net Models" (elsewhere in these proceedings).

[13] Nutt, G.J., "Evaluation Nets for Computer Systems Performance Analysis", 1972 Fall Joint Computer Conference, AFIPS Conference Proceedings, vol. 41, pp. 279-286.

[14] Nutt, G.J., "The Formulation and Application of Evaluation Nets", Ph.D. Dissertation, Dept. of Computer Science, Univ. of Washington, 1972. Available from University Microfilms, 300 Zeeb Road, Ann Arbor, MI 48106.

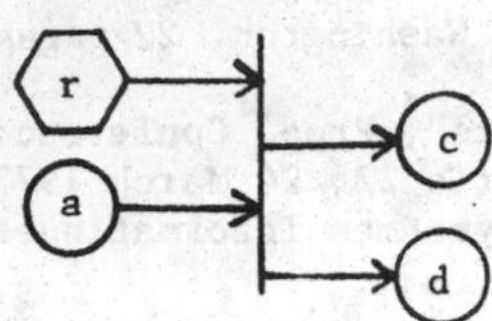

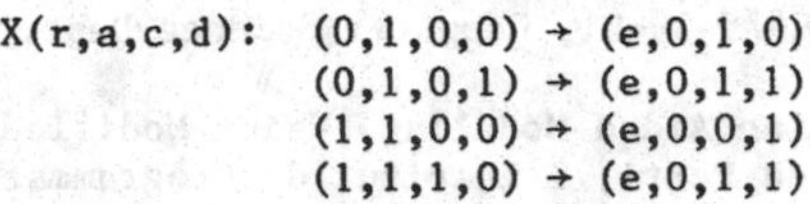

X(r,a,c,d): (0,1,0,0) → (e,0,1,0)
(0,1,0,1) → (e,0,1,1)
(1,1,0,0) → (e,0,0,1)
(1,1,1,0) → (e,0,1,1)

<u>Note</u>: "e" denotes "0" if r is an inner location; denote "Φ" (undefined) if r is a peripheral location.

X Transition

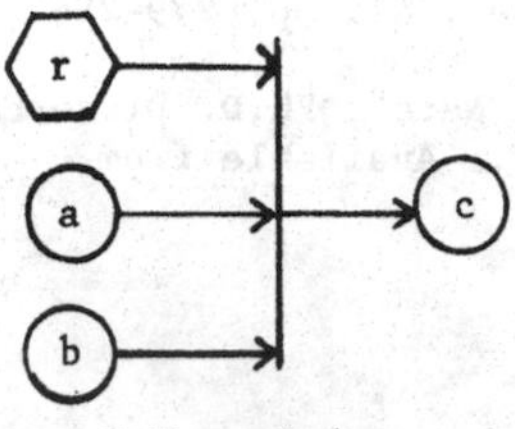

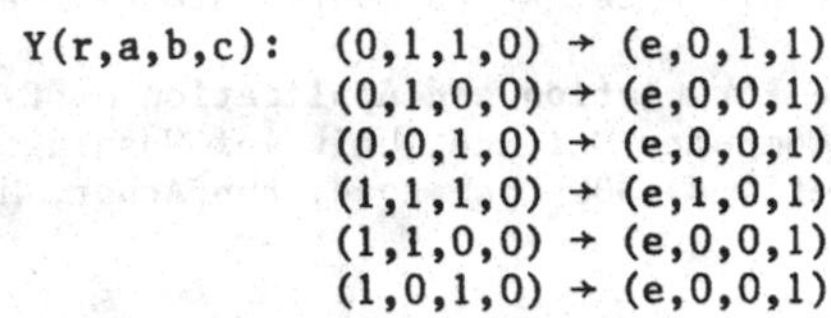

Y(r,a,b,c): (0,1,1,0) → (e,0,1,1)
(0,1,0,0) → (e,0,0,1)
(0,0,1,0) → (e,0,0,1)
(1,1,1,0) → (e,1,0,1)
(1,1,0,0) → (e,0,0,1)
(1,0,1,0) → (e,0,0,1)

Y Transition

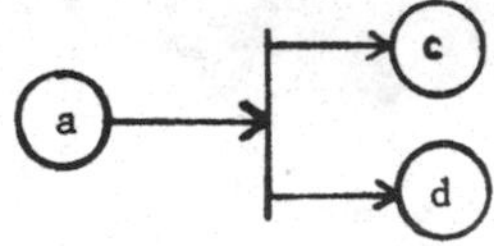

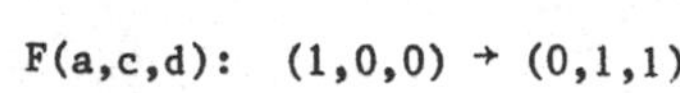

F(a,c,d): (1,0,0) → (0,1,1)

F Transition

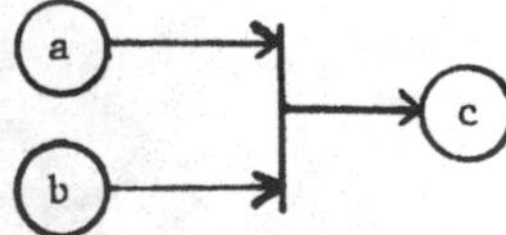

J(a,b,c): (1,1,0) → (0,1,1)

T(a,c): (1,0) → (0,1)

Figure 1. The five primitive E-Net transitions.

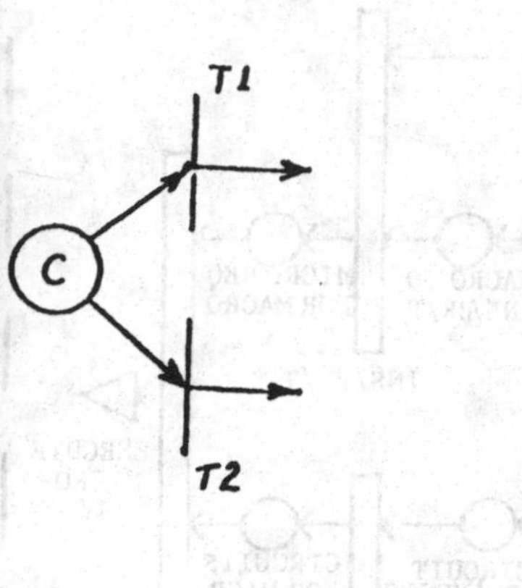

a) Separate Transitions

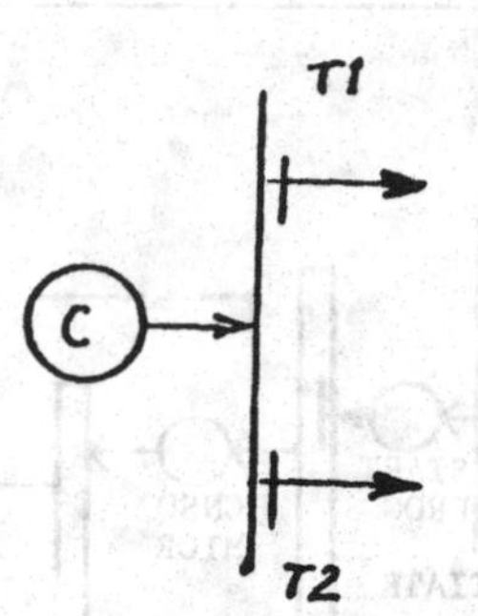

b) Coordinated Transition Options

Figure 2: Modeling Conflict with Pro-Nets: Alternative Methods

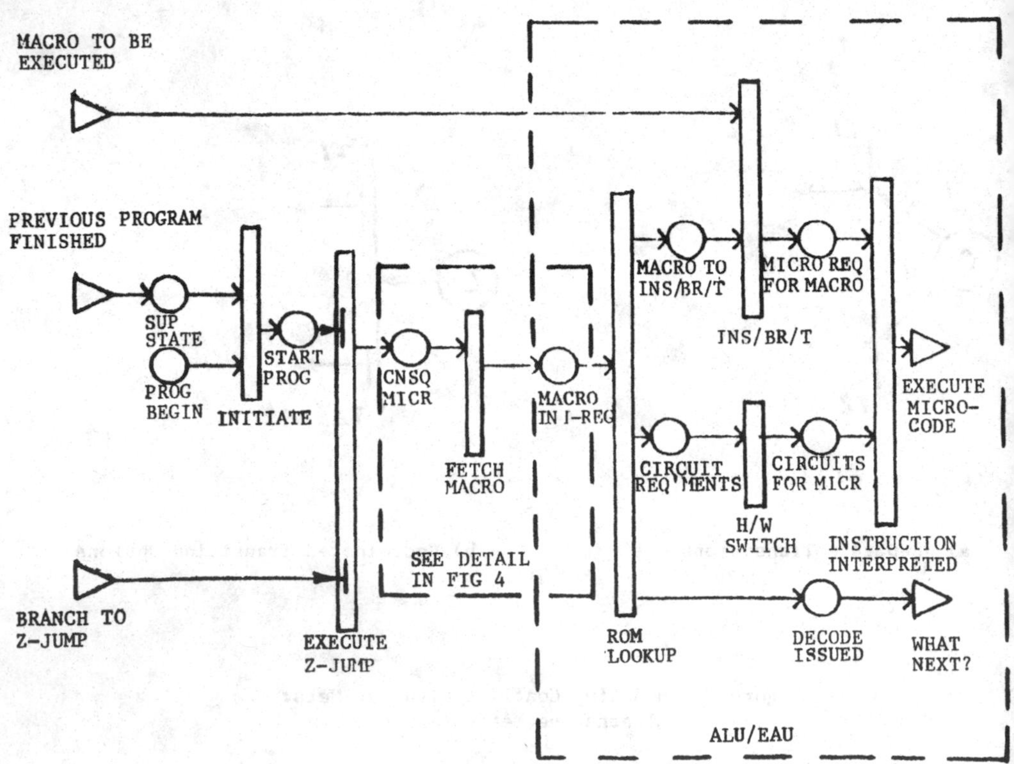

Figure 3: Pro-Net Example : Action of ALU/Effective Address Unit.

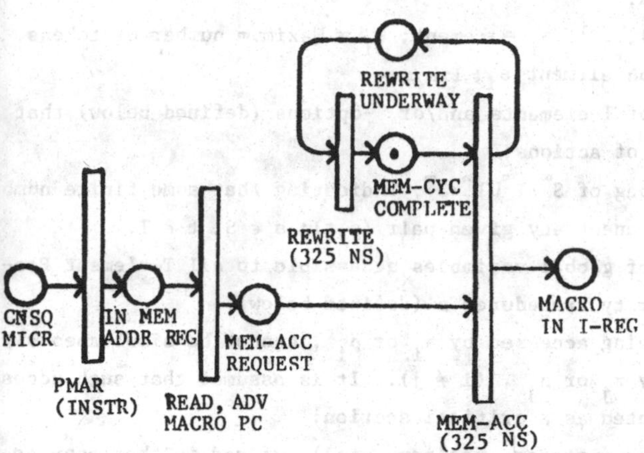

Figure 4: Pro-Net Example

Memory Functional Unit

APPENDIX A

DEFINITION OF PRO-NETS FOR MODELING PROCESSES OR PROCESSORS
(Revised July 1979)

A PRO-NET is defined as:

$\Phi = (S,T;F,V)$

where S is a finite set of S-elements with bounded markings that represent the state of the system;

$S = \{\ldots(s_i,k_i),\ldots\}$; s_i = element; k_i = Maximum number of tokens allowable on element s_i; $1 \le k_i \le \infty$

T is a finite set of T-elements and/or -options (defined below) that represent the loci of actions;

F is a finite sub-bag of $S^{\infty} \times T^{\infty} \cup T^{\infty} \times S^{\infty}$, indicating that some finite number of arcs may interconnect any given pair (s,t): $s \in S$, $t \in T$.

V is a finite set of global variables accessible to all T-element Procedures π and Priority Procedures ρ (defined below)

$v \in V$, while being accessed by π_i or ρ_i, cannot be simultaneously accessed by π_j or ρ_j, $(i \neq j)$. It is assumed that such access is implemented as a critical section.

v are of types (integer, boolean, etc.) defined in the language in which procedures, π and ρ, are expressed.

Net Marking:

M is a vector of tokens on elements of S.

A token $\mu \in M$ is defined as a marker on $s \in S$ indicating that the condition represented by the S-element exists. A token may have zero to a finite number of attributes:

$\mu = \{\alpha_1,\ldots,\alpha_n\}$; finite $n \ge 0$

α_i are to be accessed only by procedures in the T-elements connected to the S-elements marked by the tokens.

α_i are of types (integer, boolean, etc.) defined in the language in which procedures, π and ρ, are expressed.

A T-element is defined as:

$t \in T : t = (A,B,C,D,\rho,\tau,d_{min},d_{max},\Pi)$

where A,B are finite sets of input arcs with zero or more members; $A \cap B = \phi$

C,D are finite sets of output arcs with zero or more members; $C \cap D = \phi$

A is the set of "AND" logic input arcs.

B is the set of "SELECTOR" input arcs.

Partitions $\{b\}_i \subseteq B$ may exist, with $1 \le |b|_i$ and $\sum_i |b|_i = |B|$

$\{b\}_j \cap \{b\}_i = \phi \quad i \neq j$

C is the set of "AND' logic output arcs.

D is the set of "SELECTOR" output arcs.

Partitions $\{d\}_j \subseteq D$ may exist, with $1 \leq |d|_j$ and $\sum_j |d|_j = |D|$

$\{d\}_i \cap \{d\}_j = \phi \quad i \neq j$

ρ is a Priority Procedure, invoked when a T-element is (with the possible exception of marking on output places) enabled to act (defined below). The Priority Procedure may:

Access (but not modify) global variables and attributes of tokens marking vicinal input places. (The procedure may "reserve" tokens as noted below).

Select one input subset $\{b\}_i \subseteq B$;

At action initiation, mark the input tokens that are to be removed from $\{b\}_i$ as "reserved for action". (Marking and action initiation occur as an indivisible pair.)

Select $\pi \in \Pi$ associated with the T-element, and prior to enabling, cause a trial action requiring zero time. (The trial is to assess the marking state of the output S-elements.)

Postpone action, if necessary, until bounds on output S-elements permit action, or until the required input marking ceases to exist due to the action of some other T-element.

τ is a set of action times, i.e. the time delays (≥0) between initiation and completion of action of the T-element; $\tau \in T$ may be a value or an expression leading to a value;

d_{min} is the time delay (≥0) that must elapse between enabling for action and the initiation of action.

$d_{max}(\geq d_{min})$ is the maximum time delay allowed to exist between enabling and initiation of action.

Π is a finite, possibly empty, set of T-element transition Procedures.

$\pi \in \Pi$ may:

Access and modify any $v \in V$;

Read attributes of tokens marking vicinal input places;

Write values into attributes of tokens placed on vicinal output locations;

Select output locations via arcs $\{d\}_j \in D$.

Assign $\tau_k \in T$ to each arc $d_k \in \{d\}_j$. $0<k\leq|d|_j$

Assign $\tau_i \in T$ to each arc $c_i \in C$.

A <u>T-Option</u> is a part of a T-element, representing a particular case of the exclusive OR selections, and is defined as:

$t_{bd} \in T : t_{bd} = (A,\{b\}_i,C,\{d\}_j,\rho,\tau,\{\tau\}_j,d_{min},d_{max},\{\pi\})$

$\{b\}_i \in B : \{b\}_i$ is the subset of input arcs selected by ρ, the priority procedure

$\{d\}_j \in D$: $\{d\}_j$ is the subset of output arcs selected by π

$\pi \in \Pi$: π is the transition procedure selected by ρ

$\tau \in T$: τ is the action time associated with the set of arcs C

$\{\tau\}_j \in T$: $\{\tau\}_j$ is the subset of action times associated with $\{d\}_j$

A T-element is shown graphically as:

a line segment, when it is a primitive, not subject to replacement by a more detailed net;

a rectangle, in general.

An S-element $s_i \in S$ is shown graphically as a circle:

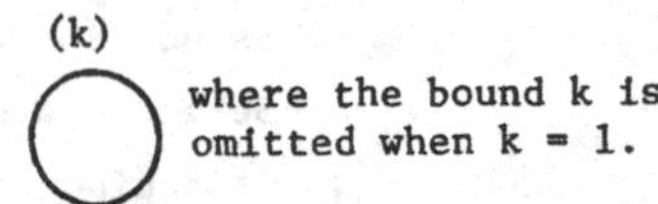

(k)
where the bound k is omitted when k = 1.

An S-element may have zero or more arcs entering or leaving it.

An <u>input S- (or T)-element</u> has only arcs leaving.

An <u>output S- (or T)-element</u> has only arcs entering.

<u>T-element Action Rules:</u>

Upon establishment of a set of input markings necessary for action, a trial action (requiring zero time) determines whether or not a T-element is enabled to act. Enabling occurs when input and output markings are permissive (see below), and local state variables defined within the Priority Procedures are permissive. After enabling, the T-element must begin action within a time bounded by d_{min} and d_{max}, unless the enabling conditions cease to exist during this delay time, in which case the T-element will not act. The criteria for action depend both upon the markings of the vicinal S-elements, and the values of state-determining variables that may exist.

<u>Marking required to initiate action.</u>

All the following must exist:

<u>Input S-element Marking</u>

A non-reserved token exists on <u>each</u> S-element connected by arc $a \in A$.

A non-reserved token exists on <u>each</u> S-element in at least one subset connected by arcs $\{b\}_i \in B$.

<u>Output S-element Marking</u>

Tokens $K_i \leq (k_i - 1)$ on <u>each</u> S-element connected by arc $c \in C$.

Tokens $K_i \leq (k_i - 1)$ on <u>each</u> S-element s_i, connected by arc d_i in the selected subset $\{d\}_j$.

Note: Token count K includes tokens on the output S-element, plus those that will be placed as a result of this action.

<u>Marking change caused by completion of T-element action.</u>

All the following take place at completion of time delay τ:

<u>Input S-element Marking</u>

The reserved token is removed from <u>each</u> place connected by $a \in A$.

<u>Output S-element Marking</u>

One token is added to <u>each</u> place connected by $c \in C$.

The reserved token is removed from each place in <u>one selected</u> subset connected by $\{b\}_i \in B$.

One token is added to each place in <u>one selected</u> subset connected by $\{d\}_j \in D$.

<u>Markings during action</u>:

During time delay τ between initiation and completion of action ($\tau \geq 0$), markings remain in pre-firing status, with the selected input tokens <u>reserved</u> so they cannot participate in enabling any other action. At end of delay, τ, new markings and variable values become effective. A second action of the same T-element can be initiated during τ if firing criteria permit.

Note: If, during action time, another T-element has placed tokens on any $c \in C$ or $d_i \in \{d\}_j$ such that bounds would be exceeded by completion of this action, one of the two T-element actions must be rescinded. The conflict must be resolved outside the model. It is possible to prevent such occurrences by proper choice of time delays and action times.

A <u>Primitive Pro-Net Element</u> is defined as a T-element that will not be further expanded in the model. It is shown with its input and output S-elements and arcs, as follows:

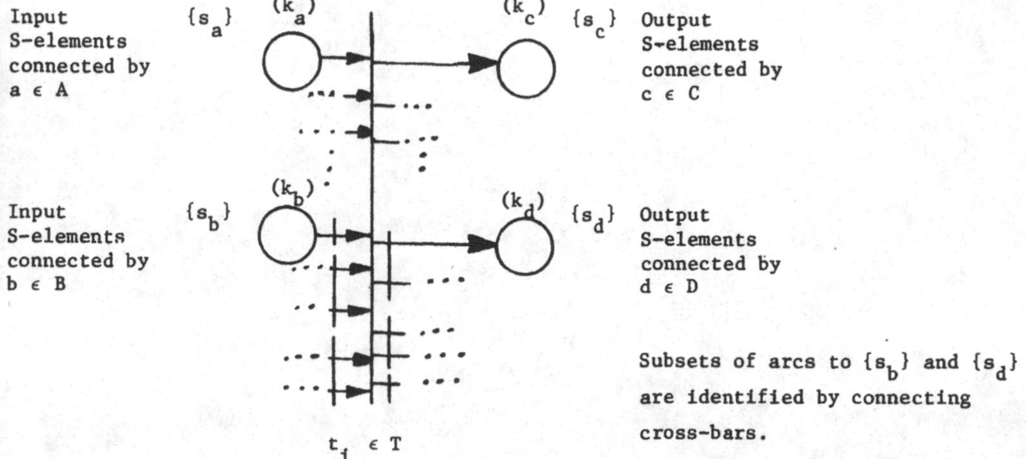

Figure A-1: A Primitive Pro-Net Element

A Pro-Net Element is defined as a T-element representing a Pro-Net consisting of a finite set of Pro-Net Elements and is shown graphically as follows:

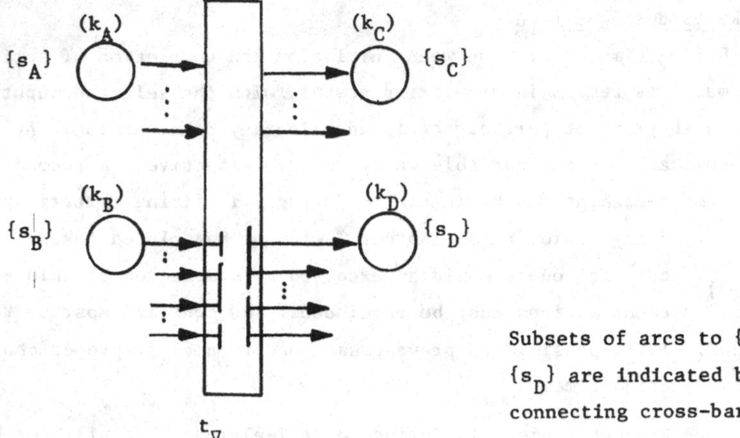

Figure A-2: A Pro-Net Element

Labels: S-elements, T-elements and arcs may have distinguishing labels.

ABSTRACTIONS OF NET MODELS

Jerre D. Noe*
Univ. of Washington, Seattle, Wa. 98195

Abstract

The representation of a detailed model by one with less detail, but preserving input/output behavior, is an essential element in understanding, designing, and analyzing large systems. This paper presents a mechanizable approach to such abstraction, for a limited class of net models. The work is based on Pro-Nets, an application-oriented outgrowth of place/transition nets.

Table of Contents

*This work was jointly supported by NSF Grant No. MCS77-22819, by the University of Washington, and by the Nederlandse Organisatie voor Zuiver - Wetenschappelijk Onderzoek (the ZWO).

1. INTRODUCTION

This deals with abstraction of net models, i.e., reduction of a detailed model t a simpler structure accompanied by some description of its internal behavior. The approach is within the context of Pro-Nets [6] and the behavioral description metho is chosen to encourage automation of its manipulation.

The terms "abstraction" and "refinement" used in this discussion are those expre sed by Horning and Randell [1]. Abstraction is the higher level, less detailed description of a process and a refinement is the lower level, more detailed version. I particular, we are here interested in projection functions, in which a subset of the state variables is selected as being observable, and all others are lost. For example, in going from a refinement to an abstraction, we wish to observe only those variables that describe inputs and outputs, plus those that store information about the internal state of the module.

The usual process during design is one of refinement. Given the definition of t input-output behavior of the module, the problem faced by the designer is to find a structure that meets these specifications. In this discussion, we are concerned wit the reverse of this usual procedure. Attention is drawn to this fact for the orientation of the reader, and by no means is to be interpreted as denying the importance of the process of designing a refinement; rather, it is believed that these are mutu ly supportive activities. Refinement is part of the top-down design process; abstra tion is more related to bottom-up design. But few, if any, systems are truly desig either top-down or bottom-up. Most design activities use both, and involve continua improvement of the design in a series of steps, and these steps include setting spec fications, interconnecting modules into subsystems, and checking the degree to which these subsystem specifications are met. Thus, abstraction is viewed as merely one c the tools important in design. With relation to nets, it should be noted that since complete analysis of general nets appears to be impossible or prohibitive, designers must think in terms of modular structures for which net models can be constructed, and that are small enough to understand and analyze. Then, one needs to concentrate on rules for combining known modules into larger structures in ways that preserve th properties of interest.

Abstraction has its role not only in design as discussed above, but also in performance improvement of an existing design. Improvement of performance usually involves identification of a significant subsystem, followed by study to understand the performance or behavior of the subsystem, then examination of the interaction of this subsystem (in abstract form) with the rest of the system. An example of this is to be found in hybrid simulation [7], in which fast moving subsystems are identified that are amenable to queueing analysis. These queueing models are then embedded in the midst of the simulation that represents the slower moving remainder of the system.

Given these reasons for an interest in abstraction, the remainder of the paper will be concerned with finding ways to abstract net models, and will describe a limited amount of progress in a specialized subset of the problems of interest.

2. THE NEED FOR MECHANIZATION

A modeling method adapted to hierarchical views needs to provide a consistent notation useable at all levels of abstraction and refinement, and should provide a mechanism to trade between structural detail and behavioral detail. It is also desirable that the modeling method allow varying degrees of precision so that, on the one hand, it can express the informal ideas that characterize the early stages of design, or of understanding, but at the other extreme, it can encompass formal specifications suitable for analysis and quantitative study. Furthermore, the modeler needs machine aid in moving from one level to another. In the context of abstraction, one needs an algorithmic way to examine a refined net and produce an abstraction of it, with suitable trade-off between structural and behavioral modeling.

One can visualize practical cases in which such an approach would be helpful. For example, suppose one had a net model of a computer's disc subsystem for which input-output behavior had been derived in some manner, e.g., simulation or analysis. Then it might be desirable to reduce this disc subsystem to a simpler representation, still retaining its input-output properties so that it could be absorbed into a larger model that included the CPU and scheduler. One would like machine aid in this reduction process. However, such an example is far too complex at this stage of development, so let us be content with a much simpler example that will help focus on the ideas involved.

3. EXAMPLE OF ABSTRACTION

As an initial exercise consider the S-module (taken from [4]) shown in Figure 1. This is a net of primitive elements combined to form a switching module that can direct an input to either two outputs, depending upon an internal state. All actions are expressed in the structure of the net, and, given the firing rules for the primitive elements, one can see the input-output behavior of the structure. An input on I-20 will result in an output on 0-10 or 0-20, depending upon the initial state as shown by the token either on L(0) or L(1). Inputs at either L-1 or L-2 will attempt to set or reset the state and an echoing or acknowledging signal will be placed on L_1^1 or L_2^1 .

A Pro-Net abstraction of this primitive net is shown in Figure 2. However, the behavior is entirely lost in the graphical abstraction, since all inputs and outputs are disjunctive, and one no longer can tell from structure alone how the module ope ates. Also shown in the figure is a program segment that describes the behavior of this abstract element relating the input and output variables. The purpose of this example, however, was to illustrate a problem: How can one derive the program describing behavior from the structural statement of behavior in the refined net? Thi writer currently sees no way to invoke machine aid to produce such a program. Furt more, think of a more complex situation, in which the refined net one wishes to abstract includes transitions that have procedures associated with them, since Pro-Ne allow both priority procedures and transition procedures. Then, the abstraction op tion would require producing a program describing the behavior of the abstraction, the input for this derivation would have to be not only the structural interconnect within the refined net, but also the segments of code associated with each T-elemen Let us instead turn to an alternate way of expressing the behavior of the abstracte element, still staying within the confines of an original module in which the T-elements have no time-delays and no transition procedures that operate upon data. This approach, discussed in the next section, will make use of Vector Addition Systems, suitably modified, and we will see that it leads to some success in a limited case.

4. ABSTRACTION USING VECTOR ADDITION SYSTEMS REPRESENTATION

When dealing only with the control structure of a Pro-Net model, making use of S-elements, T-elements, and arcs without regard to data and data-dependent procedur Vector Addition Systems (VAS) may be used to represent the nets. VAS were introduc by Karp and Miller [2] and the VAS representation was shown to be equivalent to the Petri Net by Keller, in a work in which he also introduced Vector Replacement Systen [3]. (For simplicity, we consider only nets with no self-loops, representable by V VRS, with self-loops, are easily represented by VAS).

VAS can also be used to describe control in Pro-Nets that have data-sensitive p choices if one modifies the VAS addition rules: a) recognize the effects of bounds on the number of tokens that can occupy S-elements in the net, and b) take account of state variables associated with the columns of the VAS (representing T-elements c T-options of the nets.) The state variables help select between two or more T-optic that could act simultaneously, considering only the markings on their associated S-e ments. The correspondence between nets and VAS should become clear during the discu sion of the following example.

The question may have occurred to the reader: "Why work with both the Pro-Net a the VAS representation if they are equivalent?" In answer, the net is easier for mo humans to comprehend and to see patterns and structural relationships; however, the VAS representation is easier for machine manipulation of the algorithm. For the abstract graphical version of the net, the complex T-elements show that several arcs <u>may</u> be involved in the action, but one needs a behavioral specification to show precisely <u>which</u> arcs are involved. The abstracted VAS preserves in concise form this specific behavior.

4.1 Example Containing Internal States

Let us now return to the S-Module introduced in Section 3, taken from the work by Keller. His work provides a useful point of departure for this paper because of the subject matter and because of its availability in the open literature. His paper demonstrates the need for abstraction and he makes use of it, but employs only an ad hoc representation of the abstraction since that is not the purpose of his paper. Using his work as the basis for this study is purposely limiting; it deals only with flow control. The data manipulating operations are concerned only with data sensitive choices of control signals, so there are aspects of the Pro-Net modeling method that are not used. However, it still leaves an interesting domain to explore. This example shows abstraction in two successive levels and deals only with sequential circuits. It is taken from a more detailed study involving abstraction through five levels [5] that does include very limited concurrency.

Keller defines building blocks, among them being the "S-module" and the "M-module". These are combined and used to form a larger unit, which he calls a "DC-5 module". In this example we show at "level-0" the S-module as a net of Pro-Net primitives, Figure 1. The M-module happens already to be a primitive Pro-Net T-element; it makes a selection of one or the other of two inputs to produce one output. The S-module is abstracted to a single Pro-Net T-element at "level-1" where several copies of it are interconnected and combined with an M-module to form a DC-5 module at level 1. This, in turn, is abstracted to a single T-element at "level 2".

In this simple case, the behavior of the T-elements at the most detailed level is inherent in the action rules of the primitive Pro-Net T-elements. The input-output behavior of the net is entirely determined by the structure and the basic definitions of the T-elements. Considering the primitive net as a "black box", its internal states are clearly shown by tokens residing on internal locations. The net at level-0 can also be represented by a VAS with a row for each place in the net and a column for each T-option.

When the net is abstracted and no longer consists purely of net primitives, the behavior of the complex T-element will again be described by a VAS. The purpose of the following abstraction algorithm will be to transform the VAS representation at one level (whether it be the primitive level or a higher one) to the corresponding simpler VAS describing the behavior of the complex T-element representing the abstraction. When necessary, the algorithm converts from representation of internal states by structure to representation by internal state variables used to help select columns of the VAS for firing.

4.2 Definitions Pertaining To Various Levels:

At Refined Level

R: All or part of a net. R becomes one T-element after abstraction

V(R): The vector addition system describing R.

T: The set of T-elements or T-options in R. (Column names in V(R).)

t∈E: An individual T-element or T-option in R. (Individual column in V(R).)

Y: The set of S-elements in R row names in V(R).)

y∈Y: An individual S-element in R.

$\{t\}_i \in t$: The set of T-elements or T-options that fire as a consequence of traversing path P_i (note that this may include internal cycles in the graph).

At Abstract Level

TA: The abstract T-element representing refinement R.

V(A): The vector addition system describing TA.

~V(A): The non-reduced VAS describing TA (containing S-element labels to be eliminated)

*TA: The set of input S-elements for TA.

TA*: The set of output S-elements for TA.

TA_i: The T-option for path p_i.

At Both Levels

$\{v_i\}$: The set of internal state variables within the specification of a T-element that may influence choice of the T-option involved in action.

State Label: A label associated with a T-option. Consists of the values of the internal state variables (if any) before and after action of the T-option.

P: The set of paths (P∈{*TA}X{TA*}) allowed by the structure, markings, and states.

$p_i \in P$: 1≤i≤Cardinal{P}.

$a_i \in$: {Actions that are initiated by markings of *TA that produce markings of TA*}

4.3 Abstraction Algorithm:

1) Select R such that it can be represented by a TA that is appropriate to the abstract modeling level required.
2) Form V(R). If there are state labels in V(R) (associated with the T-option labels), reduce them to the minimal set, using established minimization methods and taking into account the "don't care" cases due to restrictions on inputs and due to structural interconnections. (The penalty for not minimizing is unwanted complexity -- not abject failure.)
3) Identify *TA and TA* and P.
4) For each p_i in P:
   a) determine $\{t\}_i \in p_i$.
   b) form the vector sum of all colums t $\in\{t\}_i$. Label the result vector TA_i and provide for the later addition of associated state-labels for "before action" and "after action". Mark all vector components that became zero, due to the addition of non-zero values. Label these components $Z_i y_j$,

where y_j Y are the row labels, $(1 \le j \le \text{Cardinal } Y)$.

c) place TA_i in ~V(A) as its ith T-element column option.

5) From ~V(A) eliminate all rows containing <u>only</u> zero and $Z_i y_j$ values.

6) The remaining $Z_i y_j$ (from step 4b) are in state determining cycles. Treat them as follows: Relabel the y_j (row labels that contain the remaining $Z_i y_j$, using the temporary labels v_j. Construct the state-label for column TA_i as follows:

a) If the v_j component of TA_i contains a "-1" then label "before action" with the name v_j as a state value assignment.

b) If the v_j component of TA_i contains a "+1" then label "after action" with the name v_j as a state value assignment.

c) If the v_j component of TA_i contains a $Z_i y_j$ (i.e., a zero due to cancellation of + and - entries in $\{t\}_i$ then label both "before action" and "after action" with the name v_j as a state value assignment.

d) Eliminate from ~V(A) all the v_j rows.

7) Combine "don't care" cases:

a) If columns TA_i, TA_k ($\forall_i$ and $\forall_k$, $i \ne k$) are identical in element values and in "after action" states, label the "before action" state of TA_i with the union of the two "before action" states, and eliminate TA_k.

8) Examine all TA_i without state labels and use labels, if they exist, from V(R), chosen as follows:

a) the V(A) label "before action" is the "before action" label in V(R) for the <u>first</u> state-altering T-element in path p_i.

b) the V(A) label "after action" is the "after action" label in V(R) for the <u>last</u> state-altering T-element in path p_i.

c) (Optional) rename the state variables and the TA_i to isomorphic sets consistent with chosen terminology.

4.4 Level-0 To Level-1 Abstraction:

Figure 1 shows the S-module as a Pro-Net of primitives with no self loops. The behavior of the module can be seen from its structure, and it was also described in Section 3.

The net-model objective of the abstraction from Level-0 to Level-1 is shown in Figure 3, which preserves all the input-output places, but no longer completely specifies the action of the module. Something additional is required. That "something additional" will be a VAS representation of the action and, in order to derive it through application of the abstraction algorithm, one must first start with the VAS representation of the Level-0 net of Figure 1. This VAS is shown in Figure 4 where, for example, the first column labeled t_1 represents the action of T-element t_1 of Figure 2. The -1 at the top of the column indicates that an input token is required from S-element 1_1 and, further down, is also required from S-element L(1). With these conditions satisfied, the T-element is able to act and will absorb those tokens and place tokens where a 1 is located in the column, i.e., on row labels (corresponding to locations in Fig. 1) L_1^1 and L(0). Normally in VAS representation 0's are included where there is no interaction between row and column, e.g., at coordinates (t_1,L_2). However, for clarity in this figure, such zeros will be implicit and not shown specifically. Note also that there are no state labels in this particular case. In later abstractions, the state variables will appear. Thus Figure is a one-to-one mapping of Figure 1 at this most primitive level. This has taken us through steps 1 and 2 of the abstraction algorithm.

Step 3: (Determine the input and output S-elements and paths between them.)

$*TA = \{L_1,L_2\ I_{20}\}$; $TA* = \{L_1^1,\ L_2^1,\ 0_{10},\ 0_{20}\}$;

P $= \{p_1,\ldots p_6\}$ where:

P_1 = path from L_1 to L_1^1, given initial state L(1)

P_2 = path from L_1 to L_1^1, given initial state L(0)

P_3 = path from L_2 to L_2^1, given initial state of L(1)

P_4 = path from L_2 to L_2^1, given initial state of L(0)

P_5 = path from I_{20} to 0_{10}

P_6 = path from I_{20} to 0_{20}

Step 4(a): (Determine T-elements in Level-0 for each path.)

$\{t_1\}\epsilon p_1$; $\{t_2,t_5\}\epsilon p_2$; $\{t_9,t_8\}\epsilon p_3$; $\{t_{10}\}\epsilon p_4$;
$\{t_3,t_6\}\epsilon p_5$; $\{t_4,t_7\}\epsilon p_6$

The results of step 4(b) and 4(c) are shown in Figure 5. The result of the sixth st is shown in Figure 6, where the only rows shown are the particular ones operated up by this step of the algorithm. The final result after steps 7 and 8 (steps 8 (a,b) null in this case) is shown in Figure 7, which is the behavior of the abstract T-ele ment for the S-module that was illustrated in Figure 3.

4.5 Level-1 to Level-2 Abstraction

Now, following Keller's synthesis, five of the S-modules are interconnected an an M-module is added, to produce a larger module that he termed a "DC5". This inter connection is shown in Figure 8 and the reader will note the abstract T-element in the upper left-hand corner labeled S_1 that corresponds to Figure 3. From the nature of the interconnection, it can be seen that when S-module S_i is set to a given state its acknowledging output sets the state of S_{i+1} so this interconnection results in equating the states of successive stages.

Figure 9 shows the result of step 1 of the next application of the algorithm it is the Level-2 representation of this DC5 module. It is the objective of the remainder of the algorithm to produce the VAS that describes its precise behavior. Figure 10 shows the results of step 2 and is the complete Level-1 VAS behavior description for the module.

The remainder of the algorithm is applied as in the previous case and the fin result is shown in Figure 11, which provides the behavioral description for the complex graphical T-element shown in Figure 9.

5. SUMMARY

Hierarchical modeling is of crucial importance in handling large systems. The need for abstraction, i.e., selective elimination of detail while preserving input-output characteristics of a subsystem, is an integral part of hierarchical modeling. A modification of Petri Nets to bring them closer to expressing the information needed in modeling real systems has been described [6] and an algorithmic approach to abstraction, using some of the properties of this modeling method, has been presented. Among the longer-term motivations for this work is the potential for programming the algorithm to operate on system models developed by means of a graphical net editor. This will simplify incorporation of substructures whose properties have been determined so that they may become parts of higher level models; it will also aid checking against top-down specifications expressed in the form of net models.

Note again that the example just discussed deals only with flow of control. There are no data operations except those on the internal local variables that effect path choice. There is no parallel activity and no time delays are associated with the transitions; this is indeed a very limited situation. A more complex case, including concurrency and time delays, is now under study, but is not yet complete at this time.

REFERENCES

[1] Horning, J.J., Randell, B. "Process Structuring", Computing Surveys, V. 5, No. 1, Mar. 1973, pp. 5-30.

[2] Karp, R.M., Miller, R.E. "Parallel program schemata: a mathematical model for parallel computation", IEEE Conf. Record, 8th Annual Symp. on Switching and Automata Theory, Oct. 1967, pp. 55-61.

[3] Keller, R.M. "Vector replacement systems: a formalism for modeling asynchronous systems", TR 117, Comp. Sci. Lab, Princeton Univ., Dec. 1972.

[4] ______ "Towards a theory of universal speed-independent modules", IEEE TR Comp, Jan. 1974, pp. 21-33.

[5] Noe, J.D. "Abstraction Levels with Pro Nets: An Algorithm and Examples". TR 77-03-01, revised 9/12/77, Dept. of Computer Science, Univ. of Washington, Seattle, Wa. 98195.

[6] ______ "Nets in Modeling and Simulation" (In this proceeding).

[7] Schwetman, H.D. "Hybrid Simulation Models of Computer Systems", CACM, V.21, No. 9, Sept. 1978, pp. 718-723.

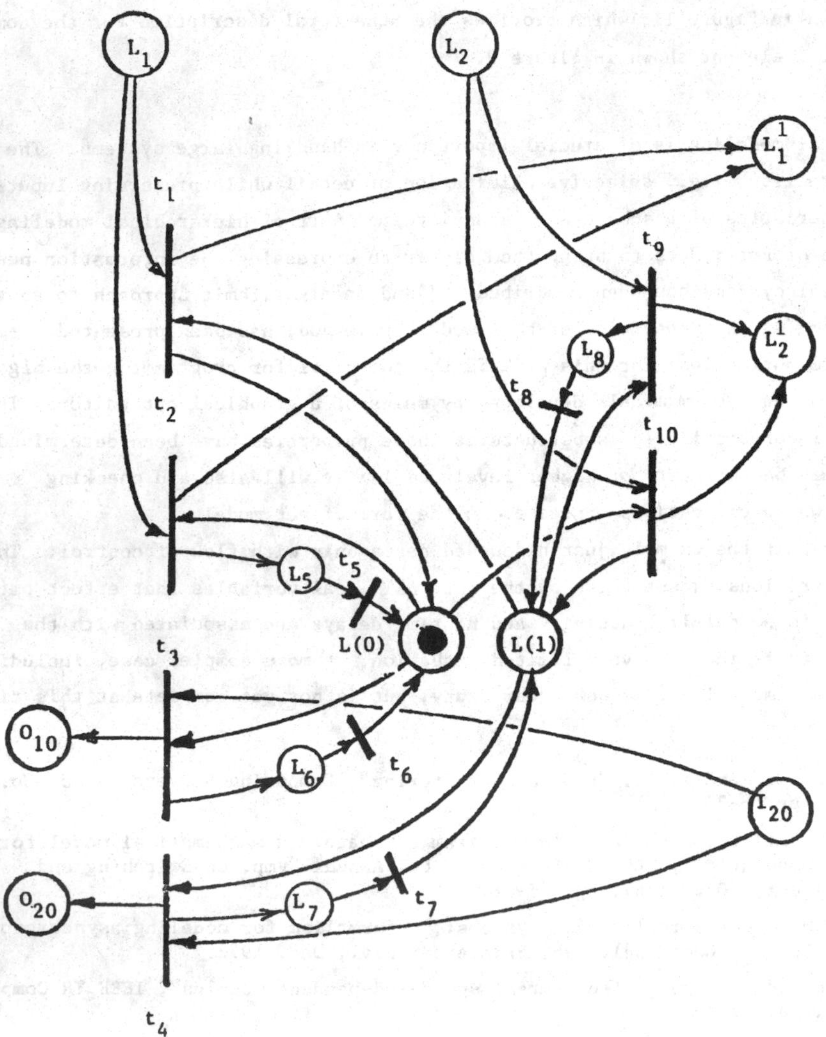

Figure 1: Level-0; S-module in Pro-Net primitives

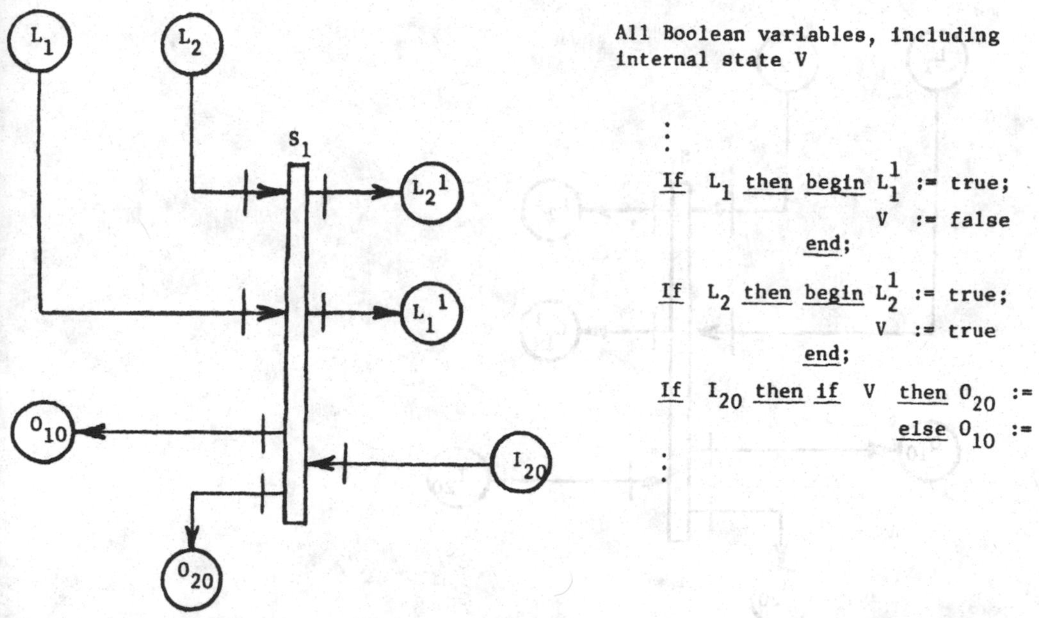

Figure 2: S-Module as an abstract Pro-Net T-element.

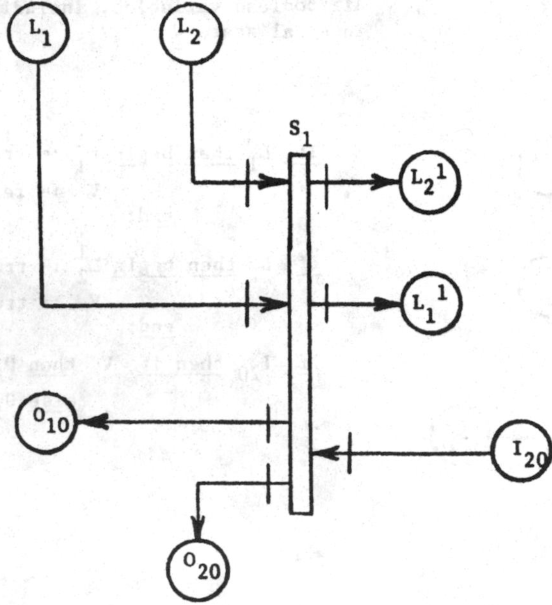

Figure 3: Level-1; Pro-Net T-element representing the abstractions of the S-module shown in Fig. 1 (Step 1 of algorithm).

	t_1	t_2	t_3	t_4	t_5	t_6	t_7	t_8	t_9	t_{10}
L_1	-1	-1								
L_2									-1	-1
L_1^1	1	1								
L_2^1									1	1
L(0)	1	-1	-1		1	1				-1
L(1)	-1			-1			1	1	-1	1
I_{20}			-1	-1						
O_{10}			1							
O_{20}				1						
L_5		1			-1					
L_6			1			-1				
L_7				1			-1			
L_8								-1	1	

Figure 4: V(R) for S-module at level-0 (algorithm step 2 in level-0 to level-1 abstraction)

States:						
Before Acting						
After Acting						
T-Options	TA_1	TA_2	TA_3	TA_4	TA_5	TA_6
L_1	-1	-1				
L_2			-1	-1		
L_1^1	1	1				
L_2^1			1	1		
$L_{(0)}$	1	0		-1	0	
$L_{(1)}$	-1		0	1		0
I_{20}					-1	-1
O_{10}					1	
O_{20}						1
L_5		0				
L_6					0	
L_7						0
L_8			0			

Note: The newly created $Z_i y_i$ are identified as "0" entries.

Figure 5: ~V(A) for S-module after step 4(c) of algorithm, (Level 0 to 1).

States						
Before Acting	v_1	v_0	v_1	v_0	v_0	v_1
After Acting	v_0	v_0	v_1	v_1	v_0	v_1
T-Options	TA_1	TA_2	TA_3	TA_4	TA_5	TA_6

$L(0) = v_0$	1	0			0		Step 6(d) eliminates these rows
$L(1) = v_1$	-1		0			0	

Figure 6: Determination of State Labels for ~V(A) of S-module (Step 6 of algorithm, Level 0 to 1).

State				
Before Acting	*	*	v_0	v_1
After Acting	v_0	v_1	v_0	v_1
T-Options	Sl_1	Sl_2	Sl_3	Sl_4
L_1	-1			
L_2		-1		
L_1^1	1			
L_2^1		1		
I_{20}			-1	-1
O_{10}			1	
O_{20}				1

Note: * Denotes either state

Figure 7: Level-1 behavior of S-module shown in Fig. 3 after application of algorithm to level-0

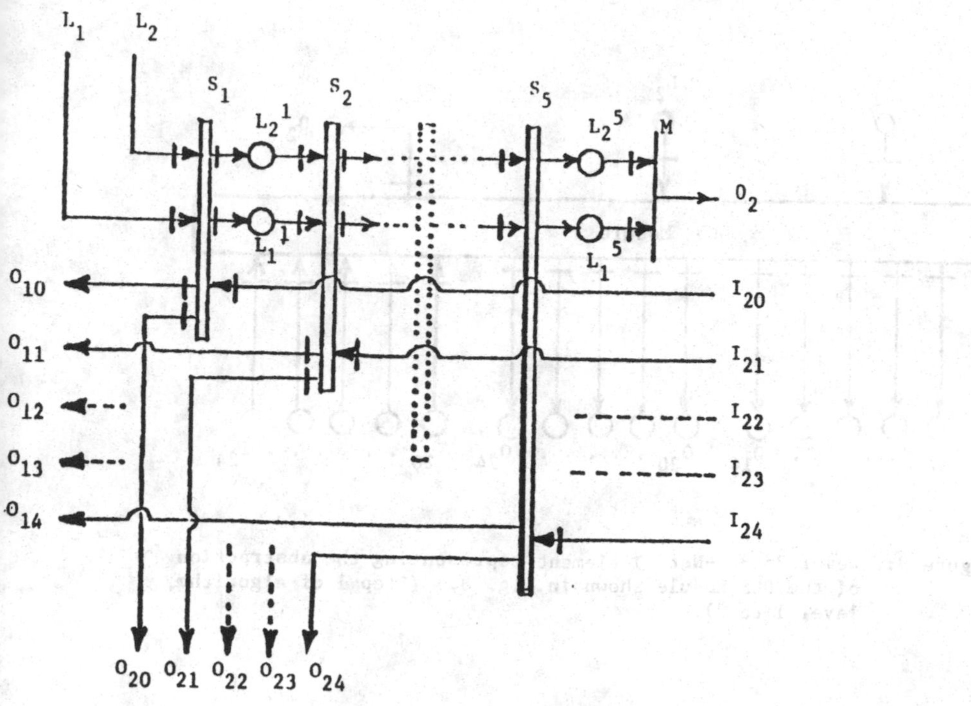

Figure 8: Level-1; five S-modules and one M-module interconnected to form a module named DC5.

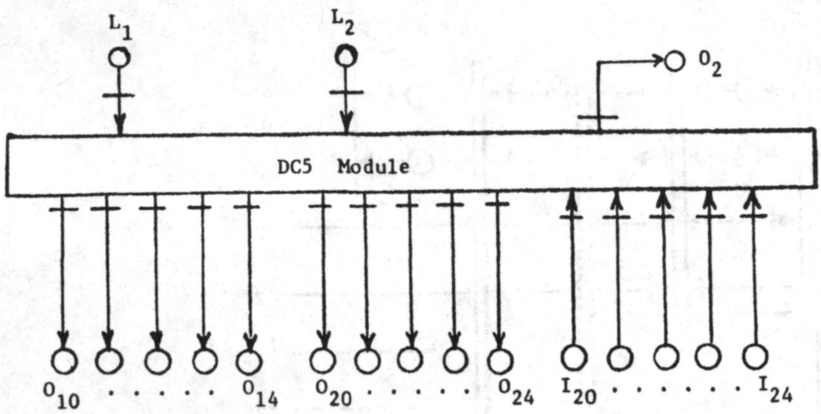

Figure 9: Level 2; Pro-Net T-element representing the abstraction of the DC5 Module shown in Fig. 8. (Step 1 of algorithm, level 1 to 2).

Notes: * denotes either state
- denotes no internal state

Module:	S1				S2				S3				S4				S5				M	
State: Before Acting	*	*	v_0	v_1	*	*	v_0	v_1	*	*	v_0	v_1	*	*	v_0	v_1	*	*	v_0	v_1	-	-
After Acting	v_0	v_1	v_0	v_1	v_0	v_1	v_0	v_1	v_0	v_1	v_0	v_1	v_0	v_1	v_0	v_1	v_0	v_1	v_0	v_1	-	-
T-Options	$S1_1$	$S1_2$	$S1_3$	$S1_4$	$S2_1$	$S2_2$	$S2_3$	$S2_4$	$S3_1$	$S3_2$	$S3_3$	$S3_4$	$S4_1$	$S4_2$	$S4_3$	$S4_4$	$S5_1$	$S5_2$	$S5_3$	$S5_4$	M_1	M_2
L_1	-1																					
L_2		-1																				
L_1^1	1				-1																	
L_2^1		1				-1																
I_{20}			-1	-1																		
O_{10}			1																			
O_{20}				1																		
L_1^2					1				-1													
L_2^2						1				-1												
I_{21}							-1	-1														
O_{11}							1															
O_{21}								1														
L_1^3									1				-1									
L_2^3										1				-1								
I_{22}											-1	-1										
O_{12}											1											
O_{22}												1										
L_1^4													1				-1					
L_2^4														1				-1				
I_{23}															-1	-1						
O_{13}															1							
O_{23}																1						
L_1^5																	1				-1	
L_2^5																		1				-1
I_{24}																			-1	-1		
O_{14}																			1			
O_{24}																				1		
O_2																					1	1

Figure 10: Level -1 V(R) for DC5 module of Figure 8 (after Step 2 of algorithm, Level -1 to -2).

Note: * denotes either state

State:												
Before Acting	*	*	v_0	v_0	v_0	v_0	v_0	v_1	v_1	v_1	v_1	v_1
After Acting	v_0	v_1	v_0	v_0	v_0	v_0	v_0	v_1	v_1	v_1	v_1	v_1
T-Options	TA_1	TA_2	TA_3	TA_5	TA_7	TA_9	TA_{11}	TA_4	TA_6	TA_8	TA_{10}	TA_{12}
L_1	-1											
L_2		-1										
O_2	1	1										
I_{20}			-1					-1				
I_{21}				-1					-1			
I_{22}					-1					-1		
I_{23}						-1					-1	
I_{24}							-1					-1
O_{10}			1									
O_{11}				1								
O_{12}					1							
O_{13}						1						
O_{14}							1					
O_{20}								1				
O_{21}									1			
O_{22}										1		
O_{23}											1	
O_{24}												1

Figure 11 : Level-2 Behavior of one DC5 module shown in Figure 9 after completion of algorithm and regrouping of columns

APPLICATIONS OF NET-BASED MODELS

Jerre D. Noe*

University of Washington, Seattle, WA., U.S.A.

Abstract Selected applications of nets by other authors are discussed, to show a range of use of the models, and to show the modifications to nets that have been adopted for specific applications. The topics include models of a parallel algorithm for lexical analysis, net augmentation to detect and correct errors, an approach to error correction in distributed systems with no central control, and modeling aids to design of properly functioning systems.

1. INTRODUCTION

The applications that have been chosen for this discussion display a range of approaches to making use of nets in addressing problems that arise in design and use of computer systems. In all but one of these examples, nets have been modified to be more adaptable to the problem at hand - in some cases to introduce concepts of time of action, in other cases to include data representation, and sometimes data-dependent decisions in flow of control. Are these modifications necessary? Perhaps not always, in the sense that equivalent models could be constructed using unmodified condition/event nets. However, the changes often prove to be particularly convenient in the context of the problems studied, and they provide clues concerning the features useful to incorporate in higher-level, or problem-oriented, net languages.

The first application, by J. L. Baer, deals with the idea of proper termination - i.e. the return of a cyclic sub-system to a state where it is prepared to repeat its task on new data.

The second, by W. L. Heimerdinger and Y. W. Han, is part of a long-term effort to provide design aids by restricting the allowable interconnections of components, and by verifying the correctness of operation at each hierarchical level.

The third topic includes the work of several people concerned with problems that arise during execution of processes - i.e. error detection and recovery.

In each case, the objective in this paper is merely to express the essence of the ideas of the individual authors. The reader will want to go to the original references if the topic proves to be of interest.

2. MODELING FOR PARALLEL COMPUTATION (J.L. Baer):

Baer [1] is concerned with modeling a class of parallel computation algorithms that "terminate" properly in the sense of finishing one set of computations and being

---

*This paper was prepared through support by NSF Grant No. MCS77-22819 and the University of Washington.

again in the initial state to begin the next. The example cited is parallel treatment of the lexical analysis phase of compilation; Petri Nets are used to model the control structure, and proper termination consists of cycling back, after recognition of a lexical entity, to an initial marking that is ready for the search for the next lexical entity.

The approach taken is to modify Petri Nets by the addition of three constructs -- exclusive OR logic, switches and token absorbers -- while taking care not to destroy desired formal properties of the model.

Baer and Ellis [2] extend and make use of the model to examine a complete compiler in a search for ways to pipeline its action with multiple processors. In so doing, they augment the control model to allow simple descriptive representations of the associated data operations, although they express some dissatisfaction with this data representation. More complex alternatives to this simple data graph can be found in Ellis' dissertation [3].

2.1 Extensions to the Control Graph -

Exclusive OR (EOR) Logic: Baer adds a transition type that may have a set of EOR input or output arcs. If more than one of the EOR input places contains a token, the firing conditions are undefined, so net structure must insure exclusive marking. Data operations associated with the control transition may be used to select the EOR output.

Switch: For the case where one wishes to embed in the network the explicit selection of control paths, Baer adds a switch. It is associated with a transition having a pair of EOR output arcs, and the switch is a special input place whose marking (or lack of) determines which output arc is used. When the transition fires, a token is removed from the switch if it was marked. This structure is essentially the X-transition introduced by Nutt [11].

Token Absorber: Proper termination often requires getting rid of tokens within a net. This is particularly true where two or more activities are concurrent and success in one obviates further activity in the others. For this purpose, a token absorber is introduced, consisting of an output arc (shown as a dashed line) from a transition to a place. When the transition fires, all tokens are removed from the place connected by this absorber arc. If no tokens were there, transition firing proceeds normally, affecting the input and other output places.

One or more absorber arcs may co-exist with output arcs having AND logic or EOR logic, but not both.

2.2 Data Operations

Rather than use a separate data graph, as in LOGOS [12], Baer and Ellis represent the data operations as special nodes with descriptive statements of the data operator and structures. The data nodes are connected to controlling transitions by arcs. No attempt is made to distinguish between single memory cells and composite structures, other than through their names.

2.3 Example: Lexical Analysis -

An example of the use of the constructs is taken from [2], and shows the lexical analysis portion of a compiler, with a scanner pipelined in front of concurrent subprocesses for reserved-word search and for hash function calculation.

Referring to Fig. 1, the first stage of the pipeline continues to scan characters until a separator or an illegal character for a word is encountered. In the second stage of the pipeline, the reserved word table is searched as long as the possibility exists that the word being scanned is a reserved word. Meanwhile the other process is calculating the hash value of the word being built. When it is determined that the word being scanned is not a reserved word, the switch is set and subsequent output from the switch transition goes to the arc labelled f rather than e and scanning continues for a keyword rather than a reserved word. When a separator is found, the scan of this lexical entity is done, the appropriate data values have been entered into the data structures represented as rectangular nodes, and the last transition removes tokens from the interior of the net so that its marking is proper for beginning the scan of the next lexical entity. Note in this net that the authors are either making use of a global variable referred to by the label "done?" on two transitions or they are implying attributes carried along on tokens to denote that a separator has been found. Neither of these aspects are discussed in their papers.

2.4 Proper Termination -

Proper termination has been informally described as leaving the marking of a net at the end of a cyclic operation in a state such that the net is ready for the next cycle. Proper termination is defined formally in [1] and Baer presents a theorem and its proof showing that there exists an effective procedure to determine if the execution of a k- safe, repetition-free net is properly terminating. He points out that the number of steps in the procedure grows exponentially with the number of places in the net and then extends a reduction procedure by Gostelow et al [4] so that it is valid for the modified nets Baer is using. This results in reducing the computational difficulty of establishing whether or not proper termination exists for a net.

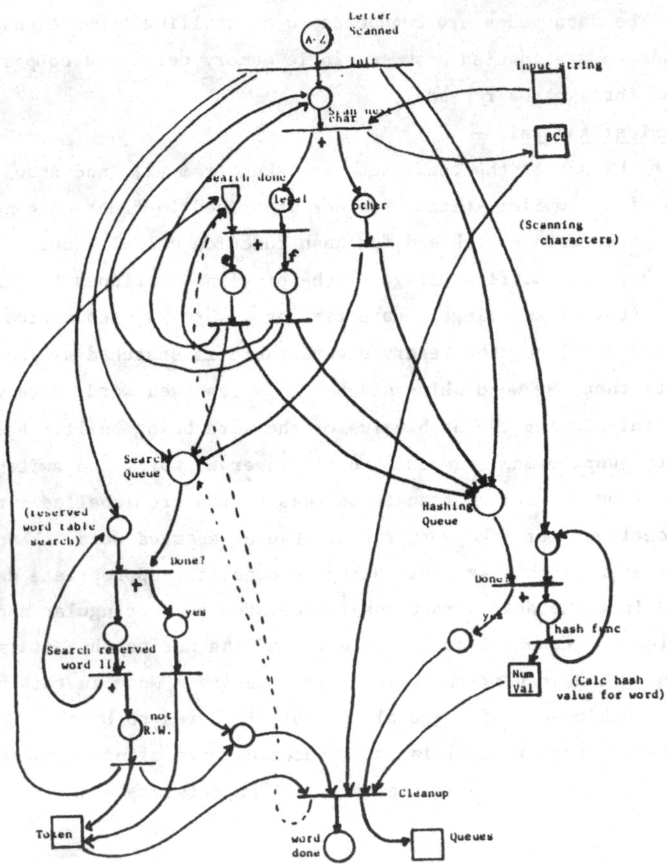

Figure 1: Expansion of LEXICAL ANALYSIS transition

3. FAULT TOLERANT DESIGN (Heimerdinger and Han)

The long-term goal of this work is to aid system design by developing mechanizabl methods to verify the correctness of system operation on a level-by-level basis in a hierarchical structure. The approach seeks ways to abstract, or reduce, net models to simpler representations, for ease in analysis. One form of analysis developed allows tracing of bad data, for prevention or correction.

In [5] the authors make use of a two-graph system separating control flow and data operations. The control graph uses Petri Nets modified to exhibit priorities among firings of simultaneously enabled transitions. Priorities are, in effect, determined by accessing global variables at the time firing is enabled in order to specify priority. The data graph they use is related to LOGOS [12] but Han and Heimerdinger use a simplified version with only two types of nodes, representing operands and operators.

To allow hierarchical modeling they develop reduction techniques for both the control graph and the data graph. These reduction techniques are applied manually by searching for patterns in each graph that can be replaced by simpler structures. The authors state that these reduction techniques can be mechanized. The three patterns in control graphs that can be so reduced are serial, parallel and pipeline. Serial refers to sequential alternation of transitions and places. Parallel refers to concurrently marked places connected by arcs between two transitions. Pipeline refers to sequential stages in which each contains a forward and a reverse path between sequential transitions. The two data graph structures that can be reduced are tree structures, and those that begin with a single operator and end with a single operator, with series and parallel combinations in between. Both reductions require that invocation of the operators occur in fixed sequences. The series parallel data graphs are those that have one data operator at the start and only one operator at the end and all paths through the subgraph go through both of these. The tree structure has one data operator as a root and one and only one directed path to all other data operators.

The authors restrict the cases to control graphs that are both consistent (non-trivial solution to C.X =0), where C is the incidence matrix, and invariant (the weighted sum of markings remains constant). Hence consistency and invariance tests are used to eliminate non-valid nets.

When reduction by inspection/replacement fails on data nets they use symbolic execution (with output variables represented as functions of input variables) in order to develop the reduced data net.

3.1 Tracing Contaminated Data

Reference [6] presents a data contamination analysis that allows one either to trace the spread of bad data or to locate the data ancestors of a particularly crutical data item. They borrow "global data flow analysis" ideas from compiler optimization (for example, the idea of "reaching definitions") and extend them to develop their methods. They first transform the control graph into a directed graph in which each node is a transition that changes from one reachability graph state to another. Each such node corresponds to an operation on data. Then the contamination-spread analysis consists of tracing through these nodes to see where variables are defined, where they are used (hence possibly redefined), and - at critical points - noting where the definition "reaching" these points could have been affected by previous definitions or alterations. A similar analysis tracing backwards is used to find ancestors of crucial operations.

The Use of Timed Nets

Reference [6] discusses the need for introducing time in order to model performance of physical systems, looks at five different alternatives for specifying the time between enabling and firing of a transition, then chooses for later work the method introduced by Merlin, in which there is a specification for each transition of the minimum and the maximum elapsed time between enabling and firing.

4.1 Application of Coding Theory to Petri Nets (Sifakis)

The problem attacked by Sifakis [13] is that of protecting a Petri Net against undetected errors that add to, or subtract from, the markings on places.

The general approach taken by Sifakis is to augment the net by adding new places, connected to some or all of the existing transitions. By then observing the markings on the augmented net, and performing a specified calculation on this marking each time a state change occurs, it is possible to detect errors or to show how they should be corrected, depending upon the design of the augmentation. The author draws upon existing techniques in Systematic Parity-Check Codes to implement this approach.

4.1.1 Systematic Parity-Check Coding: The author, Sifakis, does not review the relevant coding ideas, and it seems helpful to do so, as follows.

Given a string of information bits, $U = (U_1, U_2 \ldots U_L)$, one can establish a generator matrix G that produces a longer string of bits, X. Considering U and X as row vectors, the relationship is

$$X = UG \qquad X = (X_1, X_2 \ldots . X_N), \qquad N > L$$

With proper choice of G, X will contain the elements of U, plus additional parity-check bits that allow detection of some set of errors, and correction of a subset of them, depending on how G was chosen. The matrix G that generates parity-check codes can be manipulated, without changing its value, so that its first L rows form the unit matrix. The unit matrix "reproduces" the information bits, U, as a contiguous part of X, and the last N-L rows of G produce the "check bits". Such code are referred to as systematic parity-check codes (SPC).

In turn, a check matrix, H can be derived from G (or vice-versa, depending on where the design starts) that provides the error detection or correction information. This is accomplished by performing the multiplication $S = H^t X$ where H^t is the transpose of H and S is the syndrome, which is a vector with all zero elements if no error has been made, i.e. if X = UG.

If an error has transformed X into Y, then S will be a non-zero vector, and its value may be used to correct some errors. Note, however, that a family of errors can give the same value of S, so not all errors can be distinguished. A typical design would correct errors in single bit positions and detect multiple errors, but would not correct less-probable, higher order, multiple-bit errors.

4.1.2 Applying SPC Codes to Petri Nets: Sifakis uses SPC coding by treating the n places of a Petri Net, N, as the elements corresponding to U, the information to be encoded. This is first done generally with unbounded markings on the places, then is specialized to bounded markings, including the binary case. The net, N, has an incidence matrix C, with places corresponding to rows and transitions as columns. A generating matrix G is used that maps C into the incidence matrix GC of the augmented net N'. The markings M' of the n' places in net N' then correspond to code string X, and a check matrix H that is related to G is used to calculate the syndrome, $S = H^tM'$. The syndrome must be calculated every time the state of the net N' changes to see if an error has occurred.

Given the Net N, design of N' begins by determining the check matrix H. This, in turn depends upon the degree of protection desired, and is discussed in terms of the required Hamming distance of the incidence matrix GC. To avoid having to explore the entire marking space in order to assure that the Hamming distance is sufficient, Sifakis chooses H (and hence G) so that the <u>added</u> places in GC provide adequate distance. Coding theory provides methods to find implementable check matrices, although not necessarily optimal ones (in the minimum error probability sense).

With H determined, in the form $H^t = [-F, E_{(n'-n)}]$ where $E_{(n'-n)}$ is the unit matrix of order (n'-n), and F is the unique part of H, the generating matrix G is simply determined by $G = [{En \atop F}]$.

GC becomes the incidence matrix of the augmented net, with n' places (n'>n) and the same transitions as C.

<u>Example:</u> Given Fig. 2, a net N, with n = 5, design a system that will allow detection of single errors.

Suppose a distance d = 2 is required, and coding theory considerations lead to $H^t = [-F, E_{n'-n}] = [-1\ -1\ -1\ -1\ -1\ 1]$ as a suitable check matrix. Then G becomes

$$G = \begin{bmatrix} E_5 \\ F \end{bmatrix} = \begin{bmatrix} 1&0&0&0&0 \\ 0&1&0&0&0 \\ 0&0&1&0&0 \\ 0&0&0&1&0 \\ 0&0&0&0&1 \\ 1&1&1&1&1 \end{bmatrix} \qquad GC = G \begin{bmatrix} -1&0&0&1 \\ 1&-1&0&0 \\ 1&0&-1&0 \\ 0&1&0&-1 \\ 0&0&1&-1 \end{bmatrix} = \begin{bmatrix} -1&0&0&1 \\ 1&-1&0&0 \\ 1&0&-1&0 \\ 0&1&0&-1 \\ 0&0&1&-1 \\ 1&0&0&-1 \end{bmatrix}$$

where GC is the connectivity matrix for Fig. 2a. Note that one place was the necessary addition, and the bottom row of GC shows its interconnection with the transitions of the original net.

Now, given a marking Mo (column vector) of net N $(Mo)^t = [\,1\ 0\ 0\ 0\ 0]$

The corresponding marking Mo' of N' is $GMo = (Mo')^t = [1\ 0\ 0\ 0\ 0\ 1]$.

The syndrome is

$H^tMo' = 0$, as one would expect.

If an error occurred, changing Mo' to M_1' , where $(M_1')^t = [1\ 0\ 0\ 1\ 0\ 1\ ]$

then $S = H^TM_1' = -1$, indicating that an error occurred.

More interesting examples are shown in the original paper, including single-error correction in which S becomes a column vector whose value identifies the location and value of the error.

Discussion

Unlike Merlin's work on recoverable sets, [7], which is discussed in the next section, this approach does not directly correct errors in control. However, it can locate an incorrect marking and specify the correction to be made, at the cost of making a check calculation at each state change, and there are design trade-offs, since the degree of protection can be increased by adding more complex checking structures. It further has the advantage that the design applies to the entire net, whereas Merlin's construction must be applied to the specific place in the net that is to be error-corrected.

Sifakis' method is applicable to unmodified Petri Nets, without the addition of time constraints, but does not appear to be directly applicable to distributed systems, as treated in the following discussion of the work by Merlin and Randell, since it requires an overall concept of the state of the system in order to perform the check calculation.

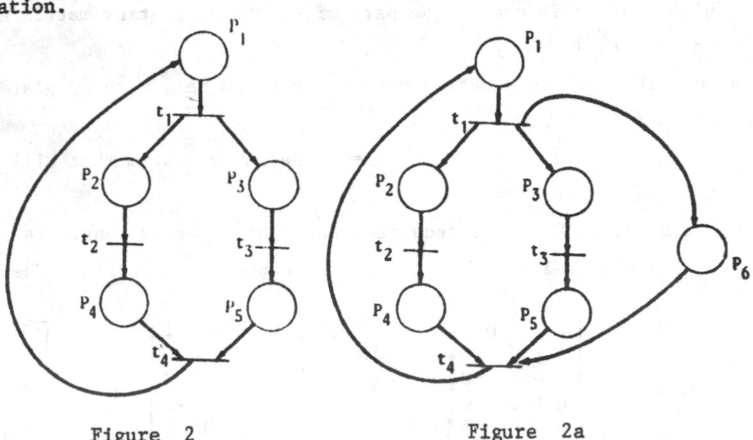

Figure 2 Figure 2a

A Net Modified for Single Error Detection

4.2 Recoverability of Computing Systems (Merlin)

This work in [7] and [8] goes beyond the concept of encoding places in order to be able to detect errors or calculate where corrections should take place and instead seeks to incorporate automatic error correction in the basic structure of the Petri Net representing control of this system. The problem addressed is: given a Petri Net and the possibility of an error caused by a loss of a token in a place, how does one construct a Petri Net that automatically recovers to the full power (i.e. having the same reachability graph) of the original Petri Net. The general approach taken is to add additional places and transitions to the net that lead one from the incorrect marking back to a marking that is legal in the original net. It would typically be applied to the "weakest link" in a system, since the construction applies to correcting the marking of one specific location.

Merlin claims however [7] that this correcting cannot be achieved with ordinary Petri Nets. His thesis presents proof that all Petri Nets that are recoverable have an "irreversible degradation", meaning that after the return to some legal state only a subset of the markings in the reachability graph can be reached. It is not the purpose of this present discussion to present the proof or rationale for that conclusion but instead to illustrate how his altered Petri Nets -- "Time Petri Nets" -- are capable of accomplishing the goal.

Merlin limits his attention to systems having finite reachability graphs. He introduces the concept of a minimum and maximum time between the existence of conditions that enable a transition to fire and its actual firing. It is guaranteed that the transition will not fire in a time less than the mimimum and will certainly fire in a time less than or equal to the maximum. This modificiation allows the addition of places and transitions that can correct for errors after expiration of a "time-out interval" that is long enough to guarantee that the added transition will not interfere with normal error-free operation. Application of his method depends upon examination of the complete reachability graph (or token machine, TM, as he calls it).

Example

In reference [8], Merlin and Farber illustrate the ideas with an application to design of a message protocol for two stations on a computer network. The example is a simplified version of the IMP to IMP protocol in the ARPANET and an error consists of losing a message during transmission. Figure 3 shows a Time Petri Net (TPN) of the protocol in which the conditions have the following meaning:

A - ready to send
M - message sent
B - ready for message
C - message received
D - message in receiver's buffer ready to absorb
K - acknowledgement sent
W - message stored, waiting for acknowledgement
E - acknowledgement received

Initially consider transition number 7 and its three arcs missing from the Petri Net; it was added to achieve the error correction. Figure 4 shows the reachability graph (or ETM - Error Token Machine) for this net. Again, initially neglect the arc representing firing of transition 7. The markings WB and DW represent illegal markings that have occurred because of a loss of the message, i.e. the marking on M. In Figure 4, addition of the arc labeled 7 will return from an illegal to a legal marking. The modifying transition 7 in the Petri Net in Figure 3 illustrates how a new message is added to correct for the error. However, note that transition 7 must be prevented from firing except in the case of error. It will be enabled during normal operation while the sending station is waiting for acknowledgement; if acknowledgment is received before transition 7 fires, transition 4 will fire and all is well. Therefore the minimum time between enabling and firing of transition 7 must be greater than the accumulated maximum time between the marking of W and the firing of transition 4. This example serves to illustrate the utility of time Petri Nets. The more elaborate example in [8] extends the same ideas to a protocol in which a sequentially numbered series of messages may be sent and received. Interestingly enough, in this example, the authors have developed a net that will recover from two types of errors, either the loss of a message or the addition of a message when none was intended. However, they do not point this out in the text and one discovers it only by working through the example.

The authors state "this paper demonstrates that there do not exist practical asynchronous recoverable communication protocols if some a priori knowledge of execution time of the events is not provided". It would be more correct to say that this is demonstrated in the original thesis [7].

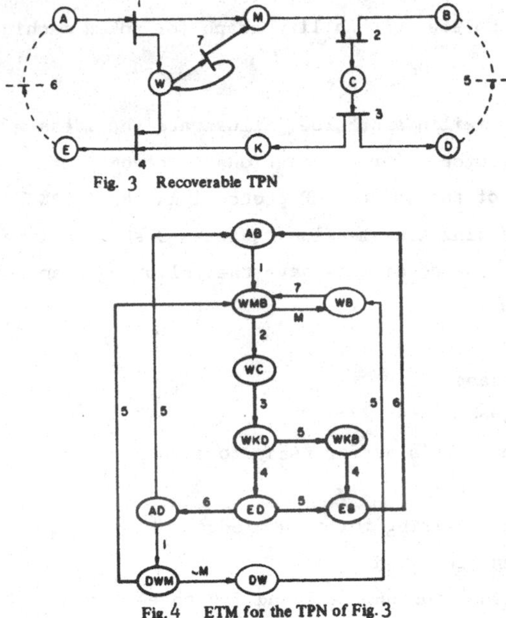

Fig. 3 Recoverable TPN

Fig. 4 ETM for the TPN of Fig. 3

4.3 State Restoration in Distributed Systems (Merlin and Randell)

Whereas Sifakis was concerned with finding out that errors had occurred, and Merlin and Farber were intent on correcting an error in a given location, the work by Merlin and Randell [9,10] concerns what to do after the error is known. The general problem attacked is how to reestablish valid processing in a distributed system after errors have been detected; no central authority is assumed in the system. The general approach makes use of checkpointing, i.e. storing state information at various times during the computation, then upon detecting error, falling back to a consistent set of such checkpoints and reestablishing the computation from there. The design compromise is to avoid excessive recomputation by dropping back too far and to avoid excessive use of memory by storing state too frequently.

The model is based on OCCURRENCE-GRAPHS (OG) that show the actual conditions and events that occur during execution. Some conditions (recovery places) are declared (temporarily) restorable and serve as checkpoints. When errors are detected the processing drops back to the recovery line (a sufficient set of recovery places). The paper is not concerned with means for error detection or for making decisions about which places to select as "restorable". Its main thrust is to present a protocol to be used by the individual processors so as to insure that the whole system will recover in spite of having no central control. Proof of the validity of the protocol is given in [9] and is not repeated in the other reference.

The protocol is nicely summarized in [10] and will not be repeated here.

References

[1] Baer, J.L., "Modelling for Parallel Computation: A Case Study", Proceedings 1973 Sagamore Computer Conference on Parallel Processing.

[2] Baer, J.L. and Ellis, C.S., "Model Design and Evaluation of a Compiler for a Parallel Processing Environment", IEEE Transactions on Software Engineering Volume SE-3, No. 6, Nov. 1977.

[3] Ellis, C.S. "The Design and Evaluation of Algorithms for Parallel Processing", Ph.D. Dissertation, University of Washington, 1979.

[4] Gostelow, K., et al, "Proper-Termination of Flow of Control in Programs Involving Concurrent Processes", SIGPLAN Notices, 7, 11, Nov. 1972.

[5] Han, Y.W. and Heimerdinger, W.L. "Theory of Fault Tolerance", Final Report, Dec 1977, Honeywell Research Systems and Research Center, ONR Contract No. N00014-75-C-0011.

[6] Heimerdinger, W.L. and Han, Y.W. "A Graph Theoretic Approach to Fault Tolerant Computing", Final Report, Sept. 12, 1977, Honeywell Systems and Research Center, 2700 Ridgeway Parkway, Minneapolis, MN 55413, AFOSR Contract No. F44620-75-C-0053.

[7] Merlin, P.M., "A Study of the Recoverability of Computing Systems", a Ph.D. Thesis, University of California, Irvine.

[8] Merlin, P.M. and Farber, D.J., "Recoverability of Communication Protocols--Implications of a Theoretical Study".

[9] Merlin, P.M. and Randell, B., "Consistent State Restoration in Distributed Systems", To appear in CACM. Also TR 113, Computing Lab., Univ. of Newcastle upon Tyne, 1977.

[10] Merlin, P.M. and Randell, B., "State Restoration in Distributed Systems", Digest of Papers, FTCS-8, Toulouse, Fr., June 1978, IEEE Comp. Soc., Catalog No. 78, Ch 1286-4C.

[11] Nutt, G.J., "Evaluation Nets for Computer Systems Performance Analysis", Proc. FJCC, AFIPS, v.41, 1972, pp 274-286.

[12] Rose, C.W. and Bradshaw, F.T., "The LOGOS Representation System", Proc. IEEE Computer Conf., 1972.

[13] Sifakis, J., "Realization of Fault-Tolerant Systems by Coding Petri Nets", To appear in Journal of Design Automation and Fault-Tolerant Computing.

THE APPLICATION OF GENERAL NET THEORY -- A PERSONAL HISTORY

R. M. Shapiro

Meta Information Applications, Inc.

ABSTRACT

The author describes his personal experience applying net-based descriptive techniques to the design of computer hardware/software systems. A hypothetical Automated Design Tool is described.

TABLE OF CONTENTS

INTRODUCTION

For the past fifteen years, I have applied net-based techniques to the analysis and solution of a variety of computer-related problems. I would like to share my personal history and conclusions on this subject.

At the outset understand that I am not a theoretician: I have designed and implemented computer applications since 1956. Theoretical work I engaged in was peripheral to my applied work. If the materials presented here have value it lies in the following areas:

(1) How to apply General Net Theory to common design problems
(2) Tools to extend the utility of General Net Theory

In what follows I explain the contribution net techniques made to the analysis in each problem area and in which ways they were deficient. The first part of the paper is a review of past work focusing on the role of 'net theory' in that work. I then describe my current work and sketch a computer-based design tool that would facilitate such work. Appendices contain examples for several of the problem areas.

HISTORICAL ORIGINS

In 1962 I developed some techniques for object code optimization as part of a compiler-generator system. I was confronted with two major representational problems:

(1) A means for describing any instance of a conventional digital computer, focusing on the instruction set and registers, for the purpose of automating the code selection phase of the compiler-generator.
(2) A representational form, adequate for modeling algorithms written in conventional programming languages, that would facilitate the application of techniques for object code optimization such as redundant subexpression elimination.

The overall project had to produce a commercially useful compiler-generator and several language/machine specific compilers. My research efforts were brief and the results described in [15].

Using the compiler-generator, compilers were produced for several machines, including the IBM 7090, CDC 1604 and Burroughs D-825. The object code was good. For the D-825, a machine which was complicated to hand program because it had a high-speed stack for intermediate results and a large number of index and limit registers, the code was remarkable.

Tree-structures played an important role in the representation employed by the compiler. They provided the domain in and over which the strategy of translation was expressed. The optimization procedures were in turn restricted to flow blocks of code represented by partial orderings. Thus, redundant sub-expression elimination and all sequencing choices occurred within this domain. Some method of representing cycles within partial orderings and analyzing them was required to provide a proper domain for optimizing conventional programs, but this did not exist.

The lack of a satisfactory representational form placed severe limitations on what could be accomplished in these areas. By satisfactory I mean:

(1) The notation must not be so far removed from the semantics of what is to be described as to make the relationship obscure and the translation unreasonable.

(2) The resulting description must be amenable to various forms of 'calculation' for such purposes as:
  - (a) cost analysis -- e.g. space/time tradeoffs as in various optimization procedures
  - (b) predicting behavior -- e.g. simulation, error analysis, proof of correctness

In pursuit of such a representational tool, I became involved in ISTP (Information Systems Theory Project).

Ω-THEORY

The outcome of the first phase of ISTP (1964-1966) was called Ω-Theory. Ω-Theory had general objectives and a guiding philosophy consonant in many ways with General Net Theory:

(1) The representation was *graphical*.
(2) The concept of *global system state* was *rejected* as a useful primitive for defining system behavior.
(3) States and transitions were regarded as deriving always from the cumulative effects of purely *local laws*.
(4) The notion of an *absolute time continuum* was *rejected*.

The formalism was never refined. Its focus was primarily *structura* and those aspects of the theory that dealt with change did not rest on a sound basis.

During this period I attempted to describe various database systems using the concepts of ϑ-Theory [1]. The intent here was to highlight th similarities and differences in these systems (ADAM, COLINGO, FFS) by using a common representational form capable of expressing both structu and change. The existing descriptions of these systems relied on infor mal techniques using words such as file, record, repeating group, etc. A comparison required some formal basis and ϑ-Theory was a start in th direction.

OCCURRENCE SYSTEMS

The outcome of the second phase of ISTP (1966-1968) was called Occu rence Systems and the principal results were:

(1) A completely different method for describing systems, based on place/transition nets [2].
(2) The application of this descriptive technique to the solution of resource-allocation problems [4].

Occurrence systems made it possible for me to overcome some of the differences I had encountered in 1962. In particular, I was able to re present an algorithm (A FORTRAN LOOP) in such a way as to:

(1) Eliminate accidental ordering constraints introduced by the sequential nature of FORTRAN.
(2) Introduce hardware ordering constraints that represented the resources provided by the instruction set and registers of the CDC 6600.

(3) Determine the optimal sequence of instructions to implement the algorithm on the CDC 6600.

The representational form permits all of this in a fairly natural way. Place/transition nets are unbiased in respect to sequencing; they do not themselves contain implicit sequencing requirements or force sequencing commitments not required by the task. They exhibit sequencing clearly and are suited to the generation of different legitimate sequences. They represent all synchrony and concurrency explicity; reductions in asynchrony are expressible in a uniform manner, and their effects are determinable. Finally, they are by their nature applicable to cyclic situations.

However, the utility of the approach was restricted by several factors:

(1) The net representation of the algorithm had to be generated 'by hand'.
(2) The hardware constraints had to be introduced 'by hand'.
(3) There were no mathematical tools for doing anything with the resulting representation, aside from actual simulation of the net. While this was practical for the particular algorithm, its general usefulness is questionable.

THE REPRESENTATION OF ALGORITHMS

In the following year (1969) I attacked the problem of automatically generating a net representation of algorithms with the partial ordering required by data-dependencies preserved and accidental ordering relations discarded. The results of this project were described in [5,6].

Procedures were developed which make possible the translation of a sequentially defined algorithm into a representation of a highly concurrent version of the algorithm. Roughly speaking, each operation may take place when:

(1) The necessary operand values are available.
(2) Enough decisions have been made to guarantee that the operation

will be required (don't perform calculations on a branch that might not be taken).

(3) Enough decisions have been made to guarantee that no logically prior claim can be made on the algorithmic parts involved (in an iterative context, preserve the iterative order; i.e. don't perform an operation for iteration 'n' until either it has been performed for iteration 'n-1' or definitely need not be performed for iteration 'n-1'.

All sequencing has been stripped out except that which is given by data-dependencies or by priorities for part use. In the process, 'control' has been dismantled and the useful information which it carried h been broken down into individual ordering relations.

The major value of this work resides in what it tells us about sequential languages and the difficulties involved in exploiting hardware with highly concurrent processing capabilities. Nets provide the basic representational medium. The particular class of nets is a Condition/ Event System. In practice net representations of algorithms can be ver complicated and their utility depends upon satisfactory calculational tools for analysis and display. These did not exist at the time.

FILE STRUCTURE DESIGN

Starting around 1966 I began to design and analyze various file structures for interactive information retrieval systems. The notation of Ω-Theory was used in an effort at producing formal descriptions of some file structures, including edge-notched card systems [1,7].

Another modeling attempt was made somewhat later, using C/E systems In [7], in the context of database design, the concepts of batching, bu fering and concurrency were explicated by the use of C/E systems. Both hardware and software were modeled, including a magnetic card random ac cess memory device and a highly concurrent version of a cross-indexing system.

In these cases the value of applying nets lay in the clarity forced on the applier in the effort to produce the net description. The descr tive techniques were a constructive force in trying to think about the semantics of the problems being studied. The resulting descriptions also served as a vehicle of communication, but their value in this regard was more dubious. To be successful they needed to make use of net morphisms and other concepts from General Net Theory of which I was unaware at that time.

NET CALCULATIONS

An early promise of net theory was the potential for performing useful calculations on net descriptions of systems and thereby discovering interesting properties of the systems. The applications described so far in no way realized this potential. The assignment and sequencing problem in coding a FORTRAN loop for the CDC-6600 did use net simulation, but this is the crudest of calculational techniques. The Representation of Algorithms contains within it an algorithm (Warshall's Algorithm) which plays a critical role in the translation process from a conventional sequential language to a highly concurrent net representation. However, the algorithm itself is derived from conventional graph mathematics rather than General Net Theory.

The difficulties involved in developing calculational techniques lie partially in the generality of net structures. Various restricted classes of nets have yielded significant results in this area (e.g. Marked Graphs). Unfortunately, modeling real problems using nets in these restricted classes has not proved so easy.

'Calculating Logical and Probabilistic Dependencies'[8], was the result of my efforts to develop a calculational tool applicable to nets which included both concurrency and choice, i.e. more general than a state machine or a marked graph. The class of nets was related to marked graphs by a straightforward mapping. It was also related to a Condition/Event system with 'conflicts' restricted to 'input' events. These C/E nets were 'live' and 'safe', but neither 'free-choice' nor 'simple'.

With a net was an associated set of boolean equations. These in turn generated a set of affine recurrence equations whose periodic solutions could be determined. However, the particular class of nets was very restrictive and has not occurred in any of the applications I have subsequently analyzed.

Useful calculational techniques for nets need to satisfy several requirements:

(1) They must be applicable to nets that arise in the context of actual systems, not special classes of nets invented because of their 'nice' properties.

(2) The computational effort must be reasonable, i.e. a significa improvement over enumerative approaches such as simulation.

I await these techniques. However, General Net Theory is of value without them, as what follows makes clear.

DESCRIPTIONS USING NET MORPHISMS

Subsequent to this effort I spent a considerable time studying the use of computers in agriculture. One outcome of this effort was an anaysis of the impact of computers in the U.S. dairy industry [9]. In the course of writing this analysis, I used nets and net morphisms as a pur ly descriptive tool. In other words, my purpose in using net-based description was strictly communicative with no expectation of other benefits such as 'interesting' calculational results. In my opinion this effort was quite successful.

DESIGN METHODOLOGY

At about the same time I utilized net morphisms, along with other concepts from General Net Theory, especially 'facts' [3], as the basis for a proposed Design Methodology for Information Systems [14]. This ap proach combined the descriptive effectiveness of Net Theory with calcul tional possibilities of a very different nature than those mentioned pr ously.

A design effort would begin by developing a formal description of t application requirements (what is to be done) which could serve, among other purposes, as a legally binding specification of what must be acco plished by the implementation. Successive refinements of this formal d scription would elaborate in detail how to meet the application require ments. At a sufficiently detailed level the description would serve as specification in the same manner as a flow chart specifies to a programmer what must be done, or a logical wiring diagram specifies to an engineer what must be built.

Having elaborated the design by this top-down approach, it would then be possible to prove (eventually by formal means involving calculation) that the design satisfies the application requirements. This would be accomplished by proceeding from the most detailed description (exactly how it is done) back up to the application requirements.

SYNCHRONIZATION AND RELIABILITY IN DISTRIBUTED DATABASES

Some of the descriptive techniques based on net morphisms were modified and used in the design and description of a reliability plan for a distributed database system [10,11,12,13]. A version of the system existed prior to the reliability study, precluding the possibility of following the Design Methodology described above. However, the inherently concurrent aspects of the existing system, involving multiple computing hosts sharing a common operating system and database, made the descriptive capabilities of General Net Theory particularly applicable. The ultimate value of using net theory was in:

(1) analyzing the problem
(2) formulating a solution
(3) communicating the solution to others, in particular the programmers responsible for implementing the reliability plan.

The descriptive form developed in the course of this effort seems particularly suited to the design of multiprocessing systems and provided the basis for an application of a significant part of the design methodology described previously. The approach defines a system in terms of a set of inter-related scenarios. A scenario itself is one or more closely related processes.

SCENARIO DESCRIPTION

(1) Scenarios are depicted as a set of clockfaces representing processes and accompanied by descriptive text. The text is organized on a per-process basis and keyed to the clockface for a

particular process by the use of clockface hour positions (e.g. one o'clock).

(2) All processes start at one o'clock and advance clockwise except when repetition is required as denoted by parenthesis and discussed in the accompanying text.

(3) Events are depicted as boxes distributed around the clockface and designated by hour and fraction of an hour. (The event at 3 is at 3 o'clock. 3.5 designates 3:30, etc.) An event denoted by a box with an "x" in it is termination of the process.

(4) Links connect events to inputs and outputs:

a) Arrows into an event depict inputs required for the event to take place and the process (clock) to advance. The source of the input is designated to aid in understanding the scenario.
b) Arrows out of an event depict output produced by the event. The destination of the output is indicated. Destination name includes, when appropriate, both the name of the process and when in that process the output is needed.
c) An undirected link serves as a shorthand for communication to another process and subsequent receipt of its reply.
d) An arrow or link connecting an event with names in the clockface center depicts an operation on the designated database or global resource, with arrow direction having the obvious meaning.
e) Links to processes in the interior of a clockface depict interactions with an internal subprocess. Exterior links depict interaction with external processes frequently (but not necessarily) running on a different computer host. Subprocesses always run on the same host as the process they are interior to. A subprocess may execute concurrently with its process, or act as an in-line subroutine. The clockface for the process specifies the manner of use of the subprocess.
f) A number on an arrow directed away from an event designates the setting of a timer on the event located at the clock position corresponding to the number (see 11 and 12).
g) A number on an arrow directed toward an event designates

the need to send timing signals to the process mentioned as an output of the event at the clock position designated by the number.

(5) A clockface name and clock position written next to an event indicate that event is identical to the designated event and joins two scenarios.

(6) Upon completion of an event, the process may advance to the next event.

(7) Occasionally, there will be several possible next events. This is depicted by the use of parentheses to denote optional groups of events. Parentheses are also used to denote possible repetition of a group of events. In that case, completion of the event immediately preceeding a closing parenthesis implies that the event immediately following the matching open parenthesis is a possible next event. When important for clarity, repetition possibilities may be explicitly designated by attaching an arrow head to a closing parenthesis and specifying the clock position of the matching open parenthesis. Possible number of repetitions may also be specified.

(8) Brackets are used to denote a choice of exactly one group of events from the parenthesized event groups within the brackets.

(9) When there are several possible next events, they are implicitly assigned priorities as a function of clockface position: the 'earlier' event has higher priority.

(10) When a process advances to an event which requires an input, the process input buffer is searched. (If there is more than one next possible event, search order is determined by the priority assignments in (9).

If an input is found, it is removed from the buffer and the corresponding event takes place. Otherwise, the process is quiescent until the process input buffer receives another input.

The input buffer is created and cleared when the process is initiated. The input buffer is released when the process terminates.

(11) There are three types of input:

a) A message, either from another process or from some host--local activity such as probing a database or accessing a global.
b) A timing signal, which is a substitute message and indicates that the source of the timing signal is attempting to complete tasks that are prerequisites for the message.
c) A timeout, which is a substitute message and indicates that neither the message nor a timing signal arrived within the time allotted.

(12) A timeout is caused by a communication failure (lost message or very slow message) or a crash or an aborted process. The appropriate remedial action is indicated in the description of the scenario.

USING SCENARIOS

In the past few months I have designed the application software for a multiprocessor system based on scenario descriptions. The steps in the design process were as follows:

(1) Produce a description of the hardware base, clearly delineating the different computer hosts.

(2) Produce high level scenarios that include the functional requirements of the application.

(3) Produce a detailed design by recursion:

a) A process at any level invokes subprocesses. These in turn are described. Stop when the implementation of a subprocess is sufficiently obvious that it need not be broken down any further.

b) Processes communicate with other processes. The details of communication are defined in the course of (3a) and in turn affect the scenarios. Communication includes:
   1) Communication with the human USER.
   2) Communication with processes on other HOSTS.
   3) Communication between superior and inferior processes on the same HØST.

c) Processes use data structures and globals. These are defined in the course of (3a) and affect the details as consideration of available resources (such as space, processing bandwidth) are introduced.

A design document is then produced for each type of host. This document has the following form:

(1) Scenario
  a) Overview
  b) Brief Descriptions
(2) Global variables
(3) Tables
(4) Communications with the USER
(5) Communications with other HOSTS
(6) Scenario Cross-Reference
(7) Scenario invocation arguments and resource utilization
(8) Scenario Detailed Description

The scenario overview is produced by a mechanical procedure. A single diagram is produced by a net morphism which maps the highest level scenari and all subprocesses invoked by it, to a level of two or three deep, into a 'role/activity' oriented diagram.

The brief descriptions are 1 to 5 line informal verbal descriptions of what each scenario accomplishes, organized by lexical order of the scenari names.

The Global Variables section is a brief discussion of each global vari able, giving its structure and purpose. Organized by lexical order of the global variable names.

The Tables section is a brief discussion of each table, giving its structure and purpose. Organized by lexical order of the Table names.

Communications with the USER describes all user dialogs, giving a detailed description of the structure of each dialog and the scenarios in which it occurs. Organized by lexical order of the Communication dialog name.

Communications with other HOSTS describes all inter-host dialogs, giving a detailed description of the structure of each dialog and the scenarios in which it occurs. Organized by lexical order of the Communication dialog names.

Scenario Cross-Reference is a mechanically produced matrix which displays for each scenario all the scenarios which it invokes as well a all the scenarios which invoke it.

Scenario Invocation Arguments and Resource Utilization describes fo each scenario the form of the arguments it expects when invoked and the names and mode of use of all globals and tables. Organized by lexical order of the scenario names.

Scenario Detailed Description consists of two pages for each scenari organized by lexical order of scenario names. The first page is a grap description of the scenario, using the clockface technique discussed pr viously. The second page is brief accompanying text which includes a d cussion of arguments of invocation, alternative event choices, and fail possibilities.

AUTOMATING THE DESIGN METHODOLOGY

In the course of doing the software design I observed what fraction of my time was required for various tasks and how mechanical they were. Some of the tasks were completely mechanical and could have been perfor by a computer with no human interaction. Some of the tasks were mostly mechanical and computer assistance would have speeded them up by a sign ficant factor. Some of the tasks were primarily creative. Much of the editing and revising, which all told took more time than anything else, was completely mechanical. From a productivity point of view there is no doubt that a set of automated tools could have reduced the design ti by a factor of 2 to 5.

Automated assistance falls into two categories:

(1) Procedures which involve no breakthroughs in terms of notation, calculational techniques, proofs.

(2) Procedures which require a sophisticated algorithmic basis, such as proofs of correctness in the spirit of 'facts', 'violations', and so forth.

I would like to focus on the first category. In the sequel I will describe an imaginary design session, using suitable computer equipment and software to assist in the production of a design document.

THE HARDWARE BASE FOR AUTOMATED DESIGN

The following components would be adequate for an automated design tool:

(1) CRT Display capable of presenting a full page of text, with some graphic capability (i.e. the ability to draw boxes and circles of various sizes, containing text).

(2) A light pen or sensitized tablet to facilitate positioning of displayed graphics and text.

(3) Two flexible disk drives (8 inch diskettes).

(4) Microcomputer with 64 Kbytes of memory.

Hardcopy output could either be included in the basic ADT (Automated Design Tool) or associated with other equipment. Diskettes prepared by the ADT could contain the already formatted output. In any case, two types of hardcopy would be desirable: relatively low quality (electrostatic) reproduction and typesetter quality, final design document.

This ADT is a stand-alone device. It could equally well be a work station of a multiprocessor system with a large shared database, or a conventional time-shared computer. I prefer to think of it as a piece of equipment much like a word-processor, perhaps even an optional package associated with an existing word processor.

USING THE ADT

The specification of a scenario is the major design input provided by the human user. The ADT would guide the designer through this process, perform basic syntactic verification, relate the process names, global names, table names, and message names to an existing and growin database for the particular design project. New names would require cc roboration; the use of existing names would imply requirements on arguments of call, message formats, etc. During the specification of a scenario the designer might want to look at other scenarios already defined, or information about the other entities in the system. Editing of the scenario would be automated, with any alterations producing a se of changes that would be propagated throughout the design database.

The ADT would maintain and produce upon demand the various cross-references and lexically ordered lists. All text in the entire design would be stored in the database and available for editing. The formal names in the text and diagrams would be accessible via various retrieva paths, and easily modified. Upon request the ADT would analyze the des for various types of completeness and consistency and conduct a dialogu with the designer. In this way, the ADT would guarantee that all scena that are not 'terminal' are defined; that the design has a sensible top logy; that patterns of usage of globals and tables makes sense, etc. U request the ADT would construct top-down overviews, starting at any lev with user assistance on depth pruning, positioning of text on the scree etc. Upon request the ADT would guide the designer through an error an sis, requiring specification of error alternatives at all places where munications take place, to deal with message loss, timeouts, failure of other hosts, etc.

During the design process the ADT would on demand produce hardcopy examination by the designers and other people on the project, including other designers, the customer, etc. Changes in the design caused by re sion of functional requirements or other causes, would be entered on th ADT using the editing facility. Automatically updated documentation wc always be available on demand.

When the design is complete, the high quality hardcopy design document would be run off, complete with date and release specifications. Subsequent changes in the design would be accomplished using the ADT, with the standard procedures for issuing new releases with cover sheets enumerating all changed sheets, inserted or deleted sheets, etc. Thus, the ADT would continue to assist in keeping the documentation up-to-date.

In addition, the ADT would function as communication device in explaining a design. The hardcopy document is a useful and necessary object, but in the process of implementing the design, a computer-aided retrieval mechanism that can rapidly display any scenario, related groups of processes, text descriptions and so forth greatly facilitates the implementation itself. An extended ADT could permit the editing and storage of computer programs using the FORMAL entities in the design as subroutine names, data object names, etc. in the program and thereby help maintain the correspondence between the high-level design document and the detailed implementation.

A SOPHISTICATED ADT

The ADT capabilities discussed so far require no breakthroughs in methodology, software or hardware. I would like to suggest a few more advanced capabilities:

(1) Guided simulation. The ADT, interacting with the designer, walks through the scenarios, allowing the use of dynamic or stored responses in all dialogs and process invocations and permitting the overall flow of the system design to be examined.

(2) Guided verification. The ADT, interacting with the designer, proceeding from the lowest level scenarios (most detailed), establishes the guaranteed properties of the system, using 'facts', 'violations', etc.

(3) Guided design of failure recovery. The ADT, interacting with the designer, enumerates failure situations in multi-host scenarios in order to arrive at a robust design.

(4) Guided timing estimates. The ADT, using time estimates for the lowest level scenarios, establishes time estimates for high-level functions.

THE VALUE OF GENERAL NET THEORY IN APPLIED WORK

For me personally, General Net Theory is first and foremost a descriptive tool. From this perspective it is essential to make use of various levels of description, related by net mappings. To do this eas in an application context requires practice. When it becomes second nature to view a complicated system in terms of the primitives of net the the utility presents itself. Whether significant calculational tools c be developed that are unique to this domain, remains to be seen. In my opinion, insufficient attention has been given to more modest calculati which take advantage of the formal basis to enhance the descriptive val of nets.

ACKNOWLEDGEMENTS

While the contents of this paper are entirely my responsibility, th ideas have a long history and it seems appropriate to mention the peopl primarily responsible for introducing them to me. Anatol Holt has been a colleague for many years and first introduced me to graphical represe tions for the description of systems. The work of Carl Adam Petri has provided the basic representational form for much of my own work. Fina Hartmann Genrich has helped me understand and apply various concepts fr General Net Theory.

APPENDIX ONE: THE REPRESENTATION OF ALGORITHMS

The Basic Schemata

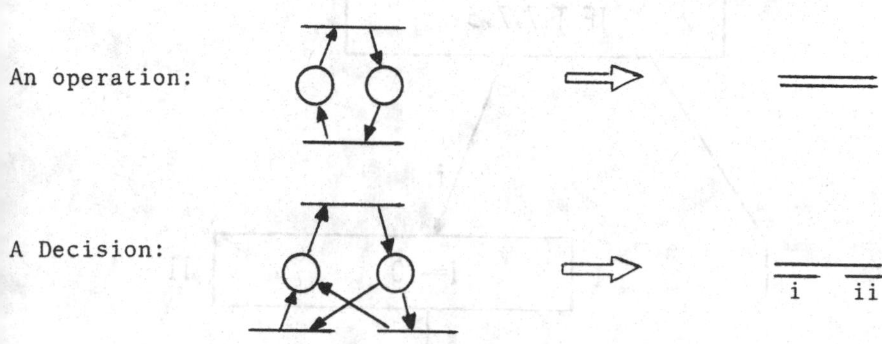

Generation and use of a result:

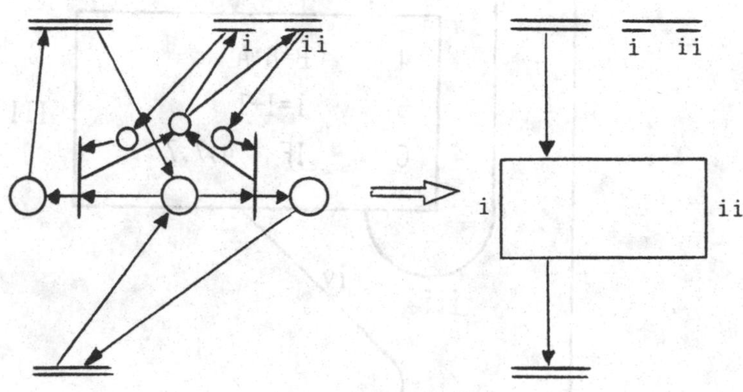

Decision outcome ii enables one use
Decision outcome i frees resource for next generation.

If at least one use after generation is guaranteed, rectangle has diagonal line in upper right corner:

If at most one use after generation, rectangle has diagonal line in lower left corner :

A Sample Algorithm to be Translated

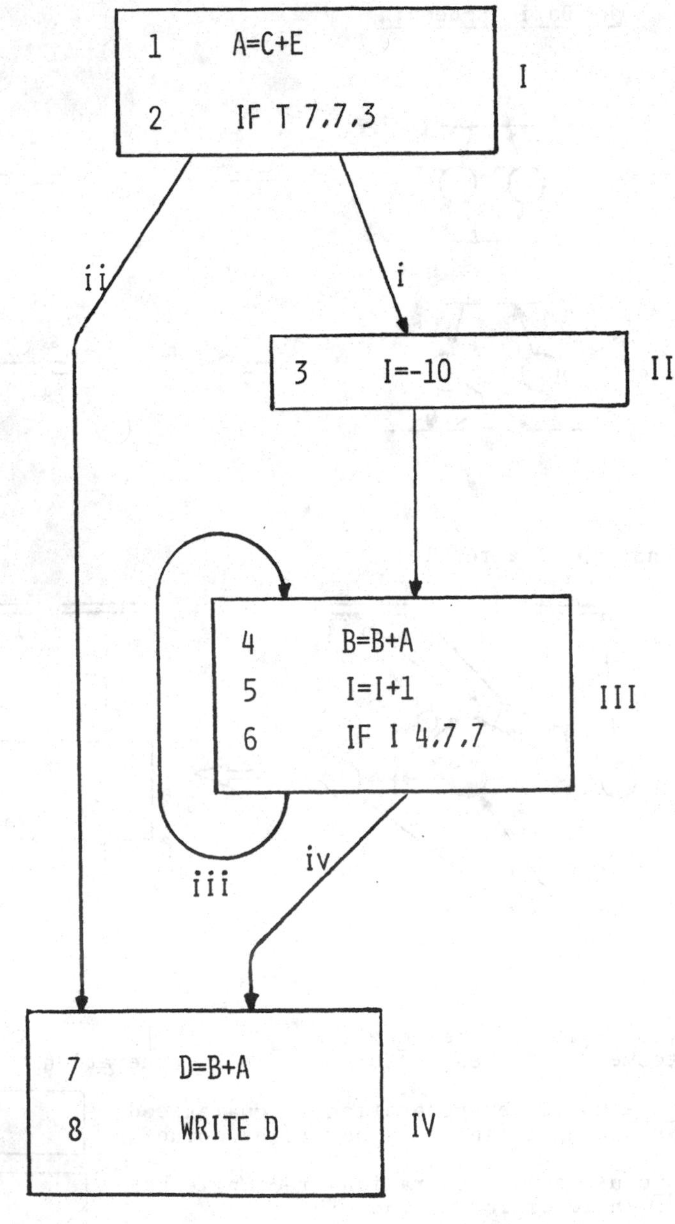

AN ANALYSIS OF THE VARIABLES USING WARSHALL'S ALGORITHM

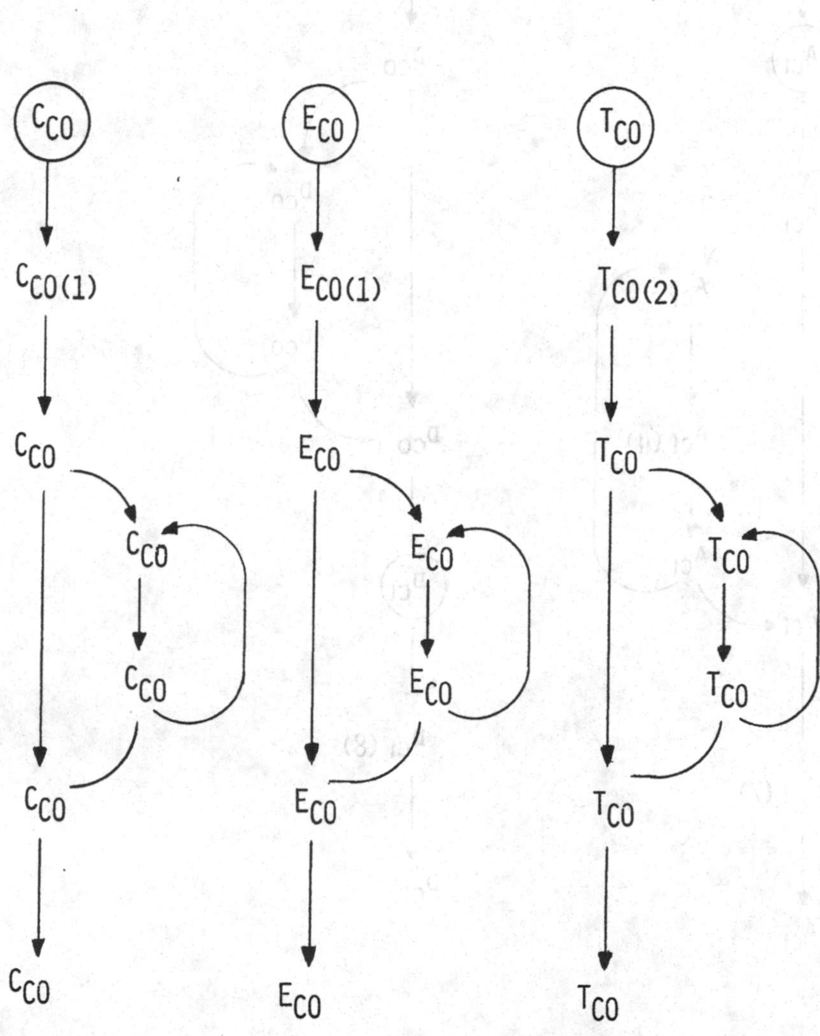

(CONTINUED):

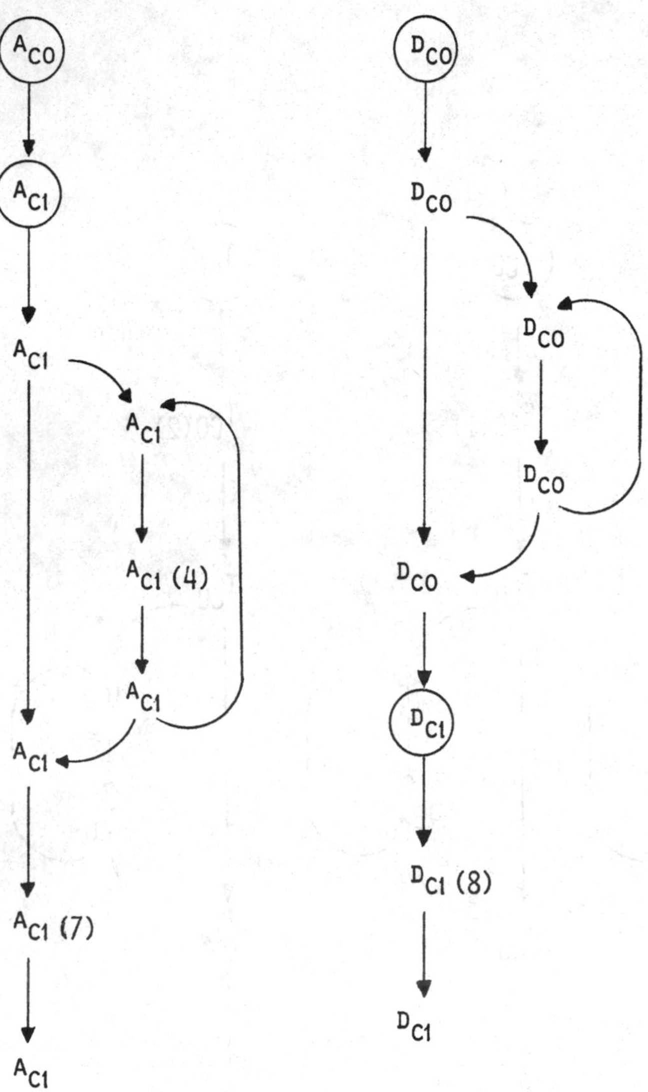
A_{C0}
A_{C1}
A_{C1}
A_{C1}
A_{C1} (4)
A_{C1}
A_{C1}
A_{C1} (7)
A_{C1}
D_{C0}
D_{C0}
D_{C0}
D_{C0}
D_{C0}
D_{C1}
D_{C1} (8)
D_{C1}

(CONTINUED)

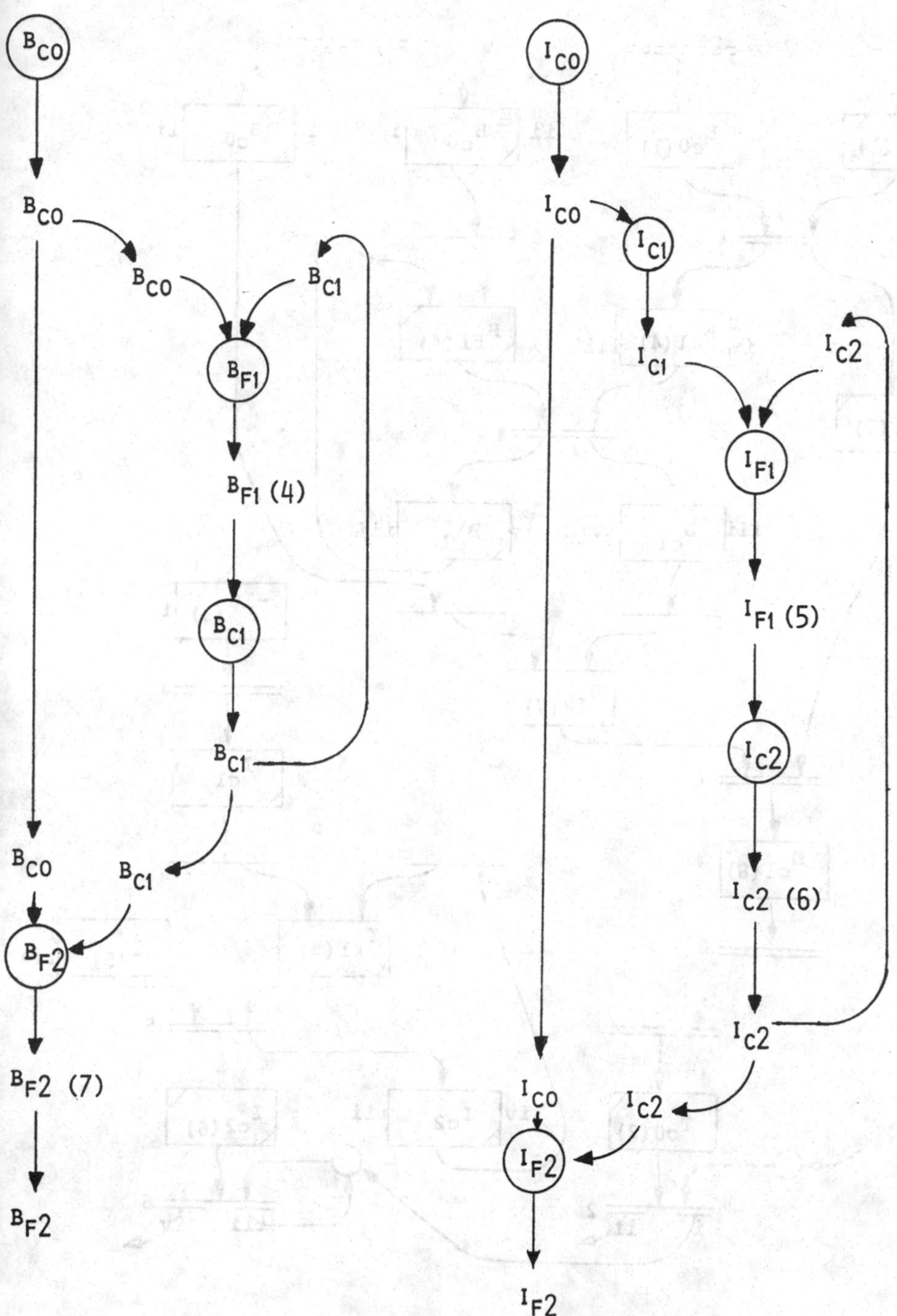
B_{C0}
B_{C0}
B_{C0}
B_{C1}
B_{F1}
B_{F1} (4)
B_{C1}
B_{C1}
B_{C0}
B_{C1}
B_{F2}
B_{F2} (7)
B_{F2}
I_{C0}
I_{C0}
I_{C1}
I_{C1}
I_{c2}
I_{F1}
I_{F1} (5)
I_{c2}
I_{c2} (6)
I_{c2}
I_{C0}
I_{c2}
I_{F2}
I_{F2}

The Translated Representation of the Algorithm

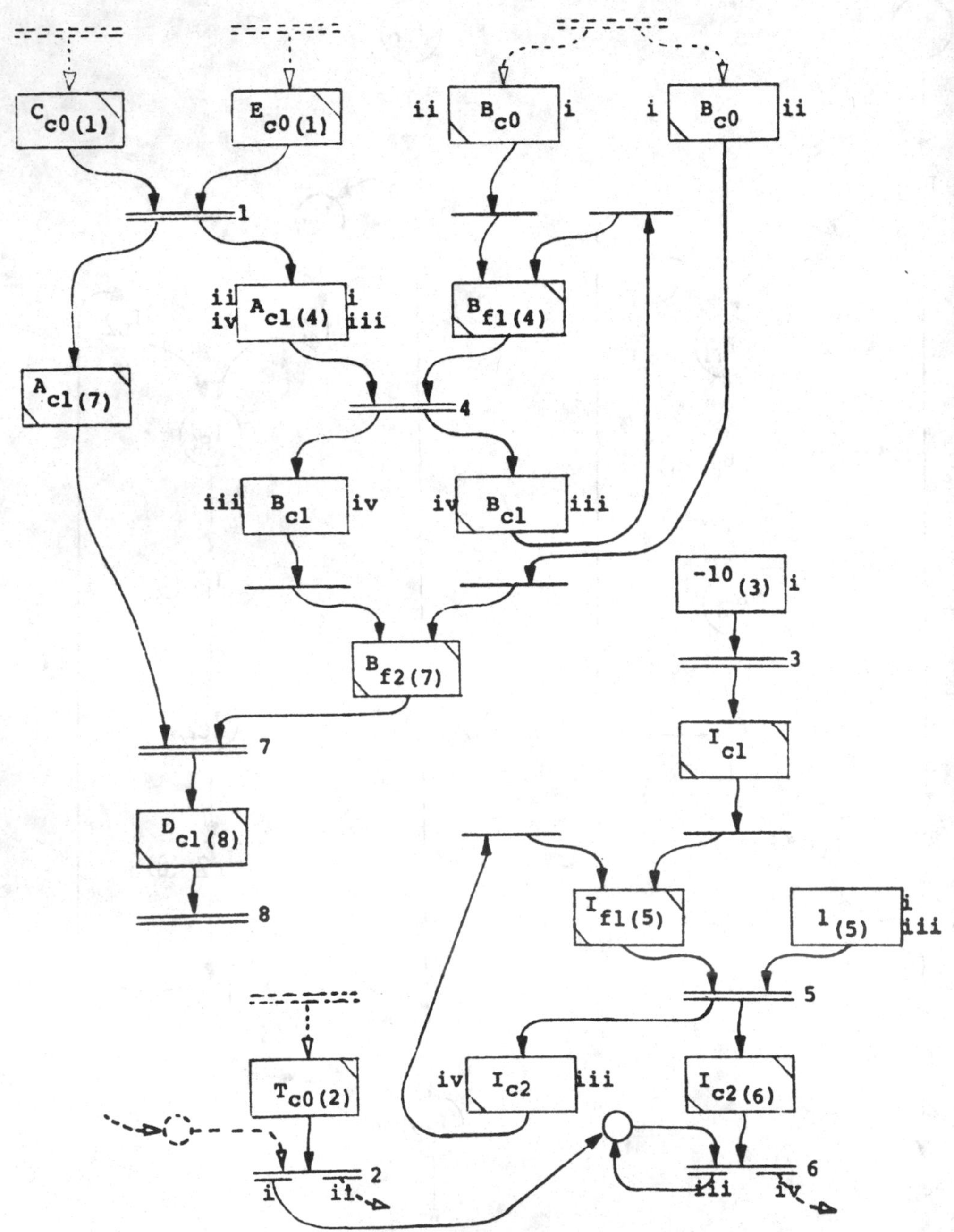

APPENDIX TWO: DESCRIPTIONS USING NET MORPHISMS

(1) The boxes represent activities of exchange, material and/or informational, between a set of participating agents. An inscription in a box designates the frequency with which that particular activity takes place (D/2 = twice a day, M = monthly, Q = quarterly, SA = semi-annually).

(2) The circles represent agents in their capacity to participate in the activities to which they are linked: the farmer, the herd, the milk storage system, a data processing form and so forth. Sometimes the names are chosen to stress the material or informational aspect of the agent. Sometimes the links are directed to stress the direction of flow of material of information.

(3) The pattern □:—Ⓧ specifies the possibility of more than one agent of type X connected to the activity. Similarly, the pattern Ⓧ:—□ specifies the possibility of more than one activity with the same exchange structure, connected to an agent of type X.

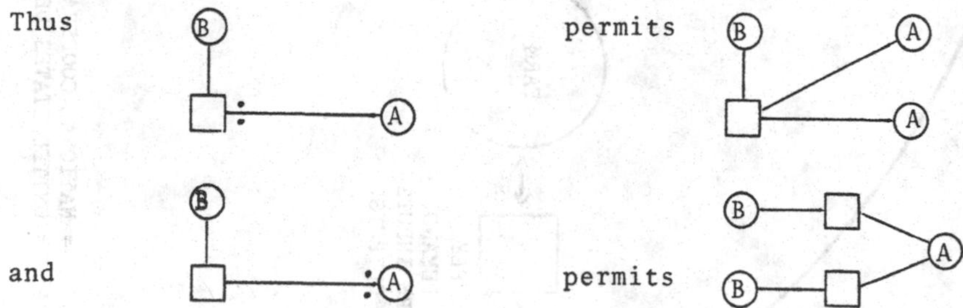

(4) The pictures portray several levels of detail. These levels are related by topological mappings known as net morphisms. A discussion of the formal basis for net description can be found in [3] .

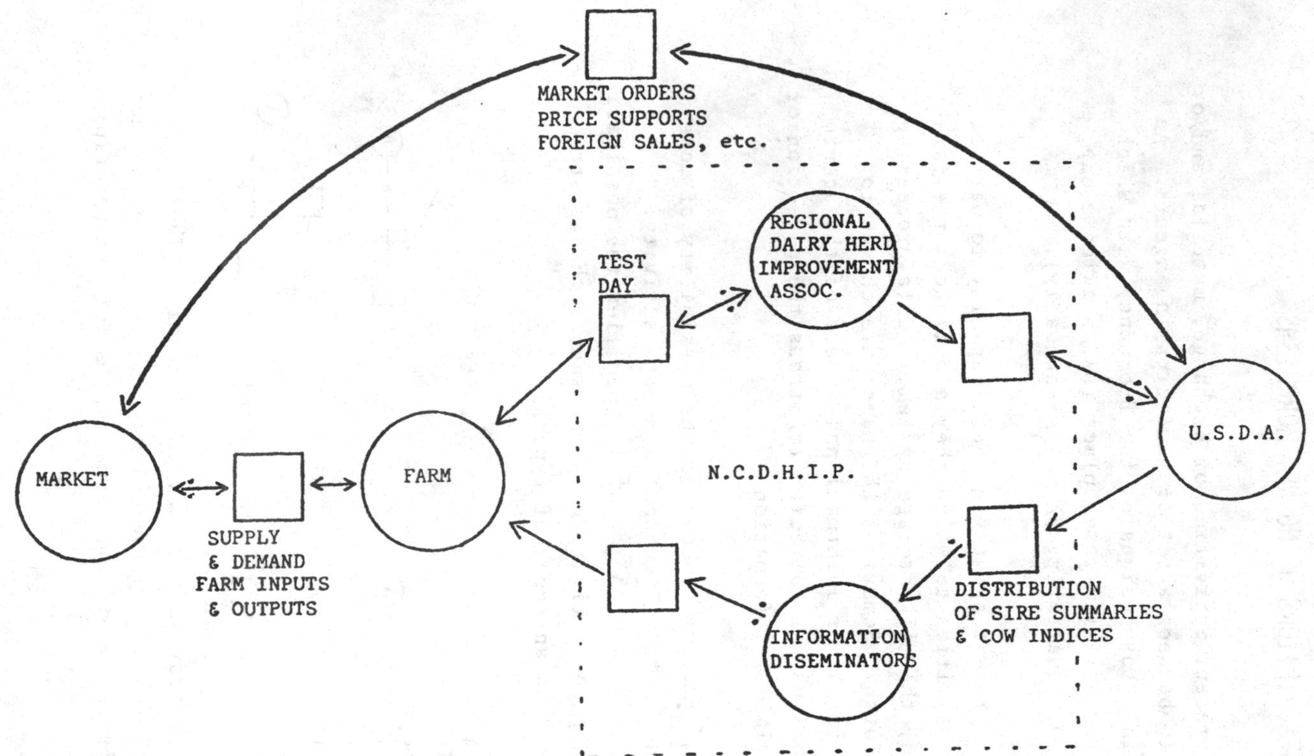

NCDHIP = NATIONAL COOPERATIVE DAIRY HERD IMPROVEMENT PROGRAM
USDA = UNITED STATES DEPARTMENT OF AGRICULTURE

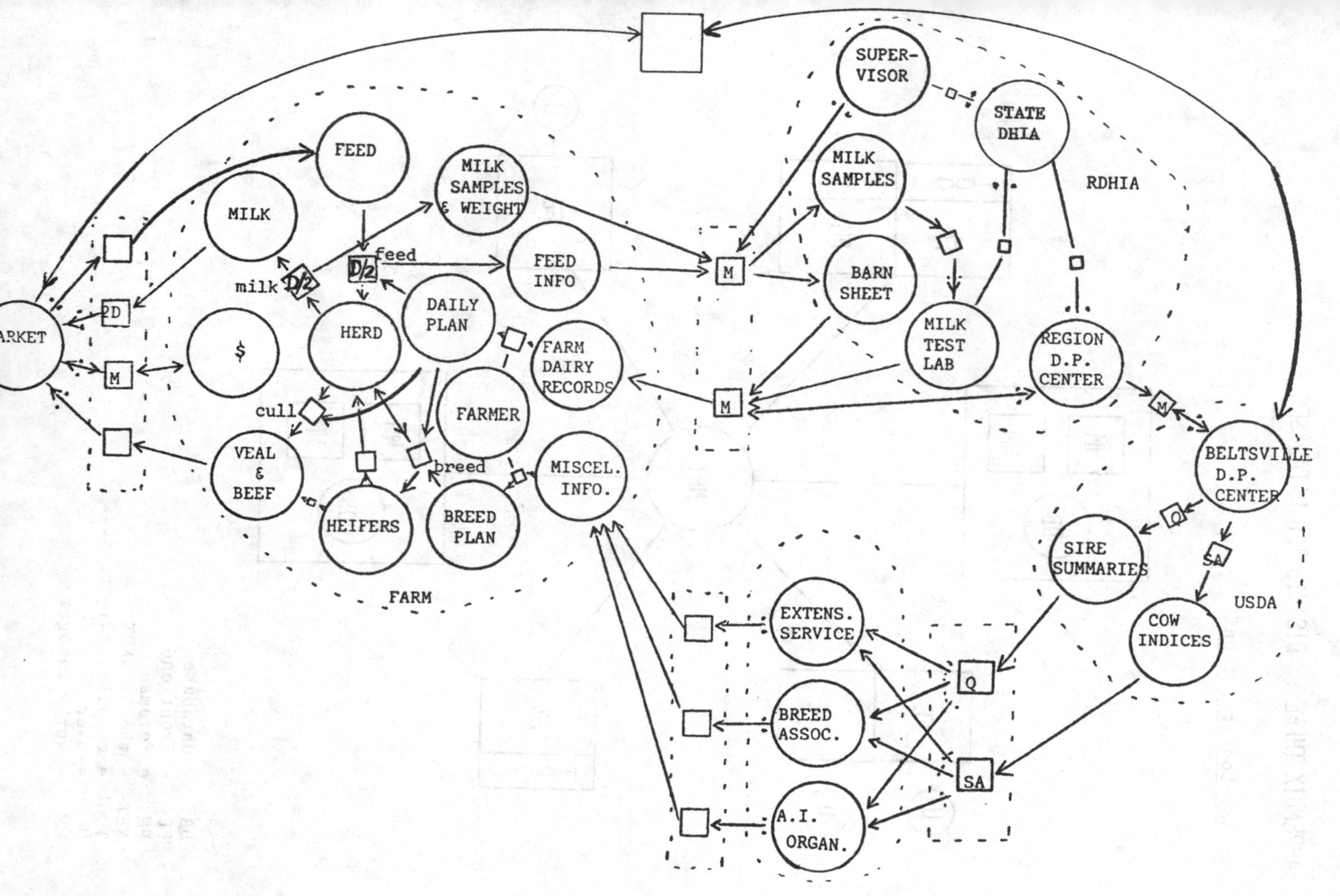

SUPER-VISOR
STATE DHIA
RDHIA
MILK SAMPLES
BARN SHEET
MILK TEST LAB
REGION D.P. CENTER
BELTSVILLE D.P. CENTER
USDA
SIRE SUMMARIES
COW INDICES
Q
SA
EXTENS. SERVICE
BREED ASSOC.
A.I. ORGAN.
M
FEED
MILK
MILK SAMPLES & WEIGHT
FEED INFO
DAILY PLAN
HERD
$
FARM DAIRY RECORDS
FARMER
MISCEL. INFO.
VEAL & BEEF
HEIFERS
BREED PLAN
FARM
feed
milk
cull
breed
D/2
D
MARKET

APPENDIX THREE : DISTRIBUTED DATABASES

An NSW Configuration

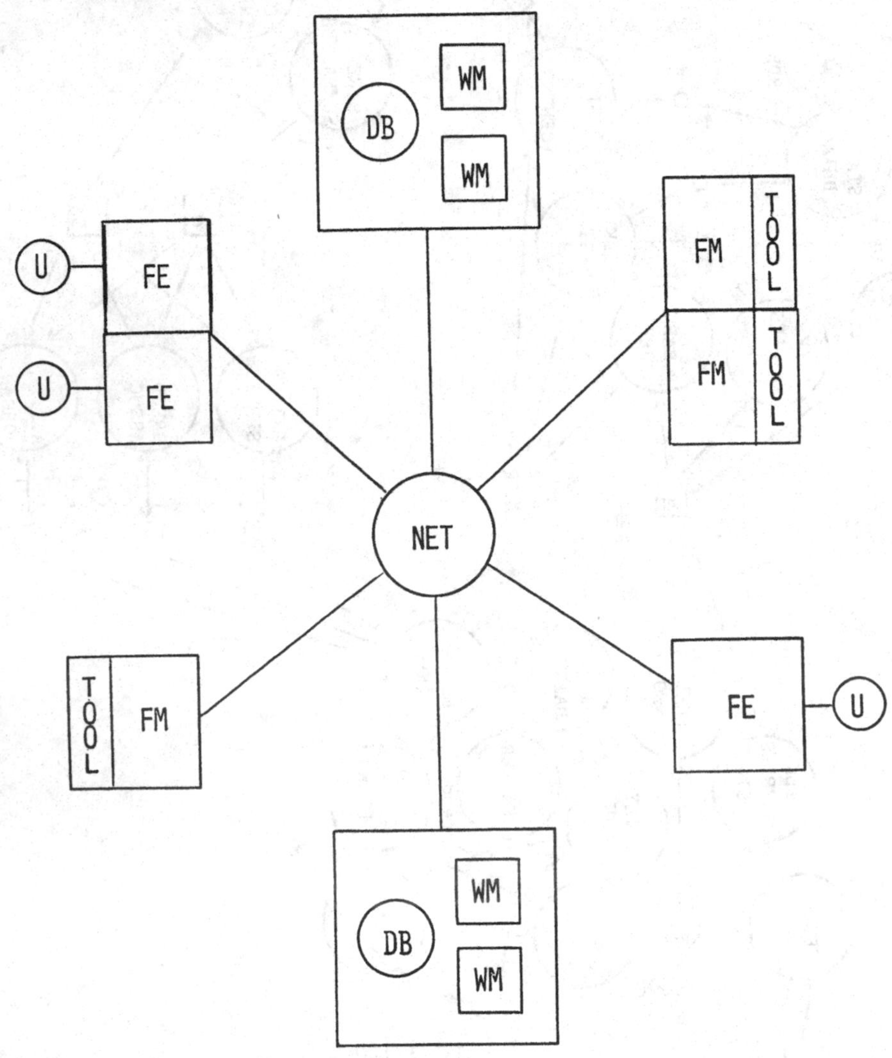

DB = database
FE = front end
FM = foreman
NET = the ARPANET
TOOL = compiler,editor,etc.
U = user
WM = works manager

FE/WM/FM 8/25/79 SCENARIO Brief Descriptions

RUNTOOL

When a user tries to run a tool, FEcontrol initiates an FEruntool scenario. If the RUNTOOL is successful, FEruntools becomes FEtoolrunning. Another outcome of success is the creation of an FMcontrol process.

The Works Manager verifies that the user has access to the tool. It creates an instance of the tool process by sending a generic message to a suitable Tool Bearing Host. The Foreman process created on that host is responsible for establishing the connection between the Foreman/tool and the Front End. The Works Manager process returns to the Front End the process name of the Foreman/tool.

A SAMPLE DOCUMENT

RUNTOOL SCENARIO

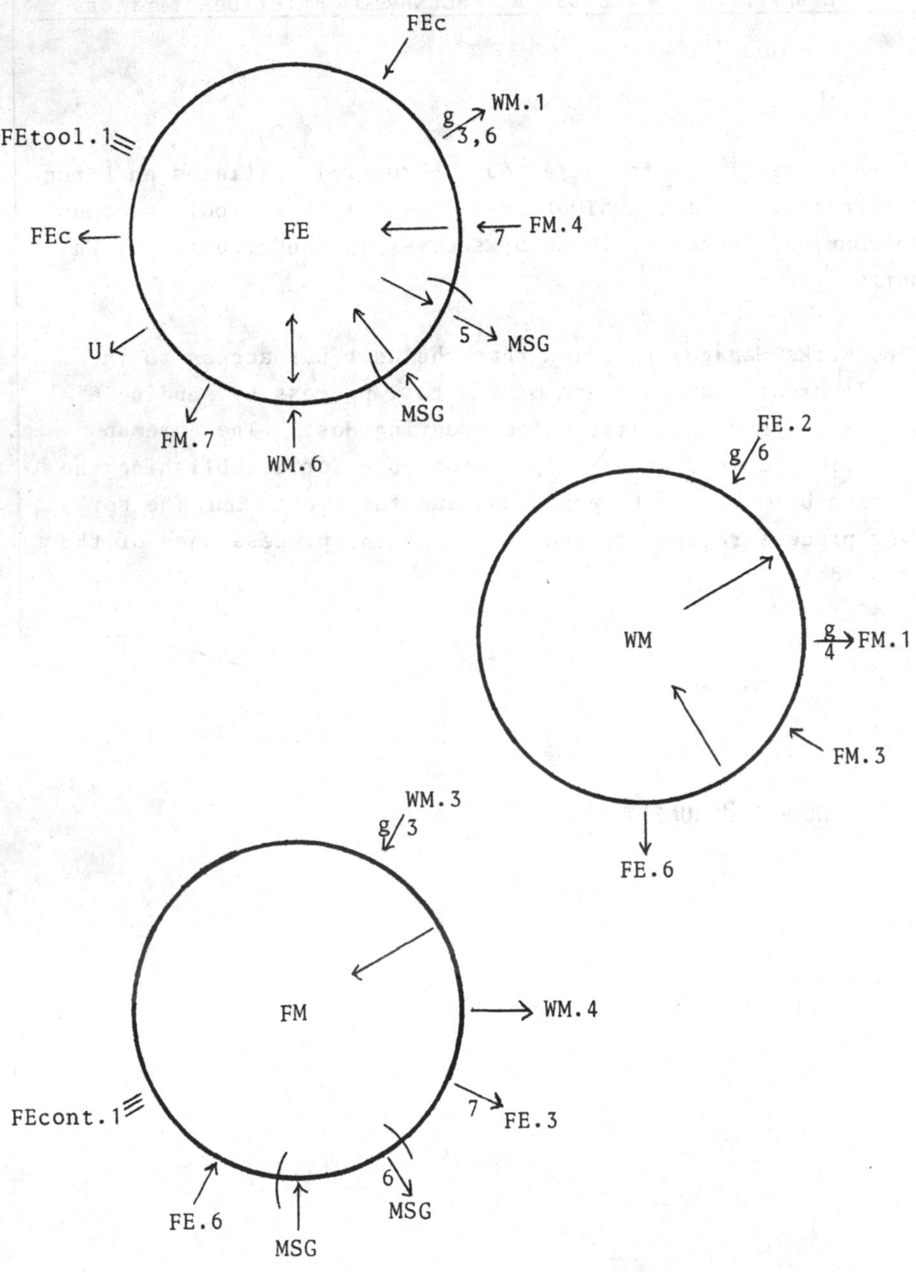

	FE		8/25/79		RUNTOOL	

FEcontrol starts Runtool scenario.	1	FEc	-
Call WM-RUNTOOL. Timers set on Foreman response at 3 and Works Manager response at 6.	2	-	WM.1
Receive message from Foreman. Success: Front End records name of Foreman process and indication of wether a direct connection is required. Error: None. Timeout: Recorded but no other action is required until the response from Works Manager at 6.	3	FM.4	DB
If required, Front End attemps to establish a direct connection by calling MSG.	4	DB	MSG
Response from MSG. Success: Front End updates local status information on tool. Error, timeout: Front End takes no special action for a timeout because it is the Foreman's responsibility to maintain the connection. Timer is restarted for response at 3.	5	MSG	DB
Return from WM-RUNTOOL. Success: This includes the specific name of the Foreman. Verify that this name agrees with the name of the Foreman from which the message at 3 was received. If not, log error and retry at 2. If the Foreman response at 3 times out, the Front End must retry at 2. Error: If a connectionwas established, break it. Prepare a suitable message for user and abandon and scenario. Timeout: If a connection has been established, break it. Retry at 2.	6	WM.6	DB
Send go-ahead message to Foreman.	7	-	FM.7
Send response to user.	8	-	U
FEcontrol informed of RUNTOOL success or error.	9		
If RUNTOOL were successful, this process becomes FEtoolrunning at clock position 1.	10		

	WM		8/25/79		RUNTOOL		
Receive call on WM-RUNTOOL.					1	FE.2	-
The user's rights are verified, and the tool descriptor located. If there are any problems, prepare error return and go to 6.					2	DB	-
Call FM-BEGINTOOL.					3	-	FM.1
Return from FM-BEGINTOOL. Success: Return includes specific name of Foreman and workspace identification. Error: Various error possibilities. Prepare error message; proceed to 6. Timeout: Choose another potential host for the tool and retry at 3. If all potential hosts are exhausted, the Works Manager prepares error return at 6.					4	FM.3	-
Information in Foreman return stored in Data Base.					5	-	DB
Send WM-RUNTOOL return.					6	-	FE.6

	FM		8/25/79		RUNTOOL		
Receive call on FM-BEGINTOOL.					1	WM.3	FM.1
Foreman establishes workspace, tool instance, etc.					2	-	DB
Send FM-BEGINTOOL response.					3	-	WM.4
Send message to the Front End to establish connection.					4	DB	FE.3
If a direct connection is required, Foreman calls MGS.					5	DB	MSG
MGS return. Success: Connection is established. Error: Similar to timeout. Timeout: Resend message at 4. If this does not succeed, Foreman logs error and disappears.					6	MSG	DB
Go-ahead message from Front End. Success: Nothing irrevocable should be preformed by the tool until this signal is received. Error: None. Timeout: If this response times out, try again at 4. If that does not succeed, log error and disappear.					7	FE.6	-
This is now the FMcontrol scenario at 1.					8		

APPENDIX FOUR: DISPLAY AD SYSTEM

Equipment Overview

TEE = Text Entry and Editing
CAM = Composition and Makeup

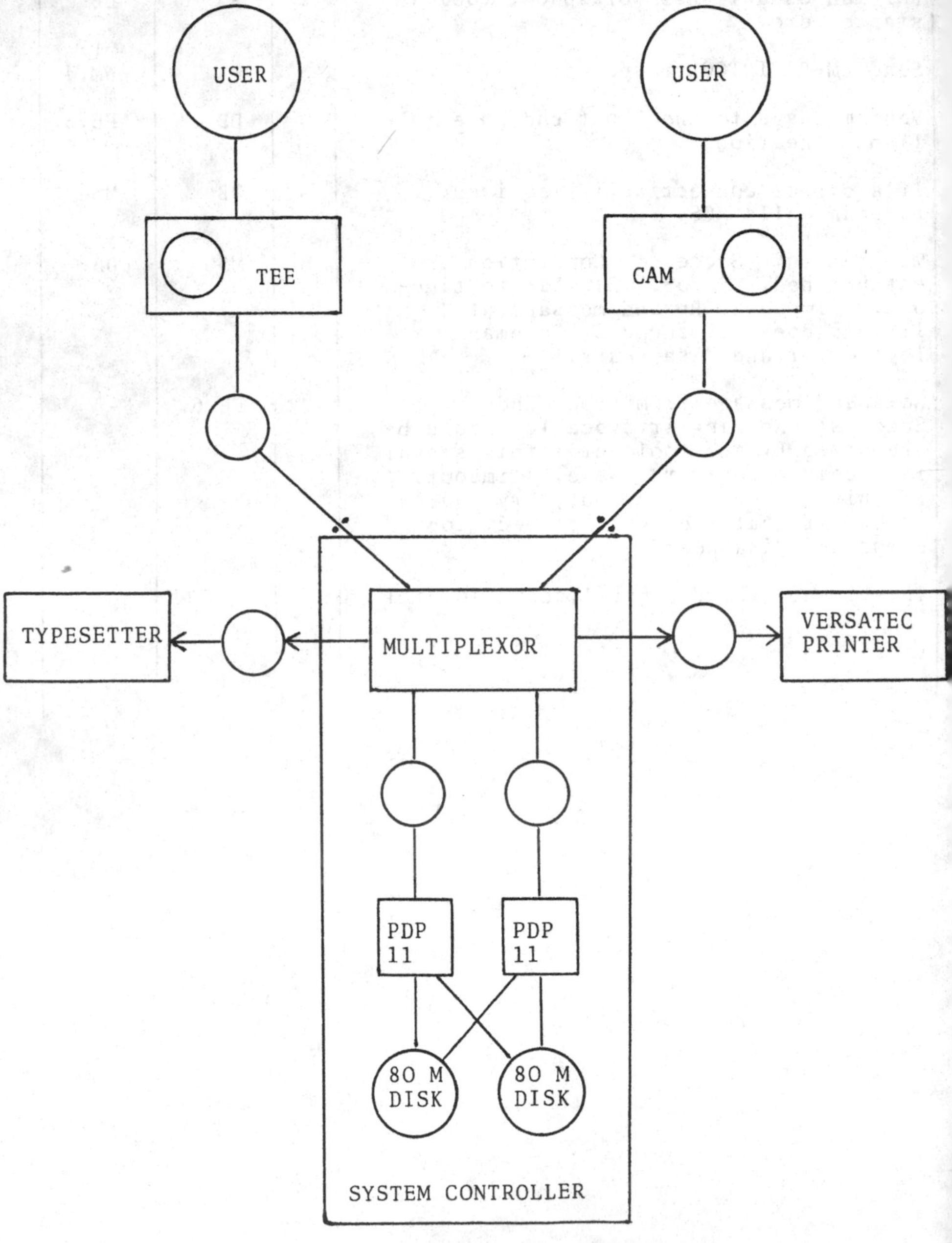

USER
USER
TEE
CAM
TYPESETTER
MULTIPLEXOR
VERSATEC PRINTER
PDP 11
PDP 11
80 M DISK
80 M DISK
SYSTEM CONTROLLER

Information Flow

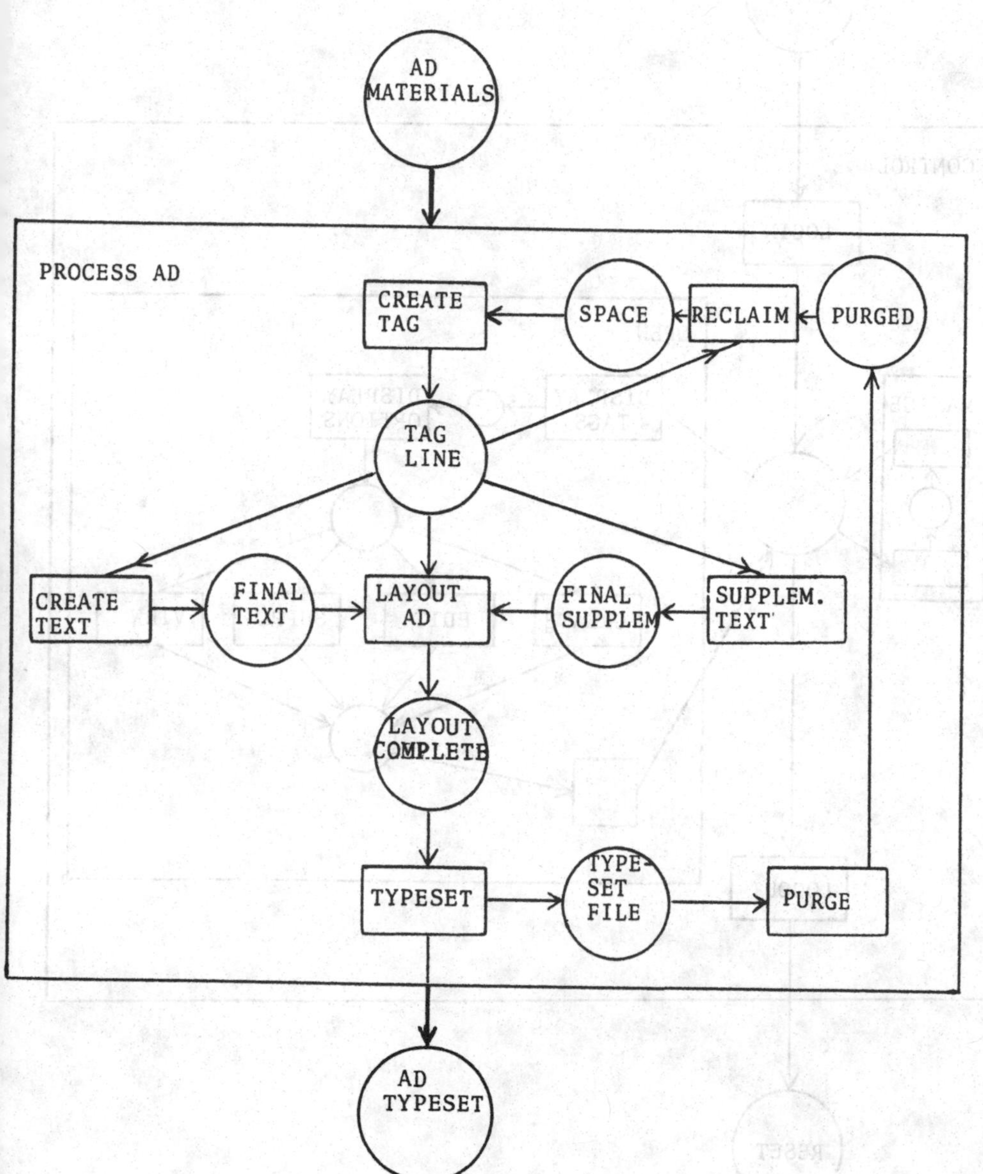

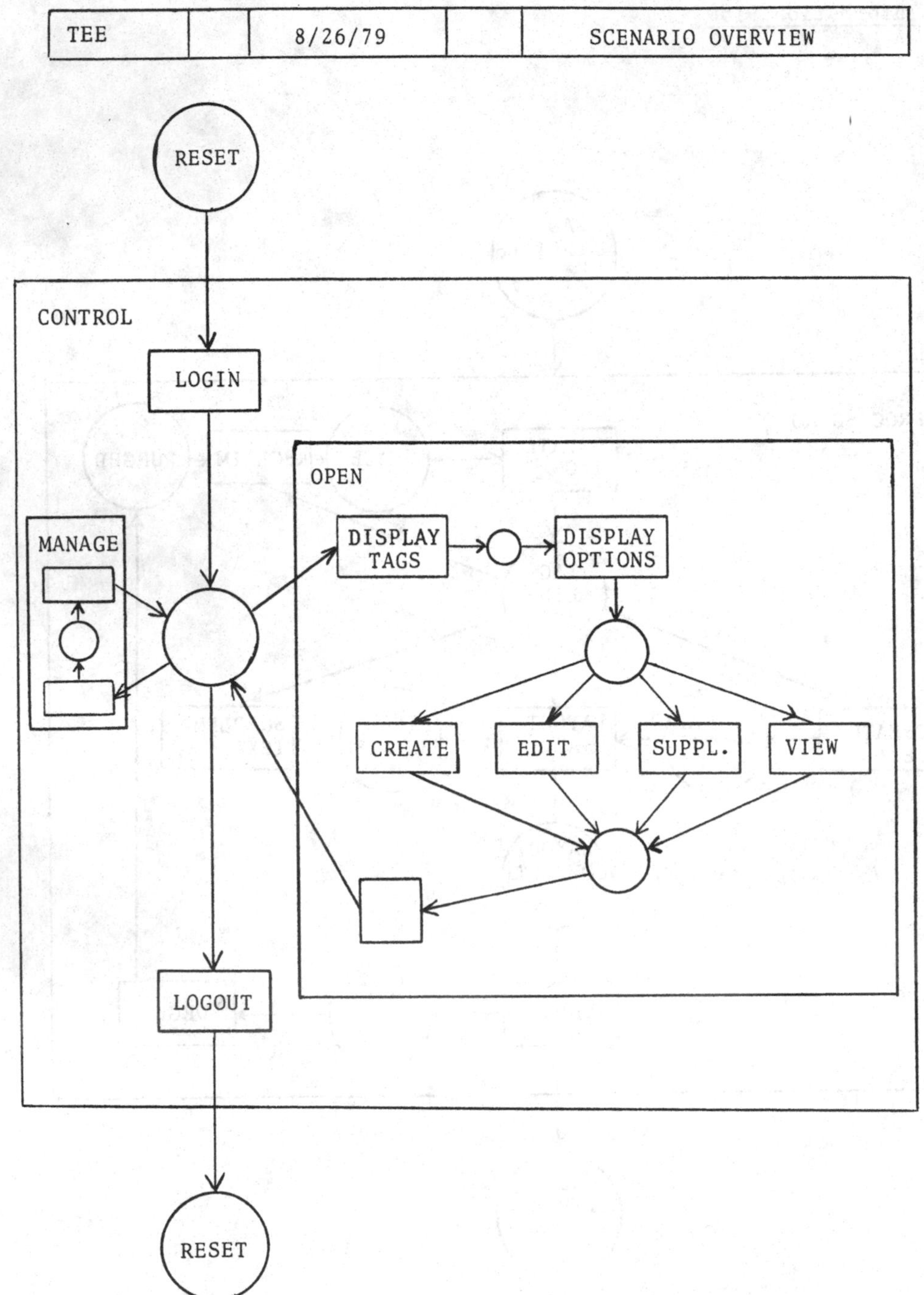
TEE
8/26/79
SCENARIO OVERVIEW
RESET
CONTROL
LOGIN
MANAGE
OPEN
DISPLAY TAGS
DISPLAY OPTIONS
CREATE
EDIT
SUPPL.
VIEW
LOGOUT
RESET

TEE/CAM

CREATE

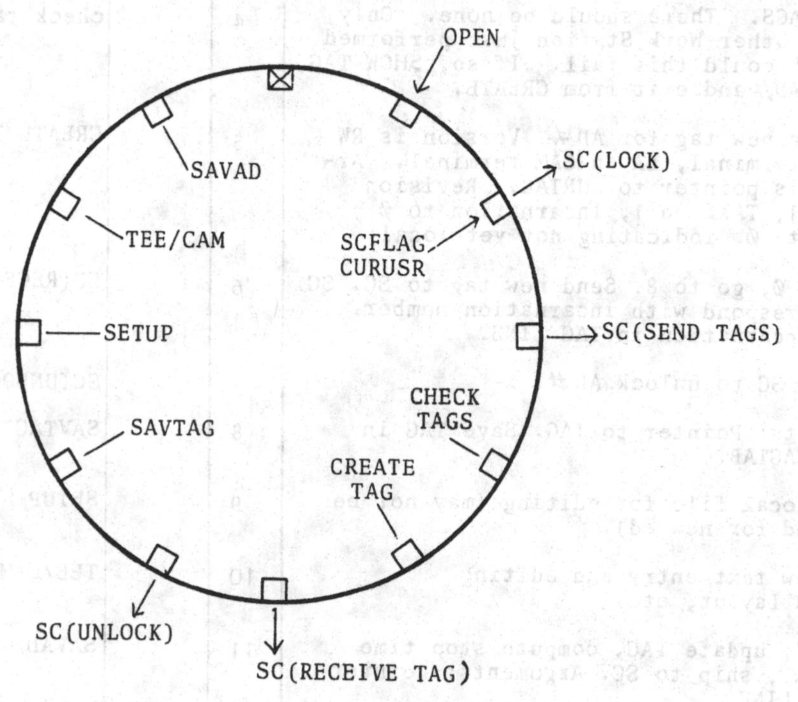

	TEE/CAM		7/23/79		CREATE

Description	Step		
Initiated from OPEN. Argument is pointer to TAG LINE.	1	OPEN	
If SCFLAG = Ø go to 5. Request SC to LOCK AD #. If lockrequest is rejected, inform User and display name of User who holds the LOCK. Wait for User ack, then terminate CREATE.	2	SCFLAG CURUSR	SC(LOCK)
Request all TAGS for this AD #. TAGS go in TAG BUFFER.	3		SC(SEND TAG)
CHECK TAGS. There should be none. Only if some other Work Station just performed a CREATE could this fail. If so, SHOW TAG, unlock AD# and exit from CREATE.	4		check tags
CREATE a new tag for AD #. Version is RW on TEE terminal, LA on CAM terminal. Argument is pointer to CURTAG. Revision set to 1, TAKE to 1, Incarnation to Ø, CURFIL to Ø, indicating not yet local.	5		CREATE TAG
If SC = Ø, go to 8. Send new tag to SC. SC should respond with incarnation number. Store incarnation in TAG LINE.	6		SC(RECEIVE)
Request SC to unlock AD #.	7		SC(UNLOCK)
Arguments: Pointer to TAG. Save TAG in local TAGTAB.	8		SAVTAG
Setup local file for editing (may not be required for new ad).	9		SETUP
TEE: Raw text entry and editing CAM: Ad Layout, etc.	10		TEE/CAM
Save Ad, update TAG, compute stop time for STAT, ship to SC. Arguments: Pointer to TAG LINE.	11		SAVAD

Error Conditions

2. If no response, reset SCFLAG, warn user, go to 5.
3. If no response, reset SCFLAG, warn user, go to 5.
6. If no response, reset SCFLAG, warn user, go to 8.
7. If no response, reset SCFLAG, warn user, go to 8.

REFERENCES

1. Holt, A.W., et al. : Information System Theory Project, Volume 1, Princeton : Applied Data Research, Inc., AD 626819 (1965)

2. Holt, A.W., et al. : Information System Theory Project, Final Report, Princeton : Applied Data Research, Inc. AD 676972 (1968)

3. Petri, C.A., : Interpretations of Net Theory, St. Augustin : Gesellschaft für Mathematik und Datenverarbeitung Bonn, Interner Bericht ISF-75-07 (1975)

4. Shapiro, R.M., Saint, H. : A New Approach to Optimization of Sequencing Decisions, In : Ann. Rev. of Automatic Programming 6, no. 5, pp. 257-288, (1970)

5. Shapiro, R.M., Saint, H. : The Representation of Algorithms, New York : Applied Data Research, Inc. AD 697026 (1969)

6. Shapiro, R.M., Saint, H. : The Representation of Algorithms as Cyclic Partial Orderings, New York : Meta Information Applications, Inc., NTIS AD 742278 (1971)

7. Shapiro, R.M., et al. : A Handbook on File Structuring, New York : Applied Data Research, Inc., NTIS AD 697025 (1969)

8. Shapiro, R.M. : Calculating Logical and Probabilistic Dependencies in a Class of Net Models, In Second Semi-Annual Technical Report for the Project 'Development of Theoretical Foundations for Description and Analysis of Discrete Information System', Wakefield, Mass. : Massachusetts Computer Associates, Inc., CADD-7503-1411 (14.03.1975)

9. Shapiro, R.M., Hardt, P. : The Impact of Computer Technology --A Case Study: The Dairy Industry, St. Augustin : Gesellschaft für Mathematik und Datenverarbeitung Bonn, Interner Bericht ISF-76-11 (10.06.1976) Also in: Computers and People*)

10. Shapiro, R.M., Millstein, R.E. : NSW Reliability Plan, Wakefield, Mass. : Massachusetts Computer Associates, Inc., CA-7701-1411 (June 10, 1977)

11. Shapiro, R.M., Millstein, R.E. : Reliability and Fault Recovery in Distributed Processing, In Oceans '77 Conference Record 2, pp. 31D-5, Los Angeles, (October 17-19, 1977)

12. Shapiro, R.M., Millstein, R.E. : Failure Recovery in a Distributed Database System. In: Spring COMPCOM '78, pp. 66-70, New York : IEEE, (1978)

13. Shapiro, R.M., Thiagarajan, P.S. : On the Maintenance of Distributed Copies of a Data Base, St. Augustin : Gesellschaft für Mathematik und Datenverarbeitung Bonn, Interner Bericht ISF-78-04 (03.07.1978)

14. Shapiro, R.M. : Towards a Design Methodology for Information Systems. In: Ansätze zur Organisationstheorie Rechnergestützter Informationssysteme, ed. Petri, C.A. , GMD-Bericht Nr. 111, pp. 107-118. R. Oldenbourg Verlag, München, Wien (1979)

*) Computers and People, 25, no. 3, pp. 8-13 (1976)

15. Warshall, W., Shapiro, R.M. : A General Purpose Table-Driven Compiler. In: Programming Systems and Languages, ed. Rosen, S., pp. 332-341, New York : McGraw Hill, 1967.
Also in : Proceedings of Eastern Joint Computer Conference, AFIPS 25, pp. 59-65, (1964)

PETRI-NETS FROM THE ENGINEER'S VIEWPOINT
LECTURE I

KONRAD ZUSE

ABSTRACT

In lecture I the different aspects of Theoreticians and Engineers are discussed. The Component-Net is a special form corresponding to the state-machine-concept of the Automata-Theory. Some special symbols are suggested. Side-conditions and side effects are well appropriate for the simulation of hardware systems, for instance for the problems of Switching Algebra.

In lecture II some applications for kinematical processes and for the control of a lift-car are explained.

INTRODUCTION

Considering the lectures of this course I have the feeling that the ideas of Petri-Nets up-to-now are seen more from the theoretical point of view. There are some aspects of this theory concerning more the practical application. I myself, as an engineer, from the beginning of my activity in the computer field endeavoured to erect bridges between theory and practice. Unfortunately, I must state that mathematicians and engineers often are following diverse ways and that they are scarcely able to understand each other.

In the following two lectures I will try to explain some ideas of Net-Theory in the language engineers may understand without using the tool of abstract formulas. Besides of that, I like to make some suggestions for some symbols which may help to describe the special features of a construction.

Following this line I concentrate my statements on the simulation of constructional problems like transportation systems, elevator-control, etc.

GENERAL CONCEPT

Petri-Nets are conceived as directed graphs with two types of nodes, the places and the transitions, with the following restrictions:
Arrows go either from places to transitions or from transitions to places.
There are no multiple arrows and no isolated nodes and no slopes.

Nets may be considered as playing boards for token games. The special rule allows every place to be marked at most by one token. So the places ar holding conditions. The general rule (weak rule) allows the marking of a place by more than one token. In the following we will prefer the special r This definition differs in some way of those proposed by Genrich and Stankiewicz-Wiechno in their paper of June 1979.

The transitions have pre-conditions (incoming arrows) and post-condition (outgoing arrows). A transition has concession for firing if all pre-conditions hold (their places are marked) and all post-conditions do not hold (their places are not marked). The operation of firing means that all pre-conditions are ending and all post-conditions are beginning. In the token game that means, that all tokens of the places for the pre-conditions are removed and the places for the post-conditions are marked by a token.

It depends on the interpretation who is the player for this token game (men, hardware-elements, etc.). The general Net-Theory normally does not ta care of this question. But the implementation of a system described by a ne depends strongly on the constructional solutions for instance of conflicts, etc.

COMPONENT-NETS

A special type of nets well suited for the engineer's problems are the nets composed by components, which correspond to state-machines of the automata theory. This definition of the term "component" differs, too, from the norm interpretation. Components may represent a constructional unit of a system. But sometimes it may be comfortable to assign separate components to functio aspects like the different drives (gears) of a transport-system.

From the view-point of the token game components are "One-token-systems". Normally, each relevant state is represented by one place in the net (complet component). In a component only one place may be marked. Within a component the arrows form "token-pathes". But this aspect serves only for the better understanding of the formal net. A special instance is the binary component with two states, which can be represented by two places. This component can be reduced to one place, representing the two states by holding a token or no On the other hand we have the "Scheffer-Component" with two places, where at most one of them may be marked.

Different components may be connected in variable ways, for instance by common places or common transitions, or by special places for communication (Fig. 1, 2, 3).

Concerning the structures of the components we can accentuate some typical extreme forms:

- The state machine decomposible net (complete component-net) composed by components with one place for every state. (But some different components may have common places.)
  From the theoretical point of view in some nets there are several different ways for segmentation. But the engineer mostly has in mind the simulation of a special system, which is represented by constructional units.
- A sepcial form of the complete component net which has binary components only. For instance, most of the logic units of computers are composed of binary elements.
- The reduced binary net, containing only reduced binary components.

In principle, it is possible to transfer every net into a complete component net by appending places. But this may be of theoretical interest only. Normally, we have mixed forms. In the net there are only the relevant states of the system represented by places. Contrary to the well-known Automata-Theory, the component-nets allow the representation of complex systems by a tolerable number of states (places).

Besides of that the nets are especially appropriate for the understanding of parallel or concurrent processes. There are four typical elementary connections of a node (place or transition):

Branch, meet, split, and wait (Fig. 4).

INTRODUCTION OF SPECIAL SYMBOLS

The following (partly already known) symbols may be advantageous for the engineer.

Normally, the arrows of a net serve two purposes: As conditions for the concession for firing of a transition, and for changing the marking of the places connected with a firing transition. We can separate these two aspects by introducing arrows with limited meaning.

Side-conditions, normally represented by dotted lines (Fig. 5). They ar good only for the concession but they do not change the marking of places wh a transition is firing.

A dotted arrow going from a place to a transition (pre-condition) represents a positive side-condition.

Negative conditions and side-conditions may be represented by a special place,for instance of a complete binary component. But there is another way. Playing the token game according to the special rule the places for the post-conditions of a transition must not be marked by a token. So we can represe a negative condition by an arrow going from a transition to a place (Fig. 6). This is possible for normal arrows as well as for dotted arrows (Negative si condition).

A typical example for a side-condition is a traffic light. It is switche on and off independently from the behavior of the receiver of the signal. Therefore, the representation of a side-condition by a slope with normal arr does not correspond to the real situation. A driver reacting on a traffic light does not change its state. Simulating this by the token game it would be a misrepresentation to move the token by taking it away and setting it ag on the place.

Disjunctive firing arrows (side effects). Contrary to the side-conditio they are good for the firing of a transition only. We will represent them by two points placed aside of an arrow. They have no influence on the concessio for firing (Fig. 7). When a transition is firing (conceded by other conditio for such arrows we have the following rule:

A preceding place (Fig. 7) is set to zero (no token) and a following plac (Fig. 8) is set into the marked state (one token) independent from the former marking-state.

Especially, in hardware-systems we often have a behavior, which correspon to the rule for such disjunctive firing arrows. An instructive example is th parallel cancelling of a set of switching elements, represented by places (Fig. 9). The rule for such side-effects corresponds also to the behavior of Data-Processing Systems. Most algorithmic languages obey the rule, that a ne calculated value is cancelling the old one.

Surely, the use of side-conditions and side-effects may require some changes or expansions of the Net-Theory. In principal, it is possible to construct nets with side-conditions and side-effects only. A dotted arrow parallel to a disjunctive one mostly has the same effect as a normal (full) arrow. Fig. 10 shows an example for the connection "meet". Using normal arrows as in Fig. 1 only one may bring a token to the place, this may result in a conflict. In Fig. 10 the two transitions t1 and t2 (if conceded by their not represented pre-conditions) may fire independently one after the other or simultaneously. This corresponds to the difference between the "exclusive or" and the "disjunctive or" of formal logic.

One-way coupling of transitions: Two transitions each with its own pre-conditions and post-conditions may be connected by a black arrow-head according to Fig. 11. If this coupling arrow-head is going from the left to the right side, the left transition is controlling the right one. That means that the left transition has the concession for firing depending only on its own conditions. Contrary, the right transition is allowed to fire only together with the left one, depending on its own conditions.

This one-way coupling, for instance is appropriate for a system controlled by a clock (Fig. 12). The transitions of the system depend on the pulses of the clock. The cycles of the clock are changing independent from the state of the controlled system.

Trigger-transition. Normally, by definition, in Petri-Nets we do not consider the time leg of the elements of the simulated system. According to the normal rule for firing of a transition the pre-conditions are ending and the post-conditions are beginning simultaneously (with the exception of side-conditions).

Contrary to that in hardware-systems and switching algebra we often have the situation that one switching element controls or triggers the switching of another one. An instance is the relais circuit shown in Fig. 13. Relais A controls relais B. But it takes some time for B to change from one state into the other. During this time A must hold its engaged state. It is possible to represent this situation with the already introduced symbols of nets, for instance by defining an additional place for the state "B changes from state zero to state one". But especially for switching diagrams a special symbol for the trigger-transition as shown in Fig. 14 may be advantageous.

Symbols for alternatives. If according to the rules of Petri-Nets only one of two conceded transitions may fire, we will call this an alternative. There are several forms:

Open alternative. In case of a connection called branch, for instance tw ways for a token are possible. We need the information of one bit to decide this alternative. This may be accentuated by a symbol shown in Fig. 15. It depends on the interpretation, where the missing information is coming from. It may be given by the outside-situation, it may lead to a conflict or it may depend on a lottery-mechanism.

Critical alternative. A typical example is the connection "meet" if the places do not all belong to the same component (more than one token, Fig. 16) We suppose that at the beginning no place is marked by a token. Normally, on of the places A or B will be marked, at first. Consequently, only one of the transitions t1 or t2 has the concession for firing. But we have a critical situation, if the places A and B are marked nearly simultaneously, or if the second place is marked before the conceded transition is firing. Only in thi case, we have a critical situation and a decision is required. Therefore, we use the symbol of the open alternative but with a half black square (Fig. 16) The term "Confusion" introduced in the theory of Petri-Nets corresponds to th critical alternative.

Closed alternative. The typical example is the connection "meet" within component (Fig. 17).

Then the alternative is decided in advance in any case. Therefore, we use the symbol of the Alternative with a full black square. Fig. 18 shows a branched net with an open and a closed alternative.

Contrary to the open alternative in the closed alternative we are gaining one bit information which is only of interest for the backward tracing of a process.

The symbols for the alternatives perhaps may be redundant. But they are facilitating the understanding of the nets. In some nets it is not appropriate to use them, for instance in the case of a decision between more than two competitive transitions. The transitions connected by an alternative may have additional pre- and post-conditions. So a "branch", too, may be decided in advance.

Signal acceptor. This is a special form of an open alternative, deciding not between two transitions but only between the firing or not of a transition depending on a signal as a side condition. This is, for instance typical for a driver approaching the traffic light at a crossing street (Fig. 19). There is a critical point for the driver for accepting a signal just changing from green to red. Fig. 20 shows the symbol of the signal acceptor and its incorporation in a net simulating the situation of Fig. 19.

The signal acceptor is well suited for separated systems controlled by a clock. Most of the signals coming from the periphery are not controlled by the clock and must be inserted into the system by Signal Acceptors. This is, for instance necessary for the information transfer between independent systems.

CONSTRUCTIONAL ASPECTS OF ALTERNATIVES AND CONFLICTS

An alternative often is leading to a conflict, which is defined as follows:

There is a conflict, if the concession for firing of a transition may be cancelled by the firing of another one. This situation requires a part of a net suited for conflicts and a special marking of its places.

In the theory of Petri-Nets we have the terms forward and backward conflict. From the engineer's viewpoint only the forward conflict is relevant. For instance, in Fig. 18 the closed alternative becomes an open one, if we play the token game in the reverse direction (heads and roots of the arrows changed). Nearly all technical processes are not reversible, that means normally it is not possible to follow them in reverse time-direction. From the engineer's viewpoint we are interested mostly in solution of the problem by technical means. For instance, in automatic telephone-exchanges there are a lot of constructional elements to switch alternative branches etc. according to the actual situation.

For this purpose, bistable elements are best suited. Fig. 21 shows the net for a signal acceptor. The component C with the places C1 and C2 is a bistable binary switch. The change from C1 to C2 is stimulated by the places A and B. They are side-conditions and in critical situations A may be switched off (by transitions not shown in this partial net) shortly after the switching on of B. From the technical viewpoint the transition from C1 to C2 then depends on the question if the energy is sufficient for the switching from C1 to C2. Fig. 22 shows an electromechanical solution. A and B are represented by contacts a and b so that Relais C is connected with the voltage u. C has a contact c1, parallel to a and b, so that C stays on voltage even after a short impuls. The relais C is the bistable element of the system. The armature of the Relais is not able to keep an intermediate position. C has a second contact c which is adjusted in relation to c1 so that it is closed some time later.

Fig. 23 shows a solution for the critical alternative between two keys T and Tb. They are acting over light switches on flip-flops A and B. The lig beams la and lb are interrupted alternatively by a rotating disk S. By this way only one key is able to switch. It should be supposed, that the frequen of the disk is much higher than the operating time for the keys. Surely, th light switches with the disk may be replaced by electronic means.

Theoretical considerations show that from the viewpoint of mathematical exactness any technical device only can give a clear decision of an alternative with a certain probability. This may be reduced by appropriate means t an arbitrary low degree but never exactly to zero. But such statements are o of theoretical interest. In practice we have a large quantity of technical devices, proved to be useful in billions of cases. A good engineer will eve find a solution with no risk especially concerning the security of involved persons.

SWITCHING ALGEBRA AND PETRI-NETS

Switching algebra, today is already a classical section of computer science. Mostly, the problem may be defined as follows: There are input-values IN and output-values OUT, mostly represented by binary elements. OUT is a function of IN, which shall be represented by a switching diagram. The attention mostly is only directed to the process of bringing the OUT-elements in the right position. Normally, for this step nobody takes care, what happens to the input-values after the switching.

Contrary to this, in Petri-Nets all participating conditions (places) are changed either by removing or by setting a token (besides of side-conditions) Another viewpoint is that the elements for the binary values may be represent in the net by various forms (complete binary component, reduced binary component, Scheffer-component). So there are multiple versions for the elementary diagrams for the three elementary propositional operations conjunction, disjunction, and negation.

Fig. 24 shows an example for the operation

$A \wedge \neg B$

and Fig. 25 for the operation

$A \vee B$.

The input-values A and B are represented by complete binary components and the output-value C by a reduced binary component.

For the conjunction we need only one transition, because this has concession only when all pre-conditions hold. For the disjunction we need three transitions for the three combinations

(A,B), $(\neg A,B)$, $(A,\neg B)$.

The number of transitions is strongly growing if there are many operands for a disjunction. In this case it is more convenient to use the disjunctive firing-arrows as shown in Fig. 26. The operation

$A \vee B \vee C \vee D =: E$

is solved there with four transitions. According to Fig. 25 we would need 15 transitions for the same problem.

The theory of Petri-Nets works with the term enlogic. By introducing, for instance dead transitions it is possible to investigate the behavior of a system concerning the global states compatible with its construction. This aspect differs from that of traditional switching algebra.

PETRI-NETS FORM THE ENGINEER'S VIEWPOINT
LECTURE II

KONRAD ZUSE

SIMULATION OF HARDWARE-SYSTEMS

In the first part of this lecture some general aspects of Petri-Nets were discussed. Especially, the concept of component-nets is well-suited for the problems of the engineer. Besides of that some additional symbols were shown for instance those for side-conditions, side-effects, and several forms of alternatives.

Such nets have some formal properties. According to the rules of the tok game the behavior of a system may be studied in an abstract form. The net may be simulating a hardware-system. The relations between the elements of t net (especially the states of places) and the constructional elements are defined by the interpretation (Fig. 27). Sometimes the constructional elements may be complemented by persons involved in the system, for instance the driver of a car. Mostly there are several variations for the coordination of system- and net-elements. For instance, the system for a driver having the option between two free parking places (Fig. 28) is simulated by the net of Fig. 29. In this net the three places for the car of Fig. 28 correspond to the places of the net in Fig. 29 and the car corresponds to the token. The symbol of the open alternative shows, that one bit information is needed (conflict) which may be supplied by the driver himself or by a parking-place-attendant. Note that the net of Fig. 29 has only one component. So it needs one token only.

Fig. 30 shows the reverse situation, where two drivers F and G are lookin for the same parking place C. In this case the conflict between the two alternatives must be decided by the competition of the two drivers or by an attendant. Fig. 31 shows again a simulation of the system, where the places of Fig. 30 correspond to the places of the net of Fig. 31 and the cars correspond to the tokens. Here the symbol of the critical alternative is best suited. But Fig. 31 does not simulate the system of Fig. 30 completely. Place C can only be interpreted "occupied by a car". Unfortunately, we have no information which car succeeded in getting the free place. Fig. 32 shows another net with two reduced components A and B and one component with three places interpreted as follows:

Co not occupied

C1 occupied by car F

C2 occupied by car G

We see, that simulating a system by a net mostly means some simplifications of the reality. A good net only represents the relevant features of a system.

The constructional parts of a hardware-system do not correspond in any case to the net-components. Mostly one constructional unit is represented by several net-components. Such units may be accentuated in the net by rectangles. In Fig. 33 we have on the right side a transportation-unit which is controlled by a control unit (left side). We need the transfer of information between these two units. In real systems for this purpose we have mechanical levers and shafts, electrical circuits or optical signals, etc. The corresponding elements in the Petri-Nets may be full arrows, side-conditions, side-effects, common places, common transitions, and one-way coupling of transitions.

The most applied form may be the electrical lead, represented in the net by a binary component with two states "on tension" and "not on tension". (Sometimes in electronic devices we have two distinct levels of tension.) In the net we have a common place for the connected units. Fig. 34 shows a net with a special place C representing the information-channel, Fig. 35 shows a net with separated but connected circles in the two units, representing the same place in the net.

In Fig. 34 the transfer of information or a signal from unit A is only possible, if place C is cancelled before by the unit B. So the unit B is controlled by unit A but A must wait until B has reacted on the preceding signal.

In Fig. 34 both units A and B are equivalent concerning the information transfer.

In Fig. 36 the unit A may proceed perfectly independent of unit B, because A1 serves only as a side-condition for B.

There are some other variations of information transfer between different units, which cannot be discussed here.

PROCESS-UNITS

In hardware-systems these are self-reliant units, proceding according to the incorporated rules, which must be started by a start-signal and which produce an end-signal after having completed their task. Fig. 37 shows a net simulating such a process unit. The start- and the end-signals are represented by places Ps and Pe. The net for the proper process is represented by a box in the form of a rectangle with rounded corners. The process begins by firing of the transition t1 and ends by firing of the transition t2. Parallel to the process we have a net-place Pa, indicating that the process is just running.

There are more complicated processes including some exchange of information with their neighbourhood. In this lecture we will confine to kinematical systems like those for transportation and handling of workpieces in a factory. Such devices have moving parts like sliding carriages, grabs, etc., which must be brought in the positions required by the program. The measures for the positions normally are analogous values. For the control we need mostly only some discret information, for instance "part A is situated between X1 and X2". Owing to the inaccurancies of a technical system the information "A is positioned at the point X1", can be given only for a small intervall, including X1.

In principle, it is possible to control the drive of a moving part so that its position corresponds every time to the demanded value, for instance by step-motors. But in practice systems with feed-back mechanisms have proved to be more reliant and flexible. Therefore, we need devices indicating the actual position. These may be read by cams, electrical contacts, light beams etc. The devices are relatively simple, if the moving parts do not oscillate within the range of the limit of an interval.

In this case we have to pay attention to the following points:

- Of two neighbouring intervals exactly one should be indicated at any time.
- The indicated position should change as quickly as possible by bistable elements.
- Going in the reverse direction the signal should change with some free space or indolence.

The Figures 38, 39, 40 show an example for the implementation of the above described system. A sliding carriage S is moving along the X-axis. At point X3 the position is changing from the interval a to the interval b. The signals for the positions do not change exactly on this point but in the case of moving to the right at point X2 and moving to the left at point X1.

We have light beams LS1 and LS2, which are interrupted by the screen B of the carriage. Fig. 39 shows the diagrams for the lights L1 and L2 and the information concerning the positions Pa and Pb. Fig. 40 shows the net with two signal-acceptors.

Fig. 41 shows a slide Sl moved by a motor M and a shaft Sh. The position is indicated by a pointer Pt. There are two distinct positions X1 and X2.

Fig. 42 shows a P-Net simulating this device. We have two places for the start Ps1 for the move from X1 to X2 and Ps2 for the reverse move from X2 to X1. These distinct positions are represented in the net by the places X1 and X2.

The state of the motor is represented by three places Mo for the stop, M+ for moving to the right, and M- for moving to the left. The transitions t1 and t2 belong to the process started by Ps1 and the transitions t3 and t4 to the process started by Ps2. The places Pa and Pe are common for the two processes.

Now let us study a system with two degrees of freedom, one for the transportation along the X-axis with the positions X1 and X2, the other for the closing of a grab (G-axis) with the positions G1 (open) and G2 (closed).

The kinematic program controls the following phases. It is supposed that at the start the system has the position X1, G1.

Phase	1	closing of the grab
"	2	transport to X2
"	3	opening of the grab
"	4	transport to X1

Fig. 43 shows the net. We need two components for the motors Mg (grab) and Mx (transport) with three states each, and five transitions t1 to t5 for the representation of the sequential process. We get a better survey using the form of Fig. 44. But now the states Mgo and Mxo are represented by two circles each, which must be combined by lines. We can avoid this by eliminating the states Mgo and Mxo (stop) in the net, reducing the representation of the components to two states (Fig. 45).

COMPLEX SYSTEMS

Most of the systems used in practice are much more complex. They have more degrees of freedom and there are several selective programs, any of them involving the same set of drives. Following the method used above we would need a separated net for each program. Besides of that the states for the drives (for instance Mx+ etc.) would appear at several places of the net each.

For a better survey and flexibility in the diagrams and nets we separate the different units of the whole system. Fig. 46 shows the net for the X-drive according to Fig. 41 with the states Mx+ and Mx- for the two directions of motion, and the places X1 and X2 for the two relevant positions. The devices for setting these positions belong to the drive. The transitions t1 and t2 are stopping the drive at the limiting points. Fig. 47 shows the diagram for the symbolic representation of this net. We have input Mx- and Mx+ for starting and outputs X1 and X2 which are side-conditions for the control.

We use a separate net for the control introducing a place for each phase of the process. Fig. 48 shows a net for the problem of Fig. 45. On the right side we have the two symbolic diagrams for the two drives G and X. On the left side we have the separated control-net with the phases Pho for the rest and Ph1 to Ph4 for the motion. The places Ps, Pa, and Pe, and the transitions t1 to t5 are equivalent to those in Fig. 45. On the right side of the transitions we have the positions of the drives as side-conditions, and the arrows going to the drives.

Fig. 49 shows a system with three degrees of freedom in a shematic view with the following parts:

HGW	horizontal guide-way
VGW	vertical guide-way
Sl	slide-carriage
Gr	grab
WP	workpiece
D1, D2	depot 1 and 2

We have three drives G, X, and Z with the distinct positions

G1 open
G2 closed
X1 left
X2 right
Z1 down
Z2 up

The motors for the drives are not shown in Fig. 49. They have the states

Mg-,(Mgo),Mg+
Mx-,(Mxo),Mx+
Mz-,(MZO),Mz+

We have two depots De1 and De2 for the workpiece WP, each with two states "free" and "occupied".

D1 Depot 1 occupied
D2 Depot 2 occupied

The job of the device is the transportation of a workpiece from depot 1 to depot 2 including the testing if depot 1 is occupied and depot 2 is free. If this is not the case then the process produces the signals

Pm1 "depot 1 free"
Pm2 "depot 2 occupied"

The process begins and ends with the positions G1, X1, Z2.

We have the following phases:

Pho rest
Ph1 testing if depot 1 is occupied
Ph2 lowering the grab
Ph3 closing the grab
Ph4 lifting the grab
Ph5 transport left to right
Ph6 testing if depot 2 is free
Ph7 lowering the grab
Ph8 opening the grab
Ph9 lifting the grab
Ph10 transport from right to left

Fig. 50 shows the net. The symbolic diagrams for these drives G, X, and Z are omitted. They correspond to Fig. 48. Comparing the nets of Fig. 48 and 50 we have in Fig. 50 two alternatives (t2, t3) and (t8, t9). They are critical, because the operations of putting a workpiece on depot 1 and of clearing depot 2 are independent of the considered process of transportation. For instance, depot 1 may just be getting occupied in the moment, when the test-phase Ph1 is on the point of signalling "not occupied".

INTERRUPT

Technical systems working partially or fully automatical need some provisions for the security. There must be some kind of an emergency brake for stopping the whole process immediately. The net of Fig. 51 represents such a system for a drive Mx.

We have the already introduced states for the drive Mx-, Mxo, and Mx+, and the states for the relevant positions X1 and X2. In addition we have the places Ala meaning Alarm and two preparatory places Nx- and Nx+. The drive is started by these places and by two transitions t1 and t2, which must have the form of signal-acceptors, because the signal "Alarm" may turn up at any moment. In this case the drive rests in the state Mxo. If the drive is already running in case of Alarm it must be stopped compulsorily. The transition t3 cancels the states Mx- or Mx+ and switches the drive to Mxo by side-effects. State Ala is a side-condition for t3, because it holds its state until it is cancelled from outside.

CONTROL OF A LIFT-CAR

The Figures 52 to 56 show an extract of the control of a lift-car, namely the stopping of the down-going car by a passenger.

Fig. 52 gives a scope of the situation. In floor 2 (Fl2) a passenger (Pas) likes to go down and presses the key T. We assume that the car (C) is just in the upper floors and going down. The question is, if the stop-signal is coming timely, so that the car is able to stop. This is only possible if the control accepts the signal within the range Z2+.

We divide the whole system into three units P, Z, and M (Fig. 56). Fig. 53 shows the unit Z for indicating the relevant positions of the car. There are the floors Fl1 to Fl3. For any floor we need the indication of the range within which the car must stop, Z0.0 to Z3.0.

But this specialisation for the floors is only relevant for the door-control, which is not investigated here. For the drive we need only the signal, that the car is stopping in the range of a floor anywhere, indicated by place Z0, representing the disjunction

$$Z0.0 \vee Z1.0 \vee Z2.0 \vee Z3.0 =: Zo$$

We do not need disjunctive firing arrows in this case, because only one of the places Z0.0 to Z3.0 may be marked. For the exception of the stop-signal for the up-going car we need the indication of the ranges Zo+, Z1+, Z2+, and for the down-going car of the ranges Z1-, Z2-, Z3- (only the latter are relevant in our example).

Fig. 54 shows the drive or motion-unit M. There are three preparatory places (see also Fig. 51)

N+	going up
N-	going down
No	stopping

For the motion we must distinguish between the ordered and the actual speed. Ordered speed

M+2	full speed up
M+1	reduced speed up
Mo	stopping
M-1	reduced speed down
M-2	full speed down

These states included the processes of accelaration and decelaration. For instance, M+2 means exactly:

"Full power on the drive going up",

and M+1

"Reduce the full speed up so that immediate stopping is possible".

Going by reduced speed the drive is stopped when the car has reached the level of a floor. Therefore, we need the indication of the actual speed by the states V+2 to V-2.

By N+ or N- the motion is initialized. The transition t1 or t2 switches directly from Mo to M+2 or M-2. The stopping is ordered by No switching the drive by the transition t3 or t4 from M+2 or M-2 to intermediate state M+1 or M-1. Now the immediate stopping is possible by the signal Zo and the transition t5 or t6.

Fig. 55 shows the proper control unit with the following interpretation o the places:

T	Key "down"
L	Lamp "down"
Pho	No order
Ph1	order accepted
Ph2	car is stopping
Ph3	car has stopped

By the key T at first the phase Ph1 is marked. The order "down" now is accepted and stored. The execution of the order is started by the signal acceptor t2 when the down-going car (V-2) is in the range Z2+. t2 is firing No and switching from phase Ph1 to Ph2. The drive-unit indicates by Z2.0 the end of the stopping-process. Transition t3 changes from Ph2 to Ph3. In this phase the doors of the lift may be opened, but this is not considered here. If the car is continuing to go down this is indicated by V-2. The transition t4 sets the control unit in the state Ph0.

Fig. 56 gives a scope of the three discussed units.

Figure 1
Coupling of components A and B
by a common place G

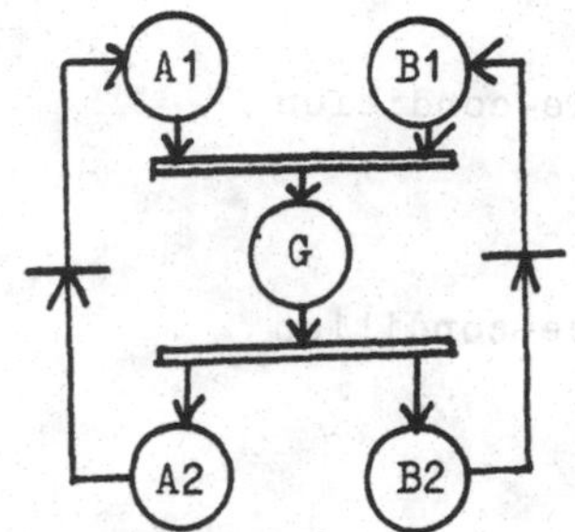

Figure 2
Coupling of components A and B
by a common transition t1

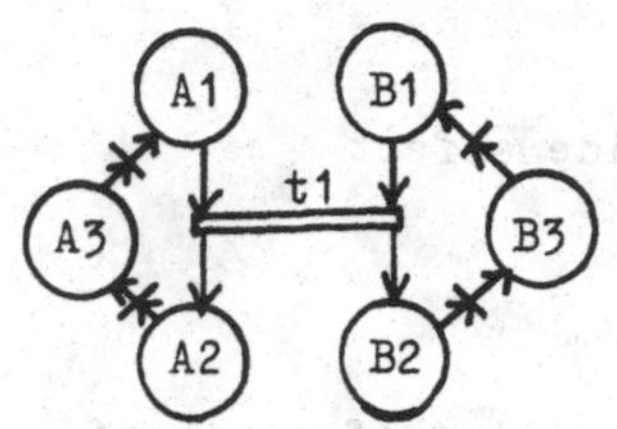

Figure 3
Coupling of comonents A and B
by a communicating place A'

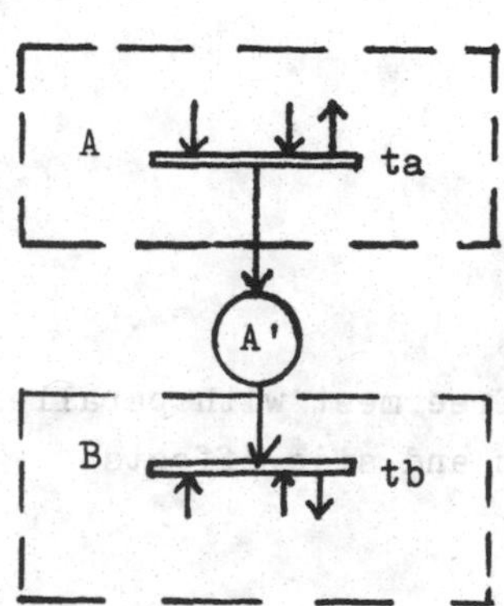

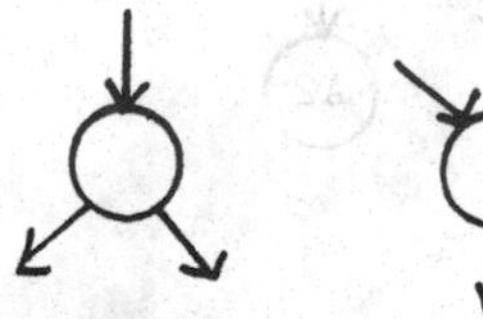

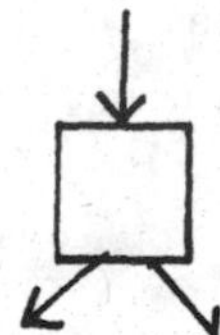

Figure 4

Branch Meet Split Wait

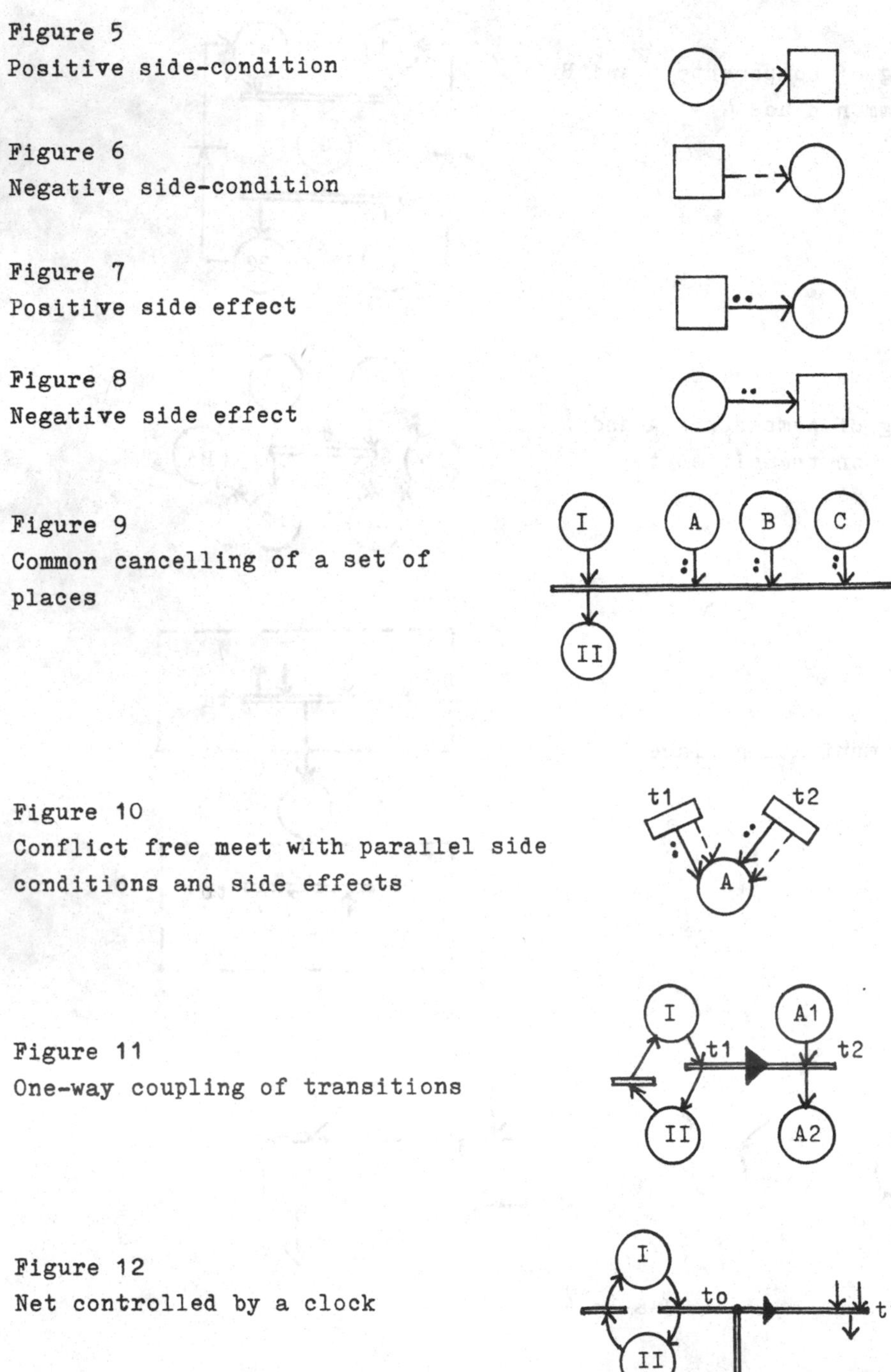

Figure 5
Positive side-condition

Figure 6
Negative side-condition

Figure 7
Positive side effect

Figure 8
Negative side effect

Figure 9
Common cancelling of a set of places

Figure 10
Conflict free meet with parallel side conditions and side effects

Figure 11
One-way coupling of transitions

Figure 12
Net controlled by a clock

Figure 13
Relais A controls Relais B

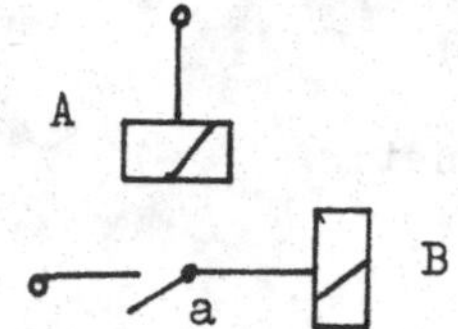

Figure 14
Trigger-transition

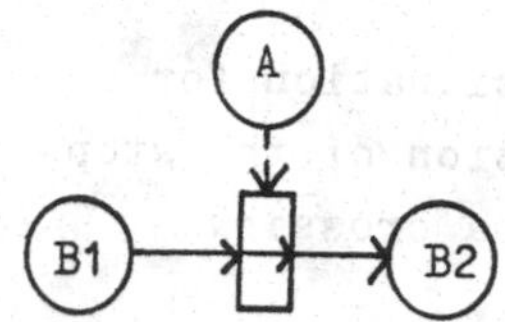

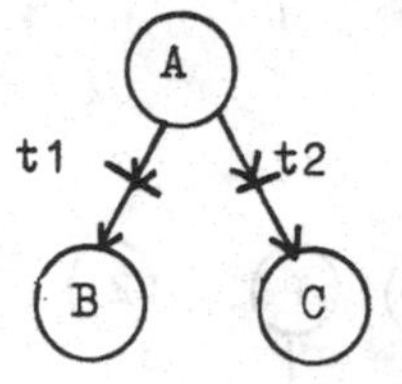

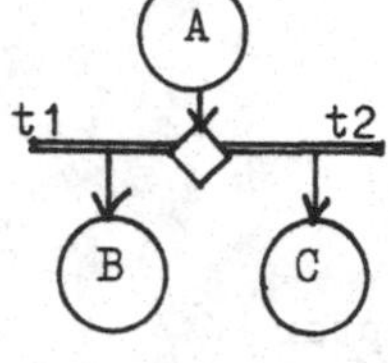

Figure 15
Open alternative (branch)

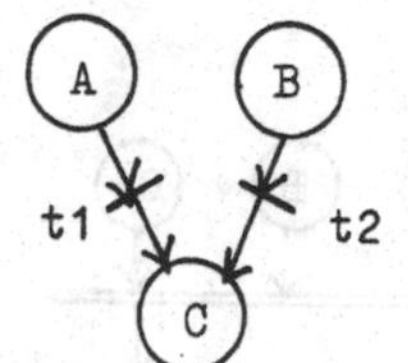

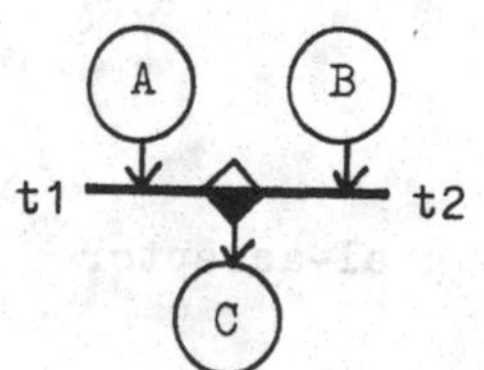

Figure 16
Critical alternative

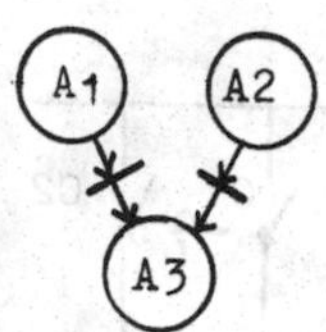

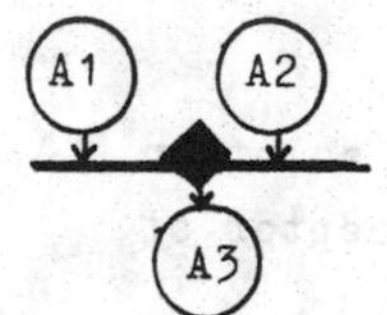

Figure 17
Closed alternative (meet)

Figure 18
Branched net

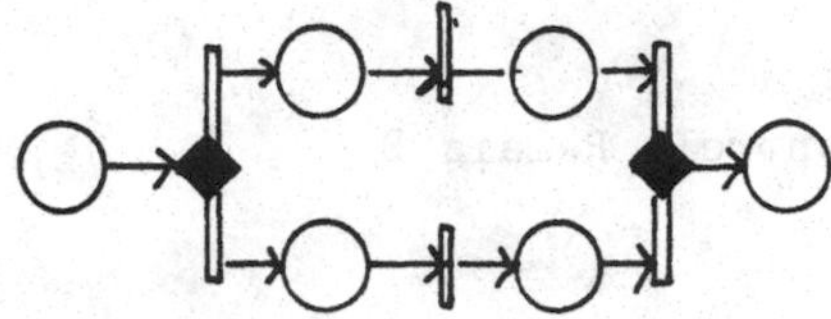

Figure 19
Critical situation for the acception of the stop-signal at a crossing

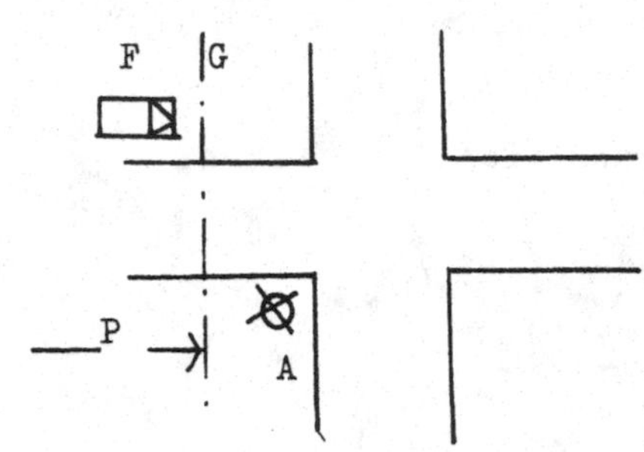

Figure 20
Net with signal acceptor according to Figure 19

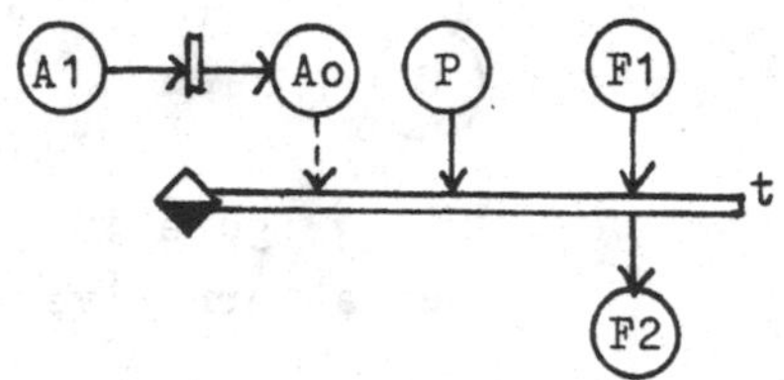

Figure 21
Petri-net for a signal-acceptor

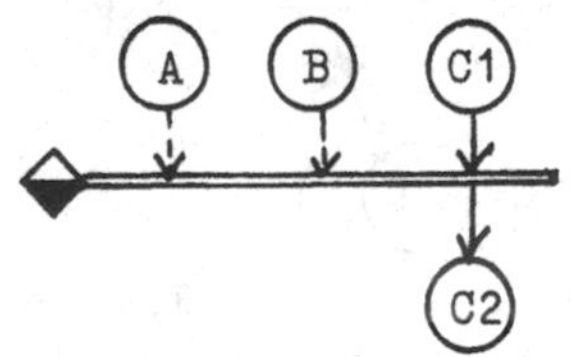

Figure 22
Electromechanical solution for the signal-acceptor of Figure 21

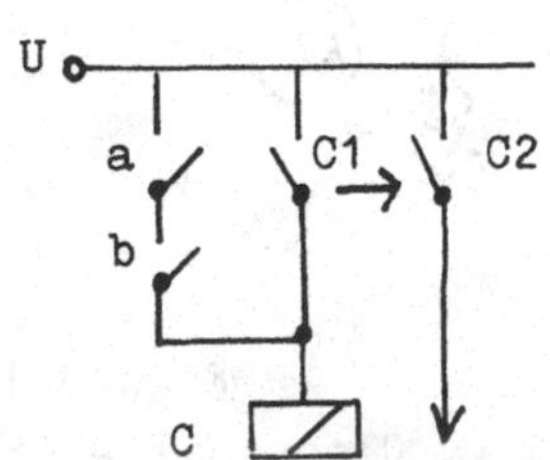

Figure 23
Alternative switching with light-beams and a rotating disk

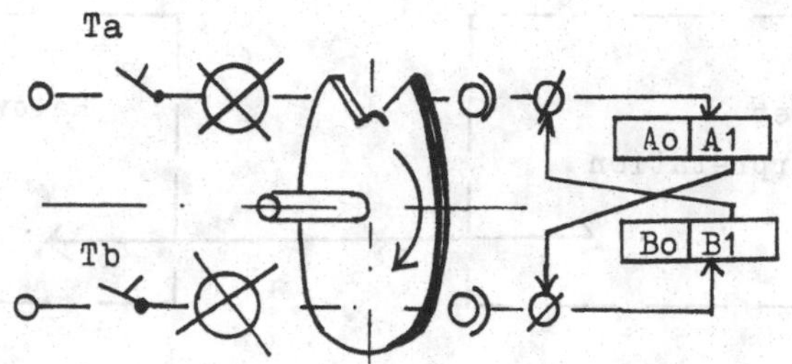

Figure 24
A∧ ¬B =: C

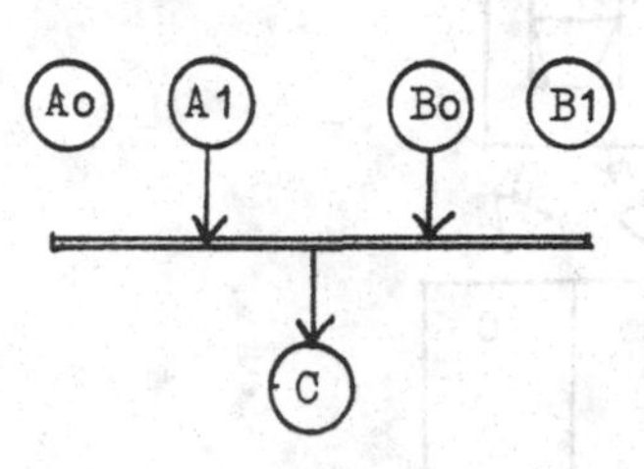

Figure 25
A∨ B =: C

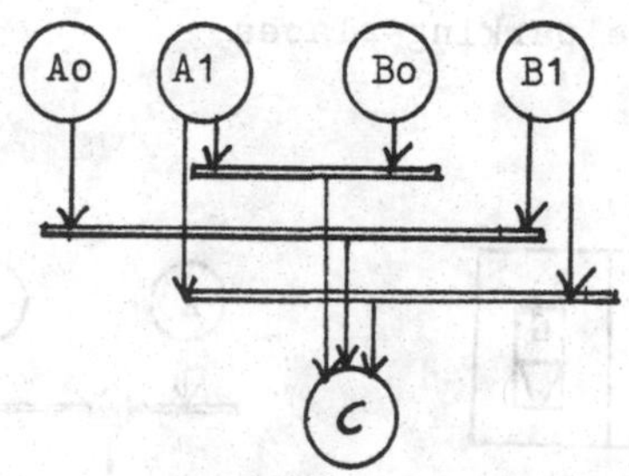

Figure 26
A∨B∨C∨D =: E

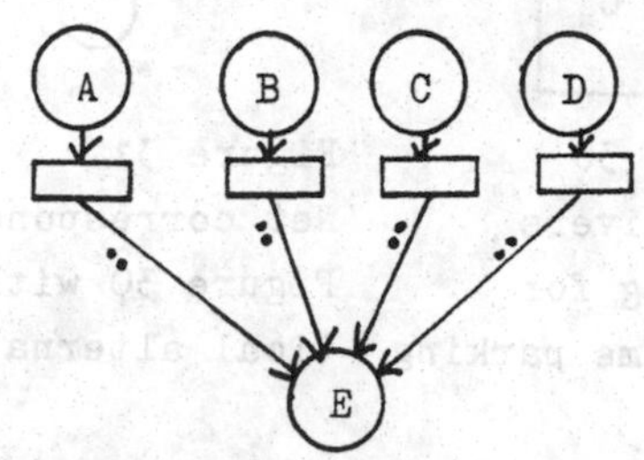

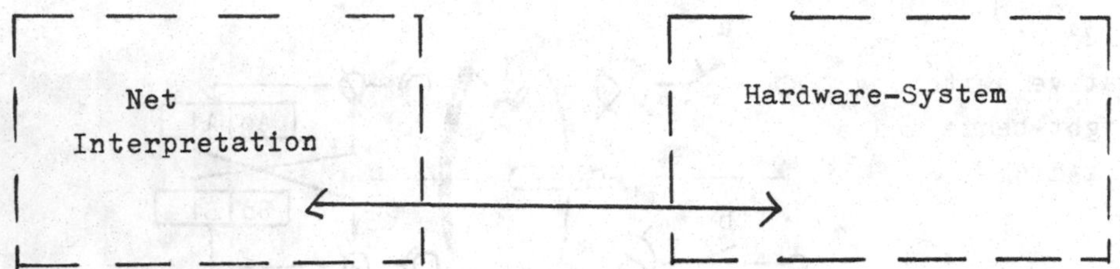

Figure 27
Relations between a hardware-system and a net

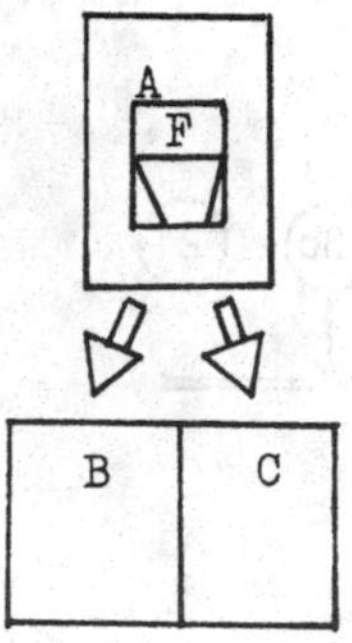

Figure 28
Driver having the choice between two free parking-places

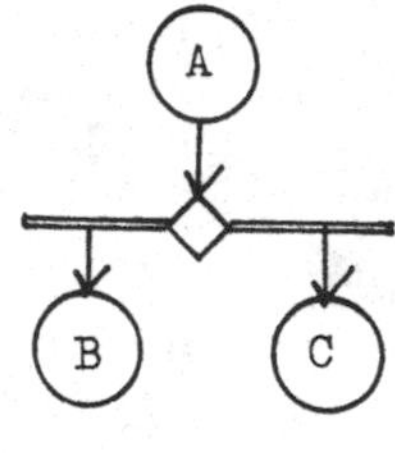

Figure 29
Net corresponding to Figure 28

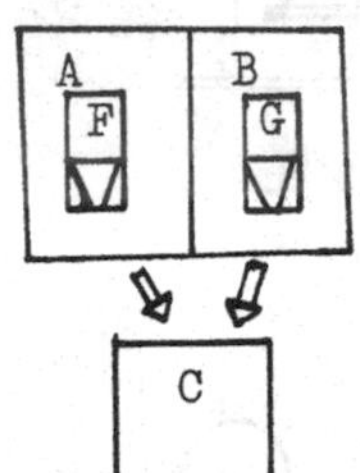

Figure 30
Two drivers hunting for the same parking place

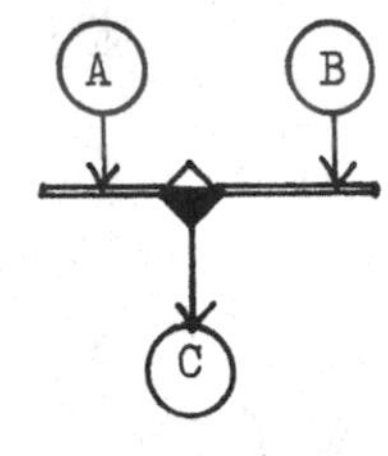

Figure 31
Net corresponding to Figure 30 with a critical alternative

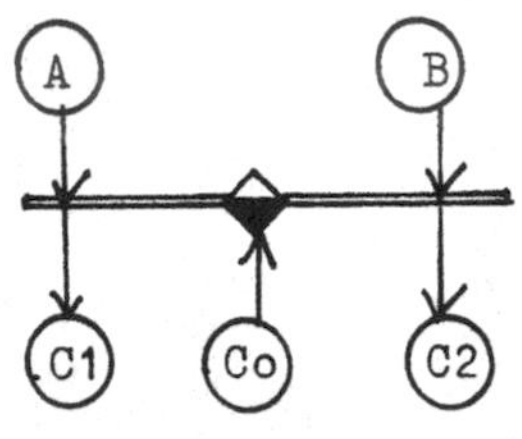

Figure 32
Net corresponding to Fig 30 but with three states for the component C

Co not occupied
C1 occupied by car F
C2 occupied by car G

Figure 33
Partition of a net for the simulation of a transport-system into a control-unit and a transport-unit

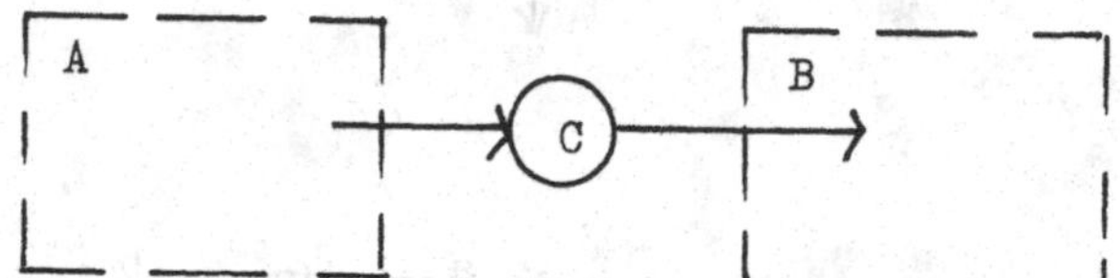

Figure 34
Transfer of information by a net-place C (channel, unilateral)

Figure 35
Transfer of information by a common net-place (bilateral)

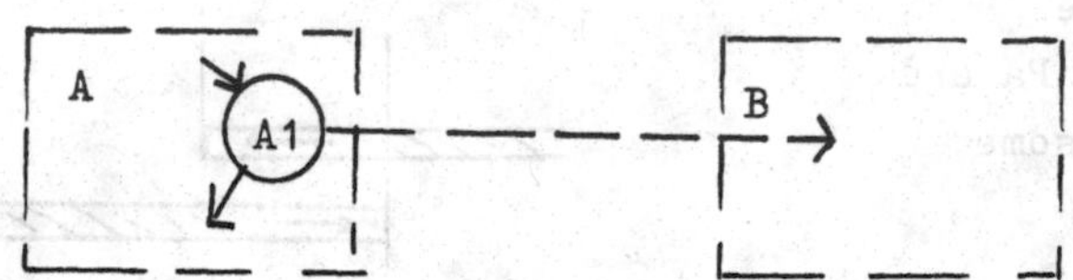

Figure 36
Transfer of information by side-condition

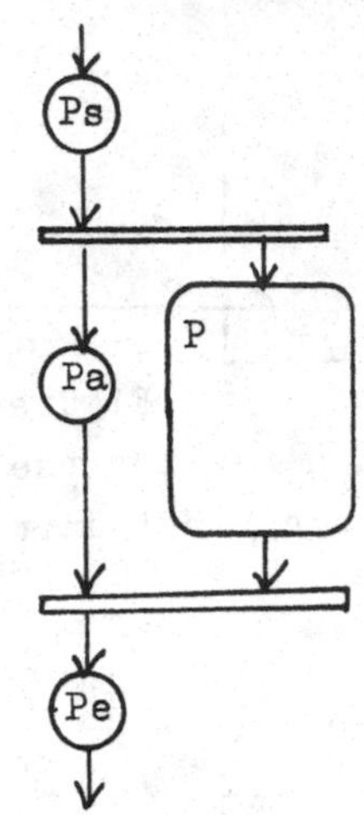

Figure 37
Net for a process P. The rectangle represents the net for the proper process

Ps Start
Pa Process is running
Pe End

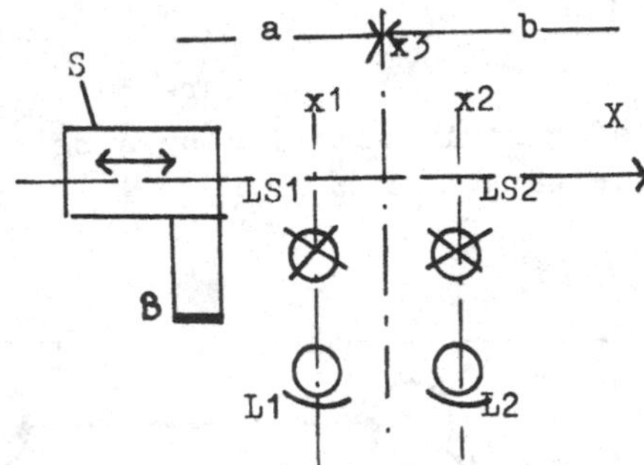

Figure 38
The slide-carriage S moving in x-direction interrupts by the screen B the light-beams LS1 and LS2

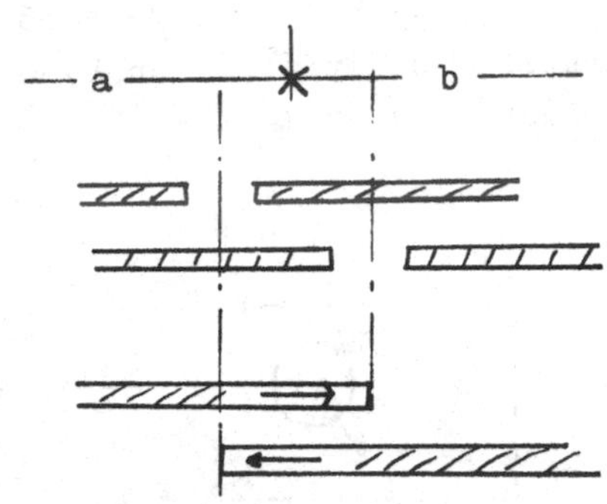

Figure 39
The ranges for the state "on" of the photocells L1 and L2 (Figure 38) and of the position indicated by Pa and Pb. They change with some indolence.

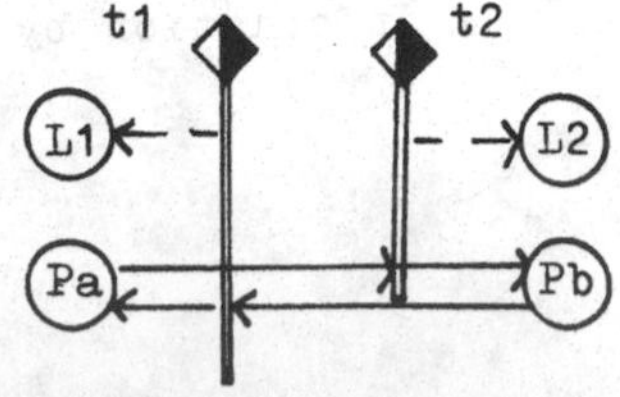

Figure 40
Net corresponding to Figure 38 and 39 with signal-acceptor.

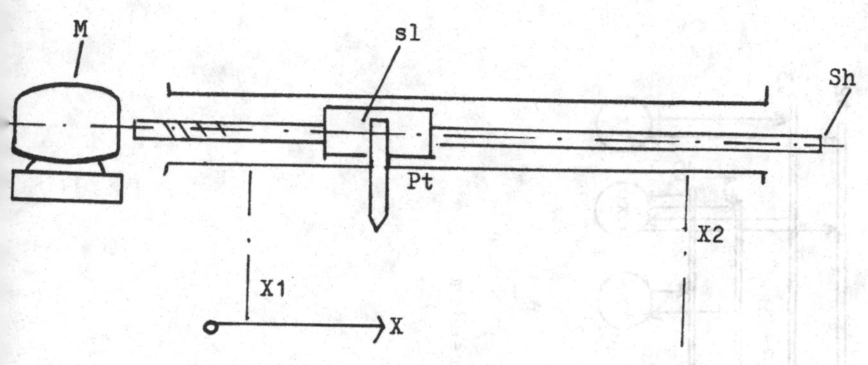

Figure 41

Drive for a slide-carriage S1

M	step motor
Sh	shaft
Sl	slide-carriage
Pt	pointer
X1, X2	relevant positions

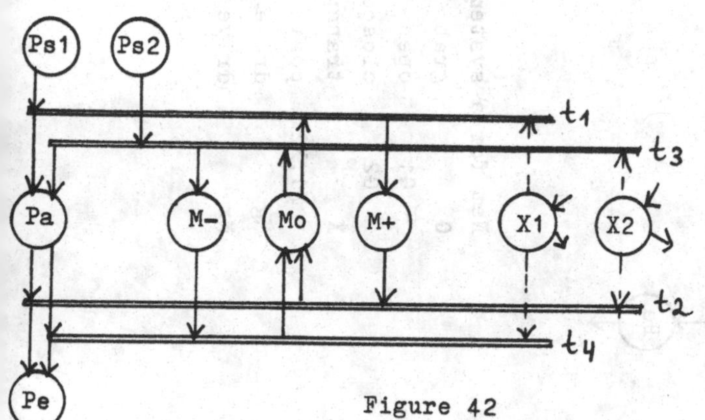

Figure 42

Net for the drive of Figure 41

Ps1	start X1 - X2
Ps2	start X2 - X1
M-,Mo,M+	states of the motor
X1,X2	relevant positions

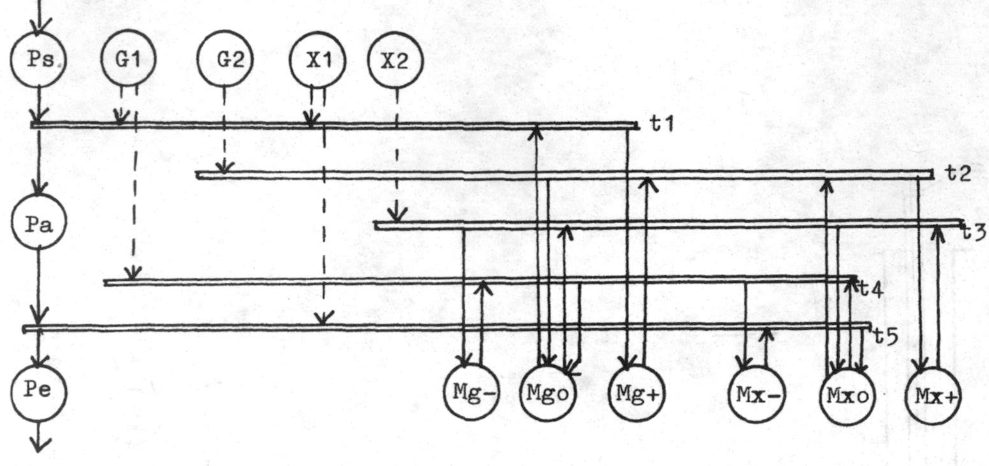

Figure 43

Net for a system with two degrees of freedom

G	grab
G1	open
G2	closed
X	transport
X1,X2	positions
Mg	drive for the grab
Mx	drive for the transport

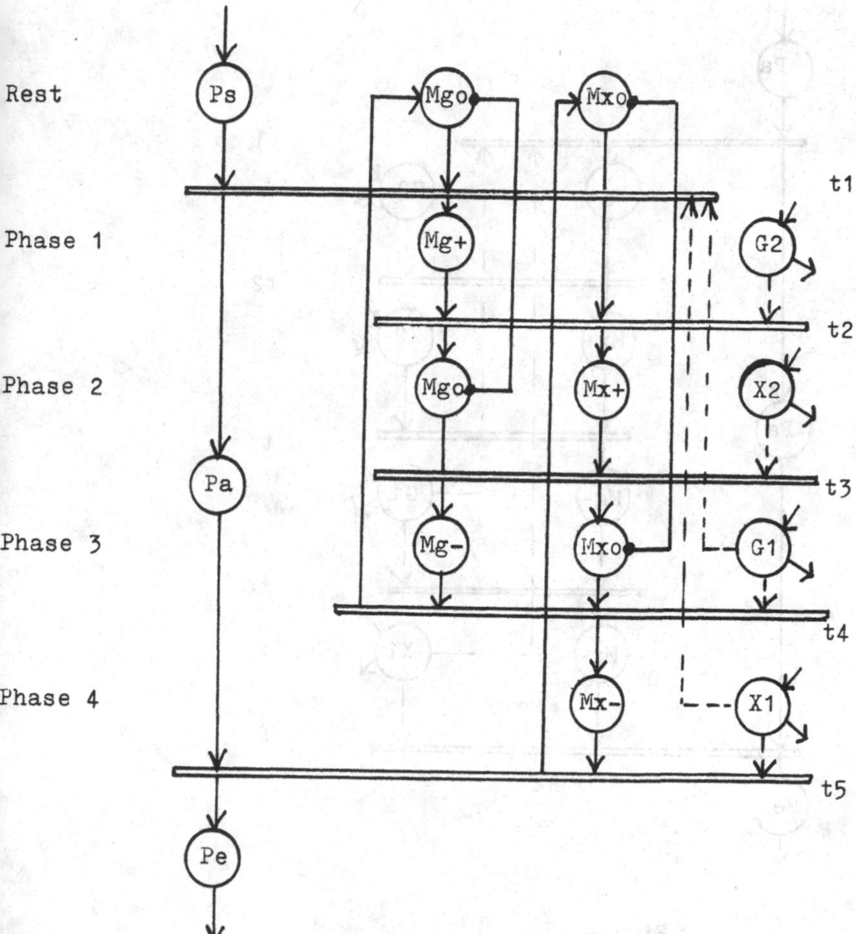

Figure 44

Variant of the net of Figure 43, giving a better survey of the different phases of the process. Note that the places Mgo and Mxo are represented twofold.

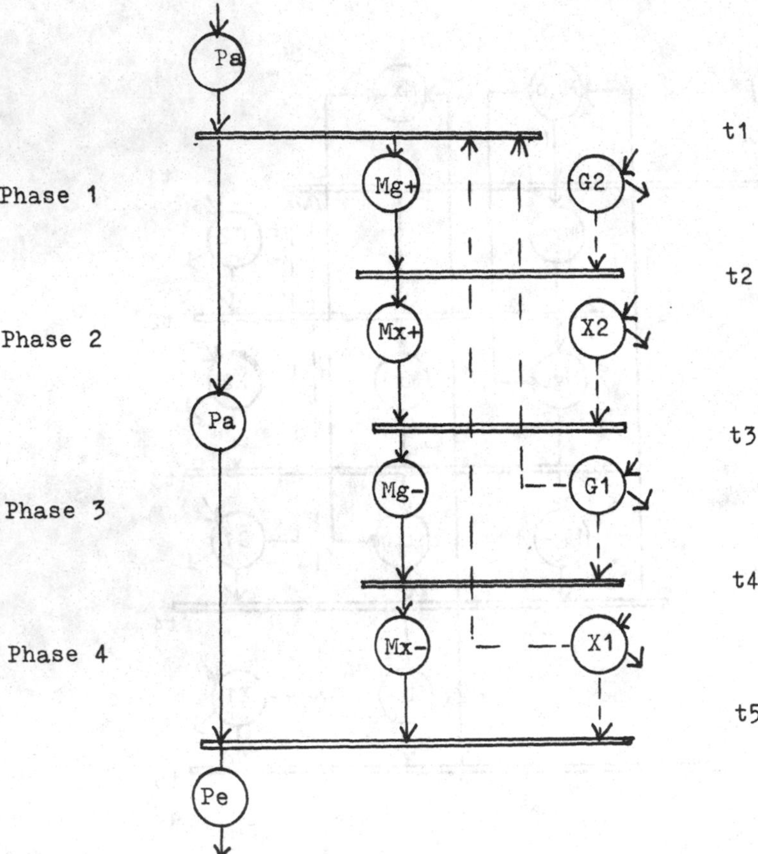

Figure 45

Variant of the net of Figure 43 and 44. Only the relevant states of the drivers (Mg-,Mg+,Mx-,Mx+) are represented.

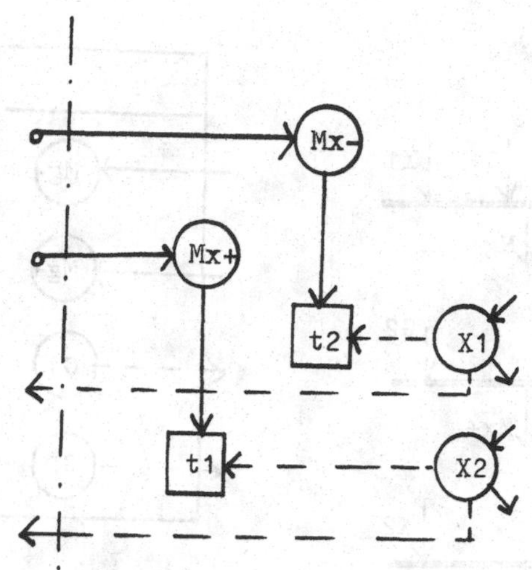

Figure 46

Net component for the drive X

Mx-	motor going right to left
Mx+	motor going left to right (started from outside)
X1, X2	positions controlled by the slide. They stop the motion and give a signal to the outside.

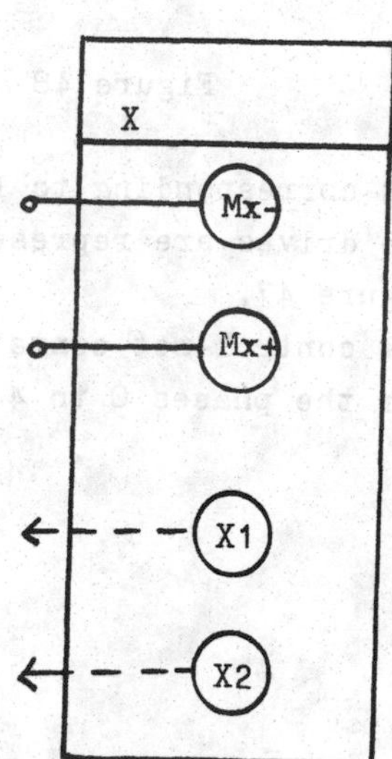

Figure 47

Symbolic diagram for the net of Figure 46.

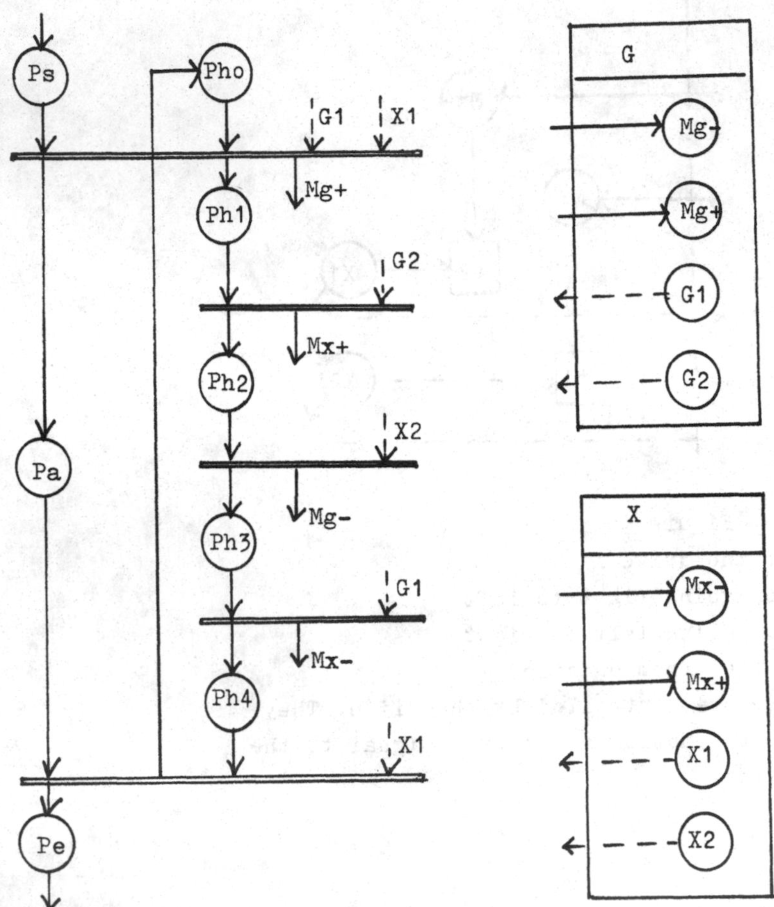

Figure 48

Net corresponding to Figure 45.
The drives are represented according to Figure 47.
The control-net contains special places for the phases 0 to 4.

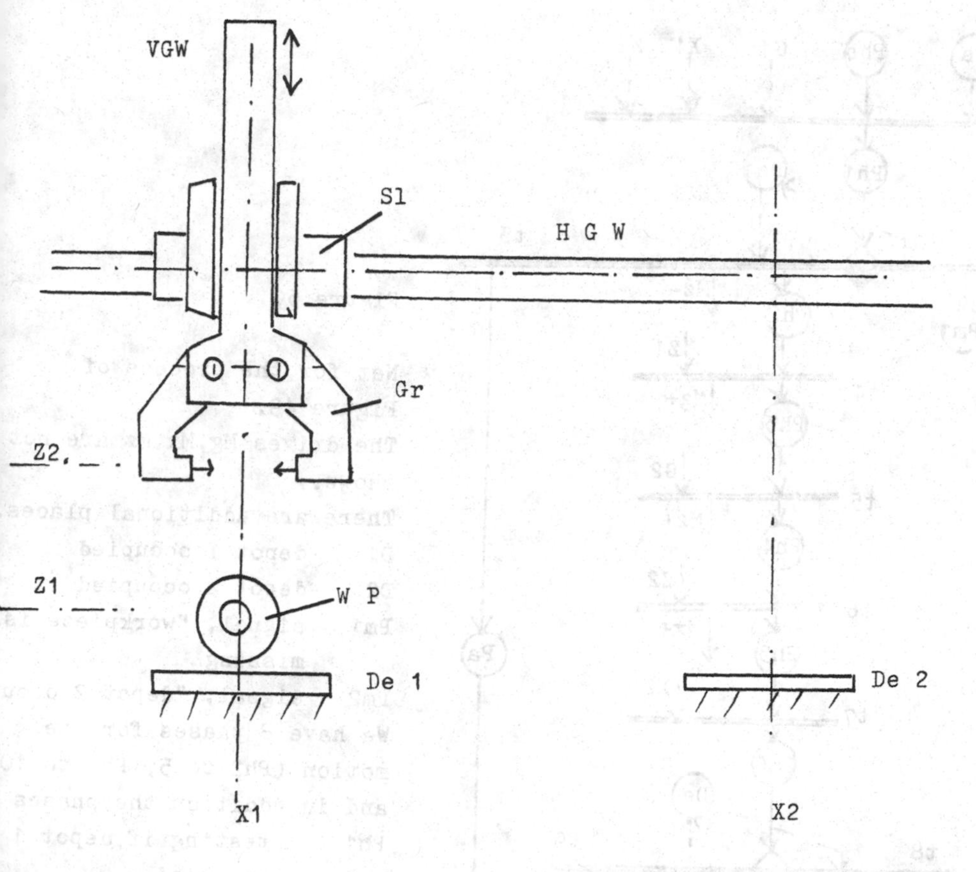

Figure 49

Handling system with three degrees of freedom Mg,Mx,Mz.
There are two depots D1 and D2 for the work-pieces.
The process transports a work-piece from D1 to D2.

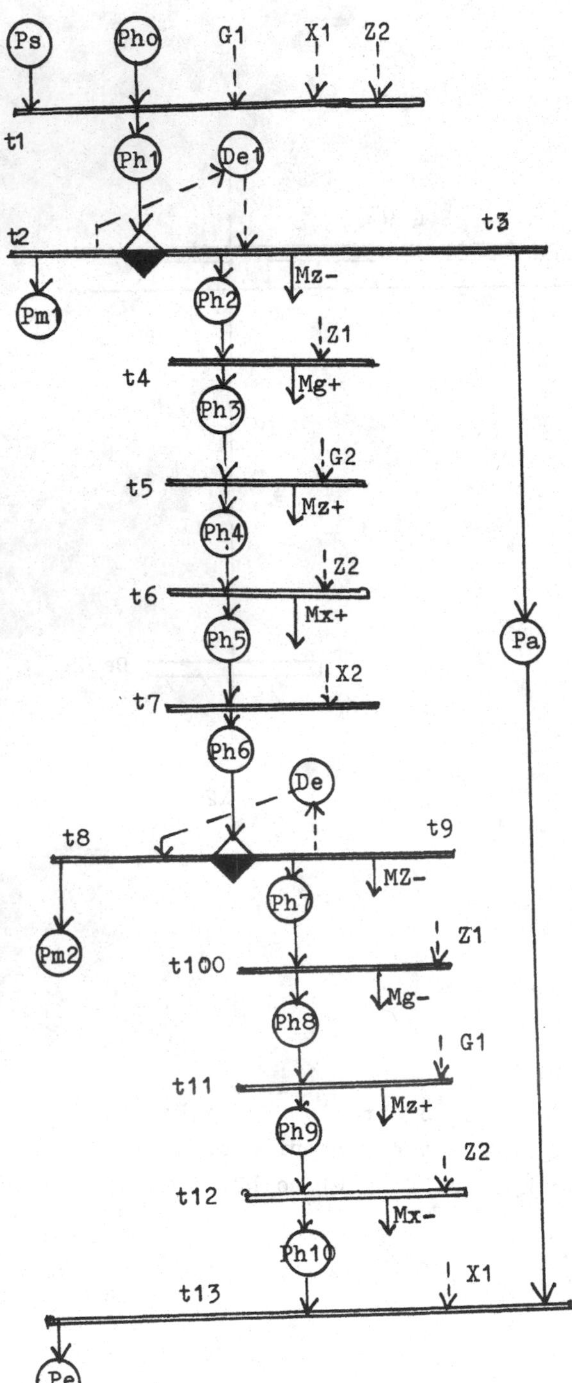

Figure 50

Net for the process of Figure 49.
The drives Mg,Mx,Mz are not shown.
There are additional places.

D1 depot 1 occupied
D2 depot 2 occupied
Pm1 signal, "workpiece is missing
Pm2 signal, "depot 2 occu

We have 8 phases for the motion (Ph2 to 5, Ph7 to 10 and in addition the phases

Ph1 testing if depot 1 occupied
Ph6 testing if depot 2 free

These tests result in branc with critical alternatives.

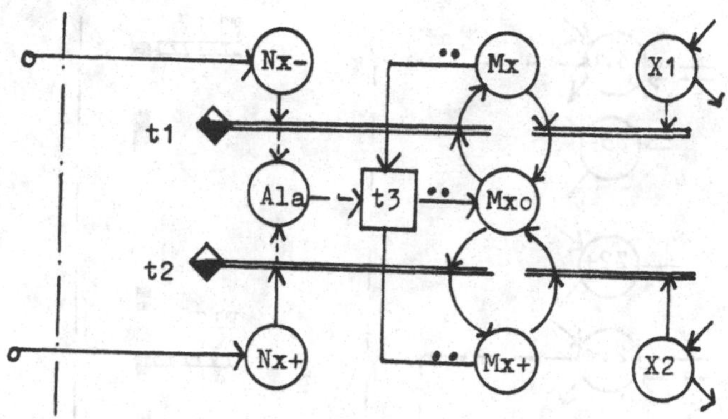

Figure 51
Net for a drive with an alarm system.

Mx-,Mxo,Mx+	states of the motion
Nx-,Nx+	Preparatory places for the start of the motion
Ala	"alarm" for instance by an emergency-brake
X1,X2	positions
t1,t2	signal-acceptors
t3	alarm-transition

In case of Ala the starting of a motion is prevented or the just going motion is stopped immediately.

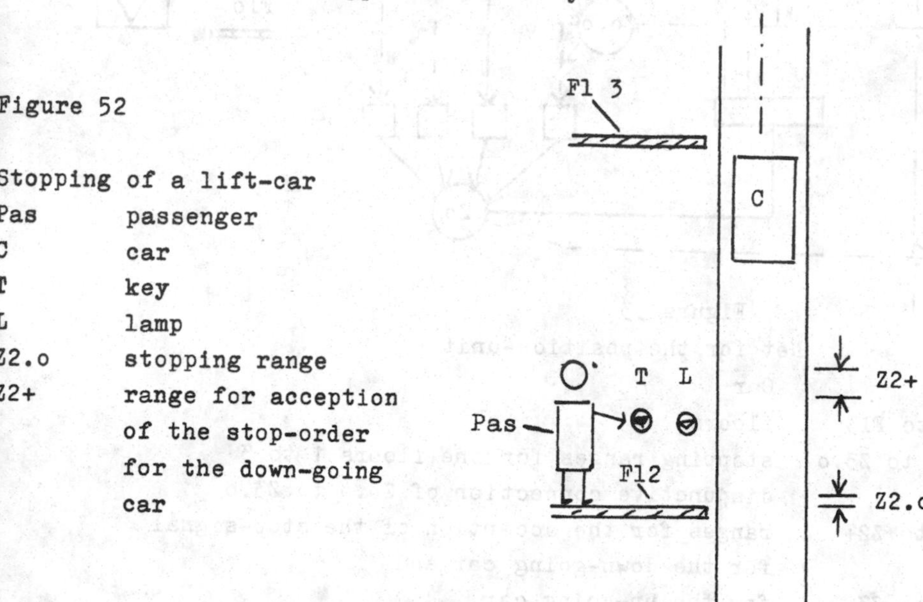

Figure 52

Stopping of a lift-car

Pas	passenger
C	car
T	key
L	lamp
Z2.o	stopping range
Z2+	range for acception of the stop-order for the down-going car

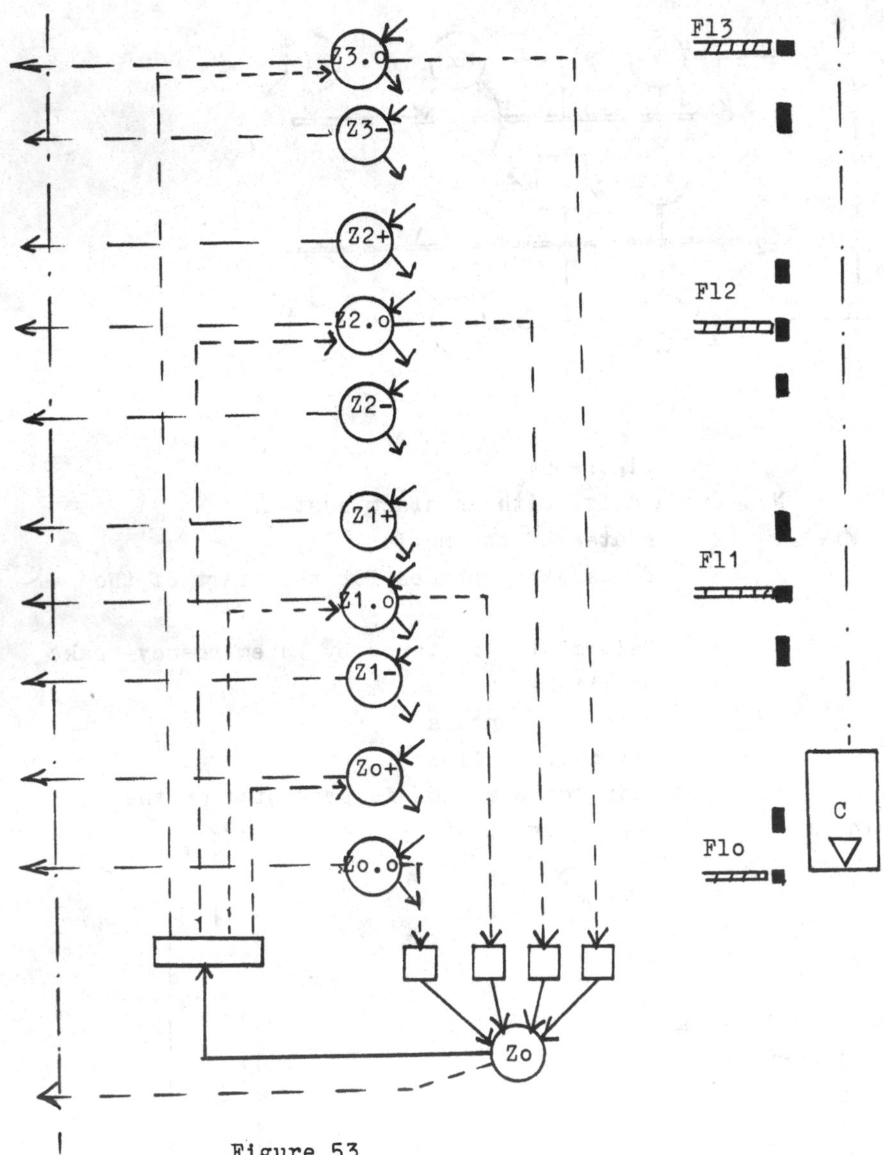

Figure 53
Net for the position-unit

C	Car
Fl1 to Fl3	floors
Zo.o to Z3.o	stopping ranges for the floors 1 to 3
Zo	disjunctive connection of Zo.o to Z3.o
Zo+ to Z2+	ranges for the acception of the stop-signal for the down-going car and
Z1- to Z3-	for the up-going car

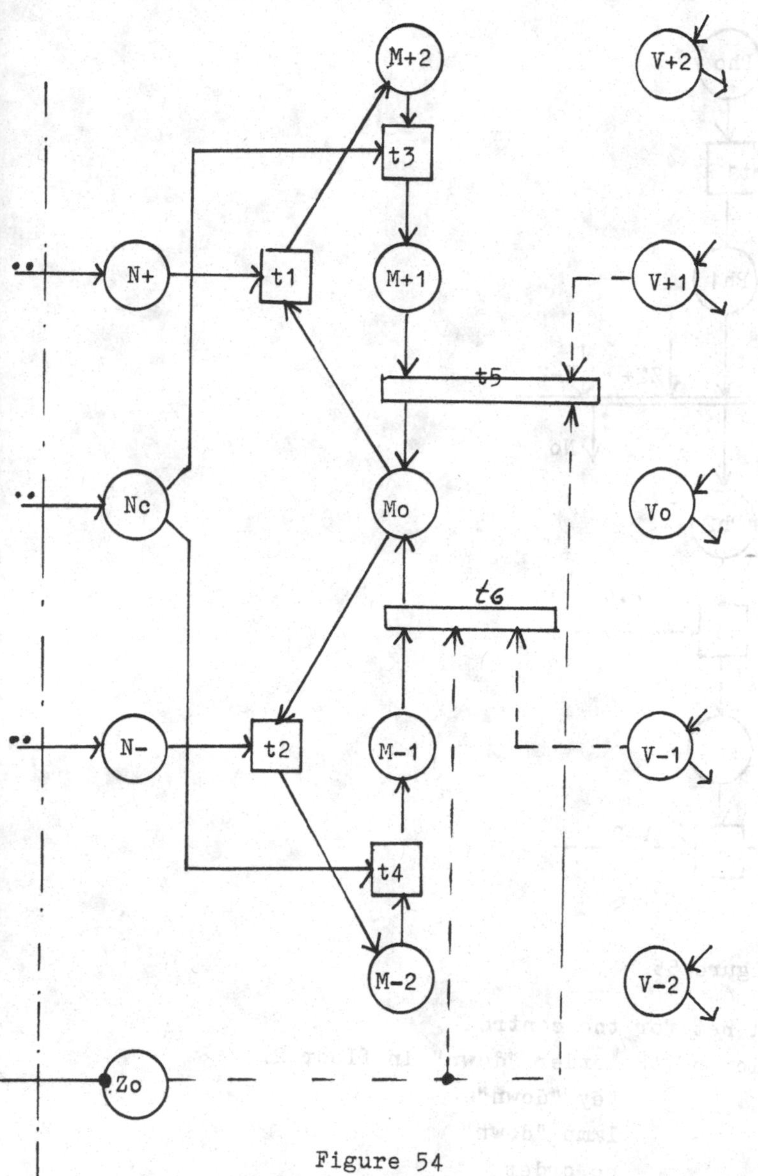

Figure 54

Net for the drive-unit

N+,No,N- preparatory places for starting
- N+ going up
- N- going down and
- No stopping

V states of actual speed of the car corresponding to M

ZO signal for the position "stopping range"

M sates of odered motion
- M+2 going up by full spe(
- M+1 going up by reduced speed
- Mo stopping
- M-1 going down by reduced speed
- M-2 going down by full speed

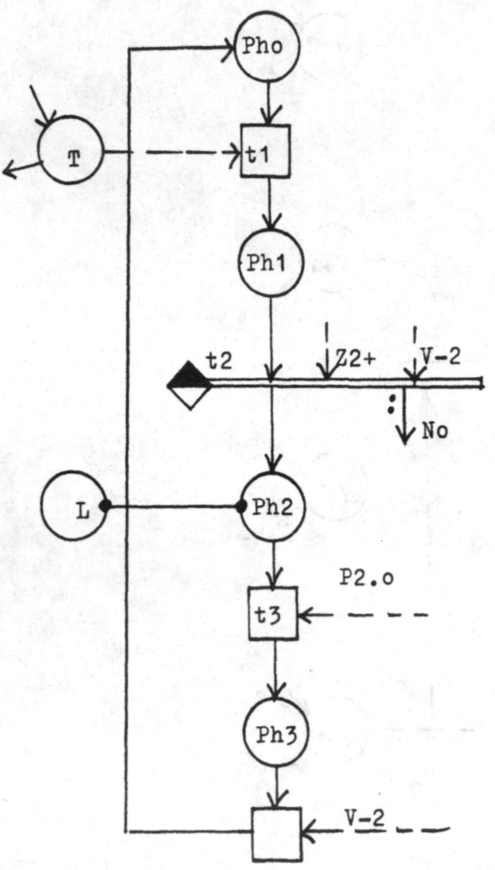

Figure 55

Partial net for the control
Acception of the order "down" in floor 2.

T	Key "down"
L	lamp "down"
Pho	no order
Ph1	order accepted
Ph2	car is stopping
Ph3	car has stopped

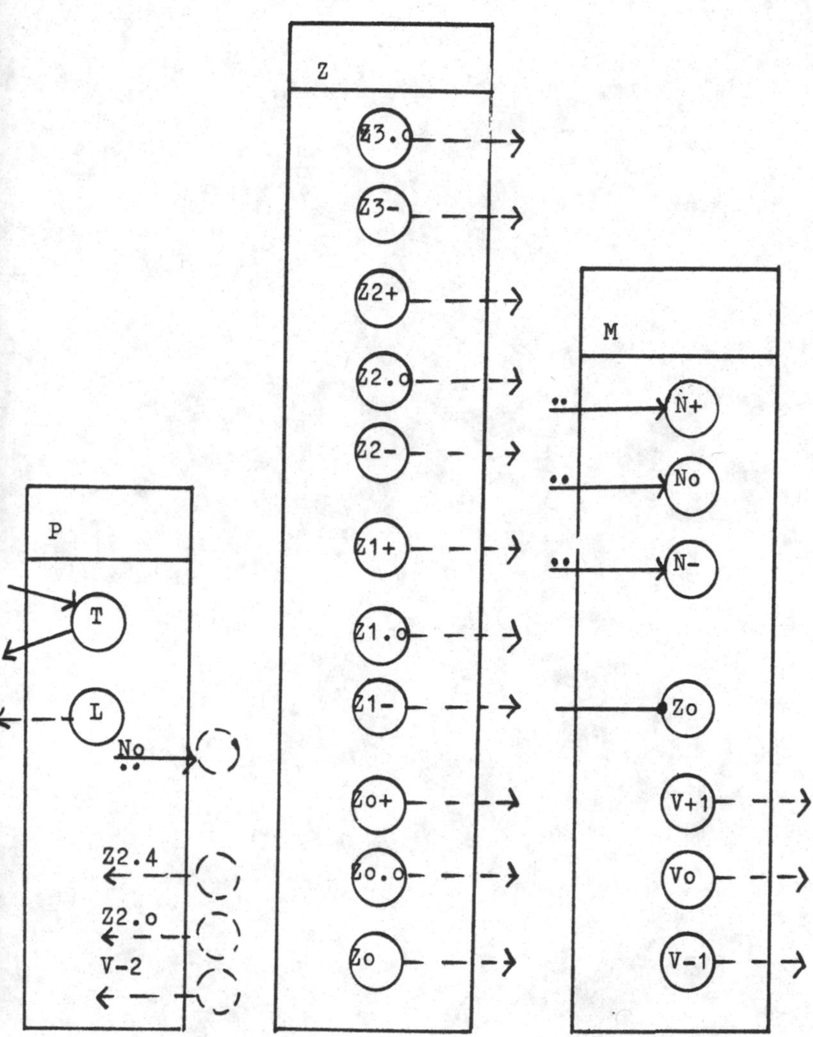

Figure 56

Scope of the 3 units for the lift-control demonstrated in Figure 52 to 55

P signal acception and control

Z position-unit

M drive

NETS AS A TOOL

IN TEACHING AND IN TERMINOLOGY WORK

Horst Oberquelle

Fachbereich Informatik, Universität Hamburg
Schlüterstr. 70, D-2000 Hamburg 13

ABSTRACT

This paper deals with some standard and non-standard applications of nets, net diagrams and net morphisms.
First, nets of channels and agencies are introduced, then nets of means and activities and nets representing relations and functions. These interpretations and the graphical representation are of great help in teaching, because they permit to represent different conceptual levels and aspects of systems to be explained by one simple formalism. The graphical representation may even be used in a naive, intuitive way to make complicated situations more transparent. This holds for static system structures, dynamic structures (processes) as well as for situations formalized by relations and functions, as is demonstrated by many examples.
In addition to teaching, the different interpretations of nets and their interrelations (expressed by net morphisms) are a suitable basis for terminology work. How the ideas of General Net Theory may help in the systematic development of a consistent terminology is demonstrated for the case of dialog systems, where phenomena on very different conceptual levels have to be covered.

CONTENTS

1. INTRODUCTION: TEACHING AND TERMINOLOGY PROBLEMS

One of the main problems in informatics is that there is not yet a widely accepted definition of the term "informatics" itself. So it is difficult to decide what the central ideas are and what is an appropriate view of information processing. Since in practice there is a clear tendency to integrate different information processing media (computers, TV, microfilm etc.) and because a lot of organizational tasks are delegated to computers, informatics should neither be only "computer" science nor "computing" science. The view of C.A. Petri that "computers are a medium for strongly organizable flow of information" shows the right direction (see [10]). In this spirit it seems appropriate to use the following preliminary definition of "informatics":

> Informatics is the science of the strongly organizable flow of information in natural and artificial systems.

This definition implies, for example, that informatics should be able to treat systems (and their behaviour at different levels of detail) independent of special realisations. It also implies that one has to consider the social environment in which information processing systems are embedded, and that one has to look for pragmatic relations (e.g. rights and duties) originating from this.
Seeing informatics in this way has consequences in teaching as well as in research.

For teaching purposes tools are needed which permit description of all kinds of systems, their components and their dynamic behaviour in a uniform, transparent way even for the beginners, i.e. without demanding too much previous knowledge.
Graphical tools have long been used for this purpose (e.g. in architecture, engine building etc.), and are especially valuable, if they are standardized and based on a formal model. Up to now many special unrelated graphical tools have been developed in informatics, often reflecting only the special realization of systems but not their abstract structure and functioning. Net diagrams are the first tool to deal with a lot of aspects in a uniform and disciplined way.

The first part of this paper reports on experiences in using net diagrams and net morphisms (see [3]) in an informal way as a vehicle to communicate important ideas, concepts, and notions to students. For this purpose standard interpretations (see [9]) as well as some new interpretations arising from teaching necessities are used, and their application is shown by means of well-known examples. The paper concentrates on applications not yet standard in informatics and excludes the whole well-established area of place/transition (PT-) nets modelling non-sequential processes.

The second part of the paper deals with terminology as a special research problem. In a young and quickly-growing branch of science like informatics, communication between researchers is complicated by the fact that even researchers in the same field speak different languages. Every "school" uses its own terminology, which is often bound to surface phenomena or to special realisations of systems.

Usually, terminology covers a wide spectrum of aspects and conceptual levels related to the same subject, for example dynamic and static aspects of systems and useful abstractions. In the long run uniformity and consistency of terminology is a necessary condition for successful communication, especially in an interdisciplinary science like informatics. This aspect of science is well established in matured branches, like physics or chemistry, in the form of terminology committees or special dictionaries written by groups of experts. In informatics hardly any effort has been made to tackle this urgent but difficult problem.

Avoiding a babel means trying to unify and standardize terminology at least for special fields in accordance with a model general enough to deal with all important phenomena under study (if such a model exists). Unification is facilitated if the underlying model allows the interrelation of different conceptual levels in a formal way.

General Net Theory (GNT) provides hope that problems of this kind can be treated now. GNT is the first (but not at all finished) approach to cover the wide spectrum from the dynamics of individual events and conditions to the static structure of systems and pragmatic relations between their components (see diagram in [9]). GNT also allows the interrelation of different conceptual levels by means of net morphisms in a formal way.

GNT has been used as a basis for a field with growing importance in practice but with chaotic terminology, namely man-computer dialogs. This example is of special interest because of its wide spectrum of conceptual levels. On the one hand, it is necessary to deal with the formal roles of persons and machines and with pragmatic relations between them on the highest conceptual level. On the other hand, one has to deal with low level phenomena of processes, even single event and condition occurences, since dialogs are unique non-sequential processes.

By using standard interpretations and tools from GNT it is possible to structure a terminology into different conceptual levels and to separate general aspects of abstract systems from special realisations. The dialog system example is given in some detail to show that unification of terminology even in a small field is a difficult task which is impracticable without a unifying view and a model for information processing, with which new terms can be explained more easily.

2. SOME HIGHER LEVEL INTERPRETATIONS

For the coarse high level description of systems the standard channel/agency interpretation and a closely related non-standard means/activity interpretation are used. A third class of interpretations allows the graphical representation of common mathematical concepts like n-ary relations, mappings and functions, and their application in complex situations.

2.1. Channel/Agency Nets

Channel/agency nets (CA-nets) are the tool for the description of the static structure of systems at any appropriate level of detail. They abstract from concrete media for the representation of messages and from concrete actors transforming messages, but stress that both kinds of functional units have to be distinguished and that both are equally important.
The components of a net are interpreted as follows:

○ (S-element): channel = functional unit,
which contains messages

□ (T-element): agency = functional unit,
which processes messages

⟶ (flow relation):

(C) ⟶ [A] : A <u>takes</u> (fetches,reads) <u>messages</u> <u>out of</u> C
(C is an <u>input</u> <u>channel</u> of A,
A is a <u>receiver</u> from C)

[A] ⟶ (C) : A <u>puts</u> (deposits,writes) <u>messages</u> <u>into</u> C
(C is an <u>output</u> <u>channel</u> of A,
A is a <u>sender</u> to C)

For ease of communication about CA-nets, it is useful to have special terms for special channel/agency configurations. For systems with two agencies communicating through channels we may classify the channels by partitioning the channels of the S-complete net (see [3]) according to the input/output channel property with respect to the agencies.

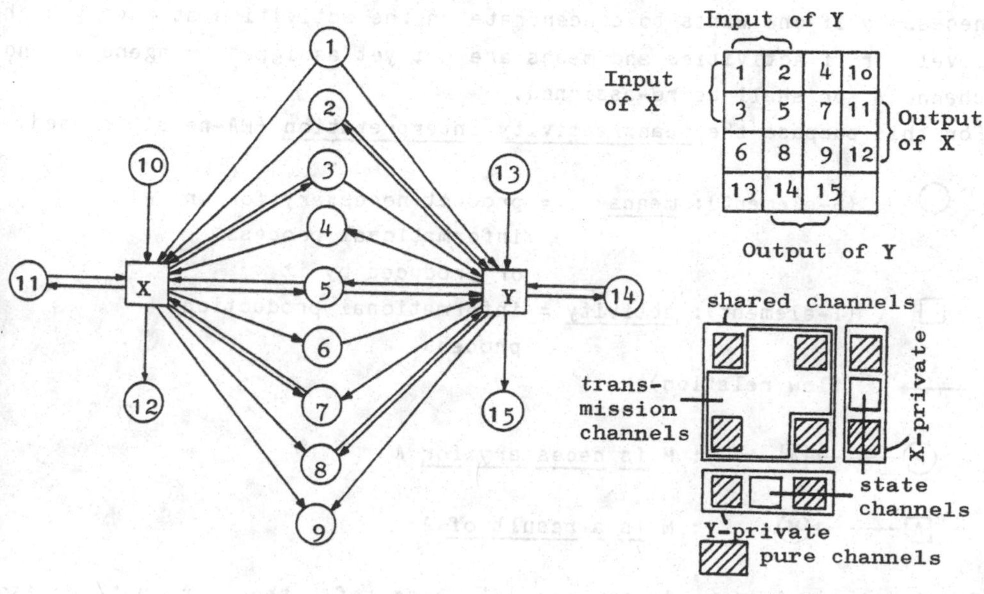

a) S-complete net b) Classification

Fig. 1. Classification of channels in a 2-agency net

Two special forms of CA-nets will be used in the following sections, which are called the <u>simple processing system</u> and the <u>conversational system</u>. The conversational system can be constructed out of two simple processing systems by a net morphism.

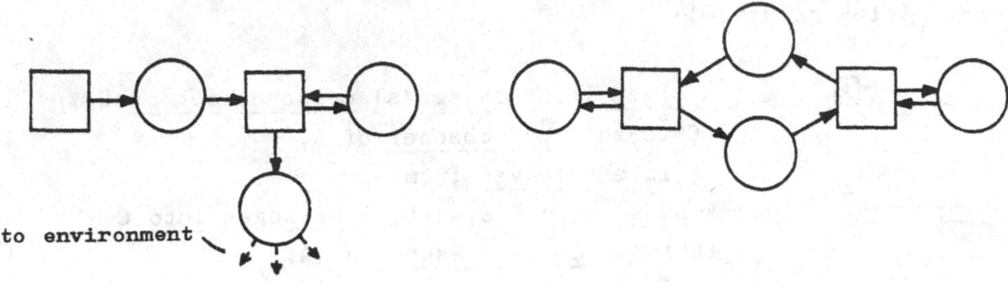

a) Simple processing system b) Conversational system

Fig. 2. Two special system structures

2.2. *Means/Activity Nets*

It is often useful to characterize information processing systems by their activities and by the means exchanged between them. This is necessary if one wants to concentrate on the activities at a very high level, or if activities and means are not yet assigned to agencies and channels, or shall be re-assigned.
For this purpose the *means/activity interpretation* (MA-nets) is used:

○ (S-element): *means* = product necessary for an informational process or produced by it

□ (T-element): *activity* = informational production process

⟶ (flow relation):

(M)⟶[A] : M *is necessary for* A

[A]⟶(M) : M *is a result of* A

This interpretation is a special case of the product/process interpretation introduced by A.W. Holt ([5]) and is closely related to the CA-interpretation:
Each agency is the carrier of one or more activities, each channel may contain one or more means. The activities of several agencies may be seen as one abstract virtual activity, the contents of many channels may be abstracted into one virtual means.

This extra interpretation is also useful for the explanation of an established terminology, since the names of channels and agencies often don't say very much about their activities or their contents .

2.3. Nets Representing Relations and Functions

Many concepts in informatics are formally described by n-ary relations and functions. A uniform visual representation of the interaction of many of them in complex situations is a valuable didactic tool, because it is much more transparent than text strings. Relations can be represented by undirected nets with labelled arcs. Let $R \subset A1 \times A2 \times \ldots \times Ak$ be a k-ary Relation. Each element $r=(a1,\ldots,ak) \in R$ can be represented by a net with the following interpretation:

○ (S-element): components of a tupel

□ (T-element): tuple formation

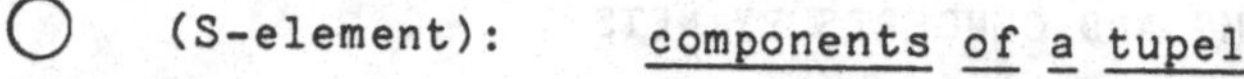

(adjacency): x is the i-th component of r

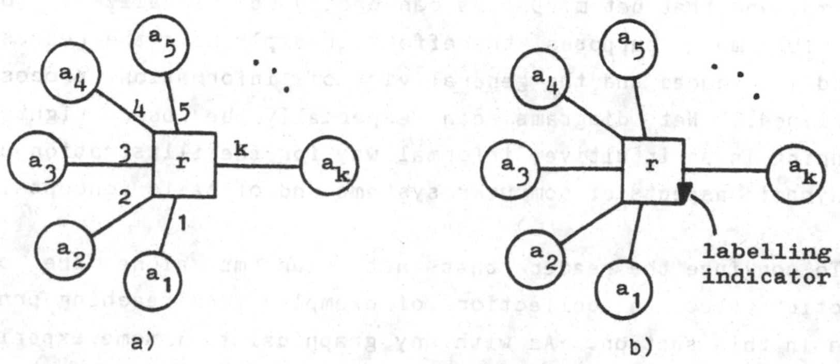

Fig. 3. Net representation of relation elements

If the labels are ordered clockwise or counter-clockwise, only a labelling indicator (as in Fig.3 b)) is used, indicating direction and start of labelling. In many contexts even this labelling indicator may be dropped. Replacing the tuple names "rj" by "R" yields a representation of the whole relation R.

The same method may be applied to show the dependencies between several relations with respect to the component sets A1,...,Ak (represented by S-elements) or with respect to special elements.

Since discrete functions are special relations, they can be represented by this method too. To show functionality directed nets may be applied, with the following interpretations of the flow relation:

(a) ——▶ [f] : a _is an argument for_ f

[f] ——▶ (a) : a _is a result of_ f

(A) ——▶ [f] : A _is a component set of the domain of_ f

[f] ——▶ (A) : A _is a component of the range of_ f .

3. EXPLANATION OF SYSTEMS AND CONCEPTS BY NETS

One of the main advantages of nets is that one can use the same formalism at different levels of detail and for different aspects of systems, and that net morphisms can easily be visualized. By using nets for many purposes, the effort in explaining the representation method is reduced and the general view of information processing is underlined. Net diagrams can especially be used right from the beginning in an intuitive, informal way for the illustration of static and dynamic aspects of computer systems and of basic concepts.

To convince the reader that net diagrams alone are of great didactic value, a collection of examples from teaching practice is given in this section. As with any graphical tool some experience in drawing and topological arrangement is necessary for successful application. Although the static structure of systems and their dynamics are closely related and should not be strictly separated in teaching, the corresponding examples are given in separate sections.

3.1. _Static structures_

The following examples show how nets and net interpretations can be used to explain complex hardware and software systems, in-the-small as well as in-the-large.
The first example shows the structure of a typical _von-Neumann-machine_ in successive refinements. This form of graphical representation is much more transparent than the somehow arbitrary drawings in traditional books on computer organization, where active and passive functional units and static and dynamic aspects are all mixed up (see e.g. Fig. 7.6. in the book of Gschwind and

McCluskey,[4]).

input channel DP-system output channel

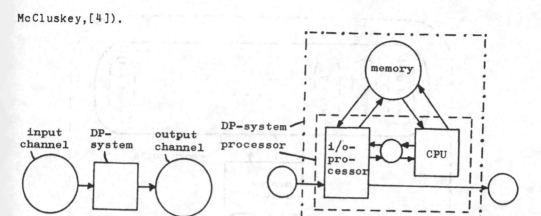

a) The most abstract view

DP-system processor memory i/o-processor CPU

b) The state-dependent machine

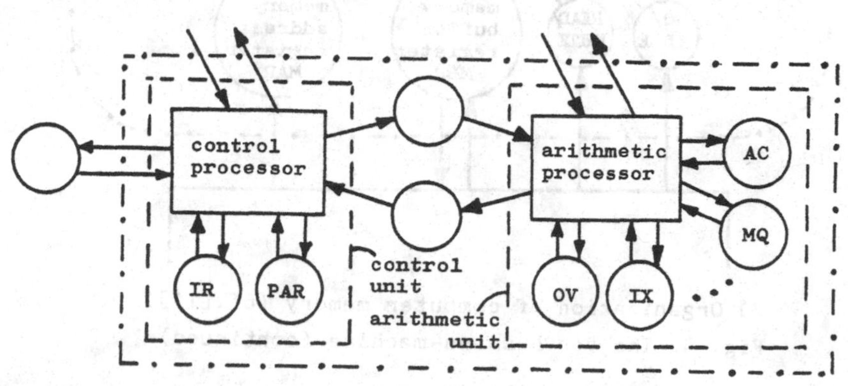

c) Organization of the CPU

Fig. 4. The von-Neumann-machine

The refinements may be carried further to show even the behaviour of the switching circuitry changing from CA-nets to PT-nets or to CE-nets.

The same method may be used to show the architecture of modern parallel machines, as for example machines with multiple independent CPU's, array processors, single CPU's with multiple functional units, pipline machines etc. (see [12] for a discussion of these architectures). It can as well be applied to hardware configurations (systems-in-the-large) as shown in the examples of Fig.5 and may be used also to show the static structure of organizations in which computer systems may be integrated as channels or agencies.

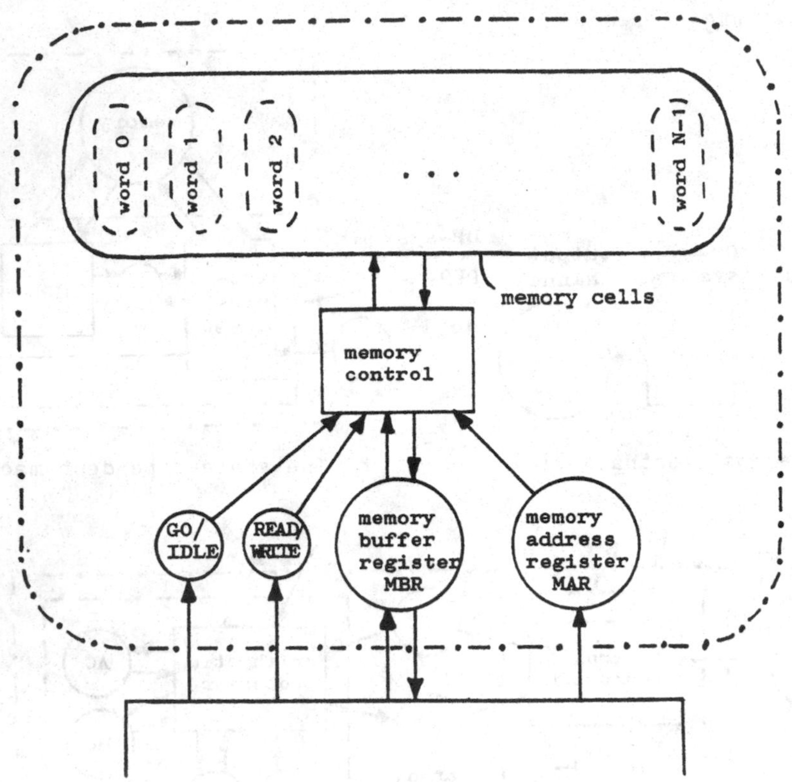

d) Organization of computer memory (cf.[11])

Fig. 4. The von-Neumann-machine (continued)

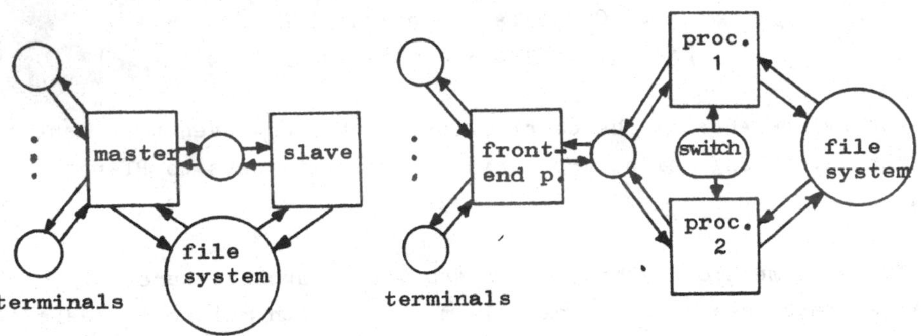

a) Master-slave configuration b) Duplex configuration with front-end

Fig. 5. Hardware configurations

Operating systems are special complex software systems and may be represented by nets on a fixed level of detail. The example of Fig. 6 shows the relevant components of a system for job processing (cf.[1]).

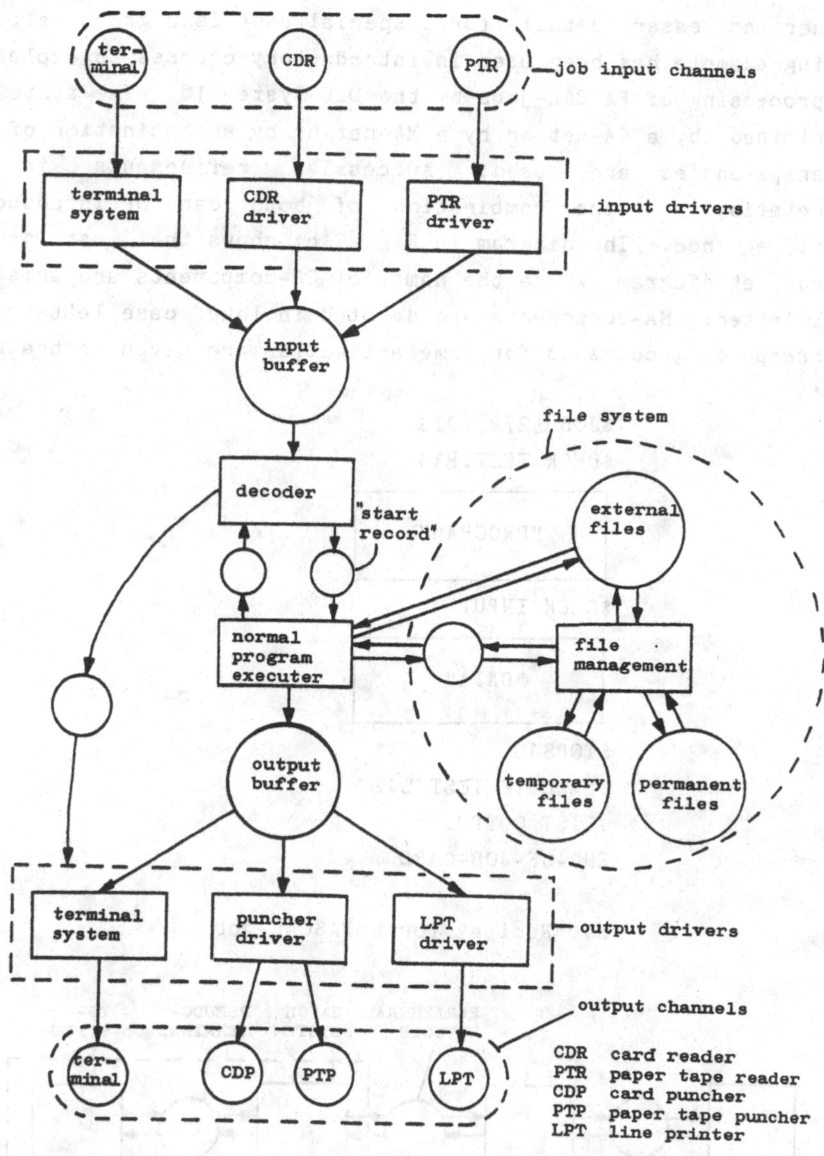

Fig. 6. Job-processing in BS3 (TR440)

CA-nets and MA-nets may be used to show the relevant system structure for the naive user, as for example beginners in programming. Usually they get a "recipe" for punching cards without enough information about the virtual system they are using, and therefore have difficulties in understanding the different printouts. In this situation a representation of the system abstracting from time-sharing and other unnecessary details for a special user is a great help. The following example has been used in introductory courses to explain the batch-processing of PASCAL-jobs by the DEC System 10. The system may be explained by a CA-net or by a MA-net or by a combination of both. If transparencies are used, successive refinements in each interpretation and the combination of both can be introduced in temporal sequence. The diagram in Fig. 7 c) shows the most detailed combined net diagram, where the names of CA-components are written in capital letters, MA-components are denoted in lower case letters, and the corresponding commands for some activities are given in brackets.

```
$JOB [272,007]
$DECK TEST.PAS
+----------------------+
|      "PROGRAM"       |
+----------------------+
$DECK INPUT
+----------------------+
|       "DATA"         |
+----------------------+
$TOPS10
.EXECUTE TEST/LIST
.LIST OUTPUT
END-OF-JOB-CARD
```

a) "Recipe" for a PASCAL-job

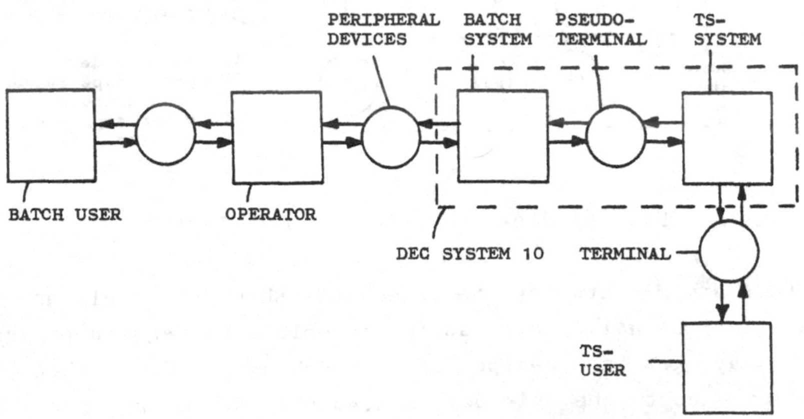

b) Coarse (partial) system structure

Fig. 7. PASCAL-job processing on a DEC System 10

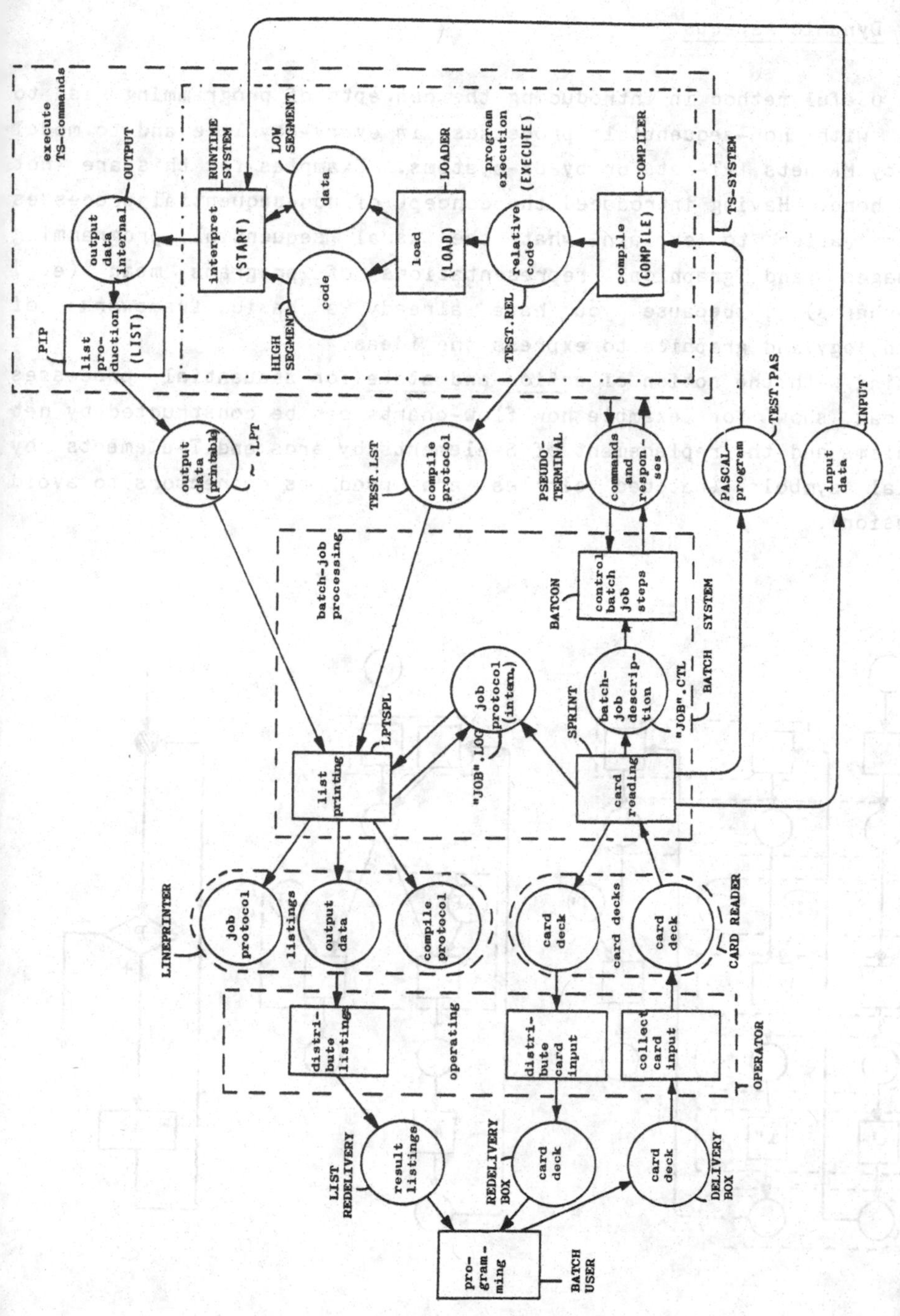

c) Fine structure (CA- and MA-net combined)

Fig. 7. PASCAL-job processing on a DEC System 10 (cont.)

3.2. Dynamic Aspects

A useful method in introducing the concepts of programming is to start with non-sequential processes in every-day life and to model them by MA-nets, PT-nets or by CE-systems. Examples for this are not given here. Having introduced the concept of non-sequential processes it is easier to explain what the usual sequential programming languages and graphical representations of programs mean (e.g. flow-charts) , because you have already a basic framework of terminology and graphics to express the ideas.
Starting with the notion of action and state for sequential processes one can show for example how flow-charts can be constructed by net morphisms and the replacement of S-elements by arcs and T-elements by special symbols (hatched circles are used as connectors to avoid confusion).

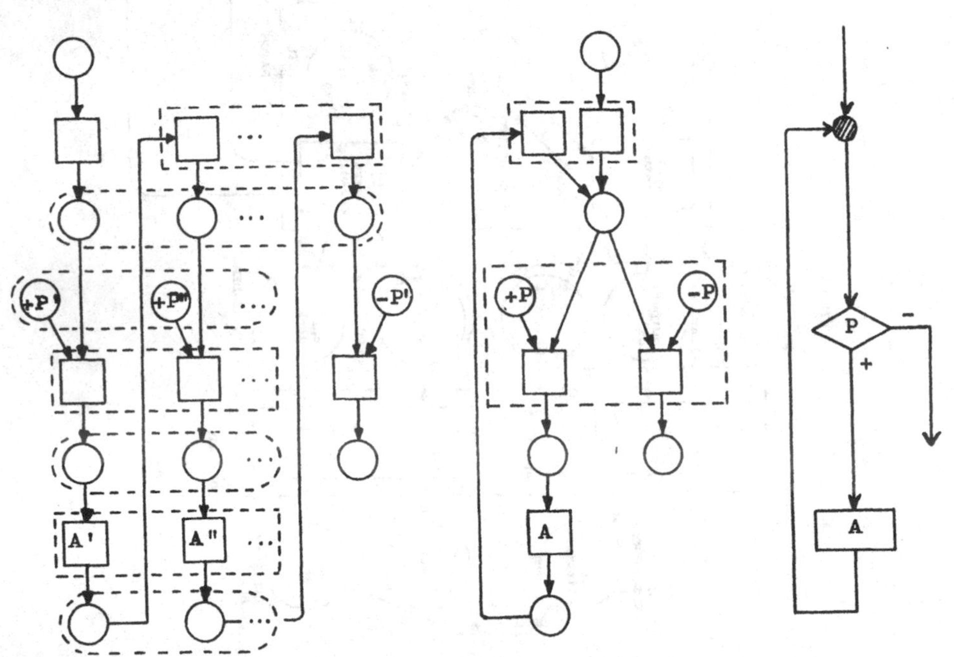

Fig. 8. Sequential processes and flow-charts

Net diagrams are not only useful for the explanation of control constructs but also for the structured representation of abstract data structures. Data Structures may be algebraically characterized by

a set $T = T1 \cup T2 \cup \ldots \cup Tn$ $(n \geq 1)$, $Ti \cap Tj = \emptyset$ for $i \neq j$,

a set $T0 = T1 \cup \ldots \cup Tk$ $(1 \leq k \leq n)$ (the type of interest),

a sequence $F = \langle f1, \ldots, fm \rangle$ $(1 \leq m)$ of functions

$$fi: Ti1 \times \ldots \times Tiz \longrightarrow Tir,$$

and a set of restrictions and axioms.

The relations between the domains and ranges of functions can be visualized by nets ('data structure diagrams',[6]), which may also be used to produce the graphical representation of correct expressions (similar to syntax diagrams) by "unfolding", for which the restrictions define forbidden subnets and for which the axioms correspond with certain net morphisms.

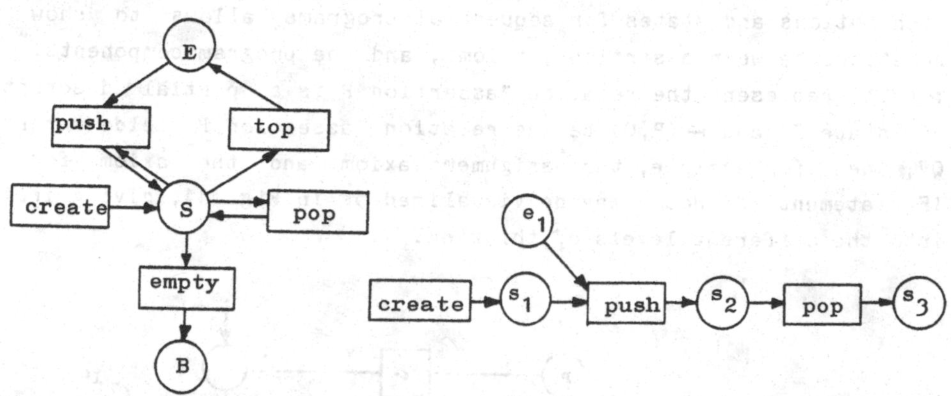

a) Data structure diagram b) A special stack

Fig.9. Net representation of stacks

An algebraic treatment of control structures by similar methods is possible (cf. [6]).

3.3 Basic Concepts

Basic concepts of informatics often deal with suitable abstractions and the combination of different levels of thinking. Some of them may be visualized by interpreted nets and net morphisms as well as by relation nets.

CA-nets and net morphisms may be used to illustrate the concept of <u>virtualisation</u>. For example, hardly any extra explanation is necessary to convey the ideas of "virtual machines" in programming.

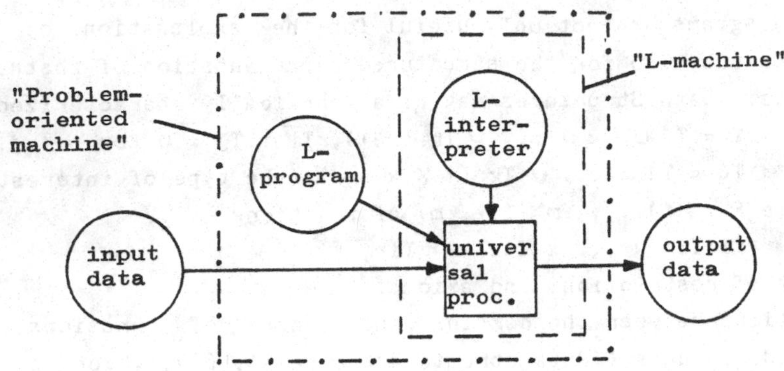

Fig. 10. Virtual machines in programming

The concept of proving the correctness of programs may be visualized by mixing flow-chart elements with net notation. Starting with actions and states for sequential programs allows to show the relations between assertions, axioms, and the program components. Let :· (P,S) represent the relation "assertion P is a partial description of state S" and ⊢ (P,Q) be the relation "assertion P yields assertion Q", then, for example, the assignment axiom and the axiom for the IF-statement of Hoare may be visualized as in Fig. 11, giving insight into the different levels of thinking.

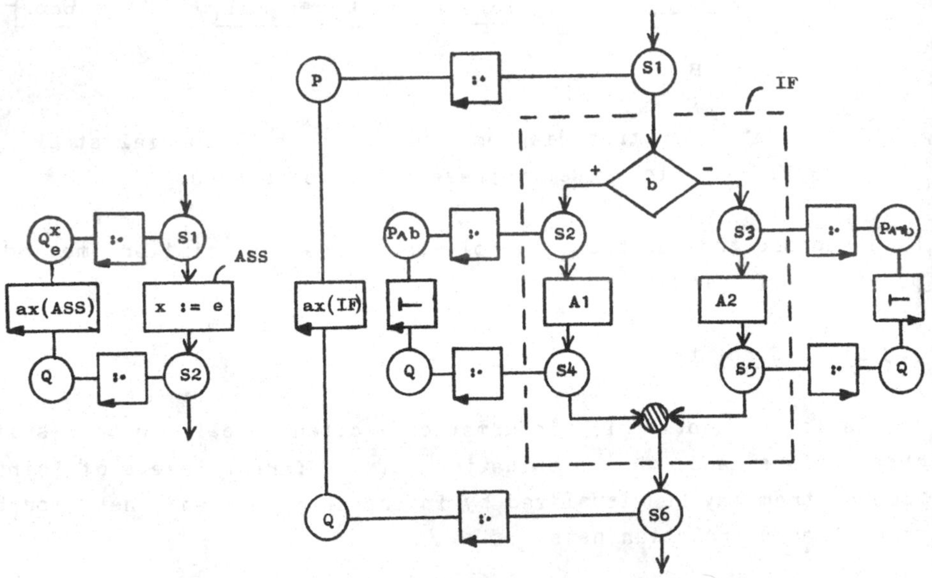

a) Assignment axiom b) IF-axiom

Fig. 11. Relations between programs and assertions

As a final example diagrams for the principle of information processing by machines using a set of relations on facts (following Kupka, [7]) is presented. The aim of information processing is to gain new information from existing information. The principle may be phrased as follows:

> "Instead of directly applying a function f to the information I(A) about a fact A to get the information I(B) about a corresponding fact B, one uses data D(A) and D(B) and a suitable function g transforming D(A) into D(B). Automation means that the problem-oriented data D(A) and D(B) are replaced by machine states M(A) and M(B) which are causally related".

This text may be illustrated by Fig. 12.

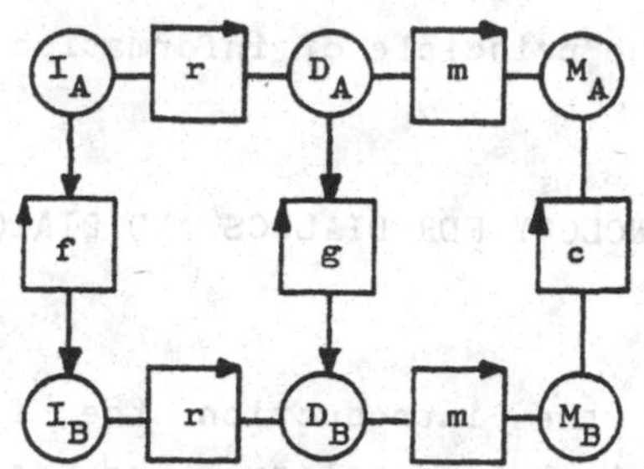

Fig. 12. Coarse relation net

On closer examination one has to recognize that the relations are context dependent and that the causal relation c is a special case of the general causal relation of a universal machine determined by a machine program MP. By introducing ternary relations mean, rep, appl and caus one gets the following extended net diagram (with contexts K_P and K_M) the details of which cannot be discussed here (cf. [7]).

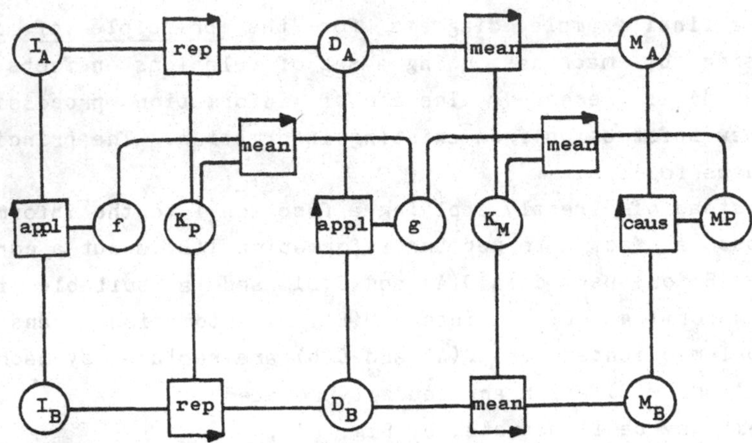

Fig. 13. The principle of information processing

4. A NET BASED TERMINOLOGY FOR DIALOGS AND DIALOG SYSTEMS

As pointed out in the introduction the field of man-computer dialogs lacks a consistent terminology. The need for a unification of terminology arose, when our research group on dialog languages tried to find out what the common dialog-specific concepts of "conversational programming languages" like APL, JOSS, BASIC etc., of command languages for time-sharing systems and of specialized application languages, e.g. for the interactive evaluation of szintigrams, are.
One main observation was that one has to consider the structure of the whole system, the language and the processes in the system in parallel to explain all relevant features, but that no terminology existed which permits discussion of all these levels and aspects in a consistent way. Even the terms "dialog language" and "dialog system" were not well defined (often "conversational" or "interactive" are used instead of "dialog", but with slightly different meaning).

There are mainly two reasons for this situation:
Firstly, in the early stages of dialog language research, the machine and its behaviour were examined in isolation. This excluded the important pragmatic relations between man and machine, which make dialogs a necessary and usefull extension of batch processing, but which lead to most of the difficulties subsequently experienced.
Secondly, without tools for the abstraction from special systems and

processes it is difficult to construct models and to develop a terminology for a broader field. GNT permits the modelling of man-machine systems and even to abstract from the special actors and media. Therefore, it is a suitable basis for terminology work.

The field of dialog languages/systems may be characterized by four main properties, which will be briefly explained in the next section. The second section concentrates on the pragmatic bindings in dialogs in general. Then it is shown how a terminology can be developed in two steps by firstly abstracting as far as possible from concrete systems to introduce general terms and by specializing and refining the terminology in cases where the internal structure and behaviour of functional units are known and must be explained. The terminology to be presented has been worked out in more dedail in a report written in German ([8]).

4.1. Dialog Characteristics

Man-computer dialogs show the following general properties which must be considered in modelling and in terminology:

(1) In general, dialogs are unique, non-sequential, non-procedural processes. Dialogs are unique because they are usually irreproducible. They are non-sequential, because the two partners and the media used may work partially in parallel and are synchronized only for communication. Dialogs are non-procedural in the sense that it is impossible or undesirable to describe the process in advance and to delegate it's execution to a computer. This is closely related to the interests of a user and his spontaneous decisions on how to continue.

(2) The roles of the partners are asymmetric. One of them usually has the initiative and gives instructions, the other one is obliged to perform specified tasks and to respond. The exchanged messages have a different pragmatic status, some are commands, others may be ignored.

(3) Dialogs are state-dependent. It is conceptually necessary to differentiate between messages exchanged between the partners and messages kept in memory (the "internal" state) and influencing the processing of the next message. The possibility of delegating the storage and retrieval of data to computers is one of the reasons for the growing importance of dialog applications.

(4) Dialogs are based on a common language for the formulation of tasks and responses.

All these characteristics can be expressed by different interpretations of nets.

4.2. Roles and Pragmatic Bindings

The roles of the dialog initiator and the dialog responder may be rendered precise by dividing a dialog into steps and each step into two parts consisting of task formation and task fulfilment on the one hand and of response construction and response evaluation on the other hand. For the first part, the terminology for task processing developed by a German standards committee (see [2]) may be adopted.

The basis of this approach is the channel/agency interpretation of nets and a simple processing system as introduced in section 2.1. One of the two agencies is called the task sender (TS), the other the task receiver (TR). The task binding may be verbally phrased as

"the obligation of a TR with respect to a TS to fulfil a certain DP-job".

Starting with these terms it is easy to specify what we mean by task description, task-description language, task formation and task fulfilment, internal and external result of task fulfilment etc. . All these terms may be explained by referring to the underlying CA-net or to the corresponding MA-net, respectively. Individual events such as start of the task ("That event by which the commencement of the task binding is defined") and end of the task may be visualized in a proper refinement of the MA-net (see Fig. 14. c)).

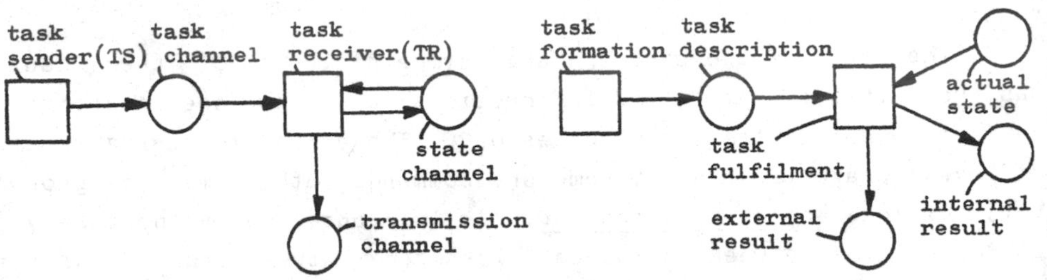

a) Simple task processing system b) MA-net for task processing

Fig. 14. Terminology for task processing

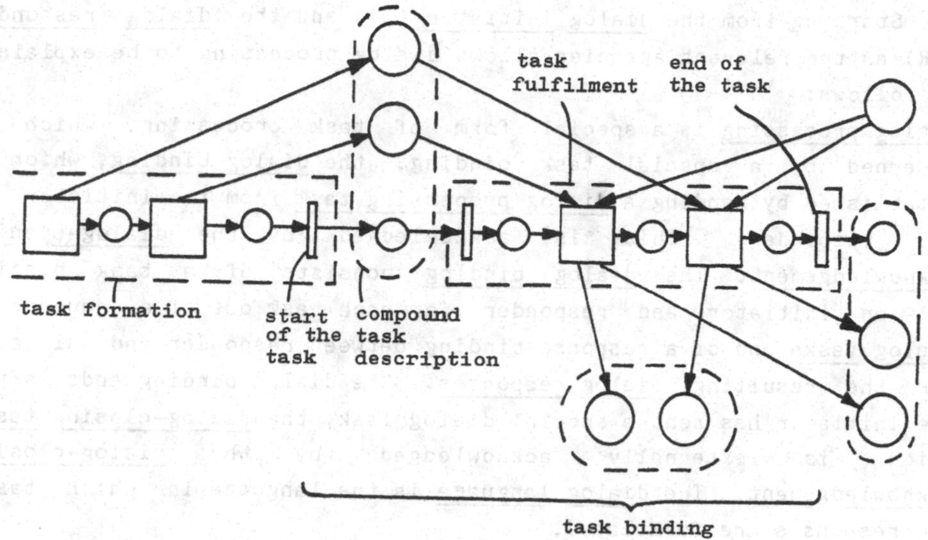

c) Individual events in task processing

Fig. 14. Terminology for task processing (continued)

The corresponding terminology for response processing can be defined using the same diagrams but starting with the response binding ("The authorization of the receiver with respect to the sender to evaluate a sent message if he wants to do so").

The role of the dialog initiator may now be characterized briefly by "task sender and response receiver" and the role of the dialog responder by "task receiver and response sender".
To make the terminology more complete, dialog processing must be embedded in task processing of a special kind, as will be explained in the next section.

4.3. Dialogs in Conversational Systems

By formally constructing an abstract conversational system out of two simple processing systems and combining task processing and response processing to get dialog processing one concentrates on the basic principles of dialogs abstracting from non-sequential processing of the two agencies and of internally active channels.

Starting from the _dialog initiator_ (DI) and the _dialog responder_ (DR) as the relevant agencies allows dialog processing to be explained as follows:
Dialog processing is a special form of task processing, which is governed by a special task binding, the _dialog binding_, which is established by sending a _dialog processing task_ from the initiator to the responder. This is acknowledged by the _dialog-opening acknowledgement_. The _dialog binding_ consists of a task binding between initiator and responder for each task out of a sequence of _dialog tasks_ and of a response binding between responder and initiator for the resulting _dialog responses_. The dialog binding ends, after the initiator has sent a special dialog task, the _dialog-closing task_, which is externally acknowledged by the _dialog-closing acknowledgement_. The _dialog language_ is the language in which tasks and responses are formulated.

The verbal explanations of special terms should be supported by net diagrams with inscriptions corresponding to suitable interpretations. Useful abstractions and connections between different interpretations may be visualized by giving the corresponding net morphisms.

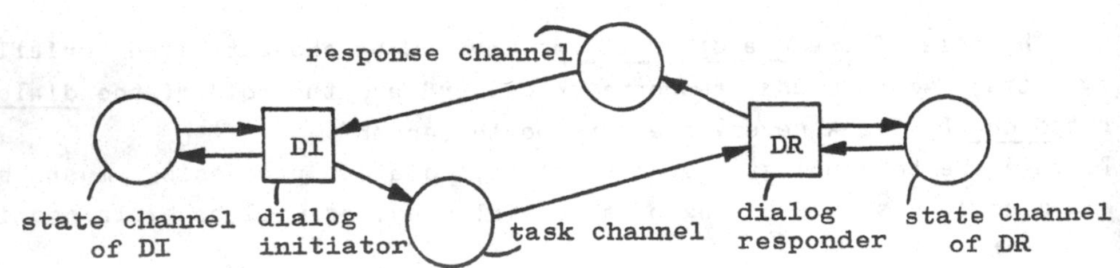

Fig. 15. Dialog processing system (CA-net)

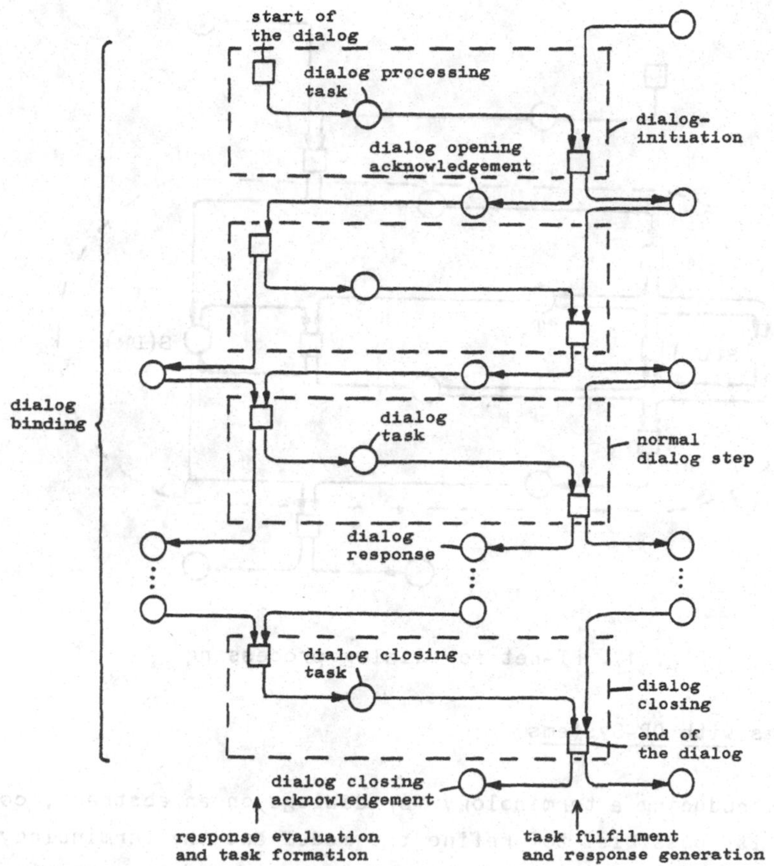

Fig. 16. MA-net of dialog processing

If one wishes to concentrate on the dynamics of dialogs alone, one may even interpret the MA-net of Fig. 16 as an occurrence net and model the repetition of normal dialog steps by repeated firings of transitions in a corresponding PT-net (see Fig. 17).

The initial marking says that the responder is ready and that the start of the dialog only depends on the initiator. The conflict given by a token on place R expresses the freedom of the initiator to continue with a normal dialog step or to close the dialog.
This net may be abstracted into a PT-net where only "dialog initiation", "being in dialog" and "dialog closing" are distinguished (dashed lines in Fig. 17.). One more step of abstraction shows again that dialog processing may be seen as a single task fulfilment, which corresponds to the firing of one transition.

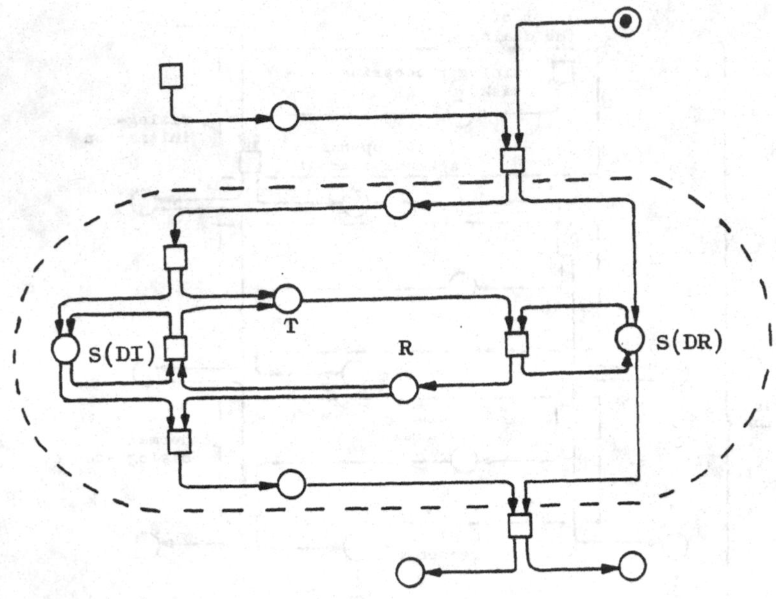

Fig. 17. PT-net for dialog processing

4.4. Dialogs with DP-Systems

After introducing a terminology for dialogs on an abstract, coarse level, it is possible to refine the model and the terminology for special cases. For example, this is necessary to explain the semantics of a dialog language of conversational systems with a DP-system as responder. The refinement may be done on the level of CA-nets, where the internal organization of the responder and state dependencies become more transparent.

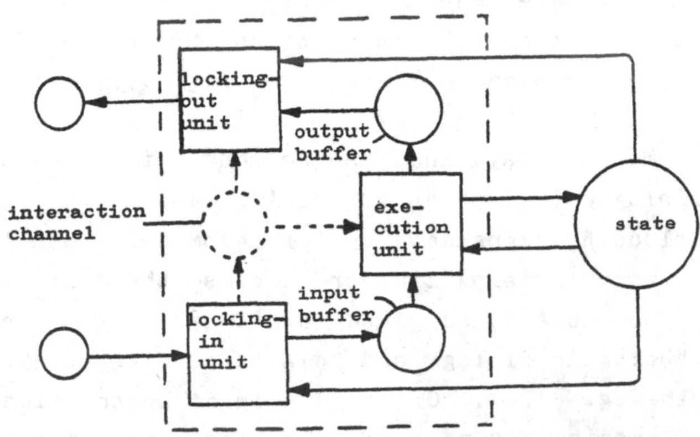

Fig. 18. DP-system as dialog responder

To explain the useful interrupt mechanism on a problem-oriented level the model may be extended by an internal interaction channel (dotted lines in Fig. 18.) and an additional interaction binding which states that a special kind of task, inserted tasks, has to be fulfilled with priority after the actual elementary task has been finished.
Even the term "user" may be defined now. The user is a person acting as dialog initiator.

Having a detailed structure of the DR and of his state, permits the definition of different classes of tasks affecting the components in different ways. Even with a rough structuring as above, one may introduce terms like declaration task, deletion task, cancellation task, suspension task, continuation task, demand task etc. .

Finally one may give a more precise definition of terms like "dialog system", "interaction system" and "communication system" with respect to dialogs.
A dialog system is a DP-system acting as dialog responder and its state. An interaction system is a dialog system with an interaction channel and interaction binding. A system is called a communication system if it is constructed out of a finite number of dialog systems which may communicate through a common shared channel.

5. CONCLUSIONS

There is no doubt that CE-systems and PT-nets are of great value in the study of non-sequential processes. Experience shows that the use of higher level nets in a naive manner or in not yet formalized areas is also very helpful.

On the one hand, nets are a simple mathematical structure with a natural mechanism for abstraction and refinement and with a nice graphical representation which can be taught to everybody in less than one hour. So little explanation of the formalism itself is necessary.

On the other hand, the same formalism has many useful interpretations which permit the explanation of rough ideas and practical experiences, as well as terminology, more precisely than by words alone. It helps in system analysis, design and concept formation and has a clean mathematical basis, on which fully formalized problems may be treated.

Two problems should be mentioned at the end. It is not always useful to use net diagrams explicitely if one is sure that other graphical representations may be explained as abbreviations of special nets. But the use of nets wherever it seems appropiate underlines the "systemic" view of informatics.
Last but not least: Drawing transparent net diagrams is a skill which can only be acquired by doing it as often as possible.

REFERENCES

1. Arbeitsgruppe für Betriebssystemnormung: Terminologie zur Beschreibung von Modellen für Rechensysteme zur Auftragsabwicklung, Teile 1 und 2, GMD, St.Augustin, 1971
2. Deutsches Institut für Normung: DIN 66200, Teil 1: Betrieb von Rechensystemen, Begriffe, Auftragsabwicklung, Berlin, Köln: Beuth, 1978
3. Genrich, H.J., Lautenbach, K., Thiagarajan, P.S.: Elements of General Net Theory, in these proceedings
4. Gschwind, H.W., McCluskey, E.J.: Design of Digital Computers, Second Edition, Berlin, Heidelberg, New York: Springer, 1975
5. Holt, A.W.: Net Models of Organizational Systems, in Theory and Practice, In Ansätze zur Organisationstheorie Rechnergestützter Informationssysteme, ed. Petri, C.A., Berichte der GMD Nr. 111, pp. 39 - 62, München, Wien: Oldenbourg, 1979
6. Kupka, I.: Structure Diagrams for Representing Semantics, Universität Hamburg, Fachbereich Informatik, IFI-HH-M-53/77, 1977
7. Kupka, I.: Ein Vorschlag zur Fortentwicklung des Informationsbegriffs, Universität Hamburg, Fachbereich Informatik, working paper, 1978
8. Oberquelle, H.: Grundbegriffe zur Beschreibung von Dialogen und dialogfähigen Systemen, Universität Hamburg, Fachbereich Informatik, IFI-HH-B-28/76, 1976
9. Petri, C.A.: Introduction to General Net Theory, in these proceedings
10. Petri, C.A.: Modelling as a Communication Discipline, In Measuring, Modelling and Evaluating Computer Systems, eds. Beilner, H., Gelenbe, E., pp. 435 - 449, Amsterdam: North-Holland, 1977
11. Stone, H.S.: Introduction to Computer Organization and Data Structures, New York: McGraw Hill, 1972
12. Tanenbaum, A.S. : Structured Computer Organisation, Englewood Cliffs,N.J.: Prentice Hall, 1976

STRUCTURED REPRESENTATION OF KNOWLEDGE BY PETRI NETS AS AN AID FOR TEACHING AND RESEARCH

M. Jantzen

University of Hamburg

Abstract

Petri nets are used to illustrate statements and dependencies in a lucid and precise way. Examples are given to indicate how this graphical representation can be used.

Introduction

Everybody knows that there is a great variety of textbooks on mathematical subjects even if one restricts attention to theoretical computer science. Each book presents the subject from a certain point of view and selects a certain logical structure which is supposed to be appropriate for the learning process of the reader. Unfortunately, most of the books do not present their underlying structure in a very clear and transparent way since the dependencies between the various statements are not explicitly shown. Of course one can find books, where the dependencies between the chapters are given by some kind of drawing. This is then a more or less informal and incomplete guideline for the reader. Figure 5 shows how a Petri net can simplify such a diagram. Another limitation is given by the fact that normally textbooks do not admit different starting points for the respective reader which are in accordance with his previous knowledge. Moreover, the reader cannot choose his personal strategy of learning since he is restricted to the special path which is presented in the book.

We are convinced that Petri nets with the interpretation of 'statements and dependencies' (see [7] for precise definitions) are suitable to give an explicit, complete, and structured representation of mathematical knowledge, as far as the logical dependency between theorems and definitions is concerned. We do not include the more complex cognitive abilities. This representation is different from that given in [2] but it may have some advantages.

There is evidence that such a representation is useful for teaching as has been partly shown in [1] , and it should be clear that an existing representation of this kind can help to prepare a course.

It is beyond the scope of this note to describe all the different applications in full detail but we hope to motivate the reader to make his own experience with this application of Petri nets.

The Basic Net Interpretation: SD-Nets

In general, a Petri net is a graph containing only two types of nodes: circles (called places) and boxes or bars (called transitions). Places and transitions are connected by directed arcs in such a way that no two nodes of the same kind are linked together. If an arc is directed from a node x to a node y then x is an input to y and y is an output of x. Tokens may be distributed over the places and can be moved around according to the following rule: If each input pla of a transition contains at least one token then exactly one token is removed from these input places and exactly one token must be added to each of the output places of this transition.

The specific interpretation of Petri nets we are going to explain i more or less equal to interpretation 3 from [7] , where the token game is not of great importance. The meaning of places and transitions can be described as follows.

Each place represents a basic unit of mathematical knowledge which is expressed by a theorem, an axiom, or a definition. So each place is in one to one correspondence with a statement which is always true.

Since theorems may have one and the same meaning but using differen notation and formulation, we have to point out that in general different formulations of the same theorem must be represented by different places. Take for example the following theorems: 'Regular sets are clo under intersection' and 'If A and B are accepted by finite automat so is $A \cap B$'. Obviously both theorems express the same fact but if we more precise we can say so only since we already know a third theorem which says: 'Every regular set is accepted by some finite automaton an vice verse'. Definitions and axioms can be considered as statements wh are true without proof.

Each transition represents a proof or trivial dependency which us the knowledge, i.e. the theorems and definitions, represented by its input places as preconditions. The output places of this transition represent the results or derived definitions. There must exist at le one output place for each transition.

Similar as for places we point out that different proofs for one the same result must be represented by different transitions, even i they have the same input places in common.

From this explanation we deduce some properties which Petri nets to satisfy in order to allow a meaningful interpretation of statemen and dependencies. For instance selfloops do not make sense under thi interpretation, so all the nets we consider are pure (convention I). Since definitions are statements which are true without a proof, one might wish that the corresponding places do not have an input transi On the other hand some definition may use another one - for instance restricting it or to derive a further one - so that it is necessary connect the corresponding places by a transition. Therefore we decid (convention II) to use at least one input transition for such a plac which it is explicitly said that the statement is true by definition Now, if one likes to construct a Petri net with this interpretation even a small part of mathematics it is obvious that this is practica impossible if one tries to incorporate all the existing mathematical sults and definitions which are necessary for a self-explanatory for lation. Therefore we include the following (convention III) : All the statements and definitions which do not appear as places in the net supposed to be already known, trivial, or standard mathematics. More over, the proofs which are represented by transitions of the net may this knowledge implicitly. The following incomplete net (figure 1) m illustrate this for the case where the set theoretic equality $\overline{A \cup B}$ $\overline{A} \cap \overline{B}$ is not represented by some other place of the net.

Figure 1.

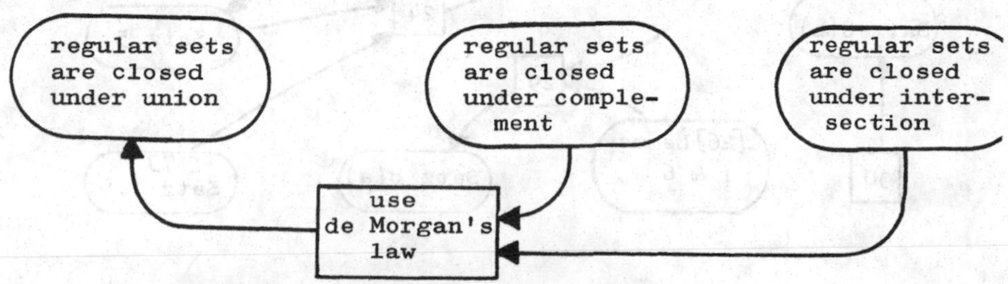

Very often proofs are used to verify only one statement at a time. If on the other hand a certain proof yields n different results then it is always possible to split the proof into n different although similar proofs, one for each result. So, for convenience only, we add the convention that each transition has exactly one output place (convention IV).

A Petri net together with an interpretation as described above and which satisfies convention I to IV will be called a SD-net.

Examples of SD-nets are given in [1,5,7] . The following SD-net (figure 2) is from [5] , where the results of one chapter together with their interconnections are shown. The inscriptions of the places ('Satz' is the german word for 'theorem') directly refer to results proved in the paper or published elsewhere. The labels of the transitions refer to the page numbers where the corresponding proofs can be found. In order to simplify the drawing definitions are not represented by places which is in accordance with our convention III.

Figure 2.

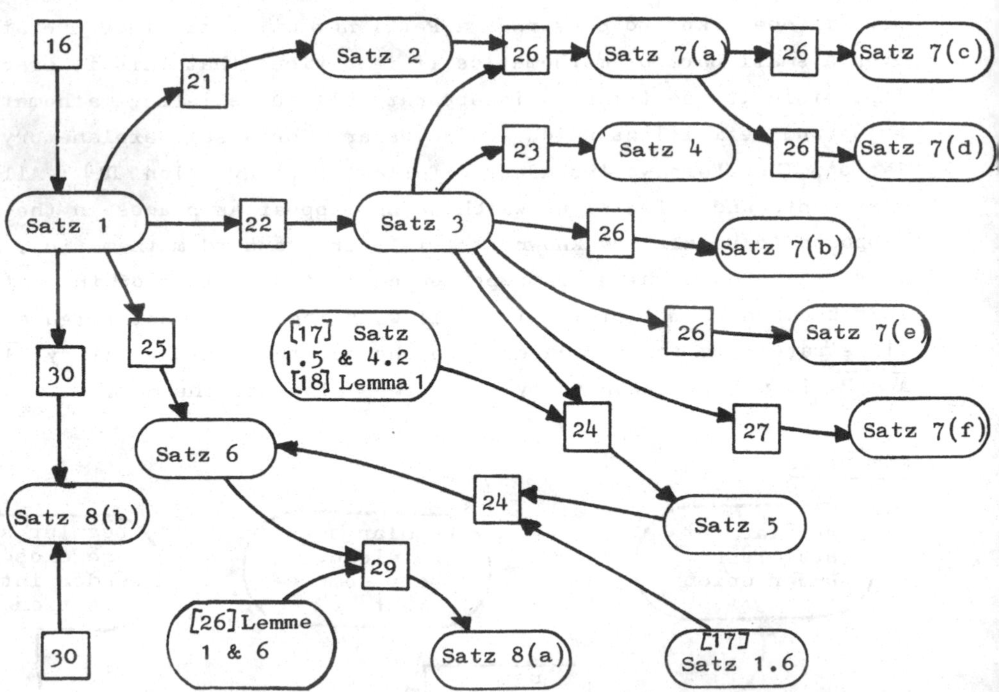

Similar Interpretations

Since the word 'statement' might be misleading we point out that the SD-nets as defined here are different from a very similar interpretation of nets, where the places represent logical statements which can be true or false, i.e. are predicates, and where transitions express implications like 'if all preconditions are true then all the postconditions are true'. An example of a Petri net with this interpretation is given by figure 3, where results about subclasses of Petri nets are vizualized. The reader is referred to [6] for proofs and definitions. All the nets N for which the predicates are formulated must be connected and every transition must have at least one input place. M is a marking of the given PT-net N. Note, that all the transitions in figure 3 are facts in the sense of [3].

Figure 3.

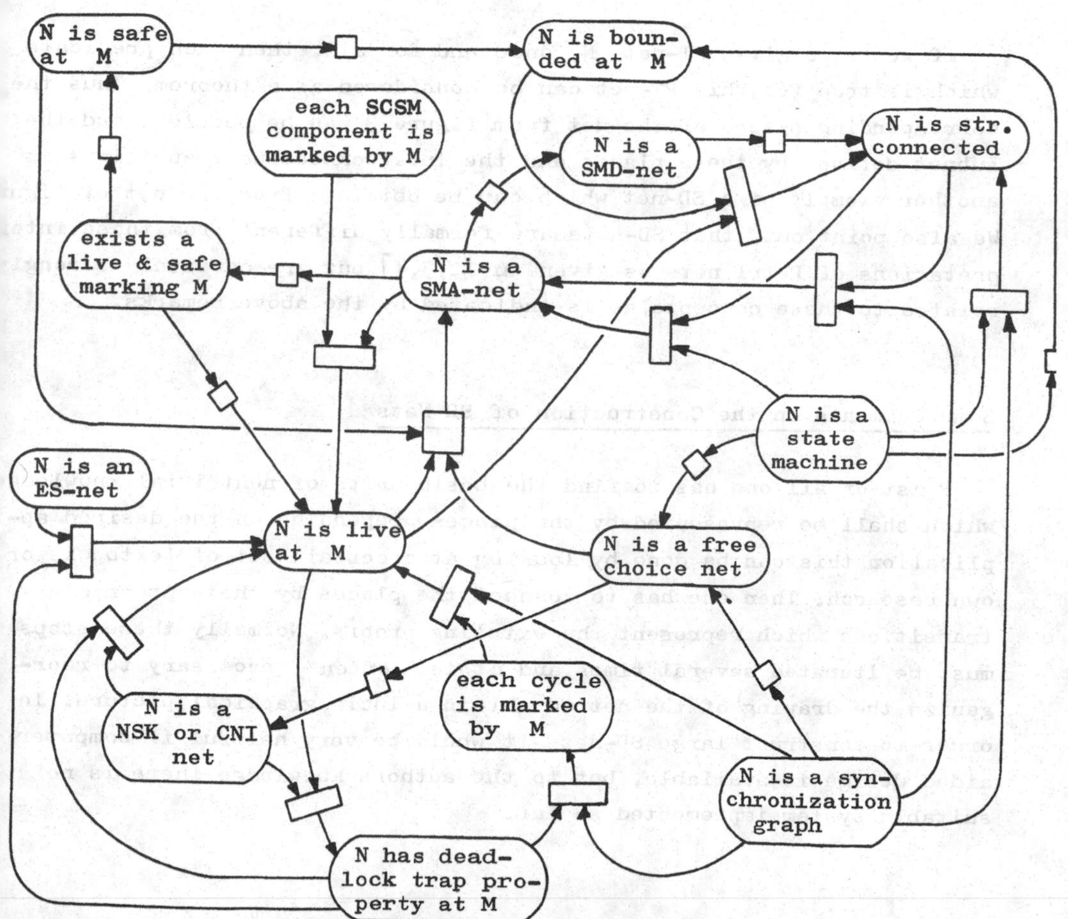

Since a predicate which is true for a given PT-net N remains true for ever as long as N is not changed, the following variant of the w known pebble game allows to derive new properties of the given PT-net from old onces.

(1) Put a pebble on those places which describe a predicate that is tr for the given PT-net N.

(2) If all the input places of a transition are pebbled then put a peb on each of its output places.

(3) If no further pebble can be put onto the net, then each place which is pebbled describes a valid property of the given PT-net N.

Obviously this interpretation of Petri nets is linked to the interpretation of statements and dependencies, since each implication of th net from figure 3 may be written as a theorem and then new theorems ca be formulated by applying the implications several times. Thus the net of figure 3 represents a collection of theorems.

If we fix a given PT-net N once and for all, then each predicate which is true for this PT-net can be considered as a theorem. Thus the corresponding places of the net from figure 3 can be pebbled, and the subnet defined by these places and the interconnecting transitions is another example of a SD-net which can be obtained from the net of figu We also point out, that SD-nets are formally different from those inte pretations of Petri nets as given in [2,3,4] but are certainly strongly related to these concepts, as is indicated by the above remarks.

Some Comments on the Construction of SD-Nets

First of all one has to find the basic units of nontrivial knowledge which shall be represented by the places. Depending on the desired application this can be done by looking at a certain set of textbooks or own research. Then one has to connect the places by the appropriate transitions which represent the existing proofs. Normally these steps must be iterated several times and it is often necessary to reorganize the drawing of the net to obtain a lucid graphical picture. In order to construct large SD-nets it would be very helpful if computer aided design is available, but to the authors knowledge there is no suitable system implemented so far.

In constructing the transitions the following situation frequently occurs (see figure 4).

Figure 4.

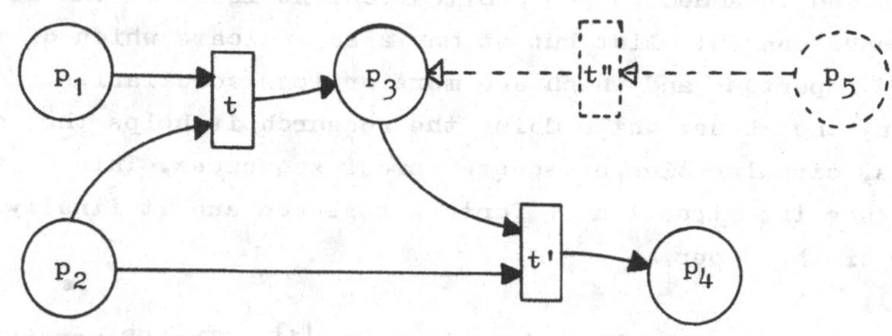

Some transition t' uses the preconditions p_2 and p_3, but p_2 is also a precondition for t , which represents a proof for p_3 , so that p_2 would be implicitly used by t' if the arc from p_2 to t' would be erased. Nevertheless, even in this case it is in general not allowed to omit the arc from p_2 to t', since it might happen in later steps of the SD-net construction that some other transition t" feeds p_3 and then there would exist a proof sequence for p_3 which does not use p_2! Only in case that the SD-net construction is completely finished one might look for those preconditions of a transition which are implicitly used in all the possible proof sequences of the other preconditions of that transition. We do not want to explain this kind of a simplifying procedure in more detail since it should be clear what we mean.

If a SD-net has been constructed one should ashure that it is complete and correct in the following sense. Each result which is represented by some place of the SD-net should admit a proof sequence which starts at those places that have an input transition without any precondition. Using the pebble game or by results about covering markings of PT-nets it can be seen that it is always decidable wether a given SD-net is complete.

Note that the reverse of a SD-net, which is obtained by reversing the direction of all the arcs, is a Petri net with a structure similar to context-free grammars, so that results about context-free derivations may be translated into results about SD-nets.

Some Hints for the Application of SD-Nets

One application has been explained by figure 2. The SD-net there is used as a complete and structured representation of results obtained by own research and is added to the publication. At least it can be used as a structured content list but it may also indicate which of the theorems are important and which are more or less corollaries. Moreover in developing the SD-net while doing the research it helps the scientist to find gaps, circularities, or shorter proof sequences. This in turn might influence the direction of further research and it finally guides the writing of the paper.

Another application has been described in [1] . The SD-net is constructed on the basis of a fixed collection of textbooks and then is used as a plan for teaching and learning similar to programmed instructions with branching facilities. The SD-net guides the learning process of a student in that he may pebble those places which represent the knowledge he already has. Some of the advantages of this approach compared with programmed instructions should be pointed out.

- There are different starting points, so that the student can choose those which are in accordance with his previous knowledge.
- Since the SD-net is a lucid, simple, and at the same time complete plan which referes to additional material, the student may not feel hampered too much.
- The SD-net offers different dependency paths, so that the student may follow his own strategy of learning. For instance he can follow some path in depth -first strategy or he may proceed in breadth-first strategy.
- The progress of the students learning process is vizualized by the marking of the places.
- Using net morphisms or colorings it is possible to define subnets and regions according to meaningful abstractions. This enables the student to classify and integrate his knowledge into a more general context.

The Petri net from figure 5 can be considered as an abstraction of an imaginary SD-net which represents the content of the entire book in full detail.

Figure 5.

The graph on the left is taken from [8] and describes different possibilities to give a course on the basis of that book. The Petri net on the right hand side shows the dependencies between the chapters of the same book. The pebble game on the Petri net yields every path which is allowed in the other graph except for the appendices.

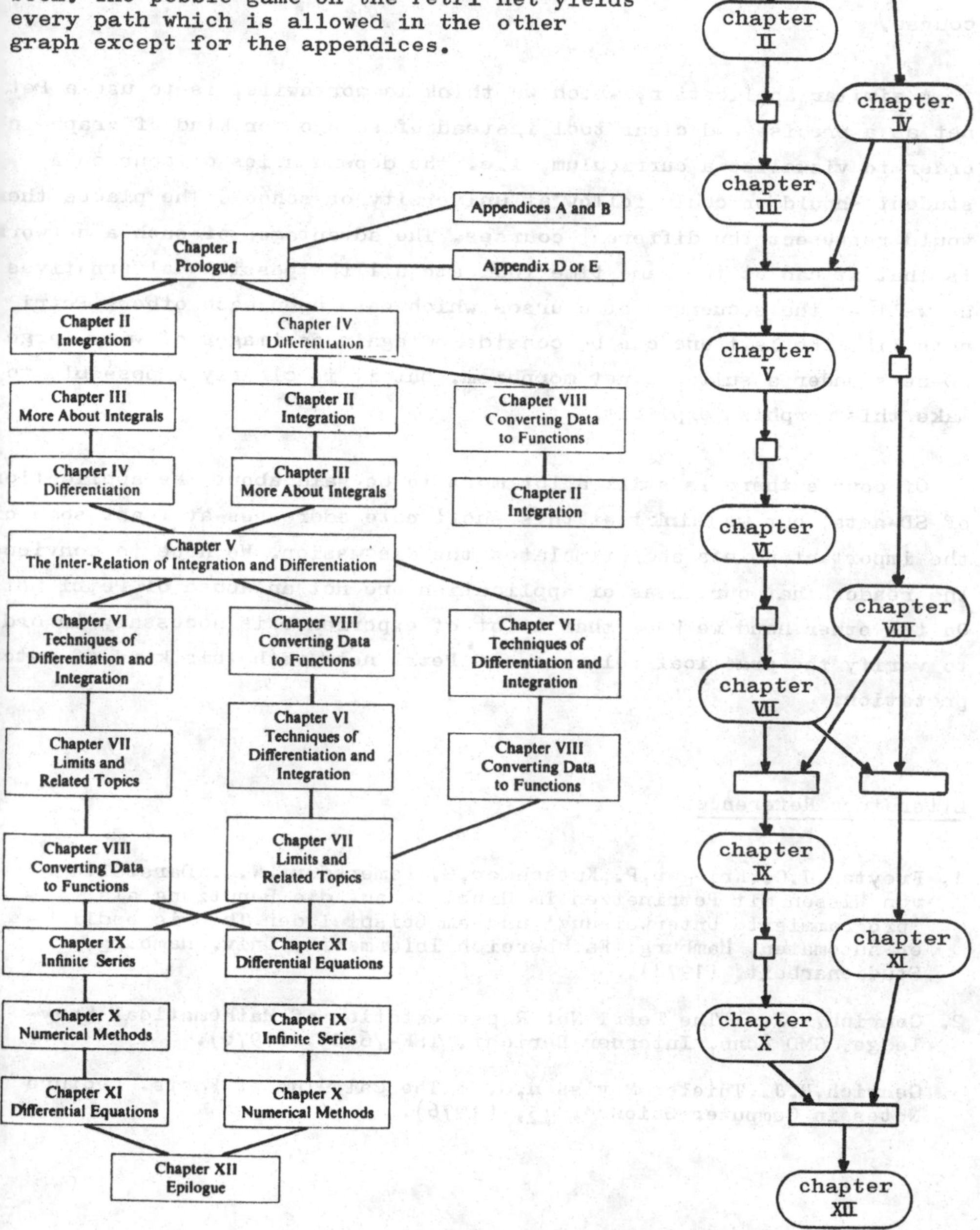

It is clear that the construction of a plan for learning on the bas of some SD-net is quite a lot of work and cannot be done by one person in short time. The work of [1] for instance not yet resulted in a fin version which could be used for teaching or learning. On the other han we made the experience that the construction of a SD-net on the basis existing textbooks is at least a very good starting point to prepare a course.

A similar application, which we think is worthwile, is to use a Pet net as a precise and clear tool instead of some other kind of graph in order to vizualize a curriculum, i.e. the dependencies of courses a student should or could follow at university or school. The places the would represent the different courses. The advantage of such a networ is that it can at the same time indicate all the possible alternatives as well as the sequences of courses which base upon each other. Petri nets like the last one can be considered again as images of very large SD-nets under a suitable net morphism, but it is clearly impossible to make this morphism explicit.

Of course there is still a lot more to be said about the applicatio of SD-nets, but we think that this short note addresses at least some o the important points and stimulates the discussion. We hope to convinc the reader that our ideas of application are not an abuse of Petri net On the other hand we know that a lot of experience is necessary in ord to verify the practical relevance of Petri nets with this kind of inte pretation.

Literature References

1. Freytag,J.C.,Krieger,P.,Kutschker,G.,Lamersdorf,W. : Darstellung von Wissen mit Petrinetzen im Hinblick auf die Benutzung als 'programmierte Unterweisung' und am Beispiel der Theorie endlicher Automaten. Hamburg, Fachbereich Informatik, Univ. Hamburg, Studienarbeit, (1978).

2. Genrich,H.J. : The Petri Net Representation of Mathematical Knowledge. GMD Bonn, Interner Bericht, ISF-76-05, (1976).

3. Genrich,H.J.,Thieler-Mevissen,G. : The Calculus of Facts. Lecture Notes in Computer Science, 45, (1976).

4. Genrich,H.J.,Lautenbach,K. : The Analysis of Distributed Systems by Means of Predicate/Transition-Nets. GMD Bonn, ISF-Report 79.01, (1979).

5. Jantzen,M. : Eigenschaften von Petrinetzsprachen. Hamburg, Fachbereich Informatik, Univ. Hamburg, Ph.D. thesis, (1979).

6. Jantzen,M.,Valk,R. : Formal Properties of Place/Transition-Nets. in these proceedings.

7. Petri,C.A. : Interpretations of Net Theory. GMD Bonn, Interner Bericht, ISF-75-07, second edition, (1976).

8. Wilson,R.L. : Much Ado About Calculus. New York, Heidelberg, Berlin, Springer, (1979).

A DICTIONARY OF SOME BASIC NOTIONS OF NET THEORY

H.J. Genrich[+], E. Stankiewicz-Wiechno[++]

[+] GMD-ISF, Schloss Birlinghoven, D-5205 St.Augustin 1

[++] Institute of Mathematics, Technical University, Warsaw

0. SOME MATHEMATICAL NOTATIONS

0.1:

$:\Longleftrightarrow$, $:=$	equivalence, equality by definition
$\bigwedge$ or $\forall$	universal quantifier
$\bigvee$ or $\exists$	existential quantifier
$\mathbb{N}$	the set of natural numbers, $\{0,1,2,\ldots\}$
$\mathbb{Z}$	the set of integers
$\mathcal{P}(A)$	the powerset of a set A
$\dot{x}$	the singleton $\{x\}$
$\|A\|$	the cardinality of a set A
ω	the cardinality of $\mathbb{N}$
$\bigcup$, $\bigcap$	generalized union, intersection
id	the identity relation

0.2: Let X,Y be sets, $R,S \subseteq X \times X$ binary relations in X, and $f: X \to Y$ a mapping of X into Y:

$xRy :\Longleftrightarrow (x,y) \in R$	x is <u>R-related</u> to y
$R^{-1} := \{y,x \mid xRy\}$	the <u>reverse</u> of R
$\overline{R} := X \times X - R$	the <u>complement</u> of R
$\mathrm{dom}(R) := \{x \mid \bigvee y: xRy\}$	the <u>domain</u> of R
$\mathrm{cod}(R) := \mathrm{dom}(R^{-1})$	the <u>codomain</u> of R
$R\|Y := R \cap (Y \times Y)$	the <u>restriction</u> of R to Y
$R[Y] := \mathrm{cod}(R \cap (Y \times X))$	the <u>R-image</u> of Y
$f[R] := \{f(x),f(y) \mid xRy\}$	the <u>f-image</u> of R
$\widehat{R} := R \cup R^{-1} \cup \mathrm{id}\|X$	the <u>symmetric and reflexive closure</u> of R
$RS := \{x,z \mid \bigvee y: xRySz\}$	the <u>composition</u> of R and S
$R^0 := \mathrm{id}\|X$	
$R^{n+1} := R^n R$	
$R^* := \bigcup R^n \mid n \in \mathbb{N}$	the <u>iteration</u> of R
$R^+ := RR^*$	the <u>transitive closure</u> of R

$\mathrm{Ken}(A,R) :\Longleftrightarrow \bigwedge x,y \in A: x\widehat{R}y \wedge \bigwedge x \in (X-A) \bigvee y \in A: x\overline{\widehat{R}}y$ A is a <u>ken</u> of R

K-dense $R :\Longleftrightarrow \bigwedge A,B: [\mathrm{Ken}(A,R) \wedge \mathrm{Ken}(B,\overline{R}) \Longrightarrow |A \cap B| = 1]$

1. NETS AND THEIR REPRESENTATION

1.1: A triple $N = (S,T;F)$ is called a *(directed) net* iff

(1) $S \cap T = \emptyset$

(2) $S \cup T \neq \emptyset$

(3) $F \subseteq (S\times T) \cup (T\times S)$

(4) $dom(F) \cup cod(F) = S \cup T$

1.2: Let $N = (S,T;F)$ be a net:

(1) $X := S \cup T$ is the set of *(S- or T-) elements* of N.

(2) F is the *flow* relation, its elements are the *arcs* of N.

(3) Between S- and T-elements of N,
$Z := F\cap(S\times T)$ is the *target* relation,
$Q := F^{-1}\cap(S\times T)$ is the *source* relation, and
$P := Z \cup Q$ is the *adjacency* relation.

(4) For an element $x\in X$, $\bullet x := \{y \mid (y,x)\in F\}$ is the set of *input* elements (the *pre-set*) and $x\bullet := \{y \mid (x,y)\in F\}$ the set of *output* elements (the *post-set*) of x; $\bullet x\bullet := \bullet x \cup x\bullet$ is the set of 'neighbours' of x.

(5) The tuples $(X;Z,Q)$, $(X;P,F)$, $(S,T;Z,Q)$ are equivalent representations of N.

(6) The tuples $(X;P)$, $(S,T;P)$ represent the *undirected net* belonging to N.

1.3: Let $N = (S,T;F)$ be a net:

(1) In the graphical representation of N, circles ○ and boxes □ represent the S-elements and T-elements, respectively; for an arc (x,y) of F, the corresponding nodes are connected by an arrow as follows:

(x)⟶[y] <==> $(x,y)\in F\cap(S\times T) = Z$

[x]⟶(y) <==> $(x,y)\in F\cap(T\times S) = Q^{-1}$

(2) A very narrow box ▯ or a stroke ┃ may be used for representing T-elements which are known to have no interior.

(3) In the graphical representation of the undirected net, arrowheads are omitted:

(x)——[y] <==> $(x,y)\in P$

1.4: Let $N = (S,T;F)$ be a net:

(1) N is called *pure* iff $Z \cap Q = \emptyset$, i.e. it does not contain subnets of shape ○⇄□.

(2) N is called <u>simple</u> iff no two elements have the same pre-set and the same post-set: $\bullet x = \bullet y \land x\bullet = y\bullet \Longrightarrow x = y$.

(3) N is called <u>S-complete</u> <u><T-complete></u> iff for any pair of sets of T-elements <S-elements> A,B with $A \cup B \neq \emptyset$ there exists an S-element <T-element> x with $\bullet x = A$ and $x\bullet = B$.

1.5: Let N = (S,T;F) be a net:

(1) N^d := (T,S;F) is called the <u>dual</u> of N.

(2) N^{-1} := $(S,T;F^{-1})$ is called the <u>reverse</u> of N.

(3) A net N' = (S',T';F') is called a <u>subnet</u> of N iff $S' \subseteq S$, $T' \subseteq T$, and $F' = F|X'$.

(4) For a set of S-elements $A \subseteq S$, the <u>subnet generated by</u> A is the net (A,T';F') with $T' = \bigcup \bullet x \bullet | x \in A$ and $F' = F|(A \cup T')$.
For a set of T-elements $A \subseteq T$, the <u>subnet generated by</u> A is the net (S',A;F') with $S' = \bigcup \bullet x \bullet | x \in A$ and $F' = F|(S' \cup A)$.

1.6: Let N = (S,T;F) be a net, and $A \subseteq X$ a set of elements of N:

(1) An element $x \in X$ belongs to the <u>surface</u> of A iff it belongs to A and is connected by an arc to an element outside of A.

(2) A is called <u>open</u> <u><closed></u> in N iff its surface is contained in S < T >.

(3) A subnet N' of N is called <u>open</u> <u><closed></u> iff the set of its elements is open <closed> in N.

(4) The set Π of open sets of elements of N is <u>the topology</u> of N; $(X;\Pi)$ is a topological space called a <u>Petri space</u>.

(5) The topology of N is structurally equivalent to the undirected net of N.

1.7: Let N = (S,T;F) be a pure finite net:

(1) The <u>incidence matrix</u> of N is a matrix $C: S \times T \rightarrow \{-1,0,+1\}$ with |S| rows and |T| columns such that

$$C(s,t) = \begin{cases} -1 & \text{iff } (s,t) \in F \\ +1 & \text{iff } (s,t) \in F^{-1} \\ 0 & \text{otherwise} \end{cases}$$

(2) C^T, the transpose of C, is the incidence matrix of the reverse dual of N.

2. NET MORPHISMS

2.1: Let $N_1 = (S_1,T_1;F_1)$ and $N_2 = (S_2,T_2;F_2)$ be nets and $f:X_1 \rightarrow X_2$ a mapping of X_1 into X_2.

(1) The triple (N_1,N_2,f) is called a net morphism iff f respects adjacency P and orientation F:

$f[P_1] \subseteq P_2 \cup id$

$f[F_1] \subseteq F_2 \cup id$

N_1 is called the source and N_2 the target of the net morphism which is denoted by $f:N_1 \rightarrow N_2$.

(2) For nets N_1, N_2 and a mapping $f:X_1 \rightarrow X_2$, the following statements are equivalent:

- (N_1,N_2,f) is a net morphism;
- f respects Z and Q: $f[Z_1] \subseteq Z_2 \cup id$ and $f[Q_1] \subseteq Q_2 \cup id$;
- f respects F and is continuous: $f[F_1] \subseteq F_2 \cup id$ and $[A \in \Pi_2 \Longrightarrow f^{-1}[A] \in \Pi_1]$.

2.2: The source N_1 of a net morphism $f:N_1 \rightarrow N_2$ is a refinement of a part of the target N_2 such that for each S-element <T-element> of N_2, the surface of its pre-image under f is contained in S < T >.

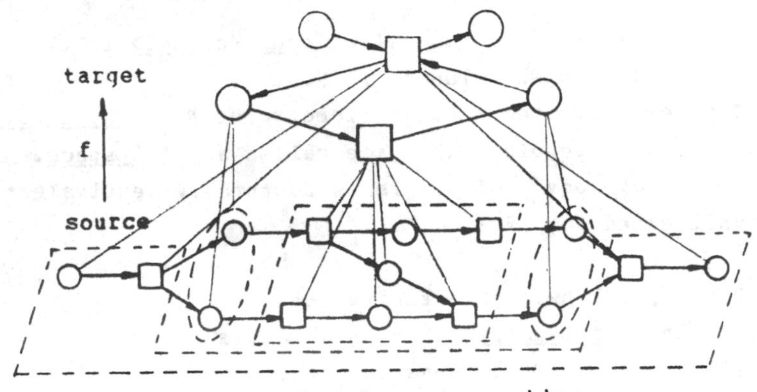

Example of a net morphism

2.3: A net morphism $f:N_1 \rightarrow N_2$ is called a quotient iff for every arc $(x,y) \in F_2$ there exists an arc $(u,v) \in F_1$ with $f(u)=x$ and $f(v)=y$. Graphically, a quotient can be represented in two ways: Either all elements of N_1 are labelled with the name of their image, or for each element of N_2 its pre-image is enclosed in N_1 by a dotted circle or box, as appropriate.

2.4: A net morphism $f:N_1 \to N_2$ is called

(1) a <u>folding</u> iff no adjacent nodes are mapped onto the same image: $f[P_1] \subseteq P_2$ [<==> $f[F_1] \subseteq F_2$] ;

(2) a <u>subnet injection</u> iff the f-image of N_1 is a subnet of N_2 and isomorphic to N_1;

(3) a <u>simplification</u> of N_1 iff it is a quotient onto a largest simple net N_2;

(4) a <u>S-completion <T-completion></u> of N_1 iff it is a subnet injection into a smallest S-complete <T-complete> net N_2.

2.5: Net morphisms may be denoted by special <u>inscriptions</u> assigned to either the source or the target net. The following examples show the splitting of diagrams and the representation of nets which show some regular structure. ⟶ denotes the corresponding morphism and ⇒ the interpretation of the inscriptions.

(1) Inter-page connection of diagrams by means of connectors

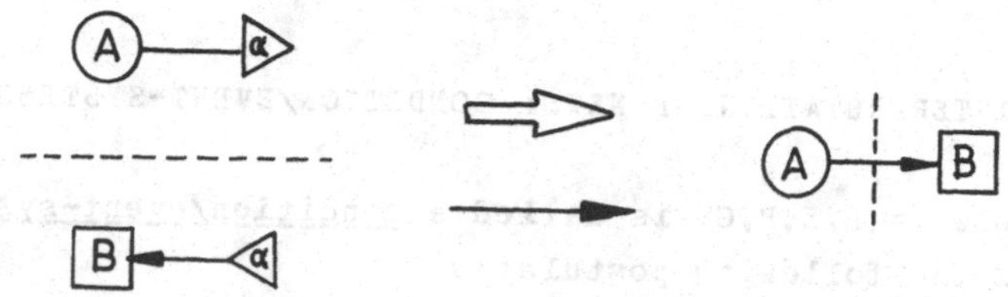

(2) Inter-page connection by means of multiple elements

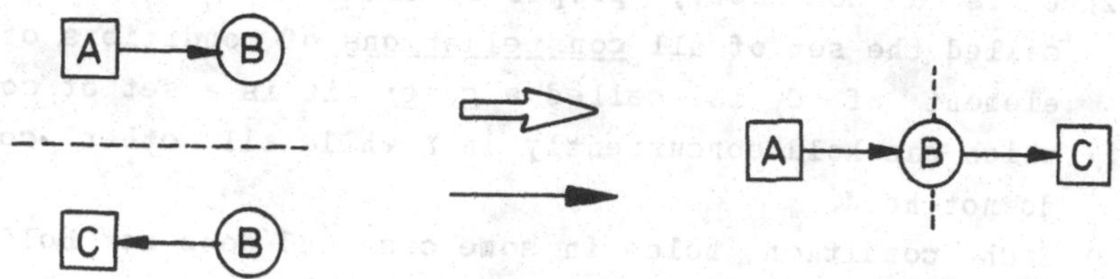

(3) Multiplication of subnets

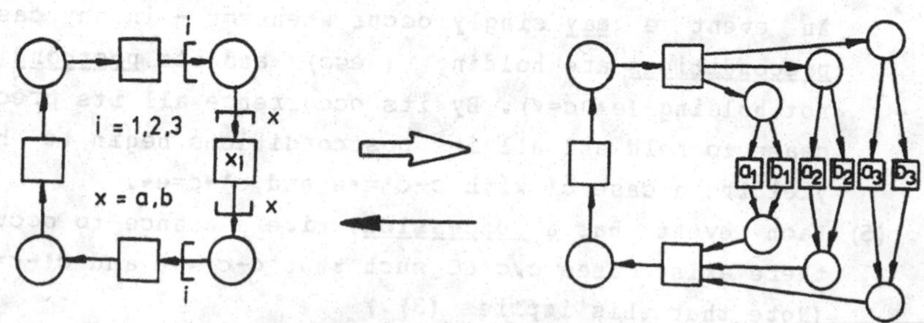

(4) (Recursive) substitution of net elements

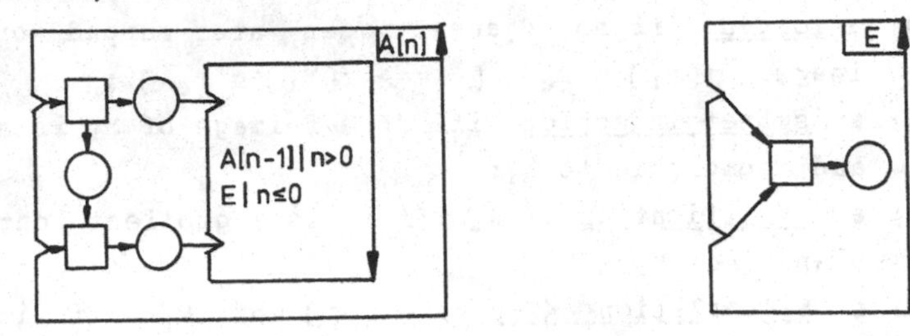

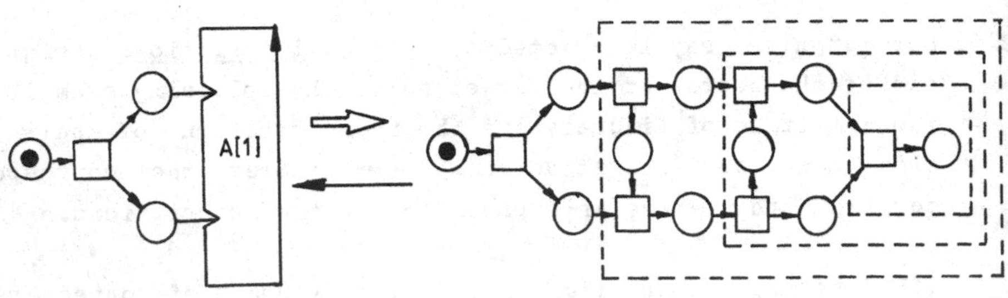

3. THE BASIC INTERPRETATION OF NETS: CONDITION/EVENT-SYSTEMS

3.1: A quadruple $\Sigma=(B,E;F,C)$ is called a <u>condition/event-system</u> iff it satisfies the following postulates:

(1) $(B,E;F)$ is a pure, simple net. The elements of B are called <u>conditions</u>, the elements of E are called <u>events</u>.

(2) C is a non-empty, proper subset of $K := \mathcal{P}(B)$, where K is called the set of all <u>constellations</u> of conditions of Σ. An element of C is called a <u>case</u>; it is a set of conditions which can hold concurrently in Σ while all other conditions do not hold.

(3) Each condition holds in some case and does not hold in some case: $\bigwedge x\in B \bigvee c,c'\in C:[x\in c \wedge x\notin c']$.

(4) The events are repeatable elementary changes in conditions. An event e <u>may</u> singly occur whenever - in any case c - its <u>preconditions</u> are holding $({}^\bullet e\subseteq c)$ and its <u>postconditions</u> are not holding $(e^\bullet \cap c=\emptyset)$. By its occurrence all its preconditions cease to hold and all its postconditions begin to hold thus yielding a case c' with $c-c'={}^\bullet e$ and $c'-c=e^\bullet$.

(5) Each event has a <u>concession</u>, i.e a chance to occur, in Σ: there exist cases $c,c'\in C$ such that $c-c'={}^\bullet e$ and $c'-c=e^\bullet$. (Note that this implies (3).)

(6) Two events may occur concurrently in one step G iff they may singly occur and have no pre- or postconditions in common. The notion step is introduced (for constellations) in the following way:

$k_1[G>k_2 :\Longleftrightarrow k_1,k_2 \in K \wedge \emptyset \neq G \subseteq E \wedge$

$\bigwedge e_1,e_2 \in G:[e_1 \neq e_2 \Longrightarrow \bullet e_1 \cap \bullet e_2 = e_1 \bullet \cap e_2 \bullet = \emptyset] \wedge$

$k_1 - k_2 = \bigsqcup \bullet e | e \in G \wedge k_2 - k_1 = \bigsqcup e \bullet | e \in G$

Note that the second line of this definition enforces the resolution of conflicts between events which may singly occur in k_1, but have preconditions or postconditions in common. "Reachability-in-one-step" is defined as

$k_1[\rightarrow k_2 :\Longleftrightarrow \bigvee G \subseteq E: k_1[G>k_2$, and "forward reachability" as

$k_1[\Rightarrow k_2 :\Longleftrightarrow k_1[\rightarrow^* k_2$

(7) C is an equivalence class of the full reachability relation R which expresses "reachability in a finite number of forward or backward steps": Ken(C,R) with $R := ([\rightarrow \cup \leftarrow])^*$.

If c is a current or an "initial" case of Σ then C is denoted by [c].

Note: (4),(5),(6) and (7) express the extensionality of the notion event in condition/event-systems: An event is fully characterized by the extension of the change in conditions effected by each of its occurrences.

3.2: In the graphical representation of condition/event-system, the holding or not holding of a condition in a given case is represented by the presence or absence of a marker ('token') on the corresponding ◯ symbol of the diagram of the net (B,E;F). The effect of the occurrence of an event is expressed by the following transition rule for case markings:

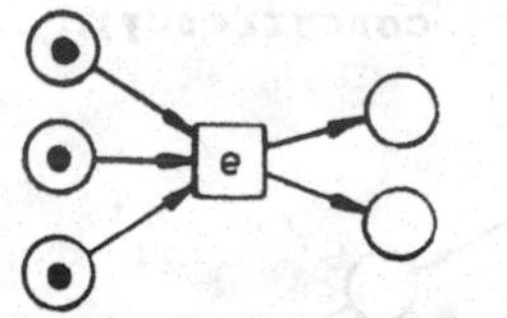

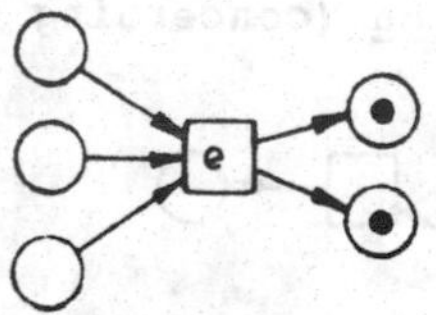

situation

before after

an occurrence of an event e

3.3: The following diagrams show examples of the four fundamental types of situation which can arise in condition/event nets:

(1) concession (of an event)

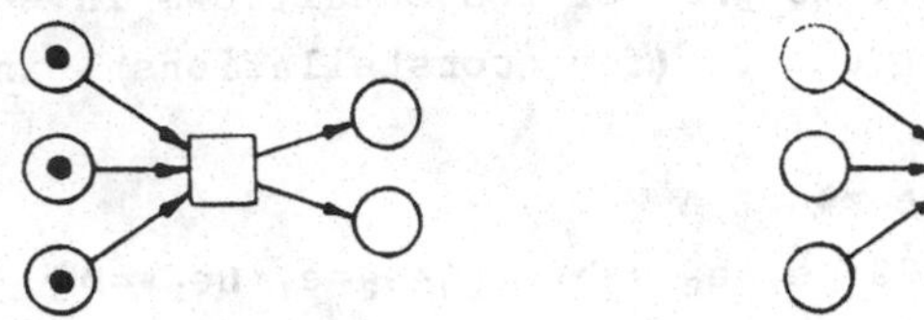

forward backward

(2) contact (of conditions, in an event)

forward backward

(3) conflict (between two events)

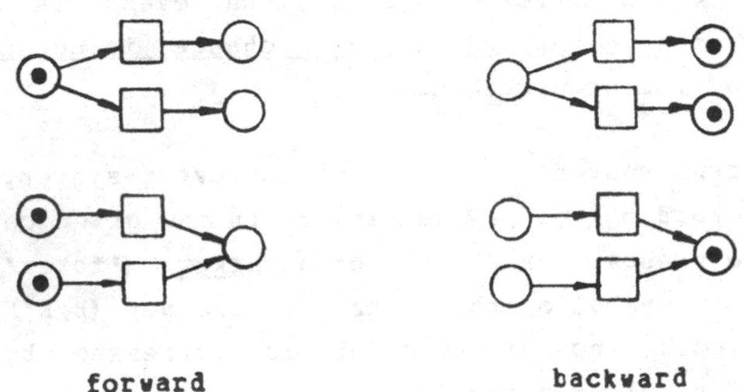

forward backward

(4) confusion (concerning conflict and concurrency)

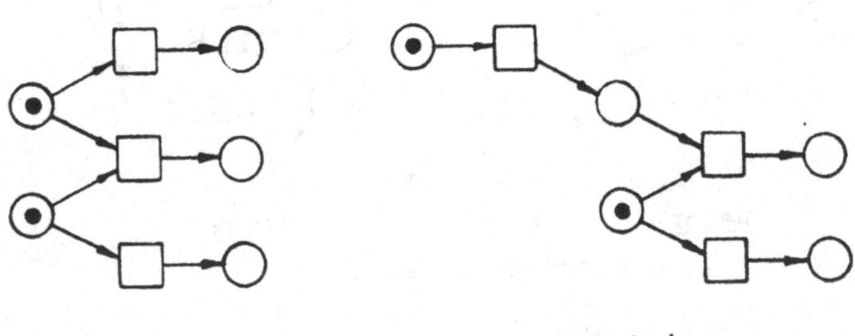

symmetric asymmetric

3.4: A condition/event-system is called <u>safe</u> iff it is free of contacts. It is called <u>conflict-free</u> iff it does not contain a conflict situation. A system is conflict-free if and only if there is no gain (forward conflict) or loss (backward conflict) of <u>information</u>. In systems with confusion, conflicts and their decisions are not <u>objective</u>, i.e. their existence does not depend on Σ alone but also on the observer, respectively simulator, who enforces sequence on occurrences which are concurrent.

4. OCCURRENCE NETS

4.1: Let $N=(S,T;F)$ be an acyclic net ($F^+ \cap id = \emptyset$) in which each S-element $s \in S$ has at most one predecessor ($|{\bullet}s| \le 1$) and at most one succesor ($|s{\bullet}| \le 1$). Then N is called an <u>occurrence net</u>. With a given occurrence net we associate the following notions:

(1)	$< \; := F^+$	<u>before</u> (a partial order)
(2)	$> \; := \; <^{-1}$	<u>after</u>
(3)	$li := \; < \cup > \cup \; id\|X$	<u>on a line</u>
(4)	$co := \overline{li} \cup id\|X$	<u>concurrent</u>
(5)	$\mathbb{C} := \{A \| Ken(A,co)\}$	the set of <u>cuts</u>
(6)	$\mathbb{L} := \{A \| Ken(A,li)\}$	the set of <u>lines</u>

4.2: Let Let $N_1=(B_1,E_1;F_1)$ be an occurrence net and $\Sigma=(B_2,E_2;F_2,C_2)$ be a condition/event-system. A net morphism $p:N_1 \to N_2$ is called a <u>process</u> of Σ iff it satisfies the following conditions:

(1) $p:N_1 \to N_2$ is a folding, i.e. $p[B_1] \subseteq B_2$ and $p[E_1] \subseteq E_2$).
A process element $x \in X_1$ is called an <u>occurrence</u> of the system element $p(x) \in X_2$.

(2) Each cut of N_1 which contains only conditions is part of an occurrence of a case of Σ: $\bigwedge c \in \mathbb{C} \cap \mathcal{P}(B_1) \bigvee c' \in C_2 : p[c] \subseteq c'$.

(3) Two occurrences of the same condition are on a line:
$\bigwedge a,b \in B_1 : [p(a)=p(b) \Longrightarrow a \; li \; b]$

(4) Two process events are occurrences of the same system event iff they effect the same changes in Σ:
$\bigwedge e \in E_1 \bigwedge f \in E_2 : [p(e)=f \Longleftrightarrow p[{\bullet}e]={\bullet}f \wedge p[e{\bullet}]=f{\bullet}]$
(Note that $(B_2,E_2;F_2)$ is simple.)

5. PLACE/TRANSITION-NETS (PETRI NETS)

5.1: A tuple $PN = (S,T;F,K,W,M_0)$ is called a <u>place/transition-net (PT-net, Petri net)</u> iff it has the following properties:

(1) $N = (S,T;F)$ is a directed net. The elements of S are called <u>places</u> and carry a variable number of <u>tokens</u>. The elements of T are called <u>transitions</u> and represent elementary changes of the distribution of tokens over the places.

(2) $K:S \to \mathbb{N} \cup \{\omega\}$ assigns to each place its, possibly infinite, token <u>capacity</u>, i.e. the maximal number of tokens it may carry.

(3) $W:F \to \mathbb{N}$ assigns to each arc its <u>multiplicity</u> or <u>token width</u>.

(4) $M_0:S \to \mathbb{N} \cup \{\omega\}$ is the <u>initial marking</u>, i.e. the initial distribution of tokens, which observes the capacities: $\bigwedge s \in S: M_0(s) \leq K(s)$.

(5) A <u>marking</u> $M:S \to \mathbb{N} \cup \{\omega\}$ may be changed under the following <u>transition rule</u>:
Let $t \in T$ be a transition with m input places, $\bullet t = \{a_1,\ldots,a_m\}$, and n output places, $t\bullet = \{b_1,\ldots,b_n\}$. An <u>occurrence</u> ('firing') of t decreases the number of tokens on each a_i by $W(a_i,t)$, and increases the number of tokens on each b_j by $W(t,b_j)$. It therefore <u>may occur</u> (has <u>concession</u>, is <u>enabled</u>) under the marking M iff all input places carry enough tokens: $M(a_i) \geq W(a_i,t)$, and all output places have enough space: $M(b_j) \leq K(b_j) - W(t,b_j)$.

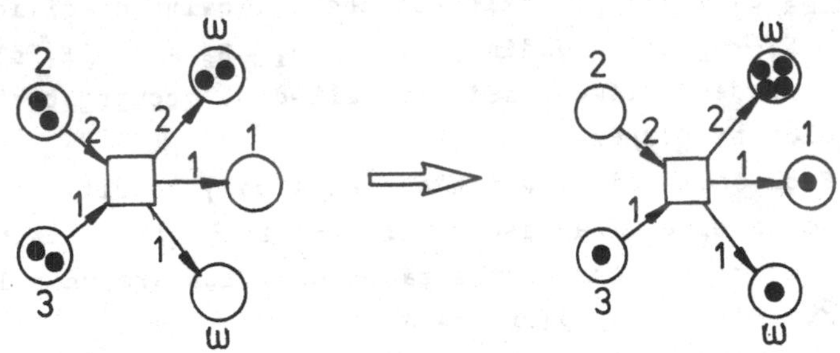

Effect of an occurrence of a transition

(6) Two transitions t_1,t_2 may occur <u>concurrently</u> (in one <u>step</u>) under M iff they may singly occur and have no adjacent places in common. A <u>step</u> U from marking M to a marking M' is therefore described as follows:

$M[U>M' :\Longleftrightarrow M,M':S\to \mathbb{N}\cup\{\omega\} \wedge \emptyset\neq U\subseteq T \wedge$
$\bigwedge t_1,t_2\in U: ({}^\bullet t_1 \cup t_1^\bullet)\cap({}^\bullet t_2 \cup t_2^\bullet) = \emptyset \wedge$
$\bigwedge s\in S: M(s), M'(s) \leq K(s) \wedge$
$\bigwedge t\in U: [[(s,t)\in F \Longrightarrow M'(s)=M(s)-W(s,t)] \wedge$
$[(t,s)\in F \Longrightarrow M'(s)=M(s)+W(t,s)]]$

(7) The set of all markings which are reachable from a given marking M by a finite number of forward steps <forward or backward steps> is denoted by $[M>$ < $[M]$ >:

$M[\to M' :\Longleftrightarrow \bigvee U: M[U>M'$

$[M> := \{M' \mid M\ [\to^* M'\}$, $[M] := \{M' \mid M\ ([\to \cup \leftarrow])^*\ M'\}$

$[M_0]$ is called the full_marking_class and $[M_0>$ the forward marking_class of PN.

5.2: Let PN = $(S,T;F,K,W,M_0)$ be a PT-net:

(1) If (S,T;F) is pure and simple and all places have capacity 1 - $K:S\to\{1\}$ - PN may represent a condition/event-system.

(2) If all places of PN have unlimited capacity - $K:S\to\{\omega\}$ - PN is called to follow the _weak_ transition rule: A transition is then enabled iff only all input places carry enough tokens. In this case, the function K may be omitted.

(3) PN is called _safe_ with respect to the given capacities K iff increasing K does not change the marking class.

(4) PN is called _bounded_ iff it follows the weak transition rule and for each place s there exists an upper bound for the number of tokens to be carried by s in the marking class (unlimited capacities can be replaced by some finite capacities without changing the marking class).

(5) PN is called _persistent_ if an enabled transition may loose its concession only by its own firing. (In case of a condition/event-net, persistency means conflict freeness.)

Note that the notions safe, bounded, and persistent depend on whether the full or the forward marking class are considered.

(6) PN is called _live_ iff for every forward reachable marking $M\in[M_0>$ and every transition t there exists a follower marking of M under which t is enabled.

5.3: Let PN = $(S,T;F,K,W,M_0)$ be a PT-net without multiple arcs ($W[F] = \{1\}$). Then PN is called

(1) a _state-machine graph_ iff all transitions have exactly one input and one output place: $t\in T \Longrightarrow |{}^\bullet t|=|t^\bullet|=1$;

(2) a synchronization graph (marked graph) iff all places have exactly one input and one output transition:
$s \in S \implies |{\bullet}s| = |s{\bullet}| = 1$;

(3) a free-choice net iff no transition with more than one input place shares an input place with some other transition:
$(s,t) \in F \implies s{\bullet} = \{t\} \vee {\bullet}t = \{s\}$;

(4) state-machine decomposable iff there exists a family of sets of places, $S_1,\ldots,S_n \subseteq S$ such that each subnet PN_i generated by S_i is a state-machine graph and each arc of PN belongs to at least one PN_i (PN is covered by the PN_i).

5.4 Let PN = $(S,T;F,K,W,M_0)$ be a pure finite PT-net:

(1) The incidence matrix of PN is a matrix $C: S \times T \to \mathbb{Z}$ with $|S|$ rows and $|T|$ columns such that

$$C(s,t) = \begin{cases} -W(s,t) & \text{iff } (s,t) \in F \\ +W(t,s) & \text{iff } (s,t) \in F^{-1} \\ 0 & \text{otherwise} \end{cases}$$

(2) The effect of the firing of a transition t to a marking M can be expressed by adding $C(-,t)$, the t-th column of C, to M (where M is treated as vector in places, and all vectors are treated as one-column-matrices).
$M[t>M' \implies M' = M + C(-,t)$

(3) Consequently, if u is the characteristic vector of a set $U \subseteq T$ then $M[U>M' \implies M' = M + C \bullet u$,
and therefore $M' \in [M] \implies \bigvee x: M' = M + C \bullet x$.

(4) An integer vector in places, $i: S \to \mathbb{Z}$, is called an S-invariant of PN iff $C^T \bullet i = 0$.
For an S-invariant i, the set of places s for which i(s) is non-zero is called the support of i, and the (closed) subnet of PN generated by it is called an S-component of PN.

(5) An integer vector in transitions, $r: T \to \mathbb{Z}$, is called a T-invariant of PN iff $C \bullet r = 0$.
For a T-invariant r, the set of transitions t for which r(t) is non-zero is called the support of r, and the (open) subnet of PN generated by it is called a T-component of PN.

5.5: Let PN be a PT-net:

(1) An impure transition (transition with a 'side condition') may be eliminated by dividing it into its begin, its being active, and its end:

v t w v 1 begin of t t being active w end of t

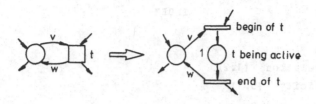

(2) In a similar way, transitions which 'take time' for their firing may be refined:

3s 1 3 s

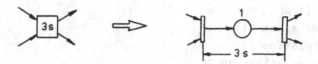

(3) A PT-net PN with strict transition rule can be transformed into a PT-net PN' with weak transition rule which is, with respect to what can happen, equivalent to PN. For each place s with finite capacity a <u>complementary place</u> s' with •s' = s• and s'• = •s is added to PN and initially marked by $K(s)-M_0(s)$.

Example:

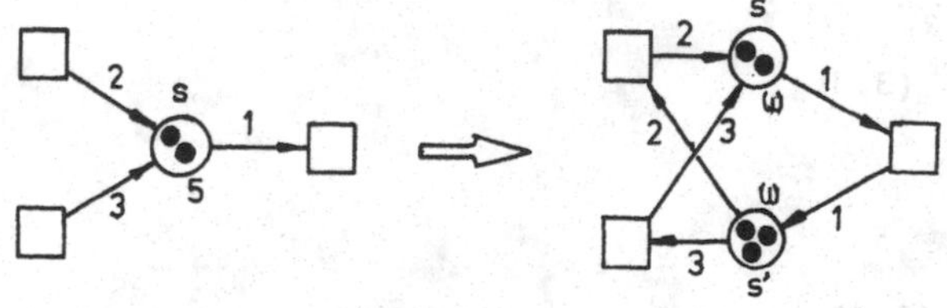

INDEX

ADDRESSES OF ALL AUTHORS

Dr. C. André
L.A.S.S.Y.
41 BD, Napoleon 3
F - 06041 Nice
France

Dr. G. Berthelot
Institut de Programmation Tour 55-65
Université Pierre et Marie Curie
4, Place Jussieu
F - 75230 Paris Cedex 05
France

E. Best
University of Newcastle upon Tyne
Claremont Tower
Newcastle upon Tyne NE1 7RU
G.B.

Dr. M. Diaz
L.A.A.S. - C.N.R.S.
Toulouse
France

Dr. H.-J. Genrich
G.M.D. - I.S.F.
Postfach 1240
Schloß Birlinghoven
D - 5205 St. Augustin 1
Germany

Prof. Dr. C. Girault
same address as Dr. G. Berthelot

Dr. M. Jantzen
Fachbereich Informatik
Universität Hamburg
Schlüterstraße 70
D - 2000 Hamburg 13
Germany

Prof. Dr. K. Lautenbach
same address as Dr. H.-J. Genrich

Dr. G. Memmi
E.C.A. Automation
F - 75230 Paris
France

Prof. Dr. J. D. Noe
Dept. of Computer Science
1122 Sieg Hall
University of Washington
Seattle - Washington 98195
U.S.A.

Dr. H. Oberquelle
same address as Dr. M. Jantzen

Dr. C. A. Petri
same address as Dr. H.-J. Genrich

Dr. G. Roucairol
same address as Dr. G. Berthelot

Robert M. Shapiro
Meta Information Applications Inc.
Box 943
Wellfleet - Massachusetts 02667
U.S.A.

Dr. J. Sifakis
Laboratoire I.M.A.G.
B.P. 53 X
F - 38041 Grenoble Cedex
France

Dr. E. Stankiewicz-Wiechno
Institute of Mathematics
Technical University
Warsaw
Poland

Dr. P. S. Thiagarajan
same address as Dr. H.-J. Genrich

Prof. Dr. R. Valk
same address as Dr. M. Jantzen

Prof. Dr.-Ing. e.H. Dr. rer. nat. h.c. Konrad Zuse
Im Haselgrund 21
D - 6418 Hünfeld
Germany

Vol. 49: Interactive Systems. Proceedings 1976. Edited by A. Blaser and C. Hackl. VI, 380 pages. 1976.

Vol. 50: A. C. Hartmann, A Concurrent Pascal Compiler for Minicomputers. VI, 119 pages. 1977.

Vol. 51: B. S. Garbow, Matrix Eigensystem Routines – Eispack Guide Extension. VIII, 343 pages. 1977.

Vol. 52: Automata, Languages and Programming. Fourth Colloquium, University of Turku, July 1977. Edited by A. Salomaa and M. Steinby. X, 569 pages. 1977.

Vol. 53: Mathematical Foundations of Computer Science. Proceedings 1977. Edited by J. Gruska. XII, 608 pages. 1977.

Vol. 54: Design and Implementation of Programming Languages. Proceedings 1976. Edited by J. H. Williams and D. A. Fisher. X, 496 pages. 1977.

Vol. 55: A. Gerbier, Mes premières constructions de programmes. XII, 256 pages. 1977.

Vol. 56: Fundamentals of Computation Theory. Proceedings 1977. Edited by M. Karpiński. XII, 542 pages. 1977.

Vol. 57: Portability of Numerical Software. Proceedings 1976. Edited by W. Cowell. VIII, 539 pages. 1977.

Vol. 58: M. J. O'Donnell, Computing in Systems Described by Equations. XIV, 111 pages. 1977.

Vol. 59: E. Hill, Jr., A Comparative Study of Very Large Data Bases. X, 140 pages. 1978.

Vol. 60: Operating Systems, An Advanced Course. Edited by R. Bayer, R. M. Graham, and G. Seegmüller. X, 593 pages. 1978.

Vol. 61: The Vienna Development Method: The Meta-Language. Edited by D. Bjørner and C. B. Jones. XVIII, 382 pages. 1978.

Vol. 62: Automata, Languages and Programming. Proceedings 1978. Edited by G. Ausiello and C. Böhm. VIII, 508 pages. 1978.

Vol. 63: Natural Language Communication with Computers. Edited by Leonard Bolc. VI, 292 pages. 1978.

Vol. 64: Mathematical Foundations of Computer Science. Proceedings 1978. Edited by J. Winkowski. X, 551 pages. 1978.

Vol. 65: Information Systems Methodology, Proceedings, 1978. Edited by G. Bracchi and P. C. Lockemann. XII, 696 pages. 1978.

Vol. 66: N. D. Jones and S. S. Muchnick, TEMPO: A Unified Treatment of Binding Time and Parameter Passing Concepts in Programming Languages. IX, 118 pages. 1978.

Vol. 67: Theoretical Computer Science, 4th GI Conference, Aachen, March 1979. Edited by K. Weihrauch. VII, 324 pages. 1979.

Vol. 68: D. Harel, First-Order Dynamic Logic. X, 133 pages. 1979.

Vol. 69: Program Construction. International Summer School. Edited by F. L. Bauer and M. Broy. VII, 651 pages. 1979.

Vol. 70: Semantics of Concurrent Computation. Proceedings 1979. Edited by G. Kahn. VI, 368 pages. 1979.

Vol. 71: Automata, Languages and Programming. Proceedings 1979. Edited by H. A. Maurer. IX, 684 pages. 1979.

Vol. 72: Symbolic and Algebraic Computation. Proceedings 1979. Edited by E. W. Ng. XV, 557 pages. 1979.

Vol. 73: Graph-Grammars and Their Application to Computer Science and Biology. Proceedings 1978. Edited by V. Claus, H. Ehrig and G. Rozenberg. VII, 477 pages. 1979.

Vol. 74: Mathematical Foundations of Computer Science. Proceedings 1979. Edited by J. Bečvář. IX, 580 pages. 1979.

Vol. 75: Mathematical Studies of Information Processing. Proceedings 1978. Edited by E. K. Blum, M. Paul and S. Takasu. VIII, 629 pages. 1979.

Vol. 76: Codes for Boundary-Value Problems in Ordinary Differential Equations. Proceedings 1978. Edited by B. Childs et al. VIII, 388 pages. 1979.

Vol. 77: G. V. Bochmann, Architecture of Distributed Computer Systems. VIII, 238 pages. 1979.

Vol. 78: M. Gordon, R. Milner and C. Wadsworth, Edinburg VIII, 159 pages. 1979.

Vol. 79: Language Design and Programming Methodolog ceedings, 1979. Edited by J. Tobias. IX, 255 pages. 1980.

Vol. 80: Pictorial Information Systems. Edited by S. K. Char K. S. Fu. IX, 445 pages. 1980.

Vol. 81: Data Base Techniques for Pictorial Applications. Pr ings, 1979. Edited by A. Blaser. XI, 599 pages. 1980.

Vol. 82: J. G. Sanderson, A Relational Theory of Computi 147 pages. 1980.

Vol. 83: International Symposium Programming. Proceedings Edited by B. Robinet. VII, 341 pages. 1980.

Vol. 84: Net Theory and Applications. Proceedings, 1979. by W. Brauer. XIII, 537 Seiten. 1980.